Word Study That Works for All Learners

WORDS THEIR WAY™

Online Course for Teachers

This self-paced, interactive, professional development workshop is designed to help teachers, reading specialists, literacy coaches, and staff development trainers master the methodology of the Words Their Way™ word study approach for their students.

The Words Their Way™ Online Course for Teachers provides:

- **Personal training**—self-paced practice on your own time.
- **Individual instructional path**—tailored path based on your grade level or role in your school.
- **Interactive practice**—classroom video, student writing samples, assessments, and activities.
- **Immediate feedback**—assessment that tracks and guides your mastery of the Words Their Way™ approach to word study.

Learn more and view the introduction at www.pearsonlearningsolutions.com/online-learning/words-their-way-online-workshop

WORDS THEIR WAY™

Training for Teachers

Words Their Way™ Training for Teachers is a three-day, face-to-face workshop that will help teachers and literacy coaches unlock the potential of word study and enhance learning in phonemic awareness, phonics, vocabulary, spelling, fluency, and comprehension. Key features include:

- High-quality training on the research-based book *Words Their Way™*, developed with the Words Their Way™ author team
- Training focused on characteristics and instruction at each developmental spelling level
- How to effectively implement the Words Their Way™ approach in your classroom

WORDS THEIR WAY™

Virtual Training for Teachers

Pearson's virtual institutes are a travel-free and schedule-friendly way to learn about implementing the Words Their Way™ word study approach. Professional development is provided in 12 sessions over 4 weeks from leading authors and experts, featuring live sessions and self-paced learning.

WORDS THEIR WAY™

Coaching and Modeling

In this job-embedded professional development, a Pearson consultant works directly with teachers and coaches to analyze data, review lessons, and address areas of student need.

Coming soon! MY ONLINE WORKSHOP: WORDS THEIR WAY™

Short self-paced online modules sold in bundles that reflect a range of developmental levels

Learn more about Pearson Professional Development at www.pearsonpd.com

The Words Their Way™ Series

Words Their Way™: Word Study for Phonics, Vocabulary, and Spelling Instruction, 5th Edition

The core Words Their Way™ book gives you the tools you need to carry out word study instruction, while complementing the use of any existing phonics, spelling, and vocabulary curricula. A new online PDToolkit for *Words Their Way*™ is now available with the fifth edition.

Words Their Way™ Companion Volumes

These 5 companion volumes are targeted to the word study instruction of an individual stage of spelling development outlined in the core book, and, with reproducible sorting pages and directions, the books provide a plan of action for motivating and engaging your students.

Words Their Way™ with English Learners

Based on the same solid research, the *Words Their Way™ with English Learners* book and companion sort books for Spanish speakers help you determine what your students bring with them from their home languages, where their instruction in English orthography should begin, and how best to move these students through their development and help them master their new language. A new online PDToolkit for *Words Their Way™ with English Learners* is now available with the second edition.

Newest additions to the Words Their Way™ series!

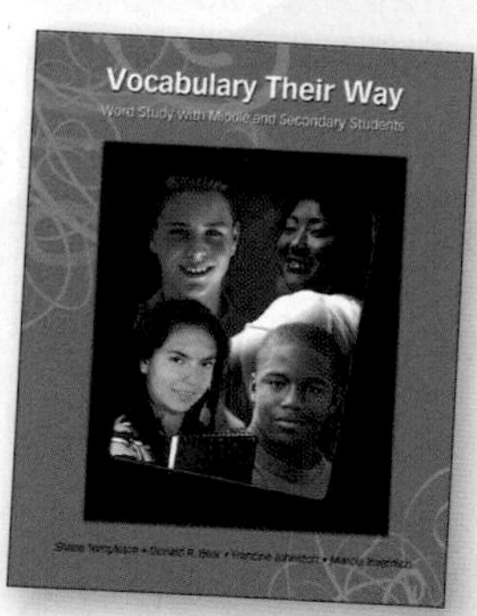

Vocabulary Their Way™: Word Study with Middle and Secondary Students

With a focus on developing vocabulary with students in intermediate, middle, and secondary grades, this new book offers research-tested ideas for helping students use word patterns to puzzle out meaning to content area vocabulary. It also provides much needed assessment information to help teachers gauge where to begin instruction as well as hands-on opportunities for teachers to keep students' attention and interest as they build vocabulary.

Words Their Way™ with Struggling Readers: Word Study for Reading, Vocabulary, and Spelling Instruction, Grades 4–12

This new resource provides specific guidance, strategies, and tools for helping struggling students catch up with their peers in literacy. The thrust is intervention—specifically, utilizing word study with its hands-on, accessible approach to aid students struggling with the vocabulary, fluency, and comprehension load of middle and secondary classrooms. This book will help you determine student needs, provide you with the strategies to guide each student toward success in content area comprehension, and even outline ideas for fitting these strategies into your crowded schedule.

Learn more at www.allynbaconmerrill.com/wordstheirway

Words Their Way™: *Word Study in Action with English Learners*

The official companion eases your classroom preparation!

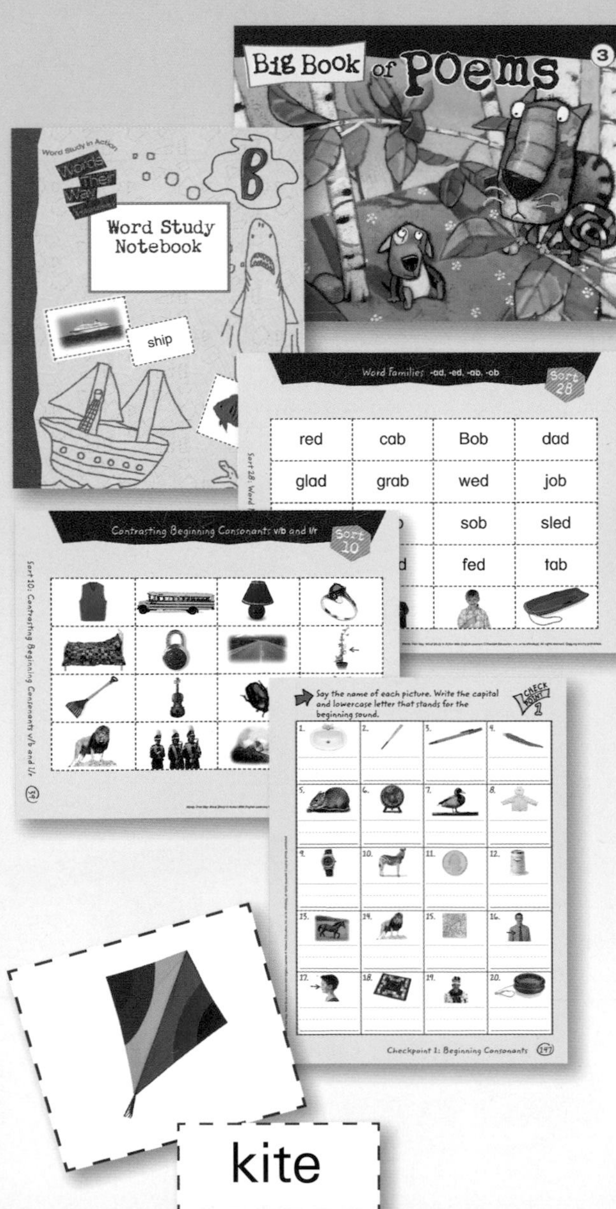

Word Study in Action with English Learners, the classroom-ready companion to ***Words Their Way***™ ***with English Learners: Word Study for Phonics, Vocabulary, and Spelling,*** is ideal for your students from diverse language backgrounds.

- Use the research-based developmental perspective to guide phonics, vocabulary and spelling instruction for Emergent, Beginning, Transitional, and Intermediate English learners.
- *Words Their Way™ with English Learners* will help you understand what English learners bring with them from their home language and *Word Study in Action* will help you guide students as they progress with literacy in English.
- 15-minute daily lessons integrate easily into literacy blocks.
- Weekly assessments monitor progress and guide instruction.
- Provide hands-on learning experiences by sorting ready-made pictures and words into specific categories such as concepts, letters, syllables, spelling patterns and sounds. Sort in your students' home language and English to tie the languages together and build upon commonalities.

Program Components

Each classroom package (Level 1, 2, 3, and 4) includes: 12 Word Study Notebooks, Teacher Resource Guide, Big Book of Poems and Resource CD-ROM.

- **Student Word Study Notebook**—Includes 36 leveled sorts based on phonics, vocabulary, and spelling.
- **Teacher Resource Guide**—Offers weekly lesson plans to guide and instruct.
- **Big Book of Poems**—Thirty-six poems that correspond to the weekly lesson.
- **Teacher Resource CD-ROM**—Includes games that correspond to the 36 sorts, sorting cards and their translations, and copy of the poems to reproduce.
- **Words Their Way™ Library**—Thirty-six books that provide additional reading and discussion opportunities. Libraries sold separately.

Words Their Way™

Words Their Way™

Word Study for Phonics, Vocabulary, and Spelling Instruction

FIFTH EDITION

Donald R. Bear
University of Nevada, Reno

Marcia Invernizzi
University of Virginia

Shane Templeton
University of Nevada, Reno

Francine Johnston
University of North Carolina at Greensboro

Boston • Columbus • Indianapolis • New York • San Francisco • Upper Saddle River
Amsterdam • Cape Town • Dubai • London • Madrid • Milan • Munich • Paris • Montreal • Toronto
Delhi • Mexico City • Sao Paulo • Sydney • Hong Kong • Seoul • Singapore • Taipei • Tokyo

Vice President, Editor in Chief: Aurora Martínez Ramos
Senior Development Editor: Max Effenson Chuck
Editorial Assistant: Katherine Wiley
Production Editor: Annette Joseph
Executive Marketing Manager: Krista Clark
Marketing Assistant: Elizabeth Mackenzie-Lamb
Marketing Manager: Danae April
Editorial Production Service: Omegatype Typography, Inc.
Manufacturing Buyer: Megan Cochran
Electronic Composition: Omegatype Typography, Inc.
Interior Design: Carol Somberg
Cover Design: Jennifer Hart
Art Director: Linda Knowles
Illustrator: Francine Johnston

Credits and acknowledgments borrowed from other sources and reproduced, with permission, in this textbook appear on appropriate page within text.

Library of Congress Cataloging-in-Publication Data

Bear, Donald R.
Words their way : word study for phonics, vocabulary, and spelling instruction / Donald R. Bear, Marcia Invernizzi, Francine Johnston.—5th ed.
p. cm.
Rev. ed. of: Words their way / Donald R. Bear . . . [et al.].
Includes bibliographical references and index.
ISBN-13: 978-0-13-703510-6 (pbk.)
ISBN-10: 0-13-703510-1 (pbk.)
1. Word recognition. 2. Reading—Phonetic method. 3. English language—Orthography and spelling. I. Invernizzi, Marcia. II. Johnston, Francine R. III. Bear, Donald R. Words their way. IV. Title.
LB1050.44.B43 2012
372.46'2—dc22

2011010231

10 9 8 7 6 5 4 3 2 1

ISBN-10: 0-13-703510-1
ISBN-13: 978-0-13-703510-6

This book is dedicated to
the memory of our teacher,
Edmund H. Henderson.

Donald R. Bear

Marcia Invernizzi

Shane Templeton

Francine Johnston

LETTER from the AUTHORS

Dear Educator,

It is an honor for the authors of ***Words Their Way*™: *Word Study for Phonics, Vocabulary, and Spelling Instruction*** to present the fifth edition of this seminal text on word study. Accompanying this significant revision is an online resource, PDToolkit for *Words Their Way*™, featuring all-new classroom video as well as easy-to-navigate word sorts and games, assessment tools, and applications all in one place. These tools will help you to effectively implement word study instruction in your classroom.

For the fifth anniversary of writing this text, our editors asked us this question:

What do you feel your book has done to change the way teachers teach word study?

Donald
Words Their Way has provided a developmental approach that guides and sharpens our teaching. The integration of phonics, vocabulary, and spelling in *Words Their Way* represents a paradigmatic shift in modern times: No longer do we have to think of these as three separate areas of instruction. Integrating phonics, vocabulary, and spelling instruction with a developmental approach has contributed, we hope, to deep and rewarding learning and teaching.

Marcia
Words Their Way has gotten teachers to think about phonics, spelling, and vocabulary instruction from a developmental perspective. Being the only assessment-driven developmental guide for word study instruction available, *Words Their Way* has taken the concept of differentiation to a whole new level. Teachers welcome our student-centered, minds-on, active approach that considers word study as an integral and integrated part of literacy development.

Shane
Words Their Way has helped teachers provide their students with the breadth and depth of exploration necessary to construct knowledge about words over time—from individual letters to sound, from groups of letters to sound, and from groups of letters to meaning. Awareness and appreciation of how children construct this knowledge has empowered and emboldened many teachers to advocate for developmental instruction in word study specifically and in literacy more generally.

Francine
Word study engages students in active critical thinking—comparing, contrasting, and forming generalizations as they sort words into categories. This is in sharp contrast to traditional phonics and spelling programs that merely ask students to memorize relationships, rules, and words. This active exploration of words appeals to teachers who want to promote inquiry and thoughtful discussions about how words work and know that "teaching is not telling."

Bring your colleagues and come join us in the most active edition of ***Words Their Way*™** yet. We wish you happy sorting with your students!

Sincerely,

Donald R. Bear   Marcia Invernizzi   Shane Templeton   Francine Johnston

ABOUT the AUTHORS

Donald R. Bear

Donald R. Bear is director of the E. L. Cord Foundation Center for Learning and Literacy in the Department of Educational Specialties, College of Education at the University of Nevada, Reno, where he and his students teach and assess students who experience difficulties learning to read and write. A former elementary teacher, Donald currently researches literacy development with a special interest in students who speak different languages and he partners with schools and districts to think about how to assess and conduct literacy instruction.

Marcia Invernizzi

Marcia Invernizzi is director of the McGuffey Reading Center in the Curry School of Education at the University of Virginia. She and her multilingual doctoral students enjoy exploring developmental universals in non-English orthographics. A former English and reading teacher, Marcia extends her experience working with children who experience difficulties learning to read and write in numerous intervention programs, such as Virginia's Early Intervention Reading Initiative and Book Buddies.

Shane Templeton

Shane Templeton is Foundation Professor of Literacy Studies in the Department of Educational Specialties at the University of Nevada, Reno. A former classroom teacher at the primary and secondary levels, he has focused his research on the development of orthographic and vocabulary knowledge. He has written several books on the teaching and learning of reading and language arts and is a member of the Usage Panel of the *American Heritage Dictionary*.

Francine Johnston

Francine Johnston is an associate professor in the School of Education at the University of North Carolina at Greensboro, where she coordinates the reading masters program and directs a reading clinic for struggling readers. Francine is a former first grade teacher and reading specialist, and she continues to work with schools as a consultant and researcher. Her research interests include current spelling practices and materials as well as the relationship between spelling and reading achievement.

BRIEF CONTENTS

CONTENTS

CHAPTER 8

ACTIVITIES

Activities for the Emergent Stage 122

Activities for the Letter Name–Alphabetic Stage 177

Activities for the Within Word Pattern Stage 225

Activities for the Syllables and Affixes Stage 261

Activities for the Derivational Relations Stage 294

PREFACE

I see and I forget. I hear and I remember. I do and I understand.

—Confucius

Word study involves "doing" things with words—examining, manipulating, comparing and categorizing—and offers students the opportunity to make their own discoveries about how words work. When teachers use this practical, hands-on way to study words with students, they create tasks that focus students' attention on critical features of words—sound, pattern, and meaning.

Words Their Way is a developmental approach to phonics, vocabulary, and spelling instruction. Using a systematic approach, guided by an informed interpretation of spelling errors and other literacy behaviors, *Words Their Way* offers a teacher-directed, child-centered plan for the study of words from kindergarten to high school. Step by step, the chapters explain exactly how to provide effective word study instruction. The keys to this research-based approach are knowing your students' literacy progress, organizing for instruction, and implementing word study.

New to This Edition

- **NEW:** The redesign of the book emphasizes coherence between the media and the book.
- **NEW:** End-of-chapter media guides summarize what media has been integrated into each chapter and where to find it in the text and on the Web.
- **NEW**: In this edition, the coverage of oral vocabulary is enhanced with activities at all stages.
- **NEW**: Secondary coverage is enhanced in the within word pattern stage and the syllables and affixes stage.
- **NEW**: Progress monitoring is a natural extension of the words their way approach. A section on monitoring progress has been added in Chapter 2 and in each stage chapter. In addition, marginal icons throughout the book indicate where monitoring progress is discussed.
- **NEW:** This edition has enhanced coverage of English learners throughout the book using marginal icons that highlight where coverage of English learners has been integrated into the text. There are also sections devoted to English learners in Chapters 4–8.
- **NEW:** Resource Connection features appear in selected chapters. They provide a list of relevant literature and URLs that support what is being discussed in the text.
- **NEW:** A newly designed marginal icon links the reader to specific videos, sorts, or assessments on the web.
- **NEW**: A new, applied feature—Resources for Implementing Word Study in Your Classroom—appears before the end-of-chapter activities in each chapter.

- **NEW:** Chapter 3 describes a continuum of support that will help teachers maximize time and manage groups for sorting.
- **NEW**: Each chapter includes new activities.
- **NEW**: Photos pulled from the video appear in the book, further enhancing the interconnectedness between the text and the media.
- **NEW:** A section in Chapter 3 called "Teacher Talk and Student Reflection" provides ideas about leading discussions after sorting.

New PDToolkit for *Words Their Way*™

Accompanying *Words Their Way*, fifth edition, there is a new website with media tools that, together with the text, provide you the tools you need to carry out word study instruction that will motivate and engage your students and help them succeed in literacy learning.

The PDToolkit for *Words Their Way*™ is available free for six months after you use the password that comes with this book. After that, it is available by subscription for a yearly fee. Be sure to explore and download the resources available at the website. Currently, the following resources are available:

- All-new video has been shot for the fifth edition. This classroom footage brings you into the classrooms of teachers using word study at all of the different stages of development.
- An assessment tool provides downloadable inventories and feature guides as well as interactive classroom composites that help teachers monitor their students' development throughout the year.
- Prepared word sorts and games for each stage will help you get started with word study in your classroom.
- A Create Your Own feature will allow you to modify and create sorts and games by selecting words or pictures to be used with the word sort and game templates.
- Word sorts that can be used in conjunction with interactive whiteboards are available.

In the future, we will continue to add other resources.

Knowing Your Students

After Chapter 1 provides you with foundational information on word study and the research in orthography and literacy development that led to this word study approach, Chapter 2 presents assessment and evaluation tools, walking you step by step through the process of determining your students' instructional level and focusing your word study instruction appropriately. After you administer one of the spelling inventories, you will be able to compile a feature guide for each of your students that will help you identify their stage and the word study features they are ready to master. Spelling inventory data can be entered electronically using the assessment tool at our website and it will automatically create a feature guide as well as a classroom composite record. The classroom composite will identify which students have similar instructional needs, allowing you to plan wisely and effectively for word study grouping.

New to this edition are progress monitoring charts and spell checks that will enable you to determine the effectiveness of instruction on a regular basis and to modify it as needed. At the PDToolkit for *Words Their Way*™ you will find assessment resources to download, including:

- Primary Spelling Inventory, feature guide, error guide, and classroom composite
- Elementary Spelling Inventory, feature guide, error guide, and classroom composite
- Upper-Level Spelling Inventory, feature guide, and classroom composite
- Spelling-by-Stage Organizational Chart
- Qualitative Spelling Checklist
- Emergent Class Record
- Word Feature Inventory
- McGuffey Qualitative Spelling Inventory
- Kindergarten Spelling Inventory and Analysis
- Progress monitoring charts
- Spell checks

Organizing for Instruction

Chapter 3 outlines the most effective ways to organize word study for classroom instruction. We suggest activities for small groups, partners, and individuals that can be incorporated into weekly routines that will help you manage leveled groups for instruction at all grade levels. In this edition we describe a continuum of support that will help you plan and implement lessons to maximize classroom time. We also have added tips for guiding discussions about words.

Implementing Word Study

Once you've assessed your students, created leveled groups, and developed routines for word study, the information and materials in Chapters 4 through 8 and the Appendixes will guide your instruction. Chapters 4 through 8 explore the characteristics of each particular stage, from the emergent learner through the advanced reader and writer in the derivational relations stage of spelling development. Each of these chapters covers the research and principles that drive instruction and the most appropriate sequence and instructional pacing.

Activities described in each chapter include concept sorts, word sorts, and games, which will help you focus instruction where it is needed to move students into the next stage of development. These word study activities promise to engage your students, motivate them, and improve their literacy skills. The activities sections have shaded tabs for your convenience, creating a handy classroom resource. New to this edition are additional vocabulary strategies for each developmental level.

Importantly, as you work with the *Common Core State Standards*, you will see how *Words Their Way* supports the Reading Foundational Skills and the Language Standards across all the grades. The depth and breadth of word knowledge developed through *Words Their Way* will also support the Common Core's emphasis on students' reading more complex literary and informational texts.

The Appendixes at the back of the book contain most of the assessment instruments described in Chapter 2, as well as word sorts, sound boards, and game templates you'll need to get your own word study instruction under way.

Companion Volumes

Additional stage-specific companion volumes provide a complete curriculum of reproducible sorts and detailed directions for the teacher. Purchase any of the following valuable professional resources at **www.allynbaconmerrill.com:**

- *Words Their Way™: Letter and Picture Sorts for Emergent Spellers* (2nd ed.), by Donald R. Bear, Marcia Invernizzi, Francine Johnston, and Shane Templeton
- *Words Their Way™: Word Sorts for Letter Name–Alphabetic Spellers* (2nd ed.), by Francine Johnston, Donald R. Bear, Marcia Invernizzi, and Shane Templeton
- *Words Their Way™: Word Sorts for Within Word Pattern Spellers* (2nd ed.), by Marcia Invernizzi, Francine Johnston, Donald R. Bear, and Shane Templeton
- *Words Their Way™: Word Sorts for Syllables and Affixes Spellers* (2nd ed.), by Francine Johnston, Marcia Invernizzi, Donald R. Bear, and Shane Templeton
- *Words Their Way™: Word Sorts for Derivational Relations Spellers* (2nd ed.), by Shane Templeton, Francine Johnston, Donald R. Bear, and Marcia Invernizzi

Other related volumes are designed to meet the needs of English learners and students in the intermediate and secondary levels:

- *Words Their Way™ with English Learners: Word Study for Phonics, Vocabulary, and Spelling* (2nd ed.), by Lori Helman, Donald R. Bear, Shane Templeton, Marcia Invernizzi, and Francine Johnston
- *Words Their Way™: Emergent Sorts for Spanish-Speaking English Learners*, by Lori Helman, Donald R. Bear, Marcia Invernizzi, Shane Templeton, and Francine Johnston
- *Words Their Way™: Letter Name–Alphabetic Sorts for Spanish-Speaking English Learners*, by Lori Helman, Donald R. Bear, Marcia Invernizzi, Shane Templeton, and Francine Johnston
- *Vocabulary Their Way™: Word Study with Middle and Secondary Students*, by Shane Templeton, Donald R. Bear, Marcia Invernizzi, and Francine Johnston
- *Words Their Way™ with Struggling Readers: Word Study for Reading, Vocabulary, and Spelling Instruction, Grades 4–12*, by Kevin Flanigan, Latisha Hayes, Shane Templeton, Donald R. Bear, Marcia Invernizzi, and Francine Johnston

Acknowledgments

We would like to thank the reviewers of our manuscript for their careful consideration and comments: Cathy Blanchfield, California State University, Fresno; Stephanie Collom, Fresno Unified School District; Lori Helman, University of Minnesota; and Maria J. Meyerson, University of Nevada, Las Vegas. Colleagues and friends are too numerous to mention here, but those who have in recent years worked with and taught us include Kelly Bruskotter, Sharon Cathey, Shari Dunn, Kevin Flanigan, Michelle Flores, Kristin Gehsmann, Ashley Gotta, Amanda Grotting, Tisha Hayes, Ryan Ichanberry, Darl Kiernan, Sandra Madura, Kara Moloney, Ann Noel, Leta Rabenstein, Kelly Rubero, Alisa Simeral, David Smith, Regina Smith, Kris Stosic, and Alyson Wilson. We would like to thank the video production team from University of Nevada, Reno, for their excellent work on the video accompanying this book as well as most of the photos in the book. The team includes Mark Gandolfo, Theresa Danna-Douglas, Maryan Tooker, and Shawn Sariti.

For this edition, we also reached out to people who are using our book or have attended our institutes and our colleagues, who comprised our Advisory Council. We would like to thank them for their contribution throughout our development process. They include Rachael Agre, Gwynne Ash, Joan Boshart, Rita Britton, Melanie Burgess, Shan Cannon, Gisele (Sue)

Cauley, Sandy Cebollero, Eileen Cirincione, Sandy Citron, Amanda Clark, Gwen Collins, Iris Comer-Day, Lindsay Comstock, Cheri Cooke, Clairin DeMartini, Maria Duron, Donna Eatinger, Leah Edwards, Amy Fogarty, Francine Fredrickson, Angela Gabaldon, Keri Glazier, Camille Grabb, Tania Hanna, Martha Harsch, Joanne Harmsen, Keitha Havey, Cathy Isbell, Anita James, Elizabeth Kauffman, Angela Kheradmand, Mary Kirkpatrick, Barbara Kruse, Jane Lemons, Amy Lindley, Michelle McKenzie-Marlin, Stacey Mersy, Sheri Miller, Kirstin New, Bobby Norman, Suzie Olson, Sheri Pentecost, Marie Peterson, Sara Reynolds, Dianna Riley, Coleen Sams, Lori Schouvieller, Mary Schroepfer, Alyssa Slater, David Smith, Regina Smith, A. J. Stevens, Eleanor Tyson, and Holli Wroblesski.

We would also like to thank the following teachers for their classroom-tested activities: Cindy Aldrete-Frazer, Tamara Baren, Margery Beatty, Telia Blackard, Janet Bloodgood, Cindy Booth, Karen Broaddus, Wendy Brown, Janet Brown Watts, Karen Carpenter, Carol Caserta-Henry, Jeradi Cohen, Fran de Maio, Nicole Doner, Allison Dwier-Seldon, Marilyn Edwards, Ann Fordham, Mary Fowler, Erika Fulmer, Elizabeth Harrison, Esther Heatley, Lisbeth Kling, Pat Love, Rita Loyacono, Barry Mahanes, Carolyn Melchiorre, Colleen Muldoon, Liana Napier, Katherine Preston, Brenda Riebel, Leslie Robertson, Geraldine Robinson, Elizabeth Shuett, Jennifer Sudduth, and Charlotte Tucker.

Finally, a very special "thank you" to the following individuals: Aurora Martínez Ramos, who conceptualized much more than a book and who resolved innumerable challenges; Vikki Myers, Molly Bagshaw, and Barbara Strickland, for support and attention to detail truly above and beyond; Karla Walsh and the rest of the Omegatype Typography team; and Max Chuck, our developmental editor for this new edition. Max has been devoted to this book, taking on extraordinary details never encountered before, and has dedicated a good portion of her life over the last couple of years to making this edition be all that we have hoped it could be. You have our eternal gratitude!

chapter 1

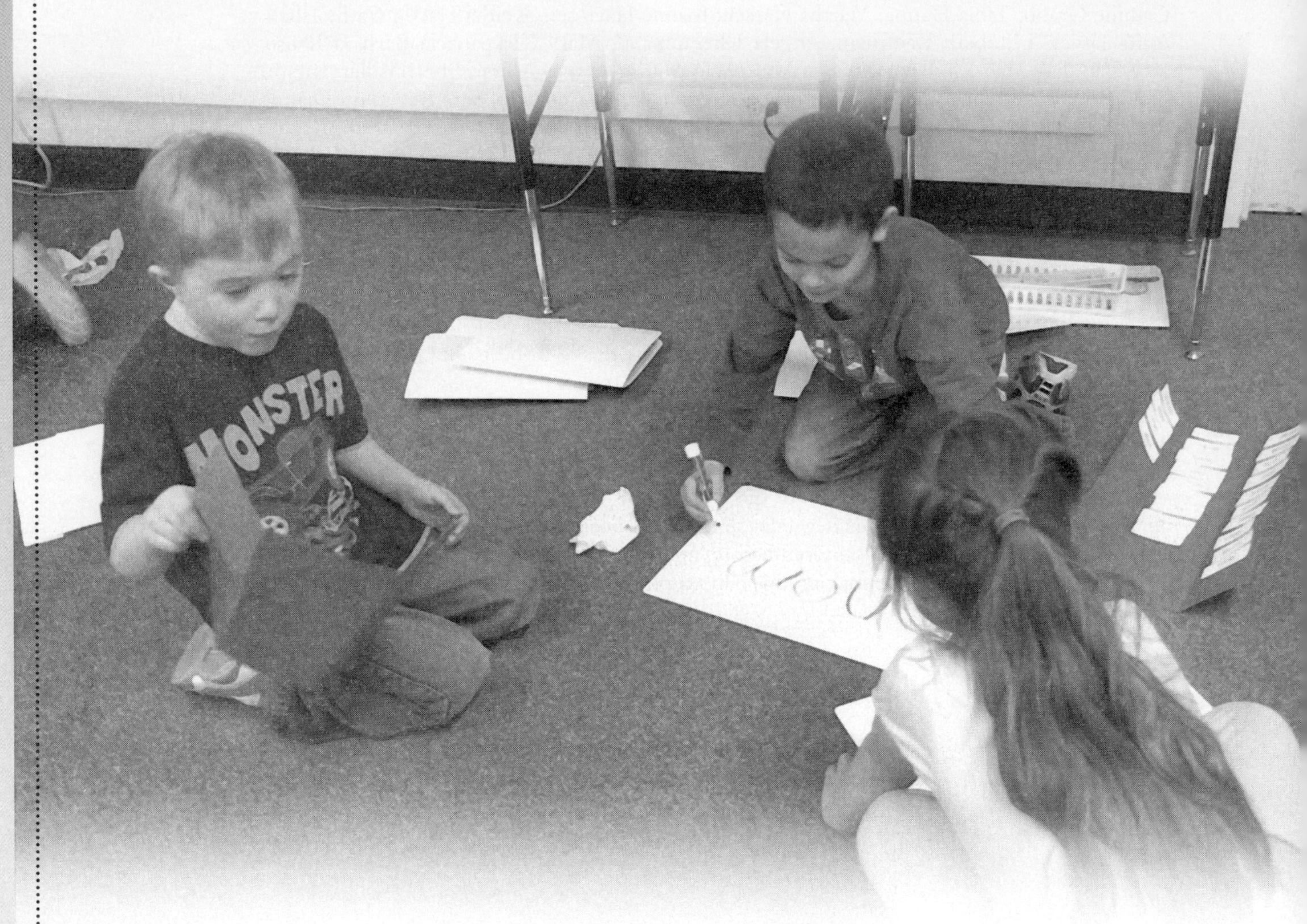

Developmental Word Knowledge

For students of all ages and languages, knowledge of the ways in which their written language represents the language they speak is the key to literacy. Understanding how the spoken word is represented in print is fundamental to this understanding: In English, for example, how do the marks on the page represent not only *sound* but also *meaning?* In this new fifth edition, we continue our exploration of how teachers can most effectively guide and support students' learning about the sounds, structure, and meanings of words—crafting our instruction so that our students learn about words *their* way. In addition to demonstrating how a developmental approach to word study best supports students' deep and long-term word learning, this new edition further explores how educators may apply this developmental model as they address the following: effective and engaging vocabulary instruction from preschool through the middle grades, ongoing progress monitoring, response to intervention, and accommodations for English learners. Whether you are a long-standing companion on this adventure or joining us for the first time, we welcome you on this continuing journey to learn and teach about words *their* way.

The Braid of Literacy

Literacy is like a braid of interwoven threads. The braid begins with the intertwining threads of oral language and stories that are read to children. As children experiment with putting ideas on paper, a writing thread is entwined as well. As children move into reading, the threads of literacy begin to bond. Students' growing knowledge of spelling or **orthography**—the correct sequences of letters in words—strengthens that bonding. The size of the threads and the braid itself become thicker as orthographic knowledge grows (see Figure 1.1).

During the preschool years, children acquire word knowledge in a fundamentally aural way from the language that surrounds them. Through listening to and talking about everyday events, life experiences, and stories, many children develop a rich speaking vocabulary. As they have opportunities to talk about and to categorize their everyday experiences, children begin to make sense of their world and to use language to negotiate and describe it. Children also begin to experiment with pen and paper when they have opportunities to observe parents, siblings, and caregivers writing for many purposes. They gradually come to understand the forms and functions of written language. The first written words students learn are usually their own names, followed by those of significant others. Words such as *Mom, cat, dog,* and phrases like *I love you* represent people, animals, and ideas dear to their lives.

FIGURE 1.1 Braid of Literacy

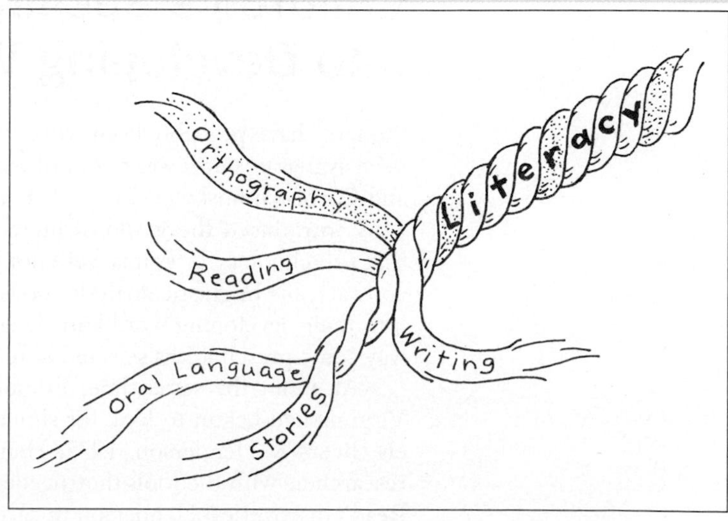

As students grow as readers and writers, print becomes a critical medium for conceptual development. When purposeful reading, writing, listening, and speaking take place, vocabulary is learned along the way. Even more words are acquired when students explicitly examine word spellings to discover relationships among words and how these relationships represent sounds and meanings.

A major aim of this book is to demonstrate how an exploration of spelling or orthographic knowledge

FIGURE 1.2 Student Sorting Words

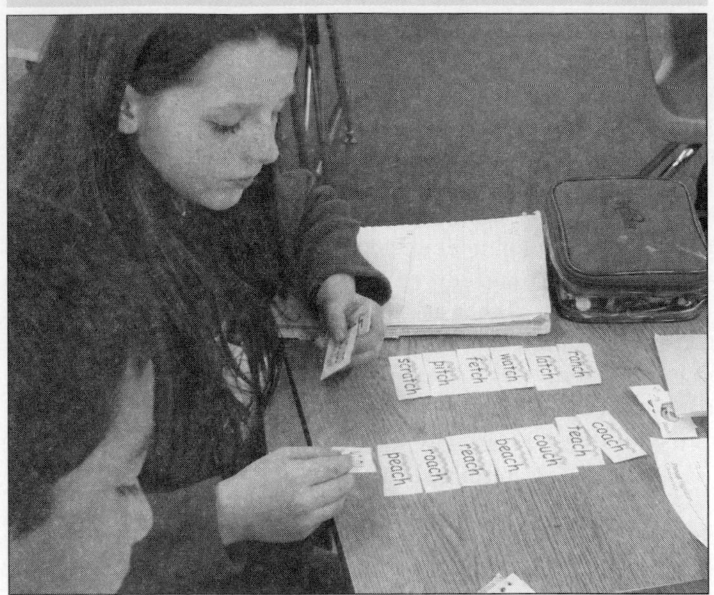

can lead to the lengthening and strengthening of the literacy braid. Teachers must know a good deal about the ways in which these threads intertwine to create this bond so that they can direct children's attention to words *their* way.

There are similarities in the ways learners of all ages expand their knowledge of the world. It seems that humans have a natural interest in finding order, comparing and contrasting, and paying attention to what remains the same despite minor variations. Infants learn to recognize Daddy as the same Daddy with or without glasses, with or without a hat or whiskers. Through such daily interactions, we categorize our surroundings. Similarly, our students expand their vocabularies by comparing one concept with another. Gradually, the number of concepts they analyze increases, but the process is still one of comparing and contrasting. They may first call anything with four legs "doggie" until they attend to the features that distinguish dogs, cats, and cows, and later terriers, labrador retrievers, border collies, and greyhounds. In the process they learn the vocabulary to label the categories.

Word study, as described in this book, occurs in hands-on activities that reflect basic cognitive learning processes: comparing and contrasting by categorizing word features and then discovering similarities and differences within and between categories. For example, by sorting words according to whether they end in *ch* or *tch*, as the student is doing in Figure 1.2, students can discover a consistent pattern that goes with each. Single short vowels are followed by *tch* and vowel pairs are followed by *ch*. Under the guidance of a knowledgeable teacher, the logic of the spelling system is revealed when students sort words into categories.

During word study, words and pictures are sorted in routines that require children to examine, discriminate, and make critical judgments about speech sounds, spelling patterns, and meanings. Just as *Math Their Way* uses concrete manipulatives to illustrate principles of combining and separating (Baretta-Lorton, 1968), *Words Their Way* uses concrete pictures and words to illustrate principles of similarity and difference.

Children's Spellings: A Window into Developing Word Knowledge

Students have probably been "inventing" their own spelling ever since paper and pencil have been available, but it was not until the early 1970s that research by Charles Read (1971, 1975) and Carol Chomsky (1971) took a serious look at young children's spelling attempts. Their work introduced the world of literacy to the notion of invented spelling. Read understood that preschoolers' attempts were not just random displays of ignorance and confusion. To the contrary, his linguistic analysis showed that children's invented spellings provided a window into their developing word knowledge. These "inventions" revealed a systematic logic to the way some preschoolers selected letters to represent sounds.

At about the same time, Edmund Henderson and his colleagues at the University of Virginia had begun to look for similar logic in students' spellings across ages and grade levels (Beers & Henderson, 1977; Henderson & Beers, 1980). Read's findings provided these researchers with the tools they needed to interpret the errors they were studying. Building on Read's discoveries, Henderson unearthed an underlying logic to students' errors that changed over time, moving from using but confusing elements of sound to using but confusing elements of pattern and meaning (Henderson, Estes, & Stonecash, 1972). The Virginia spelling studies corroborated and extended Read's findings upward through the grades and resulted in a comprehensive model of developmental word knowledge (Henderson, 1990; Templeton & Bear, 1992; Templeton & Morris, 2000).

Subsequent studies have confirmed this developmental model across many groups of students, from preschoolers (Ouellete & Sénéchal, 2008; Templeton & Spivey, 1980) through adults (Bear, Truex, & Barone, 1989; Massengill, 2006; Worthy & Viise, 1996), as well as across socioeconomic levels, dialects, and other alphabetic languages (Bear, Helman, & Woessner, 2009; Cantrell, 2001; He & Wang, 2009; Helman, 2009; Helman & Bear, 2007; Yang, 2005). The power of this model lies in the diagnostic information contained in students' spelling inventions that reveal their current understanding of how written words work (Invernizzi, Abouzeid, & Gill, 1994; McKenna & Picard, 2006). In addition, the analysis of students' spelling has been explored independently by other researchers (e.g., Bissex, 1980; Ehri, 1992; Holmes & Davis, 2002; Nunes & Bryant, 2009; Richgels, 1995, 2001; Treiman, 1993).

Henderson and his students not only studied the development of children's spelling, but also devised an instructional model to support that development. They determined that an informed analysis of students' spelling attempts can cue timely instruction in phonics, spelling, and vocabulary that is essential to move students forward in reading and writing. By using students' spellings as a guide, teachers can efficiently differentiate effective instruction in phonics, spelling, and vocabulary. We call this efficient and effective instruction **word study.**

Why Is Word Study Important?

Becoming fully literate is absolutely dependent on fast, accurate recognition of words and their meanings in texts and fast, accurate production of words in writing so that readers and writers can focus their attention on making meaning. Understanding of phonics and spelling patterns, high-frequency-word recognition, decoding strategies, and insight into word meanings are among the attributes that form the basis of written word knowledge. Designing a word study approach that explicitly teaches students necessary skills and engages their interest and motivation to learn about how words work is a vital aspect of any literacy program. Indeed, how to teach students these basics in an effective manner has sparked controversy among educators for nearly two hundred years (Balmuth, 1992; Carnine, Silbert, Kame'enui, & Tarver, 2009; Mathews, 1967; Schlagal, 2002; Schlagal, 2007; Smith, 2002).

Many phonics, spelling, and vocabulary programs are characterized by explicit skill instruction, a systematic scope and sequence, and repeated practice. However, much of the repeated practice consists of drill and memorization, so students have little opportunity to discover spelling patterns, manipulate word concepts, or apply critical thinking skills. Although students need explicit skill instruction within a systematic curriculum, it is equally true that "teaching is not telling" (James, 1899/1958).

Students need hands-on opportunities to manipulate word features in ways that allow them to generalize beyond isolated, individual examples to entire groups of words that are spelled the same way (Joseph, 2002; Juel & Minden-Cupp, 2000; Templeton, Smith, Moloney, Van Pelt, & Ives, 2009; White, 2005). Excelling at word recognition, spelling, and vocabulary is not just a matter of memorizing isolated rules and definitions. The best way to develop fast and accurate perception of word features is to engage in meaningful reading and writing and to have multiple opportunities to examine those same words and word features out of context. The most effective instruction in phonics, spelling, and vocabulary links word study to the texts students are reading, provides a systematic scope and sequence of word-level skills, and provides multiple opportunities for hands-on practice and application. In a sense, word study teaches students how to look at words so that they can construct an ever-deepening understanding of how spelling works to represent sound and meaning. We believe that this word study is well worth 10 to 15 minutes of instruction and practice daily.

What Is the Purpose of Word Study?

The purpose of word study is twofold. First, students develop a *general* knowledge of English spelling. Through active exploration, word study teaches students to examine words to discover generalizations about English spelling. They learn the regularities, patterns, and conventions of English orthography needed to read and spell. This general knowledge is conceptual in nature and reflects what students understand about the nature of our spelling system. Second, word study increases *specific* knowledge of words—the spellings and meanings of individual words.

General knowledge is what we access when we encounter a new word, when we do not know how to spell a word, or when we do not know the meaning of a specific word. The better our knowledge of the system, the better we are at decoding unfamiliar words, spelling correctly, or guessing the meanings of words. For example, if you have knowledge of short vowels and consonant **blends** (two consonants occurring together that each retain their individual sounds), you would have no trouble attempting the word *crash* even if you have never seen or written it before. The spelling is unambiguous, like so many single-syllable short vowel words. Knowledge of how words that are similar in spelling are related in meaning, such as *compete* and *competition*, makes it easier to understand the meaning of a word like *competitor*, even if it is unfamiliar. Additional clues offered by context also increase the chances of reading and understanding a word correctly.

To become fully literate, however, we also need specific knowledge about individual words. The word *rain*, for example, might be spelled *rane*, *rain*, or *rayne*—all are orthographically and phonetically plausible. However, only specific knowledge will allow us to remember the correct spelling. Likewise, only specific knowledge of the spelling of *which* and *witch* makes it possible to know which is which! The relationship between specific knowledge and general knowledge of the system is reciprocal; that is, each supports the other. Conrad (2008) expressed this idea in observing that "the transfer between reading and spelling occurs in both directions" (p. 876) and that "the orthographic representations established through practice can be used for both reading and spelling" (p. 869).

The purpose of word study, then, is to examine words in order to reveal the logic and consistencies within our written language system and to help students achieve mastery in recognizing, spelling, and defining specific words.

What Is the Basis for Developmental Word Study?

Word study evolves from three decades of research exploring developmental aspects of word knowledge with children and adults (Henderson, 1990; Henderson & Beers, 1980; Templeton, 2011; Templeton & Bear, 1992). This line of research has documented the convergence at certain developmental stages of specific kinds of spelling errors that tend to occur in clusters and reflect students' uncertainty over certain recurring orthographic principles. These "clusters" have been described in terms of (1) errors dealing with the alphabetic match of letters and sounds (FES for *fish*), (2) errors dealing with letter patterns (SNAIK for *snake*) and syllable patterns (POPING for *popping*), and (3) errors dealing with words related in meaning (INVUTATION for *invitation*—a lack of recognition that *invite* provides the clue to the correct spelling). The same cluster types of errors have been observed among students with learning disabilities and dyslexia (Sawyer, Lipa-Wade, Kim, Ritenour, & Knight, 1997; Templeton & Ives, 2007; Treiman, 1985; Worthy & Invernizzi, 1989), students who speak in variant dialects (Cantrell, 1990), and students who are learning to read in different alphabetic languages (Bear, Templeton, Helman, & Baren, 2003; Helman, 2004; Yang, 2004). Longitudinal and cross-grade-level research in developmental spelling has shown that developmental progression (with associated stage-related errors) occurs for all learners of written English in the same direction and varies only in the rate of acquisition (Invernizzi & Hayes, 2004).

Word study also comes from what we have learned about the orthographic structure of written words. Developmental spelling researchers have examined the three layers of English orthography (Figure 1.3) in relation to the historical evolution of English spelling as well as developmental progressions from *alphabet* to *pattern* to *meaning* among learners of English. Each layer builds on the one before. In mature readers and writers, there is interaction among the layers.

FIGURE 1.3 Three Layers of English Orthography

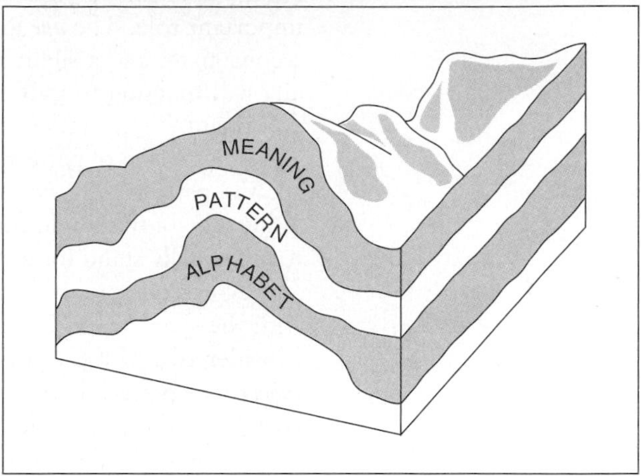

Alphabet

Our spelling system is **alphabetic** because it represents the relationship between letters and sounds. In the word *sat*, each sound is represented by a single letter; we blend the sounds for *s*, *a*, and *t* to read the word *sat*. In the word *chin*, we still hear three sounds, even though there are four letters, because the first two letters, *ch*, function like a single letter, representing a single sound. So we can match letters—sometimes singly, sometimes in pairs—to sounds from left to right and create words. This **alphabetic layer** in English spelling is the first layer of information at work.

The alphabetic layer of English orthography was established during the time of Old English, the language spoken and written by the Anglo-Saxons in England between the Germanic invasions of the sixth century C.E. and the conquest of England by William of Normandy in 1066 (Lehr, 2009). Old English was remarkably consistent in letter–sound correspondence and used the alphabet to systematically represent speech sounds. The long vowels were pronounced close to the way they are in modern Romance languages today, such as Spanish, French, and Italian.

The history of the alphabetic layer reflected in the story of Old English is relevant to teachers today because beginners spell like "little Saxons" as they begin to read and write (Henderson, 1981). Armed with only a rudimentary knowledge of the alphabet and letter sounds, beginning spellers of all backgrounds use their alphabet knowledge quite literally. They rely on the sound embedded in the names of the letters to represent the sounds they are trying to represent (Read, 1971). This strategy works quite well for consonants when the names do, in fact, contain the correct corresponding speech sounds (*Bee, Dee, eF, eS*, and so forth). It works less well for letters that have more than one sound (*C, G*), and it does not work at all for consonants with names that do not contain their corresponding speech sounds (*W*: *double you; Y*: *wie;* and *H*: *aitch*). Short vowel sounds are particularly problematic for novice spellers because there is no single letter that "says" the short vowel sound. As a result, beginning readers choose a letter whose name, when pronounced, is closest to the targeted short vowel sound (Beers & Henderson, 1977; Read, 1975). For example, beginning readers often spell the short *e* sound in *bed* with the letter *a* (BAD) and the short *i* sound in *rip* with the letter *e* (REP).

Pattern

Why don't we spell all words in English "the way they sound"—at the alphabetic level, in other words? If we did, words like *cape, bead,* and *light* would look like *cap, bed,* and *lit*—but these spellings, of course, already represent other words. The **pattern layer** therefore overlies the alphabetic layer. Because there are 42 to 44 sounds in English and only 26 letters in the alphabet, single sounds are sometimes spelled with more than one letter or are affected by other letters that do not stand for any sounds themselves. When we look beyond single letter–sound match-ups and search for **patterns** that guide the groupings of letters, however, we find surprising consistency (Hanna, Hanna, Hodges, & Rudorf, 1966; Venezky, 1999).

Take, for example, the *ape* in *cape;* we say that the final *e* makes the preceding vowel letter, *a,* stand for a long vowel sound. The *e* does not stand for a sound itself, but it plays an important role. The *ape* group of letters therefore follows a pattern: When you have a vowel, a consonant, and a silent *e* in a single syllable, this letter grouping forms a pattern that usually will function to indicate a long vowel. We refer to this pattern as the consonant-vowel-consonant-silent *e* (CVCe) pattern—one of several high-frequency long vowel patterns.

The notion of pattern helps us talk more efficiently about the alphabetic layer as well. In a CVC pattern (*sat, chin, crash*), note that, regardless of how many consonant letters are on either side of the single vowel, the fact that there is but one vowel letter in that pattern means it will usually stand for a short vowel sound.

Words of more than one syllable also follow spelling patterns. These patterns are described with the same V and C symbols and also relate to the vowel sound within each syllable. Let's consider two of the most common syllable patterns. First is the VCCV pattern, such as in *robber* (the pattern is vowel and consonant to the left of the syllable break and consonant and vowel to the right). When we have this pattern, the first vowel is usually short. Second is the VCV syllable pattern, as in *robot, pilot,* and *limit.* This pattern will usually signal that the first vowel is long, but in a few cases, such as *limit,* the first vowel may be short. Overall, knowledge about patterns within single syllables and syllable patterns within words will be of considerable value to students in both their reading and their spelling.

Where did these patterns originate? The simple letter–sound consistency of Old English was overlaid by a massive influx of French words after the Norman conquest in 1066. Because these words entered the existing language through bilingual Anglo-Norman speakers, some of the French pronunciations were adopted, too. Also, because the scribes who wrote the new words were biliterate, they applied French orthographic conventions to the spellings of some English words as well. Old English was thus overlaid with the vocabulary and spelling traditions of the ruling class, the Norman French. This complex interaction of pronunciation change on top of the intermingling of French and English spellings led to a proliferation of different vowel sounds represented by different vowel patterns. The extensive repertoire of vowel patterns today is attributable to this period of history, such as the various pronunciations of the *ea* vowel pair in words like *bread* and *thread, great* and *break, meat* and *clean.* It is uncanny that students moving out of the beginning phase spell like "little Anglo-Normans" when they write *taste* as TAIST or *leave* as LEEVE.

Meaning

The third layer of English orthography is the **meaning layer.** When students learn that groups of letters can represent meaning directly, they will be much less puzzled when encountering unusual spellings. Examples of these units or groups of letters are prefixes, suffixes, and Greek and Latin roots. These units of meaning are called **morphemes**—the smallest units of meaning in a language.

As one example of how meaning functions in the spelling system, think of the prefix *re-;* whether we hear it pronounced "ree" as in *rethink* or "ruh" as in *remove,* its spelling stays the same because it directly represents meaning. Why is *composition* not spelled *compusition* since the second vowel sounds more like *uh* than *o?* Because it is related in meaning to *compose.* The spelling of the second vowel in the related words, *comp<u>o</u>se* and *comp<u>o</u>sition,* stays the same even though the pronunciation of the second syllable is different. Likewise, the letter sequence *photo* in *photograph, photographer,* and *photographic* signals spelling–meaning connections among these words, despite the changes in sounds that the letter *o* represents.

How did Greek roots like *photo* enter into English orthography? The explosion of knowledge and culture during the Renaissance required a new, expanded vocabulary to accommodate the growth in learning that occurred during this time. Greek and Latin were used by educated people throughout Europe and classical roots had the potential to meet this demand for meaning. Greek roots could be combined (for example *autograph* and *autobiography*) and prefixes and suffixes were added to Latin roots (*in<u>spect</u>, <u>spect</u>ator,* and *<u>spect</u>acular*). So, to the orthographic record of English history was added a third layer of meaning that built new vocabulary out of elements that came from classical Greek and Latin.

The spelling–meaning relations inherent in words brought into English during the Renaissance have important implications for vocabulary instruction today as students move through the intermediate grades and beyond (Templeton, 2004). As students explore how spelling visually preserves the meaning relationships among derivationally related words (for example *bomb* and *bombard*, *mental* and *mentality*), vocabulary and spelling instruction become closely related. The seemingly arbitrary spelling of some words—in which silent letters occur or vowel spellings seem irrational—is in reality central to understanding the meanings of related words. For example, the "silent" *c* in *muscle* is "sounded" in the related words *muscular* and *musculature*—all of which come from the Latin *musculus*. Such words, through their spellings, carry their history with them (Venezky, 1999).

Learning the Layers of English Orthography

Organizing the phonics, spelling, and vocabulary curriculum according to historical layers of alphabet, pattern, and meaning provides a systematic guide for instruction and places the types of words to be studied in an evolutionary progression that mirrors the development of the orthographic system itself. Anglo-Saxon words, the oldest words in English, are among the easiest to read and the most familiar. Words like *sun*, *moon*, *day*, and *night* are high-frequency "earthy" words that populate easy reading materials in the primary grades. Anglo-Saxon words survive in high-frequency prepositions, pronouns, conjunctions, and auxiliary verbs (for example *have*, *was*, *does*) although the pronunciation is now quite different. More difficult Norman French words of one and two syllables—words like *chance*, *chamber*, *royal*, *guard*, and *conquer*—appear with great frequency in books suitable for the elementary grades. The less frequent, more academic vocabulary of English—words like *calculate*, *maximum*, *cumulus*, *nucleus*, *hemisphere*, *hydraulic*, and *rhombus*—are of Latin and Greek origin and appear most often in student reading selections in the middle grades and beyond.

Alphabet, pattern, and meaning represent three broad principles of written English and form the layered record of orthographic history. Students' spelling attempts mirror the richness and complexity of this history. As students learn to read and write, they appear to reinvent the system as it was itself invented. As shown in Figure 1.4, beginners invent the spellings of simple words quite phonetically, just as the Anglo-Saxons did in 1000 C.E. As students become independent readers, they add a second layer of complexity by using patterns, much as the Norman French did. Notice the overuse of the silent *e* at the ends of all of Antonie's words, much like Geoffrey Chaucer's! Intermediate and advanced readers invent conventions for joining syllables and units of meaning, as was done during the Renaissance when English incorporated a large Classical Greek and Latin vocabulary (Henderson, 1990; Templeton, Bear, Invernizzi, & Johnston, 2010). As Figure 1.4 shows, both Julian and Elizabeth I struggled with issues relating to consonant doubling where syllables meet.

In this book, we suggest that orthographic knowledge plays a central role in a comprehensive language arts program that links reading and writing. Word knowledge accumulates as students develop orthographic understandings at the alphabetic level, the pattern level, and the meaning level in overarching layers of complexity. Students

FIGURE 1.4 Historical Development of English Orthography: Sound, Pattern, and Meaning from Past to Present

	Anglo-Saxon	**Letter Name–Alphabetic**
Alphabet	WIF (wife) TODAEG (today) HEAFONUM (heaven) **(Lord's Prayer, 1000)**	WIF (wife) TUDAE (today) HAFAN (heaven) **(Tawanda, age 6)**
	Norman French	**Within Word Patterns**
Pattern	YONGE (young) SWETE (sweet) ROOTE (root) CROPPE (crop) **(Chaucer, 1440)**	YUNGE (young) SWETE (sweet) ROOTE (root) CROPPE (crop) **(Antonie, age 8)**
	Renaissance	**Syllables & Meaning**
Meaning	DISSCORD (discord) FOLOWE (follow) MUSSIKE (music) **(Elizabeth I, 1600)**	DISSCORD (discord) FOLOWE (follow) MUSSIC (music) **(Julian, age 14)**

Source: Adapted from "Using Students' Invented Spellings as a Guide for Spelling Instruction That Emphasizes Word Study" by M. Invernizzi, M. Abouzeid, & T. Gill, 1994, *Elementary School Journal, 95*(2), p. 158. Reprinted by permission of The University of Chicago Press.

discover the basic principles of spelling—alphabet, pattern, and meaning—when they read and write purposefully and are also provided with explicit, systematic word study instruction by knowledgeable teachers. Word study should give students the experiences they need to progress through these layers of information.

- For students who are experimenting with the alphabetic match of letters and sounds, teachers can contrast aspects of the writing system that relate directly to the representation of sound. For example, words spelled with short *e* (*bed, leg, net, neck, mess*) are compared with words spelled with short *o* (*hot, rock, top, log, pond*).
- For students experimenting with pattern, teachers can contrast patterns as they relate to vowels. For example, words spelled with *ay* (*play, day, tray, way*) are compared to words spelled with *ai* (*wait, rain, chain, maid*).
- For students experimenting with conventions of syllables, affixes (prefixes and suffixes), and other meaning units, teachers can help students become aware of the stability of these elements across variations. Students will see that words with similar meanings are often spelled the same, despite changes in pronunciation. For example, *admiration* is spelled with an *i* because it comes from the word *admire*.

The Development of Orthographic Knowledge

When we say word study is developmental, we mean that the study of word features must match the level of word knowledge of the learner. Word study is not a one-size-fits-all program of instruction that begins in the same place for all students within a grade level. One unique quality of word study, as we describe it, lies in the critical role of differentiating instruction for different levels of word knowledge.

Research spanning over 30 years has established how students learn the specific *features* of words as well as the *order* in which they learn them. Knowledgeable educators have come to know that word study instruction must match the needs of the child. This construct, called **instructional level,** is a powerful determinant of what may be learned. Simply put, we must teach within each child's zone of understanding (Harre & Moghaddam, 2003; Vygotsky, 1962). To do otherwise results in frustration or boredom and little learning in either case. Just as in learning to play the piano students must work through book A, then book B, and then book C, learning to read and spell is a gradual and cumulative process. Word study begins with finding out what each child already knows and then starting instruction there.

One of the easiest and most informative ways to know what students need to learn is to look at the way they spell words. Students' spellings provide a direct window into how they think the system works. By interpreting what students do when they spell, educators can target a specific student's instructional level and plan word study instruction that this student is conceptually ready to acquire. Furthermore, by applying basic principles of child development, educators have learned how to engage students in learning about word features in a child-centered, developmentally appropriate way.

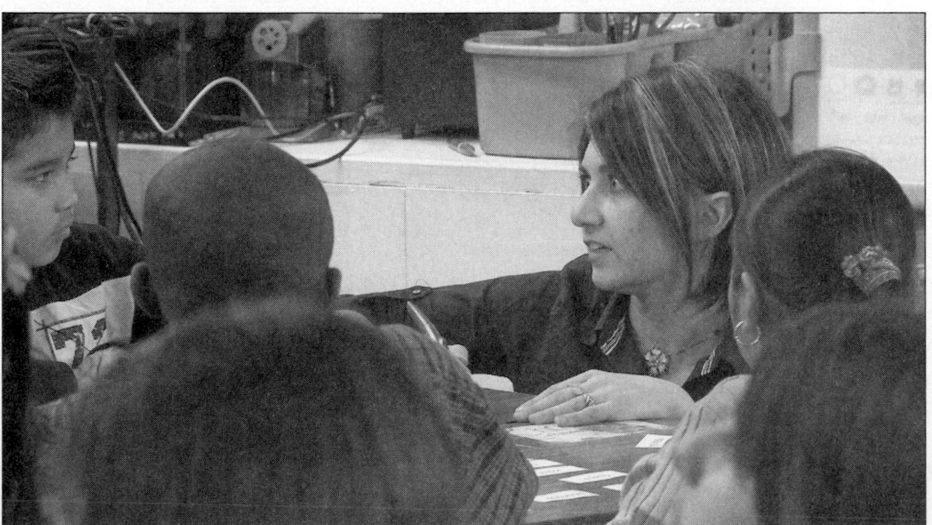

When students are instructed within their own zone of understanding or **zone of proximal development (ZPD)**—studying words *their* way—they are able to build on what they already know, to learn what they need to know next, and to move forward. Zone of proximal development was first described by Vygotsky (1962); the "zone" refers to the span between what a learner knows and is able to do independently and what she is able to do with support and guidance. With direct instruction and ongoing support, word features that were previously omitted or confused become incorporated into an ever-increasing reading and writing vocabulary.

Stages of Spelling Development

As we have described, students move from easier one-to-one correspondences between letters and sounds, to more difficult, abstract relationships between letter patterns and sounds, to even more sophisticated relationships between meaning units as they relate to sound and pattern. Developmental spelling research describes this growth as a continuum or a series of chronologically ordered stages or phases of word knowledge (Ehri, 2005; Nunes & Bryant, 2009; Steffler, 2001; Templeton, 2011). In this book, we use the word *stage* as a metaphor to inform instruction. In reality, as students grow in conceptual knowledge of the three general layers of information and of specific word features, there is often an overlap in the layers and features students understand and use.

Stages are marked by broad, qualitative shifts in the types of spelling errors students make as well as changes in the way they read words. It is not the case that students abandon sound once they move to the use of patterns, or abandon patterns once they move to the use of meaning units or **morphology**. Rather, the names of the stages capture the key understandings that distinguish them among the layers of English orthography and among the levels of students' general knowledge of the orthography (Bryant, Nunes, & Bindman, 1997; Ehri, 1997, 2006; Templeton, 2002, 2003). Over the years, the labels used to describe the five stages of spelling development have changed somewhat to reflect what research has revealed about the nature of developmental word knowledge and to represent most appropriately what occurs at each level.

Because word study is based on students' level of orthographic knowledge, the word study activities presented in this book are arranged by stages of spelling. Knowing each student's stage of spelling will determine your choices of appropriate word study activities. This chapter presents an overview of these stages (see Figure 1.5), which guides you to the instructional chapters. Teachers can use the guidelines discussed in this chapter and the assessment procedures described in Chapter 2 to determine the spelling stages of their students. By conducting regular spelling assessments, perhaps three times a year, teachers can track students' progress and development. An important prerequisite, however, is to know the continuum of orthographic development.

For each stage, students' orthographic knowledge is defined by three functional levels that are useful guides for knowing when to teach what (Invernizzi et al., 1994):

1. What students do correctly—an independent or easy level
2. What students use but confuse—an instructional level at which instruction is most helpful
3. What is absent in students' spelling—a frustration level in which spelling concepts are too difficult

Studying the stages of spelling development has important implications for a scope and sequence of word study. In Vygotskian terms (1962), focus on the student's zone of

FIGURE 1.5 Spelling and Reading Stages, Grade Levels, and Corresponding Instructional Chapters

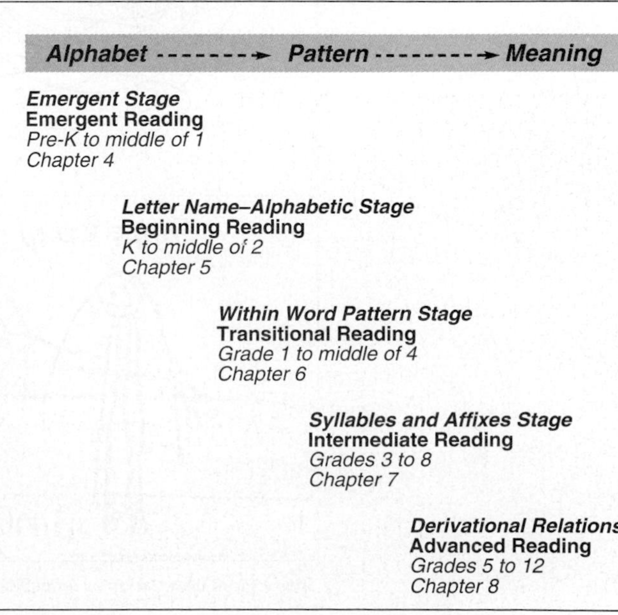

proximal development by determining what the student uses but confuses. In this way, you will learn which orthographic features and patterns to explore, because this is where instruction will most benefit the student.

Emergent Spelling

Emergent spelling encompasses the writing efforts of children who are not yet reading conventionally and in most cases have not been exposed to formal reading instruction. Emergent spellers typically range in age from 2 to 5 years, although anyone not yet reading conventionally is in this stage of development. Most toddlers and preschoolers are emergent spellers, as are most kindergartners and even some first-graders at the beginning of the year. Emergent spelling may range from random marks to legitimate letters that bear a relationship to sound. However, most of the emergent stage is decidedly **prephonetic,** which means there is little if any direct relationship between a character on the page and an individual sound.

Emergent spelling may be divided into a series of steps or landmarks. In the early emergent stage, students may produce large scribbles that are basically drawings. The movement may be circular, and children may tell a story while they draw. At the earliest points in this stage there are no designs that look like letters and the writing is undecipherable from the drawing. As you can see in Figure 1.6(A), Haley has drawn large scribble-like circles and simply called it writing, asserting that it says, "All the birdies." There is little order to the direction in Haley's production; it goes up, down, and around, willy-nilly.

Gradually, and especially when sitting next to other children or adults who write, children begin to use something that looks like script to "tell" about the picture. In the middle of the emergent stage, pretend writing is separate from the picture, although there is still no relationship between letters and sound. Writing may occur in any direction but is generally linear. In Figure 1.6(B), the child labeled his drawing to the left of the picture as "Cowboy."

FIGURE 1.6 Early Emergent Writing

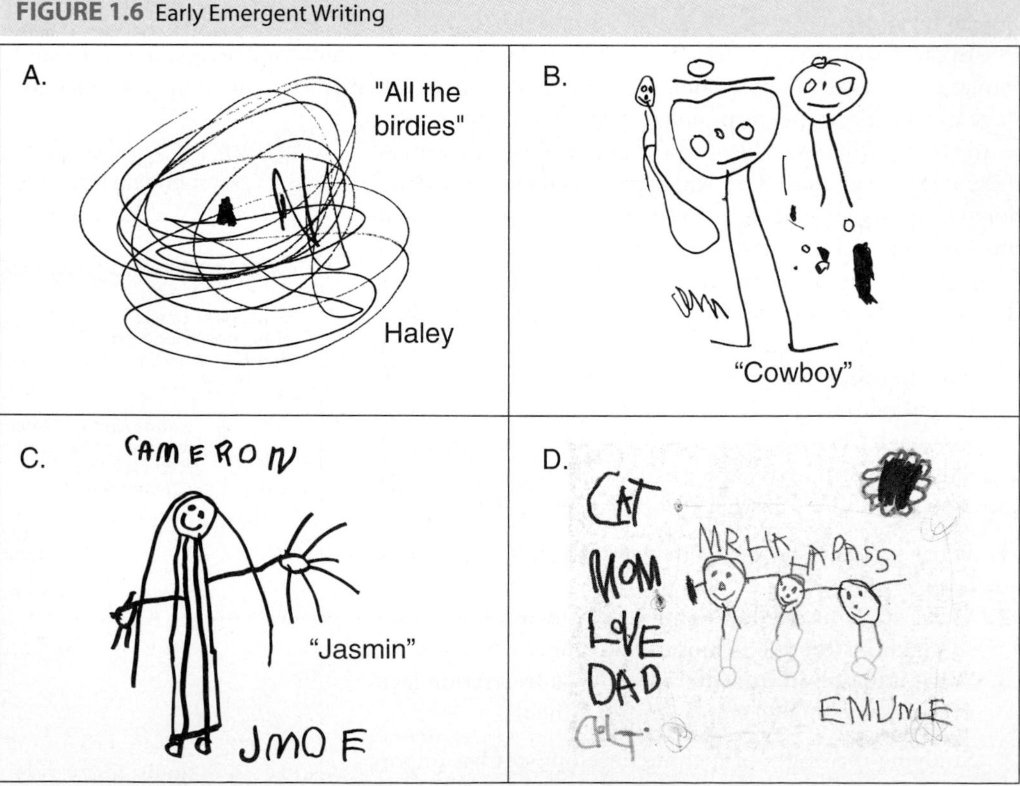

Source: From dissertation by Janet Bloodgood (1996). Adapted with permission.

Throughout the emergent stage, children begin to learn letters, particularly the letters in their own names, and begin to pay attention to the sounds in words. Toward the end of the emergent stage, their writing starts to include the most prominent sounds in a word. The ability to make a few letter–sound matches is evident in Figure 1.6(C), in which *Jasmin* is spelled JMOE. Toward the end of emergent spelling, students start to memorize some words and write them repeatedly, such as the *cat, Mom, love,* and *Dad* in Figure 1.6(D). The movement from this stage to the next stage hinges on learning the **alphabetic principle:** Letters represent sounds in a systematic way, and words can be segmented into sequences of sound from left to right.

Letter Name–Alphabetic Spelling

The **letter name–alphabetic spelling stage** is the second stage in the developmental model and encompasses that period of time during which students are formally taught to read, typically during the kindergarten and first grade years and extending into the middle of second grade. Most letter name–alphabetic spellers are between the ages of 5 and 8 years, although a beginning reader at age 55 also can be a letter name–alphabetic speller (Bear, 1989; Massengill, 2006; Viise, 1996). Early in this stage, "letter name" is students' dominant approach to spelling; that is, they use the *names* of the letters as cues to the sounds they want to represent (Read, 1975). In Ellie's early letter–name alphabetic spelling shown in Figure 1.7, she used the letter *Y* to represent the /w/ sound at the beginning of the word *when,* because the first sound in the pronounced letter name *Y* ("wie") matches the first sound in the word *when.* The letter name for *N* includes the "en" sound to finish off the word *when.* Ellie used *R* and *U* to represent the entire words *are* and *you,* another early letter name strategy.

FIGURE 1.7 Early Letter Name–Alphabetic Spelling: Ellie's Note to Her Sister, Meg—"When Are You Coming?"

We divide this letter name–alphabetic stage into early, middle, and late periods because of the rapid and dramatic growth during this time. As students move through this stage, they learn to segment the sounds or **phonemes** within words and to match the appropriate letters or letter pairs to those sequences.

EARLY LETTER NAME–ALPHABETIC SPELLING. Early in the letter name–alphabetic stage students apply the alphabetic principle primarily to consonants, as Ellie did in Figure 1.7. Often, students spell the first sound and then the last sound of single-syllable words. For example, *when* may be spelled Y or YN. The middle elements of syllables, the vowels, are usually omitted. Typically, only the first sound of a two-letter consonant blend is represented, as in FT for *float.*

Students at this stage find matches between letters and the spoken word by how the sound is made or articulated in the mouth. For example, students may confuse the /b/ and /p/ sounds because they are made with the lips in the same way except for the **voiced** sound produced by the vocal cords vibrating to make the /b/. An early letter name–alphabetic speller might spell the word *pat* as BT.

Early letter name–alphabetic writing often lacks spacing between words, which makes it hard to decipher unless you know something about the writer's message. This type of writing is **semiphonetic** because only some of the sounds are represented.

MIDDLE TO LATE LETTER NAME–ALPHABETIC SPELLING. In her note in Figure 1.8, Kaitlyn shows mastery of most beginning and ending consonants. She spells many high-frequency words correctly, such as *will, love, have,* and *you.* What clearly separates her from the

FIGURE 1.8 Middle to Late Letter Name–Alphabetic Spelling: Kaitlyn's Farewell Note to Her First-Grade Teacher

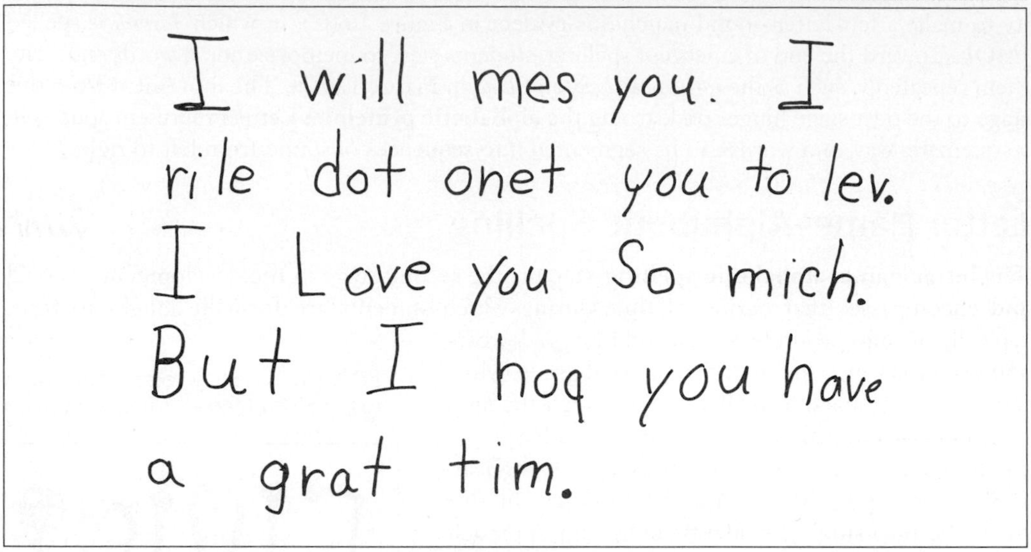

I will mes you. I
rile dot onet you to lev.
I Love you So mich.
But I hoq you have
a grat tim.

early letter name speller is her consistent use of vowels. Long vowels, which "say their name," appear in TIM for *time* and HOP for *hope*, but silent letters are not represented. Short vowels are used but confused, as in *miss* spelled as MES and *much* as MICH.

In the middle letter name–alphabetic stage, students are also learning to segment both sounds in a consonant blend and begin to represent the blends correctly, as in GRAT for *great.* Kaitlyn has also correctly represented the /ch/ digraph in *much.* A **digraph** is two consonant letters that together stand for a single sound. Because middle letter name–alphabetic spellers can segment and represent most of the sound sequences heard within single-syllable words, their spelling is described as **phonetic.**

LATE LETTER NAME–ALPHABETIC SPELLERS. By the end of this stage, late letter name–alphabetic spellers are able to consistently represent most regular short vowel sounds, digraphs, and consonant blends because they have full **phonemic awareness.** The letters *n* and *m* as in *bunk* or *lump* are referred to as **preconsonantal nasals** (nasal sounds that come before a consonant) and are generally omitted by students throughout this stage, as when they spell them as BUK or LUP. Kaitlyn omitted the nasal in her spelling of *don't* as DOT and used an interesting strategy to get the *n* in *want* by spelling it as *one* + *t.*

Henderson (1990) recognized that the correct spelling of the preconsonantal nasal was a reliable and important watershed event that heralds the onset of the next stage of orthographic knowledge. By the end of the stage, students have firmly established the alphabetic layer of English orthography and will now begin to use but confuse silent long vowel markers such as the silent *e*, spelling *rain*, for example, as RANE.

Within Word Pattern Spelling

Students entering the **within word pattern spelling stage** can read and spell many words correctly because of their automatic knowledge of letter sounds and short vowel patterns. This level of orthographic knowledge typically begins as students transition to independent reading toward the end of first grade. It expands throughout the second and third grades, and even into the fourth grade. Although most within word pattern spellers typically range in age from 7 to 10 years, many low-skilled adult readers remain in this stage. Regardless, this period of orthographic development lasts longer than the letter name–alphabetic stage, because the vowel pattern system of English orthography is quite extensive.

The within word pattern stage begins when students can correctly spell most single-syllable short vowel words correctly, as well as consonant blends, digraphs, and preconsonantal nasals. Once these basic phonics features have been mastered, within word pattern spellers can work at a more abstract level than letter name–alphabetic spellers (Snowling, 1994; Zutell, 1994). They move away from the linear, sound-by-sound approach of the letter name–alphabetic spellers and begin to include patterns or chunks of letter sequences. Within word spellers can think about words in more than one dimension; they study words by sound and pattern simultaneously. As the name of this stage suggests, within word pattern spellers take a closer look at vowel patterns within single-syllable words (Henderson, 1990).

FIGURE 1.9 Early Within Word Pattern Spelling: Kim's Soccer Game

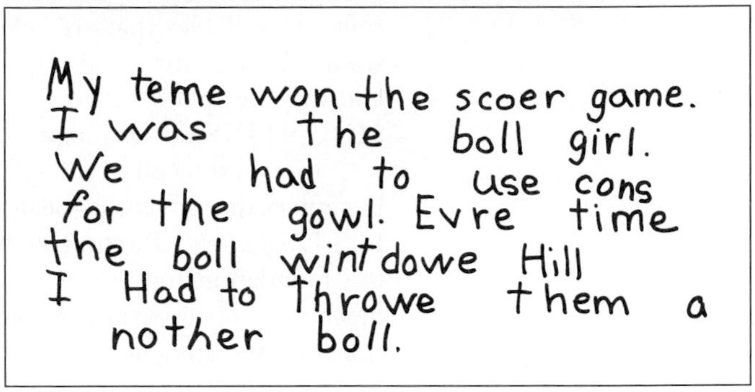

My teme won the scoer game.
I was the boll girl.
We had to use cons
for the gowl. Evre time
the boll wint dowe Hill
I Had to Throwe them a
nother boll.

Kim's writing in Figure 1.9 is that of an early within word pattern speller. She spells many short vowel and high-frequency words correctly, such as *hill, had, them, girl,* and *won.* She also spells some common long vowel patterns correctly in CVCe words like *time* and *game.* Kim hears the long vowel sounds in words like *team, goal,* and *throw,* but she selects incorrect patterns, spelling them as TEME, GOWL, and THROWE. She omits the silent *e* in *cones.* These are good examples of how Kim is using but confusing long vowel patterns.

During the within word pattern stage, students first study the common long vowel patterns (long *o* can be spelled with *o*-consonant-*e* as in *joke, oa* as in *goal,* and *ow* as in *throw*) and then less common patterns such as the VCC pattern in *cold* and *most.* The most difficult patterns are **ambiguous vowels** because the sound is neither long nor short and the same pattern may represent different sounds, such as the *ou* in *mouth, cough, through,* and *tough.* These less common and ambiguous vowels may persist as misspellings into the late within word pattern stage.

Although the focus of the within word pattern stage is on the pattern layer of English orthography, students must also consider the meaning layer to spell and use **homophones,** words such as *bear* and *bare, deer* and *dear,* and *hire* and *higher.* Because these words sound the same but have different spellings and meanings, sound, pattern, and meaning must be considered when spelling. Homophones introduce the spelling–meaning connection explored in the next two stages of spelling development.

Syllables and Affixes Spelling

The **syllables and affixes stage** is typically achieved in the upper elementary and middle school grades, when students are expected to spell many words of more than one syllable. This represents a new point in word study when students consider spelling patterns where syllables meet and meaning units such as affixes (prefixes and suffixes). Students in this fourth stage are most often between 9 and 14 years, though many adults can also be found in this stage.

In Figure 1.10, a fourth-grader in the early syllables and affixes stage has written about his summer vacation. Xavier spelled most one-syllable short and long vowel words correctly (*went, west, drove, last*). Many of his errors are in two-syllable words and fall at the places where syllables and affixes meet. Xavier has used—but confused—the conventions for preserving vowel sounds when adding **inflectional endings** in *stopped* and *hiking,* spelled as STOPED and HIKEING. The principle of doubling the consonant at the **syllable juncture** to keep the vowel short is used in LITTEL for *little,* but is lacking in his spelling of *summer* as SUMER.

FIGURE 1.10 Syllables and Affixes Spelling: Xavier's Account of His Summer Adventures

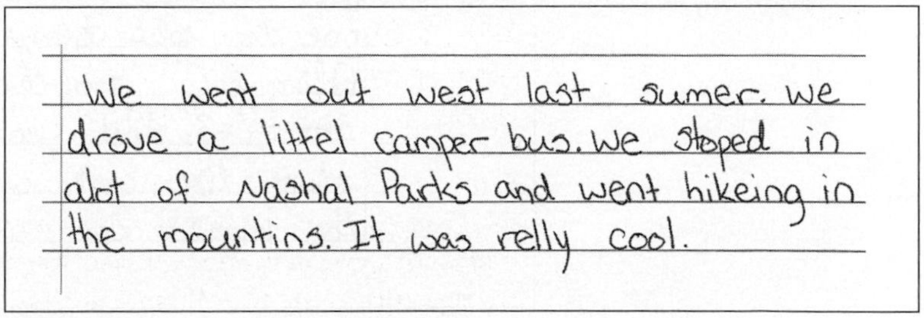

We went out west last sumer. we
drove a littel camper bus. We stoped in
alot of Nashal Parks and went hikeing in
the mountins. It was relly cool.

Syllable juncture patterns include the open first syllable in *hu-mor* (V/CV usually signals a long vowel in the first syllable) and closed first syllable in *sum-mer* and *cam-per* (VC/CV usually signals a short vowel sound in the first syllable). The term **open syllable** refers to syllables that remain "open" because they end with a long vowel sound; the term **closed syllable** refers to syllables that are "closed" by a consonant or consonants, resulting in a short vowel sound. Unaccented final syllables give students difficulty because the vowel sound is not clear and may be spelled different ways, as shown in Xavier's spellings of LITTEL for *little* and MOUNTINS for *mountains.*

Toward the end of the syllables and affixes stage, students explore spelling patterns involving affixes that affect the meanings of words—for example, DESLOYAL for *disloyal* and CAREFULL for *careful.* By studying base words and affixes as meaning units, students are constructing the foundation for the next stage, derivational relations, in which they study the spelling–meaning connections of related words (Templeton, 2004). By studying base words and derivational affixes, students learn more about English spelling as they enrich their vocabularies.

Derivational Relations Spelling

The **derivational relations spelling stage** is the final stage in the developmental model. Although some students may move into the derivational stage as early as grade 4 or 5, most derivational relations spellers are found in middle school, high school, and college. This stage continues throughout adulthood, when individuals continue to read and write according to their interests and specialties. This stage of orthographic knowledge is known as *derivational relations* because this is when students examine how many words may be *derived* from base words and word roots. Students discover that the meanings and spellings of meaningful word parts or morphemes remain constant across different but derivationally related words (Henderson & Templeton, 1986; Henry, 1988; Nunes & Bryant, 2009; Schlagal, 1989; Templeton, 2004). Word study in this stage builds on and expands knowledge of a wide vocabulary, including thousands of words of Greek and Latin origin. We refer to this level as the **generative** level of spelling and vocabulary instruction, because as students explore and learn about the word formation processes or morphology of English they are able to *generate* knowledge of literally thousands of words (Kirk & Gillon, 2009; Nunes & Bryant, 2006; Templeton, Bear, Invernizzi, and Johnston, 2010).

Early derivational relations spellers like sixth-grader Kaitlyn (Figure 1.11) spell most words correctly. However, some of her errors reflect a lack of knowledge about derivations. For example, *favorite* is spelled FAVERITE and does not show its relationship to *favor;* and *different* is spelled DIFFRENT and lacks a connection to *differ.* Her errors on final suffixes, such as the *-sion* in *division* and the *-ent* in *ingredients* are also very typical of students in this stage.

FIGURE 1.11 Derivational Relations Spelling: Kaitlyn's Sixth Grade Math Journal Reflection

Math is not my faverite subject and
I don't always enjoy it. Math homework
is usually ok. It's been mostly easy and
some challaging. The hardest part of math class
for me is devisun because it's hard for
me to split things up into diffrent numbers.
Also big problems are hard for me, like
368 ÷ 7 = ?. Last year the 6th graders did cool
stuff like cook and make recipes with half of
the ingredence.

A frequent type of error at this level is the spelling of the unaccented or **reduced vowel** in derivationally related pairs. When *competition* is derived from the base word *compete*, adding the suffix *-ition* has the effect of reducing the vowel in the second syllable to a schwa sound. The **schwa** sounds like a short *u* with no "oomph" behind it and is often misspelled any number of ways: Students in the earlier part of the derivational relations stage might spell *competition* as COMPUTITION or COMPOTITION or even COMPITITION. A student who misspells *competition* may see the correct spelling more easily by going back to the base, as in *compete*, in which the long vowel gives a clear clue to spelling. Knowing that the word *competition* is derivationally related to the word *compete* will help these students spell the derived form correctly.

Students' spelling errors often have to do with using but confusing issues of consonant doubling in **absorbed (assimilated) prefixes,** the convention of changing the last consonant of a prefix to the first consonant of the base word or word root (for example, *in* + *mobile* = *immobile*). Students may spell *immobile* as IMOBILE or *correspond* as CORESPOND. Other aspects of affixation students negotiate in the derivational relations stage involve changing adjectives to nouns (*brilliant* to *brilliance; adolescent* to *adolescence*). It is not uncommon to find students using but confusing these derivational endings (for example, INDEPENDANCE and DEFENDENT).

The logic inherent in this lifelong stage can be summed up as follows: Words that are related in meaning are often related in spelling as well, despite changes in sound (Templeton, 1979, 1983, 2004). Spelling–meaning connections provide a powerful means for expanding vocabulary.

The Synchrony of Literacy Development

The scope and sequence of word study instruction presented in Chapters 4 through 8 is based on research describing the developmental relationship between spelling and reading behaviors. When teachers conduct word study with students, they are addressing learning needs in all areas of literacy because development in one area relates to development in other areas. This harmony in the timing of development has been described as the **synchrony** of reading, writing, and spelling development (Bear, 1991b; Bear & Templeton, 1998). All three advance in stagelike progressions that share important conceptual dimensions.

Working independently, other researchers have described a remarkably similar progression of reading phases covering the range from prereading to highly skilled, mature reading (Chall, 1983; Ehri, 2005; Frith, 1985; Juel, 1991; Spear-Swerling & Sternberg, 1997). There is converging evidence that reading, writing, and spelling development are integrally related. Figure 1.12 compares other researchers' descriptions of reading development to the spelling stages.

Individuals may vary in their rate of progress through these stages, but most tend to follow the same order of development. The synchrony that is observed makes it possible to bring together reading, writing, and spelling behaviors to assess and plan differentiated instruction that matches students' developmental pace. The following discussion centers on this overall progression with an emphasis on the synchronous behaviors of reading and writing with spelling.

Emergent Readers

During the emergent stage, the child may undertake reading and writing in earnest, but adults will recognize their efforts as more pretend than real. Students often write with scribbles, letterlike forms, or random letters that have no phonetic relationship to the words they confidently believe they are writing. These students may "read" familiar books from memory using the pictures on each page to cue their recitation of the text. Chall (1983) called this stage of development *prereading* because students are not reading in a conventional sense. Emergent

FIGURE 1.12 Spelling and Reading Stages

Alphabet ⟶ **Pattern** ⟶ **Meaning**

Emergent Spelling
Emergent Reader

Prereading *(Chall, 1983)*
Logographic *(Frith, 1985)*
Prealphabetic *(Ehri, 1997)*
Selective Cue *(Juel, 1991)*

Letter Name–Alphabetic Spelling
Beginning Reader

Stage 1: Initial Reading & Decoding *(Chall, 1983)*
Alphabetic *(Frith, 1985)*
Partial-to-Full Alphabetic *(Ehri, 1997)*
Phonetic Cue *(Spear-Swerling & Sternberg, 1997)*

Within Word Pattern Spelling
Transitional Reader

Stage 2: Confirmation & Fluency *(Chall, 1983)*
Orthographic *(Frith, 1985)*
Consolidated Alphabetic *(Ehri, 1997)*
Automatic Word Recognition *(Spear-Swerling & Sternberg, 1997)*

Syllables and Affixes Spelling
Intermediate Reader

Stage 3: Reading to Learn *(Chall, 1983)*
Strategic Reading *(Spear-Swerling & Sternberg, 1997)*

Derivational Relations Spelling
Advanced Reader

Stage 4: Multiple Viewpoints *(Chall, 1983)*
Stage 5: Construction & Reconstruction *(Chall, 1983)*
Proficient Adult Reading *(Spear-Swerling & Sternberg, 1997)*

readers may call out the name of a favorite fast food restaurant when they recognize its logo, but they are not systematic in their use of any particular cue.

During the emergent stage, children lack an understanding of the alphabetic principle or show only the beginning of this understanding. Ehri (1997) designated this as the **prealphabetic phase;** children's use of logos led Frith (1985) to name it the logographic stage. Juel (1991) uses the term selective cue to describe how children select nonalphabetic visual cues like the two *os* in *look* to remember a word.

During the emergent stage, children can become quite attached to selected letters that they notice in their names. On entering preschool, Lee realized that other children's names on their cubbies had some of the same letters that were in her name. Perplexed and somewhat annoyed, she pointed to one of the letters also in her name. "Hey, that's MY letter!" she insisted. Children in the emergent stage also begin to see some letters from their names in environmental print. Walking around the grocery store, Lee pointed to the box of Cheer detergent and said, "Look, Mommy! There's my name!" Lee's special relationship with the letters in her name is a living embodiment of the prealphabetic, logographic, and selective-cue strategy these researchers describe.

Beginning Readers

Understanding the alphabetic nature of our language is a major hurdle for readers and spellers. The child who writes *light* as LT has made a quantum conceptual leap, having grasped that there are systematic matches between sounds and letters that must be made when writing. The early letter name–alphabetic speller has moved from pretend reading to the beginning of real reading, starting to use systematic letter–sound matches to identify and store words in memory.

Just as early attempts to spell words are partial, so too beginning readers initially have limited knowledge of letter sounds as they identify words by phonetic cues. Ehri (1997) describes these readers and writers as being in the **partial alphabetic phase.** The kinds of reading errors students make during this phase offer insights into what they understand about print. Using context as well as partial consonant cues, a child reading about good things to eat might substitute *candy* or even *cookie* for *cake* in the sentence, "The cake was good." Readers in this stage require much support in the form of predictable, memorable texts.

As readers and writers acquire more complete knowledge of letter sounds in the later part of the letter name–alphabetic stage, they will include, but often confuse, vowels in the words they write and read. Students who spell BAD for *bed* may make similar vowel errors when they read *hid* as *had* in "I hid the last cookie." These students resemble Ehri's (1997) **full alphabetic** readers who begin to use the entire letter string to decode and store sight words. Nevertheless, the reading of letter name–alphabetic spellers is often disfluent—that is, choppy and often word by word, unless they have read the passage before or are otherwise familiar with it (Bear, 1992). If you ask such spellers to read silently, the best they can do is to whisper. They need to read aloud to vocalize the letter sounds and usually fingerpoint as they read.

Readers in this stage continue to benefit from repeated readings of predictable texts, but also from the reading of text with many phonetically regular words. These "decodable" texts support the development of decoding strategies and the acquisition of sight words (Juel & Roper-Schneider, 1985; Mesmer, 2006). Chall (1983) referred to this stage as a period of *initial reading and decoding* when students are "glued to print."

Transitional Readers

Transitional readers and spellers move into the within word pattern spelling stage when single letter–sound units are consolidated into patterns or larger chunks and the spellings of most consonant digraphs and blends are internalized. Longitudinal research on spelling development has identified the progressive order in which students appear to use these larger chunks. After mastering basic letter sounds in the **onset** position (initial consonants, consonant blends, and consonant digraphs), students focus on the vowel and what follows (Ganske, 1994; Invernizzi, 1992; Viise, 1996; White, 2005). The spellings of short vowel **rimes**—the vowel sound and what follows in a single syllable—are learned first with consonants and consonant blends in the context of simple **word families** or **phonograms** such as *h-at, ch-at,* or *fl-at.* Phonogram chunks such as *at* come relatively easily in the letter name–alphabetic stage, probably as a result of their frequency in one-syllable words. Other stage models of reading acquisition describe this chunking phenomenon as an orthographic stage in which readers use progressively higher-order units of word structures to read and spell (Chall, 1983; Frith, 1985; Gibson, 1965). Ehri and McCormick (1998) call this the **consolidated alphabetic phase,** in which students' reading is supported by familiarity with frequently occurring letter pattern units. Having solidified the rime/phonogram unit as a chunk, however, students still use but confuse the various long vowel patterns of English (Invernizzi, 1992).

From the beginning to the end of this stage, students move from needing support materials and techniques to being able to pick from various texts and reading them independently—from the Sunday comics to easy chapter books such as *Freckle Juice* and *Superfudge,* both by Judy Blume, and *Ramona the Pest,* by Beverly Cleary. With easy, **independent-level** material, students stop fingerpointing and, for the first time, begin to read silently (Bear, 1982; Henderson, 1990).

Their reading moves from halting word-by-word reading to more expressive phrasal reading, and they can read fluently at their instructional level (Zutell & Rasinski, 1989).

During this stage, students integrate the knowledge and skills acquired in the previous two stages, as Chall (1983) describes by calling this stage one of confirmation and fluency. Advances in word knowledge affect students' writing, too. Their sizable sight word vocabulary allows them to write more quickly and with greater detail. Writing and reading speeds increase significantly from the beginning letter name–alphabetic stage to the transitional within word pattern stage (Bear, 1992; Invernizzi, 1992).

Intermediate and Advanced Readers

The stages of word knowledge that characterize intermediate readers and advanced readers are called *syllables and affixes* and *derivational relations*, as shown in Figure 1.13. These two periods of literacy development are generally accompanied by increased abilities to solve abstract problems and to reflect metacognitively on experiences. Students at these stages have relatively automatic word recognition, leaving their minds free to think as rapidly as they can read. They use reading as a vehicle for learning new information from texts, and their vocabulary grows with their reading experience. Intermediate and advanced readers are also fluent writers. The content of their writing often displays complex analysis and interpretation, reflecting a more sophisticated, content-oriented vocabulary. The degree to which they write at this level, however, often depends on the quality of the writing instruction they receive.

Intermediate students read most texts with good accuracy and speed, both orally and silently. For these students, success in reading and understanding is related to familiarity and experience with the topic being discussed. Through plenty of practice, students in this intermediate stage acquire a repertoire of reading styles that reflects their experience with different genres. They may obsess about reading fantasy or historical fiction and voraciously consume all of the books in a series, such as the Harry Potter books by J. K. Rowling or the His Dark Materials series by Philip Pullman. The same is true for writing. Intermediate students may focus on a particular type of writing: persuasive essays, editorials, poetry, or their own versions of fantasy or realistic fiction.

Advanced readers have a broader experience base that allows them to choose from a variety of reading styles to suit the text and their purposes for reading. They read according to their own interests and needs and seek to integrate their knowledge with the knowledge of others. The same picture is evidenced in their writing. With purpose and practice, derivational relations students develop and master a variety of writing styles.

These two stages of word knowledge correspond roughly to Chall's (1983) *multiple viewpoints* and *construction and reconstruction* stages. Others refer to this period as one during which students learn to become *strategic readers* and ultimately become *proficient adult readers* (Spear-Swerling & Sternberg, 1997). Still others lump these two stages of reading together as the *automatic* stage (Gough & Hillinger, 1980), even though much is still not automatic. For example, syllables and affixes spellers may be uncertain about how to pronounce the name of the main character in *Caddie Woodlawn*, sometimes calling her "Cadie." Derivational relations spellers may have seen the word *segue* in print but never have heard it pronounced, and read it as *seck* or *seck-que*.

Vocabulary and word use play a central role in the connections that intermediate and advanced readers forge between reading and writing. From adolescence on, most of the new vocabulary students learn—except perhaps for slang—comes from reading and reflects new domains of content-specific knowledge that students explore (Beck, McKeown, & Kucan, 2002; Zwiers, 2008). Studying spelling–meaning connections is central to maximizing this vocabulary growth (Nunes & Bryant, 2006; Templeton, 2004).

Research to Support the Synchrony of Spelling and Reading

Significant correlations between spelling and various measures of word recognition and decoding have been reported. For example, Ehri (2000b) reviewed six correlational studies in

FIGURE 1.13 The Synchrony of Literacy Development

Layers of the Orthography

ALPHABET/SOUND

PATTERN

MEANING

Reading and Writing Stages:

Emergent	Beginning	Transitional	Intermediate	Advanced
Pretend read	Read aloud; word-by-word, fingerpoint reading	Approaching fluency, phrasal, some expression in oral reading	Read fluently, with expression. Develop a variety of reading styles. Vocabulary grows with reading experience.	
Pretend write	Word-by-word writing; writing moves from a few words to paragraph in length	Approaching fluency, more organization, several paragraphs	Fluent writing, build expression and voice, experience different writing, styles and genre, writing shows personal problem solving and personal reflection.	

Spelling Stages:

	Emergent→			Letter Name–Alphabetic→			Within Word Pattern→			Syllables and Affixes→			Derivational Relations→		
	Early	*Middle*	*Late*	*Early*	*Middle*	*Late*	*Early*	*Middle*	*Late*	*Early*	*Middle*	*Late*	*Early*	*Middle*	*Late*
Examples of spellings:															
bed	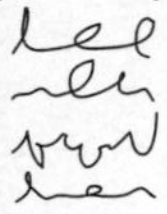	*MST*	*E*	*bd*	*bad*		*bed*								
ship		*TFP*	*S*	*sp*	*sep*	*shep*	*ship*								
float		*SMT*	*F*	*ft*	*fot flot*	*flott*	*flowt floaut*	*flote*	*float*						
train		*FSMP*	*G*	*jn jan*	*tan chran*	*tran*	*teran traen*	*trane*	*train*						
bottle			*B*	*bt*	*botl*	*bodol*		*botel*	*botal*	*bottel*	*bottle*				
cellar			*S*	*slr*	*salr*	*celr*	*seler*	*celer*	*seler*	*celler*	*seller*	*cellar*			
pleasure			*P*	*pjr*	*plasr*	*plager*	*plejer*	*pleser*	*plesher*	*pleser*	*plesher*	*plesour*	*plesure*	*pleasure*	
confident										*confadent*		*confiednet*	*confedent*	*confendent*	*confident*
opposition										*opasishan*		*oppasishion*	*opositian*	*oposision*	*opposition*

which students of various ages (first grade through college) were asked to read and spell words. These studies reported correlations ranging from .68 to .86.

In other studies, spelling measures have accounted for as much as 40 to 60 percent of the variance in oral reading measures (Zutell, 1992; Zutell & Rasinki, 1989). Intervention studies exploring the added value of supplemental spelling instruction have repeatedly found better performance on reading tasks such as oral reading, silent reading comprehension, and other reading-related measures in addition to spelling (Bear & Smith, 2009; Berninger et al., 1998; Goulandris, 1992; Graham, Harris, & Chorzempa, 2002; Joseph & Schisler, 2009; McCandliss, Beck, Sandak, & Perfetti, 2003; Torgesen, 2004; Vellutino, Scanlon, Small, & Fanuele, 2006). Notably, Perfetti (1997) observed that practice at spelling helps reading more than practice at reading helps spelling.

Students' spelling attempts also provide a powerful medium for predicting reading achievement (Cataldo & Ellis, 1988). Morris and Perney (1984) found that first-graders' invented spellings were a better predictor of end-of-grade reading than a standardized reading readiness test. In a two-year study following students from first through third grade, Ellis and Cataldo (1992) indicated spelling to be the most consistent predictor of reading achievement. Sawyer et al. (1997) reported that a child's score on a developmental spelling inventory (Ganske, 1999) was a more powerful predictor of decoding than phonemic awareness tasks such as segmentation. Moreover, the spelling inventory identified the exact word elements students had already mastered and those currently under negotiation. Thus, establishing levels of development in spelling and reading has enormous potential for guiding instruction.

Integrated Phonics, Spelling, and Reading Instruction

Henderson (1981) devised the concept of word study because he was convinced that understanding how children learn to spell words could also provide insight on how they read them. He believed that children's growing word knowledge encompasses information about *phonology* or sound, *syntax* or grammatical relationships and word order, *semantics* or meaning, and *orthography*. He believed that categorizing written words through **word sorts, word hunts,** and **writing sorts** enables learners to sort out the relationships between these different types of information. His work, and the work of his colleagues and students, demonstrated that written word knowledge is developmental and advances progressively and in synchrony in relation to cognitive development, exposure to print, and instruction.

Research by other investigators over the last several years has confirmed that the development of word knowledge follows a developmental continuum. A debate continues, however, regarding the degree to which this development may be described in terms of developmental stages or phases (Chliounaki & Bryant, 2007; Conrad, 2008; Deacon, Conrad, & Pacton, 2008; Sharp, Sinatra, & Reynolds, 2008; Templeton, 2003). Yet there is agreement on the fundamental observation that learning the conventional spellings of words in the English language and the processes that determine conventional spelling occur over the course of the school years. This knowledge evolves from productions first at the alphabetic level, then the pattern level, and eventually includes spelling–meaning or morphological relationships (Berninger, Abbott, Nagy, & Carlisle, 2009; Ehri, 2005; Ehri & McCormick, 2004; Nunes & Bryant, 2009; Reed, 2008; Templeton & Bear, 1992).

As you saw on page 19, Figure 1.13 presents an integrated model of how reading, writing, and spelling progress in synchrony. In parent–teacher conferences, teachers often refer to this figure when they discuss a student's development. They explain to the parent how the child's spelling level corresponds to her reading level, as well as the types of writing we may expect from a child at that particular **developmental level.**

Word study activities in this book are organized around this model. Chapter 2 will help you identify your students by the stages of reading, writing, and spelling. You will then know which chapters contain the activities that are most relevant to their development, as shown in Figure 1.5 on page 9.

As described throughout this chapter, developmental spelling theory provides a window through which we can discern a child's knowledge of how written words work. Specific kinds of spelling errors at particular levels of orthographic knowledge reflect learners' developing understanding of word elements that determines how quickly they can read words and how easily they can write them. Insight into students' conceptual understanding of these word elements will help you better guide and support your students as they learn to read and spell. Figure 1.14 illustrates the theory of developmental word knowledge and shows how word study links reading and writing.

FIGURE 1.14 Word Study: Reading and Writing

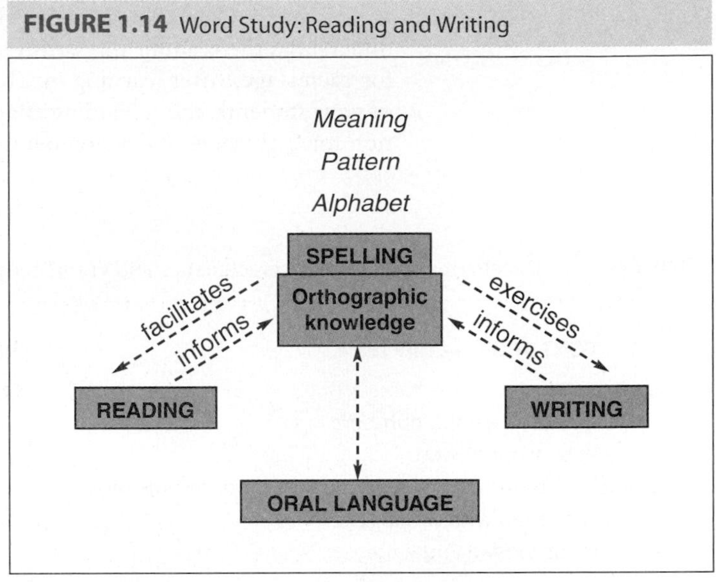

Where Do I Begin Word Study?

Students acquire word knowledge implicitly as they read and write and also through explicit instruction orchestrated by the teacher. It is impossible to know exactly what to teach and when to teach it, however, until we have a living child before us. An informed interpretation of students' reading and writing attempts shows us which words they can read and spell, and of those, which they might learn more about. There is more to pacing instruction than plugging students into a sequence of phonics or spelling features. Instructional *pacing* must be synonymous with instructional *placing*. That is, we must fit our instruction to what our students are using but confusing. How do we know what they are using but confusing? A good deal of what students understand about orthography is revealed in their uncorrected writing. Using the spelling inventories described in the next chapter as a guide, you will be able to place students and pace the content of word study instruction for phonics, spelling, and vocabulary.

Words Their Way

To help students explore and learn about words their way, instruction must be sensitive to two fundamental tenets:

1. Students' learning of phonics, spelling, and vocabulary is based on their developmental or instructional level.
2. Students' learning is based on the way they are naturally inclined to learn: through comparing and contrasting word features and discovering consistencies.

When these two tenets are honored, students learn *their* way—building from what is known about words to what is new. Rather than rote memorization activities designed only to ensure repeated mechanical practice, word study encourages active exploration and examination of word features that are within a student's stage of literacy development. Word study is active, and by making judgments about words and sorting words according to similar features, students construct their own understandings about how the features work. Active, thoughtful practice helps students internalize word features and become automatic in using what they have learned.

Figure 1.15 summarizes the characteristics of each stage of development to help you understand the reading and writing context for the word study instruction that is appropriate for each stage. After learning in Chapter 2 how to assess the developmental word knowledge of your students, the remaining chapters offer more detail about planning word study instruction for each stage of development.

FIGURE 1.15 Developmental Stages, Characteristics, and Word Study Instruction

I. EMERGENT STAGE—CHAPTER 4

Characteristics

1. Scribbles letters and numbers
2. Lacks concept of word
3. Lacks letter–sound correspondence or represents most salient sound with single letters
4. Pretends to read and write

Reading and Writing Activities

1. Read to students and encourage oral language activities
2. Model writing using dictations and charts
3. Encourage pretend reading and writing

Word Study Focus

1. Develop oral language with concept sorts
2. Play with speech sounds to develop phonological awareness
3. Plan activities to learn the alphabet
4. Sort pictures by beginning sound
5. Encourage fingerpoint memory reading of rhymes, dictations, and simple pattern books
6. Encourage invented spelling

II. LETTER NAME–ALPHABETIC STAGE—CHAPTER 5

EARLY LETTER NAME–ALPHABETIC

Characteristics

1. Represents beginning and ending sounds
2. Uses letter names to invent spellings
3. Has rudimentary or functional concept of word
4. Reads word by word in beginning reading materials

Reading and Writing Activities

1. Read to students and encourage oral language activities
2. Secure concept of word by plenty of reading in predictable books, dictations, and simple rhymes
3. Record and reread individual dictations
4. Label pictures and write in journals regularly

Word Study Focus

1. Collect known words for word bank
2. Sort pictures and words by beginning sounds
3. Study word families that share a common vowel
4. Study beginning consonant blends and digraphs
5. Encourage invented spelling

MIDDLE TO LATE LETTER NAME–ALPHABETIC STAGE

Characteristics

1. Correctly spells initial and final consonants and some blends and digraphs
2. Uses letter names to spell vowel sounds
3. Spells phonetically, representing all salient sounds in a one-to-one, linear fashion
4. Omits most silent letters and preconsonantal nasals in spelling (*bop* or *bup* for *bump*)
5. Fingerpoints accurately and can self-correct when off track
6. Reads aloud slowly in a word-by-word manner

Reading and Writing Activities

1. Read to students
2. Encourage invented spellings in independent writing, but hold students accountable for features and words they have studied
3. Collect two- to three-paragraph dictations that are reread regularly
4. Encourage more expansive writing and consider some simple editing procedures for punctuation and high-frequency words

Word Study Focus

1. Sort pictures and words by different short vowel word families
2. Sort pictures and words by short vowel sounds and CVC patterns
3. Continue to examine more difficult consonant blends with pictures and words
4. Study preconsonantal nasals and digraphs at ends of words
5. Sort pictures comparing short and long vowel sounds
6. Collect known words for word bank (up to 200)

III. WITHIN WORD PATTERN STAGE—CHAPTER 6

Characteristics

1. Spells most single-syllable short vowel words correctly
2. Spells most beginning consonant digraphs and two-letter consonant blends
3. Attempts to use silent long vowel markers
4. Reads silently and with more fluency and expression
5. Writes more fluently and in extended fashion
6. Can revise and edit

FIGURE 1.15 Continued

Reading and Writing Activities

1. Continue to read aloud to students
2. Guide silent reading of simple chapter books
3. Write each day, writers' workshops, conferencing, and publication

Word Study Focus

1. Complete daily activities in word study notebook
2. Sort words by long and short vowel sounds and by common long vowel patterns
3. Compare words with *r*-influenced vowels
4. Explore less common vowels, diphthongs (*oi, oy*), and other ambiguous vowels (*ou, au, ow, oo*)
5. Examine triple blends and complex consonant units such as *thr, str, dge, tch, ck*
6. Explore homographs and homophones

IV. SYLLABLES AND AFFIXES—CHAPTER 7

Characteristics

1. Spells most single-syllable words correctly
2. Makes errors at syllable juncture and in unaccented syllables
3. Reads with good fluency and expression
4. Reads faster silently than orally
5. Writes responses that are sophisticated and critical

Reading and Writing Activities

1. Plan read-alouds and literature discussions
2. Include self-selected or assigned silent reading of novels from different genres
3. Begin simple notetaking and outlining skills, and work with adjusting reading rates for different purposes
4. Explore reading and writing styles and genres

Word Study Focus

1. Examine plural endings
2. Study compound words
3. Study consonant doubling and inflectional endings
4. Study open and closed syllables and other syllable juncture issues
5. Explore syllable stress and vowel patterns in the accented syllable, especially ambiguous vowels
6. Focus on unaccented syllables such as *er* and *le*
7. Explore unusual consonant blends and digraphs (*qu, ph, gh, gu*)
8. Study base words and affixes
9. Focus on two-syllable homophones and homographs
10. Join spelling and vocabulary studies; link meaning and spelling with grammar and meaning
11. Explore grammar through word study
12. Sort and study common affixes (prefixes and suffixes)
13. Study stress or accent in two-syllable words

V. DERIVATIONAL RELATIONS—CHAPTER 8

Characteristics

1. Has mastered high-frequency words
2. Makes errors on low-frequency multisyllabic words derived from Latin and Greek
3. Reads with good fluency and expression
4. Reads faster silently than orally
5. Writes responses that are sophisticated and critical

Reading and Writing Activities

1. Include silent reading and writing, exploring various genres
2. Develop study skills, including textbook reading, note-taking, adjusting rates, test taking, report writing, and reference work
3. Focus on literary analysis

Word Study Focus

1. Focus on words that students bring to word study from their reading and writing
2. Join spelling and vocabulary studies; link meaning and spelling with grammar and meaning
3. Examine common and then less common roots, prefixes, and suffixes (e.g., *ion*)
4. Examine vowel and consonant alternations in derivationally related pairs
5. Study Greek and Latin word roots and stems
6. Focus on abstract Latin suffixes (*ence/ance; ible/able; ent/ant*)
7. Learn about absorbed or assimilated prefixes
8. Explore etymology, especially in the content areas
9. Examine content-related foreign borrowings

chapter 2

Getting Started: The Assessment of Orthographic Development

ffective teaching cannot begin until you understand what students already know about words and what they are ready to learn. Likewise, instructional adjustments cannot be made until you evaluate the results of your teaching. This chapter presents an informal assessment process that will enable you to do the following:

1. Informally observe your students' orthographic knowledge
2. Select and administer a qualitative spelling inventory
3. Score and analyze the spelling inventory and identify specific features students need to study
4. Determine students' developmental stage of word knowledge or **instructional level**
5. Group students for differentiated instruction
6. Use supplemental assessments for a wide array of instructional needs
7. Set goals and monitor students' growth in orthographic knowledge over time
8. Interpret the orthographic knowledge of your English learners

Informal Observations to Assess Orthographic Knowledge

There is synchrony in the development of reading, writing, and spelling, and informal observation of students' synchronous literacy behaviors provides rich information for planning instruction. Flexibility of strategy use in reading and writing are related to students' increased levels of orthographic knowledge (Sharp et al., 2008). Because of these interactions, we look to what students do as they write and as they read.

Observe Students' Writing

Teachers have daily opportunities to observe students as they write for a variety of purposes. These observations help to reveal what students understand about words. The following example demonstrates what you might learn about a kindergartner's literacy development. Sarah called this her "first restaurant review." Although it appears to be a menu, she posted it on the wall the way she had seen reviews posted in restaurants.

What Sarah Wrote	How She Read What She Wrote
1. CRS KAM SAS	First course, clam sauce
2. CRS FESH	Second course, fish
3. CRS SAGATE	Third course, spaghetti
4. CRS POSH POPS	Fourth course, Push Pops

This writing tells a lot about Sarah: She sees a practical use for writing and she enjoys displaying her work. She has a good grasp of how to compose a list and she is even beginning to understand menu planning! When we look for what Sarah knows about spelling, we see that she represents many consonant sounds and some digraphs (the /sh/ in *fish* and *push*), but blends are incomplete (as in KAM for *clam*). She has placed a vowel in all but one syllable; however, she is using but confusing short vowels. In spelling *fish* as FESH, Sarah uses a vowel, but she confuses *e* and *i*. In the word *course*, spelled as CRS, the letter *r* represents the /r/ and the vowel sound. According to the sequence of development presented in Chapter 1, Sarah is considered a middle letter name–alphabetic speller who would benefit from instruction emphasizing short vowel sounds and the spelling of blends.

In Figure 2.1, we see a writing sample from Jake, an older student. The writing is readable because many words are spelled correctly and the others are close approximations. When we look for what Jake knows, we see that he has mastered most consonant relationships—even the three-letter blend in SCRAPPED—but not the complex *tch* unit in STICHES. Most long

FIGURE 2.1 Jake's Writing Sample

My Acident

Last year I scrapped my chian. I was shacking and my mom was too. My Dad met us at the docters offises. And I had to have stiches. Then my Dad bout me an ice crem cone. And we went home. I didn't go to school the nexs day. I was to tird.

and short vowels are correctly represented, as in *had, have, went, cone, home,* and *day*. When we look for what Jake uses but confuses, we see that he confuses the *-ck* and *-ke* ending in SHACKING for *shaking*. He inserts an unnecessary extra vowel when he spells *chin* as CHIAN but omits some vowel markers where they are needed, as with CREM for *cream*. He has spelled the *r*-influenced vowel in *tired* as TIRD and the ambiguous vowel in *bought* as BOUT. Based on the vowel errors, Jake is considered a within word pattern speller who would benefit from the study of vowel patterns. We will take another look at Jake's word knowledge when we examine his spelling inventory later in this chapter.

Student writings, especially unedited rough drafts, are a gold mine of information about their orthographic knowledge. Many teachers keep a variety of student writing samples to document students' needs and growth over time. The Qualitative Spelling Checklist in Appendix A and on the website provides a systematic way to analyze your students' writing samples for the specific orthographic features included. Relying entirely on writing samples has drawbacks, however. Some students are anxious about the accuracy of their spelling and will only use words they know how to spell. Others will get help from resources in the room, such as word walls, dictionaries, and the person sitting nearby, and thus their writing may overestimate what they really know. On the other hand, when students concentrate on getting their ideas on paper, they may not pay attention to spelling and make excessive errors. Some students write freely with little concern about accuracy and need to be reminded to use what they know. Knowing your students through daily observations will help you to determine not only their orthographic knowledge but also their habits and dispositions.

Go to PDToolkit for *Words Their Way*, click on the Assessment Tools tab, then type "Qualitative Checklist."

Observe Students' Reading

Important insights into orthographic knowledge can also be made when we observe students' reading. Their reading and spelling are related but not mirror images because the processes differ slightly. In reading, words can be recognized with many types of textual supports, so the ability to read words correctly lies a little ahead of students' spelling accuracy (Bear & Templeton, 2000; Templeton & Bear, 2011). For example, within word pattern spellers, who are also transitional readers, may read many two-syllable words like *shopping* and *bottle* correctly but spell those same words as SHOPING and BOTEL.

Spelling is a conservative measure of what students know about words in general. If students can spell a word, then we know they can read the word. It seldom works the other way around except in the emergent and early letter name stages, in which students might generate spellings they don't know how to read (Invernizzi & Hayes, 2010; Rayner, Foorman, Perfetti, Pesetsky, & Seidenburg, 2001). When students consult reference materials such as a spell checker or dictionary, the spelling task becomes a reading task; we all know the phenomenon of being able to recognize the correct spelling if we just see it.

Like spelling errors, reading errors show us what students are using but confusing when they read and certain errors can be expected of students in different stages. Teachers who understand students' developmental word knowledge will be in a good position to interpret students' reading errors and to make decisions about the appropriate prompt to use (Brown, 2003). A student who substitutes *bunny* for *rabbit* in the sentence "The farmer saw a rabbit" is probably a beginning reader and an early letter name–alphabetic speller. The student uses the picture rather than knowledge about sound–symbol correspondences to generate a logical response. For students at this partial alphabetic or **semiphonetic** stage, drawing attention to the first sound can teach them to use their consonant knowledge. The teacher might point to the first letter and say, "Can that word be *bunny?* It starts with an *r.* What would start with *rrrrr?*"

Further in development, assessments of oral reading substitutions show a different level of word knowledge. A transitional reader who substitutes *growled* for *groaned* in "Jason groaned when he missed the ball" is probably attending to several orthographic features of the word. The student appears to use the initial blend *gr*, the vowel *o*, and the *-ed* ending to come up with a word that fits the meaning of the sentence. Because this student has vowel knowledge, a teacher might direct the student's attention to the *oa* pattern and ask him to try it again.

Our response to reading errors and our expectations for correcting such errors depend on a number of factors, one of which is knowing where students are developmentally. For example, it would be inappropriate to ask students in the early letter name–alphabetic stage to sound out the word *flat* or even to look for a familiar part within the word in the hope that they might use their knowledge of *-at* words by analogy. Emergent and early letter name–alphabetic spellers may be able to use the beginning letters and sounds of words to help but frequently must also turn to context clues to read the words on the page (Adams, 1990; Biemiller, 1970; Johnston, 2000). They simply don't know enough words or patterns to apply analogy. However, students in the latter part of the letter name–alphabetic stage could be expected to sound out *flat* because they know other written words that sound and look the same and they know something about blends and short vowels. Having students read at their instructional levels means that they can read most words correctly and when they encounter unfamiliar words in text, their orthographic knowledge, combined with context, will usually help them read the words. Flanigan et al. (2011) provide comprehensive guidelines for recording and analyzing oral reading errors that include an inventory of orthographic features paralleling those we assess in the spelling development inventories (p. 85).

Although observations made during writing and reading offer some insight into students' development, assessments should also include an informal qualitative spelling inventory. Together, reading, writing, and spelling inventories provide a rich collection of information to understand students' knowledge of orthography. Use the Synchrony of Literacy Development model in Figure 1.13 by reading from top to bottom across the literacy behaviors of reading, spelling, and writing. Look for corroborating evidence to place students' achievement along the developmental continuum. This model helps to generate expectations for student development using an integrated literacy approach. A student's reading behaviors should be in synchrony with his or her range of writing behaviors.

Qualitative Spelling Inventories

Spelling inventories consist of lists of words specially chosen to represent a variety of spelling features at increasing levels of difficulty. The lists are not exhaustive in that they do not test all spelling features; rather, they include orthographic features that are most helpful in identifying a stage and planning instruction. Students take an inventory as they would a spelling test. The results are then analyzed to obtain a general picture of their orthographic development.

The Development of Inventories

The first inventories were developed under the leadership of Edmund Henderson at the University of Virginia. One of the best-known early inventories is the McGuffey Qualitative Inventory of Word Knowledge (Schlagal, 1992), consisting of eight graded lists, as described in more detail later in the chapter. Several of Henderson's students developed simpler inventories that consisted of a continuous list of words sampling a range of spelling features characteristic of each stage (Bear, 1982; Ganske, 1999; Invernizzi, 1992; Invernizzi, Meier, & Juel, 2003; Morris, 1999; Viise, 1994). The same developmental progression has been documented through the use of these inventories with learning disabled students (Invernizzi & Worthy, 1989), students identified as dyslexic (Sawyer, Wade, & Kim, 1999), and functionally literate

Table 2.1 *Words Their Way™* **Spelling Assessments**

SPELLING INVENTORIES	GRADE RANGE	DEVELOPMENTAL RANGE
Primary Spelling Inventory (PSI) (p. 315)	K–3	Emergent to late within word pattern
Elementary Spelling Inventory (ESI) (p. 319)	1–6	Letter name to early derivational relations
Upper-Level Spelling Inventory (USI) (p. 322)	5–12	Within word pattern to derivational relations

for Words Their Way™

Go to PDToolkit for *Words Their Way* and click on the Assessment Tools tab and Assessment Materials. Scroll to the inventories.

adults (Worthy & Viise, 1996). Spelling inventories have also been developed and researched for other alphabetic languages as well (Gill, 1980; Temple, 1978; Yang, 2005).

Although there are multiple spelling checklists, inventories, scoring guides, and classroom organization forms that may be used with a broad range of students in preschool, primary, intermediate, and secondary classrooms (see Table 2.4 later in this chapter for examples), in this chapter we start by focusing on the three inventories shown in Table 2.1: the Primary Spelling Inventory (PSI), the Elementary Spelling Inventory (ESI), and the Upper-Level Spelling Inventory (USI). Each can be found in Appendix A or printed from the website that accompanies this book.

Using Inventories

Spelling inventories are quick and easy to administer and score, and they are reliable and valid measures of what students know about words. Many teachers find these spelling inventories to be the most helpful and easily administered literacy assessments in their repertoires. Use of these spelling inventories requires four basic steps summarized here and discussed in detail in the sections that follow. All lists and forms can be found in the appendixes and on the website.

1. Select a spelling inventory based on grade level and students' achievement levels. Administer the inventory much as you would a traditional spelling test, but do not let students study the words in advance.
2. Analyze students' spellings using a **feature guide.** This analysis will help you identify what orthographic features students know and what they are ready to study as well as their approximate stage.
3. Organize groups using a **classroom composite** form and/or the **spelling-by-stage classroom organization chart.** These will help you plan instruction for developmental groups.
4. Monitor overall progress by using the same inventory up to three times a year. Weekly spelling tests and unit spell checks will also help you assess students' mastery of the orthographic features they study.

SELECTING AN INVENTORY. The best guide to selecting an inventory is the grade level of the students you teach. However, you may find that you need an easier or harder assessment depending on the range of achievement in your classroom. Table 2.1 is a guide to making your selection. Specific directions are provided in Appendix A for each inventory, but the administration is similar for all of them.

Some teachers begin with the same list for all students and after 10 or 20 words, shift to small-group administration of other lists. For example, a second grade teacher may begin with the Primary Spelling Inventory and decide to continue testing a group of students who spelled most of the words correctly using the Elementary Spelling Inventory. A key point to keep in mind is that students must generate a number of errors for you to determine a spelling stage. The three spelling inventories described in this chapter can cover the range of students from primary to high school and college.

Primary Spelling Inventory. The Primary Spelling Inventory (Appendix A, page 315) consists of a list of 26 words that begins with simple CVC words (*fan, pet*) and ends with inflectional endings (*clapping, riding*). It is recommended for kindergarten through early third grade because it assesses features found from the emergent stage through the within word pattern stage. The PSI has been used widely along with the accompanying feature guide and is a reliable scale of developmental word knowledge. The validity of the PSI bas been established using the California Standards Tests (CST) for English Language Arts (ELA) (Sterbinsky, 2007).

For kindergarten or with other emergent readers, you may only need to call out the first five words. In an early first grade classroom, call out at least 15 words so that you sample digraphs and blends; use the entire list of 26 words for late first, second, and third grades. For students who spell more than 20 words correctly, you should use the Elementary Spelling Inventory.

Elementary Spelling Inventory. The Elementary Spelling Inventory (Appendix A, page 319) is a list of 25 increasingly difficult words that begins with *bed* and ends with *opposition.* The ESI surveys a range of features throughout the elementary grades (first through sixth) and can be used to identify students up to the derivational relations stage. If a school or school system wants to use the same inventory throughout the elementary grades to track growth over time, this inventory is a good choice, but we especially recommend this inventory for grades three through five. By third grade, most students can try to spell all 25 words, but be ready to discontinue testing for any students who are visibly frustrated or misspell five in a row. Students who spell more than 20 words correctly should be given the Upper-Level Spelling Inventory.

The words on the ESI present a reliable scale of developmental word knowledge. As with the PSI, the validity of the ESI has also been established using the California Standard Tests (CST) for English Language Arts (ELA) (Sterbinsky, 2007). Moderate-to-strong relationships between scores on the ESI teachers' stage analysis and standardized reading and spelling test scores are shown in Table 2.2.

Table 2.2 **Reliability and Validity of the *Words Their Way*™ Spelling Inventories**

	PSI ($n = 647$)	ESI ($n = 862$)	USI ($n = 442$)	KSI ($n = 473$)
Reliability				
Inter-rater	.76–.95*	.70–.95*	.82–.89*	.89*
Test–retest	.76–.95**	.74–.97**	.82–.89**	.99**
Internal consistency	.93	.92	.91	.91
Validity				
Concurrent	.48–.74*	.38–.69**	.46–.66**	.56–.79**
Predictive	.53–.73*	.43–.71**	.48–.65**	.87**

*p < .01
**p < .001

Upper-Level Spelling Inventory. The Upper-Level Spelling Inventory (Appendix A, page 322) can be used in upper elementary, middle, and high school. The USI is also suitable for assessing the orthographic knowledge of older students at the college and university levels as well as adults in general equivalency diploma (GED) programs. List words were chosen because they help identify, more specifically than the ESI, what students in the syllables and affixes and derivational relations stages are doing in their spelling.

For efficiency, this inventory combines the former Intermediate and Upper-Level inventories into one list of 31 words, arranged in order of difficulty from *switch* to *succession*. The USI is highly reliable; for example, scores of 183 fifth graders on the USI significantly predicted their scores on the Word Analysis subtest of the CST four months later (Sterbinsky, 2007). With normally achieving students, you can administer the entire list, but stop giving the USI to students who have misspelled five of the first eight words—the words that assess spelling in the within word pattern stage. The teacher should use the ESI with these students to identify within word pattern features that need instruction.

PREPARING STUDENTS FOR THE SPELLING INVENTORY. Unlike weekly spelling tests, these inventories are not used for grading purposes and students should not study the particular words either before or after the inventory is administered. Set aside 20 to 30 minutes to administer an inventory. Ask students to number a paper as they would for a traditional spelling test. For younger children, you may want to prepare papers in advance with one or two numbered columns. (Invariably, a few younger students write across the page from left to right.) Very young children should have an alphabet strip on their desks for reference in case they forget how to form a particular letter.

Students must understand the reason for taking the inventory so they will do their best. They may be anxious, so be direct in your explanation:

> "I am going to ask you to spell some words. You have not studied these words and will not be graded on them. Some of the words may be easy and others may be difficult. Do the best you can. Your work will help me understand how you are learning to read and write and how I can help you."

Teachers often tell students that as long as they try their best in spelling the words, they will earn an A for the assignment. Once these things are explained, most students are able to give the spelling a good effort. You can conduct lessons such as described in Figure 2.2 to prepare younger students for the assessment or to validate the use of invented spelling during writing. Lessons like these are designed to show students how to sound out words they are unsure of how to spell. Sometimes it is easier to create a relaxed environment working in small groups, especially with kindergarten and first grade students. Children who are in second grade and older are usually familiar with spelling tests and can take the inventory as a whole class. If any students appear upset and frustrated, you may assess them individually at another time or use samples of their writing to determine an instructional level with the Qualitative Spelling Checklist.

Copying can be a problem when students are working close together. Sometimes students copy because they are accustomed to helping each other with their writing or because they lack confidence in their own spelling. Students in the earlier stages of development often enunciate the sounds in the word orally or spell them aloud, which can give cues to those around them. Some students will try to copy if they feel especially concerned about doing well on a test. Creating a relaxed atmosphere with the explanation suggested above can help overcome some of the stress students feel. Arrange seating to minimize the risk of copying or hand out cover sheets. Some teachers give students manila folders to set up right around their papers to create personal workspaces. There will be many opportunities to collect corroborating information, so there is no reason to be upset if primary students copy. If it is clear that a student has copied, make a note to this effect after collecting the papers and administer the inventory individually at another time.

ADMINISTER THE INVENTORY. When administering a spelling inventory, call the words aloud by pronouncing each word naturally without drawing out the sounds or breaking it into

FIGURE 2.2 Spelling the Best We Can: Lessons to Encourage Students to Spell

To help young students feel more comfortable attempting to spell words, conduct a few lessons either in small groups or with the whole class using the theme "How to Spell the Best We Can." You might do this to prepare young students for taking the inventory or to encourage them to invent spellings during writing. If you want students to produce quality writing, they need to be willing to take risks in their spelling. Hesitant writers who labor over spelling or avoid using words they can't spell lose the reward of expressing themselves.

A Discussion to Encourage Invented Spelling

"We're going to do a lot of writing this year. We will write nearly every day. We will write stories and write about what we see and do. When we want to write a word, and we don't know how to spell it, what might we do?" Student responses usually include:

"Ask the teacher."
"Ask someone."
"Look it up."
"Skip it."

If no one suggests the strategy of listening for sounds, you can tell your students, "Write down all the sounds you hear when you say the word and spell it the best you can."

Spell a Few Words Together

"Who has a word they want to spell?"

Following a lesson on sea life, a student may offer, "Sea turtle."

"That's a great one. Can we keep to the second word, *turtle?*" Assuming they agree, ask students to say the word *turtle.* Encourage them to say it slowly, stretching out the sounds and breaking it into two syllables (*turrr–tlllle*). Model how to listen for the sounds and think about the letters that spell those sounds: "Listen. *T-t-t-turtle.* What's the first sound at the beginning of *turtle?* What letter do we use to spell that /t/ sound?"

"Turtle. *T.*"

On the board or an overhead transparency, write a *T.* Then ask a few students for the next sounds they "hear" and "feel."

Depending on the level of the group, you may generate a range of possible spellings: TL, TRTL, TERDL, and TERTUL.

Finally, talk about what to do if the student can only figure out one or two sounds in a word. "Start with the sound at the beginning. Write the first letter and then draw a line." Here, write *T* with a line.

T__________

Occasionally, a student will be critical about another student's attempt: "That's not the right way to spell it!" Be careful to handle this criticism firmly. You might say, "The important thing is that you have written your word down and you can reread what you have written." Remind students that they are learning; there will be times when they do not know how to spell a word and it is okay to spell it the best they can. Encourage them by saying, "You will see your writing improve the more you write. At the end of the year, you will be surprised by how much more you can write."

Model Spelling Strategies over Time

One lesson to discuss spelling will not suffice, so plan to conduct similar lessons over time. Of course, if you do interactive writing activities in which you "share the pen" (described on page 141 in Chapter 4), you will model the spelling process every time you write together. Keep in mind the following points.

- Have students reread their writing to be sure they can read their words and also to add to or correct their spelling efforts.
- In addition to sounding out words, model other self-help strategies such as looking at posted word lists, using simple beginning dictionaries, or checking word banks.
- Value your students' efforts to spell words, but also push them constantly to listen for additional sounds and to use what they have been taught.

syllables. Leave this for students to do. Say each word twice and use it in a sentence if context will help students know what word is being called. For example, use *cellar* in a sentence to differentiate it from *seller.* Sentences are provided with the word lists in Appendix A. For most words, however, offering sentences is time-consuming and may even be distracting.

Move around the room as you call the words aloud to monitor students' work and observe their behaviors. Look for words you cannot read due to poor handwriting. Without making students feel that something is wrong, it is appropriate to ask them to rewrite the word or to read the letters in the words that cannot be deciphered. Students using cursive whose writing is difficult to read can be asked to print.

Occasionally, if there is time, students are asked to take a second try at spelling words about which they may have been unsure. Through this reexamination, students show their

willingness to reflect on their work. These notations and successive attempts are additional indicators of the depth of students' orthographic knowledge.

KNOW WHEN TO STOP. As you walk around the room or work with a small group, scan students' papers and watch for misspellings and signs of frustration to determine whether to continue with the list. With younger students who tire quickly, you might stop after the first five words if they do not spell any correctly. For older students in groups, who can usually take an entire inventory in about 20 minutes, it is better to err on the side of too many words than too few. Rather than being singled out to stop, some students may prefer to "save face" by attempting every word called out to the group even when working at a **frustration level.** In Figure 2.3, you can see that Jake missed more than half the words on the inventory but continued to make good attempts at words that were clearly too difficult for him. However, his six errors in the first fifteen words identify him as needing work on vowel patterns, and testing could have been discontinued at that point. Sometimes teachers are required to administer the entire list in order to have a complete set of data for each child. In this case, tell students before you start that the words will become difficult but to do the best they can.

Score and Analyze the Spelling Inventories

Once you have administered the inventory, collect the papers and set aside time to score and analyze the results. Scoring the inventories is more than marking words right or wrong. Instead, each word has a number of orthographic "features" that are counted separately. For example, a student who spells *when* as WEN knows the correct short vowel and ending consonant and gets points for knowing those features even though the complete spelling is not correct. The feature guides will help you score each word in this manner. This analysis provides *qualitative* information regarding what students know about specific spelling features and what they are ready to study next.

FIGURE 2.3 Jake's Spelling Inventory

Jake		September 8 9/25	
1. bed		14. caryes	carries
2. ship		15. martched	marched
3. when		16. showers	shower
4. lump		17. bottel	bottle
5. float		18. faver	favor
6. train		19. rippin	ripen
7. place		20. selar	cellar
8. drive		21. pleascher	pleasure
9. brite	bright	22. forchunate	fortunate
10. shoping	shopping	23. confdant	confident
11. spoyle	spoil	24. sivulise	civilize
12. serving		25. opozishun	opposition
13. chooed	chewed		

ESTABLISH A POWER SCORE. Begin by marking the words right or wrong. It is helpful to write the correct spellings beside the misspelled words as was done in the sample of Jake's spelling in Figure 2.3. This step focuses your attention on each word and the parts of the words that were right and wrong (key to the qualitative **feature analysis**). Scoring in this way also makes it easier for other teachers and parents to understand students' papers. Calculate a raw score or *power score* (nine words correct on Jake's paper in Figure 2.3). This will give you a rough estimate of the student's spelling stage. Table 2.3 lists the power scores on the three major *Words Their Way*™ inventories in relation to estimated stages and their breakdown by early, middle, or late stage designations. As can be seen, Jake's power score of 9 on the ESI places him in the late within word pattern stage.

Previous research on grade-level spelling lists such as the McGuffey Spelling Inventory revealed a relationship between the power score (total number of words correct) and the quality of spelling errors that students committed (Henderson, 1990; Morris, Nelson, & Perney, 1986; Schalgal, 1989). The relationship between power scores and specific features is also relevant for the inventories in this book. The ESI, for example, consists of groups of words containing spelling features negotiated in successive spelling stages. In Figure 2.3, for example, you can see that the first five words tap easy spelling patterns such as beginning and ending consonant sounds, short vowels (*bed, ship, when*), consonant digraphs (***sh**ip, **wh**en*), preconsonantal nasals (*lu**m**p*), and consonant blends (***fl**oat*)—all features acquired during the letter name–alphabetic stage. Jake would be considered "independent" at this stage.

His spelling of *float* transitions into the next set of words, all tapping long vowel patterns (*fl**oa**t, tr**ai**n, pl**ace**, dr**ive**,* and *br**igh**t*)—the primary features acquired during the within word pattern stage of spelling development. Although Jake spells the first four long vowel pattern words correctly, he commits his first error in this set on the word *bright* (BRITE). Because Jake spells most of the long vowel pattern words correctly (*float, train, place, drive*) and only one incorrectly (BRITE), we can speculate that he needs only a brief review of long vowel patterns.

The next five words tap late within word and early syllables and affixes features as well as other vowel patterns including diphthongs (*sp**oi**l*), schwa-plus-*r* (*s**er**ving*), and lower-frequency vowel patterns (*ch**ew**ed*) in addition to a variety of inflections (*serv**ing**, chew**ed**, carr**ies**,* and *march**ed***). We see Jake using but confusing these features, getting some of them right (*serving*) and others wrong (SPOYLE, CHOOED, CARYES, MARTCHED), so this set would be considered within Jake's instructional range. However, the final ten words, tapping syllable and affixes features (*shower, bottle, favor, ripen, cellar*) and derivational relations elements (*pleasure, fortunate, confident, civilize,* and *opposition*), were all misspelled. Because Jake got these words wrong, we can determine that the two stages represent his frustration level. In planning instruction for Jake, we analyze the features he uses but confuses on his instructional level—the within word pattern.

SCORE THE FEATURE GUIDES. Feature guides help analyze student errors and confirm the stage designations suggested by the power score. The feature guides that accompany each inventory are included in Appendix A. Jake's spellings are presented as an example in Figure 2.4 (on page 35) to guide you in the scoring process. Use the following steps to complete the feature guide. Alternatively, the assessment application on the website gives you an electronic format for scoring student feature guides.

Go to PDToolkit for *Words Their Way*, click on the Assessment Tools tab, then type "Student Feature Guides."

1. To score by hand, make a copy of the appropriate feature guide for each student and record the date of testing. The spelling features are listed in the second row of the feature guide and follow the developmental sequence observed in research.
2. Look to the right of each word to check off each feature of the word that is represented correctly. For example, because Jake spelled *bed* correctly, there is a check for the beginning consonant, the final consonant, and the short vowel for a total of three feature points. Jake also gets a point for spelling the word correctly recorded in the far right column. For the word *bright*, which he spelled as BRITE, he gets a check for the blend but not for the *igh* spelling pattern. Notice on Jake's feature guide in Figure 2.4 how the vowel patterns he substituted have been written in the space beside the vowel feature to show that Jake is using but confusing these patterns. Every feature in every word is not scored; however, the features sampled are sufficient to identify the stages of spelling.
3. After scoring each word, add the checks in each column and record the total score for that column at the bottom as a ratio of correct responses to total possible features. (Adjust this ratio and the total possible points if you do not have a student spell all of the words.) Notice how Jake scored six out of six under Digraphs, seven out of seven for Blends, and four out of five under Long Vowels. Add the total feature scores across the bottom and the total words spelled correctly. This will give an overall total score that can be used to rank order students and to compare individual growth over time. If you use the

TABLE 2.3 Power Scores and Estimated Stages

INVENTORY	EMERGENT	LETTER NAME			WITHIN WORD PATTERN			SYLLABLES & AFFIXES			DERIVATIONAL RELATIONS		
		E	*M*	*L*	*E*	*M*	*L*	*E*	*M*	*L*	*E*	*M*	*L*
Primary Spelling Inventory	0	0	2	6	8	13	17	22					
Elementary Spelling Inventory		0	2	3	5	7	9	12	15	18	20	22	
Upper-Level Spelling Inventory					2	6	7	9	11	18	21	23	27

assessment application on the website, it will calculate the total feature scores and the overall inventory score for you.

COMMON CONFUSIONS IN SCORING. To ensure consistency in scoring students' spelling, keep the following points in mind. Letter reversals, such as writing *b* as *d*, are not unusual in young spellers, but questions often arise about how to score them. Reversals should be noted, but in the qualitative analysis, reversals should be seen as the letters they were meant to represent and not counted as wrong. These might be considered handwriting errors rather than spelling errors. For example, a **static reversal,** such as the *b* written backward in *bed* or the *p* reversed in *ship*, should be counted as correct. There is space in the boxes of the feature analysis to make note of these reversals. Record what the student did, but add the check to give credit for representing the sound. Letter reversals occur with decreasing frequency through the letter name–alphabetic stage.

Confusions can also arise in scoring **kinetic reversals** when the letters are present but out of order. For example, beginning spellers sometimes spell the familiar consonant sounds and then tag on a vowel at the end (e.g., FNA for *fan*). This can be due to their extending the final consonant sound or to repeating each sound in the word *fan* and extracting the short *a* after having already recorded the FN. In cases like this, give credit for the consonants and the vowels. However, do not give the bonus point for correct spelling.

Early beginning spellers sometimes spell part of the word and then add a random string of letters to make it look longer (e.g., FNWZTY for *fan*). Older students will sometimes add vowel markers where they are not needed (as in FANE for *fan*) or will include two possibilities when in doubt (as in LOOKTED for *looked* or TRAINE for *train*). In these cases, students should get credit for what they represent correctly. In the case of FANE for *fan* or TRAINE for *train*, the student would get credit for the consonants and vowel features but would not get the extra point for spelling the word correctly. In general, give students credit when in doubt and make a note of the strategy they might be using. Such errors offer interesting insights into their developing word knowledge. FANE for *fan* may be incorrect but it represents a more sophisticated attempt than FN.

PDToolkit for Words Their Way™

Go to PDToolkit for *Words Their Way* and click on the Assessment Tools tab and Assessment Application, where you will be able to enter inventory results electronically.

IDENTIFY FEATURES FOR INSTRUCTION. The feature guide should be used to determine a starting place for appropriate instruction. Looking across the feature columns from left to right, *instruction should begin at the point where a student first makes two or more errors on a feature.* Consider the totals along the bottom of Jake's feature guide. Ask yourself what he knows and what he is using but confusing. His scores indicate that he has mastery of Consonants and Short Vowels, so he does not need instruction there. Jake only missed one of the Long Vowels (*igh* in *bright);* this can be considered an acceptable score. However, he missed two of the Other Vowels, so this is the feature that needs attention during instruction.

FIGURE 2.4 Jake's Feature Guide for the Elementary Spelling Inventory

Student's Name *Jake Fisher* Teacher *T. Atkinson* Grade *5* Date *September*

Words Spelled Correctly: *9*/25 *Feature Points:* *43*/62 *Total:* *52*/87 *Spelling Stage:* *Late Within Word Pattern*

SPELLING STAGES →	EMERGENT LATE	LETTER NAME–ALPHABETIC EARLY	MIDDLE		LATE	WITHIN WORD PATTERN EARLY	MIDDLE	LATE	SYLLABLES AND AFFIXES EARLY	MIDDLE	LATE	DERIVATIONAL RELATIONS EARLY	MIDDLE		
Features →	**Consonants Initial**	**Consonants Final**	**Short Vowels**	**Digraphs**	**Blends**	**Common Long Vowels**	**Other Vowels**	**Inflected Endings**	**Syllable Junctures**	**Unaccented Final Syllables**	**Harder Suffixes**	**Bases or Roots**	**Feature Points**	**Words Spelled Correctly**
1. bed	b ✓	d ✓	e ✓										3	1
2. ship		p ✓	i ✓	sh ✓									3	1
3. when			e ✓	wh ✓									2	1
4. lump	l ✓		u ✓		mp ✓								3	1
5. float		t ✓			fl ✓	oa ✓							3	1
6. train		n ✓			tr ✓	ai ✓							3	1
7. place					pl ✓	a-e ✓							2	1
8. drive		v ✓			dr ✓	i-e ✓							3	1
9. bright					br ✓	igh *i-e*							1	
10. shopping			o ✓	sh ✓				pping					2	
11. spoil					sp ✓		oi *oy*						1	
12. serving							er ✓	ving ✓					2	1
13. chewed				ch ✓			ew *oo*	ed ✓					2	
14. carries							ar ✓	ies	rr				1	
15. marched				ch ✓			ar ✓	ed ✓					3	
16. shower				sh ✓			ow ✓			er ✓			3	
17. bottle									tt ✓	le			1	
18. favor									v ✓	or			1	
19. ripen										pen				
20. cellar									ll	ar ✓			1	
21. pleasure											ure	pleas ✓	1	
22. fortunate							or ✓				ate ✓	fortun	2	
23. confident											ent	confid		
24. civilize											ize	civil		
25. opposition											tion	pos		
Totals		7/7	5/5	6/6	7/7	4/5	5/7	3/5	2/5	2/5	1/5	1/5	43	9

DETERMINE A DEVELOPMENTAL STAGE. The continuum of features at the top of the feature guide shows gradations for each developmental level. A student who has learned to spell most of the features relevant to a stage is probably at the end of that stage. Conversely, if a student is beginning to use the key elements of a feature but still has some misspellings from the previous stage, the student is at an early point in that new stage. Tables in each instructional chapter (Chapters 4–8) provide additional information about how to determine where students are within each stage (early, middle, late). These gradations make the assessment of orthographic knowledge more precise than simply an overall stage designation, and this precision will be useful in designing a word study curriculum.

Developmental levels should be circled in the shaded bar across the top that lists the stages. For example, Jake spelled all of the Short Vowels and most Long Vowel features correctly, and he was also spelling some of the words in the Other Vowels category, so Jake is at least in the middle of the within word pattern stage. This has been circled in the top row. These stage designations can be used to complete the Spelling-by-Stage form described later in this chapter that will help you create instructional groups. Knowing the student's developmental stage is a guide to the instructional chapter for word study. In Jake's case, refer to Chapter 6 for activities.

Colleagues who teach together may not always agree on a student's stage. The gradations within each stage clarify the distance between ratings and make it possible to resolve scoring differences between raters. For example, a teacher who may have noted that a student is in the late letter name–alphabetic stage is quite close to a teacher who has determined that the student is an early within word pattern stage speller.

You do not need to make the discrimination within stages too weighty a decision. When it comes to planning instruction, take a step backward to choose word study activities at a slightly easier level than the stage determination may indicate. It is more effective to introduce students to sorting routines when they are working with familiar features and known words; moreover, it is easier to move students up to a higher group than to move them back to a lower group.

Spelling inventory results should be compared to what we know about students' orthographic knowledge from their reading and writing. Referring back to Jake's writing in Figure 2.1, we see similar strengths and weaknesses. His mastery of Short Vowels and his experimentation with Long Vowels and Other Vowels is what we would expect of a student in the middle to late within word pattern stage of spelling. When Jake reads he may confuse words like *through* and *thought*. These errors in word identification will be addressed in word study when he examines the Other Vowels. His spelling inventory, writing sample, and reading errors offer corroborating evidence that we have identified his developmental stage and the features that need attention.

Some students are out of synchrony in their development, such as the one who is notoriously poor at spelling but is a capable reader. When there is a mismatch between reading and spelling development, you can help improve spelling and obtain synchrony by pinpointing the stage of spelling development and then providing instruction that addresses the student's needs. Using these assessments and the developmental model, you can establish specific curricular goals and plan for small-group instruction accordingly.

Sample Practice

The spelling examples of five students in Figure 2.5 can be used to practice analyzing student spellings and determining a developmental stage if you do not have a class of children to assess or if you want to try analyzing a broad spectrum of responses. Make a copy of the ESI feature guide for each student. Determine both the developmental stage of the speller and the place you would start instruction. After you are finished, check the results at the bottom of the page. Were you close in the stages you selected? If you scored the spelling in terms of the three gradations within a stage, you may find that although your assessment may differ by a stage name, it is possible that the difference is just between the latter part of one stage and the early part of the next.

FIGURE 2.5 Examples of Students' Spelling in September

Spelling Words	GREG (Grade 1)	JEAN (Grade 1)	REBA (Grade 2)	ALAN (Grade 3)	MITCH (Grade 3)
bed	bd	bed	bed	bed	bed
ship	sp	sep	ship	ship	ship
when	yn	whan	when	when	when
lump	lp	lop	lump	lump	lump
float	fot	flot	flote	flote	float
train		tran	trane	train	train
place		plac	plais	place	place
drive		driv	drive	drive	drive
bright		brit	brite	brigt	bright
shopping		sopng	shopen	shoping	shopping
spoil			spoal	spoale	spoil
serving			serving	serveing	serving
chewed			chud	choued	chewed
carries			cares	carres	carries
marched			marcd	marched	marched
shower				shouer	shower
bottle				bottel	bottle
favor				favir	favor
ripen				ripen	ripen
cellar				seller	celler
pleasure					pleshur
fortunate					forchenet
confident					confedent
civilize					civilize
opposition					oposition

RESULTS:

Greg Early letter name–alphabetic
Review consonants, study short vowel word families, digraphs, and blends

Jean Middle letter name–alphabetic
Study short vowels

Reba Middle within word pattern
Study long vowel patterns

Alan Late within word pattern
Study long vowels and other vowel patterns

Mitch Early derivational relations
Study roots and unaccented final syllables

Group Students for Instruction

Your spelling analysis as discussed in the previous section will pinpoint students' instructional levels and the features that are ripe for instruction. In most classrooms, there will be a range in students' word knowledge. For example, in a second grade class there will be students in the letter name–alphabetic stage who need to study short vowels and consonant blends whereas others are in the syllables and affixes stage and ready to study two-syllable words. After

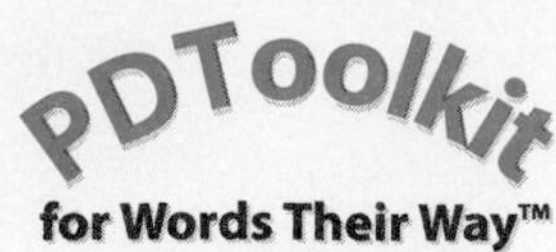

Go to PDToolkit for *Words Their Way,* click on the Videos tab, then type "Professional Development with 2nd Grade Teachers" and listen to a literacy coach talk with teachers about development and instructional plans.

analyzing students individually, you can create a classroom profile by recording the individual assessments on a single chart.

We present two ways to record information about the class: the classroom composite to group students by features and the spelling-by-stage classroom organization chart to group students by developmental levels. These charts show you the instructional groups at a glance. Before we discuss them, however, let's consider the importance of grouping for instruction in word study.

Grouping to Meet Students' Diverse Needs

Grouping for instruction is a challenge for teachers and there are reasons to be suspicious of ability grouping. There may be stigmas associated with grouping and sometimes the lower-ability groups receive inferior instruction (Allington & Cunningham, 2006; Morris, 2008). However, students benefit from differentiated instruction. Experience has shown that when students study a particular orthographic feature, it is best if they are in groups with students who are ready to study the same feature. For example, it is difficult to study long vowel patterns when some of the students in the group still need work on digraphs or blends and may not even be able to read the words that contain the long vowel patterns. When students are taught at their instructional levels in spelling (even when instruction is below grade level), they will make more progress than with materials that are too difficult for them (Morris, Blanton, Blanton, Nowacek, & Perney, 1995).

Many teachers organize three or more small groups by instructional level for reading. Word study can be incorporated in these small-group reading lessons, especially in the lower grades where students work with words under the teacher's supervision and then complete other activities at their desks or workstations. In other classes, especially in the upper grades, word study may occur at a separate time of the day, but still two to four groups are generally needed to meet students' needs.

Groups should be fluid. If students are frustrated or not challenged by the activities, then they should be placed in a different group. If you are using the progress monitoring described later in the chapter there should be many opportunities to refine your groups.

Classroom Composite Chart

Go to PDToolkit for *Words Their Way* and click on the Assessment Tools tab and Assessment Application, which will allow you to create a class composite electronically.

After administering an inventory and completing a feature guide for each student, transfer the individual scores in the last row of the form to a Classroom Composite Chart (Figure 2.6) to get a sense of the group as a whole. If you use the electronic assessment application on the website the Classroom Composite Chart will be created automatically. The following steps will help you do this manually.

1. Begin by stapling each student's spelling test and his or her feature guide together.
2. Sort student papers by the power score (or number of words correct) or by the total feature score and record students' names from top to bottom on the composite form on the basis of this rank order.
3. Next, record scores from the bottom row of each student's feature guide in the row beside his or her name on the composite chart.
4. Highlight cells in which students are making two or more errors on a particular feature and column. For example, a student who spells all but one of the short vowels correctly has an adequate understanding of short vowels and is considered to be at an **independent level.** However, students who misspell two or three of the short vowels need more work on that feature. Highlighted cells indicate a need for sustained instruction on a feature. Do not highlight cells in which students score a zero because this indicates frustration level rather than using but confusing a feature. Focus instead on features in columns to the left of any zero levels that need attention first.
5. Look for instructional groups. If you rank order your students in completing the composite chart, you can find clusters of highlighted cells that can be used to assign students

to developmental stages and word study groups. For example, the fifth grade class composite in Figure 2.6 shows that many students fall under the syllables and affixes stage of development because this is where they are making two or more spelling errors (students 3 through 16). John, Maria R., and Patty, who missed more than two words in vowel patterns, might join this group or might go in a lower group, but should be carefully monitored. A smaller group of students fall under the middle-to-late within word pattern stage (students 17 through 25) and should begin word study by looking at single-syllable word patterns for long vowels and then other vowel patterns. One student (Mike) needs individualized help, beginning with short vowels as well as digraphs and blends. At the upper end of the class composite are two children in the derivational relations stage who should be further assessed with the USI to gather more information about particular features to study.

Spelling-by-Stage Classroom Organization Chart

When you know students' developmental stages, you can also form groups with the Spelling-by-Stage Classroom Organization Chart (see Figure 2.7). Many teachers find this easier to use than a class composite when planning groups. Refer to the stage circled in the shaded bar with the developmental stages on each student's feature guide. Students' names are recorded underneath a spelling stage on the chart, differentiating among those who are early, middle, or late. (To determine early, middle, and late designations, refer to each chapter for further information.) Once the names are entered, begin to look for groups. In each of the classroom examples in Figure 2.7 three or four groups have been circled.

You can see different ways to organize word study instruction in the three classroom profiles presented in Figure 2.7. The first profile is of a first grade class with many emergent spellers. The four circled groups suggested for this class are also the teacher's reading groups.

In the third grade and sixth grade examples, you can see where teachers have used arrows to reconsider the group placement of a few students. Inventory results are considered along with other observations of students' reading or writing. The arrows indicate students who might place slightly higher or lower as the groups take shape. Some of the group placement decisions are based on social and psychological factors related to self-esteem, leadership, and behavior dynamics.

The teacher in the sixth grade classroom could consider running two groups at the upper levels or combining them as one group. The three students in the letter name–alphabetic stage will need special attention because they are significantly behind for sixth-graders. Ideally, these students will have additional instruction with a literacy specialist or in a tutoring program to review and practice activities that are appropriate for the letter name–alphabetic spelling stage.

Factors to Consider When Organizing Groups

The Classroom Composite Chart and the Spelling-by-Stage Classroom Organization Chart help to determine word study groups for instruction. Groups of six to eight make it easier for students to listen to each other and for you to observe how they sort. While students work on different features and with different words, they can still work side by side during many of the follow-up word study routines that occur after the initial small-group discussion. Different schemes for managing class, group, and individual word study are discussed in Chapter 3.

If there is a wide range of achievement to be considered when forming groups, some students may not be placed exactly at their developmental stages. Although you will certainly try to accommodate them, your best spellers are not likely to be negatively affected with grade-level word study activities that might be easy for them. However, your less able spellers will probably suffer if they are working at a frustration level in which they will not make progress.

FIGURE 2.6 Example of Elementary Spelling Inventory Classroom Composite Chart

Teacher ______________ School ______________ Grade ________ Date ________

SPELLING STAGES →	EMERGENT LATE	EARLY	LETTER NAME–ALPHABETIC MIDDLE	LATE	EARLY	WITHIN WORD PATTERN MIDDLE	LATE	EARLY	SYLLABLES AND AFFIXES MIDDLE	LATE	EARLY	DERIVATIONAL RELATIONS MIDDLE		
↓ Students' Names	Consonants	Short Vowels	Digraphs	Blends	Common Long Vowels	Other Vowels	Inflectional Endings	Syllable Junctures	Unaccented Final Syllables	Harder Suffixes	Bases or Roots	Correct Spelling	Total Rank Order
Possible Points	**7**	**5**	**6**	**7**	**5**	**7**	**5**	**5**	**5**	**5**	**5**	**25**	**87**
1. Stephanie	7	5	6	7	5	7	5	5	5	4	3	23	82
2. Andi	7	5	6	7	5	7	5	4	4	3	2	21	76
3. Henry	7	5	6	7	5	7	5	4	3	3	2	20	74
4. Molly	7	5	6	7	5	7	4	4	3	2	2	20	72
5. Jasmine	7	5	6	7	5	7	3	3	3	2	2	19	69
6. Maria H.	7	5	6	7	5	7	3	3	2	3	2	19	69
7. Mike T.	7	5	6	7	5	6	3	3	2	2	1	17	64
8. Lee	7	5	6	7	5	6	2	2	1	2	1	15	59
9. Beth	7	5	6	7	5	7	2	2	1	1	2	14	59
10. Gabriel	7	5	6	7	5	6	2	2	1	1	2	14	58
11. Yamal	7	5	6	7	4	6	2	2	1	1	0	12	53
12. Elizabeth	7	5	6	7	4	6	2	2	1	0	0	11	51
13. John	7	5	6	7	3	5	2	2	1	1	0	10	49
14. Patty	7	5	6	7	3	5	2	2	1	0	0	11	49
15. Maria R.	7	5	6	7	3	4	2	2	1	0	0	11	48
16. Sarah	7	5	6	7	4	4	2	1	0	1	0	9	46
17. Jared	7	5	6	7	2	3	1	1	1	1	0	9	43
18. William	7	5	6	7	3	3	2	0	1	0	0	8	42
19. Steve	7	5	6	7	3	3	2	1	0	0	0	8	42
20. Anna	7	5	6	6	4	3	1	1	0	0	0	8	41
21. Nicole W.	7	4	6	6	3	3	1	1	0	0	0	8	39
22. Robert	7	5	5	7	3	3	2	0	0	0	0	6	38
23. Celia	7	4	6	6	2	3	1	0	0	0	0	7	36
24. Nicole R.	7	4	5	6	2	3	2	0	0	0	0	7	36
25. Jim	7	5	5	6	2	2	1	0	0	0	0	7	35
26. Mike A.	7	3	4	5	1	0	1	0	0	0	0	4	25
Highlight for instruction*		1	1	1	12	13	22	16	15	13	10		

*Highlight students who miss more than 1 on a particular feature; they will benefit from more instruction in that area.

FIGURE 2.7 Examples of Spelling-by-Stage Classroom Organization Charts

First Grade Spelling-by-Stage Classroom Organization Chart

SPELLING STAGES→	Emergent			Letter Name–Alphabetic			Within Word Pattern			Syllables and Affixes			Derivational Relations		
	Early	Middle	Late	Early	Middle	Late	Early	Middle	Late	Early	Middle	Late	Early	Middle	Late
	Gerald	Buck	Tammy	Milo	Brandi										
	Doug	Felicia 7	Kristy	Jennifer	Matthew										
	Danielle	Brad	Brandon	Jerrilynn	5										
	5 Jon	Shaun	J.J.												
	Jennifer	Luis													
	Jona														
	Adam 6														
	Caritha														
	Reyche														

Third Grade Spelling-by-Stage Classroom Chart

SPELLING STAGES→	Emergent			Letter Name–Alphabetic			Within Word Pattern			Syllables and Affixes			Derivational Relations		
	Early	Middle	Late	Early	Middle	Late	Early	Middle	Late	Early	Middle	Late	Early	Middle	Late
							Josh B.	Dominique	Elizabeth	Jamie	Zac				
							Dustin	Ian	Craig	Daniel					
								Emily	Melanie -->	Eric 7					
								Brenner	Melissa	Sare					
									Josh						
								8	Paula -->						
									<-- Erik						
									Josh C.						
									Joshua 8						
									Sarah						
									<-- Cliff						
									Camille						

Sixth Grade Spelling-by-Stage Classroom Organization Chart

SPELLING STAGES→	Emergent			Letter Name–Alphabetic			Within Word Fattern			Syllables and Affixes			Derivational Relations		
	Early	Middle	Late	Early	Middle	Late	Early	Middle	Late	Early	Middle	Late	Early	Middle	Late
				Victoria	Juan 3	Mike		Jon	Elizabeth -->	Nicole	Phong	Sean	Steve	Desiree	
										<-- Arcelia	Ray	Maro	Sheri	Eric	
											Scott	Christi		5 Mary	
										9	Don	Jonna 6	11		
											<-- Rashid	Heather			
												Esther			

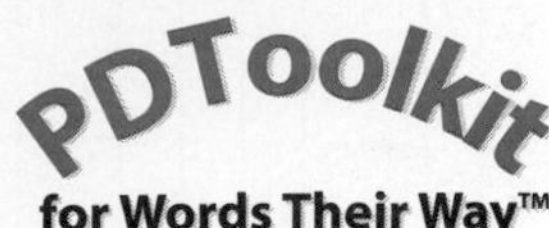

Go to PDToolkit for *Words Their Way,* click on the Videos tab, then type "The Assessment Process" to hear four teachers (K, 1, 2, 5, 7) discuss the results of the spelling inventories and the growth of students over the year.

In many classrooms, there are students at each end of the developmental continuum who, in terms of word study and orthographic development, are outliers. For example, Zac in the third grade class in Figure 2.7 is the only student in the middle syllables and affixes stage and it would be impractical to place him in a group by himself. He has been placed in the closest group for instruction. The teacher can work to accommodate Zac, however, by asking him to work with a different, more difficult set of words sharing the same features that the early syllables and affixes spellers are studying, such as harder words with open and closed syllables. Less advanced students, such as Jon in the sixth grade example in Figure 2.7 for example, may work with partners who can help them read and sort the group's words, such as one-syllable words with long vowel patterns. English language learners also benefit from sorting with partners who can clarify the pronunciations and meanings of the words.

Interpreting feature guides, determining stages, and then creating and monitoring groups involve ongoing assessment, observations, and teacher judgment. It cannot be reduced to a simple formula. Be assured that over time you will gain expertise and satisfaction in being able to accurately identify and meet the instructional needs of your students.

Other Assessments

Go to PDToolkit for *Words Their Way* and click on the Assessment Tools tab and Assessment Materials. Scroll to the PDFs that you would like to print.

There are other assessments and forms that teachers may find useful as supplements or, on occasion, alternatives to the Primary, Elementary, or Upper-Level Spelling Inventories. For example, it is beneficial to have a systematic way of assessing your students' application of their growing word knowledge in their writing. For teachers of emergent learners, it is helpful to have emergent class records and a shorter assessment. Other teachers may want to have grade-level assessments for reporting grade-level achievement. Finally, many teachers prefer to have a single, continuous feature inventory that can be used across all grade levels. The alternate assessments described in this section and listed in Table 2.4 can meet all of these needs. These assessments can be found online and printed out for use in your classroom.

Table 2.4 Alternative Assessments

SPELLING INVENTORIES	GRADE RANGE	DEVELOPMENTAL RANGE
Qualitative Spelling Checklist	K–8	All stages
Emergent Class Record	Pre-K–K	Emergent to letter name–alphabetic
Kindergarten Spelling Inventory (KSI)	Pre-K–K	Emergent to early letter name–alphabetic
McGuffey Spelling Inventory	1–8	All stages
Viise's Word Feature Inventory (WFI)	K–12+	Letter name to derivational relations
Spell Checks	K–12	Early letter name–alphabetic to early derivational relations
Goal-Setting/Progress Monitoring Charts	K–12	Early letter name–alphabetic to early derivational relations

Qualitative Spelling Checklist

When you look at students' writing in their journals or in the first drafts of their reports and stories, you can use the Qualitative Spelling Checklist to verify what types of orthographic features students have mastered, what types of features they are using but confusing, and the degree to which they are applying their spelling knowledge in actual writing. The checklist offers examples of spelling errors students make and matches these errors to stages of spelling. Through a series of 20 questions, you check off the student's progress through the stages. Consider what features are used consistently, often, or not at all. The checklist is set up to be used at three different points during the school year and can serve as a record of progress over time.

Emergent Class Record

The Emergent Class Record is used to assess daily writing or spelling inventory results of pre-K or kindergarten children or other emergent spellers. Making a copy of the PSI feature guide for each student may seem like a waste of paper when many will record only a few initial and final consonants. The Emergent Class Record can be used as an alternative with the entire class represented on one form. It captures the prephonetic writing progression (from random marks to letters) that is missing on the other feature guides and covers the range from emergent through letter name–alphabetic spelling that would be expected in many kindergarten classes at the beginning of the year. Emergent assessments are described in Chapter 4 and available to print from the website.

Kindergarten Spelling Inventory

The Kindergarten Spelling Inventory (KSI) has been used widely with thousands of children as part of Virginia's Phonological Assessment and Literacy Screening (PALS) (Invernizzi, Juel, Swank, & Meier, 2006). Carefully chosen after extensive research, each of five three-phoneme words is scored for the number of phonemes represented in a student's spelling. A feature guide is provided, but unlike the feature guides described so far, students get credit for identifying phonemes and representing those sounds with phonetically logical letters, even if those letters are actually incorrect. As a result, the KSI is a reliable measure of phonemic awareness development, letter–sound correspondences, and the gradual development of conventional spelling (Invernizzi, Justice, Landrum, & Booker, 2005). KSI scores in kindergarten predict children's end-of-year reading standards scores as much as three years later (Invernizzi, Juel, Swank, & Meier, 2008). Table 2.2 on page 29 summarizes the technical adequacy of the KSI, along with the PSI, the ESI, and the USI.

McGuffey Spelling Inventory

The McGuffey Qualitative Inventory of Word Knowledge (QIWK) (Schlagal, 1992) is useful for conducting individual testing and for obtaining grade-level information. The inventory spans grades 1 through 8 with from 20 to 30 words in each level. Instructional spelling levels are found when a student's power score falls above 50 percent but below 90 percent on a graded list (Morris, Blanton, Blanton, & Perney, 1995; Morris et al., 1986). After administering the grade-level list, you will need to give the list from the previous grade level to students who fall below 50 percent and use the list from the next higher grade level for students who score above 90 percent.

The McGuffey Inventory is especially useful when teachers want to report spelling achievement in terms of grade levels. The words in these lists present plenty of opportunities to observe a student's spelling across a variety of features. For example, for the teacher who wishes to obtain a fuller assessment of prefixes, suffixes, and roots, Levels 5 and 6 would offer a larger number of derivational words with prefixes and suffixes to analyze.

Because a feature guide has not been developed for the McGuffey Inventory, you must analyze errors yourself to determine which features and patterns students know and which they are using but confusing.

Viise's Word Feature Inventory

The Word Feature Inventory (WFI) developed by Neva Viise is another qualitative inventory (Viise, 1996; Worthy & Viise, 1996). The WFI is divided into four achievement levels corresponding to four of the five stages of developmental word knowledge: letter name–alphabetic, within word pattern, syllables and affixes, and derivational relations. The words on each level are divided into groups of five, each subgroup probing the student's treatment of a specific word feature such as short vowel, consonant blend, long vowel pattern, and so on. As with the PSI, ESI, and USI, an assessment of students' spellings of the words on this list will indicate the features that have already been mastered and pinpoint the level at which instruction must begin. The WFI is a continuous measure and can be used across all grade levels.

Set Goals and Monitor Student Growth over Time

There is increasing attention to monitoring the progress of students in response to our instruction over time. Brief, ongoing assessment alerts us to the need to adjust the content and pacing of our instruction to meet student needs and to arrange additional instruction for students who may need extra help in meeting long-term goals.

Use a Variety of Assessments to Monitor Growth

Teachers have been monitoring the progress of their students for years through the use of weekly spelling tests that provide immediate feedback regarding students' short-term retention of specific words that have been studied. But few teachers give consideration to long-term retention, the generalization of the spelling patterns students have learned to other words they may not have studied, or the application of students' orthographic word knowledge in their writing. Below, we discuss four ways you can monitor progress in orthographic development in the short term and the long run, in spelling lists, and in writing.

Go to PDToolkit for *Words Their Way,* click on the Videos tab, then type "Professional Development with 2nd Grade Teachers" to listen to teachers describe how they interpret and use their word study assessments.

WEEKLY SPELLING TESTS AND UNIT TESTS. We recommend weekly tests at most grade levels as a way to monitor mastery of the studied features and to send a message to students and parents alike that students are accountable for learning to spell the words they have sorted and worked with in various activities all week. Students will usually be very successful on these weekly tests when they are appropriately placed for instruction. If they are incorrectly spelling more than a few words, it may mean that you need to adjust your instruction. They may either need to spend more time on a feature or are not ready to study the feature and should work on easier patterns first. You may also want to periodically give a review test or unit test—without asking students to study in advance—to test for retention. Simply select a sample of words from previous lessons and call them aloud as you would for any spelling test.

SPELLING INVENTORIES. Students may be given the same spelling inventory three times during the year to assess progress and to determine whether changes need to be made in groups or instructional focus. You can even use the same paper several times if you fold back previous results and ask students to record their latest effort in the next column. In Figure 2.8, you will see Benny's spelling inventory results at three different times during the first grade year recorded on the same form. He has made noticeable progress during the year, moving from early letter name–alphabetic spelling to the within word pattern. However, don't expect such dramatic progress in one year beyond the primary grades. Some students will take two years to master the within word pattern stage. Therefore, teachers in upper elementary, middle school, and high school may find that assessing students only at the beginning and end of the year is sufficient.

Using the same spelling inventory each time is recommended so that you can compare progress on the same words. In Benny's inventory results, we can track the qualitative changes in his spelling over time. Don't be too surprised if students sometimes spell a word correctly one time and later spell the same word incorrectly. Because students are sometimes inventing a spelling for a word that they do not have stored in memory, they may invent it correctly one time and not the next. Or they might master short vowel sound matches but later use but confuse silent vowel markers as Benny did in his spelling of *fan* as FANE.

FIGURE 2.8 Samples of Benny's Spelling Errors at Three Times in First Grade

	September	January	May
1. fan	FNA	fan	fane
2. pet	PT	pat	pet
3. dig	DKG	deg	dig
4. hope	HOP	hop	hope
5. wait	YAT	wat	wayt
6. sled	SD	sed	sled
7. stick	SK	stek	stike
8. shine	HIN	shin	shine

Remember that you should not have students directly study the words on the inventory, although the words may naturally show up in word study activities that you plan. If students study the lists in advance, assessment results will be inflated and you will lose valuable diagnostic information. Using the same inventory more than three times a year may also familiarize students with the words enough to inflate the results. In between administrations of the spelling inventories, use the spell checks described next to monitor progress within and across stages.

SPELL CHECKS. Spell checks are mini-inventories that can be used over shorter periods of time than spelling inventories to monitor students' generalization of specific features over and beyond what they may have demonstrated on weekly spelling tests. Spell checks serve several purposes: (1) to fine-tune placement, (2) as a pretest for a feature or unit of study before instruction to determine what students already know, (3) as a posttest after instruction to determine what students have learned, and (4) as a delayed posttest administered several weeks after instruction to determine what students have retained over time.

Like inventories, spell checks are organized by sequential groups of developmental phonics features and spelling patterns, but each spell check includes more features and more words for each feature within a stage. Because spell checks are more thorough, they can be used to confirm the stage designation and placement determined by the spelling inventories. If students misspell only one or two words in a feature category on the inventory, you may want to do some further assessment using the spell checks. In Jake's case, we might want to gather some more information about his knowledge of less common long vowel patterns because he misspelled *bright*. If Jake were to spell at least eight (out of ten) words correctly on the spell check for less common long vowel patterns, you would have additional assurance that he is ready to move on to the study of *r*-influenced vowels, the next set of features in the scope and sequence toward the latter part of the within word pattern stage.

Spell checks can also be used as pretests to confirm the appropriateness of the next unit of instruction. Jake might be given a pretest on *r*-influenced vowels, in which a score of 30 to 70 percent would suggest that he is using but confusing this feature, making it an area ripe for instruction.

Spell checks are also used to monitor progress and refine the focus and pacing of instruction for individuals or small groups. Figure 2.9 shows Omar's spell checks for short vowels and preconsonantal nasal sounds. The first is a pretest on which he scored 30 percent. The second, using a different form on which he scored 90 percent, was given after he had spent several weeks working on that feature in his word sorts. Several weeks later, his teacher assessed his retention of this feature by administering another form of the same spell check.

Go to PDToolkit for *Words Their Way* and click on the Assessment Tools tab then Assessment Materials. Scroll to the PDFs you would like to print.

FIGURE 2.9 Omar's Spell Checks for Preconsonantal Nasals

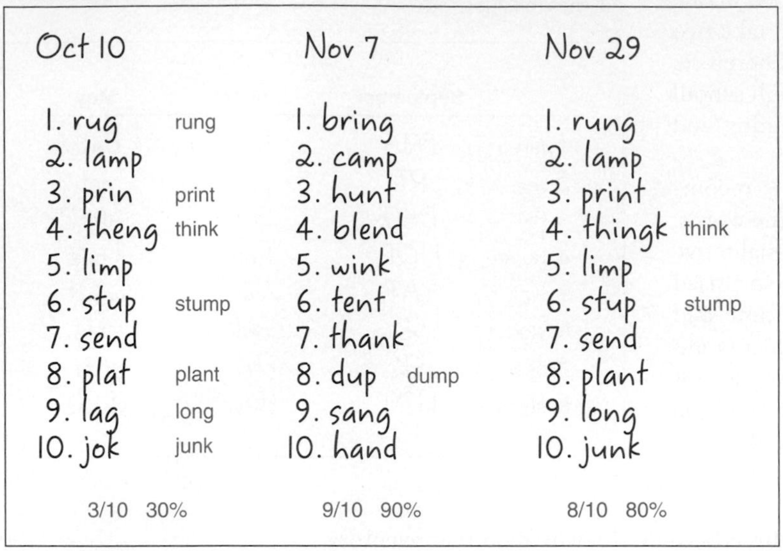

Oct 10		Nov 7		Nov 29	
1. rug	rung	1. bring		1. rung	
2. lamp		2. camp		2. lamp	
3. prin	print	3. hunt		3. print	
4. theng	think	4. blend		4. thingk	think
5. limp		5. wink		5. limp	
6. stup	stump	6. tent		6. stup	stump
7. send		7. thank		7. send	
8. plat	plant	8. dup	dump	8. plant	
9. lag	long	9. sang		9. long	
10. jok	junk	10. hand		10. junk	
3/10 30%		9/10 90%		8/10 80%	

Although Omar misspelled two words in the delayed posttest, eight out of ten words spelled correctly is still a good indication of mastery. His teacher recorded all these scores on the progress monitoring chart for late letter name–alphabetic spellers (Figure 2.10). If Omar had scored less than 80 percent on the delayed posttest, some targeted review would be needed. In his case it appears that the *ump* pattern is a problem and words like *jump* and *stump* might be compared to words like *cup* and *pup* in which there is no preconsonantal nasal.

QUALITATIVE SPELLING CHECKLIST. Teachers can use the qualitative checklist on page 312 to identify progress through the stages of spelling development based on students' use of specific spelling features in their writing. Look carefully at students' uncorrected writing samples and, using the qualitative checklist, note instances of correct or invented spellings for specific features. Collecting a variety of writing samples across the curricular areas is a great way to verify students' application and transfer of their word study instruction.

Develop Expectations for Student Progress

Spelling inventories, spell checks, and qualitative checklists are used to identify students' developmental stages, to determine the features that need instruction, and to form and reform instructional groups. At the same time, teachers need to set long-term goals and objectives for student growth within grade levels. Although it true that all students do not develop at the same rate despite the very best instruction, it is helpful to articulate end-of-grade expectations in terms of stages of development (see Table 2.5). Teachers should know the typical range of development within grade levels so that they can provide additional instruction and intervention for students who lag below that range. Teachers should also know where students must be at the end of the year if they are to succeed in subsequent grades and meet standards in reading and writing.

Table 2.5 Spelling Stage Expectations by Grade Levels

GRADE LEVEL	TYPICAL SPELLING STAGE RANGES WITHIN GRADE	END-OF-YEAR SPELLING STAGE GOAL
K	Emergent—Letter name–alphabetic	Middle letter name–alphabetic
1	Late emergent—Within word pattern	Early within word pattern
2	Late letter name—Early syllables & affixes	Late within word pattern
3	Within word pattern—Syllables & affixes	Early syllables & affixes
4	Within word pattern—Syllables & affixes	Middle syllables & affixes
5	Syllables & affixes—Derivational relations	Late syllables & affixes
6 +	Syllables & affixes—Derivational relations	Derivational relations

Goal-Setting/Progress Monitoring Charts

The stage expectations listed by grade level in Table 2.5 are long-term goals. Setting short-term goals is also important so that you and your students can see what it is that must be learned. Goal-setting charts are useful for establishing short-term goals that will ultimately lead you to the long-term expectations outlined in Table 2.5. Generally speaking, long-term goals reflect your stage expectation whereas short-term goals indicate the features necessary to study and learn to reach the designated long-term stage goal (Flanigan et al., 2011). The goal-setting/progress monitoring charts make explicit what must specifically be learned to reach the ultimate long-term goal.

Go to PDToolkit for *Words Their Way,* click on the Assessment Tools tab, then type "Goal-Setting/Progress Monitoring Charts."

You will find it motivating for your students in the upper elementary grades and beyond to be involved in their own short-term goal setting for progress in spelling. Older students will want to understand exactly what they need to learn to become stronger readers and writers. It may not be important for them to remember the name of the stage they are in or even their numerical power scores, but it's reassuring for them to hear the specifics of what features they already know and what features they need to learn next to move forward.

For older students, we recommend that you meet with them individually to share the results of the inventory or spell checks and set goals together. Then students can keep a record of their own weekly assignments, tests, and spell checks to chart their own progress. This is especially helpful for students who are struggling with reading, writing, and spelling and may feel overwhelmed with all they need to learn. The goal setting/progress monitoring helps students define a set of goals that are within reach—within their zone of proximal development.

Goal-setting/monitoring charts can be used to track student progress and to guide your conferences with specialists, parents, and students from early letter name to late syllables and affixes. (Charts are not provided beyond the early derivational relations stage because mastery continues throughout adulthood.) Use the results from one of the inventories to determine which chart is most appropriate. As shown in Figure 2.10, Omar's teacher has checked off each feature when Omar consistently used the feature correctly. Omar is making good progress; he could identify short vowels in September and spelled them correctly in CVC words, in words with blends and digraphs, and in words with preconsonantal nasals by November. Progress monitoring charts help students define a set of goals that are within reach, within their zone of proximal development.

Changing Groups in Response to Progress

When considering whether a student should be moved to a group studying more advanced features, multiple pieces of evidence should be sought.

1. First, look at the student's spelling samples from the spelling inventories and the spell checks. Consider both the power scores and the feature scores.

FIGURE 2.10 Omar's Goal-Setting/Progress Monitoring Chart

10. Spell short vowels with preconsonantal nasals *Pretest* *3/10 30%*	ing ✓ ang ✓ ong ✓ ung ✓ amp ✓✓ ump XX imp ✓ ant ✓ int ✓ ent ✓ unt ✓ and ✓ end ✓✓ ank ✓ ink ✓X unk ✓
Criterion Met ✓	Spell Check 10 *Form A 11/7 90%* *Form B 11/29 80%*

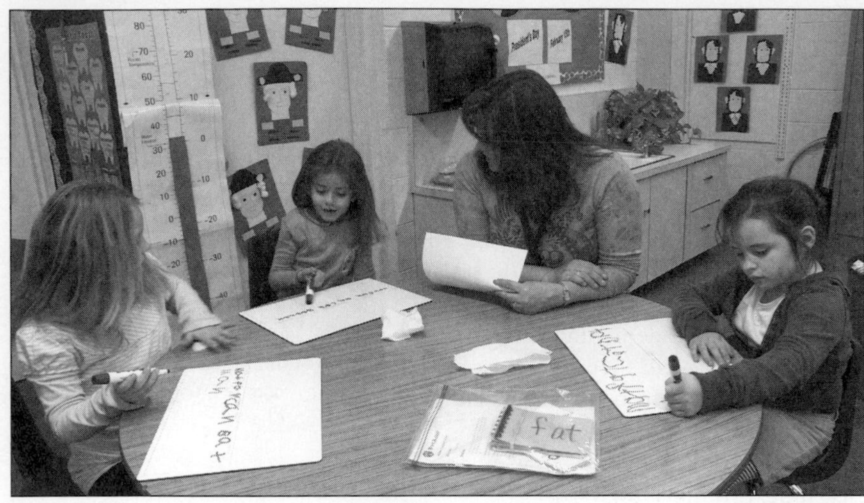

2. Next, look at several uncorrected writing samples using the qualitative checklists. If students are ready to be moved they should be correctly applying the features they have studied in their independent, unedited writing. The goal-setting/progress monitoring charts should confirm these sources of evidence.
3. Finally, look at the big picture, the synchrony of literacy development. Table 2.6 shows the concordance of developmental spelling stages with reading stages and approximate levels of reading achievement. If you want to move a student from a late letter name word study group to an early within word pattern group, look to see if the student can read on at least a first grade level. Orthographic knowledge develops in synchrony with reading and writing. When development is out of synch, this is often an indication that there has been a mismatch of instruction (Invernizzi & Hayes, 2010).

Sharing Progress with Parents and Other Teachers

Spelling inventories, spell checks, and goal-setting/progress monitoring charts are valuable artifacts to add to students' portfolios and use in parent conferences to discuss individual needs and progress. Benny's parents should be able to appreciate the growth he has made over his first grade year, as shown in Figure 2.8. It is reassuring for parents to see their child's earlier invented spellings give way to greater accuracy in writing. Benny has made good progress moving from early letter name–alphabetic spelling to early within word pattern spelling across the year. In looking at the end-of-grade expectations chart in Table 2.5, we see that Benny is right on target.

Unlike some literacy skills, spelling results are very visible, and with a little explanation parents can understand how you are using spelling errors to plan instruction. Parents who are accustomed to seeing their children bring home lists of spelling words taken from thematic units and content materials are sometimes a little dismayed when they see word lists designed for their children's developmental level. In one case, second-graders were given words like *butterfly*, *chrysalis*, and *caterpillar* to memorize for a test each week. When their third grade teacher designed word study based on a spelling inventory, the parents thought the words (*drew*, *flew*, *blow*, *snow*) were too easy and that their children were not being challenged enough. The teacher responded by explaining the spelling inventory and showing parents the results; the students consistently used but confused long *o* and long *u* patterns. The parents then understood and appreciated that the teacher was teaching their children *how to spell* and not just assigning them words to memorize and forget.

In many schools, literacy specialists meet with teachers in grade-level meetings to review assessment results, discuss grouping, and plan for word study instruction. Many schools are using spelling inventory results as universal screening tools to help identify students who need intervention services. Spell checks and goal-setting/progress monitoring charts are then used to gauge how well students respond to classroom instruction and additional interventions. The end-of-grade-level expectations chart in Table 2.5 can be useful in this regard. Often spelling inventories are administered at all grade levels and each year the results are put in students' permanent records and serve as an important part of the school's cumulative literacy assessment. Next year's teachers and specialists have access to these records and can use them to place students and plan instruction.

Table 2.6 Concordance of Spelling and Reading Stages across Grade Levels

GRADE LEVEL	SPELLING STAGE	POWER SCORES			READING PHASE	READING STAGE AND LEVEL		BOOK LEVELS	
		PSI	*ESI*	*USI*				*Letters*	*Numbers*
Pre-K	Early emergent	—	—	—	Pre-alphabetic	Early emergent	Readiness	—	—
K	Early to middle emergent	0	0	N/A	Pre-alphabetic	Early to middle emergent	Readiness	A	1
K / 1st	Middle to late emergent	0	0	N/A	Pre-alphabetic	Middle to late emergent	Readiness	B	2
K / 1st	Late emergent to early letter name	0–6	0–3	N/A	Partial alphabetic	Late emergent to early beginning	PrePrimer 1	C	3
1st	Early to middle letter name–alphabetic	0–2	0–2	N/A	Partial alphabetic	Early to middle beginning	PrePrimer 2	D	4
1st	Middle letter name–alphabetic	2	2	N/A	Partial alphabetic	Middle beginning	PrePrimer 3	E	6 & 8
1st	Late letter name–alphabetic	6	3	N/A	Full alphabetic	Late beginning	Primer	F & G	10 & 12
1st / 2nd	Early within word pattern	8–17	5–9	2–7	Full alphabetic	Early transitional	First	H & I	14 & 16
2nd	Middle within word pattern	13	7	6	Consolidated alphabetic	Middle transitional	Second	J & K	18 & 20
2nd / 3rd	Late within word pattern	17	9	7	Consolidated	Late transitional	Second	L & M	24 & 28
3rd / 4th	Early syllables & affixes	22–26	12–18	9–18	Consolidated	Early intermediate	Third	M, N, O, P	30, 34, 38
4th	Middle syllables & affixes	N/A	15	11	Automatic	Middle intermediate	Fourth	P, Q, R	40
5th	Middle syllables & affixes to early derivational relations	N/A	15–20	11–21	Automatic	Intermediate to advanced	Fifth	S, T, U	50
6th	Middle syllables & affixes to middle derivational relations	N/A	15–22	11–23	Automatic	Intermediate to advanced	Sixth	V & up	60
7th	Early to middle derivational relations	N/A	18–25	15–28	Automatic	Early to middle advanced	Seventh	Y/Z	70
8th	Middle derivational relations	N/A	18–25	18–28	Automatic	Middle advanced to advanced	Eighth +	Z & up	80+

Assessing the Spelling Development of English Learners

for **English Learners**

for Words Their Way™

Go to PDToolkit for *Words Their Way*, click on the Videos tab, then type "The Assessment Process" to hear teachers talk about the spelling errors of English learners.

To obtain a complete understanding of the word knowledge of students who are learning English, explore their literacy knowledge in the primary or first language. A spelling inventory in students' spoken language can indicate their literacy levels in the primary language and more specifically, show which orthographic features they already understand. *Words Their Way™ with English Learners* discusses spelling development, assessment, and instruction for English learners in depth (Helman, Bear, Templeton, Invernizzi, & Johnston, 2012) and also provides inventories in several languages.

Bilingual learners rely on knowledge of their primary language to spell words in a second language (Fashola, Drum, Mayer, & Kang, 1996; Nathenson-Mejia, 1989; Shen & Bear, 2000; Yang, 2005; Zutell & Allan, 1988). For example, Spanish speakers take the 22 sounds of Spanish and match them to the roughly 44 sounds of English, making some logical substitutions along the way. By assessing their orthographic knowledge using the assessments described in this chapter teachers can observe whether students are applying the rules of phonology and orthography from the written form of their primary language to English or vice-versa (Estes & Richards, 2002; Helman, 2004, 2010).

Predictable Spelling Confusions

Because students are expected to learn the orthography of English, it is very useful to administer one of the inventories from Table 2.1 to see what they know and are ready to learn. The responses will also reveal some of the predictable confusions students may make. Bear et al. (2003) have identified which English consonant sounds are problematic for Spanish speakers, who make a variety of substitutions that can be traced to the influence of Spanish on their spelling. Examples include spelling *that* as DAT and *ship* as CHAP because the digraphs /th/ and /sh/ do not exist in Spanish. Because the silent *h* in Spanish can be spelled with a *j*, *hot* may be spelled JAT. Spellers use the nearest equivalents in their attempts to spell English. Short *a*, *e*, *i*, and *u* do not occur in Spanish, and the sound we call short *o* is spelled with the letter *a*, so we can expect many confusions about how to represent these short vowel sounds.

FIGURE 2.11 Rosa's Spelling

1. bed	bed
2. ship	shep
3. when	wan
4. lump	lamp
5. float	flowt
6. train	trayn
7. place	pleays
8. drive	kids
9. bright	brayt
10. shopping	shapen
11. spoil	spoyo
12. serving	sorven
13. chewed	shod
14. carries	cares
15. marched	marsh
16. shower	showar
17. cattle	cadoto
18. favor	fayvr
19. ripen	raypn
20. cellar	sallar

The spelling sample of a second-grader in Figure 2.11 shows how a student's spoken Spanish can affect her English spelling. Several of Rosa's attempts follow the logical substitutions that are seen from English-speaking students in the letter name–alphabetic stage—that is, SHEP for *ship* and WAN for *when*. Other errors make good sense in relation to patterns of Spanish. For example, given the lack of short *u* in Spanish, her substitution of LAMP for *lump* is understandable. In a reversal, she replaces the *ch* in *chewed* with *sh* (SHOD). Rosa is also trying to find a spelling for the long *i*, shown by *ay* in three of her spellings. The long *i* is really two vowels ("eye-ee"—a diphthong), with the *y*, pronounced as a long *e* in Spanish, used to spell the second half of the combination ("ee"). In *spoil* as SPOYO, Rosa seems to be using the /y/ sound as in *yes* to help spell *oil.*

The Influences of Students' Primary Languages

As Rosa's spelling illustrates, English learners' invented spellings are logical and interesting. As you listen to the speech and oral reading of English language learners, notice the influences of their first languages on pronunciation and look for spelling errors that may be explained by a primary language or dialect. For example, one teacher learned about the influence of different East Indian dialects when she noticed confusions of /p/ for *f* and /sh/ for *s*. Another teacher noted her Korean students consistently confusing *r* for *l* and vice-versa. In spoken Korean, /r/ and /l/ are not different sounds and are represented with the same letter in Hangul, the Korean writing system (Yang, 2005).

Through observing English learners' native languages, teachers can better understand their literacy development in English. Look in each of the instructional chapters for specific guidance on the interrelatedness of students' home languages and English.

Conclusion

Looking at a child's spelling gives us a window into that child's word knowledge, the information he or she uses to read and write words. The word *assessment* comes from the Latin word *assidere*—"to sit beside." Spend some time sitting beside your students and looking through the window that their spellings provide. Learn to assess what they know about how words work by administering one of the spelling inventories provided in this book or on the website for this book.

You may refer to the developmental sequence inside the front cover, as well as the detailed sequences of word study in the instructional chapters for this book. You will also find specific types of features to explore in word study activities throughout the instructional chapters. Remember that the inventories only sample the most common features. At each stage there is a considerable body of knowledge that students should master before they move on to the next stage.

Keep your fingers on the pulse of development by monitoring progress over time using the spell checks and the goal-setting/progress monitoring tools discussed in this chapter and printable from the website. And always keep in mind the synchrony of literacy development.

MEDIA GUIDE ***Getting Started: The Assessment of Orthographic Knowledge***

SECTION	PAGE	GO TO PDTOOLKIT FOR *WORDS THEIR WAY*™
Videos		
Group Students for Instruction	38	Click on the Videos tab, then type "Professional Development with 2nd Grade Teachers."
Factors to Consider When Organizing Groups	42	Click on the Videos tab, then type "The Assessment Process."
Use a Variety of Assessments to Monitor Growth	44	Click on the Videos tab, then type "Professional Development with 2nd Grade Teachers."
Assessing the Spelling Development of English Learners	50	Click on the Videos tab, then type "The Assessment Process."
Assessment Tools		
Observe Students' Writing	26	Click on the Assessment Tools tab, then type "Qualitative Checklist."
The Development of Inventories	28	Click on the Assessment Tools tab, click on Assessment Materials, and scroll to the inventories.
Score and Analyze the Spelling Inventories	33	Click on the Assessment Tools tab, then type "Student Features Guides."
Score and Analyze the Spelling Inventories	34	Click on the Assessment Tools tab, then type "Student Features Guides."
Factors to Consider When Organizing Groups	42	Click on the Assessment Tools tab, and then select Assessment Materials. Scroll to the PDFs that you would like to print.
Use a Variety of Assessments to Monitor Growth	44	Click on the Assessment Tools tab, and then select Assessment Materials. Scroll to the PDFs that you would like to print.
Goal-Setting/Progress Monitoring Charts	47	Click on the Assessment Tools tab, then type "Goal-Setting/Progress Monitoring Charts."

chapter 3

Organizing for Word Study: Principles and Practices

Once you have ascertained the developmental level of each of your students as described in Chapter 2, you are ready to organize your classroom for word study. In this chapter we will describe the basic activities for word study, how to create and organize materials, and how to set up weekly routines that will facilitate effective and efficient word study. We will address related issues such as expectations for editing and grading before ending with a review of guiding principles of word study and a table of resources. To illustrate the details that make up this chapter, let us first visit the classroom of Mrs. Zimmerman as she introduces a group of her students to *r*-influenced vowels.

Earlier in the year, Mrs. Zimmerman assessed her third-graders and divided them into three instructional groups for word study. On Mondays she meets with each group for about 15 to 20 minutes to go over the words, model the word sort for the week, and help her students make discoveries about the particular group of words she has chosen. After getting her students started on independent reading and journal writing, Mrs. Zimmerman calls her first group together on the carpet. She has a set of words written on cards that she lays out for everyone to see. She begins by saying, "Let's read over these words to be sure everyone knows how to read them and what they mean." After discussing *mare,* which Julio defines as a "mother horse," she picks up *bear* and *bare* and reads both. "Who remembers what words like these are called? That's right, they are homophones." She holds up *bear* and asks who knows what it means.

"It's an animal and I saw one last summer when we went camping," offers Shannon.

"What about this *bare?*" asks Mrs. Zimmerman, as she holds up the word. Rayshad explains that it means "having no hair, like being bald."

"Right," says Mrs. Zimmerman, "or you might go barefooted without shoes. There is another set of homophones here. Can anyone find them?" Mason finds *hair* and *hare* and again they talk about the meaning of each. They recall that they have heard the word *hare* in the story *The Hare and the Tortoise,* which they read during a unit on fables.

Mrs. Zimmerman continues the lesson by saying, "We are going to begin today by thinking about the sounds in these words. I am going to put *cart* here as one of our key words and *care* over here for the other. Listen to the middle sounds in each: *caaarrrt, caaarrrre.*" Then she picks up and reads the word *farm.* "Does the middle sound like *cart* or *care?* Right! We will put it under *cart.* How about *chair?* Does the middle sound like *cart* or *care?*" After sorting several more words, Mrs. Zimmerman hands out the rest of the word cards and calls on students to read and sort each word by its vowel sound. After sorting all the words, the students read down each column to verify that the words all have the same sound in the middle. The final sort by sound looks like Figure 3.1.

FIGURE 3.1 Mrs. Zimmerman's Sound Sort

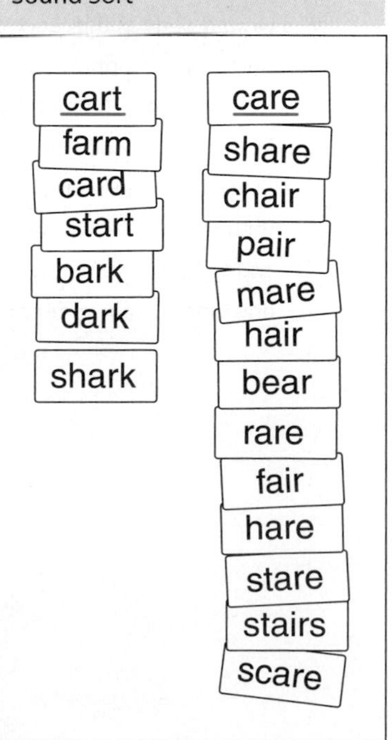

Next, Mrs. Zimmerman directs her students' attention to the spelling patterns. "How are all the words in the first column alike?" she asks. Lisa replies that they all have an *a* and *r* in them. "That's right," says Mrs. Zimmerman, "and what about the words under *care?*" William volunteers that they all have an *ar* also, but sometimes there is an *e* at the end or an *i* in the middle. "Can we put these words into two separate categories?" asks Mrs. Zimmerman. "What shall we use as headers?" The students agree to keep *care* as one header and to use *chair* for the other, and these words are underlined. Mrs. Zimmerman passes out the word cards and students take turns placing each word under *care* or *chair.*

"I have an oddball!" calls out Tan, and she places the word *bear* off to the right.

"I am glad you caught that," says Mrs. Zimmerman. "Why is it an oddball?"

"It is the only one with an *ea,*" explains Tan.

FIGURE 3.2 Mrs. Zimmerman's Pattern Sort

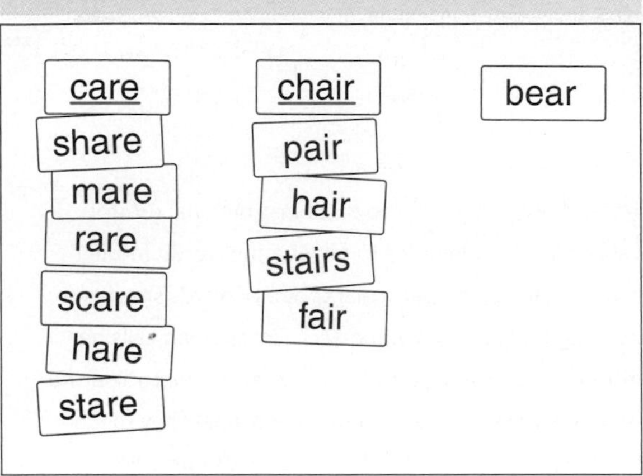

After sorting the words as shown in Figure 3.2, Mrs. Zimmerman asks her students to tell her how the words in each column are alike, and they read the words once more to verify that they all have the same sound as well as the same pattern. Mrs. Zimmerman then asks her students if the patterns remind them of other words they have studied. Brian points out that *ai* and *a* with an *e* on the end are patterns that go with long *a.* "Are these long *a* words?" probes Mrs. Zimmerman. "Listen: *caaaare, chaaair.*" The children agree that they can hear the sound of /ā/ in those words. "What about the *a* in *cart?* Does that sound like an *a?*" asks Mrs. Zimmerman. This time there is some discussion as students come to the conclusion that they cannot even hear a vowel! Mrs. Zimmerman tells the students that over the next few weeks they will look at more words with an *r* after the vowel and they should keep these ideas in mind. To end the lesson Mrs. Zimmerman asks students to reflect on what they have learned and she records their summary: The sound "air" can be spelled *air* and *are.*

Before they return to their seats, Mrs. Zimmerman gives each student a handout of word cards to cut apart for sorting independently at their seats. She reminds them to draw colored lines down the back to mark their set of words and then underline the key words before cutting them apart. They are to sort first by sound (naming each word quietly as they sort) and then by pattern as they did in their final group sort. Two volunteers agree to illustrate the homophones for the class homophone dictionary.

After Mrs. Zimmerman meets with her next word study group, she quickly checks in with each student in the first group to look at his or her sort. As she moves around the room, she asks individual students to read a column of words and explain how they are alike. On Tuesday she will ask all her students to sort their words once more and then to write the words by categories in word study notebooks. On other days they will work with partners to sort and to find more words that fit the sound and/or pattern. On Friday, Mrs. Zimmerman assesses all three groups at one time by calling out a word in turn for each group to spell.

This classroom vignette illustrates several key principles of developmental word study:

1. *A step backward is a step forward.* Students in this group had already studied the fairly consistent *ar* sound in words like *car* and *star.* In this sort those sounds are reviewed and a new sound is introduced that is spelled with two different patterns.
2. *Use words students can read.* Mrs. Zimmerman began this lesson by going over the words, reading and discussing their meanings.
3. *Sort by sound and sight.* Mrs. Zimmerman began by comparing two sounds before leading a visual sort in which spelling patterns were compared. Even when students sort by pattern it is important for them to "say it" as they "lay it."

4. *Don't hide exceptions.* In this sort the word *bear* was included as an **oddball,** a word that has the same sound but a different spelling pattern. Words like *pear* and *wear* might have been included as well. These so-called exceptions reveal that there is a small subset of words with the same long *a* sound spelled with an *ear* pattern.
5. *Work for automaticity.* Students will sort the same set of words repeatedly throughout the week to ensure accuracy and fluency as measures of mastery.

The Role of Word Sorting

Throughout this book you will see many examples of games and activities, but the simple process of sorting words into categories, like the word sort described in Mrs. Zimmerman's class, is the heart of word study. Categorizing is a fundamental way that humans make sense of the world. It allows us to find order and similarities among various objects, events, ideas, and words that we encounter. When students sort words, they are engaged in the active process of searching, comparing, contrasting, and analyzing. Word sorts help students organize what they know about words and form generalizations that they can then apply to new words they encounter in their reading (Gillet & Kita, 1979).

Go to PDToolkit for *Words Their Way,* click on the Videos tab, then select Word Study Activities to see teachers conducting word sorts.

Because sorting is such a powerful way to help students make sense of words, we will take some time here to discuss it in depth. We recommend this same categorization routine for students in all stages studying a variety of word features. At first, emergent and beginning readers learn to pay attention to sounds at the beginnings of words by sorting pictures (Figure 3.3). By the time they are transitional readers, enjoying their first Frog and Toad books (by A. Lobel), students benefit from sorting written words by vowel sounds and vowel patterns. In later grades, students enhance their spelling and vocabulary through sorting words by prefixes and suffixes. In middle school and high school, students sort words by Greek and Latin roots that share common meanings. As children progress in word knowledge, they learn how to look at and think about words in different ways.

Teaching New Word Knowledge through Sorting

Word sorting offers the best of both constructivist learning and teacher-directed instruction. The teacher begins by "stacking the deck" with words that can be contrasted by sound, pattern, or meaning. In the process of sorting, students have an opportunity to make their own discoveries and form their own generalizations about how the English spelling system works. Notice that Mrs. Zimmerman avoids telling the students any rules or generalizations herself, but instead leads them to some conclusions through careful questioning. Over the next few weeks, they will continue to explore *r*-influenced vowels through a series of sorts and will discover that *r* often "robs" the vowel of the sounds we normally associate with it. Rather than simply memorizing 20 words each week for a spelling test, students have the opportunity to construct their own word knowledge that they can apply to reading and writing. Through sorting, students acquire and integrate new word knowledge that is extended and refined through the activities we describe. In addition to learning how to spell, read, understand, and use new words, students develop productive habits of mind (Marzano, 1992).

FIGURE 3.3 Beginning Sound Sort

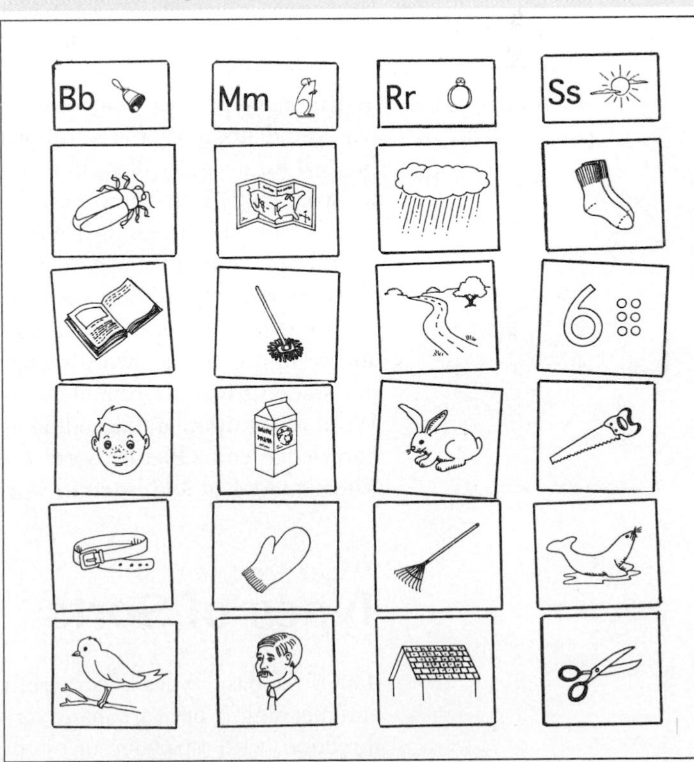

Teaching Phonics through Sorting

Picture and word sorting differ from other phonics approaches in some important ways. First, word sorts are interesting and fun for students because they are hands-on and manipulative. The process of sorting requires students to pay attention to words and to make logical decisions about sound, pattern, and/or meaning as they place each one in a column. Consider the ancient proverb: "I hear and I forget, I see and I remember, I do and I understand." Word sorts help students learn by doing (Morris, 2008).

Second, students work with words or the names of pictures that they can already pronounce. In this way, processing words from the known to the unknown while sorting through a set of cards, children concentrate on analyzing the sounds or patterns within each word. This is not possible if students cannot first name the words. Because learning to spell involves making associations between the spelling of words and their pronunciations, it is important that children know and can already pronounce most of the words to be sorted.

A third way in which sorting differs from some other phonics approaches is that sorting is analytic, whereas many phonics programs take a synthetic approach. In both approaches, students are taught letter–sound correspondences. However, in a **synthetic phonics** approach, students are expected to sound out words phoneme by phoneme. This makes reading tedious and can detract from meaning and engagement. An **analytic phonics** approach uses known words and then examines their parts. Analytic phonics supports the synthetic skill necessary to decode new words when reading and to encode words when writing.

A fourth way in which sorts differ from most phonics and spelling programs is that sorting does not rely on rote memorization or the recitation of rules prior to an understanding of the underlying principles. During sorting, students determine similarities and differences among targeted features as they utilize higher-level critical thinking skills to make categorical judgments. When students make decisions about whether the middle vowel sound in *cat* sounds more like the medial vowel sound in *map* or *top*, independent analysis and judgment are required. Memorization *is* necessary to master the English spelling system. One simply must remember that the animal is spelled *bear* and the adjective is spelled *bare*, but memorization is easier when served by knowledge and understanding of the principles of English spelling. Likewise, rules are useful mnemonics for concepts already understood.

Efficiency in terms of time and cost is a fifth factor to consider. Word sorting offers more concentrated practice than most phonics programs. Instead of filling in worksheets or workbook pages students can sort a set of picture or word cards in a matter of minutes with a set that can be used for a variety of sorting activities throughout the week. The low cost of preparing sorts for word study instruction leaves a larger chunk of the budget for children's books.

Finally, because of the simplicity of sorting routines, teachers find it easier to differentiate instruction among groups of learners. Sorting is infinitely adaptable and the process involved in categorizing word features lends itself to cooperative learning.

One central goal of word study is to teach students how to spell and decode new words and to improve their word recognition speed in general. To accomplish this goal, we teach our students how to examine words to learn the regularities that exist in the spelling system. Word recognition and decoding as well as phonics and spelling are two sides of the same word knowledge coin. Picture sorts and word sorts are designed to help students learn how and where to look at and listen to words.

Types of Sorts

The three basic types of sorts reflect the three layers of English orthography: sound, pattern, and meaning. There are many variations of these sorts that students can do under the teacher's direction, with a partner, or by themselves for additional practice.

Sound Sorts

Sound is the first layer of English orthography that students must negotiate to make sense of the alphabetic nature of English spelling. Pictures are naturally suited for sound sorts: The picture begs to be named, yet there is no printed form of the word for reference. As students sort each picture, they must pay attention to the phonemes contained in the word. Picture sorting is particularly suited for students in the emergent, letter name–alphabetic, and early within word pattern stages of spelling development who do not have extensive reading vocabularies. At different points in development, students sort pictures by rhyme, initial sounds, consonant blends or digraphs, rhyming word families, or vowel sounds. Advanced spellers may sort by unaccented syllables, the number of syllables, and even by syllable stress when they compare such words as *pro' duce* versus *pro duce'*.

Teachers first model picture sorts, such as the one shown in Figure 3.3, as they work with students who are learning initial consonants. Working as a group, students say the names of the pictures as they place them under the letters and **key pictures** they associate with the initial sound. At the end of this guided activity, students work independently to sort similar sets of pictures into the same categories. For variety, small objects can be used instead of pictures, especially with very young children, like a penny, pencil, and pin for sorting by beginning /p/ sound. English learners will need extra time and support to learn the names of the objects and pictures before sorting them by sound.

for **English Learners**

Printed words, too, can be sorted for sound, as Mrs. Zimmerman did using the key words *cart* and *care*. Because sound is the first aspect of a word that a speller has for reference, sound sorts are very important. For example, only after the long *a* in *tape* is identified can the speller consider which of several spelling patterns might be used. (Is it *taip* or *tape?*) Not all word sorts involve a sound contrast, but many do.

Pattern Sorts

When students use the printed form of the word, they can sort by the visual patterns made by groups of letters or letter sequences. Letter name–alphabetic spellers sort words into word families (*hat, rat, pat* versus *run, fan, tan*). Students in the within word pattern stage sort their words into groups by vowel patterns (*wait, train, mail, pain* versus *plate, take, blame*). More advanced spellers will sort by the pattern of consonants and vowels at the syllable juncture (*button, pillow, ribbon* versus *window, public, basket*) or by patterns of constancy and change across derivationally related words (e.g., *divine–divinity, mental–mentality*).

Pattern sorts often follow a sound sort as we saw in the lesson with Mrs. Zimmerman. The words under *care* were subdivided into two pattern groups: words spelled with *air* and words spelled with *are*. Because certain patterns go with certain categories of sound, students must be taught to first listen for the sound and then to consider alternative ways to spell that sound.

Sometimes a new feature is best introduced with a pattern sort to reveal a related sound difference. Consider the words in Figure 3.4 that have been sorted by the final *ch* or *tch* pattern. The final sound in all the words is the same, so a sound sort would not help to differentiate their spellings. However, now that the words are sorted by the final consonant patterns, read down each column to see if you notice anything about the vowel sounds within each column. What did you discover? The *tch* pattern is associated with the short vowel sound whereas *ch* is associated with the long vowel sound. Exceptions are *rich* and *such*, which should be moved to a new column of **oddballs** or exceptions and remembered as such. In either case, the visual patterns of words are best remembered when associated with categories of sound.

FIGURE 3.4 Word Sort by Final *ch* and *tch* Patterns

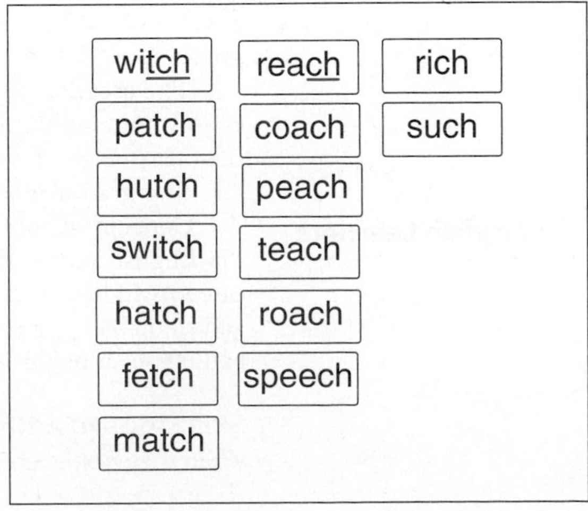

Word sorts with printed word cards are the mainstay of pattern sorts and are useful for all students who have a functional sight word vocabulary. **Key words** containing the pattern under study are designated to label each category. Students sort word cards by matching the pattern in each word to the pattern in the key word at the top of the column. **Headers** are used to describe the recurring patterns such as the abbreviated code that stands for the pattern of consonants and vowels in the feature of study. With C representing consonants and V representing vowels, the abbreviation CVC is specified as a column header for patterns of short vowel words such as *cat, stop,* or *ship* and CVVC is the column header for the pattern in long vowel words such as *rain, coat, suit,* or *green.* Students can sometimes create headers as part of the word sorting lesson to summarize a generalization.

Although pictures cannot teach patterns, using pictures to head a column reminds students to think about sound. For the same reason, it is sometimes a good idea to mix a few pictures into a pattern word sort. Because it is easier to sort words by visual pattern, students can lose sight of the fact that certain patterns go with certain sounds. By mixing a few pictures in with a stack of word cards, students are challenged to be flexible in their word analysis and capitalize on the pattern-to-sound regularities of English spelling.

Meaning Sorts

Sometimes the focus of a sort is on meaning. The two major types of **meaning sorts** are concept sorts and meaning sorts related to spelling.

FIGURE 3.5 Word Sorts Based on *Stuart Little*

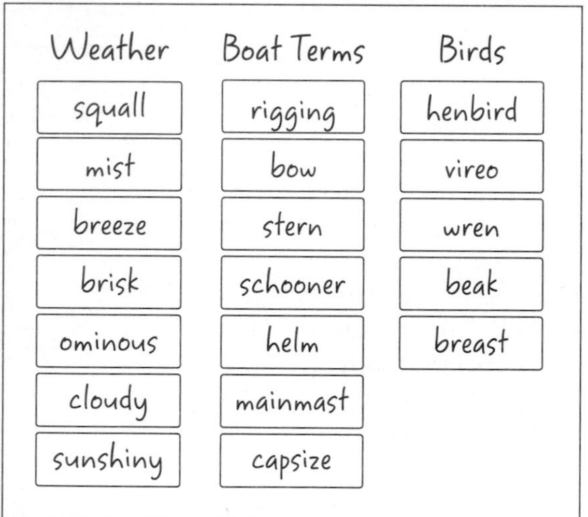

Weather
Boat Terms
Birds
squall
rigging
henbird
mist
bow
vireo
breeze
stern
wren
brisk
schooner
beak
ominous
helm
breast
cloudy
mainmast
sunshiny
capsize

CONCEPT SORTS. Sorting objects, pictures, or words by concepts or meaning is a good way to link vocabulary instruction to students' conceptual understanding. Concept sorts are appropriate for all ages and stages of word knowledge and should be used regularly in the content areas. Pictures of mammals, mathematical formulas, geometric shapes, or social studies vocabulary words all can be sorted into conceptual categories for greater understanding.

Concept sorts can be used for assessing and building background knowledge before embarking on a new unit of study. A science unit on matter, for example, might begin by having children categorize the following words into groups that go together: *steam, wood, air, ice cube, rain, metal, glue, paint, plastic, smoke, milk,* and *fog.* A discussion of the reasons behind their conceptual groupings would probably be most revealing. As the unit progresses, this sort can be revisited and used to review and assess core concepts and vocabulary. Having students categorize examples under the key words *solid, liquid,* and *gas* will help them sort out the essential characteristics for each state of matter. Concept sorts are effective for dealing with new words in novels, too. While reading *Stuart Little* (by E. B. White), a group of Mrs. Birckhead's third-graders sorted some of the vocabulary they encountered, as shown in Figure 3.5.

The creative possibilities for concept sorts are endless. They can be advanced organizers for anticipating new reading or revisited and refined after reading. As tools for writing they can be used to organize ideas before composing. Concept sorts are even useful for teaching grammar when words are sorted by parts of speech.

for **English Learners**

Concept picture sorts are particularly beneficial for English learners. Without knowing the English terms, they can sort pictures of a dog, a cat, a duck, and so on into an animal category. These can be contrasted with pictures of a flower, a tree, a cornfield, a pumpkin, and so on—all examples of plants. English vocabulary is expanded as students repeat the sort, naming each picture and category with help from a teacher or peer.

SPELLING-MEANING SORTS. Students see that meaning influences the spelling of words when they first encounter sound-alike **homophone** pairs like *by* and *buy* or *to* and *too.* Students enjoy homophones because they are interesting, and it makes sense that words with different meanings take different spelling patterns. When teachers teach homophones through word sorting, students expand their vocabularies and learn about spelling patterns at the same time, as demonstrated by the discussion of *bare* in Mrs. Zimmerman's class. **Homographs** are words that are spelled the same but pronounced differently, depending on part of speech: We *record* our sorts so that we will have an ongoing *record* of them. By sorting homographs into grammatical categories by part of speech, students enrich their vocabularies while learning how to pay attention to syllable stress.

Advanced spellers learn how words that are related in meaning often share similar spellings. This spelling–meaning connection in derivationally related words provides a rich arena for meaning sorts that build on Greek and Latin elements. Spellers who are learning derivational relations will sort words by similarities in roots and stems such as the *spect* in *spectator, spectacle, inspect,* and *spectacular* versus the *port* in *transport, import, portable,* and *port-o-john.*

A Continuum of Support When Introducing Sorts

Instruction in word study, as in comprehension and other areas of the curriculum, should follow a gradual release model (Fisher & Frey, 2008) that begins with teacher modeling and explicit explanations (Duffy, 2009) and moves to guided practice and then to independent work. Each week students get a new set of words to work with and teachers need to decide how best to introduce those words so that students are led to form generalizations about how a feature works. Introductory lessons can range from **teacher-directed sorts** to student-centered sorts done independently. Which level of support you select depends on several factors:

1. How familiar students are with the sorting process
2. Whether a new feature is being introduced
3. The amount of time available for sorting
4. How well students can work independently

Different levels of support are summarized in Table 3.1 and described in the following subsections, but the infinite variations of these allow you to adapt word sorting to your own tastes and situation. Open-ended questions that require students to do their own thinking and form their own generalizations are used at all levels but you should always be ready to model your own thinking when they are unable to articulate a generalization.

Mrs. Zimmerman chose a teacher-directed group sort to introduce the new feature of *r*-influenced vowels in the vignette at the beginning of this chapter. Such a lesson can take 20 minutes or more. The next week she might ask students to sort the words on their own before coming to the group because she knows that they are experienced sorters who will be thinking about sounds and patterns as they sort. She may only need five to ten minutes of group time in which the students quickly re-sort their words, check the sort, and reflect on what they discovered.

Teacher-Directed Closed Sorts

The highest level of support and explicit instruction is offered in teacher-directed **closed sorts.** Teachers define the categories in advance using key words and/or headers in closed sorts and make it clear how to conduct the sort (Gillet & Kita, 1979). For example, in a beginning sound phonics sort, the teacher isolates the beginning sound to be taught and makes an explicit connection to the letter that represents it using a key word to designate the category. The teacher might think aloud like this: "*Shhhhhoe, shhhhell.* I hear the same sound at the

Table 3.1 Continuum of Support for Introducing Word Sorts

	FOR NOVICE SORTERS OR TO INTRODUCE NEW FEATURES		FOR EXPERIENCED SORTERS OR TO ASSESS	
	Teacher-Directed Closed Sort	*Teacher-Directed Guess My Category*	*Student-Centered Closed Sort*	*Student-Centered Open Sort*
Materials	One set of words for group to focus on using a pocket chart, overhead, interactive whiteboard, or other method. Students bring their own set of words already cut apart to the group or are given a set at the end of group work to take back to their seats to cut apart and sort.		Students get their own set of words with key words and/or headers.	Students get their own set of words with no key words or headers.
Introduce the Sort	Read through all the words and talk about any that students might not know. Introduce each category with a header and a key word and explicitly describe the features students are to look for.	Read through the words and talk about any that are unfamiliar. Set up the categories with key words but do not describe the feature or put up headers.	Read through the words and talk about any that are unfamiliar. Students can also do this on their own, putting aside any words they don't know to discuss and sort later.	Students work on their own to read through words and put aside any words they don't know.
Sorting	Demonstrate how to sort two or three words in each category and describe explicitly why each word goes there. Students help to complete the sort and justify their placements.	Model by sorting several words in each category but do not explain the reasons. Students are then invited to try sorting the rest of the words.	Students use headers and key words to set up categories and sort independently.	Students determine categories and sort their own words. They explain to you or each other why they sorted as they did.
Check and Reflect	Model how to check the columns and create a generalization with student help. Be ready to model as needed to summarize what the sort has revealed. Sort again at this point if time allows to reinforce the features and reflect once more.	Ask students to describe the features in each category and then check each column. Create a generalization with students' help. Supply headers at this point or label key words.	Call group together or check in individually for students to describe the features and talk about any unfamiliar words. Everyone checks.	"Close" the sort. Establish key words so everyone sorts the same way. Check and talk once more about generalizations. Supply or label headers.
Sort Individually	Students sort their own set of words in the group under your supervision or at their seats. Monitor, remind students to check, and ask each student to state generalizations.	Students sort their own set of words using the key words and headers in the group or independently. Monitor and check in during or after students sort.		

beginning of *shoe* and *shell*, so I am going to put the picture of the shell under *shoe*. They both begin with /sh/, the sound made by the letters *s–h*."

After modeling several words this way, the teacher gradually releases the task to the students' control as they finish the sort under her supervision. As they work, teacher and students discuss the characteristics of the words in each column and develop a generalization based on the selected feature. Students may then sort independently or collaboratively in pairs under the teacher's guidance. This practice is carefully monitored and corrective feedback is provided.

The teacher-directed sort is the most commonly used approach to introduce a new sort to a group, providing a model of direct instruction that is explicit and systematic, yet sensitive to individual variation. The teacher-directed lesson plan includes four components: demonstrate, sort and check, reflect, and extend.

DEMONSTRATE. Introduce the sort using key pictures or words.

1. Look over the words or pictures for items that are potentially difficult to identify or that may be unfamiliar to students. You should name the pictures. ("This is a picture of a yard.") Do not make naming the pictures into a guessing game. Tell your students the names of the pictures immediately. Word sorts may contain unfamiliar vocabulary or words with multiple meanings. Be ready to pronounce and define the words as well as use them in sentences. ("Does anyone know what a hutch is? It is a kind of wooden cage up on legs. Pet rabbits often live in hutches.") Keep dictionaries handy and ask selected students to look up words and report back to the group. ("A hutch is a pen for animals but also a piece of furniture.") Supply pictures when possible to develop new meanings and revisit vocabulary throughout the week. Your English learners will especially benefit from picture dictionaries and a discussion of vocabulary.

for **English Learners**

2. Next establish the categories. Open-ended questions such as "What do you notice about these words?" or "How might we sort these words?" can be used to get students thinking about categories. If you have stacked the deck with words that share common patterns or sounds and your students are familiar with categorizing, they should notice common features fairly quickly. If not, then define the categories for them directly as Mrs. Zimmerman did with the two *r*-influenced vowel sounds in *cart* and *care*.

3. Introduce letter cards, key pictures, key words, or headers with pattern cues such as CVC to indicate the categories. If you are working with sounds, you can emphasize or elongate them by stretching them out. If you are working with patterns, you can think aloud as you point out the spelling pattern. If you are working with syllables, affixes, or derivational relations, you can explicitly point out the unit you are using to compare and contrast.

4. Shuffle the rest of the cards and be very explicit as you model the sort: "We are going to listen for the sound in the middle of these words and decide if they sound like *map* or like *duck*. I'll do a few first. Here is a rug. *Ruuuuug, uuuug, uuuuuuh*. *Rug* has the "uh" sound (/ŭ/) in the middle, so I'll put it under *duck, uuuuck, uuuuh*. Here is a flag. *Flaaaaag, aaaag, aaaa*. I'll put *flag* under *maaaap*. *Flag* and *map* both have the /ă/ sound in the middle; the /ă/ sound is made by the vowel letter *a*."

5. After modeling several words, turn the task over to students. Display the rest of the pictures or words, pass them out, or continue to hold them up one at a time. Students even enjoy taking turns and the anticipation of turning over a word in the stack. Students should name the picture or read the word aloud and then place it in a category, explaining why it goes there. If students make a mistake at the very beginning, correct it immediately. Simply say: "*Sack* would go under *map*. Its middle sound is /ă/." Then model how to segment the phonemes to isolate the medial vowel: /s/–/ă/–/k/.

for Words Their Way™

Go to PDToolkit for *Words Their Way*, click on the Videos tab, then type "Whole Class Reading and Picture Sort" and watch as Mrs. Smith reviews the beginning sounds.

SORT AND CHECK. Model how to check the sort by reading down each column to listen for sound or look for the pattern. Oddballs may be revealed and discussed at this point and you may move to the reflection portion of the lesson, or you may ask students to sort their own set of words cooperatively or independently under your supervision. Unless your students are in the last two levels of word knowledge (syllables and affixes or derivational relations), ask them to name each word or picture aloud as they sort. If someone does not know what to call a picture, tell the student immediately. If someone cannot read a word, lay it aside to consider later.

During a second, repeated sort, do not correct your students, but when they are through, have them name the words or pictures in each column to check themselves. When students make mistakes it is sometimes useful to find out why they sorted a picture or word in a particular way. Simply asking, "Why did you put that there?" can provide further insight into a student's word knowledge. If mistakes are made during the second sort, your students will learn more if you guide them to finding and correcting the mistake on their own. You might say, "I see one word in this column that doesn't fit."

REFLECT. Compare and declare. It is important to have students verbalize what the words or pictures in each column have in common. The best way to initiate such a discussion is to say, "What do you notice about the words in each column?" Guide them to consider sound, pattern, and meaning with open-ended questions such as, "How are the sounds in these words alike? What kind of pattern do you notice? Are any of these words similar in meaning?" Avoid telling rules, but help students shape their ideas into generalization statements, such as, "All of these words have the letter *u* in the middle and make the 'uh' sound," or "The words with an *e* on the end have the /ā/ sound in the middle." Be sure to talk about oddballs and why they are placed in another category and return to any words that students were not able to read. With the generalization or "big idea" now stated they may be able to apply it to the decoding of unfamiliar words. During the reflection part of the lesson, students are asked to declare their knowledge about sound, pattern, and meaning.

EXTEND. After the group demonstration, sorting, and reflection, students participate in a number of activities at centers, with partners, as seatwork, and for homework to reinforce and extend their understanding. They continue to sort a number of times individually and with partners. They hunt for similar words. They draw and label pictures, add to word charts, complete word study notebooks, and play games. Extensions are described in more detail later in this chapter.

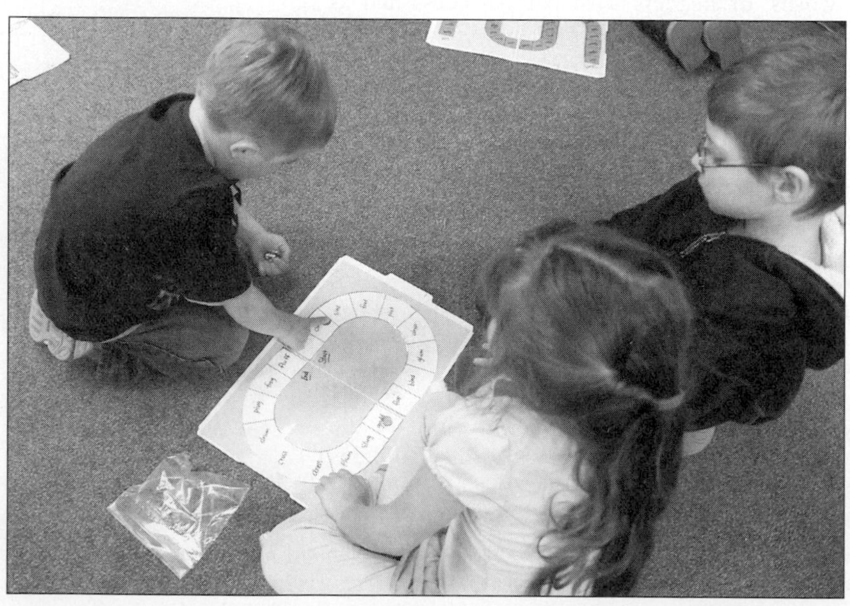

A Teacher-Directed Sort: Guess My Category

When children are comfortable with sorts, you can introduce any new area of study with a collection of objects, words, or pictures in a variation of the teacher-directed sort called Guess My Category. Set up key words or pictures as in a closed sort but do not offer any explanation of the categories. Rather, it will be the job of your students to develop hypotheses about how the things in each category are alike. Begin by sorting two or three pictures or words into each group. When you pick up the next picture or word, invite someone to guess where it will go. Continue doing this until all the pictures or words have been sorted. Try to keep the children who have caught on to the attributes of interest from telling the others until the end. Look at the words below sorted under the key words *dead*, *street*, and *reach*. Can you guess the categories and decide where to sort *speak*, *bread*, and *sweet?*

dead	*street*	*reach*
head	queen	dream
breath	trees	beach

After sorting, check the sort and guide a reflection as you would for the teacher-directed sort above. Students get their own words to sort and are assigned follow-up activities to do throughout the week.

Guess My Category is particularly useful in small groups for exploring content-specific vocabulary while also stimulating creative thinking. Give small groups sets of words, pictures, or objects that might be grouped in a variety of ways. Ask each group to come up with their own categories working together. Allow them to have a Miscellaneous designation for those things that do not fit the categories they establish. After the groups are finished working, let them visit each other's sorts and try to guess the categories that were used. For example, pictures of animals might be sorted into groups according to body covering, habitat, or number of legs.

Student-Centered Sorts

As students become sorting pros, student-centered sorts increase the cognitive demand and can reduce the amount of teacher-directed group time. In many classrooms, students are given their words for the week on Monday morning, and they sort their words independently in anticipation of the categories they will be sorting later in teacher-directed groups. The handout for a closed sort, such as the example in Figure 3.6, provides the headers and key words students need to complete the sort on their own. They have some support, but must still read each word and think about sounds and patterns as they make their own decisions about where to sort. Remind students to watch out for oddballs. Oddballs present an enjoyable challenge for students that forces them to test the hypotheses they form about the words.

The student-centered **open sort** is really our favorite, demanding the highest level of independent effort and thought because students are not given any clues to the categories or features—only a set of words to sort. Open sorts are often the most satisfying for students as well because they present a puzzle to solve. Pass out a handout that has no headers or key words, such as Figure 3.7, and ask students to create their own categories. (If you are using prepared sorts that come with headers and key words, as in Figure 3.6, cut them off.) Students can be asked to compare their categories with a partner to begin the reflection part of the lesson and come up with their own generalizations before sharing with the larger group.

Even with student-centered sorts you should still meet with the students individually or in a group to discuss the sort and check it for accuracy as described previously. In the case of an open sort you may find that some students have sorted the words in ways that do not reveal a generalization or the "big idea." For example, your students may sort the words in Figure 3.7 by the number of letters, by vowel sounds (long or short), by rhyming words, or by beginning consonants (with a blend

FIGURE 3.6 Closed Sort Handout for *tch* and *ch* Patterns with Headers and Key Words

tch	ch	
witch	teach	catch
coach	each	patch
hutch	rich	switch
much	hatch	reach
fetch	much	match
peach	screech	sketch

FIGURE 3.7 Open Sort Handout for *tch* and *ch* Patterns

witch	teach	catch
coach	each	patch
hutch	rich	switch
much	hatch	reach
fetch	much	match
peach	screech	sketch

or no blend). After acknowledging that the words could be sorted that way you should "close the sort" by identifying the categories. At this point you might give students the headers and key words that were cut off the sort, but having them create their own headers provides a way they can summarize the features as part of the reflection process. In the final sort (see Figure 3.4 on page 57) the *tch* and *ch* endings have been underlined to identify both key words and headers. The same headers should be used each time students sort.

Student-centered sorts are particularly useful for students already accustomed to sorting who are adept at finding commonalities among words. These sorts are also diagnostic in nature because they reveal what students know about examining the orthography when they work independently. Open sorts provide opportunities for students to test their own hypotheses and they often come up with unexpected ways to organize words. These open sorts are interesting for the teacher to observe and to discover what students already understand or misunderstand. Some of the most productive discussions about orthography come when students explain *why* they sorted the way they did in an open sort.

Extensions and Follow-Up Routines

After an introductory sort, students are assigned a variety of follow-up activities designed to reinforce generalizations and their memory of words, connect to reading and writing, and build speed and accuracy. Sorting activities develop productive habits of looking for and thinking about word attributes. They give students plenty of individual practice and experience manipulating and categorizing words until they can sort quickly and accurately. Repeated sorts and variations like buddy sorts, blind sorts, writing sorts, word hunts, and speed sorts can serve a variety of instructional purposes.

Repeated Sorts

To become fluent readers, students must achieve fast, accurate recognition of words in context. The words they encounter in context are made of the same sounds, patterns, and meaning units they examine out of context, in word study. One of the best ways to achieve **automaticity** (Samuels, 1988) in word recognition is to build fast, accurate recognition of these spelling units. To meet that goal, it is necessary to have students do a given picture or word sort more than one time. In Mrs. Zimmerman's class, students sort individually after the group lesson, again on Tuesday, and Wednesday with partners. They are also expected to take their words home to sort several days a week for homework. All this adds up to sorting the same words six to eight times throughout the week.

Buddy Sorts

for **English Learners**

Students love to work cooperatively. In a buddy sort, they can sort together, read the words or name the pictures in each column to check the sort, and then talk to each other about the generalization covered by the sort. The sorting can take place in tandem, side by side with two sets of words, or alternating turns, with one set of words. Buddy sorts can provide support for students who are not sure of how to name pictures (often the case for English learners) or read words. Two sorts that work well with buddies are blind sorts and blind writing sorts.

Blind Sorts

Completing sorts without seeing the words is particularly valuable because sorting words by sound prevents the printed form of the word from "giving away" the category (as when short *a* words are compared with short *u*). In a **blind sort,** headers or key words are used to establish categories, but then the teacher or a partner shuffles the word cards and calls each word aloud without showing it. The student indicates the correct category by pointing to or naming the header. The response is checked and corrected immediately when the printed word is revealed and put in place. Buddies can work together by taking turns either reading the words or indicating where they should go. Take time to model how to do a blind sort as a group activity on the overhead or interactive whiteboard before expecting children to work together productively.

FIGURE 3.8 Word Study Notebook

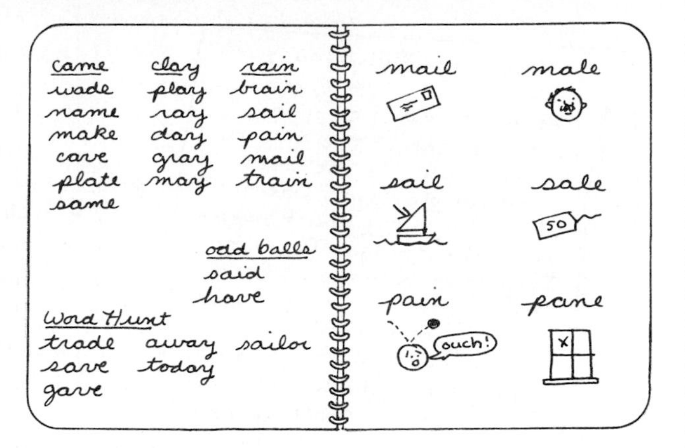

Writing Sorts

Writing words as a study technique for spelling is well established. Undoubtedly the motoric act reinforces the memory for associating letters and patterns with sounds and meanings. However, the practice of assigning students to write words five or more times is of little value because it can become simply mindless copying. Where there is no thinking, there is no learning.

Writing words into categories demands that students attend to the sounds or patterns of letters and to think about how those characteristics correspond with the established categories cued by the key word, picture, or pattern at the top of the column. **Writing sorts** encourage the use of analogy as students consider the key word as a clue for the spelling of words that have the same sound, pattern, or meaning. Start by writing key words or headers to label each category. The words are then put in appropriate categories as in Figure 3.8, in which words have been written under the keywords *came*, *clay*, and *rain*. A student can sort individually by copying a previous sort done with word cards or by turning over one word at a time from his or her collection and writing it down.

Blind Writing Sorts

A variation of the blind sort, a **blind writing sort** requires students to write each word in the correct category before seeing the word. In a blind writing sort, students must rely on the sound they hear in the word as well as their memory for the letters associated with it, cued by the key word at the top of the column. This is what spelling is all about. Blind writing sorts are an established weekly routine in many classrooms once students have had the chance to practice the sort several times. Some teachers conduct them in a group using the overhead projector, saying the word aloud and letting the students write it before they lay the word down to be checked. This sort is important for students who need to attend less to visual patterns and more to the sounds. Blind writing sorts can help identify what words need more attention and can serve as a pretest for the final assessment.

Blind writing sorts done with a buddy or for homework are a good way to prepare for a weekly test. Partners take turns calling the words aloud for each other to write and then immediately show the word to check the spelling and placement. Writing sorts are also an instructionally sound way to construct spelling tests. Key words are written and then students write and sort the words as they are called.

Word Hunts

Students do not automatically see the relationship between spelling words and reading words. Word hunts help them make this important connection. In **word hunts**, students hunt through their reading and writing for words that are additional examples of the sound, pattern, or meaning unit they are studying. They see, for example, the many short *a* words

FIGURE 3.9 Word Hunt in Story Summary

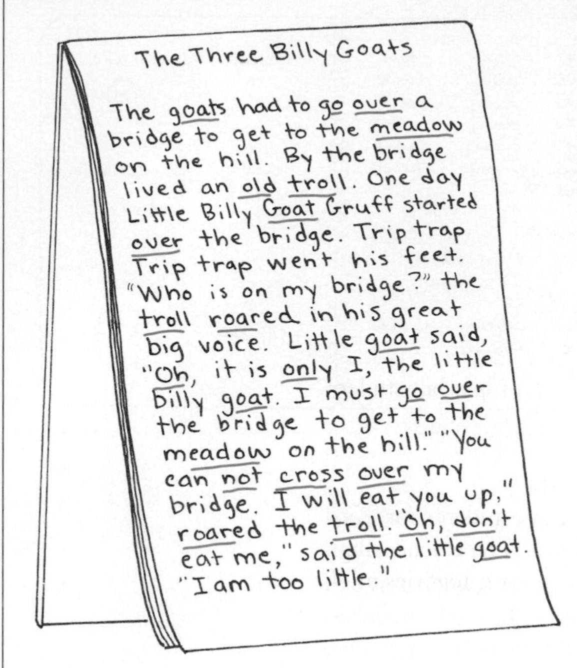

or that *le* is much more common at the ends of words than *el*. Some patterns are found in virtually every text again and again, whereas others are harder to find; thus, word hunts are more appropriate for some features than others.

The Three Billy Goats
The goats had to go over a
bridge to get to the meadow
on the hill. By the bridge
lived an old troll. One day
Little Billy Goat Gruff started
over the bridge. Trip trap
Trip trap went his feet.
"Who is on my bridge?" the
troll roared in his great
big voice. Little goat said,
"Oh, it is only I, the little
billy goat. I must go over
the bridge to get to the
meadow on the hill." "You
can not cross over my
bridge. I will eat you up,"
roared the troll. "Oh, don't
eat me," said the little goat.
"I am too little."

MODELING AND RECORDING WORD HUNTS. Before students are expected to do word hunts, the teacher should model the activity. This can be done with a portion of text copied onto chart pages, copies of text on overhead transparencies, a big book, or simply a book being used for instruction. Working line by line, teachers demonstrate how to locate words that fit the categories under study and how to record those words into categories. After the teacher demonstration, students return to familiar texts to hunt for other words that contain the same features. These words are then added to written sorts under the corresponding key word. See Figure 3.8 for words added to the long *a* categories at the bottom of the notebook page. It is important that students not confuse skimming for word patterns with reading for meaning. The teacher asks the students to use familiar books or already-read portions of the books they are currently reading.

Figure 3.9 shows an example of a word hunt conducted on a chart summary by a small group of students in Mrs. Fitzgerald's third grade class during a unit on folktales. After working with long *o* and short *o* in word study, students found and charted more words from *The Three Billy Goats Gruff*. After this sound sort, students sorted the words by patterns and organized them in their word study notebooks. Three words, including *gobble*, were added to the short *o* column. *Groaned* and *goat* were added to the *oa* column, *home* to the *o*–consonant–*e* column, and *meadow* was added to the *ow* column. A new pattern of open, single long *o* spellings was discovered with *so*, *go*, and *over*. Students debated where to put *too* and *who* before classifying them as oddballs.

This word hunt in *The Three Billy Goats Gruff* summary added more examples for students to consider and created new categories. Word hunts connect word study to other literacy contexts and can also extend the reach to more difficult vocabulary such as *meadow* and *gobble*. With these words, students are able to generalize the pattern within one-syllable words to two-syllable words. Word hunts thus provide a step up in word power.

FIGURE 3.10 Cooperative Group Word Hunt

CONDUCTING WORD HUNTS. Word hunts can be conducted in small groups, with partners, or individually for seatwork or homework. Figure 3.10 shows students gathered around a large sheet of paper on which key words have been written. Students skim and scan pages of books that they have already read, looking for words that match the key words according to the feature under study. Much discussion may ensue as to whether a word contains the spelling feature in question. Often students consult the dictionary, particularly to resolve questions of stress, syllabication, or meaning.

When conducting word hunts with emergent to beginning readers, teachers should have children scan texts that are guaranteed to contain the phonics features targeted in their search. Many core reading programs provide **phonics readers** that are simple books organized around specific phonics features that repeat in the text. Other companies create similar books for emergent readers containing recurring phonics elements as well. Two examples are *Ready Readers* by Pearson Learning Group and the phonics readers by Creative Teaching Materials. Although such texts may not be the heart of your reading program, they offer children a chance to put into practice what they are learning about words and to see many words at the same time that work the same way.

Brainstorming

Although word hunts in text can extend the number of examples to consider, students may also supply additional examples through brainstorming. Brainstorming might be considered a word hunt through one's own memory. The teacher may want to ask for more words that rhyme with *cat*, words that describe people ending in *er*, or words that have *spir* as a root. Word hunts in current reading materials are not always productive when it comes to some features. It is unlikely, for example, that a word hunt would turn up many words with the Latin root *spir*, but students may be able to brainstorm derived words they already know, such as *inspire* or *perspire*. Words brainstormed by students can be added to established categories listed on the board, a chart, or a word study notebook.

Brainstorming can also be used to introduce a sort. The teacher may ask students for words that have particular sounds, patterns, or roots and write them on the board. The teacher might write words in categories as they are given, as in a Guess My Category sort, or categories might be determined by discussion. These words might then be transferred to word study sheets for weekly word sorting routines. After one student raised a question about why the word *sleeve* had an *e* on the end when it already had the *ee*, Mrs. Zimmerman asked her students to think of other words that ended in either *ve* or *v*. After listing their brainstormed words on the board, students sorted them into two groups—those that had a long vowel sound and needed the *e* to mark the vowel (*stove*, *alive*, *cave*) and those that did not (*give*, *love*, *achieve*). After awhile, students realized that there were no words that ended in plain *v*. An *e* always came after *v*, whether the vowel needed it or not.

Speed Sorts

Students are highly motivated to practice their sorts in preparation for **speed sorts.** Some teachers do speed sorts as a quick whole-class activity by displaying a timer (possibly projecting a timer downloaded from the Internet) or simply calling the seconds aloud from the classroom clock. Everyone sets up their headers and then shuffles the rest of their words (students in different groups will have different words). When the teacher says "go" everyone begins to sort. As they finish, students record their times. After checking, the speed sort can be repeated immediately as well as on other days so students can attempt to beat their own times. To encourage accurate sorting, seconds may be added for incorrectly placed words.

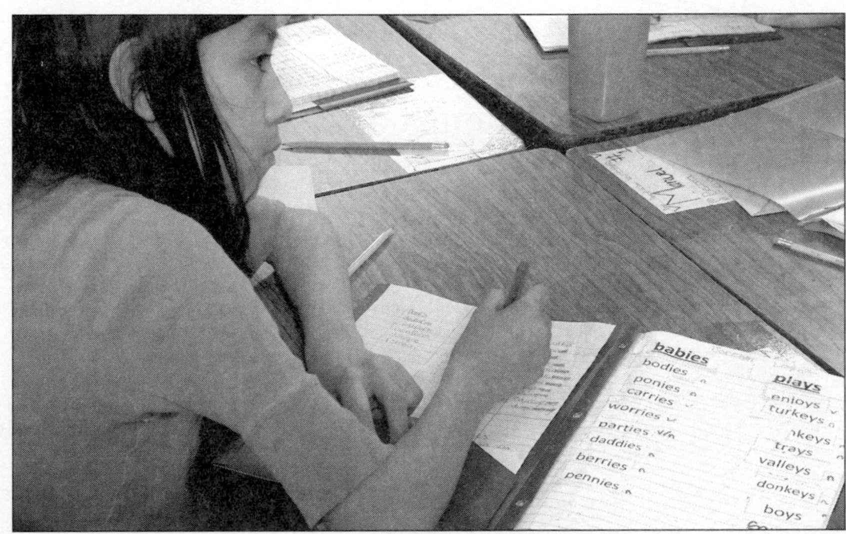

Students can also be paired to time each other using a stopwatch and chart their progress over time. Throughout the day, partners go back to the "sorting table" at ten-minute intervals to sort their word cards for accuracy and speed. One child times the other with a stopwatch kept at the table and then checks for correctness against an answer sheet. We do not recommend pitting students against each other in a competitive mode,

FIGURE 3.11 Draw and Label Activity

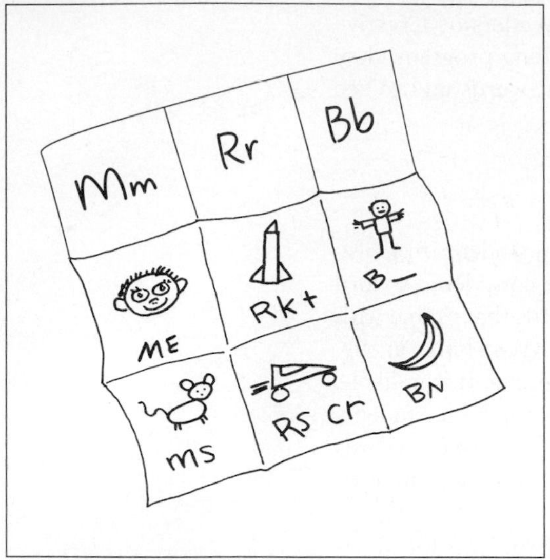

however; instead, students should compare their speeds with their own earlier speeds and work toward individual improvement.

Draw and Label/Cut and Paste

Drawing is particularly useful for teaching emergent and letter name–alphabet spellers initial consonant sounds, as it encourages them to brainstorm other words that begin with the same sounds. Some teachers provide paper that has been divided into columns headed by a key letter (see Figure 3.11). Each column is divided into boxes so that students can see where to draw, how big to draw, and how many to draw. Students brainstorm other words that start with the same sound, illustrate the word in a box under the appropriate key letter and picture, and then label the picture with their best writing. Students are held accountable for spelling the initial sound correctly, but they are encouraged to invent the rest if they do not know how to spell the entire word.

Draw and label is a good activity at a variety of levels to demonstrate the meanings of words. See for example the second page of the word study notebook in Figure 3.8 (page 65). Multiple meanings for words like *block* can be illustrated, for example, as a toy, a section of a neighborhood, and a sports play. Homophones like *bear* and *bare* are made more memorable through drawings, and creating an ongoing class homophone book, as shown in Figure 3.12, is a popular activity. Even advanced spellers in the derivational relations stage might illustrate the meanings of words like *spectacles*, *spectators*, and *inspector*.

FIGURE 3.12 Class Homophone Book

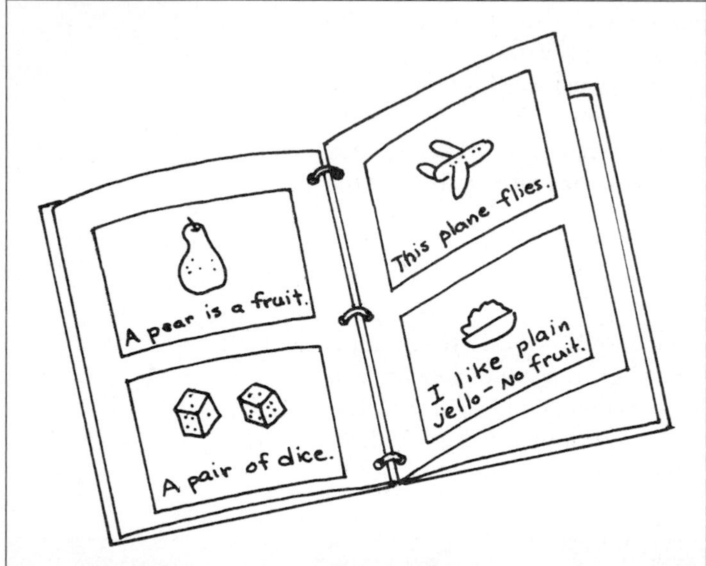

A variation of draw and label, the **cut and paste activity** is like a word hunt using pictures instead of written words, making it appropriate for emergent and letter name–alphabetic spellers. Students hunt through old catalogs and magazines for pictures beginning with a certain sound and then cut out the pictures to paste them in the appropriate column. They then label the pictures as indicated. Pictures that have been used for sorting can also be pasted on a sheet of paper and labeled. Some teachers have their students paste word sorts as well.

Games and Other Activities

At the end of each chapter that follows you will find a number of games and other activities that provide additional practice with words and generalizations for each stage of spelling. Classrooms are busy places and there is not much time for games, but most of these are designed to move quickly in cooperative settings. Games can be used during the week to reinforce a particular sort and also kept available over time to provide review.

Teacher Talk and Student Reflection

Student reflection is a critical part of word study instruction. Students identify and discuss the big ideas from each word study lesson in response to teachers asking *why* they put certain words in the same category. Teachers can encourage student reflection by modeling teacher talk about *position*, *frequency*, and *related words*. Some spelling patterns are often found at the ends of words (like the *oy* in *toy* and *enjoy*) and others in the middle (like the *oi* in *soil* or *choice*). By asking students to reflect on where certain patterns occur within words, teachers can lead students to consider position as they learn to read and spell. Frequency of occurrence is also worthy of reflection. For example, word hunts will reveal that words ending in *er* are much more common than *or* or *ar*. Once students are clued into the frequency of certain spelling patterns they can use the "best bet" approach to spelling unfamiliar words. Finally, reflecting on related words will extend their insights to other words—a major goal of word study. Words with similar roots and affixes are related in both spelling and meaning. The word *cover*, for example, is related to *discover*, *uncover*, *recover*, *discovery*, *recovery*, and so on. Through teacher talk, students can reflect on how their study of words helps them with reading, writing, spelling, and vocabulary. The following questions can assist you in getting this kind of talk about words going in your classroom:

- What do you notice about these words? How are they alike?
- Where in the word do you find the spelling pattern?
- In your word hunts, which pattern did you find more frequently? Which pattern has the most words in the column? The fewest?
- If you're not sure how to spell a word with a long *a* sound, how would you know which pattern to use? What would be your best bet? Why?
- Can you divide the word into parts? What is the base word? Are there any prefixes or suffixes?
- Do the word parts give you information about the word's meaning?
- Can you think of other words that have the same sound (or root, base word, etc.)?
- What did you learn that might help you be a better speller or a better reader?

Now that we have described the rationale for sorting, provided directions for introducing and discussing sorts, and shown a variety of ways to sort, we will focus next on how to prepare sorts.

Guidelines for Preparing Word Sorts

After identifying spelling stages and grouping students for instruction as described in Chapter 2, you must decide on what orthographic features to study and prepare collections of words or pictures for sorting. The particular feature you choose to study should be based on what you see students using but confusing on an inventory or in their writing. No matter what the feature is, when preparing word lists for sorting, collect sets of words that offer a contrast between at least two sounds, patterns, or meaning categories. Compare *b* to *s*, compare short *a* to short *i*, compare words that double the final consonant before adding *-ing* with those that do not. By carefully setting up contrasts in a collection of words, you are stacking the deck so that students can make discoveries and form generalizations as they sort.

Resources for Sorts and Words

The website that accompanies this book offers a collection of prepared picture and word sorts to get you started, and the *Words Their Way*™ companion volumes provide a complete curriculum for each stage, with prepared sorts and spell checks for each unit. (See a list of these resources at the end of this chapter.) However, there are also times when you may want to modify existing sorts or create your own. Only you can be sure of what words your students can already read and thus use for sorting. It is unlikely that any prepared collection of sorts or sequence of study will be just right for your students. The following resources are valuable for determining features to study and finding words:

Go to PDToolkit for *Words Their Way*, click on the Sorts and Games tab, then search for sorts by stages of development. You can also click on the Create Your Own button to make your own sorts.

- Chapters 4 through 8 have guidelines for features to study at each stage and the end matter provides pictures in Appendix C and word lists in Appendix E.
- Word lists can be found in *The Reading Teacher's Book of Lists* (Fry & Kress, 2006), *The Spelling Teacher's Book of Lists* (Phenix, 1996), and *The Spelling List and Word Study Resource Book* (Fresch & Wheaton, 2004).
- Special dictionaries such as the *Scholastic Rhyming Dictionary* (Young, 1994) list words by rhymes and vowel patterns. Regular dictionaries are good for finding words with such beginning features as blends, digraphs, and prefixes. Online dictionaries can be used to search for internal spelling patterns such as vowel digraphs or root words. To search for an internal pattern, you usually use an asterisk or a question mark before or after the pattern. Using a question mark as in "??ar?" or "?ar??" would yield five-letter words with *ar* in the middle. Using an asterisk, as in "*ar*," would yield all the words in the dictionary with *ar* in them.

  Some websites have excellent vocabulary enrichment activities such as a "Word of the Day" with information about the origins and use of different words. Take some time to explore sites like those in the following list:

www.yourdictionary.com	www.etymonline.com
www.wordcentral.com	www.wordnik.com
www.allwords.com	www.onelook.com

- The spelling features introduced across grade levels in basal phonics and spelling programs generally follow the same progression of orthographic features outlined in Chapters 4 through 8 of this textbook (e.g., Templeton & Bear, 2006). One difference, however, is that basal phonics or spelling programs often present only one sound or spelling pattern at a time in lists that offer no contrasts. For example, one unit may be on words ending with the /ch/ phoneme spelled with the *tch* pattern (*patch*, *itch*, *fetch*, etc.). Without a contrast in vowel sound, students are not able to discover that the final /ch/ phoneme in single-syllable words is spelled with the *tch* pattern (*match*, *pitch*, *scotch*) or the *ch* pattern (*coach*, *teach*, *pooch*) depending on the medial vowel sound: short, long, or other.

Making Sorts Harder or Easier

Students in different stages and with different levels of skill will be more successful when sorts are developed with certain factors in mind. For example, English learners often need fewer words while they learn to pronounce and master the meanings of words and pictures. The difficulty of sorts can be adjusted in several ways:

- The more contrasts that a sort provides the more challenging it will be. If children are young or inexperienced, starting with two categories is a good idea. As they become adept at sorting, step up to three categories and then four. Even after working with four categories or more, however, you may want to go back to fewer categories when you introduce a new unit of study.
- The difficulty of the sort also depends on the contrasts you choose. It is easier to compare the sounds for /b/ and /s/ than for /b/ and /p/, for example, because the letter names *b* and *s* are made in different parts of the mouth. Likewise, it is easier for students to learn the short sound for *i* when it is contrasted with the short sound of *a* or *o* than with *e*. Start with obvious contrasts before moving to finer distinctions.
- The level of difficulty can be increased or decreased by the actual words you choose as examples within each category. For example, adding words with blends and digraphs (*black*, *chest*, *trunk*) to a short vowel sort can make those words more challenging than simple words like *tap* and *set*. Ideally, children should be able to read all of the words in a word sort. In reality, however, this may not always be the case. The more unfamiliar

words in a given sort, the more difficult that sort will be. This caveat applies to both being able to read the word and knowing what the word means. A fifth-grader studying derivational relations will need easier words to study than a tenth-grader in that same stage, simply because the fifth-grader will have a more limited vocabulary. If there are unfamiliar words in a sort, try to place them toward the end of the deck so that known words are the first to be sorted. Unfamiliar words can be set aside, but revisit them later and encourage your students to compare the new spelling with the known words already sorted in the columns to arrive at a pronunciation.

- Including a miscellaneous or oddball column with "exception" words that do not fit the targeted letter–sound or pattern feature can increase the difficulty of a sort.

Oddballs

Words that are at odds with the consistencies within each category will inevitably turn up in word hunts and should be deliberately included in teacher-developed sorts. These words go into a miscellaneous category known as Oddballs, as distinct from irregular words. The word *work*, for example, would be an oddball in a sort with other *r*-influenced *o* words like *fork*, *corn*, and *sport*, but is not really irregular or an exception. It fits a small but regular category of words that start with *wor*: *world*, *worm*, *worse*, and *word*. Oddballs are often high-frequency words such as *have*, *said*, *was*, and *again*. Such words become memorable from repeated usage, but are also memorable because they are odd. They stand out in the crowd. Such words should be included in the sorts you prepare, but not too many. One to three oddballs per sort are plenty, so that they do not overshadow the regularity you want students to discover.

The oddball category is also where students may place words if they are simply not sure about the sound they hear in the word. This often happens when students say words differently due to dialectical or regional pronunciations that vary from the "standard" pronunciation. For example, one student in Wise County, Virginia, pronounced the word *vein* as *vine* and was correct in placing *vein* in the oddball column as opposed to the long *a* group. To this student, the word *vein* was a long *i*. Sometimes students detect subtle variations that adults may miss. Students often put words like *mail* and *sail* in a different sound category than *maid*, *wait*, and *paid*, because the long *a* sound is slightly different before liquid consonants like *r* and *l*. *Mail* may sound more like /mā-əl/.

Preparing Your Sorts for Cutting and Storing

Word study does not require great monetary investment because the basic materials are already available in most classrooms. Access to a copier and plenty of unlined paper will get you well on your way.

SORTS FOR STUDENTS. Copies of word sheets or picture sheets as in Figure 3.13 are available from the website or in the companion books listed on page 89. They can also be created by hand using the templates and pictures in this book, the Create Your Own feature on the accompanying website, or by using the "tables" format on your computer and setting all margins at 0 inches. You may want to have the handouts ready first thing Monday morning so the sorts can be cut apart and ready for group activities or you may want to pass the word sheets out after the group time and assign students to cut them apart at their seats.

Show students how to use a magic marker or crayon to draw three vertical lines down the backside of their paper or scribble over it quickly to distinguish their word cards from others in case they should end up on the floor or get mixed up in some way. Older students may initial their words or mark them in some other unique way. Next, model how to cut words apart efficiently using three long vertical cuts before stacking them and cutting them horizontally. Eliminating any borders by enlarging the sort before copying can reduce cutting

Go to PDToolkit for *Words Their Way*, click on the Videos tab, then type "How to Cut and Glue in Primary Classroom."

FIGURE 3.13 Sample Word Study Handouts

time and paper waste. The words or pictures can be stored in an envelope or plastic bag that is reused each week. Sometimes the cut-up words and pictures are kept for review, sometimes they are pasted into a notebook or onto paper, and sometimes they may be simply discarded. Take the time to teach these routines explicitly so that students complete them quickly and independently.

With younger children or when cutting is too time-consuming, you may want to have prepared sets of pictures and words already cut for sorting. Make sets of pictures by copying the pictures in Appendix C onto card stock and coloring them. Laminating the card stock is optional, as the material is quite durable. One or more sets of these pictures can be stored by beginning sounds or by vowel sounds in library pockets or in envelopes. They can then be used for small-group work or for individual sorting assignments. For example, you may find that you have one student who needs work on digraphs. You can pull out a set of *ch* and *sh* pictures, mix them together, and then challenge the student to sort them into columns using the pocket as a header. The **sound boards** in Appendix B can be copied, cut apart, and used to label the picture sets. Resource teachers often create word card sets that can be stored in envelopes and reused from year to year.

Some teachers make manila sorting folders for seats or centers as shown in Figure 3.14. File folders are divided into two to five columns with key words or pictures for headers glued in place. Words or pictures for sorting are stored in the folder in library pockets or plastic bags and students sort directly on the folder. You may want to avoid laminating, which makes the sorting surface slippery, unless you anticipate heavy use. Once the folders have been developed, teachers can individualize word study fairly easily by pulling out the folders that target the exact needs of their students.

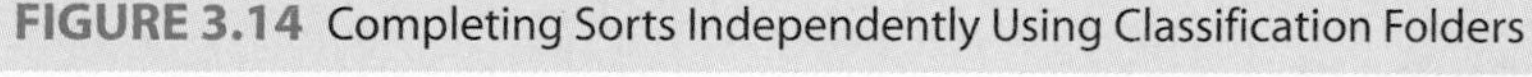

FIGURE 3.14 Completing Sorts Independently Using Classification Folders

SORTS FOR TEACHER MODELING. For group time you will need your own set of words that students can see as you direct a sort. In small groups, you may simply use the same cutout words students have as you model on a table or rug. For larger groups you may want to model sorts using an overhead projector (make a transparency of the handout and cut it apart), or enlarge the pictures or word cards to use in a pocket chart. Advances in technology make it possible to sort easily with document cameras, interactive whiteboards, and interactive tables. Students may even get their own handheld devices for sorting—the possibilities are exciting to consider for word sort activities, which lend themselves to electronic applications.

Preparing Word Study Games for Extension and Practice

Games appeal to children, encouraging them to practice in more depth and apply what they have learned in new situations. Games can be left out for several weeks after a related sort to provide review. This book contains many ideas for the creation of games, and you will want to begin making these to supplement the basic word or picture sorts as you have time. Look for generic games in the activity section of each chapter first, as many of them can be used with a variety of word features you will study across the year. For example, the follow-the-path game being played by the boys in Figure 3.15 can be laminated before labeling the spaces so that new letters can be substituted as they become the focus of study. Label the spaces with a washable overhead projector pen. Over time you can create more specific games.

FIGURE 3.15 Follow-the-Path Game for Initial Consonants

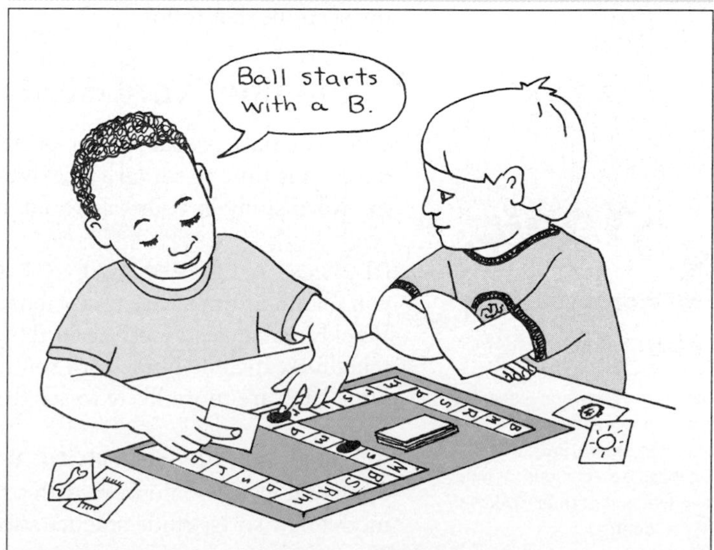

Preparing Your Room

Classroom space is needed for group work, individual work, and partner work. Separate areas for word sorting and discussion are needed to convene a group on the floor or at tables in one part of the classroom while

Table 3.2 Word Study Materials

FROM THE SUPPLY ROOM	FROM THE BOOKSTORE	FROM THE COPY ROOM
Copy paper for sorts	Student dictionaries	Photocopied picture cards
Card stock	Rhyming dictionary	Photocopied word cards
Word study notebooks	Etymological dictionary	Student sound boards
Manila folders	Homophone books	Poster sound boards
Game board materials	Alphabet books	
Spinners and dice	Phonics readers	
Storage containers		
Library pockets		
Chart paper		
Stopwatches		
Scissors		

other children continue to work at their desks or in other areas of the room. Students' desks provide a surface for individual word sorting. In addition, centers or workstations can be set up where students work individually or with partners to sort or play games. A stopwatch is needed for speed sorts and can be placed in the word study center. Many teachers also post chart-sized sound boards in this area. Table 3.2 summarizes what you might need, depending on the age and range of developmental word knowledge in your classroom.

Implementation of Word Study Instruction

What does a word study classroom look like? How can you differentiate instruction within a heterogeneous classroom? How much time does it take? What exactly do students do on different days? These questions and more about organizing for word study are answered in the sections that follow.

Managing Word Study in the Classroom

Once you have prepared your word sorts and introduced your students to basic sorting procedures, it is time to set up a weekly schedule and develop predictable routines. When scheduling word study in your classroom, consider the following.

Go to PDToolkit for *Words Their Way,* click on the Videos tab, then type "Classroom Organization in the Syllables and Affixes Stage" to see Ms. Bruskotter establish expectations for independent and partner work with her students.

DEVELOP A FAMILIAR WEEKLY ROUTINE WITH DAILY ACTIVITIES. Routines will save you planning time, ease transitions, and make the most of the time you devote to word study. Weekly schedules described in this chapter will give you ideas about how to create your own schedules. Include homework routines as well. When parents know what to expect every evening, they are more likely to see that the work gets done.

SCHEDULE TIME FOR GROUP WORK WITH THE TEACHER. Students at the same developmental level should work with a teacher for directed word study. During this time, teachers model new sorts, guide practice sorts, and lead discussions that help students develop and test hypotheses and reach conclusions. Chapter 2 offers assessment-driven guidelines on grouping students for instruction.

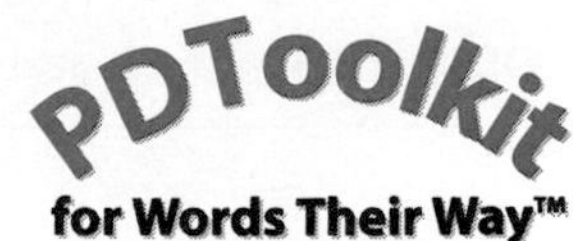

Go to PDToolkit for *Words Their Way,* click on the Videos tab, then type "Weekly Schedules and Activities in the Within Word Pattern Stage, Part 1." Watch how Ms. Flores includes word study with her guided reading groups.

KEEP IT SHORT. Word study should be a regular part of daily language arts, but it need not take up a great deal of time. Teacher-led introductory lessons take the most time, but subsequent activities take little time and do not require a lot of supervision once students understand the routines. Word study can fit easily into odd bits of time during the day. Children can play spelling games right before lunch or sort their words one more time before they pack up to go home. Try a quick word hunt through already-read pages following a guided reading lesson—search for and share words from the reading that fit the categories under study.

PLAN TIME FOR STUDENTS TO SORT INDEPENDENTLY AND WITH PARTNERS. Students need time to sort through words on their own and make decisions about their attributes. Teachers build this independent work into seatwork and center activities. Word study also lends itself nicely to many cooperative activities. Working together in pairs and in groups allows students to learn from each other.

Scheduling Time for Word Study

It is essential that you find time in your instructional day for word study at all grade levels because orthographic knowledge promotes fluent reading and writing—critical goals for academic success. There are many ways to do this. Some teachers conduct word study lessons as part of their reading groups. Other teachers work with two to three separate word study groups and may rotate their students from small-group time with the teacher to individual seatwork and workstation or center times. Still others use a block of time that incorporates differentiated word study. Some teachers conference individually with students in a largely independent workshop routine. In all settings, the focus of word study should be on active inquiry and problem solving in which students are engaged in their own learning.

WORD STUDY AS AN EXTENSION OF THE READING GROUP. Because spelling and reading development are so closely aligned, it makes good sense for word study instruction to occur as an extension of the reading group whenever possible. You can move quite seamlessly from the reading lesson into word study by asking students to look back through certain pages to find words that contain the feature you are about to introduce. After reading *The Cat on the Mat* (by B. Wildsmith) for shared reading, go back and find words in the *at* family as a way to introduce a sort. After reading a chapter in *Frindle* (by A. Clemmons), ask students to find words that end in *ed* as an introduction to a unit on inflectional endings. On other days introduce a word sort and have your students repeat the sort under your supervision. Additional word study activities might be assigned during group time to be completed as seatwork or for homework. This organizational setup is efficient and integrates word study into the total reading and language arts program.

SEPARATE WORD STUDY GROUPS IN A CIRCLE–SEAT–CENTER ROTATION. Figure 3.16 shows a five-day schedule that accommodates word study for three groups rotating through a circle–seat–center instructional plan. This plan works well if your word study groups are separate from the reading groups. The teacher introduces a new sort during **circle time** to a group of students who are at the same developmental level. Half of the remaining students work independently or in buddy pairs for **seatwork,** while the other half work at stations for **center time.** After about 15 to 20 minutes, the groups rotate. Students at the centers join the teacher at the circle table, students who were working at their seats go to the centers, and students who had been with the teacher return to their seats to work independently or with buddies. Counting transition time, three word study groups rotate through all three instructional formats in about an hour. A second slightly longer rotation

FIGURE 3.16 Circle–Seat–Center Schedule

		9:00–9:25	9:25–9:30	9:30–9:55	9:55–10:00	10:00–10:25	
	Group 1	Circle		Seat		Center	Evaluation and Break
Whole Class Review of Schedule & Activities	Group 2	Center	Evaluation and Break	Circle	Evaluation and Break	Seat	
	Group 3	Seat		Center		Circle	Whole Class Activities

occurs also for reading groups. This organization scheme works well in schools in which the entire morning is devoted to reading and language arts.

WORD STUDY BLOCK. Some teachers set aside a separate word study block on Mondays to meet with each developmental group and then schedule a short follow-up each day of the week. All students may cut and sort their words at the same time, but the words they are sorting and the word features they are categorizing are different. Across the week, students during this block of time will engage in different follow-up activities each day. This organizational plan works well for teachers who prefer everyone to be doing the same thing at the same time, yet allows for differentiation of instruction within the word study block.

for Words Their Way™

Go to PDToolkit for *Words Their Way,* click on the Videos tab, then type "Word Study Intervention in the Letter Name–Alphabetic Stage" to see students work with an aide in intervention group.

INDIVIDUALIZED WORD STUDY IN INTERVENTION SETTINGS. Resource teachers who work with small groups of students identified with special needs may have only short sessions with mixed-ability groups, making it challenging to implement word sorts. However, these are usually the very students who need differentiated word study the most! In these settings we recommend that you have appropriate sorts selected and cut out in advance. Form groups when possible but pockets of prepared picture or word cards or word study folders described earlier can be given out to individual students to use independently as you circulate to talk about words, check sorts, and lead students to make generalizations. Students might complete follow-up activities under your supervision on other days of the week or they might take their sorts back to the regular classroom setting and engage in the same activities as their classmates using their own word cards.

INDIVIDUALIZED STUDENT CONTRACTS IN UPPER ELEMENTARY, MIDDLE SCHOOLS, AND HIGH SCHOOLS. Reading and the English language arts are often taught in a readers' workshop environment in the upper grades, in which students may be reading self-selected books as part of literature circles (Daniels, 2002) or book clubs (Raphael, Pardo, Highfield, & McMahon, 1997). The workshop environment allows teachers to meet individually with groups and individuals to give direct instruction in word study and provide feedback as necessary.

One- or two-week contracts are particularly useful at the secondary level. Students contract in advance to complete a certain amount of work in different areas and to turn in that work by a certain date. Figure 3.17 shows a sample student contract that reflects the importance of activities that examine word meanings. Student contracts "spell out" exactly

FIGURE 3.17 Sample Student Work Contract

WORD STUDY CONTRACT

Name ______________________________ **Date** ______________

Feature of Study ______________________________________

Directions: Select activities to earn up to 100 points toward your word study grade. Complete all written work in your word study notebook and turn in along with this contract for final grading.

Required Activities

____ Sort, record, and reflect (30 pts)	____ Work with a partner to complete at least one spelling activity.
	Partner signs here: ________________

Explore Spelling (10 pts each)

____ Repeat sort 2 times	____ Sort a different way and record
____ Blind sort with partner	____ Word hunt (find at least 5 words)
____ Blind writing sort with partner	____ Speed sorts
____ Play a game with partner	Record times: ____________

Explore Meaning (20 pts each—select at least one)

____ Define 7 words	____ Brainstorm or hunt for additional words
____ Use 7 words in sentences	____ Report etymologies for 7 words
____ Illustrate 7 words	____ Make up new words and define them
____ Create a comic strip using 5 words	____ Create your own game
____ Complete a word tree or root web	____ Other

Total Points ______ **Test Grade** ______

what is expected of students in terms of assignments and how much they have to do to earn various grades. The feature of study may be determined by the goal-setting charts described in Chapter 2.

An important decision that a teacher makes is how to schedule word study activities over the course of a week. In the following section, we describe several possible schedules but encourage you to adapt these to your own setting. In the examples, all of the teachers begin with a small-group word study lesson.

A Weekly Schedule for Students Working with Picture Sorts

Betty Lee, a first grade teacher from Montgomery County, Maryland, introduces her emergent to letter name–alphabetic spellers to picture sorts at circle time, working with about a third of the class at the same developmental level. Another third of the class works at their seats and the remaining students are stationed at different centers in which they work with partners. All the activities can be organized in a five-day routine as summarized in Figure 3.18 and described in the following paragraphs, or this routine can be shortened into a three-day plan for students who are reviewing and need to move more quickly.

Go to PDToolkit for *Words Their Way*, click on the Videos tab, then type "Weekly Schedules and Activities in the Letter Name–Alphabetic Stage." Notice the organizational plan Ms. Kiernan uses with her first-graders.

FIGURE 3.18 Betty Lee's Weekly Schedule of Word Study with Pictures

BETTY LEE'S SCHEDULE				
Monday	**Tuesday**	**Wednesday**	**Thursday**	**Friday**
Picture Sorting	Drawing and Labeling	Cutting and Pasting	Word Hunts Word Banks	Games

Figure 3.19 shows an individual pocket folder for this level to keep materials organized and guide students to the daily routines. Students can keep their cutout pictures in the envelope until they are pasted down or discarded. Each folder has a sound board (one of three sound charts that can be found in Appendix B) to use as a reference and a record of progress. Students simply color the boxes lightly with crayon to indicate which sounds they have worked with.

MONDAY—PICTURE SORT. The teacher models a picture sort with a letter as a header to help students develop a strong association between the beginning sound of a word and the letter or letters that represent it. Each picture is named and compared with the key picture to listen for sounds that are the same. The sort might be repeated several times in the circle as a group or with partners. During their center or seat time, students do the same picture sort again on their own or with a partner.

TUESDAY—DRAW AND LABEL. Students sort again at their seats or in a center and then extend the feature through drawing and labeling activities that ask students to think of other words that have the same beginning sound, as in Figure 3.11 on page 68. Students are encouraged to write as much of the word as they can, using invented spelling to label their drawing. Teachers can assess these spellings to judge student progress in hearing and representing sounds.

WEDNESDAY—CUT AND PASTE. After sorting several times students can paste the picture sort into categories and label them. Or children can look through old catalogs and magazines

FIGURE 3.19 Pocket Folder for Organizing Materials

for pictures that begin with a particular sound. These pictures are cut out, pasted into categories or into an alphabet book (as in Activity 4.25 in Chapter 4), and labeled.

THURSDAY—WORD AND PICTURE HUNTS. Children reread nursery rhymes and jingles and circle words that begin with the same sounds they have been categorizing all week. These words can be added to their word banks and sorts. (Word bank activities are described in more detail in Chapter 5.) Students can also go for word hunts in alphabet books or beginning dictionaries. Keep a variety on hand to teach students rudimentary research skills. Their findings can be recorded as an additional draw and label activity.

FRIDAY—GAME DAY AND ASSESSMENT. Children delight in the opportunity to play board or card games and other fun activities for further practice. Assessment at this level is primarily informal as the teacher watches for automaticity and accuracy during sorting and how well students label pictures or use initial sounds in writing.

A Weekly Schedule for Students in the Elementary and Middle Grades

The next schedule works well for children who are readers and able to spell entire words. Sorting words in a variety of contexts and completing assignments in a word study notebook comprise most of the schedule summarized in Figure 3.20.

Word study notebooks, mentioned earlier in the chapter, provide a built-in, orderly record of activities and progress. Composition books with stiff cardboard covers and sewn pages last all year. Many teachers grade the notebooks as part of an overall spelling grade. Figure 3.21 is a list of the expectations and grading criteria used by Kathy Ganske when she taught fourth grade. This chart can be reproduced and pasted inside the cover of the notebook. Possible assignments such as the following can be completed in the notebook. You may want to distinguish "required" activities, such as writing the sort, and "choice" activities, such as draw and label. There is no need to do each activity every week and some are more valuable at times than others. Other ideas for word study notebooks are noted in the chapters that follow.

- *Write word sorts.* Students write the words into the same categories developed during hands-on sorting using the same key words or headers. They can also be asked to write a generalization or the big idea about this word sort.
- *Select five to ten words to draw and label.* Even older students enjoy the opportunity to illustrate words with simple drawings that reveal their meanings. Encourage students to think about multiple meanings of even simple words like *park* or *yard.*
- *Word operations.* Children change a letter (or letters) of a selected word to make new words. Initial letters, or orthographic units, might be substituted to create lists of words

FIGURE 3.20 Suggested Schedule for Students Who Sort Words

Monday	Tuesday	Wednesday	Thursday	Friday
Sort introduced; students sort at least once independently	Re-sort and Writing Sort; first Speed Sort	Re-sort and Blind Buddy Sorting	Re-sort; second Speed Sort and Word Hunt	Testing and games
Homework: Sort again	Homework: Re-sort and Writing Sort	Homework: Blind Sort	Homework: Blind Writing Sort	

FIGURE 3.21 Expectations for Word Study Notebooks

Word Study Notebooks

Weekly activities for this notebook include:

1. Written sorts
2. Draw and label
3. Sentences
4. Words from word hunts
5. Timed sorts

You are expected to:

1. Use correct spelling of assigned words
2. Use complete sentences
3. Use your best handwriting
4. Make good use of word study time

You will be evaluated in this manner:

★ Excellent work
✓ Good work but could be improved
R You need to redo this assignment

that rhyme. For example, starting with the word *black*, a student might substitute other consonant blends or digraphs to generate *stack*, *quack*, *track*, *shack*, and so on. Students studying more complex words might substitute prefixes, suffixes, or roots—for example, using *graph* to generate *autograph*, *biography*, *photograph*, and *photography*.

- *Select five to ten words to use in sentences.* Meaning and usage are important as children begin the study of homophones, inflected words (*ride*, *rides*, *riding*), and roots and suffixes. Challenge students to use two or more words from their sort, especially derivationally related words. (I will need new *spectacles* to *inspect* the *spectacular* new *specimens*.)
- *Record words from word hunts in trade books and response journals.* Students add new words from their reading and writing to the written sorts in their notebooks.
- *Record times from speed sorts.* When students are timed early in the week and then again after repeated sorting, they are likely to show improvement.
- *Record a blind writing sort.* Led by a partner or the teacher, a blind writing sort is a written record of student knowledge.

MONDAY—INTRODUCE THE SORT. Words are introduced and sorted according to one of the levels of support described in Table 3.1 on page 60. Many teachers like to keep each group's attention on one set of word cards used for modeling and guided practice. Then students sort their own words individually in the group, at their seats, and for homework. The teacher then repeats this procedure with the next group, focusing on a different feature. Each group has different words, depending on the students' stage of development. After meeting with a second and third group, teachers often circulate around the room to check in with students sorting at their desks.

If you do not want to take a large block of time on Monday to do all the introductory small-group sorts, you can spread them across the week by meeting with one group a day on Monday, Tuesday, and Wednesday, with each group's independent work operating on an "offset" schedule (see Figure 3.22). In such a schedule, students with the least ability get the most practice, but everyone does similar activities by Thursday and Friday. An alternative would be to give all groups a five-day schedule and test on different days of the week.

TUESDAY—PRACTICE THE SORT, INITIAL SPEED SORT, AND WRITING SORT. Students sort again, often at their seats as the teacher circulates and asks students to read the

FIGURE 3.22 "Offset" Weekly Plan

	Monday	Tuesday	Wednesday	Thursday	Friday
Lowest Group	Meet with teacher Sort again	Re-sort and Writing Sort	Buddy Sorting	Re-sort and Word Hunt	Testing and games
Middle Group	Sort independently	Meet with teacher Re-sort and Writing Sort	Buddy Sorting	Re-sort and Word Hunt	Testing and games
Highest Group		Sort independently	Meet with teacher Re-sort and Writing Sort	Re-sort and Word Hunt	Testing and games or buddy work and test on Monday

words and explain their thinking. If more support is needed students can bring their words to sort under the teacher's supervision in a brief session or as part of a guided reading group. Students are assigned a writing sort for seatwork or for homework. Speed sorts might also be planned for Tuesday. This can be a whole-group activity in which everyone sorts their own words at the same time or students can be paired up and follow a posted schedule of times and partners.

WEDNESDAY—BLIND SORTS AND WRITING SORTS. Students work in pairs to do blind sorts as described earlier in this chapter. After each partner has had a turn to lead the sort, the pair might do a blind writing sort in which partners take turns calling words aloud for the other to write into categories. This can also be a homework assignment.

Go to PDToolkit for *Words Their Way*, click on the Videos tab, then type "Weekly Schedules and Activities in the Syllables and Affixes Stage," where Ms. Bruskotter has students call each other's spelling words aloud for a blind sort.

THURSDAY—SECOND SPEED SORT AND WORD HUNTS. Thursday is a good day to sort again for speed as students try to beat their times from earlier in the week. Word hunts are conducted in groups, with partners, or individually. All students in the class can be engaged at the same time by convening in their respective groups. The teacher circulates from group to group to comment and listen in on students' discussions. The teacher asks group members to provide reasons for the agreed groupings. Afterward, words from the hunt are recorded in each member's word study notebook. For homework that night, students find additional examples to add to their notebooks from the books they are reading at home.

FRIDAY—GAMES AND ASSESSMENT. Although games can be played anytime, Fridays might be reserved for them. Games from previous weeks provide ongoing review and you need not provide a game for every sort. Students pair up with partners or join small groups according to their developmental levels during center time or a designated word study time.

A traditional spelling test format can be used for assessment. If you have two or three groups, simply call one word in turn for each group. This may sound confusing, but children will recognize the words they have studied over the week and rarely lose track. It is not necessary to call out every word studied during the week (ten words may be enough); teachers may even call out some bonus or transfer words that were not among the original list to see whether students can generalize the orthographic principles to new words. In this way, the generalization is emphasized, as opposed to rote memorization of a given list of words. It is particularly effective to conduct the spelling test as a writing sort, having students write each word as it is called out into the category where it belongs. One point can be awarded for correct category placement and one point for correct spelling. Spelling tests conducted as writing sorts reinforce the importance of categorization and press students to generalize from the specific word to the system as a whole.

Some teachers are expected to assign grades for spelling, or spelling may be part of an overall language arts or writing grade. Ideally such a grade should include more than an average of Friday test scores. Figure 3.23 offers a more holistic assessment using a form that can be adapted for other grade levels. Some teachers may wish to add a section for students to rate themselves. The form in the illustration might be used with students in upper elementary grades who can be expected to spell most words correctly.

Friday completes the cycle for the week. If students have been appropriately placed and engaged in a variety of activities throughout the week they should score well on the Friday test (90% or better). Results of the Friday test and observations made during the week influence the teacher's plans for the next week. If scores are low, the teacher may decide that students need to revisit a feature or compare it with another feature. Group membership may also change depending on a given child's pace and progress.

Scheduling for Students in the Secondary Grades

Because secondary English classes are not usually as heterogeneous as elementary classrooms, students are more likely to have similar word study needs. Still, the typical

FIGURE 3.23 Grading Form for Word Study

NAME ______________________ GRADING PERIOD __________

	Excellent Effort	*Good Effort*	*Needs Improvement*
Weekly Word Study Word sorts			
Word study notebook			
Partner work			
Final tests			
Editing Written Work Spells most words right			
Finds misspelled words to correct			
Assists others in editing work			
Uses a variety of resources to correct spelling			
A = Excellent work in most areas B = Good work in most areas C = Needs improvement in most areas Recommended Grade __________			

Comments:

Go to PDToolkit for *Words Their Way,* click on the Videos tab, then type "Classroom Organization across the Grades" and listen to each teacher on the video describe her word study routine and organization.

secondary English teacher plans instruction for students in at least two different stages of word knowledge. If you work with students reading below grade level in middle school or high school, we recommend *Words Their Way™ with Struggling Readers: Word Study for Reading, Vocabulary, and Spelling Instruction, Grades 4–12* (Flanigan, Hayes, Templeton, Bear, Invernizzi, & Johnston, 2011) as a resource to help you organize and carry out word study.

Secondary students in middle and high school often change classes every 50 minutes, or if they have block scheduling, every 1 hour and 40 minutes. Either way, the constraints of periods or blocks limit the way word study is conducted. Some teachers find that a two-week cycle works well. Students have more time to work with a set of words and word hunts can go on for days instead of taking time on a particular day. One way to organize word study instruction in secondary classrooms is through the use of contracts or individualized assignment plans, as described previously. However, you must still find time to meet with students to introduce new sorts, provide corrective feedback, and discuss generalizations either individually or in groups.

If students are in the late syllables and affixes stage or the derivational relations stage, it is less important for them to physically sort word cards. Instead, sorts can be conducted in writing, using a worksheet format in which students write the words listed at the top or bottom of the sheet into the appropriate category. All of the other word study activities may also be conducted as paper-and-pencil tasks and organized in a word study section of a three-ring binder.

FIGURE 3.24 Parent Letter

Dear Parents,

Your child will be bringing home a collection of spelling words weekly that have been introduced in class. Each night of the week your child is expected to do a different activity to ensure that these words and the spelling principles they represent are mastered. These activities have been modeled and practiced in school, so your child can teach you how to do them.

Monday Remind your child to *sort the words* into categories like the ones we did in school. Your child should read each word aloud during this activity. Ask your child to explain to you why the words are sorted in a particular way—what does the sort reveal about spelling in general? Ask your child to sort them a second time as fast as possible. You may want to time them.

Tuesday Do a *blind sort* with your child. Lay down a word from each category as a header and then read the rest of the words aloud. Your child must indicate where the word goes without seeing it. Lay it down and let your child move it if he or she is wrong. Repeat if your child makes more than one error.

Wednesday Assist your child in doing a *word hunt,* looking in a book they have already read for words that have the same sound, pattern, or both. Try to find two or three for each category.

Thursday Do a *writing sort* to prepare for the Friday test. As you call out the words in a random order your child should write them in categories. Call out any words your child misspells a second or even third time.

Thank you for your support. Together we can help your child make valuable progress!

Sincerely,

Word Study Homework and Parental Expectations

Classrooms are busy places and many teachers find it difficult to devote a lot of time to word study, so homework can provide additional practice time. A letter such as the one shown in Figure 3.24 is a good way to encourage parents to become involved in their children's spelling homework. Parents are typically firm believers in the importance of spelling because it is such a visible sign of literacy, and many are even taking political action to see it reinstated. Unfortunately, invented spelling is often a scapegoat because parents, politicians, and even some teachers unfairly associate the acceptance of invented spelling with lack of instruction and an "anything goes" expectation regarding spelling accuracy in children's writing at all grade levels. Communicate clearly to parents that their children will be held accountable for what they have been taught. Homework assignments help them see what is being taught in phonics and spelling.

Go to PDToolkit for *Words Their Way,* click on the Videos tab, then type "Weekly Schedules and Activities in the Letter Name–Alphabetic Stage." Listen to what Ms. Kiernan says about how she involves parents. Also type "Prefix Assimilation (*com*-), Day 2" to watch Ms. Rubero assign students to go on word hunts for homework.

Starting Your Weekly Routines

For students who are not familiar with the process of sorting and for teachers who are hesitant about implementing a brand new organizational scheme, we offer some recommendations about how to gradually transition into fully differentiated word study.

1. *Begin with the whole group and teach the routines.* Start with one to three weeks of whole-class sorts that will be relatively easy for everyone in the class. Use a teacher-directed closed sort for maximum support so you can model and offer explicit directions. Teach students the basic routines that you want them to apply throughout the week. Role-play buddy activities such as blind sorts or writing sorts by having students observe as you

partner with a child, demonstrating how to lead the sort and take turns. Show students how to cut words out quickly and neatly.

2. *Teach students how to talk about the sorts.* Students will need to be shown how to think about words, how to reflect, and how to form generalizations that summarize their new learning. Use open-ended questions to promote critical thinking. If students have trouble responding to questions, model your own thinking with phrases like "I notice that . . ." or "I learned that . . ." Ask students to begin their reflections the same way and give them the language to formulate statements until they can do it for themselves. ("This week we learned about how two-syllable words sometimes have double letters in the middle and short vowel sounds in the first syllable.") Ask students to turn and talk to a partner before sharing in the group to increase verbal practice.
3. *Begin to differentiate.* Once routines are well established, you can begin to work with two and then three groups of students. Because your lowest students need the most help, create that group first as the other students continue to work together. Then split that group. Observe how students sort, how they do on spell checks, and how they work together to modify groups as needed. See Chapter 2 for ideas about organizing groups.
4. *Introduce student-centered sorts.* With experience students gain skill and independence, which makes it easier for you to manage the groups in a more timely fashion or to move to the offset schedule in Figure 3.22. Model how to do both closed and open sorts by thinking aloud as you sort before you assign them to students.

for Words Their Way™

Go to PDToolkit for *Words Their Way,* click on the Videos tab, then type "Weekly Schedules and Activities in the Syllables and Affixes Stage" and watch as Ms. Bruskotter prints out a bookmark of the weekly routines.

Shari Dunn and Tamara Baren suggest introducing the sorting process to young children by using objects or pictures, beginning with just two categories in a closed concept sort (such as animals/not animals or animals/birds). Objects with obvious attributes will be easier for young children to sort than abstract sounds. Also teach routines students will be using such as draw and label or cut and paste. When children are familiar with the sorting process, introduce sound sorts such as two rhyming categories or two initial sounds.

Integrating Word Study into Reading, Writing, and the Language Arts Curriculum

The weekly schedules described in this chapter provide examples of how to integrate spelling instruction into the language arts classroom, implementing routines that are central to both reading and writing. Students return again and again to trade books they have already read to analyze the reading vocabulary. Poetry lessons might begin with reference to a word study lesson on syllable stress. In a writing lesson, students might discuss comparative adjectives from a previous word study lesson that focused on words ending in *er.* During a lesson on parts of speech, students can be asked to sort their week's spelling words into categories of nouns, verbs, and adjectives. Whatever scheduling scheme you choose, your sequence of activities must fit comfortably within your reading/writing/language arts block of instruction.

The features and strategies that students learn during word study should also be applied to decoding strategies during reading and to spelling strategies during writing. If students get stuck on a word while reading, prompt them with a word study cue. Cover up part of the word with your finger to highlight a specific orthographic unit. You can also point out the similarity between the orthographic features in that particular word to the spelling features they have been sorting. The more frequently you make connections between word study and decoding strategies, the more often your students will use them. This is equally true for writing, and many teachers use the features students are categorizing during word study for targeted proofreading.

Teachers and parents often complain that students get perfect scores on their spelling tests only to misspell those same words in their writing assignments the following week.

To ensure transfer of the big ideas gained during word study, students must be engaged in activities that specifically require them to apply their growing word knowledge through wide reading and writing. Using techniques such as the following promote the connection between writing and word study.

DICTATED OR SILLY SENTENCES. Select several words from the weekly word sort and dictate a sentence for the student to write. For example, following an *at* and *an* rhyming family word sort, letter name spellers might be asked to write "The fat cat sat in the tan van" (Johnston, Invernizzi, Juel, & Lewis-Wagner, 2010). Derivational spellers might be asked to write "The competitor competed in the competition" following a vowel alternation sort involving derivational pairs. Some teachers include dictations or silly sentences as part of their weekly routines as well as for assessment.

RELATIONS AMONG RELATED RELATIVES. Provide a word root such as *divide* and ask students to write related words like *division, divisive, divisor,* or *dividend.* Interesting discussions about students' thinking as they spelled these related words are likely to follow, including lots of talk about the meaning as well as about sound and spelling patterns.

COVER AND CONNECT. The teacher writes a word on the board and demonstrates how to cover up word parts, saying the remaining portion and then connecting that segment with the rest of the word when it is uncovered (O'Connor, 2007). The parts that are covered vary according to developmental stage of word knowledge. For letter name–alphabetic spellers, consonant digraphs, consonant blends, or the short vowel rhyming family can be covered and then connected (e.g., *fl-at*). For within word pattern spellers, long vowel patterns can be covered and connected to the remaining consonant blends or digraphs (e.g., *sn-ake*). For syllables and affixes spellers, prefixes and suffixes can be covered and connected to base words, or syllables can be covered and connected one to the next (e.g., *re-read-ing; in-ter-est-ing*). When students encounter a word they don't know in their reading, they can be prompted to use this cover and connect strategy for decoding.

WORD DISPLAYS. Charts of word families or Latin roots, new vocabulary from units of study in science or social studies, word hunt results, and other word displays posted around the room announce to students, parents, and visitors that words are valued and celebrated. Word displays call attention to the richness and power of a versatile vocabulary and provide a ready reference for writing. Word walls (Cunningham, 2009) are widely used in primary classrooms as a way to display high-frequency words needed for reading and writing but can also be used for many other categories of words that deserve recognition and can help students develop a richer vocabulary:

- Onomatopoeia words (*boo-hoo, cockadoodledoo*)
- Oxymorons (*plastic silverware*)
- Multiple meanings (*bat, run, draw*)
- Brand names that now represent a generic product (*Kleenex* for tissue)
- Homophones and homographs
- Collective nouns (*batch of brownies, gaggle of geese*)
- Acronyms (LASER, SCUBA)
- Eponyms (Louis Pasteur—*pasteurization*)
- Spanish–English cognates (*content–contento*)
- Palindromes (*mom*)
- Idioms (*pulling your leg*)
- Puns (*an artist who could really draw a crowd*)
- Similes (*smiling like an angel*)
- Alliteration (*big bad Bruce*)

Resources such as *The Reading Teacher's Book of Lists* (Fry & Kress, 2006) will give you more ideas about interesting categories of words, but it is important that students are involved as much as possible in the creation of such lists for them to be useful and meaningful. For example, in the activity "Said is dead," students help brainstorm lists of words (i.e., *shouted, jeered, whispered, lisped*) to use in their writing instead of that overworked verb (*said*) or a list of contractions can be constructed from examples they come across in their reading. In addition, you need to be mindful of referring to such displays on a regular basis if you want students to benefit from them. For example, when you add a new word, go back over the list of previous words.

Selecting Written Word Study Activities: A Caveat Regarding Tradition

There are many long-standing activities associated with spelling that teachers often assign their students, such as writing words five times, listing them in alphabetical order, and copying definitions of words from the dictionary. Think critically about whether assignments like these fulfill the purpose of spelling instruction, which is not only to learn the spellings of particular words but also to understand generalizations about the spelling system itself and to cultivate a curiosity about words. Writing a word five times is a rote, meaningless, and ineffective activity (Templeton & Morris, 2000), whereas writing words into categories requires the recognition of common spelling features and the use of judgment and critical thinking. Writing words in alphabetical order may teach alphabetization, but it will not teach anything about spelling patterns. Alphabetizing words might be assigned occasionally as a separate dictionary skill, but children will be more successful at it when they can first sort their word cards into alphabetical order before writing them.

Students do need to associate meanings with the words they are studying, particularly in upper-level word study dealing with syllables and affixes and derivational relations. It is reasonable to ask students to look up the meanings of a few words they do not know or to find additional meanings for words, but asking students to write out the definitions of long lists of words whose meanings they already know is boring and not likely to encourage dictionary use.

Writing words in sentences can also be overdone. You might ask students to choose 5 to 10 words (out of 20 to 25) each week to write sentences in their word study notebooks. For example, students like the challenge of using two or more in the same sentence. This is a more reasonable assignment than writing 25 isolated sentences with the weekly spelling list. Many teachers employ sentence writing to work on handwriting, punctuation, and grammar (see the expectations in Figure 3.21). Writing sentences is more useful for some features than others. For example, sentences will help students show that they understand homophones or the tenses of verb forms when studying inflectional endings such as *ed* and *ing*.

Be wary of other traditional assignments that take up time and may even be fun, but have little value in teaching children about spelling. Activities such as Hangman, word searches, and acrostics may keep students busy, but they impart little or no information about the English spelling system. Spelling bees reward those children who are already good spellers and eliminate early the children who need practice the most.

Word study can be fun, but make good use of the time available and do not overdo it. Remember that word study activities should be short in duration so that students can devote most of their attention and time to reading and writing for meaningful purposes.

Spelling Expectations

Invented spelling, or spelling as best you can, frees children to write even before they can read during the emergent stage, and children should be free to make spelling approximations when writing rough drafts at all levels. Invented spellings also offer teachers diagnostic information about what children know and what they need to learn. But that does not mean that teachers do not hold children accountable for accurate spelling. Knowing where children are in terms of development level and considering which word features they have studied enable teachers to set reasonable expectations for accuracy and editing. Typical third-graders in the within word pattern stage can be expected to spell words like *jet*, *flip*, and *must*, but it would be unreasonable to expect them to handle multisyllabic words like *leprechaun* or *celebration*. Just as students are gradually held more and more accountable for conventions of writing such as commas and semicolons, so, too, they are gradually held more accountable for spelling accuracy.

Teachers need to direct students to a range of spelling resources and help students learn to use them: word displays, word banks, personal dictionaries, sound boards, and dictionaries. Even first-graders can use simple dictionaries appropriate for their level, such as the *American Heritage First Dictionary* and *Curious George's Dictionary* to look up some special words. However, that does not mean you can expect them to look up all the words they need to use. A study by Clarke (1988) found that first-graders who were encouraged to use invented spellings wrote more and could spell as well at the end of the year as first-graders who had been told how to spell the words before writing. The report of the National Reading Panel (2000) also underscored the importance of encouraging children to apply their knowledge of letter–sound relationships in their writing. This suggests that children are not marred by their own invented spellings nor do they perseverate with errors over time. However, unless teachers communicate that correct spelling is valued, students may develop careless habits.

Many teachers wonder when they should make the shift from allowing children to write in invented spelling to demanding correctness. The answer is "from the start." Teachers must hold students accountable for what they have been taught. What they have not been taught can be politely ignored. For example, if a child has been taught consonant sound-to-letter correspondences, the teacher would expect the child to spell those sounds correctly, as in PGS LK MD (*Pigs like mud*); however, if the child has not yet been taught the short vowel sounds needed in *pigs* and *mud*, these attempts should be allowed to stand as is. Because the sequence for phonics and spelling instruction is cumulative and progresses linearly from easier features such as individual letter sounds to harder features such as Latin-derived *tion*, *sion*, and *cian* endings, there will always be some features that have not yet been taught. Thus, children (and adults also) will always invent a spelling for what they do not yet know.

Ten Principles of Word Study Instruction

A number of basic principles guide the kind of word study described in *Words Their Way*™ (you were introduced to some of these at the beginning of the chapter as they related to Mrs. Zimmerman's class). These principles set word study apart from many other approaches to the teaching of phonics, spelling, or vocabulary.

LOOK FOR WHAT STUDENTS USE BUT CONFUSE. Students cannot learn things they do not already know something about. This is the underlying principle of Vygotsky's (1962) zone of proximal development (ZPD) and the motivating force behind the assessment described in Chapter 2. By analyzing invented spellings, a zone of proximal development may be identified and instruction can be planned to address features the students are using but confusing instead of those they totally neglect (Invernizzi et al., 1994). Take your cue from the students to teach developmentally.

A STEP BACKWARD IS A STEP FORWARD. Once you have identified students' stages of developmental word knowledge and the orthographic features under negotiation, take a step backward and build a firm foundation. Then, in setting up your categories, contrast something

FIGURE 3.25 Doubling Sort: Comparing Words That "Do" with Words That "Don't"

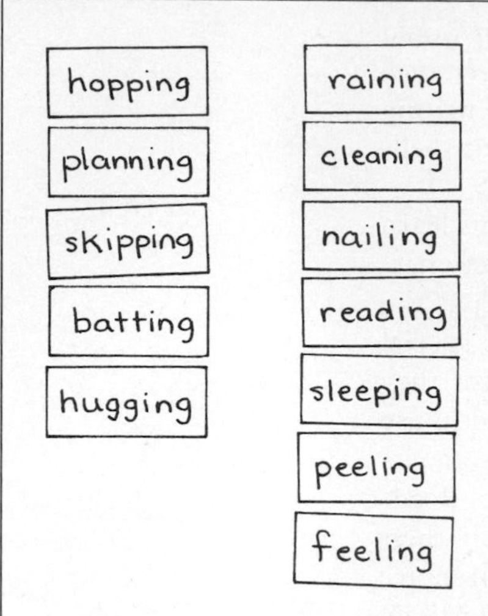

new with something that is already known. It is important to begin word study activities where students will experience success. For example, students in the within word pattern stage who are ready to examine long vowel patterns begin by sorting words by short vowel sounds, which are familiar, and long vowel sounds, which are being introduced for the first time. Then they move quickly to sorting by pattern. A step backward is the first step forward in word study instruction.

USE WORDS STUDENTS CAN READ. Because learning to spell involves achieving a match between the spoken language and the orthography, your students should analyze words that they can readily pronounce. It is easier to look across words for consistency of pattern when the words are easy for students to pronounce. Known words come from any and all sources that students can read: language experience stories, recent readings, poems, and phonics readers. As much as possible, choose words to sort that students can read out of context.

COMPARE WORDS THAT "DO" WITH WORDS THAT "DON'T." To learn what a Chesapeake Bay retriever looks like, you have to see a poodle or a bulldog, not another Chesapeake Bay retriever. What something *is* is also defined by what it is *not;* contrasts are essential to students' building of categories. Students' spelling errors suggest what contrasts will help them sort out their confusions. For example, a student who is spelling *stopping* as STOPING will benefit from a sort in which words with consonants that are doubled before adding *ing* are contrasted with those that do not take doubled letters, as in Figure 3.25.

SORT BY SOUND AND SIGHT. Students examine words by how they sound and how they are spelled. Both sound and visual pattern are integrated into students' orthographic knowledge. Too often, students focus on visual patterns at the expense of how words are alike in sound. The following sort illustrates the way students move from a sound sort to a visual pattern sort. First, students sort by the differences in sound between hard and soft *g*. Then students subdivide the sound sort by orthographic patterns. See what you can discover from this sort.

First Sort by Sound of g

Soft	*Hard*
edge	bag
cage	twig
huge	slug
judge	drug
stage	leg
badge	flag
page	
lodge	

Second Sort by Pattern

dge	*ge*	*g*
edge	cage	bag
judge	huge	twig
badge	stage	slug
lodge	page	flag
		drug
		leg

BEGIN WITH OBVIOUS CONTRASTS. When students begin the study of a new feature, teachers choose key words or pictures that are distinctive. For example, when students first examine initial consonants, teachers do not begin by contrasting *m* with *n*, which are both nasals and visually similar. It is better to begin by contrasting *m* with something totally different at first—*s*, for example—before working toward finer distinctions as these

RESOURCES FOR IMPLEMENTING WORD STUDY *in Your Classroom*

Throughout this text you will see references to the PDToolkit for *Words Their Way*™, which includes all-new video, sample word sorts and games, as well as a Create Your Own feature. The content in the following list further enriches our book. We also list our companion books that offer a complete curriculum of word sorts for each stage.

PDToolkit for *Words Their Way*™

PDToolkit for *Words Their Way*™, the website that accompanies this text, prepares you for word study by examining successful classroom instruction—from assessment to organization to implementation across grade levels. You'll hear teachers explain the process, watch students master skills, and see how a successful word study approach is established and managed.

Words Their Way™ *with English Learners: Word Study for Phonics, Vocabulary, and Spelling,* Second Edition, by L. Helman, D. R. Bear, S. Templeton, M. Invernizzi, and F. Johnston

Based on the same research and developmental model, this companion volume focuses on using word study to enhance literacy learning for English learners.

Each of the following stage-specific companion volumes provides reproducible sorts and detailed directions for the teacher. You'll find extensive background notes about the features of study and step-by-step directions on how to guide the sorting lesson. Organizational tips and follow-up activities extend lessons through weekly routines.

Words Their Way™*: Letter and Picture Sorts for Emergent Spellers,* Second Edition, by D. R. Bear, M. Invernizzi, F. Johnston, and S. Templeton

Teachers in pre-K through grade 1 will find ready-made sorts as well as rhymes and jingles for emergent readers.

Words Their Way™*: Word Sorts for Letter Name–Alphabetic Spellers,* Second Edition, by F. Johnston, D. R. Bear, M. Invernizzi, and S. Templeton

Primarily for students in kindergarten through grade 3, the 50 blackline masters include picture sorts for beginning consonants and for digraphs and blends, word families with pictures and words, and word sorts for short vowels.

Words Their Way™*: Word Sorts for Within Word Pattern Spellers,* Second Edition, by M. Invernizzi, F. Johnston, D. R. Bear, and S. Templeton

Teachers of grades 1 through 4 will find 50 reproducible sorts that cover the many vowel patterns.

Words Their Way™*: Word Sorts for Syllables and Affixes Spellers,* Second Edition, by F. Johnston, M. Invernizzi, D. R. Bear, and S. Templeton

This text includes 56 sorts for syllables and affixes spellers in grades 3 to 8.

Words Their Way™*: Word Sorts for Derivational Relations Spellers,* Second Edition, by S. Templeton, F. Johnston, D. R. Bear, and M. Invernizzi

Teachers in grades 5 to 12 will find 60 upper-level word sorts that help students build their vocabulary as well as spelling skills. Lots of additional words are provided to modify or create new sorts.

categorizations become quite automatic. Move from general, gross differences to more specific discriminations.

DON'T HIDE EXCEPTIONS. Exceptions arise when students make generalizations. Do not hide these exceptions. By placing so-called irregular words in a miscellaneous or oddball category, new categories of consistency sometimes emerge. For example, in looking at long vowel patterns, students find exceptions like *give*, *have*, and *love*, yet it is no coincidence that they all have a *ve*. They form a small but consistent pattern of their own. True exceptions do occur (e.g., was, women, laugh) and become memorable by virtue of their rarity.

AVOID RULES. Rules with many exceptions are disheartening and teach children nothing. They may have heard the long vowel rule, "When two vowels go walking, the first one does the talking," but this rule is frequently violated in words like *head*, *boot*, or *soil*. Learning about English spelling requires students to consider sound and pattern simultaneously to discover consistencies in the orthography. This requires both reflection and continued practice. Students discover consistencies and make generalizations for themselves. The teacher's job is to stack the deck and structure categorization tasks to make these consistencies explicit and to instill in students the habit of looking at words, asking questions, and searching for order. Rules are useful mnemonics if you already understand the underlying concepts at work. They are the icing on the cake of knowledge. But memorizing rules is not the way children make sense of how words work. Rules are no substitute for experience.

WORK FOR AUTOMATICITY. Accuracy in sorting is not enough; accuracy *and* speed are the ultimate indicators of mastery. Acquiring automaticity in sorting and recognizing orthographic patterns leads to the fluency necessary for proficient reading and writing. Your students will move from hesitancy to fluency in their sorting. Keep sorting until they do.

RETURN TO MEANINGFUL TEXTS. After sorting, students need to return to meaningful texts to hunt for other examples to add to the sorts. These hunts extend their analysis to more words and more difficult vocabulary. For example, after sorting one-syllable words into categories labeled *cat*, *drain*, and *snake*, a student added *tadpole*, *complain*, and *relate*. Through a simple word hunt, this child extended the pattern-to-sound consistency in one-syllable words to stressed syllables in two-syllable words.

These ten principles of word study boil down to one golden rule of word study instruction: *Teaching is not telling* (James, 1958). In word study, students examine, manipulate, and categorize words. Teachers stack the deck and create tasks that focus students' attention on critical contrasts. Stacking the deck for a discovery approach to word study is not the absence of direct instruction. On the contrary, a systematic program of word study, guided by an informed interpretation of spelling errors and other literacy behaviors, is a teacher-directed, child-centered approach to vocabulary growth and spelling development. The next five chapters will show you exactly how to provide effective word study instruction.

MEDIA GUIDE *Word Study: Principles and Practices*

SECTION	PAGE	GO TO PDTOOLKIT FOR *WORDS THEIR WAY*™
Videos		
The Role of Word Sorting	55	Click on the Videos tab, then click Word Study Activities to see teachers conducting word sorts.
Teacher-Directed Closed Sorts	61	Click on the Videos tab, then type "Whole Class Reading and Picture Sort."
Preparing Your Sorts for Cutting and Storing	71	Click on the Videos tab, then type "How to Cut and Glue in Primary Classroom."
Managing Word Study in the Classroom	74	Click on the Videos tab, then type "Classroom Organization in the Syllables and Affixes Stage."
Scheduling Time for Word Study	75	Click on the Videos tab, then type "Weekly Schedules and Activities in the Within Word Pattern Stage, Part 1."
Scheduling Time for Word Study	76	Click on the Videos tab, then type "Word Study Intervention in the Letter Name–Alphabetic Stage."
A Weekly Schedule for Students Working with Picture Sorts	77	Click on the Videos tab, then type "Weekly Schedules and Activities in the Letter Name–Alphabetic Stage."
A Weekly Schedule for Students in the Elementary and Middle Grades	81	Click on the Videos tab, then type "Weekly Schedules and Activities in the Syllable and Affixes Stage."
Scheduling for Students in the Secondary Grades	82	Click on the Videos tab, then type "Classroom Organization across the Grades."
Word Study Homework and Parental Expectations	83	Click on the Videos tab, then type "Weekly Schedules and Activities in the Letter Name–Alphabetic Stage." Also type "Prefix Assimilation (*com-*), Day 2."
Starting Your Weekly Routines	84	Click on the Videos tab, then type "Weekly Schedules and Activities in the Syllables and Affixes Stage."

chapter 4

Word Study for Learners in the Emergent Stage

This chapter describes the literacy development that occurs during the emergent stage, a period in which young children imitate and experiment with the forms and functions of print: directionality, the distinctive features of print, the predictability of text, and how all of these correlate with oral language. The emergent stage lies at the beginning of a lifetime of learning about written language. Emergent students do not read or spell conventionally and they score 0 on spelling inventories like those in Chapter 2 because they have very tenuous understandings of how units of speech and units of print are related. Nevertheless, children are developing remarkable insights into written language, and with the help of caregivers and teachers they learn a great deal. Before we go into a thorough description of the emergent stage, we will visit a classroom where 23 kindergartners explore literacy under the guidance of their teacher, Mrs. Regina Smith.

During a unit on animals, Mrs. Smith shares a big book, *Oh, A-Hunting We Will Go,* by John Langstaff. This book is based on the traditional song, "Oh, a-hunting we will go, a-hunting we will go. We'll catch a fox and put him in a box and then we'll let him go." The pattern repeats with various animals and places substituting for *box* and *fox*. After reading several pages, Mrs. Smith begins pausing to allow students to guess the name of the place using their sense of rhyme and picture cues. When several students sing out that the *whale* would be put in a *bucket,* Mrs. Smith acknowledges that the picture could be called a bucket or a pail. She then points to the word *pail* on the page and says, "Is this word *pail* or *bucket?* What does *bucket* start with? Listen: *b-b-b-bucket.* What does this word start with? *Pail* starts with *P* and the sound is *p-p-p.* Does *pail* rhyme with *whale*? Does *bucket* rhyme with *pail?*" Later Mrs. Smith holds up the pail at the sand table and reminds students that it could be called a bucket or a pail. She poses the question, "What are things that you might carry in a bucket or pail?" and she asks the children to respond in full sentences such as, "I can carry sand in a pail or bucket."

In this fashion, Mrs. Smith introduces a new book with her children as they enjoy the silliness of the rhymes and pictures. In the process she draws her students' attention to letters and sounds and models pointing to words as she reads. She also finds an opportunity to highlight vocabulary. After enjoying the big book version, she plans a number of follow-up activities to further develop emergent literacy skills.

Mrs. Smith has created a chart with the first five lines of patterned text. She has also written them on sentence strips and placed them in order in a pocket chart. After the children have read the lines several times chorally on the chart, Mrs. Smith passes out the strips. As a group they put the sentences back in order by comparing them to the chart.

On another day, word cards for *fox, box, catch, go,* and *we* are held up one by one as volunteers come up to find the words on the chart or sentence strips. Mrs. Smith observes carefully to see which children are beginning to point accurately as they recite. She makes sure the book, chart, strips, and words are left out where everyone can practice freely with them during the day.

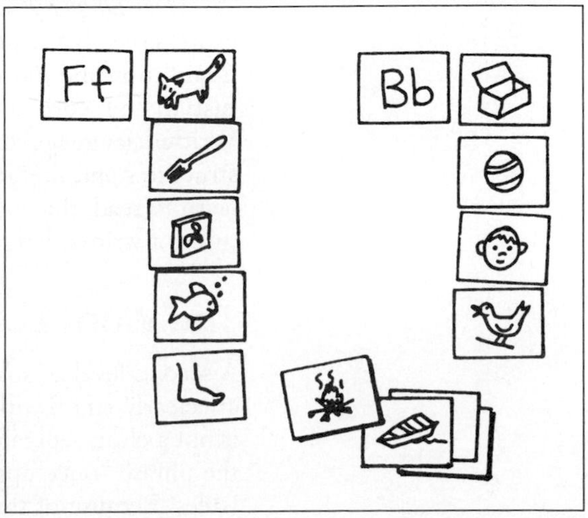

Most of the students in Mrs. Smith's class are studying initial consonants. In previous lessons they have compared words that start with *s* and *m*. Now they look for words that start with *b* and *f* on the five-line chart and find *fox* and *box.* Mrs. Smith writes those words on cards as the key words for a picture sort. She brings out a collection of pictures that start with *b* and *f* and puts up a picture of a box and a fox as headers in a pocket chart (see Figure 4.1). After naming all the

FIGURE 4.1 Picture Sort for Comparing *f* and *b*

pictures, she models how to sort several by beginning sound before inviting the children to take turns sorting the rest. This sort is repeated by the group, and on subsequent days all the children have a number of opportunities to sort on their own, to hunt for more pictures in alphabet books and magazines beginning with *b* and *f*, and to draw and label pictures with those sounds. After the students compare the sounds for *b* and *f* in several ways, the pictures are combined with *m* and *s* for a four-category sort. The students work with all four letters and sounds for several days before moving on to a new contrast.

Go to PDToolkit for *Words Their Way*, click on the Videos tab, and type "Whole Class Reading and Picture Sort" to see Ms. Smith using *Oh, A-Hunting We Will Go.*

Mrs. Smith uses a core book as the basis for teaching a variety of emergent literacy skills in a developmentally appropriate fashion starting with a whole text and working down to the parts (sentences, words, letters and sounds). Her word study activities address issues critical to emergent literacy in the context of shared reading and playful language lessons.

From Speech to Print: Matching Units of Speech to Print

Learning to read and spell is a process of matching oral and written language structures at three different levels: (1) the global level, at which the text is organized into phrases and sentences, (2) the level of words, and (3) the level of sounds and letters within words and syllables. For someone learning to read, there is not always an obvious match between spoken and written language at any of these levels. Mismatches occur because of the fixed nature of print versus the flowing stream of speech it represents. Learning to match between speech and print is a gradual process, but is essential in learning how to read.

The Global Level

In oral language, the global level is characterized as **prosodic.** This first level is the "musical" level of language, usually consisting of sentences or phrases. Within these phrases, speakers produce and listeners hear intonation contours, expression, and tone of voice, all of which communicate ideas and emotions. For example, a rising note at the end of a statement often indicates a question; precise, clipped words in a brusque tone may suggest irritation or anger.

Oral language is a direct form of communication accompanied by gestures and facial expressions that takes place in a shared context. *Written language* is an indirect form of communication and must contain complete, freestanding messages to make meaning clear. Punctuation and word choice are the reader's only cues to the emotions and intent of the writer. Written language tends to be more formal and carefully constructed, using recognizable structures and literacy devices such as "happily ever after" to cue the reader. When children learn to read, they must match the prosody of their oral language to these more formal structures of written language.

The Word Level

A second level of structures that students negotiate are the units called *words.* In print, words are clearly set off with spaces between a string of letters. In speech, words are not distinct; there is not a clear, separable unit in speech that equates perfectly to individual words. For example, the phrase "once upon a time" represents a single idea composed of four words and five syllables. Because of this, when children try to match their speech to print, they often miss the mark, as Lee does in her elephant story in Figure 4.5 (page 99). It takes practice and instruction to match words in speech to written words (Flanigan, 2006; Morris, 1980; Roberts, 1992).

This mismatch of meaning units between speech and print is most clearly illustrated through an instrument called a spectrograph. An acoustic representation of speech reveals a surprising thing: Humans do not speak in words! There are no "spaces" between individual words when a person is talking. The only break in a spectrograph coincides with phrases and pauses for breathing. *Word* is a term specific to print, and cultures that have no written language have no word for *word* (Malinowski, 1952). This remarkable state of affairs creates an enormous challenge for individuals learning to read, which is why Mrs. Smith is careful to point to words as she reads.

Sounds in Words

Sounds and letters make up the third level of analysis. In learning to read, students must segment the sounds or phonemes within words and match them to the letters in print. In speech, the phonemes (consonants and vowels) are interconnected and cannot be easily separated (Liberman & Shankweiler, 1991). Yet the alphabet and letter sounds must be understood as discrete units that match in systematic ways. This is the basis for the alphabetic principle, which is essential for learning to read and spell English.

Characteristics of the Emergent Stage of Reading and Spelling

Some emergent children may have well-developed language skills and know a great deal about stories and books; others may not. However, it is not necessary for children to develop a certain amount of oral language *before* learning the alphabet or seeing printed words tracked in correspondence to speech. To withhold these essential components of the learning-to-read process would put them in double jeopardy. Besides putting them behind in language and story development, they also would be behind in acquiring the alphabetic principle. Children can develop oral language, learn about stories, *and* learn about words, sounds, and the alphabet simultaneously as teachers model reading and writing and encourage children to imitate and experiment.

Emergent Reading

Can children in the emergent stage read? Yes, but not in a conventional way. The reading of the emergent child is best described as pretend reading, or reading from memory. Both are essential practices for movement into literacy. **Pretend reading** is basically a paraphrase or spontaneous retelling at the global level that children produce while turning the pages of a familiar book. In pretend reading, children pace their retelling to match the sequence of pictures and orchestrate dialogue and the voice and cadence of written language (Sulzby, 1986).

Memory reading is more exacting than pretend reading. It involves an accurate recitation of the text accompanied by pointing to the print in some fashion. Reading from memory helps children coordinate spoken language with print at the level of words, sounds, and letters. Emergent children's attempts to touch individual words while reading from memory are initially quite inconsistent and vague. Children gradually acquire **directionality,** realizing that they should move left to right, top to bottom, and end up on the last word on the page. However, the units that come in between are a blur until the systematic relationship between letters and sounds is understood. The ability to fingerpoint or track accurately to words in print while reading from memory is a phenomenon called **concept of word (COW).** It is a watershed event that separates the emergent reader from the letter name–alphabetic beginning reader (Henderson, 1981; Morris, 1981).

FIGURE 4.2 Late Emergent Writing without Word Boundaries

IKSKP

"I like housekeeping"

FIGURE 4.3 Early Letter Name–Alphabetic Spelling with Word Boundaries

i K hskpen

"I like housekeeping"

When children lack a COW, word boundaries are also obscured in their writing, even if some phoneme–grapheme correspondences have been made. Note how the words all run together in Figure 4.2. However, words gradually begin to evolve as distinct entities with their boundaries defined by beginning and ending sounds and fingerpointing becomes more exact. Children's early letter name–alphabetic writing provides evidence of this understanding, as illustrated in Figure 4.3.

Emergent readers are in what Ehri (1997) calls the prealphabetic phase of reading. They may learn to identify a few words such as their names and the names of friends and family. They might also identify signs in their environment, but their strategy is to look for nonalphabetic cues such as the shape of a stop sign. They may identify a large retail store because it starts with a big red *K*, but they are not systematic in their selection of any particular cue. During the emergent stage, children lack an understanding of the alphabetic principle or show only the beginning of this understanding.

Emergent Writing

Like emergent reading, early emergent writing is largely pretend. Regardless of most children's cultural backgrounds or where they live, this pretend writing occurs spontaneously wherever writing is encouraged, modeled, and incorporated into play (Ferreiro & Teberosky, 1982). The child's first task as a writer is to discover that scribbling can represent something and, thereafter, to differentiate drawing from writing and representation from communication. The child must come to realize that a drawing of a flower does not actually say "flower." Writing is necessary to communicate the complete message. The top row of Figure 4.4 presents a progression of drawings and their accompanying utterances that show a clear differentiation between picture and writing.

There are many similarities between infant talk and emergent writing. When babies learn to talk, they do not begin by speaking in phonemes first, followed by syllables, words, and finally phrases. In fact, it is quite the opposite. They begin by cooing in global, prosodic contours that approximate the music of their mother tongue. Likewise, children begin to write by approximating the broader contours of the writing system; they start with the linear arrangement of print (Ferreiro & Teberosky, 1982). This kind of pretend writing has been called **mock linear** (Clay, 1975; Harste, Woodward, & Burke, 1984). The bottom row of Figure 4.4 shows the movement from mock linear writing (bottom left) to real writing (bottom right) that uses letters to represent speech sounds.

When babies move into what is conventionally recognized as baby talk, they give up their melodious cooing to concentrate on smaller segments, usually stressed syllables. "Dat!" is hardly as fluid as cooing "Ah-ha-ah-ha," but these awkward exclamations will be smoothed out in time. Likewise, global knowledge of writing and letterforms is temporarily abandoned as children concentrate their attention on the specifics of letter formation and the representation of the most **salient** sounds of speech. Such attention sometimes leads children to spit out parts of words on paper, often using single consonants to stand for entire syllables as in Figure 4.2.

FIGURE 4.4 The Evolution of Emergent Writing

The message is often indecipherable because children do not understand the purpose or need for spaces and they tend to run their syllables and words together on paper.

Here is where the similarity between spoken and written language breaks down. Humans do not actually talk in words, and there is no such thing as an isolated phoneme. Words and phonemes are artifacts of print and do not naturally coincide with acoustic realities such as syllables. Children become aware of them as a consequence of learning to read and write. The concepts of word and phoneme must be taught; both will emerge as children gradually acquire the alphabetic principle and coordinate the units of speech with printed units on the page.

There are dramatic changes as children develop across the emergent stage that can be characterized as early, middle, and late emergent behaviors, as shown in Table 4.1.

EARLY. In the early emergent stage, children learn to hold a pencil, marker, or crayon and to make marks on paper (or windows, walls, or floors). These marks are best described as scribbles that lack directionality and may not serve a communicative function. Sometime during this early emergent stage, scribbles evolve into more representational drawings and children learn that print is distinct from drawings, as can be seen in the right-hand box of the top row of Figure 4.4. This frame shows the drawing as distinct from the writing, which is assigned a specific message: "A flower for my Mom."

MIDDLE. In the middle emergent stage, children begin to approximate the most global contours of the writing system: the top-to-bottom linear arrangement. They experiment with letterlike forms that resemble the separate circles and lines of manuscript writing or the connected loops of cursive. As letters of the alphabet and numbers are learned, they begin to show up in letter strings or a "symbol salad," as in the spelling of *macaroni* in Figure 4.4. The child

Table 4.1 Characteristics of Emergent Spelling

	WHAT STUDENTS DO CORRECTLY	WHAT STUDENTS USE BUT CONFUSE	WHAT IS ABSENT
Early Emergent	Mark on the page Hold the writing implement	Drawing and scribbling for writing	Letters Directionality
Middle Emergent	Linear movement across page Clear distinction between writing and drawing Letterlike forms	Letters and numbers Letter strings Directionality	Phonemic awareness Sound–symbol correspondences
Late Emergent SKP for *housekeeping* D for *duck*	Consistent directionality Use of letters Some letter–sound matches	Substitutions of letters that sound, feel, and look alike: *B/P, D/B* Salient phonemes	Complete sound–symbol correspondence Spacing between words

may identify his or her efforts as writing and announce that it is a "note for Daddy." Parents may be challenged at this point when children come to them with their pretend writing and say, "Read this to me, Mommy" or "What does this say?" What is exciting and significant is that young children recognize that print carries a message that can be read by others.

LATE. By the late emergent stage, children are beginning to use letters to represent speech sounds in a systematic way, as shown in the last box in Figure 4.4. These partially phonetic spellings represent four critical insights and skills.

1. To produce a spelling, children must know some letters—not all, but enough to get started.
2. They must know how to form or write some of the letters they know.
3. They must know that letters represent sounds. Again, they do not have to know all of the letter sounds; indeed, if they know the names of the letters, they might use those as substitutes.
4. They must attend to the sounds or phonemes within spoken words and syllables and match those sound segments to letters.

The ability to divide oral speech into the smallest units of sound is called **phonemic awareness.** Matching these units of sounds to letters is the beginning of **phonics,** the consistent relationship between sounds and letters. To create a spelling, a child must have some degree of phonemic awareness and some knowledge of letter sounds. By the time children gain insight into all four listed aspects of sound and print, they are at the end of the emergent stage.

Beginning to Match Sounds to Letters

As emergent readers learn their letters and develop some phonemic awareness, they use their alphabetic knowledge to represent the units of sound they perceive. If children are able to discern only the most prominent sound, then they usually will put down only one letter: *D* for *dog*, *S* for *mouse*, *N* for *and.* Until terms about language segments like "beginning sound" are sorted out, emergent children rely on the feel of their mouths as they analyze the speech stream. Say the phrase "once upon a time" aloud while paying attention to what your tongue and lips are

FIGURE 4.5 Lee's Elephant Story

1spntm	Once upon a time
Lft. T. f	the elephant went to the fair.
pplsm. et. sk	The people saw him eating strawberry cake.
nobDsMg	And nobody saw him again.
Vn	The end

doing. The tongue touches another part of the mouth only for the /s/ sound of *once*, the /n/ sound of *upon*, and the /t/ sound of *time*. The lips touch each other twice: for the /p/ sound in the middle of *upon* and for the /m/ sound at the end of *time*. It is not surprising, therefore, that Lee wrote "once upon a time" as 1SPNTM in Figure 4.5. Late emergent spellers pay attention to those tangible points of an utterance in which one part of the mouth touches another, or to the most forcefully articulated sounds that make the most vibration or receive the most stress. If some letters are known, they will be matched to these prominent sounds.

Figure 4.5 illustrates Lee's phonemic analysis of words and phrases in her elephant story relative to her knowledge of the alphabet and letter sounds. As children begin to achieve a concept of word, they become better able to pay attention to sounds that correspond to the beginnings and ends of word units. If children know their letters and how to write them, their spelling will reflect this phonemic awareness. Such children will usually put down one or two letters, as in F for *fair* or TM for *time*. As the spellings in Lee's elephant story depict, the phonemes represented are always the most prominent, but the most prominent are not always at the beginnings of words; she spelled *went* as T and *him* as M. Notice her confusion with word boundaries and how she tries to help herself with periods. When letter names are coordinated with word boundaries in a consistent fashion, the student is no longer an emergent speller. Spelling that honors word boundaries consistently is early letter name–alphabetic.

Teaching students letters of the alphabet and the sounds they represent is absolutely essential during the emergent stage, but children do not have to get them all straight before they begin to read and write. As with oral language learning, written language learning involves forming and testing hypotheses as new bits of knowledge are perceived and internalized. Like the incessant chatter of the growing child, it is the extensive practice in approximating the writing system that extends the child's reach. Pretend writing and pretend reading must come first, and as they evolve, real reading and real writing will follow.

The Context for Early Literacy Learning

To move from emergent to beginning reading, students must have many opportunities to see and experiment with written language. They must see their own spoken language transcribed into print and must be encouraged to write, even if this writing is little more than scribbles.

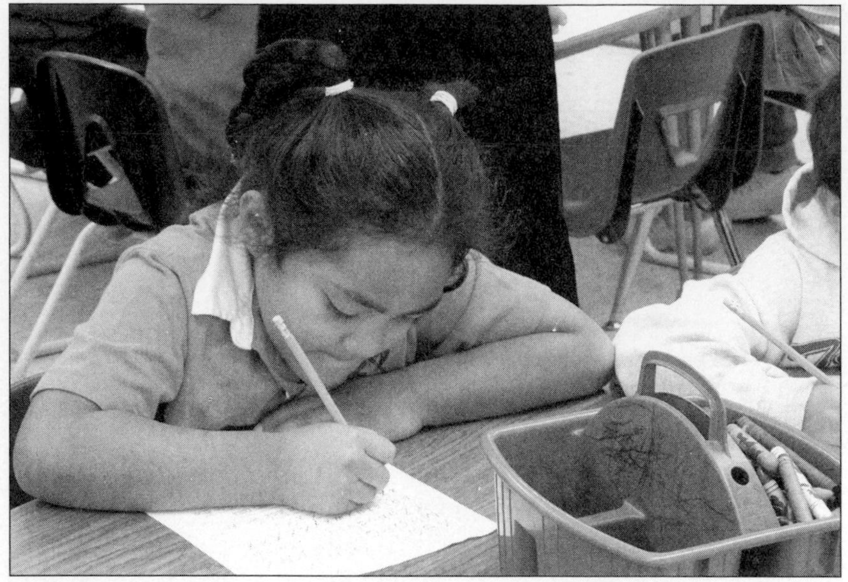

They must also be supported in their efforts to pretend read or read from memory, making the speech-to-print match. The most important condition for emergent literacy to blossom is the opportunity to practice, and children's approximations must be encouraged and celebrated.

Supporting Emergent Writing

The mere act of leaving one's mark on paper has been called the "fundamental graphic act" (Gibson & Yonas, 1968)—an irresistible act of self-fulfillment. Young children will write, or pretend to write, well before they learn to read, provided they are encouraged to do so. The trick in developmental literacy instruction is how to give that encouragement. As the teacher, you should provide immediate and ready access to implements of writing (markers, crayons, pencils, chalk) and model how to use writing in centers: a grocery store play area where grocery lists are drawn and labeled; a restaurant where menus are offered and orders are written; a block center with cardboard shapes for making signs; a writing center with a variety of paper, alphabet stamps, markers, and pictures cut from magazines. Outfitted and supported accordingly, writing will happen spontaneously and well before children can spell conventionally or properly compose (Richgels and McGee, 2007; Strickland & Morrow, 1989).

It is important to provide a visible model of the forms and functions of print when teachers write with children. This can take place as they record children's ideas in student dictations or during interactive writing when they make the writing process explicit by talking aloud about how to spell and compose (Aram & Biron, 2004; Button, Johnson & Furgerson, 1996). Children should also be given journals in which they are encouraged to write. Samples of Lee's daily journal entries are shown in Figures 4.4 and 4.5. For many young writers their first efforts may be drawings accompanied by labels such as Kaitlyn's journal entry in Figure 4.6.

FIGURE 4.6 Kaitlyn's Kindergarten Journal in October

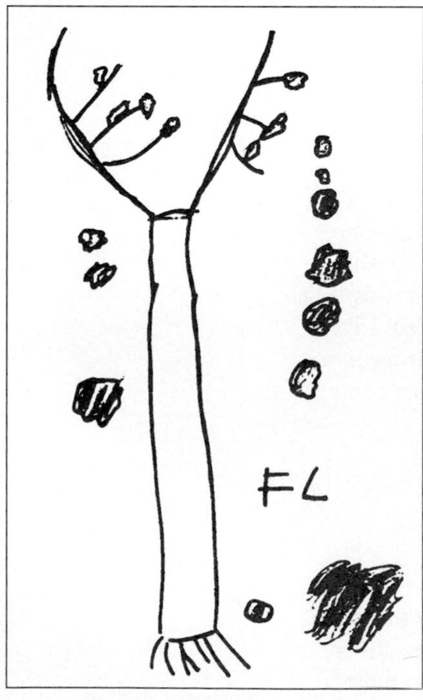

In addition, writing extensions to other literacy activities and thematic studies should be modeled and encouraged. Children might record their observations of seeds growing, write about a field trip, or record a prediction. Expect these efforts to range from scribbles to partial phonetic writing, as shown in Figure 4.4. What matters is engaging children in the process as the first step and as an incentive for learning more about the process.

Supporting Emergent Reading

There are two kinds of reading formats for emergent learners: "reading to" children, which includes interactive read-alouds with children's literature, and "reading with" children, which includes shared reading. **Interactive read-alouds** (Barrentine, 1996) promote oral language discussions around vocabulary, ideas, and concepts related to the content and genre of a book. During **shared reading** (Holdaway, 1979) teachers read with children from enlarged texts like big books and charts on which children can see the print and join in chorally on rereadings. Both formats provide a supportive social context and opportunities to talk about the forms and functions of print, but shared reading, in which children's attention is directed to enlarged print, is particularly powerful. Teachers

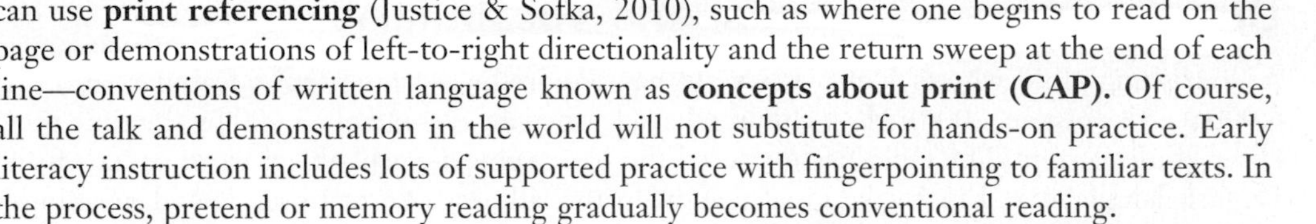

can use **print referencing** (Justice & Sofka, 2010), such as where one begins to read on the page or demonstrations of left-to-right directionality and the return sweep at the end of each line—conventions of written language known as **concepts about print (CAP).** Of course, all the talk and demonstration in the world will not substitute for hands-on practice. Early literacy instruction includes lots of supported practice with fingerpointing to familiar texts. In the process, pretend or memory reading gradually becomes conventional reading.

PDToolkit for Words Their Way™

Go to PDToolkit for *Words Their Way,* click on the Videos tab, and revisit "Whole Class Reading and Picture Sort" to see Ms. Smith work with sentence strips.

The reading materials best suited for shared reading with emergent readers are simple predictable books, familiar nursery rhymes, poems, songs, jump rope jingles, and children's own talk written down. Familiarity with songs and rhymes helps bridge the gap between speech and print and cultivates the sense that what can be sung or recited can be written or read. Recording children's own language in the form of picture captions and dictations also nurtures the notion that print is talk written down. The ownership that comes with having one's own experiences recorded in print is a powerful incentive to explore the world of written language.

Although in the emergent stage children are heavily supported by memory in their first efforts to read, these attempts are nonetheless valuable. The best way to create a reader is to make reading happen, even if it is just pretend. Useful techniques for fostering early literacy development include the **whole-to-part model** (McCracken & McCracken, 1995), which begins with the shared reading of familiar rhymes and jingles (whole texts). Then follow-up activities move to the parts (sentences, words, letters, and sounds) as children rebuild the text with sentence strips in pocket charts and match word cards to individual words on the sentence strips as an explicit way to direct attention to words in print. This can then be followed by sorting pictures and words by beginning sounds to draw attention to letter–sound correspondences.

The Literacy Diet for the Emergent Stage

This section examines the wondrous ways in which emergent spellers analyze speech and construct an understanding of how print works. Bear in mind, however, that emergent understandings of how units of speech correspond to units of print operate within a larger context of concept, language, and vocabulary development (Kaderavek & Justice, 2004; Purcell-Gates, Jacobson, & Degener, 2004; Snow, 1983).

Through reading and writing activities, word study instruction for the emergent reader must aim toward the development of six main components of the learning-to-read process:

1. Oral language, concepts, and vocabulary
2. Phonological awareness (PA)
3. Alphabet knowledge
4. Letter–sound knowledge
5. Concepts about print (CAP)
6. Concept of word in text (COW)

These six components constitute a comprehensive "diet" for early literacy learning and instruction (Invernizzi, 2002). If all components are addressed on a daily basis, no matter how far along the emergent continuum a child may be, conventional reading and writing should inevitably follow.

Oral Language, Concepts, and Vocabulary

A flourishing child who is 4 or 5 years old has acquired a working oral vocabulary of over 5,000 words (Justice, 2006). Most children have learned an average of 13,000 by the time they enter kindergarten. The child has mastered the basic subject–verb–object word order of the English language and may take great delight in the silliness of word sounds and meanings. Many children have learned to recite the days of the week, and some, the months of the year, but they do not fully understand the relationships between them. When asked to name the months of the year, nine out of ten will name the seasons instead. Ask kindergartners to tell you what season of the year December falls in, and many will no doubt tell you "Christmas." Young children use many words whose meanings they do not fully comprehend (Carey, 2001). Their knowledge of words is only partially formed by the information gleaned from their few years of life. To extend their partial understandings of words, and to acquire new word meanings, children must have language experiences, such as conversations and being read to, that allow them to hear new vocabulary as well as complex sentence constructions.

Children come to school with widely varying language experiences (Biemiller & Slonim, 2001). In a classic study, researchers estimated that by 3 years of age, some children had heard 3 million more words than other children, and by the time they enter school, some children have heard 30 million more words than others (Hart & Risley, 1995).

A well-developed vocabulary is an essential part of school success (Cunningham & Stanovich, 2003), and vocabulary instruction needs to be a part of instruction for students at all ages (Biemiller, 2001, 2004). There are many strategies to introduce, contextualize, and exercise oral language. Adults should engage children in conversation at every opportunity and consciously use language that includes new vocabulary and complex sentences. Students with lower language skills benefit from conversation with children who have better language skills (Mashburn, Justice, Downer, & Pianta, 2009). Classroom environments that are well managed and positively oriented invite peer interaction that results in greater language use, a primary goal in early language and literacy development (Mashburn et al., 2009).

DEVELOPING VOCABULARY THROUGH INTERACTIVE READ-ALOUDS. Interactive read-alouds play a critical role in the development of vocabulary, language, and concepts. Books expose children to new words and more complex sentence structures, and they provide background and conceptual knowledge that children may not have experienced first-hand. Teachers should read from a variety of genres and select storybooks that offer rich language and themes appropriate for young children. For example, nonfiction about seasons, weather, transportation, and how seeds grow provides new vocabulary and develops background information, especially when read for units of study. Folktales offer strong plots that help children develop a sense of story and poetry offers rhyme and playful language. Reading to children should be an interactive process that stimulates lots of responses from children who ask questions and provide comments such as pointing out things they notice in the illustrations (Barrentine, 1996).

Although simply reading aloud to children will expose them to a wide range of new words, teachers need to develop the meanings of particular words in more depth to ensure vocabulary growth. When new words are introduced, children should be asked to repeat them and say them in phrases and sentences. After reading about how a little bear *hustled* after his mother (*Blueberries for Sal* by Robert McCloskey), the teacher might pause briefly to draw attention to the word and then follow up later with more discussion: "Say the word *hustle.* What do you think it means? Would you hustle to catch the bus? Would you hustle fast or hustle slow? Tell your partner how you would fill in this sentence: I hustled to ______." Beck, McKeown, and Kucan (2002, 2008) describe how to plan repeated exposure to words in different contexts to help students learn the meanings and uses of new vocabulary words.

Word selection is important. It is easy and tempting to simply look for hard words, but the most difficult examples may not be the words children are most likely to retain and use on their own. Four criteria are important in selecting target words: (1) utility, (2) concreteness, (3) repetition in text, and (4) relatedness to themes or topics of study.

Utility. When thinking about utility, consider words that can be used regularly in the classroom or words that will show up in other books. For example, the book *Corduroy* by Don Freeman includes "amazing, admiring, and enormous." After focusing on these words during the read-aloud, make a point of using them in other contexts. Instead of saying, "I like the drawing you did," substitute with "I admire your drawing. The colors are amazing and that house is enormous!"

Concreteness. Concrete words are more likely to be illustrated in the story (such as the *elevator* in *Corduroy*). Many denote concepts that children can act out, like *hustled.* Abstract words like *imagined* will take more work to develop.

Repetition in Text. Also consider words that are used more than once in the story, because these will offer repeated exposure in a meaningful context. The word *hustled* occurs several times in *Blueberries for Sal.*

Thematic or Topical Relatedness. When considering thematic or topical relatedness, choose words that can be clustered in a semantic category (Whitehurst, 1979). The words *buds, blooms,* and *blossoms* for example, all relate to the growing seeds motif in *The Tree* (A First Discovery Book). From the same book, other concrete selections that form clusters for repetition include *seed, roots,* and *sapling.*

An outline for planning and conducting an interactive read-aloud with a focus on vocabulary development is presented in Figure 4.7. Interactive read-alouds take additional time to implement because you want children to have the opportunity to engage in a lot of oral language. At the same time, excessive interruptions can disrupt the flow of the text, so it is important to strike a balance between stopping and reading. Sometimes you may want to read a book with few if any interruptions and sometimes you may use a second reading to stimulate language

FIGURE 4.7 Planning an Interactive Read-Aloud with Vocabulary Development

1. *Preparation.* Select books with rich language that are age appropriate for your listeners. Preview the book, looking for new vocabulary and conceptual understanding that will extend children's background knowledge. For example, rural children might not be familiar with the escalator mentioned in *Corduroy* by Don Freeman. Select three to five words using the criteria we describe and prepare child-friendly definitions. (You might model the use of a picture dictionary occasionally, and even use it yourself to develop definitions, but dictionaries often do not provide clear examples or explanations.)
2. *Before reading.* Introduce the book by reading the title and naming the author and illustrator. Look at the cover and at least the first few pages to elicit a prediction. ("What do you think this book will be about?") The prediction sets a purpose for reading. ("Let's read and find out if you are right.") Build background knowledge as needed and try to introduce the target words conversationally, perhaps pointing to a picture (such as the escalator) or supplying a brief definition. ("Escalators are stairs that move.") Ask the children to listen for the words as you read.
3. *During reading.* Make the read-aloud interactive by inviting comments and questions from the children. Encourage them to connect with the characters and theme. ("Have you ever worn overalls like Corduroy's?") Expand on children's brief utterances ("lost button") to model more complex language. ("Yes, Corduroy had lost a button but he did not realize it.") Point out the targeted words when they occur in context and have children say the words with you.
4. *After reading.* Invite personal responses to the story and then revisit the targeted words as you model their use, pose questions, and elicit children's responses. ("Why do you think Corduroy admired the furniture in the store?" "What is something that you admire?" "Turn to your partner and use the word *admire* in a sentence.")

and to focus on words. To increase opportunities to talk, you might want to use the "turn and talk" technique described in the activity section. Children talk with assigned partners to answer a question, share a response, or make a prediction. Turn and talk techniques multiply the opportunities for individuals to articulate their own ideas and are especially beneficial for children who are shy or learning to speak English.

EXPERIENCES AND CONVERSATION. Reading aloud to children provides virtual experiences that can stimulate oral language and vocabulary learning, but real experiences with cooking, science experiments, special visitors, classroom pets, and field trips are particularly engaging and provide direct opportunities for verbal interactions. These experiences will be particularly important for English learners, but the immediacy of real life is engaging for all young children. It is easy to think that experiences and conversations just happen, and to a certain extent they do, but *planned* experiences with careful attention to vocabulary, language, and concepts are more likely to be fruitful. Even better, combining read-alouds with experiences supports the necessary repetition of targeted vocabulary and promotes linkages that facilitate learning. Because it is important for children to encounter new words and concepts in different contexts, planning experiences that promote vocabulary learning and help maintain that vocabulary over time is critical.

for **English Learners**

Let's say you have conducted a series of read-alouds on animals that make good pets, and you have decided to get a hamster for the classroom. Some of the concepts and vocabulary that you could develop and sustain include *hamster, male, female, habitat, nutrition, diet, exercise, bedding, gnaw,* and *nocturnal.* These words represent conceptual understandings you can develop about hamsters that children can then use in their daily conversations about hamsters.

Use the same criteria outlined earlier to select words: utility, concreteness, opportunities for repetition, and relatedness to theme. An experience like caring for a classroom pet can lead to lots of reading and writing activities as well. You might create labels with the students' help for the *cage, water bottle, exercise ball,* and so on. Students might dictate their observations and insights about hamsters in the language experience approach described beginning on page 119 or participate in an interactive writing activity described on page 137. In addition, you might ask students to illustrate and write about hamsters in their own journals.

Planned Extensions. Extensions to the read-aloud offer opportunities for children to interact with peers and apply their understanding of concepts and vocabulary through planned activities in cooperative learning formats or centers (Wasik, Bond, & Hindman, 2006). Prompting children to retell what they heard in the read-aloud encourages them to use new words and more complex sentence constructions in hands-on, engaging activities (Ward, 2009).

Retellings and Dramatic Play. After students have heard a story several times, they can be asked to retell the story and in the process use new vocabulary and language forms. First and foremost, reread favorites and then always keep books available so students can pick them up during free time to explore on their own. Retellings should be modeled for students as in the following example: "When you have a chance to look at this book on your own, try to retell the story. Watch how I do that by looking at the pictures." Proceed to retell the story using the pictures and your memory of the words.

An intervention known as dialogic reading is a well-researched approach to reading aloud that is designed to stimulate oral language and dialogue while enhancing children's ability to retell stories (Whitehurst, Arnold, Epstein, Angell, Smith, & Fischel, 1994). Studies of dialogic reading have demonstrated growth in expressive and receptive language when used by parents and teachers of at-risk preschoolers (Justice & Pullen, 2003; NELP, 2008). Instructional guidelines to enhance children's ability to retell stories through questioning, modeling, and recitation are described in Activity 4.2 at the end of this chapter. Children love to hear themselves on audio and you might find that they are even happier to do a retelling when they can also record themselves and listen to it afterward.

Use dramatic play to act out stories or parts of stories under adult direction to get lots of children actively involved as actors or audience. Brainstorm with children about which characters are needed and what each one will do and then walk through the dramatization by posing questions and prompting oral responses. You can also stimulate retellings by supplying props like puppets, flannel board cutouts, objects used in the story (such as three bowls for the three bears), or plastic figures. Stick puppets are easy to make by simply copying pictures of characters or objects from the book, adding some color, cutting around them, and gluing them to popsicle sticks. After modeling the use of props or puppets as a group activity, they can be placed in a center or made available during free time.

CONCEPT SORTS. The human mind appears to work by using a compare-and-contrast categorization system to develop concepts and relationships among objects and attributes. By recognizing similarities among items, it is possible to create groups or categories according to meaningful associations, the foundation of critical thinking (Gillet & Kita, 1979). The ability to categorize demonstrates maturing hierarchical and associative thinking, but needs to be coupled with conversation about why and how objects and pictures are being categorized. **Concept sorts** can be used at all levels of development as students categorize objects, pictures, words, or phrases.

Concept sorts can develop deeper understanding about words and how they relate to other words within a semantic field. For example, most 5-year-olds know about tables, chairs, sofas, beds, ovens, refrigerators, microwaves, and blenders, but in their minds, these may be all undifferentiated "things in a house." Teachers can help to expand children's understanding of "things in a house" by introducing two different conceptual categories—*furniture* (tables, chairs, sofas, and beds) and *appliances* (refrigerators, ovens, microwaves, and blenders). By comparing and contrasting the functional attributes of these "things in a house," teachers can expand children's word knowledge to include new vocabulary that describes their relationship. Discussion can focus on how appliances are different from furniture, such as the fact that appliances require "electricity" and need to be plugged into "receptacles." Basic concept development tasks are a surprisingly simple way to provide such experiences, and they are also a good way to engage English learners and get them involved in verbal interactions (Bear & Helman, 2004).

Concept sorts can be used to extend read-alouds and provide additional exposure to new vocabulary. For example, after listening to Ruth Heller's book *Chickens Aren't the Only Ones*, children might be provided picture cards to sort into groups of birds, mammals, and reptiles. In this way, children build on a simple conceptual understanding of where eggs come from to include other attributes of the animal kingdom. Concept sorts based on daily life experiences and information gleaned from books develop and expand children's understandings of their world and the language to talk about it. For example, during a unit on animals, a teacher could introduce children to a concept sort such as the one shown in Figure 4.8.

for Words Their Way™

Go to PDToolkit for *Words Their Way*, click on the Sorts and Games tab, and select Emergent Stage and then Concept Sorts to find four prepared picture sorts: Work and Play, Clothes and Body Parts, Creatures, and Transportation.

The concept sorts described in the activities section of this chapter are all variations on the theme of categorization tasks. In addition to basic sorting, concept development activities are generally followed by draw-and-label or cut-and-paste procedures as described in Chapter 3. As always, we recommend having children write at every possible opportunity during or following the concept sorts. As a culminating activity for a unit on animals, one kindergarten teacher helped her children create their own books in which they drew pictures of their favorite animals. When asked to label these pictures or write briefly about the animals her children's efforts ranged from scribbles and random letters to readable approximations such as "I LIK THE LINS N TGRS."

FIGURE 4.8 Concept Sort with Farm Animals and Zoo Animals

If the pictures used in concept sorts reflect words that are new to students, they need to be directly taught. It will be important to talk about the meaning of the word and use it repeatedly each time it appears in sorting. For example, when sorting birds and animals, it may

for **English Learners**

be a good time to stop and talk about the meaning of *claw* or *hoof*. English learners will need to learn the names of more common objects, like *cup*. Students should be encouraged to name the pictures as they sort to provide additional practice saying and hearing others pronounce new words, and they should also be asked to describe their categories.

ASSESSING AND MONITORING VOCABULARY GROWTH. Instructional activities to extend the read-alouds such as retellings and concept sorts can also be used to measure progress in children's vocabulary growth. Teachers can note increases in word use or tally the number of ideas, facts, or concepts expressed in the retelling or in the explanation of the sort. Retell assessments have been shown to be authentic, valid, and reliable means of assessing understanding (Fuchs, Fuchs, & Maxwell, 1988). Noting the number of objects, pictures, or items correctly sorted into conceptual categories can also yield a reliable means of assessing depth of receptive vocabulary (Ward, 2009). Other developmentally appropriate ways of assessing receptive vocabulary growth in emergent learners include pointing to pictures that answer direct questions (e.g., Which picture is the veterinarian?) or answering sets of yes/no questions (e.g., Is an acorn a seed? Do plants grow from seeds? Do all seeds look the same?).

Phonological Awareness (PA)

The ability to pay attention to, identify, and reflect on various sound segments of speech is known as phonological awareness. It is the umbrella term for a range of understandings about speech sounds, including syllables, rhyme, and a sense of alliteration. Phonemic awareness is a subcategory of phonological awareness and refers to the ability to identify and reflect on the smallest units of sound: individual phonemes. The ability to segment *sit* or *thick* into three sounds (/s/-/i/-/t/ or /th/-/i/-/ck/) is an example of phonemic awareness. Children can hear and use individual phonemes easily at a tacit level—they can talk and can understand when others talk to them. But bringing tacit, subconscious awareness of individual phonemes to the surface to be examined consciously and explicitly is not easily achieved.

A certain amount of phonological awareness is critical to future reading success, and participation in phonological awareness activities has a positive influence on beginning reading (Ball & Blachman, 1988). However, phonological awareness does not have to precede or follow alphabet knowledge or other components of emergent literacy instruction. Research suggests that phonological awareness develops concurrently with students' growing understanding of how the spelling system works to represent sound (Stahl & McKenna, 2001). Although children do need a certain amount of phonological awareness to grasp the alphabetic nature of English, understanding of beginning sounds will get them started. Thereafter, phonological awareness, word recognition, decoding, and spelling will continue to develop in a symbiotic fashion. Growth in one area stimulates growth in another (Ehri, 2006; Morris et al., 2003; Perfetti, Beck, Bell, & Hughes, 1987). Although phonological awareness is essential, related activities need not be conducted as isolated tasks, nor do they need to take up a lot of time. According to some estimates, an entire year of phonemic awareness instruction need not exceed 20 hours (Armbruster, Lehr, & Osborn, 2001).

Phonological awareness develops gradually over time and progresses from a sensitivity to big chunks of speech sounds, such as syllables and rhyme, to smaller parts of speech sounds, such as individual phonemes (Pufpaff, 2009; Pullen & Justice, 2003). Early emergent readers need to participate in phonological awareness activities that focus attention on syllables and rhyming words whereas middle emergent readers learn alliteration by sorting pictures that begin with the same sound. Phonological awareness activities in preschool and primary classrooms can be engaging whole-group language activities that benefit all students, using a variety of instructional strategies that have been identified as successful and effective (Blachman, 1994; Lundberg, Frost, & Peterson, 1988; Smith, Simmons, & Kame'enui, 1995). The activity section of this chapter has many suggestions and additional resources are listed in Resource Connections: Resources for Phonological Awareness on the next page.

▶ Resources for Teaching Phonological Awareness

Adams, M. J., Foorman, B. A., Lundberg, I., & Beeler, T. (1998). *Phonemic awareness in young children.* Baltimore, MD: Paul H. Brookes.

Blevins, W. (1997). *Phonemic awareness activities for early reading success.* New York: Scholastic.

Ericson, L., & Juliebo, M. F. (1998). *The phonological awareness handbook for kindergarten and primary teachers.* Newark, DE: International Reading Association.

Fitzpatrick, J. (1998). *Phonemic awareness: Playing with sounds to strengthen beginning reading skills.* Cypress, CA: Creative Teaching Press.

Opitz, M. F. (2000). *Rhymes and reasons: Literature and language play for phonological awareness.* Portsmouth, NH: Heinemann.

Yopp, H. K., & Yopp, R. E. (2000). *Oo-pples and boo-noo-noos.* Portsmouth, NH: Heinemann.

Partial phonemic awareness is achieved at the very end of the emergent phase of literacy development when children are able to isolate consonant sounds at the beginnings (and sometimes ends) of words. Development of full phonemic awareness is achieved during the letter name–alphabetic stage as children become able to isolate vowels and tightly meshed blends. We can see this progression in children's spelling of *slide* as it moves from partial (S or SD) to developing (SID or SLD) to full (SLID).

SYLLABLES AND WORDS. Young children are very concrete thinkers, so it is not surprising that they associate the length of a word with the size of its referent. Although *caterpillar* is a fairly long word, it refers to a relatively small insect, and so it is common to find that children think the word *caterpillar* is smaller than the word *cat*, because cats are bigger than caterpillars. This is no "small" confusion because to learn to read it is necessary to pay attention to the word's sound independently of its meaning.

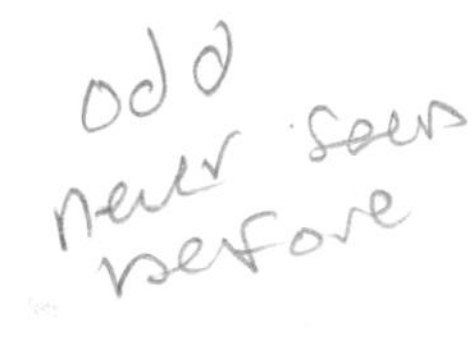

Building phonological sensitivity in young children is complicated by the fact that words are made up of more than one **syllable.** A first step in leading children to an awareness of spoken words as a unit is to take two concrete "short" words and make them into one "long" *compound word* (for example: *snow, man, snowman*). Although the emphasis in building phonological sensitivity is on the sounds of words, there can be a productive interplay between sound and meaning.

RHYMES, JINGLES, AND SONGS. Rhyme awareness activities are an easy, natural way for children to play with words and to begin to focus on speech sounds. Songs, jingles, nursery rhymes, and poems fill children's ears with the sounds of rhyme. Many children develop a sense of rhyme easily, whereas others need more structured activities that draw their attention specifically to rhyming words. The easiest approach is to talk about the rhyming words in favorite and familiar books and poems. Some books and poems lend themselves to an activity in which you simply pause and let the children supply the second rhyming word in a couplet. When picture books such as *Oh, A-Hunting We Will Go* by J. Langstaff or *Is Your Mama a Llama?* by Deborah Guarina are used, children have the support of the illustrations to help them out. Some other favorite rhyming books are listed in the activities section at the end of this chapter.

Go to PDToolkit for *Words Their Way,* click on the Sorts and Games tab, then type "Rhymes" to find several ready-to-use rhyme sorts.

Rhyming book read-alouds can be followed by picture sorts for rhymes. For example, a rhyming **sort** extension to *Oh, A-Hunting We Will Go* is to match up pictures of animals and the places they will go (fox/box, mouse/house, goat/boat, etc.). To make it easier for beginners, lay out just two pictures that rhyme along with one that does not. This odd-one-out

FIGURE 4.9 Odd-One-Out with Rhyming Words

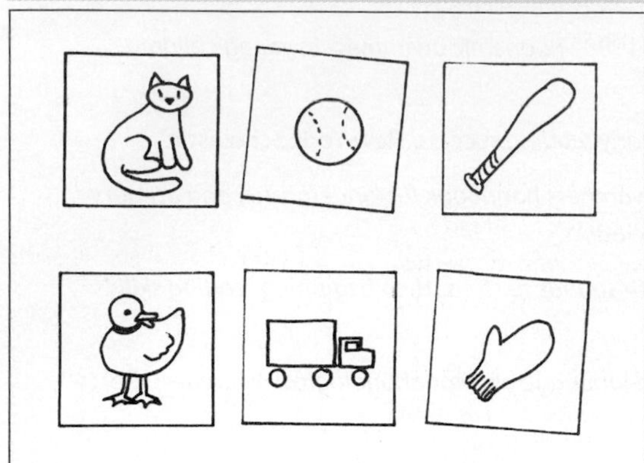

setup, shown in Figure 4.9, enables children to identify more readily the two rhyming pictures. They have only to pick up an animal and the rhyming object.

Songs are naturally full of rhythm and rhyme and hold great appeal for children. Several songs recorded by Raffi, a popular singer and songwriter for children, are particularly well suited for language play. For example, rhyme is featured prominently in the song "Willoughby Wallaby Woo" from the taped collection *Singable Songs for the Very Young*. The song features a rhyme starting with *W* for everyone's name and can be easily adapted for the children in your class. The teacher sings the initiating phrase ("Willoughby Wallaby Wackie"), changing the first letter of a name to *W*, and children sing the next phrase, naming the appropriate child ("An elephant sat on Jackie"). A stuffed elephant can be passed to the child to add to the fun. The song can be changed to focus on alliteration by holding up a particular letter to insert in front of every word. *B*, for example, would result in "Billaby Ballaby Boo," and *F* would produce "Fillaby Fallaby Foo."

for **English Learners**

English learners may not understand rhyming in English. In Spanish, for example, rhyming focuses on the stress and vowels in words, whereas in English rhyming focuses more on word endings. Expect that developing a sense of rhyme in English may take a little longer to master for English learners than native speakers.

As children become more adept at listening for rhymes, they can play a variety of categorization and matching games. Traditional games such as Bingo, Lotto, and Concentration, in which picture cards are matched to other picture cards that rhyme, are always winners. More ideas for rhyming games and activities can be found in the activity section of this chapter.

ALLITERATION AND BEGINNING SOUNDS. Children must become aware that speech can be divided into smaller segments of sound—phonemic awareness—before they will advance in literacy. They must also learn some of the terminology used to talk about these sounds. Without this knowledge, instruction in phonics or letter–sound correspondences will have little success. Children have no trouble hearing sounds, but directions such as "Listen for the first sound" may mystify them. In response to the question "What sound does *cow* start with?" one puzzled child tentatively replied, "Moo?" Without a stable concept of word in text, "first sound" is a relative notion. Phonemic awareness activities at the emergent level should help students attend to sounds and learn to label and categorize these sounds in various ways.

Activities that play with **alliteration** focus children's attention on the beginning sounds that mark word boundaries in print. This awareness of beginning sounds supports children as they learn to separate the speech stream into individual words. A number of activities help promote children's understanding of beginning sounds, starting with ABC books such as *Dr. Seuss's ABC*, which celebrates alliteration in the famous Seuss style. Beginning-sound segmentation games can be played with puppets or stuffed animals that have a funny way of talking. The puppet teaches the children how to isolate the initial phoneme from the remaining portion of the word. The children are then asked to repeat what the puppet said. The children get to manipulate the puppet themselves as they segment words given by the teacher. For example, Pat the Puppet first says "p–ig," and the students repeat by saying "p–ig." Then the teacher says "pick" and asks the students to say the word like Pat the Puppet would say it in "puppet talk." The children respond with "p–ick" (Treiman, 1985).

Teachers can use hints in games such as I Spy or I'm Thinking of Something to accentuate the initial sound. "This thing I'm thinking of begins with *mmmmm*. This thing is small and gray. It is an animal." As the children respond "mouse" or "mole," the teacher asks them to exaggerate the beginning sound. As children become proficient at playing this game, they create their own riddles. By encouraging students to emphasize the beginning sounds of the words, children learn about first sounds as part of guessing the answers to the riddles.

Alliteration is further developed as children sort pictures by beginning sound under a corresponding letter, an activity that will be described shortly. At this point, oral language activities designed to teach phonemic awareness cross over into the learning of letter–sound correspondences. This is known as **phonics.**

ASSESSING AND MONITORING PHONOLOGICAL AWARENESS. The research on the development of phonological awareness identifies two ways of understanding sound units as significantly related to reading outcomes: (a) rhyme awareness and (b) individual phoneme awareness (Swank, 1991; Yopp, 1988). Two assessments are provided on the website to gather information about these. The assessment for rhyme asks children to identify two rhyming pictures from a set of three (*duck*, *ball*, and *truck*). The Beginning Sounds Assessment is an alliterative matching task in which children are asked to find the picture that begins with the same sound. They are given a key picture such as *sun* and three choices such as *book*, *soap*, and *jet*.

PDToolkit for Words Their Way™

Go to PDToolkit for *Words Their Way*, click on the Assessment Tools tab, select Assessment Materials, and then type "Rhyme and Beginning Sounds."

Phonological awareness tasks similar to these have been scientifically validated by Invernizzi and her colleagues with thousands of children screened in Virginia with Phonological Awareness Literacy Screening (PALS) (Invernizzi et al., 2006) assessments at the preschool and kindergarten levels. Monitoring the development of phonological awareness during kindergarten helps to identify children who need additional instruction.

Alphabet Knowledge

Among the reading readiness skills that are traditionally studied, the one that appears to be the strongest predictor of later reading success on its own is letter naming (NELP, 2008; Snow, Burns, & Griffin, 1998). There is a great deal to learn about the alphabet. Letters have names, a set sequence, sounds, and upper- and lowercase forms. They must be written in particular ways, and directional orientation is vital. In the three-dimensional world, a chair is a chair whether you approach it from the front or the back, from the left or the right. Not so with letters: A *b* is a *b* and a *d* is a *d*. Print is one of the few things in life in which direction makes a difference and young children lack this directionality. They also confuse letters that share visual features: *S* may be mistaken for *Z*, *E* for *F*, *h* for *n*, and so forth (Clay, 1975; Ehri & Roberts, 2006). In addition, children must learn to recognize the salient stable characteristics of letters across different fonts, sizes, shapes, and textures, as shown in Figure 4.10. It is from seeing such variations and encountering *B* in many contexts that an abstract concept of *B* is formed.

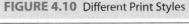

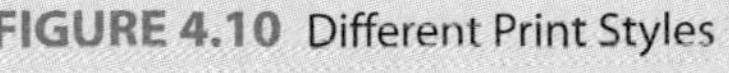
FIGURE 4.10 Different Print Styles

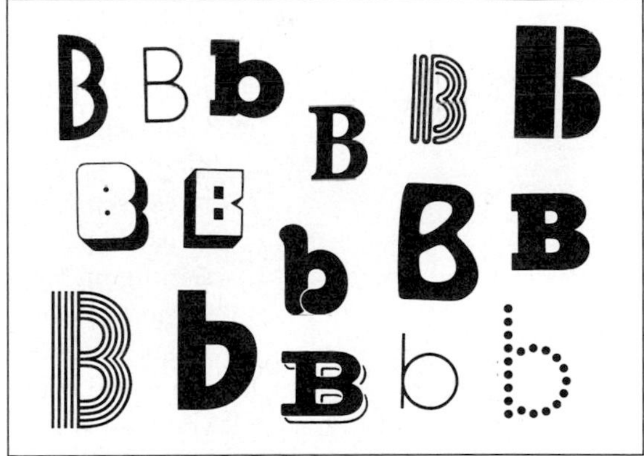

Learning the names of the letters is an important first step toward learning the sounds associated with the letters. Most of the letters have names that include a sound commonly associated with it and can serve as mnemonic devices for remembering the sounds (Kim, Petscher, Foorman, & Zhou, 2010). *B* (bee), *K* (kay), and *Z* (zee) have their sounds at the beginnings of their names, whereas *F* (eff), *L* (ell), and *S* (ess) have their sounds at the end. The names of the vowels are their long sounds. Only *H* (aitch), *W* (doubleyou), and the consonant *Y* (wie) have no sound association, and not surprisingly these letters are often the most difficult to learn. Letter names serve as the first reference point many children use when writing and explain some of the interesting invented spellings they create during the letter name–alphabetic stage, discussed more in the next chapter.

Most mainstream middle-class children take five years to acquire this alphabet knowledge at home and in preschool. Magnetic letters on the refrigerator door, alphabetic puzzles, and commercial alphabet games are staples in many middle-class homes (Adams, 1990). Truly advantaged youngsters also have attentive parents at the kitchen table modeling letter formation and speech segmentation as they encourage their child to write a grocery list or a note to Grandma. Yet many of these children also require the direct instruction provided by formal schooling to fully understand the complexity of the alphabet. Other students have less preparation. The best way to share five years of accumulated alphabet knowledge with those who have not been privy to this information is to teach it directly, in as naturalistic, fun, and gamelike a manner as possible (Delpit, 1988).

TEACHING THE ALPHABET. The alphabet is learned the same way that concepts and words for concepts are learned—through active exploration of the relationships between letter names, the sounds of the letter names, their visual characteristics, and the motor movement involved in their formation. Alphabet games and activities are designed to develop all aspects of alphabet knowledge including letter naming, letter recognition (both uppercase and lowercase), letter writing, and letter sounds. Many alphabet activities begin with the child's name, building it with letter tiles, cutting it out of play dough, or matching it letter for letter with a second set. Writing or copying their own names and the names of other family members or friends is alluring to emergent writers, making a great introduction to the alphabet as well as to writing. Letters take on personalities: *K* is Katie's letter and *T* is Tommy's letter.

The following list provides some general routines for teaching children about the forms and functions of the alphabet. See the activity section at the end of this chapter for more detail about these activities as well as games that include traditional formats like Bingo and Concentration.

Go to Go to PDToolkit for *Words Their Way,* click on the Sorts and Games tab, then type "Alphabet" to find several ready-to-use font sorts.

- To teach the letter sequence, sing the alphabet song daily until children know it by heart. In addition, point to the letters as they sing and then give students a copy of the alphabet strip so they can practice pointing individually. Use the strip to ask students to find and touch letters you name or to tell you what comes before or after a letter.
- Share alphabet books with children, pointing out the capital and lowercase forms and naming the pictures that begin with a letter. Children typically learn capital letters first, but by kindergarten, lowercase letters are needed and both can be taught together along with the sounds associated with them. See a list of books and more ideas in the activity section.
- Make alphabet books available for children to explore on their own but teach children how to use them independently. Tell them to say something like this: "Here is the capital *B* and the lowercase *b*. *Bear* and *bowl* begin with *b*."
- Children's names provide a meaningful context for the study of specific letters (Cunningham, 2005). Studying a name each day is a more appropriate pace than letter of the week (see Activity 4.23). Set up your classroom so that children need to use their names to participate in daily activities—signing in each day for attendance and lunch choices or signing up for centers or popular tasks like feeding the fish. Start by providing preprinted name cards but move toward expecting children to write out their names.
- Point out letters on signs, in book titles, on charts, and all around the school. The modern world is full of letters, but teachers need to draw children's attention to them. When you read and write with children there are endless opportunities to talk about letters; this helps children understand the many functions letters serve.
- Create an alphabet center where children have access to puzzles and games that are changed on a regular basis. Also, provide an alphabet strip and a variety of writing implements (markers, chalk, rubber stamps) and surfaces (paper, card stock, chalkboards, whiteboards, Magna Doodles, etc.) to encourage children to write and form their letters. Create letter sorts with both upper- and lowercase letters in a variety of fonts and print styles (see Activity 4.30).

PDToolkit
for Words Their Way™

Go to PDToolkit for *Words Their Way,* click on the Assessment Tools tab, select Assessment Materials, then type "Alphabet" to find several assessments.

- Letter formation is an important and often neglected component of early literacy instruction (Graham, Harris, & Fink, 2000). Teach children how to write the letters and provide a variety of ways to create letters out of clay, pipe cleaners, or cookie dough. Children can trace textured letters, make letters in trays filled with sand, or glue down rice, pasta, or beans in the shapes of letters. In teaching letter formation, it is a good idea to be consistent about spatial matters such as where to start and directionality. Have children vocalize these movements as they form their letters (e.g., "up, down, up, down" for *M;* "around" for *O*) and also repeat the letter names as they trace them.

ASSESSING AND MONITORING GROWTH IN ALPHABET KNOWLEDGE. To determine how much instruction is needed for learning letters, teachers need to use a variety of tasks. Students may be asked to point to and recite the letters in order as a first step. Watch out for how they handle *LMNOP:* Sometimes it becomes one letter! Both capital and lowercase letters should also be presented in random order to assess letter recognition. Alphabet recognition assessments are included on the website. Letter production is easily assessed by calling out letters, in or out of order, for students to write. According to research conducted with hundreds of thousands of kindergartners in the Commonwealth of Virginia, kindergartners should be able to recognize and name a minimum of 12 lowercase letters (presented in random order) in the fall of the year and nearly all of them by the end of kindergarten (Invernizzi et al., 2006). Alphabet learning is easy to monitor and teachers should assess regularly to adjust the content and intensity of their instruction and to plan additional instructional opportunities for students who are not making progress.

MONITORING PROGRESS

Letter–Sound Knowledge

Go to PDToolkit for *Words Their Way,* click on the Sorts and Games tab, then type "Beginning Consonant Picture Sorts" to find ready-to-use sorts.

During the emergent stage, children learn their letters, attend to speech sounds, and begin to make connections between letters and sounds. Toward the end of the emergent stage, many children will begin producing partial phonetic spellings that contain one or two letters for each syllable (see Figure 4.3, page 96). This is the beginning of the alphabetic principle, the idea that letters and letter combinations are used to represent phonemes in the orthography. Picture sorting by beginning sounds secures these tentative efforts and moves children along in acquiring more knowledge of letter–sound correspondences through a gamelike, manipulative phonics activity.

Some teachers choose *M* and *S* for students' first consonant contrast because both letters have continuant sounds that can be isolated and elongated without undue distortion (*mmmmoon* and *ssssun*). The sounds also feel very different in the mouth during articulation, which makes it easier for children to judge the categories while sorting. The sound for *B* (/b/) cannot be elongated or isolated without adding a vowel to it (*buh*), but it is still fairly easy to learn, perhaps because it has a distinctive feel as the lips press together and also because it is one of the earliest consonantal phonemes acquired during oral language development (Pense & Justice, 2008). However, to contrast *B* and *P* in an early sort would be confusing because they are both **articulated** the same way (Purcell, 2002). The only difference is that the /b/ sound causes the vocal cords to vibrate whereas /p/ does not. Try placing two fingers on your larynx and feel the difference in voiced /b/ and unvoiced /p/ as you say *bay* and *pay*.

A pronunciation chart of consonants is shown in Table 4.2. Read across each row saying the sound of the letter (i.e., /p/, /b/, /m/) to see how those sounds share the same place of articulation (i.e., lips together). Compare the voiced and unvoiced pairs such as /f/ and /v/ or /t/ and /d/. Notice how the nasal sounds of /m/, /n/, and /ng/ pass through the nose rather than the mouth. Understanding something about articulation may seem unnecessarily complicated, but it explains so many of the interesting things children do in their invented spellings during the emergent and letter name–alphabetic stages. Use the chart to see the logic in the invented spelling JP for *chip,* VN for *fan,* and PD for *pet.* In each case the substitutions vary only because one is voiced and the other is unvoiced. Otherwise, they are articulated exactly the same way. Knowledge of articulation also helps teachers make decisions about setting up picture sorts. The letters in any row will feel very much alike and are best not contrasted in the very first letter–sound sorts. Remember the sixth principle of word study highlighted in Chapter 3: Begin with obvious contrasts!

Go to PDToolkit for *Words Their Way,* click on the Additional Resources tab, then type "Word Study in Spanish in the Letter Name–Alphabetic Stage," where you will find prepared sorts.

English learners are often unfamiliar with many of the sounds of English and will substitute sounds and letters closest to their primary languages and alphabets. Many English learners will not articulate some sounds for awhile, but their substitutions are logical. For

Table 4.2 Pronunciation Chart of Consonant Sounds

UNVOICED	VOICED	NASALS	OTHER	PLACE OF ARTICULATION
p	b	m		lips together
wh	w			lips rounded
f	v			teeth and lips
th (thin)	th (the)			tip of tongue and teeth
t	d	n	l	tip of tongue and roof of mouth
s	z			tongue and roof of mouth
sh			y	sides of tongue and teeth
ch	j		r	sides of tongue and roof of mouth
k	g	ng		back of tongue and throat
h				no articulation—breathy sound

for **English Learners**

example, Spanish speakers may use the letter *v* to represent the /b/ sound. The logic behind the misspellings of English learners was discussed in Chapter 2 and more detail will be provided in Chapter 5.

GUIDELINES FOR BEGINNING SOUND PICTURE SORTS. There are a number of factors to keep in mind when organizing sorts for beginning letter sounds.

- *Start with meaningful text.* Choose several sounds to contrast that represent key words from a familiar rhyme, patterned book (such as *Oh, A-Hunting We Will Go*), or dictation. One advantage of teacher-directed word study over packaged programs is that teachers can integrate phonics and the variety of printed materials used in emergent classrooms.
- *Make sorts easier or harder as needed.* Start with two obvious contrasts and then add one or two for up to four categories. Look for fast and accurate picture sorting before moving on. Be ready to drop back to fewer categories if a child has difficulty.
- *Use a key picture* and *a letter as headers.* Using a key picture and a letter as a header helps students associate the letter and the sound. The headers may be letters or words selected from familiar text. Suggested key pictures can be found on the sound boards in Appendix B. Whatever key word you select, be consistent and use the same one every time.
- *Begin with teacher-directed sorts.* Discuss both the sound and the letter name, and model the placement of two or three pictures in each category. Be explicit about why you sort the way you do. Say, for example, "Foot, fffoot, ffffox. *Foot* and *fox* start with the same sound, *ffff.* I will put *foot* under the letter *F.*" Over time, as children catch on to what it is they are to attend to, you can use fewer directives. Figure 4.1 on page 93 shows how this sort would look after several pictures are sorted. Pictures for sorting can be found in Appendix C. These can be enlarged for group modeling.
- *Use sets of pictures that are easy to name and sort.* Introduce the pictures to be sure that children know what to call them. Use easily identified pictures that do not start with consonant blends or digraphs. Single-syllable words are better than two-syllable words because they have fewer sounds that need attention.

- *Correct mistakes on the first sort but allow errors to wait on subsequent sorts.* Show children how to check their sorts by naming the pictures down the columns, emphasizing the beginning sounds. Then ask if there are any pictures that need to be changed. Tell children to check their own work using the same process and praise them when they find their own errors. If they do not, prompt them by saying, "There is a picture in this row that needs to be changed. Can you find it?"
- *Vary the group sorting.* Start by putting out all the pictures face up and let children choose one that they feel confident in naming and sorting correctly. Ask them to name the picture and the letter by saying "_____ begins with the _____ sound and goes under the letter _____." Another time pass out the pictures and call on children to come up and sort the card they were given. Then turn the pictures face down in a stack or spread them out on the floor and let children turn over the picture they will sort. Children enjoy the anticipation of not knowing which picture they will get.
- *Plan plenty of time for individual practice.* After group modeling and discussion, put sets of pictures in centers or create copies of picture sets for children to cut apart for more sorting. Sheets of pictures for sorting can be created by copying pictures from this book, cutting them apart, and pasting them in a mixed-up fashion on a template.
- *Plan follow-up activities.* Cut-and-paste, draw and label, and word hunts through familiar chart stories, nursery rhymes, or little books are helpful follow-up activities. They require children to recognize, or recall, the same beginning sounds and to judge whether they fit the category.
- *Encourage pretend writing and invented spelling.* In the process of inventing spellings, children exercise their developing phonemic awareness and letter–sound knowledge in a meaningful activity (Clarke, 1988; NRP, 2000; Snow et al., 1998). To get students started, demonstrate how to use letters to represent sounds as you write with children during interactive writing (see the Morning Message described in Activity 4.40). Asking young children to "write a story" may loom as an impossible task when their concept of a story is a picture book! Asking them to label their drawings or to write just a sentence about something is a good way to get writing started.

ASSESSING AND MONITORING GROWTH IN LETTER–SOUND KNOWLEDGE. There are several ways to assess children's abilities to match beginning consonant sounds to the appropriate letters. Observing children's daily efforts to write using invented spelling provides ongoing and authentic information. The Emergent Class Record found on the website will help you analyze children's writing across the emergent stage. There is also a Beginning Consonant Sounds and Letters assessment on the website that asks children to circle a picture that begins with a given letter. A simple five-word spelling assessment such as the Kindergarten Spelling Inventory (KSI), also found on the website, is particularly appropriate for late emergent spellers. You might also call out a few of the words on the earliest inventory described in Chapter 2.

Go to PDToolkit for *Words Their Way,* click on the Assessment Tools tab, select Assessment Materials, then type "Emergent Spelling Class Record."

Longitudinal research indicates that kindergarten children should be aware that letters are associated with speech sounds and be able to provide at least 4 letter sounds in the fall of the year and at least 20 letter sounds in the spring (Invernizzi et al., 2005). Students should be assessed formally at least three times a year and informally all the time using daily writing. For children receiving additional instructional interventions, more frequent monitoring is recommended to gauge their progress (Invernizzi, 2009).

Concepts about Print (CAP)

Children are surrounded by print on signs, package labels, magazines, and television—even on the clothes they wear; however, children need adults to talk about the purposes print serves and the special ways in which the visual forms of print are organized. For example, when you print the words to "Where Is Thumbkin" on chart paper and point to them as the children sing along, you are helping them understand concepts of print. It happens when you stop to

for Words Their Way™

Go to PDToolkit for *Words Their Way,* click on the Videos tab, and type "Whole Class Reading and Picture Sort" to see Ms. Smith using *Oh, A-Hunting We Will Go* with sentence strips to develop concept of word. See "Small Group Reading and Sorting" for follow-up activities.

point out the *X* in the exit sign and explain what it means. It happens when you show a book cover and remind children that they have heard other stories written and illustrated by Tomie dePaola. The key is to be conscious of the many ways we use print and to think aloud as we draw children's attention to it in explicit ways; Justice and Ezell (2004) call this *print referencing*.

PRINT REFERENCING. When teachers have been trained to use a print referencing style during read-alouds, such as naming and pointing out letters or asking questions about print and pointing to words as they read, children have shown growth on measures of concepts about print, letter recognition, and name writing (Justice, Kaderavek, Fan, Sofka, & Hunt, 2009). Reading with children during read-alouds or shared reading, and writing with children during interactive writing and as you take dictations, provides abundant opportunities to develop concepts about print. Table 4.3 provides a list of the functions and forms of print and offers an example of print referencing that a teacher might use.

Table 4.3 CAP and Print Referencing Examples

FUNCTIONS OF PRINT	PRINT REFERENCING DURING READING AND WRITING
Print is speech written down and once written down it does not change	I'm going to write down what you say and then we can read it back.
Print is different from illustrations	You look at the picture while I read what it says over here.
Print carries a message	Here are the words to "Humpty Dumpty." Can you find the box that says "scissors"?
Print serves many purposes	Here is the recipe for cookies. Let's read and find out what ingredients we need.

FORMS OF PRINT	PRINT REFERENCING DURING READING AND WRITING
Book-handling skills—Start with the cover and turn from front to back	Let's look at the cover of the book to see what it is about.
Directionality—Print is oriented left to right with a return sweep and top to bottom	This is the top of the page where I will start reading. Then I will go to the next line. Show me where to go next.
Language related to units of print—Letters (capital and lowercase), numbers, words, sentences, lines	There are four letters in this word. Let's name them. The first letter is a capital because it is a person's name.
Language related to books—Title, author, illustrator, title page, dedication, poem, song, beginning, end	We have read another book by this author. Where do we look for the author's name?
Language related to phonological sensitivity—Syllable, sound, beginning and ending sound	This is a long word. Let's clap the syllables in *caterpillar.* Can this word be *rug?* What is the first sound in *rug?*
Punctuation and special print—Periods, question marks, exclamation marks, quotation marks, bold print, italics	Listen to how I read this sentence. It ends with an exclamation point so I want it to make it sound exciting.
Concept of word—Words are composed of a string of letters; words are separated by spaces	Watch while I point to the words in this sentence. We need to leave a space here before we write the next word.
Word identification—Words can be identified in different contexts	Here is the word *cat.* Can you find the word again on this page? What will you look for?

Source: Adapted from Justice et al., 2009.

Teachers can reference specific forms and functions of print during tasks that encourage children to write their own names, such as sign-up procedures. When print is incorporated into dramatic play centers such as restaurants, doctors' offices, and so on, children use writing as they pretend to be waiters writing down a dinner order, doctors writing a prescription, and the like. In the process they learn that print takes many forms and serves many functions.

ASSESSING AND MONITORING GROWTH IN CAP. Marie Clay (1985) first developed a formal protocol for assessing concepts about print using a series of questions while sharing a book with a child. Many variations of this exist; in fact, state and local standards for early literacy may include a checklist of questions regarding children's development in CAP. Concepts about print can be informally assessed all the time as you read and write with children by posing questions such as "Who can point to a capital letter *D*?" or "What do we put at the end of a sentence?" Concepts about print can also be observed in children's efforts to write their names. Their efforts, which may range from scribbles to letterlike forms mixed with numbers to recognizable signatures, can predict later literacy achievement (Welsch, Sullivan, & Justice, 2003).

Concept of Word in Text (COW)

The ultimate concept about print is achieving a concept of word in text (COW), the ability to fingerpoint or track accurately to printed words in text while reading from memory. Reaching this milestone depends on the ability to isolate the beginning consonant sounds of spoken words and activate letter–sound correspondences. Incorporating concept of word activities into daily literacy practice not only strengthens students' speech-to-print matching, but it also solidifies their alphabet knowledge, their emerging phonemic awareness, and their knowledge of words in print. Prior to achieving a concept of word in text, emergent children, as well as emergent adults, have great difficulty identifying individual phonemes within words (Morais, Cary, Alegria, & Bertelson, 1979). There is an interaction between alphabetic knowledge, the ability to match speech to print, and phonemic awareness (Flanigan, 2006; Morris et al., 2003; Tunmer, 1991). However, achieving a concept of word in text is not an all-or-nothing affair—there is a developmental continuum.

The concept of word continuum includes developing, rudimentary, and firm levels. Emergent stage learners move from the developing level to a rudimentary concept of word. Students with a firm concept of word in text are no longer considered emergent and are discussed in the next chapter on letter name–alphabetic spellers. You can determine where your students are on the concept of word continuum by examining the accuracy of their fingerpoint reading to memorized rhymes and jingles, their ease of identifying words in context, and their ability to remember words in isolation that were viewed previously in context (Blackwell-Bullock, Invernizzi, Drake, & Howell, 2009; Flanigan, 2007; Morris, 1993).

DEVELOPING COW. Children who are just developing a COW will have some orientation to the page, moving from the top to the bottom but perhaps not from left to right. What they point to on the page as they recite does not coincide with printed word units at all. Like the babbling infant imitating the intonation contours of speech, the preliterate child points in a rhythmic approximation of the memorized text with little attention to word boundaries or even, perhaps, direction on the page.

Through teachers' demonstrations, children's fingerpointing behaviors change. Left-to-right movement becomes habitualized, though children may not routinely use letter or word units to guide their tracking. As white spaces are noted children begin to track rhythmically across the text, pointing to words for each stressed beat. For example, when tracking the traditional five-word ditty, "Sam, Sam, the baker man," they may point four times: Sam/Sam/the-baker/man, as if keeping time on a drum. An article (*the, a, an*) may be treated as part of the noun that follows it.

for **English Learners**

Learners with limited English will benefit from practicing fingerpointing using materials in their primary languages. Rhymes and jingles in Spanish can be found in *Words Their Way*™:

FIGURE 4.11 Trying to Match Voice to Print

Emergent Sorts for Spanish-Speaking English Learners (Helman, Bear, Invernizzi, Templeton, & Johnston, 2009) and *Words Their Way™: Letter Name–Alphabetic Sorts for Spanish-Speaking English Learners* (Helman, Bear, Invernizzi, Templeton, & Johnston, 2009).

RUDIMENTARY COW. As children become aware that print has something to do with sound units such as syllables, their fingerpointing becomes more precise and changes from a gross rhythm to a closer match. This rudimentary COW works well for one-syllable words, but not so well for words of two or more syllables. When they track "Sam, Sam, the baker man," they may now point six times: Sam/Sam/the/ba/ker/man. When they pronounce "ker," the second syllable of *baker*, they point to the next word, *man*. Figure 4.11 illustrates the phenomenon of getting off track on two-syllable words.

As children learn the alphabet and the sounds associated with the letters, beginning sounds will anchor the children's fingerpointing more directly to the memorized recitation. They realize that when they say the word *man*, they need to have their finger on a word beginning with an *m*. If they do not, then they must start again. These self-corrections signal a rudimentary COW. Figure 4.12 shows the progression of fingerpointing accuracy in relation to children's writing development during the emergent to early letter name–alphabetic stage of word knowledge. Students with a rudimentary concept of word will begin to remember a few written words. This is a sign that these children are on their way to becoming the beginning readers or the early letter name–alphabetic spellers described in the next chapter.

Some children will have difficulty simply memorizing the rhyme or jingle that you plan to use for assessing and teaching concept of word in text. Such students will benefit from memorizing and tracking just one or two lines of a jingle.

FINGERPOINT READING AND TRACKING WORDS. The best way for children to move from a developing to a rudimentary concept of word is to have them point to the words as they reread memorized text and to draw their attention to letters and sounds when they get off track. These texts might be picture captions, dictated experience stories, poems, songs, simple patterned books, or excerpts from a favorite story printed on sentence strips or chart paper. Once these texts become familiar, children can be encouraged to read them from memory, pointing to each word as it is spoken. In this way, children learn how to find the words on the page—an important prerequisite to acquiring a sight vocabulary.

Rhythmic texts are particularly appealing to use when children are developing a COW but may throw children off in their tracking. An eventual move to less rhythmic, less predict-

FIGURE 4.12 Voice-to-Print Match in Relation to Spelling Development

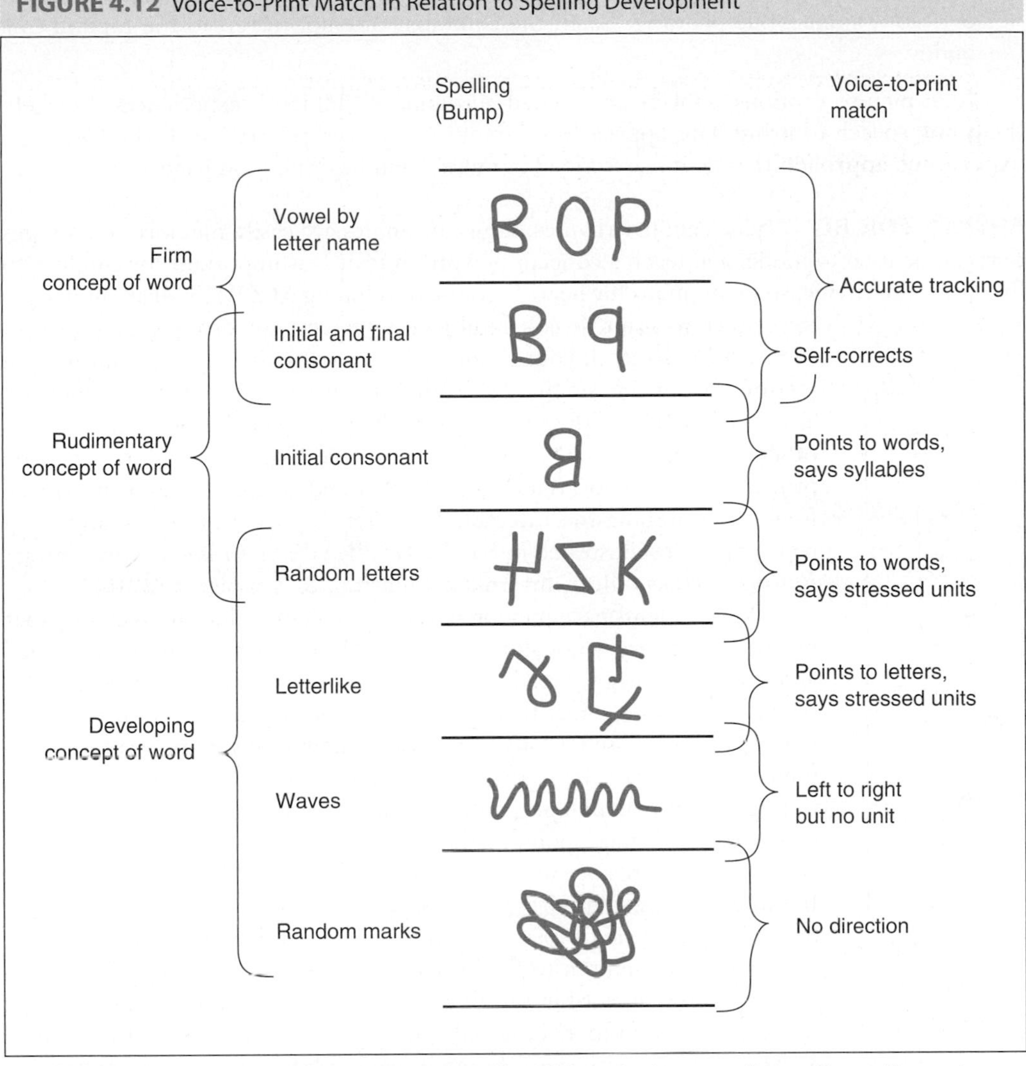

Source: Gill (1992). Focus on research: Development of word knowledge as it relates to reading, spelling, and instruction. *Language Arts, 69,* 6, 444–453. Adapted with permission.

able texts may be in order (Cathey, 1991). No matter what the source of text, the important idea from a word study point of view is to focus on individual words within the text as well as the letters and sounds at the beginnings of words.

DICTATIONS. One of the best ways to help children make connections between speech and print is to record what children say in a dictation and then to read it back. Picture captions can be quick and easy forms of dictation.

- First have the children draw a picture such as their favorite toy or Halloween costume and encourage them to include as much detail as possible.
- While they are finishing their drawings, walk around and ask each child to tell something about his or her picture. Choose a simple phrase or sentence from the child's description and write it verbatim beneath the picture (see Figure 4.13). Say each word as you write it, drawing attention to the sounds and letters and asking questions of the child when appropriate such as "What sound do you hear first?"

FIGURE 4.13 Drawing with Dictated Caption

- Read the caption by pointing to each word. Ask the child to read along with you and then to read it alone while pointing. Later, the child may attempt to reread the caption to a buddy.

Like picture captions, spoken or dictated accounts of children's experiences also help them link speech to print. This approach has traditionally been referred to as the **language experience approach** (LEA). It is described in more detail beginning on page 119.

RHYMES FOR READING. Familiar rhymes, songs, or jingles are easily memorized passages that can be used to model and teach a concept of word in text. It is important for children to first learn the rhyme, song, or jingle "by heart" because developing a COW is all about matching speech to print. It is helpful to use pictures for prompts as shown in Figure 4.14. To teach your children to memorize the rhyme, point to each picture frame while singing or reciting the line that goes with it, repeating as needed. Some children may only be able to memorize two lines whereas others can handle four or six. The Resource Connections box has some printed resources for traditional rhymes and jingles. They can also be found by searching the Internet. Many nursery rhymes, songs, and jump rope jingles are illustrated in *Words Their Way*™*: Letter and Picture Sorts for Emergent Spellers* (Bear, Invernizzi, Johnston, & Templeton, 2010).

FIGURE 4.14 Rhymes for Reading

Once students have memorized the rhyme, introduce it on chart paper printed in text large enough for all to see. Model how to fingerpoint "read" and invite students to "read" with you chorally (in unision) or using echo reading (you read a line, then they read the same line again, fingerpointing). If you have used a song, it is time to slow it down and read it at this point. After at least three passes (modeling, choral, echo), call on students to fingerpoint read independently, touching each word as they say it. After many rounds of fingerpoint reading, see whether students can find one or two targeted words per line. Point to a word and ask, "What's this word?" If a student doesn't know the word, show her how to start at the beginning of the line to reread or *voice point* up to the word in question. Alternatively, you might ask children to find a word in a particular line by providing a beginning sound. "I'm thinking of a word in this line that starts just like the word *ball.* What word am I thinking of? Can you point to it? How did you know that was the word I was thinking of? Yes! *Box* and *ball* both begin with the /b/ sound; they both begin with the letter *b!*"

Later, give students their own copy of the rhyme on a single sheet of paper so that they can get more practice pointing to the words as they read chorally and individually. You might also give them sentence strips to cut apart and rebuild the text, or individual word cards to match to the same words in context. When children have their own copies of the rhyme, they can highlight or underline the words you ask them to find. Words that students remember without having to voice point can be added to their beginning sound sorts. A detailed whole-to-part, five-day lesson plan for teaching a concept of word in text using memorable rhymes or jingles is described in Activity 4.41.

RESOURCE CONNECTIONS

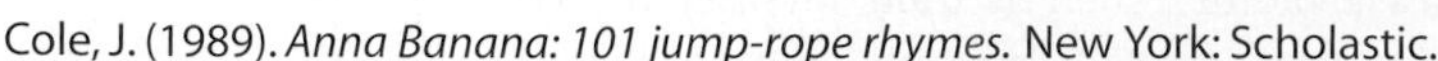

▶ Resources for Traditional Rhymes and Jingles

Cole, J. (1989). *Anna Banana: 101 jump-rope rhymes.* New York: Scholastic.

Cole, J., & Calmenson, S. (1990). *Miss Mary Mack and other children's street rhymes.* Illustrated by Alan Tiegreen. New York: Morrouno.

Schwartz, A. (1989). *I saw you in the bathtub.* New York: HarperCollins.

Sierra, J., & Sweet, M. (2005). *Schoolyard rhymes: Kids own rhymes for rope jumping, hand clapping, ball bouncing, and just plain fun.* New York: Knopf.

ASSESSING AND MONITORING GROWTH IN COW. Concept of word is easily assessed by asking children to point to individual words in a familiar piece of text, such as a nursery rhyme or jump rope jingle. "One, Two, Buckle My Shoe" or "Humpty Dumpty" work well because they have words of more than one syllable. Observe how children point to words on the page using the descriptors in Figure 4.12. After several rounds of fingerpoint reading, ask children to name the words that you point to in context or more randomly as described previously and observe their strategies. Do they reread an entire line and count up the memorized words to identify it? Or do they identify it immediately? Ask, "How did you find that word?" or "How did you know that word?" Students who can tell you that a word starts with a *w* are using developing letter–sound knowledge to track words in text. This is a necessary precursor to the acquisition of sight words, which is discussed in the next chapter. The COW assessment on the website can be used to monitor progress toward achieving a rudimentary COW across the year.

MONITORING PROGRESS

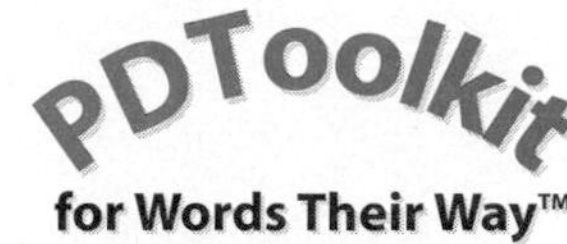

for Words Their Way™

Go to PDToolkit for *Words Their Way*, click on the Assessment Tools tab, select Assessment Materials, then type "Concept of Word Assessment."

The Language Experience Approach (LEA)

The six components of emergent literacy development—vocabulary, language, and concept development; phonological awareness; alphabet and letter–sound knowledge; concepts about print; and developing a COW—are all highly intercorrelated. One way to develop and integrate all of these components is through language-rich, hands-on experiences that engage students' attention and help them connect these abstract, decontextualized school-acquired concepts to everyday life. Students' narrative accounts of these experiences can be written down and used to develop emergent word knowledge. Developed by Stauffer (1980) and refined by Allen (1976) and others (Hall, 1980; Henderson, 1981; Nessel & Jones, 1981), the language experience approach (LEA) to reading is based on the premise that what one says can be written and what one writes can be read. The motivation and engagement that results from using students' self-generated language has revitalized an interest in LEA, especially for emergent learners and for students learning English as another language (Dorr, 2006). Experience is the best teacher!

Field trips, cooking activities, playground events, and class pets provide opportunities for shared experiences in which new vocabulary and the children's own language abounds. Students' observations and comments can then be written next to each child's name during a group dictation, as shown in Figure 4.15, or children can dictate individual accounts. In an activity described by McCabe (1996) called "Tell a story to get a story," the teacher tells a simple two-to-three-sentence story and then asks the children if they know a similar story: "Has anything like that happened to you?" Children tell their own stories, which the teacher records as dictations.

Children's own language should be recorded as closely as possible so that they will be able to read it back. Corrections to grammar should be approved by the child with prompts like "Good idea, can we say it this way?" When the dictation is completed, it should be read and reread many times. With this format, attention to words and their boundaries can be highlighted in a meaningful context. For example, a child may be asked to locate his or her own name in the group dictation or to find a word that starts with the same letter as his or her own name. Each child should get a personal copy of the dictation to practice fingerpointing while reading together chorally and from memory. These copies can be collected into a notebook called a *personal reader* (described in more detail in the next chapter). A second copy of the dictation can be cut apart into sentence strips or individual words to match back to the original.

FIGURE 4.15 Dictated Language Experience Chart

The Fire Station

Amanda said, "We went to the fire station yesterday."

Jason said, "We rode on a big orange bus."

Clint said, "I liked the ladder truck. It was huge!"

D. J. said, "The firemen told us how to be safe."

Beth said, "Firemen wear big boots and a mask."

The steps for LEA whole-to-part teaching are as follows:

- Teacher plans a hands-on experience such as a simple science experiment or feeding a baby animal. Students and teacher exchange thoughts and observations orally. New vocabulary is introduced and used.
- Students dictate a narrative account of the experience and their observations while the teacher records student statements on a chart—one statement per line for emergent learners. While writing, include print referencing.
- Students reread the dictated account several times until it becomes very familiar.
- Students get their own copy of the dictation to illustrate and use for voice pointing practice. Teacher uses whole-to-part teaching to develop concepts and vocabulary, alphabet knowledge, letter–sound correspondences, print concepts, and a concept of word in print.

Children in the late emergent stage with a rudimentary COW can begin to select words to include in a word bank of known words. Word banks are described in the next chapter.

WORD STUDY *Routines and Management*

The research in emergent literacy suggests that a comprehensive approach to instruction and early intervention is the most effective procedure (Pressley, 2006). A comprehensive approach includes attention to the six components of the literacy "diet" described in this chapter.

These essential components of emergent literacy can be integrated into major organizational time units during which teachers Read To, Read With, Write With, do Word Study, and Talk With (RRWWT). During *read to* time, teachers read aloud literature that offers exposure to new vocabulary and literary language. During *read with* time, children engage in shared reading and rereading of familiar texts. When teachers model how to write by stretching out the sounds in words and matching them to letters, they are *writing with* children, who will, in turn, write for themselves. *Word study* includes direct instruction in phonological awareness, the alphabet, and letter sounds. Finally, a comprehensive program provides students with ample opportunities to *talk with* teachers and peers about the books and experiences they have shared.

Combining these activities into a cohesive RRWWT routine is important so that the activities and materials flow together in a logical way and serve multiple purposes. Recall how Mrs. Smith introduced an engaging core book and used it to draw attention to letters and sounds, to highlight vocabulary, to offer children practice tracking familiar text, and to sort pictures by rhyme and beginning sounds. *Words Their Way™: Letter and Picture Sorts for Emergent Spellers* (Bear et al., 2010) offers examples of how these components can be integrated and provides prepared sorts as well as rhymes and jingles for reading.

Emergent Literacy Daily Management Plan

The daily management of emergent literacy instruction should include whole groups, small groups, and literacy centers, as outlined in Table 4.4. For example, Mrs. Smith first introduced a core book in which she modeled fingerpoint reading and other concepts about print for the whole group and then called a small group to introduce a picture sort of initial sounds that children later practiced independently.

Whole-group activities emphasize reading to and with children, teacher modeling, listening, and vocabulary development. Multiple opportunities for print referencing arise with whole-group instruction. Read-alouds serve many purposes and teachers of emergent children often plan two or more whole-group sessions during the day when they read aloud from a

Table 4.4 Emergent Literacy Plan

WHOLE-GROUP ACTIVITIES	SMALL-GROUP/CIRCLE TIME DIFFERENTIATED ACTIVITIES	SEAT/CENTER DIFFERENTIATED ACTIVITIES
"Read To": Read-alouds for thematic units and vocabulary work Introduce concept sorts	Concept sorts Retelling and dramatization	Practice concept sorts Retell using picture books, puppets, etc.
"Read With": Shared reading of big books, rhymes, songs, dictations Memorize "whole" texts such as nursery rhymes and jingles	Reread familiar texts until memorized "Parts"—Work with sentence strips, word cards, etc.	Partner or individual work with sentences and words
"Word Study": Sing and recite alphabet Share alphabet and language play books Name of the Day	Introduce differentiated sorts: rhyme, font, initial consonants	Practice sorts Letter and sound hunts Games and puzzles for rhyme, alphabet, initial consonants
"Write With": Modeled and interactive writing Morning Message	Language experience dictations	Picture captions Draw and label Journal writing

Note: "Talk With" happens throughout all the activities.

variety of genres, including information books related to thematic studies, alphabet books, and books with language play such as rhyme. Whole-group time can be used to sing songs while pointing to the words, practice the alphabet song, model writing, and introduce shared reading activities designed to facilitate CAP and COW. This is where the "whole" of the whole-to-part model takes place, with some attention to the parts.

Small groups or "circle time" is where students can participate actively under close adult supervision. This is the place to implement differentiated instruction according to assessed needs. Small groups can be formed initially on gradations of alphabet knowledge and phonological awareness but also on concept of word (developing vs. rudimentary). For example, some children will need to focus on alphabet recognition and look for letters in familiar texts, whereas children who already know their letters and have a rudimentary concept of word may be ready to acquire some sight words from repeated readings of familiar text. The small group is where the "parts" of the whole-to-part lesson format are addressed in depth, such as rhyming picture sorts or picture sorts for beginning sounds.

Independent work provides additional practice. Once students have been introduced to activities and sorts in small groups they can do them independently, sometimes with partners, in centers or "seats." Betty Lee's weekly word study routines described in Chapter 3 are designed for independent work. Games and puzzles, such as described in the Activities section that follows, should be first introduced and modeled in groups and then placed in centers. Writing can be an independent activity as children work in journals or draw and label pictures based on sorts.

RESOURCES FOR IMPLEMENTING WORD STUDY *in Your Classroom*

There are a number of materials available to help you implement word study with students in the emergent stage:

1. Pictures to create sound sorts for rhyme, initial sounds, and so on are in Appendix C and can be used with the template on page 397 to create your own sorts. See the directions and lists of rhyming pictures on pages 329 and 330.
2. Assessments, prepared sorts, and games are available on the website. With the Create Your Own feature you can drag pictures into a variety of game board templates.
3. *Words Their Way™: Letter and Picture Sorts for Emergent Spellers* (Bear et al., 2010) offers a complete curriculum of sorts including concept sorts, rhyme sorts, alphabet font sorts, and beginning consonant sorts. There are also 34 reading selections—ready-to-print illustrated copies of short rhymes and jingles to use for developing concept of word.
4. *Words Their Way™: Emergent Sorts for Spanish-Speaking English Learners* (Helman et al., 2009) provides many prepared sorts to develop concepts and vocabulary as well as sound sorts with different contrasts.

ACTIVITIES FOR THE EMERGENT STAGE

This section provides specific activities arranged by the six components of early literacy instruction. Within each, the activities are roughly in order of increasing difficulty. However, as noted earlier in this chapter, it is not the case that concept sorts must precede sound awareness, which in turn must precede alphabet. In reality, these develop simultaneously and constitute the "literacy diet" during the emergent years, with many activities that cut across the categories. Some of the games are generic to all stages of developmental word knowledge as indicated by the Adaptable for Other Stages symbol used throughout the book.

Oral Language, Concepts, and Vocabulary

Activities that include read-alouds, retellings, and concept sorts.

4.1 Using Read-Alouds to Develop Vocabulary

Books provide the best exposure to new vocabulary for young children, but simply reading is not enough. Teachers need to draw attention to words and plan ways to ensure that new words are acquired and used.

PROCEDURES

1. Select a book with rich language that is age appropriate for your listeners. Preview the book, looking for new vocabulary and conceptual understandings that will extend children's background knowledge. Select three to five words based on (1) utility, (2) concreteness, (3) repetition, and (4) relatedness to themes or topics of study. Prepare child-friendly definitions.

2. Introduce the book by reading the title and naming the author and illustrator. Look at the cover and at least the first few pages to elicit a prediction ("What do you think this book will be about?") and to set a purpose for reading. Build background knowledge as needed and try to introduce the target words conversationally, perhaps pointing to a picture or supplying a brief definition. Ask the children to listen for the words as you read.
3. Make the read-aloud interactive by inviting comments and questions from the children during reading. Encourage them to connect with the characters and theme. Expand on children's brief utterances with complete sentences to model more complex language. Point out the targeted words when they occur in context and have children say the words with you.
4. After reading, invite children to respond to the story in personal ways and then revisit the targeted words as you model their use, pose questions, and elicit children's responses. Use the new words in questions about the story, ask children to use them in sentences, or find other applications for them to engage children.

4.2 PEER—Retellings through Dialogic Reading

In this activity described as "dialogic reading" by Whitehurst and colleagues (1994) children learn how to talk about and retell a storybook with the guidance and prompting of the teacher. The children are gradually given more responsibility for retelling the story until they can do so with little or no assistance. Parents can be trained in this technique and teachers can send books home that have been read and discussed in school. The adult uses the PEER sequence (Morgan & Meier, 2008) to stimulate oral language and help the child become the teller of the story.

PROCEDURES Begin by reading a book aloud and then follow up with small-group or individual rereadings before engaging in a prompted discussion. The prompt sequence is repeated several times using the PEER guidelines:

P Prompt the child to say something about the book using open-ended questions. (Point to a picture of a mouse and say, "What is he doing?" The child says, "Running.")
E Evaluate the child's response. ("That's right!")
E Expand the response by rephrasing or adding information to it. ("The mouse is running away from the cat.")
R Repeat the prompt and ask the child to expand on it. ("Tell me what the mouse is doing." The child says, "He is running away from the cat.")

Additional prompts such as the following can be used to stimulate talk: (1) Ask what, when, where, why, and how questions. (2) Leave a blank at the end of a sentence for the child to fill in. (3) Ask children to retell what has happened so far or to retell the ending. (4) Ask for descriptions of what children see happening in pictures. (5) Ask children to make connections with their own experiences.

4.3 Turn and Talk

A good way to increase the opportunities for oral interaction and vocabulary use in your classroom is to ask students to turn and talk to an assigned partner during a discussion. Rather than calling on one child, everyone has a chance to respond to a question, to share an experience, to make a prediction, to summarize, and so on. Turn and talk is a good way to encourage children who might be reluctant to speak in front of the whole group. This includes English learners as well as shy or less verbal children.

PROCEDURES

1. Model your expectations for "turn and talk" with another adult. Demonstrate how both partners need a chance to speak and suggest ways to encourage a reluctant talker. ("Tell me what you think. It's your turn now." Or "You go first this time.") You can also ask

two children who do a particularly good job together to model for the rest of the group. Children should not move about during turn and talk but instead turn "knee to knee and eye to eye" and talk softly so as not to disturb others.

2. Partners should be selected before the read-aloud or other shared experience begins. You may allow children to pick their own partners on the way to the group and then sit down together. Or you may select partners, taking into consideration children's language competence and confidence. A more verbal child may provide a model for a less verbal child, but he or she might also dominate the conversation, so watch to see how pairs work out and be ready to intervene with suggestions about ways to give the less verbal child an equal opportunity. The same partners can be established for a week or longer to save organizational time.
3. Bring turn and talk time to a close by offering a countdown warning. One way to do this is to silently hold up five fingers and then lower each finger in turn. As children notice they should imitate you down to the final fist when everyone should be done talking. How much time you allow will vary but bring turn and talk time to a close before children lose their focus and get off the assigned topic.
4. As children talk to each other, listen in to monitor their conversations. When the group is back together you might call on one or two children to report what they talked about. Because less verbal or shy children have had a chance to rehearse their ideas, they should be better able to speak before a larger group after turn and talk time.

4.4 Paste the Pasta and Other Concrete Concept Sorts

FIGURE 4.16 Paste the Pasta

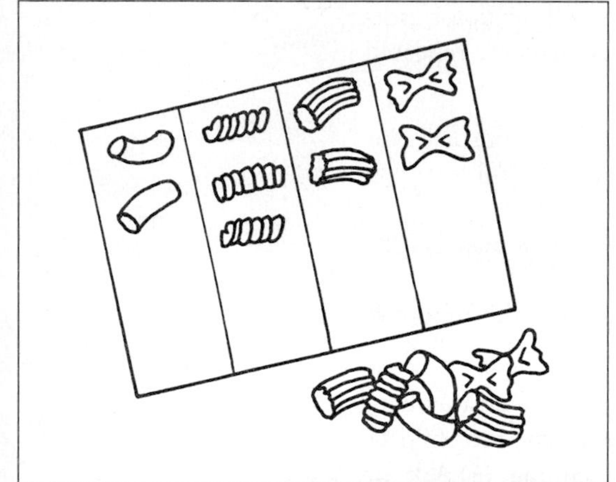

Categorizing pasta by size, shape, and color is a good hands-on activity that introduces the idea of sorting to young children. Ann Fordham developed this sort at the McGuffey Reading Center. Many early childhood curricula include the study of pattern, but being able to categorize by particular attributes must come first. It is difficult for young children to stay focused on a single attribute of interest. They may begin sorting by color and then switch to shape in midstream. They will need many activities of this kind, sorting real, concrete objects that have different features.

MATERIALS You will need three to six types of pasta that vary in size and shape. You may find pasta of various colors or you can dye your own by shaking the pasta in a jar with a tablespoon of alcohol and a few drops of food coloring. Lay it out on newspaper to dry. If you dye your own, make sure that any one color encompasses a variety of shapes and sizes. Two or three colors are enough. Children can sort onto paper divided into columns, as shown in Figure 4.16, or simply into piles.

PROCEDURES

1. Prepare a mixture of the dried pasta and give each child a handful and a sorting paper.
2. Begin with an open sort in which you invite the students to come up with their own way of grouping. This will give you an opportunity to evaluate which children understand attribute sorting and who will need more guidance. Ask the children to share their ideas and show their groups. Discuss the different features or attributes by which they can sort.
3. Ask them to re-sort using a category different from their first one. You might end this activity by letting the students glue the pasta onto their sorting sheets by categories and then labeling their chosen sorts.

VARIATIONS There is no end to the concrete things you can sort with your students as you explore the different features that define your categories, as in the following suggestions.

Children—male/female, hair color, eye color, age, favorite color
Shoes—girls'/boys', right/left, tie/Velcro/slip-on

Mittens and gloves—knit/woven, right/left
Coats—short/long, button/zip, hood/no hood
Buttons—two holes/four holes/no holes, shape, color, size
Bottle caps—size, color, plastic/metal, plain/printed, ribbed/smooth
Lunch containers—boxes/bags, plastic/metal/nylon
Legos—color, shape, number of pegs, length
Blocks—shape, color, size
Toys—size, color, purpose, hardness
Food—sweet, sour, bitter, salty, fruits, vegetables, grains

4.5 Concept Books and Concept Sorts

Simple concept books designed for young children make great beginnings for concept sorts. Examples include *Is It Red? Is It Yellow? Is It Blue?* and other books by Tana Hoban and *My Very First Book of Shapes* by Eric Carle. Topics include shapes, colors, textures, types of clothing, animals, opposites, and so on.

PROCEDURES

1. Because concept books have little text, engage children in discussing what they see and supplying appropriate labels. "This is a book about colors. Here is a picture of a toy dump truck. What color is the dump truck? Yes, the dump truck is red. Now it's your turn. Tell me what you see here."
2. Collect objects or pictures of objects that can be used for sorting. In the case of colors you can probably find real objects around the room such as books, markers, toys, and so on. Explain to the children that they are going to help you sort the objects by color. Use complete sentences to model: "Here is a red ball. I will put the ball with the other things that are red." After sorting help students make generalizations such as "How are all these things alike? Yes, all the things in this category are red."
3. Make labels for each category of your sort with help from the students: "I am going to write *red* on this card to label this category. Listen, *rrrr-ed.* What letter do I need to write down first?"
4. Put sorts where students can use them on their own and encourage them to talk as they sort. Students can look for more pictures in magazines or catalogs that fit the categories or they can draw pictures, cut them out, and paste them into categories. They should be encouraged to label their own sorts with invented spellings.

VARIATIONS Other concept sorts might be developed along the same lines. The following list of categories represents some that are frequently confused by preschool, kindergarten, and first grade children.

- Real/imaginary
- Smooth/rough
- Big/little
- Plastic/wood/metal
- Hard/soft

Of course any book can be the starting point for a concept sort. In the next chapter we describe a food sort based on *Gregory the Terrible Eater* by Marjorie Sharmat.

4.6 All My Friends Photograph Sort

Another example of an open-ended sort involves guessing each other's categories. Pat Love, from Hollymead Elementary School in Charlottesville, Virginia, developed this idea.

MATERIALS You can use photocopies of the children's school photographs made into a composite sheet or take digital pictures of your students. Each small group gets a set of pictures to cut apart and sort. The students will also need a sheet of construction paper to divide into columns for sorting.

PROCEDURES Brainstorm with the children some of the ways that the pictures might be grouped (hair length, hair color, clothing, boys/girls, facial expressions). Have students work in groups to sort by these or other categories they discover. After pasting their pictures into the columns on their paper, each group can hold up their effort and ask the others in the class to guess their categories. The category labels or key words should then be written on the papers.

VARIATIONS Photographs from home may be sorted according to places (inside/outside, home/vacation), number of people in the photograph (adults, sisters, brothers), number of animals in the photograph, seasons (by clothing, outside trees/plants), age of people in the photograph, and so forth. As children learn to recognize their classmates' names, have them match the names to the pictures. Later, these names may be sorted by beginning letter and then placed under the corresponding letter of an ABC wall strip to form a graph.

4.7 Transportation Unit

Teachers of young children often organize their curriculum into thematic units of study. Such units frequently lend themselves to concept sorts, which will review and extend the understandings central to the goals of the unit. The example described uses a transportation theme.

MATERIALS You will need a collection of toy vehicles (planes, boats, cars, and trucks) or pictures of vehicles (a prepared picture sort is on the website). Books featuring transportation could be used to introduce the sort.

FIGURE 4.17 Transportation Draw and Label

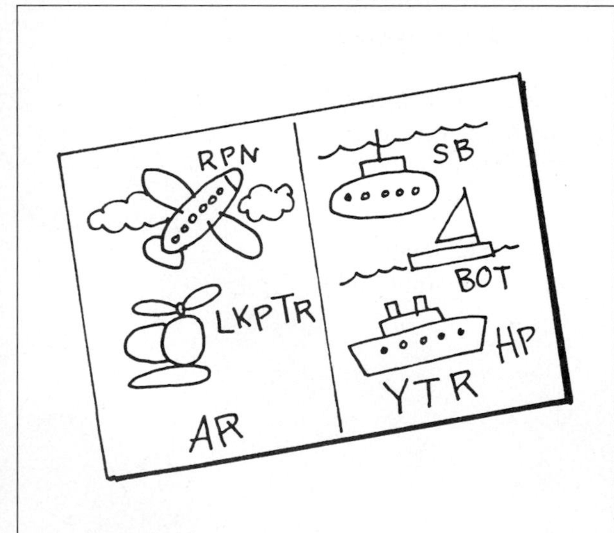

PROCEDURES

1. Lay out the pictures on the floor or table and invite the children to think of which ones might go together. Encourage them to think up a variety of possibilities that will divide everything into only two or three categories. This is an open sort because the children are providing the categories.
2. After each suggestion, sort the vehicles by the identified attributes, talking about the categories and how things are sorted: "A truck has wheels so I will put it with the car and the bicycle." Record the ideas for different sorts on a chart or chalkboard. Some possibilities include plastic/metal, big/little, old/new, one color/many colors, windows/no windows, wheels/no wheels, and land/air/water.
3. After exploring this open sort thoroughly, have the children select the suggestion they like the best. They can then be given construction paper to label their categories and draw or cut out pictures for each. As always, encourage them to label the pictures and the categories with invented spelling, as shown in Figure 4.17.

Phonological Awareness (PA)

Phonological awareness consists of an array of understandings about speech sounds that includes a sensitivity to syllables, rhyme, alliteration, and phonemes. Syllables, rhyme, and alliteration are the best places to start with emergent learners and many activities for developing these are included here. The Morning Message (4.40) and Start with Children's Names (4.23) also include phonological awareness instruction in the context of reading and writing.

4.8 Two for One! Long Words, Short Words

Emergent learners have difficulty attending to the sound structure of a spoken word apart from its meaning. One way to sensitize children to the phonological aspects of words is to build compound words. The following activity focuses on the concept that some words are long and some are short, and the difference between long and short words has nothing to do with the size of their referent.

MATERIALS Consult the list of compound words in Appendix E. Pick concrete two-syllable compound words that are easily illustrated. The words *bedroom*, *blackbird*, *doorbell*, *eyeball*, *fireman*, *football*, *doghouse*, *mailman*, *rainbow*, *raincoat*, *snowman*, and *snowball* are good choices for starters. Pictures for many of the words can be found in Appendix C.

PROCEDURES

1. Take a picture of snow and another picture of a man. After discussing the meaning of each word separately, place the two pictures side by side and ask children to say each word in succession: "snow-man." Talk about how the one word *snowman* is made of two words, *snow* plus *man*.
2. Replace the two separate pictures of snow and a man with one picture of a snowman and discuss again how the word *snowman* is made up of two words: *snow* and *man*. However, because a *snowman* might not be "as big" as a real man, it is necessary to take this exercise one step further to develop the idea of word size in terms of sound as opposed to meaning.
3. Hold up the picture of snow and ask children to clap as they say the word *snow*. Next, hold up the picture of the man and ask the children to clap as they say the word *man*. Finally, hold up the picture of the snowman and ask the children to clap for each word in *snowman*.
4. Discuss how the word *snowman* is longer than either the word *snow* or the word *man* because *snowman* has two claps whereas *snow* and *man* have only one! *Snowman* has more claps, so it is a longer word.

VARIATIONS Hold up the printed word *snow* and compare it to the printed word *snowman*. Count the letters and talk about which word has more letters. Say, "I'm going to say two short words and you tell me what long word those two short words make. Ready? *Bath* (pause) *room*. What longer word do those two smaller words make? Yes, they make the word *bathroom!* Let's clap out the syllables in *bathroom* (clap clap). Ready for another one?" Repeat with the other concrete (picturable) words.

4.9 Whose Name Is Longer? Let's Clap to Find Out!

Once children develop sensitivity to syllables through clapping out compound words, move on to clapping out the syllables in everyone's names. Tie this in with Activity 4.23 (Start with Children's Names).

PROCEDURES Choose two students whose first names differ in the number of syllables. Say each name and have your students clap to each syllable as they pronounce it. "Whose name is longer? Which name has more claps? *Shamika* has three claps; *Charles* has only one." Go around the classroom clapping out the syllables in everyone's name. Have children move into groups by the number of "claps" in their names.

4.10 Rhyme in Children's Books

Filling children's heads with rhyme is one of the easiest and most natural ways to focus their attention on the sounds of the English language. Books written with rhyme provide one way to do this. As you read these books aloud, pause to allow the children to guess the rhyming word. *I Can't, Said the Ant* is an old favorite that invites student participation, with each line cued by an illustration.

Douglas Florian has written a series of books, including *A Beach Day* and *A Winter Day*, that feature only two or three rhyming words on a page. These books can also be used to introduce concept sorts in which summer/winter and city/country can be contrasted. After hearing these books read aloud two or three times, young children may be able to recite the words or track the print successfully for themselves, which will provide them with great satisfaction from the feeling that they can read.

Many of the books enjoyed by children in the emergent stage feature rhymes. You may already have some of the following suggestions in your library.

- Ahlsberg, J., & Ahlsberg, A. (1978). *Each Peach Pear Plum: An "I Spy" Story.* New York: Scholastic.
- Cameron, P. (1961). *I Can't, Said the Ant.* New York: Putnam Publishing.
- Crews, D. (1986). *Ten Black Dots.* New York: Greenwillow.
- Degan, B. (1983). *Jamberry.* New York: Harper.
- Florian, D. (1987). *A Winter Day.* New York: Scholastic; (1990). *A Beach Day.* New York: Greenwillow.
- Guarina, D. (1989). *Is Your Mama a Llama?* Illustrated by Steven Kellogg. New York: Scholastic.
- Slate, J. (1996). *Mrs. Bindergarten Gets Ready for Kindergarten.* New York: Scholastic.
- Strickland, P., & Strickland, H. (1994). *Dinosaur Roar!* New York: Scholastic.
- Walton, R. (1998). *So Many Bunnies: A Bedtime ABC and Counting Book.* New York: Scholastic.

4.11 Match and Sort Rhyming Pictures

After reading rhyming books aloud, you can follow up with an activity in which the children sort or match rhyming pictures.

MATERIALS Three rhyming picture sorts are ready to print from the website. Appendix C of this book contains pictures grouped by initial sounds and by vowels. These can be copied, colored lightly, and glued to cards to make sets for sorting. The lists on pages 329 and 330 of Appendix C will help you find rhyming sets. You can create sets of matching pairs or sets of three or more pictures that can be sorted by rhyme.

PROCEDURES Display a set of pictures and model how to sort them by rhyme. Say something like "*Boat* rhymes with *coat*, so I will put it with the picture of the coat. Can you find two pictures that rhyme?" To make it easier for beginners, put out three pictures at a time: two pictures that rhyme and one that does not. Name the pictures and ask children to find the two that rhyme: "Listen. *Boat, train, coat.* Which pictures rhyme?" After sorting pictures as a group, put the pictures in a center for children to match on their own or create a rhyming sort handout so that each child can have his or her own sort.

VARIATIONS Set up two or more categories and lead the children in sorting pictures by rhyming sound. For example, lay down *cat* and *bee* as headers and sort other pictures in turn under the correct header.

4.12 Invent Rhymes

Nonsense rhymes and books with rhyme and word play are delightful ways to cultivate awareness of sounds. Word play directs children's attention to the sounds of the English language and can stimulate them to invent their own words. Jan Slepian and Ann Seidler's *The Hungry Thing* tells of a creature who comes to town begging for food but has trouble pronouncing what he wants; *shmancakes* (pancakes), *feetloaf* (meatloaf), and *hookies* (cookies) are among his requests. Only a small boy can figure out what he wants. After reading the book, children can act it out. As each takes the part of the Hungry Thing, they must come up with a rhyming word for the food they want, such as *moughnut*, *bandwich*, or *smello*. The story continues in *The Hungry Thing Returns*.

Making up one's own rhymes is likely to come after the ability to identify rhymes. Thinking up rhyming words to make sense in a poem is quite an accomplishment, requiring a good sense of rhyme and an extensive vocabulary. Children need supported efforts to create rhymes, and a good place to start is pure nonsense. No one was a greater master of this than Dr. Seuss. *There's a Wocket in My Pocket* takes readers on a tour of a young boy's home in which all kinds of odd creatures have taken up residence. There is a *woset* in his closet, a *zlock* behind the clock, and a *nink* in the sink. After reading this to a group, ask children to imagine what animal would live in their cubby, under the rug, or in the lunchroom. Their efforts should rhyme, to be sure, but anything will do: a *rubby*, *snubby*, or *frubby* might all live in a cubby.

Patterned text can also be used to create rhymes. The rhyming pattern in *Ten Black Dots* by Donald Crews can be extended to 11, 12, and so on: "Twelve dots can make ice cream cones or the buttons to dial a __________." In the supportive framework of a familiar patterned sentence, children are likely to be more successful at creating their own rhymes.

4.13 Use Songs to Develop a Sense of Rhyme and Alliteration

Earlier we mentioned how appropriate works by the singer/songwriter Raffi are for young children. Teaching these songs by Raffi, some of which are available in books, can lead to inventive fun with rhymes and sounds.

"Apples and Bananas" (from *One Light, One Sun*)
"Spider on the Floor" (from *Singable Songs for the Very Young*)
"Down by the Bay" (also available from *Singable Songs for the Very Young*)

Another song that features names, rhyme, and alliteration is "The Name Game," originally sung by Shirley Ellis. It has apparently passed into the oral tradition of many neighborhoods and may be known by some children in your class. Sing the song over and over, substituting the name of a different child on every round, as in the following two examples:

Sam Sam Bo Bam, Banana Fanna Bo Fam, Fee Fi Mo Mam, Sam!
Kaitlyn Kaitlyn Bo Baitlyn, Banana Fanna Bo Faitlyn, Fee Fi Mo Maitlyn, Kaitlyn!

Encourage children to share with you any playground songs and chants they might already know. Generations of children have made up variations of "Miss Mary Mack" and a new generation with a taste for rap is creating a whole new repertoire. You can take an active role in teaching these jingles to your students—or letting them teach you! Write them down to become reading material.

4.14 Rhyming Bingo

Bingo is a game that can be adapted to many features.

Go to PDToolkit for *Words Their Way*, click on the Sorts and Games tab, then type "Rhyme Bingo" for a ready-to-use game.

MATERIALS Prepare enough Bingo game boards for the number of children who will participate (small groups of three to five children are ideal). An appropriate game board size for young children is a 6-by-6-inch board divided into nine 2-by-2 squares; for older students, the game board can be expanded to a 4-by-4 or 5-by-5 array. Copy sets of pictures from Appendix C and form rhyming groups such as those listed on pages 329 and 330. Paste all but one of each rhyming group in the spaces on the game boards and then laminate them for durability. Each game board must be arranged differently.

Prepare a complementary set of cards on which you paste the remaining picture from each rhyming group. These will become the deck from which rhyming words are called aloud during the game. You will need some kind of marker to cover the squares on the game board. These may be as simple as two-inch squares of construction paper, plastic chips, bottle caps, or pennies.

PROCEDURES

1. Each child receives a game board and markers to cover spaces.
2. The teacher or a designated child is the caller who turns over cards from the deck and calls out the name of the picture.
3. Each player searches the game board for a picture that rhymes with the one that has been called out. Players can cover a match with a marker to claim the space.
4. The winner is the first player to cover a row in any direction or the first player to fill his or her entire board.

4.15 Rhyming Concentration

MATERIALS This game for two or three children is played like traditional Concentration or the more current Memory game. Assemble a collection of six to ten rhyming pairs from the pictures in Appendix C. Paste the pictures on cards and laminate for durability. Be sure the pictures do not show through from the backside.

PROCEDURES Shuffle the pictures and then lay them face-down in rows. Players take turns flipping over two pictures at a time. If the two pictures rhyme, the player keeps the cards to hold to the end of the game. A player who makes a match gets another turn. The winner is the child who has the most matches at the end of the game.

VARIATIONS This can be adapted to use with beginning sounds. Put letters on one set of cards and paste a picture of something that begins with that letter on another.

4.16 Pamela Pig Likes Pencils: Beginning Sounds and Alliteration

Alliteration refers to the occurrence of two or more words in a phrase having the same beginning sound. Sensitivity to beginning consonant sounds is essential for children to move out of the emergent phase and begin to learn to read. The following activity helps children focus their attention on beginning consonant sounds in sequences of spoken words. You might introduce this by reading *A My Name Is Alice*, by Jane Bayer and illustrated by Steven Kellogg.

MATERIALS You will need a variety of animal puppets that can be named with matching beginning consonant sounds, such as Bob Bear, Donald Dog, Cass Cat, or Pamela Pig. Try to pick names and animals beginning with just one single consonant sound—not a blend or consonant digraph. Although Charles starts with the letter *C*, it doesn't start with the initial *c* sound (/s/ or /k/); it sounds with a /ch/ sound instead. You want both the name and the animal to have the same beginning sound. Puppets may be store bought, but they can also be simple pictures of an animal like a bear or a cat cut out and fastened to the end of a stick to hold up.

PROCEDURES

1. Hold up your puppet and introduce it. Emphasize the beginning consonant sound as you introduce the name and the animal name. Say something like, "This is Pamela. She is a pig named Pamela. We call her Pamela Pig."

2. Explain that Pamela Pig like things that start with the same sound as her name, /p/. So Pamela likes *pencils* because *pencils* start with the /p/ sound just like *Pamela* and *pig*.
3. Display an assortment of pictures (see Appendix C) or objects, some of which start with a /p/ sound (pen, paper, paint, pan, pin, pear) and some of which don't. (See the *P* pictures in Appendix C.) Pick two at a time (one that starts with a /p/ sound and one that doesn't) and ask, "Which one would Pamela Pig like?"

VARIATION Have children brainstorm other things that Pamela Pig would like. They may volunteer such things as parties, plays, or parks. Have children jump rope to the familiar jump rope jingle that plays on alliteration: "Chant (initial sound) my name is (child's name) and my friend's name is (name). We live in (place) and we sell (item)."

4.17 It's in the Bag—A Phoneme Blending Game

MATERIALS You will need a paper bag (gift bags are attractive) and an assortment of small objects collected from around the classroom, from outside, or from home: chalk, pen, paper clip, tack, key, rock, stick, and so on. You might use a puppet to add interest.

PROCEDURES Lay out a dozen or so objects and name them with the children. Explain that you will use them to play a game. Introduce the puppet. The puppet will name an object in the bag, saying it very slowly, and the children will guess what it is saying.

VARIATIONS Use objects or pictures related to a topic of study. For example, if you are teaching a unit on animals, you could put toy animals or pictures of farm animals in the bag. This can be a sensory activity by letting children reach into the bag, figure out an object by touch, and then say it slowly for the other children to guess. Objects that begin with the same beginning sounds can also be put into the bag to sort.

4.18 Incorporate Phonological Skills into Daily Activities

Teachers of emergent children can incorporate sound play into many daily activities and routines.

1. Lining up, taking attendance, or calling children to a group: Call each child's name and then lead the class in clapping the syllables in the name. Announce that everyone whose name has two syllables can line up, then one syllable, three, and so on. Say each child's name slowly as it is called. Make up a rhyme for each child's name that starts with a sound of interest: Billy Willy, Mary Wary, Shanee Wanee, and so on. Substitute the first letter in everyone's name with the same letter: Will, Wary, Wanee, Wustin, and so on.
2. During read-alouds: Pause to let children fill in a rhyming word, especially on a second or third reading. If they have trouble, say the first sound for them with a clue: "It rhymes with *whale* and starts with *p*." Draw attention to a long word by repeating it and clapping the syllables: "That's a big word! Let's clap the syllables: *hip-po-pot-a-mus*, five syllables!" You might also pause while reading and say a key word very slowly before asking the children to repeat it fast: "The next day his dad picked him up in a red . . . *jeeeep*. What's that? A jeep, right." You might point to the letters as you do this.

Alphabet Knowledge

The following activities are designed to develop all aspects of alphabet knowledge, including letter recognition (both uppercase and lowercase), letter naming, letter writing, and letter sounds. You may notice that these activities address more than one letter at a time: For children who have not cut their teeth on alphabet letters and picture books, one letter per week is not enough. We must teach more than one letter at a time.

FIGURE 4.18 Alphabet Link Letters

4.19 The Alphabet Song and Tracking Activities

Every early childhood classroom should have an alphabet strip or chart at eye level. Too often these strips are put up out of the children's reach. The best locations for the strips are desktops or tabletops for easy reference. Activities such as the following can make active use of these charts.

MATERIALS Commercial or teacher-made alphabet strips for both wall display and for individual children.

PROCEDURES

1. Learn the ABC song to the tune of "Twinkle, Twinkle, Little Star." Sing it many times.
2. Model pointing to each letter as the song is sung or the letters are chanted. Then ask the children to fingerpoint to the letters as they sing or chant.
3. Play "find the letter" by naming a letter for children to touch on their strip. Ask them to name the letter that comes before or after the target letter.
4. When students know about half of the alphabet, they can work on putting a set of letter cards, tiles, or linking letters in alphabetical order. Use uppercase or lowercase letters, or pair the two (see Figure 4.18). Keep an ABC strip or chart nearby as a ready reference.

4.20 Share Alphabet Books

Share alphabet books with a group as you would other good literature and plan follow-up activities when appropriate. Some books are suitable for toddlers and merely require the naming of the letter and a single accompanying picture, such as Dick Bruna's *B Is for Bear.* Others, such as Graeme Base's *Animalia*, will keep even upper elementary children engaged as they try to name all the items that are hidden in the illustrations. Look for alphabet books such as the ones listed here to draw children's attention to beginning sounds through alliteration.

- Base, G. (1986). *Animalia.* New York: Harry Abrams.
- Bayer, J. (1984). *A My Name Is Alice.* Illustrated by Steven Kellogg. New York: Dial.
- Berenstain, S., & Berenstain, J. (1971). *The Berenstain's B Book.* New York: Random House.
- Cole, J. (1993). *Six Sick Sheep: 101 Tongue Twisters.* New York: Morrow.
- Seuss, Dr. (1963). *Dr. Seuss's ABC.* New York: Random House.

Many ABC books can be incorporated into thematic units, such as Jerry Pallotta's ABC books featuring insects and animals or Mary Azarian's *A Farmer's Alphabet.* Some alphabet books present special puzzles, such as Jan Garten's *The Alphabet Tale.* Children are invited to predict the upcoming animal by showing just the tip of its tail on the preceding page. Following is a list of some outstanding ABC books for school-age children.

- Anglund, J. W. (1960). *In a Pumpkin Shell.* (Alphabet Mother Goose). San Diego, CA: Harcourt Brace Jovanovich.
- Anno, M. (1975). *Anno's Alphabet.* New York: Crowell.
- Azarian, M. (1981). *A Farmer's Alphabet.* Boston: David Godine.
- Baskin, Leonard. (1972). *Hosie's Alphabet.* New York: Viking Press.
- Ernst, L. C. (1996). *The Letters Are Lost.* New York: Scholastic.
- Ernst, L. C. (2004). *The Turn-Around Upside-Down Alphabet Book.* New York: Simon & Schuster.
- Fain, K. (1993). *Handsigns: A Sign Language Alphabet.* New York: Scholastic.
- Falls, C. B. (1923). *ABC Book.* New York: Doubleday.
- Folsom, M. (2005). *Q Is for Duck: An Alphabet Guessing Game.* San Anselmo, CA: Sandpiper.
- Gág, W. (1933). *The ABC Bunny.* Hand lettered by Howard Gág. New York: Coward-McCann.
- Hague, K. (1984). *Alphabears: An ABC Book.* Illustrated by Michael Hague. New York: Holt, Rinehart & Winston.
- Horenstein, H. (1999). *Arf! Beg! Catch! Dogs from A to Z.* New York: Scholastic.
- McPhail, D. (1989). *David McPhail's Animals A to Z.* New York: Scholastic.
- Musgrove, M. (1976). *Ashanti to Zulu: African Traditions.* Illustrated by Leo and Diane Dillon. New York: Dial.
- Pallotta, J. (1989). *The Yucky Reptile Alphabet Book.* Illustrated by Ralph Masiello. New York: Bantam Doubleday, Dell. (There are many more in this series, such as *The Dinosaur Alphabet Book.*)
- Shannon, G. (1996). *Tomorrow's Alphabet.* Illustrated by Donald Crews. New York: Greenwillow.

4.21 Alphabet Book Follow-Ups

PROCEDURES

1. Discuss the pattern of the books, solve the puzzle, and talk about the words that begin with each letter as you go back through the books a second time.
2. Focus on alliteration by repeating tongue twisters and creating a list of words for a particular letter. Brainstorm other words that begin with that letter, and write them under the letter on chart paper.
3. Make individual or class alphabet books. You might decide on a theme or pattern for the book. Refer back to the alphabet books you have read for ideas. One idea might be a noun–verb format—for example, ants attack, bees buzz, cats catch, and dogs doze.
4. Look up a particular letter you are studying in several alphabet books or a picture dictionary to find other things that begin with that sound. This is an excellent introduction to using resource books.

4.22 Chicka Chicka Boom Boom Sort

Martin and Archambault's *Chicka Chicka Boom Boom* is a great favorite and provides a wonderful way to move from children's books to alphabet recognition. After reading this delightful book with her children, Pat Love matches foam "Laurie Letters," one at a time, to the letters printed in the book. Pat's boom boards (see Figure 4.19) can be used for sorting letters and pictures by beginning sounds.

FIGURE 4.19 Chicka Chicka Boom Boom Board

Other teachers have created a large coconut tree on the side of their filing cabinet so that children can act out the story and match uppercase and lowercase forms using magnetic letters.

4.23 Start with Children's Names

Names are an ideal point from which to begin the study of alphabet letters because children are naturally interested in their own names and their friends' names. We like the idea of a "name of the day" (Cunningham, 2005) so much better than a "letter of the week," because many more letters are covered in a much shorter time.

MATERIALS Prepare a card for each child on which his or her name is written in neatly executed block letters. Put all the names in a box or gift bag. Have additional blank cards ready to be cut apart as described. A pocket chart is handy for displaying the letters.

PROCEDURES

1. Each day, with great fanfare, a name is drawn and becomes the name of the day. The teacher begins with a very open-ended question: "What do you notice about this name?" Children will respond in all sorts of ways depending on what they know about letters: "It's a short name." "It has three letters." "It starts like Taneesh's name." "It has an *o* in the middle."
2. Next children chant or echo the letters in the name as the teacher points to each one. A cheer led by the teacher is lots of fun:

Teacher: "Give me a *T*."	Children: "*T*"
Teacher: "Give me an *O*."	Children: "*O*"
Teacher: "Give me an *M*."	Children: "*M*"
Teacher: "What have we got?"	Children: "Tom!"

3. On an additional card, the teacher writes the name of the child as the children recite the letters again. Then the teacher cuts the letters apart and hands out the letters to children in the group. The children are then challenged to put the letters back in order to spell the name correctly. This can be done in a pocket chart or on a chalkboard ledge. After several repetitions, the cut-up letters are then put into an envelope with the child's name and picture on the outside. The envelope is added to the name puzzle collection. Children love to pull out their friends' names to put together.
4. All the children in the group should attempt to write the featured name on individual whiteboards, chalkboards, or pieces of paper. This is an opportunity to offer some handwriting instruction as you model for the children. Discuss the details of direction and movement of letter formation as the children imitate your motions.
5. Each day the featured name is added to a display of all the names that have come before. Because they are displayed in a pocket chart, they can be compared to previous names and used for sorting activities.
   - Sort the names by the number of letters or syllables.
   - Sort the names that share particular letters; for example, find all the names with an *e* in them.
   - Sort the names that belong to boys and girls.
   - Sort the names by alphabetical order.

VARIATIONS Create a permanent display of the names and encourage children to practice writing their own and their friends' names. If you have a writing center, you might put all the names on index cards in a box for reference. Children can be encouraged to reproduce names not only by copying the names with pencils, chalk, and markers, but also with rubber stamps, foam cutout letters, link letters, or letter tiles. The display of children's names becomes an important reference tool during writing time.

4.24 One Child's Name

Learning the letters in one name is a good starting point for children in the early emergent stage. Use the following approach: Spell out a child's name with letter cards, tiles, foam, or plastic letters using both uppercase and lowercase. Spell it with uppercase letters in the first row and ask the child to match lowercase letters in the row below, as shown in Figure 4.20. Ask children to touch and name each letter. Scramble the top row and repeat. Play Concentration with the set of uppercase and lowercase letters needed to spell a child's name.

FIGURE 4.20 Brandon's Name Puzzle

4.25 Alphabet Scrapbook

MATERIALS Prepare a blank book for each child by stapling together sheets of paper. (Seven sheets of paper folded and stapled in the middle is enough for one letter per page.) Children can use this book in a variety of ways (see Figure 4.21).

PROCEDURES

1. Practice writing uppercase and lowercase forms of the letter on each page.
2. Cut out letters in different fonts or styles from magazines and newspapers and have children paste them into their scrapbooks.
3. Draw and label pictures and other things that begin with that letter sound.
4. Cut and paste magazine pictures onto the corresponding letter page. These pictures can be labeled, too.
5. Add sight words as they become known to create a personal dictionary.

FIGURE 4.21 Alphabet Scrapbook

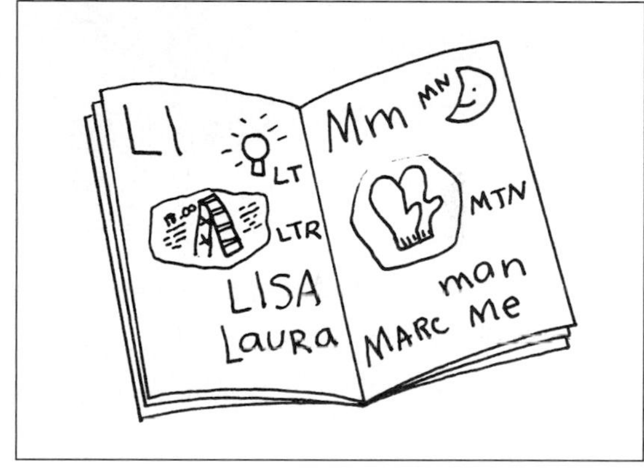

4.26 Alphabet Eggs

MATERIALS Create a simple set of puzzles designed to practice the pairing of uppercase and lowercase letters. On poster board, draw and cut out enough four-inch egg shapes for each letter in the alphabet. Write an uppercase letter on the upper half and the matching lowercase letter on the lower portion (see Figure 4.22). Cut the eggs in half using a zigzag line. Make each zigzag slightly different so the activity is self-checking. Students should say the letters to themselves and put the eggs back together by matching the uppercase and lowercase form.

Go to PDToolkit for *Words Their Way,* click on the Sorts and Games tab, then type "Alphabet Eggs" for ready-to-use eggs.

VARIATIONS There are many other shapes that can be cut in half for matching. In October, for example, pumpkin shapes can be cut in two and in February, heart shapes can be cut apart the same way. There is no end to matching possibilities. Acorn caps can be matched to bottoms, balls to baseball gloves, frogs to lily pads, and so on. These matching sets can also be created to pair letters and a picture that starts with that letter, rhyming words, contractions, homophones, and so on.

4.27 Alphabet Concentration

This game works just like Concentration with rhyming words as described in Activity 4.15. Create cards with uppercase and lowercase forms of the letters written on one side. Be sure they cannot be seen from the backside. Use both familiar and not-so-familiar letters. Do not try this with all 26 letters at once, or it may take a long time to complete; eight to ten pairs are probably enough.

FIGURE 4.22 Alphabet Eggs

VARIATIONS To introduce this game or to make it easier, play it with the cards face up. As letter sounds are learned, matching consonant letters to pictures that begin with that letter sound can change the focus of this game.

4.28 Letter Spin

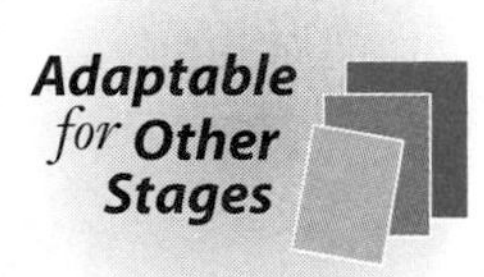

Alison Dwier-Seldon created this fast-paced game to practice upper- and lowercase letter recognition.

MATERIALS Make a spinner with six to eight spaces, and label each space with a capital letter. If you laminate the spinner before labeling, you can reuse it with other letters. Print the letters with a grease pencil or nonpermanent overhead transparency pen. Write the lowercase letters on small cards, creating five or six cards for each letter (see Figure 4.23). See Appendix F for tips on making a spinner.

Go to PDToolkit for *Words Their Way,* click on the Sorts and Games tab, then type "Alphabet Spin" for the game template.

PROCEDURES

1. Lay out all the lowercase cards face-up.
2. Each player in turn spins and lands on an uppercase letter. The player then picks up one card that has the corresponding lowercase form, orally identifying the letter.
3. Play continues until all the letter cards have been picked up.
4. The winner is the player with the most cards when the game ends.

VARIATIONS Students can be asked not only to name but also to write the uppercase and lowercase forms of the letter after each turn. This game can be adapted to any feature that involves matching—letters to sounds, rhymes, vowel patterns, and so on.

4.29 Alphabet Cereal Sort

MATERIALS For this sorting activity created by Janet Brown Watts, you will need a box of alphabet cereal—enough to give each child a handful. Prepare a sorting board for each child

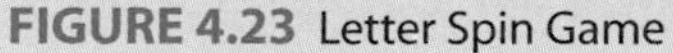

FIGURE 4.23 Letter Spin Game

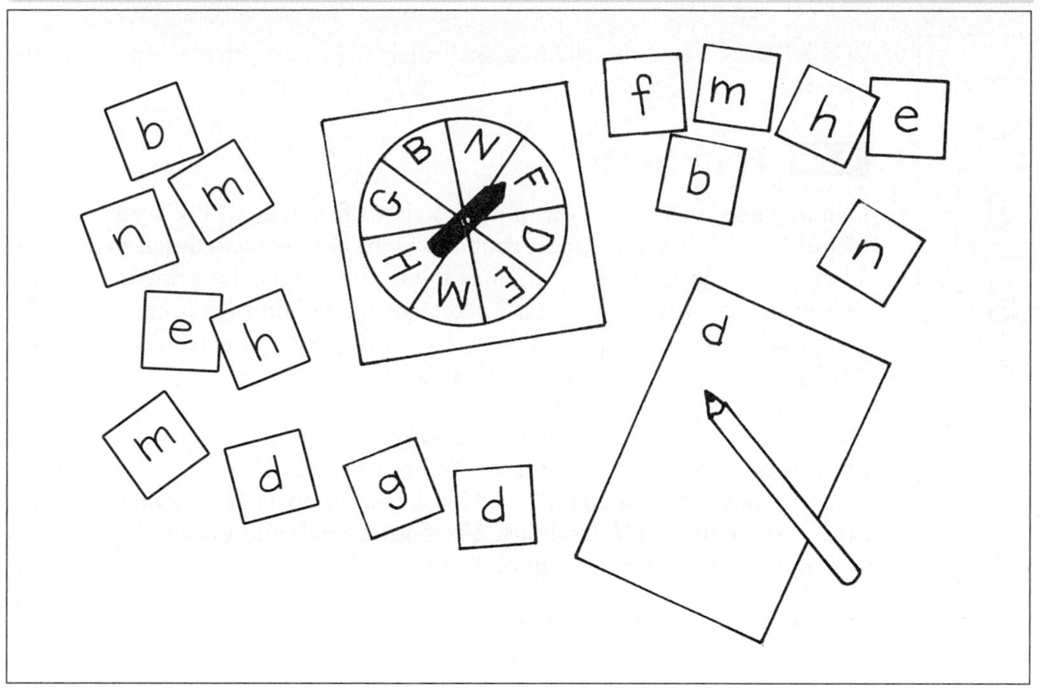

by dividing a paper into 26 squares. Label each square with an uppercase or lowercase letter. Other three-dimensional letters would work just as well as cereal.

PROCEDURES Allow the children to work individually or in teams to sort their own cereal onto their papers (see Figure 4.24). Discard (or eat) broken or deformed letters. After the children are finished, they can count the number of letters in each category (e.g., *A*-8, *B*-4).

FIGURE 4.24 Cereal Sort

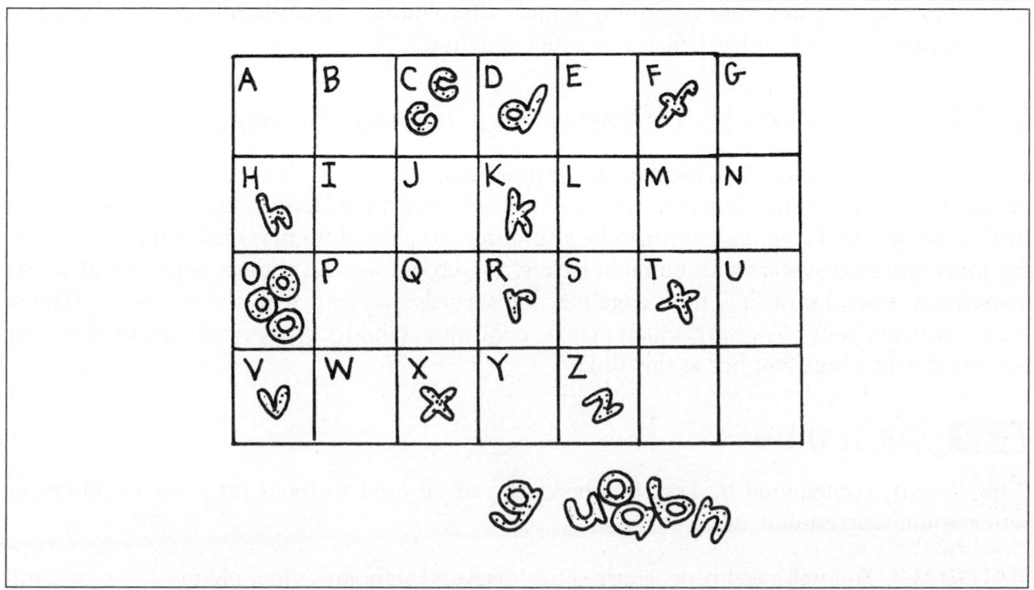

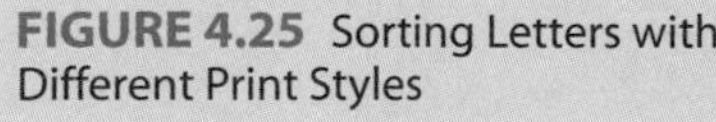

FIGURE 4.25 Sorting Letters with Different Print Styles

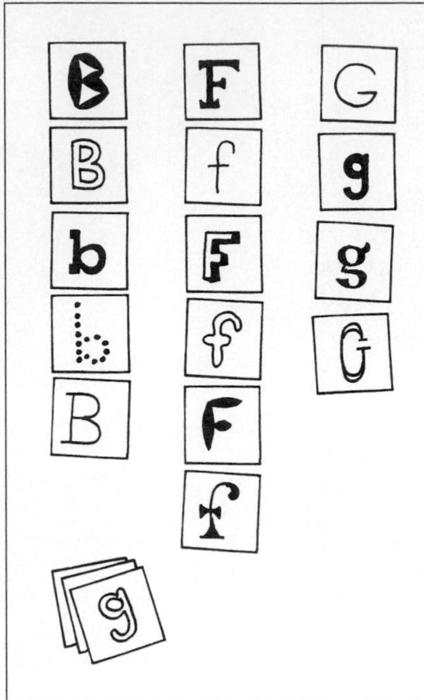

This could become a graphing activity. Finally, eat the cereal! (Or glue it down.)

VARIATIONS Have the children spell their names or other words using the cereal.

4.30 Font Sorts

Children need to see a variety of print styles before they will be readily able to identify their ABCs in different contexts. Draw children's attention to different letter forms wherever you encounter them. Environmental print is especially rich in creative lettering styles. Encourage the children to bring in samples from home—like the big letters on a bag of dog food or cereal—and create a display on a bulletin board or in a class big book.

MATERIALS Cut out different styles of letters from newspapers, catalogs, magazines, and other print sources. You can also search your computer fonts and print out letters in a large size. Cut the letters apart, mount them on small cards, and laminate for durability. Use both capitals and lowercase, but avoid cursive styles for now (see Figure 4.25).

PROCEDURES After modeling the sort with a group of children, place the materials in a center where the children can work independently. Avoid putting out too many different letters at one time—four or five are probably enough, with 8 to 12 variations for each.

VARIATIONS If you have created alphabet scrapbooks (Activity 4.25), children can paste in samples of different lettering styles.

Letter–Sound Knowledge

Specific guidelines for creating and using picture sorting for initial sounds are described earlier in this chapter and general guidelines are presented in Chapter 3. Picture and word sorts are at the heart of word study and the procedures will be revisited throughout this book. Games can be used to review beginning sounds after children have already practiced categorizing targeted sounds in basic picture sorting activities.

4.31 Use Books to Enhance Beginning Sounds

Because alphabet books often include one or more examples of words that start with a targeted letter, they are a natural choice when teaching beginning sounds. Such books can be used to introduce an initial sound or they can be a resource for a word hunt as children go searching for more words that start with targeted letters. Watch out for the choices authors and artists sometimes make, however. The *C* page may have words that start with the digraph *ch* (*chair*), hard *c* (*cat*), and soft *c* (*cymbals*), which may be confusing. Children will eventually need to sort out these confusions, but not at this time.

4.32 Soundline

This activity, contributed by Leslie Robertson, can be used to focus on letter matching or letter–sound correspondences.

MATERIALS You will need rope, clothespins, markers, tagboard, glue, pictures, scissors, and laminating film.

PROCEDURES Write uppercase and lowercase letters on the top of the clothespins. Glue a picture beginning with each letter on a square of tagboard and laminate. Students can match the picture card to the clothespin and hang it on the rope (see Figure 4.26).

FIGURE 4.26 Soundline

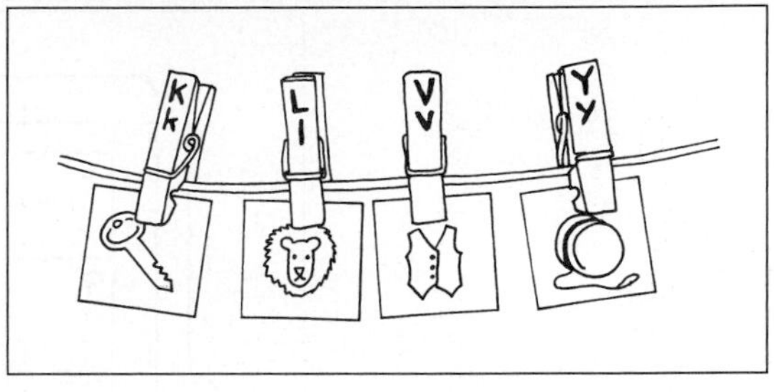

4.33 Letter Spin for Sounds

This is a good game to review up to eight beginning sounds at a time. It is a variation of the letter spin described in Activity 4.28.

MATERIALS You will need a spinner divided into four to eight sections and labeled with beginning letters to review. A large cube could be used like a die instead of a spinner. You will need a collection of picture cards that correspond with the letters, with at least four pictures for each letter. Follow the procedures for the letter spin activity.

PROCEDURES

1. Lay out all the pictures face-up.
2. Two to four players take turns spinning and then selecting one picture that begins with the sound indicated by the spinner. After selecting, the player's turn is over and the next person spins. If there are no more pictures for a sound, the player must pass.
3. Play continues until all the pictures are gone. The winner is the one with the most pictures at the end.

4.34 Sort Objects by Sounds

Divide a large sheet of poster board into squares and label each one according to the initial sounds you want to review. Collect miniature toys and animals or small objects (a button, bell, box, rock, ring, ribbon, etc.) that begin with the sounds of interest. Children are asked to sort the objects into the spaces on the board.

4.35 Initial Consonant Follow-the-Path Game

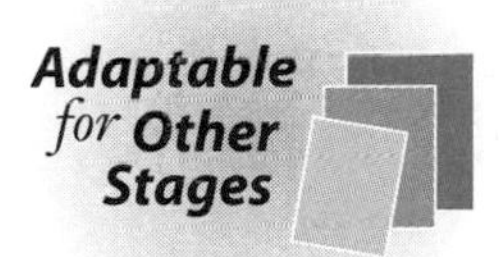

This game is simple enough that even preschoolers can learn the rules. It can be used throughout the primary grades to practice a variety of features. You will see this game adapted in many ways in Chapters 5 and 6.

MATERIALS You will need to copy the two halves of a follow-the-path game board found in Appendix F and on the website. To keep the game in a folder that can be easily stored, paste each half on the inside of a manila folder (colored ones are nice) leaving a slight gap between the two sides in the middle (so the folder can still fold). Add some color and interest with stickers or cutout pictures to create a theme such as "Trip to the Pizza Parlor" or "Adventures in Space." Label each space on the path with one of the letters you want to review, using both uppercase and lowercase forms (see Figure 4.27). Sets of three to six letter sounds at a time work best. Reproduce a set of picture cards that correspond to the letters. Copy them on card stock or glue cutout pictures to cards. You will need two to four game pieces to move around the board. Flat ones like bottle caps or plastic disks store well. Keep the pictures and playing pieces in a labeled plastic zip-top bag inside the folder.

PROCEDURES

1. Turn the picture cards face-down in a stack. Players go in alphabetical order.
2. Each player draws a picture in turn and moves the playing piece to the next space on the path that is marked by the corresponding beginning consonant.
3. The winner is the first to arrive at the destination.

Go to PDToolkit for *Words Their Way,* click on the Sorts and Games tab, then type "Follow the Path" for the game template.

VARIATIONS Pictures can be placed in each space for a "Follow The Pictures" game. Students roll a die or spin a spinner marked with letters to move to the appropriate space. The

FIGURE 4.27 Follow-the-Path Game

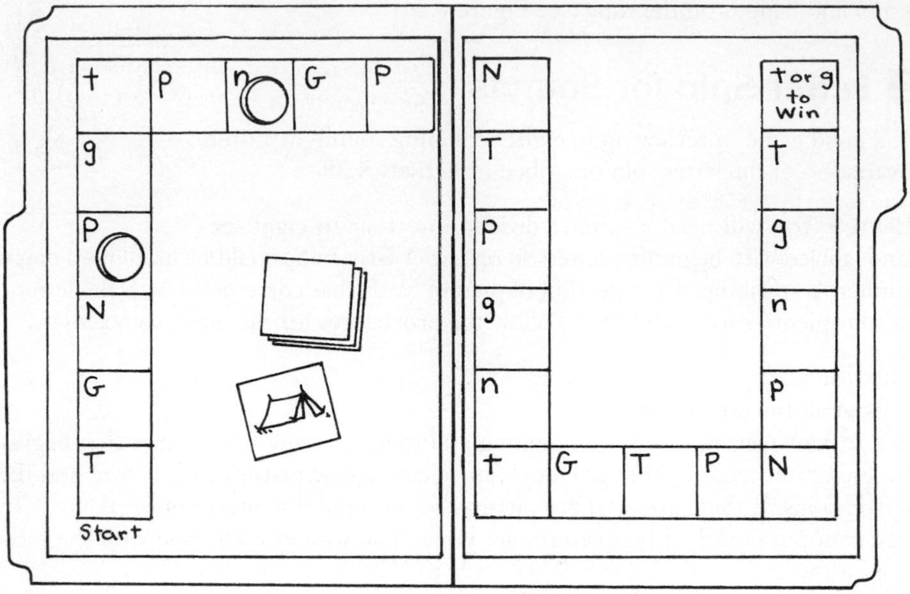

Create Your Own program on the website allows you to drag and drop pictures for any combination of letter sounds into follow-the-path templates.

Concepts about Print (CAP)

Concepts of print are best learned in the context of reading and writing. Songs that you sing, poems and jingles that you learn, and portions of longer books with catchy memorable refrains (such as "I'll huff and I'll puff and I'll blow your house down") can be put on charts for easy reference and used for print referencing and to develop concept of word.

4.36 "Who Can Find?"

This works best with a big book, chart story, or poem you have read several times. It can also be used after creating a dictation or other writing. Simply ask children questions such as "Who can find a period? Who can find a capital *A?* Who can find the last word in the first sentence? Who can find the title? Who can find a word that rhymes with *can?*" Call children forward to point to the features of print you name. It is easy to differentiate this activity for children at various points of development so that it offers just the right challenge. Some children might be asked to find letters, whereas others are asked to find words.

4.37 Explore the World of Logos

Children can learn to "read" their environment in the prealphabetic or logographic stage in which they attend to shapes, colors, and logos to distinguish words. Teachers should draw children's attention to these forms of print to emphasize the many functions print serves and the different forms it can take.

MATERIALS Collect commercial labels and logos from cereal boxes, advertisements, signs, and so on. Encourage your students to bring in examples from home. Mount these on card stock.

PROCEDURES Hold up an example such as the label on a fast food bag and ask children if they can "read it." Talk about what it says and where it came from. Create a sentence strip for a pocket chart: "I can read ______." Insert the logo in the empty space. Put these in a center for children to use on their own after introducing it in a group.

4.38 What Were You Saying?

Many concepts about print can be directly taught by writing in speech bubbles—especially speech bubbles connected to children's own pictures.

MATERIALS You will need a digital camera to take photos of your students. If you don't have a digital camera, find pictures of children engaged in an activity such as kicking a ball to a friend or licking an ice cream cone.

PROCEDURES

1. Print or project a picture that shows children. Ask questions to engage your students in recounting the event.
2. Draw a speech bubble coming out of one child's mouth. Explain that the pictures only *show* what is happening, but you can *write* what the child actually said in the speech bubble. Prompt by saying something like "What do you think she is saying in this picture?"
3. Write down what the children say in the speech bubble (see Figure 4.28). You can reference various aspects of print as you do the writing, such as letter–sound matches, capitals, and punctuation.
4. Read what it says in the speech bubble while pointing to individual words. Point out once again that the picture *shows* what happened, but the writing in the speech bubble tells what was actually *said.* Ask individual children to come up and read their own speech bubbles.

VARIATIONS Read comic strips, comic books, and children's books that feature speech bubbles, such as one of the following.

- Peggy Rathman's *10 Minutes till Bedtime* (1999) and *Goodnight Gorilla* (1994). New York: Scholastic.
- Susan Meddaught's *Martha Speaks* (1992). Boston: Houghton Mifflin.
- Mo Willems's *Don't Let the Pigeon Drive the Bus, Nuffle Bunny,* and their sequels. New York: Hyperion Books.
- Easy to read comics known as TOON books. New York: RAW Junior, LLC.

FIGURE 4.28 Using Speech Bubbles to Teach Concepts about Print

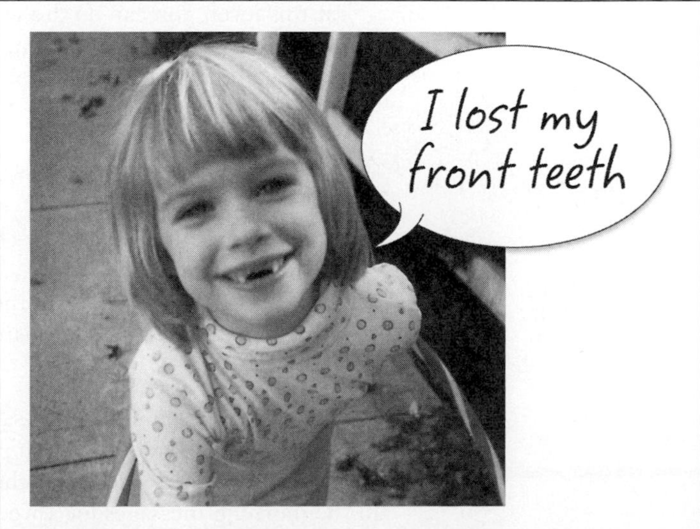

4.39 Share the Pen during Interactive Writing

The act of writing for children offers teachers the opportunity to model the use of the alphabet, phonemic segmentation, letter–sound matching, concept of word, and conventions such as capitalization and punctuation, all in the context of a meaningful group activity. As the teacher writes on the chalkboard, chart paper, or an overhead transparency, children see their own ideas expressed in oral language transformed into print, allowing many opportunities for print referencing. See Table 4.3 on page 114 for ideas.

During interactive writing, children share the pen and are invited to come forward to add a letter, a word, or a period. Such writing can take place any time of the day and for any reason—for example, to list class rules, to make a shopping list, to record observations from a field trip, to create a new version of a familiar text, or to list questions for a classroom visitor. Morning Message is a favorite form of group writing in which the teacher and children compose sentences that report on daily home and school events that are of importance to the class. The same steps can be used for any writing.

4.40 The Morning Message

Each morning the teacher talks with the entire group to discover bits of news that can be part of the morning message. In preschool or early kindergarten, this may be only one sentence, but over time, it can grow to be as long as the teacher and children desire. Keep a lively pace and be sure all children are engaged. Give each child a lap-sized whiteboard, chalkboard, or clipboard so everyone can participate in listening for sounds, handwriting, and the use of punctuation.

MATERIALS You will need a large sheet of chart paper and white tape for covering mistakes or a chalkboard with markers or chalk.

PROCEDURES

1. Chat with children informally, sharing news from home or the classroom. This is a time for generating lots of talk so do not rush through this step too quickly.
2. Select a piece of news to record in the form of a single sentence such as "We will go to PE." Recite the sentence together with the children to decide how many words it contains, holding up a finger for each word. Then draw a line for each word on the board or chart (see Figure 4.29).
3. Repeat each word, emphasizing the sounds as they are written, and invite the group to make suggestions about what letters are needed: "The first word we need to write is *we. Wwwwwweeeeee.* What letter do we need for the first sound in *wwweee?*" A child might suggest the letter *Y*. "The name of the letter *Y* does start with that sound. Does anyone have another idea?" Every letter in every word need not be discussed at length. Focus on what is appropriate for the developmental level of your students.
4. Let children take turns coming forward to write, usually just one child per letter or word at this level. You can do the writing in the beginning, but as children learn to write their letters you can share the pen. White tape is used to cover any mistakes made on paper. Model and talk about concepts about print such as left to right, return sweep, capitalization, punctuation, and letter formation. Clap the syllables in longer words, spelling one syllable at a time.
5. After the sentence is completed, read it aloud to the group, touching each word and then have them read with you. If your sentence contains a two- or three-syllable word, touch it for every syllable, helping children see how it works. Invite children to come forward and fingerpoint as they read.
6. Repeat steps 2 to 5 for another sentence. Keep in mind the attention span of the students when deciding how many sentences to write. One sentence may be enough at the beginning.

VARIATIONS The morning message should be left up all day and children should be encouraged to read it on their own. You might want to use it for some activities in the next section, such as Cut-Up Sentences or Be the Sentence or for the whole-to-part lessons. A collection of all the morning messages for a week can be sent home on Friday as a summary of class news that most children will be able to proudly read to their parents.

FIGURE 4.29 Morning Message

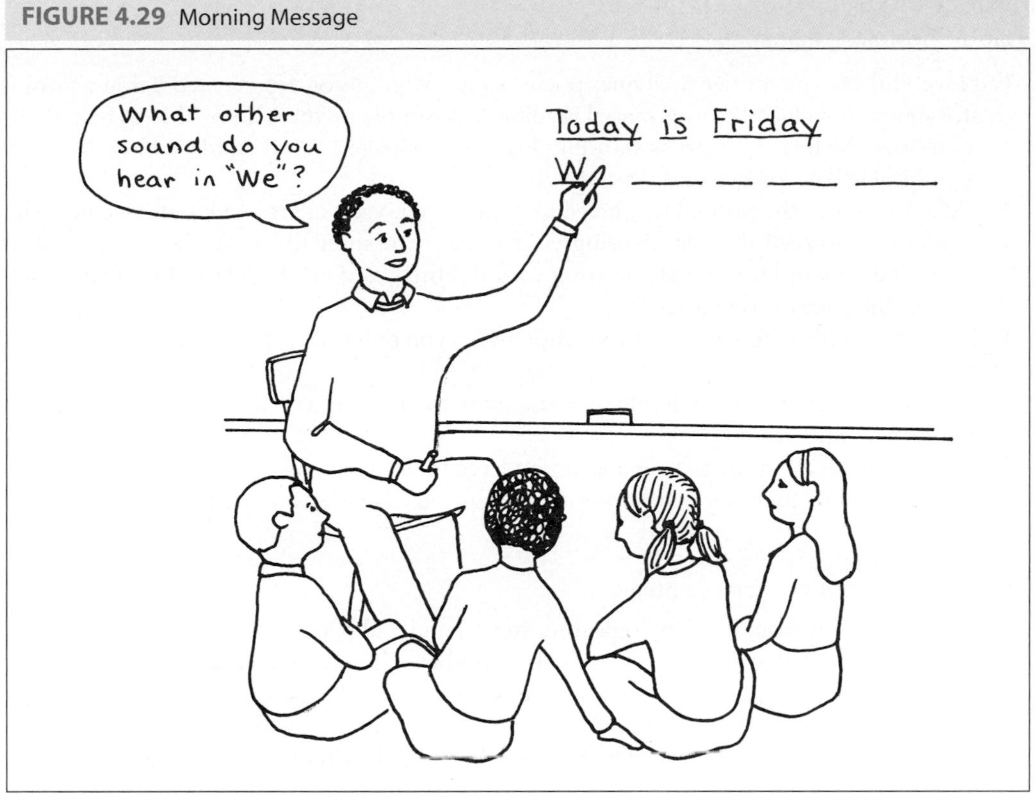

Concept of Word in Text (COW)

When children are learning about letters and sounds at the same time they are fingerpoint reading from memory, there is a complementary process at work. Learning one will give logic and purpose to learning the other. Fingerpoint reading to familiar rhymes and pattern books followed by deliberate attention to words in and out of context is the best way to achieve a COW.

4.41 The Concept of Word Whole-to-Part Five-Day Lesson Framework

The following five-day format can be used with any kind of text—language experience dictations, poems, rhymes, jingles, songs, or parts of a simple patterned book. The key is to limit the text to no more than two to eight lines that students will be able to memorize after repeated readings. The procedures described move from the introduction of a whole text to the parts. Activities on days 2 to 5 can vary, depending on the skill of your students and the time you have.

MATERIALS You will need chart paper, a pocket chart, sentence strips, envelopes, and word cards. Record the text on chart paper using print large enough for all to see and/or prepare two sets of sentence strips with individual lines from the text. Have word cards ready to record selected words. In addition, photocopy or type several lines from the text to give children their own single-sheet copy. These can be glued into personal readers made from newsprint or blank white paper stapled together. Leave out the chart, sentence strips, and word cards for children to use independently as a center activity.

PROCEDURES

Day 1. Introduce the whole.

1. Have children memorize a rhyme, poem, song, or jingle or a patterned refrain from a storybook introduced during shared reading. Use simple pictures if possible to help them memorize the lines by heart as shown in Figure 4.14 (page 118). If children have difficulty memorizing four or five lines, cut back to two.
2. Next, introduce the printed text on chart paper or a pocket chart—one sentence per line. Model how to read the text by using your finger or pointer to touch every word as you say it. Talk about how you are starting with the first *word* on the left and touching each *word* in the *sentence* as you say it.
3. Invite the children to say it with you (chorally) as you point to each word again in a second reading.
4. Ask the children to read each sentence exactly as you do after you have read it (echo). This will be the third reading.
5. Invite individual students to come up and recite as much of it as you think they are capable of while pointing to each word. Be prepared to guide as needed to ensure accurate pointing.

Day 2. Work with the parts (sentences).

1. Review the text from day 1 by repeating steps 4 and 5 above.
2. Hand out sentence strips and ask students to find which sentence it matches in the pocket chart and place it there. Discuss how they knew it was the same—prompt for specifics like "starts with" or "the word . . ." Rebuild the text with and without a model for reference. Simple pictures like those in Figure 4.14 can help children get the sentence strips in order.
3. Pass out individual copies of the rhyme. Read this together as every child tracks the print. Glue it into their personal readers.
4. Pair students up with a buddy and have them practice reading the rhyme to each other while fingerpointing. Ask the nonreading buddy to make sure his or her partner is saying and pointing to each word. Have each partner read twice.

Day 3. Work with the parts (words).

1. Repeat steps 4 and 5 from day 1 above.
2. Pass out individual word cards for each sentence and have children come up and find a word and place it on top of its match in the pocket chart. Discuss how they knew it was the same word. (Prompt for letters and beginning sounds.)
3. Pass out the sentence strips along with envelopes containing that particular sentence cut up into individual words. Have children rebuild the sentence word by word.
4. See Cut-Up Sentences (Activity 4.42) and Be the Sentence (Activity 4.43).

Day 4. Work with the parts (letters and sounds).

1. Use the chart copy or pocket chart to reread and then say, "I'm thinking of a word in this line that starts with the same sound as ______. What word am I thinking of? How did you know?" Or ask children to find words.
2. Children reread their own copies. Name words (or letters for children still learning the alphabet) for them to find and talk about how they found it (what letter or sounds they used.) They can highlight or underline the words you ask them to find.
3. Pass out envelopes of word cards with three to ten words you have selected from the rhyme (the number will depend on your judgment of what your students can handle and may vary from child to child). Have the children work with partners using the word cards to find the same word in their own copy of the rhyme and identify it. Partners can also call out words for each other to find.
4. Select two to four letter sounds or rhyming words to use as the basis for the picture sorting activity described on page 112.

Day 5. Review the whole and assess the parts.

1. Children reread using the chart or personal copies.
2. Pass out the word card envelopes again and see whether children can recognize any of them out of context. If not, repeat step 3 above. An alternative is to have children select words for a word bank, described in the next chapter.
3. Have children illustrate their rhymes in their personal readers as a reward for all their hard work.
4. Assess using the guidelines described on pages 143 and 144. Ask individual students to read the rhyme as they point to the words. Observe how accurately they track and whether they self-correct when they get off track. Point to a few words for the child to name or hold up word cards in isolation to name.

VARIATIONS

1. Periodically have children reread charts done throughout the year and all the pages in their personal readers. Personal readers can go home so children can share their developing skills. Be sure that parents understand that they will read from memory but should try to touch each word as they read.
2. On day 3 or 4, ask children to "read" from the chart or pocket chart but this time cover up one word per line, leaving only the beginning letter visible to use as a phonemic clue for figuring out what word you've left out—for example, *Four little monkeys jumping on the b___.* Uncover the *ed* to see if they were right. Ask them how they knew *bed* comes next (saw the *b*, starts with a /b/ sound, etc.). Choose concrete words that start with a consonant sound.
3. On day 5, play "Which Word Did I Change?" Going back to the chart or pocket chart, change one word per line and see whether they can find it. In the little monkeys example above, you might change *bed* to *table.* If someone can find the changed word, ask how they knew that was the one you changed (e.g., *bed* starts with a /b/ sound or a *b*, but that word starts with a *t*).

4.42 Cut-Up Sentences

Write sentences or phrases from a familiar piece of text on a sentence strip. Sentences might come from a book or a poem the group has read together. The sentences can then be used in the group to rebuild the text in order using a pocket chart. Individual copies of text can be cut apart so that each child gets to practice.

A further step is to ask the students to cut apart the words in the sentence and then challenge them to reconstruct the sentence. Hand out scissors and call out each word as the children cut it off. The spaces between words are not obvious to emergent children so be prepared to model for them. Demonstrate how to find the words in order to rebuild the sentence: "What letter would you expect to see at the beginning of *swam?*" Leave the word cards and model sentence strips with a pocket chart in a center for children to practice in their spare time. Put individual words into an envelope with the sentence written on the outside (see Figure 4.30). These can be sent home with the children to reassemble for homework. They can also be pasted down under a drawing done by the child.

FIGURE 4.30 Cut-Up Sentences

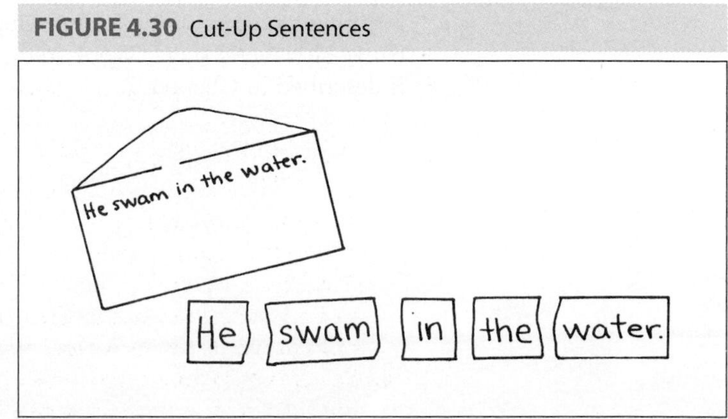

4.43 Be the Sentence

Children can also rebuild familiar sentences by pretending to be the words themselves. Write a familiar sentence on a chart or on the board. Start with short sentences such as "Today is Monday" or "I love you." Then write each word from the sentence on a large card. Give each word to a child, naming it for him or her. "Stephanie, you are the word *Monday;* Lorenzo, you are the word *is*." Ask the children to work together to arrange themselves into the sentence. Have another child read the sentence to check the direction and order. Try this again with another group of children and then leave the words out for children to work with on their own.

4.44 Stand Up and Be Counted

As children build a repertoire of known songs, nursery rhymes, and jump rope jingles, post them around the room and use them for oral concept of word activities that integrate phonological awareness with concept of word in print.

MATERIALS You will need a memorized nursery rhyme or jump rope jingle posted on the wall at an appropriate level. Be sure there is some floor space for everyone to sit in a circle.

PROCEDURES

1. Sitting in a circle, recall the nursery rhyme or jump rope jingle and recite it. Point out the written copy on the wall or chart.
2. Go around the circle, having students stand up for each word in the nursery rhyme. One student would stand up for *Hey*, another for *Diddle*, and a third for the next *Diddle*, and so on. Watch to see whether two students stand up for a two-syllable word like *Diddle* or *over*.
3. After everyone is finished standing up for each word, have everyone sit down and say, "I think we made some mistakes. Did anyone notice?" Some students will notice. Ask them to explain.
4. Say, "Yes, two people stood up for the word *over* but *over* is one word. It has two syllables, but it means one thing—over (motion with your hands jumping over something). Let's clap the word *over*. See? *Over* has two claps, but it's only one word. Go to the chart or wall poster and point out the word *over*. (You might note that it starts with an *o*.)
5. Repeat the exercise.

VARIATIONS Have students recite a sentence or rhyme and add a Lego or Unifix cube for each word as it is recited. Count the cubes (words). Compare sentences or lines. Which sentence is longer? How can you tell? (Longer sentences have more words—Legos or Unifix cubes.)

The word study activities for the emergent stage promote concept and vocabulary development, awareness of sounds, concepts about print and of word, and the alphabetic principle. These activities spring from and return to children's books and are extended through writing. Once children achieve a concept of word in print and can segment speech and represent beginning and ending consonant sounds in their spelling, they are no longer emergent but beginning readers. This is also when they move into the next stage of spelling, the letter name–alphabetic stage. Word study for the letter name–alphabetic speller/beginning reader is described in Chapter 5.

MEDIA GUIDE *Word Study for Learners in the Emergent Stage*

SECTION	PAGE	GO TO PDTOOLKIT FOR *WORDS THEIR WAY™*
Videos		
Introduction	94	Click on the Videos tab, then type "Whole Class Reading and Picture Sort."
Supporting Emergent Reading	101	Click on the Videos tab and revisit "Whole Class Reading and Picture Sort."
Concepts about Print (CAP)	114	Click on the Videos tab, then type "Whole Class Reading and Picture Sort." For follow-up activities, in the Videos tab, type "Small Group Reading and Sorting."
Sorts and Games		
Oral Language, Concepts, and Vocabulary	105	Click on the Sorts and Games tab and select Emergent Stage and Concept Sorts, where you will find four prepared picture sorts: Work and Play, Clothes and Body Parts, Creatures, and Transportation.
Phonological Awareness (PA)	108	Click on the Sorts and Games tab, then type "Rhymes" to find several ready-to-use rhyme sorts.
Alphabet Knowledge	110	Click on the Sorts and Games tab, then type "Alphabet" to find several ready-to-use font sorts.
Letter–Sound Knowledge	111	Click on the Sorts and Games tab, then type "Beginning Consonant Picture Sorts" to find ready-to-use sorts.
Activities for the Emergent Stage	129	Click on the Sorts and Games tab, then type "Rhyme Bingo."
Activities for the Emergent Stage	135	Click on the Sorts and Games tab, then type "Alphabet Eggs" for ready-to-use eggs.
Activities for the Emergent Stage	136	Click on the Sorts and Games tab, then type "Alphabet Spin" for the game template.
Activities for the Emergent Stage	139	Click on the Sorts and Games tab, then type "Follow the Path" for the game template.
Assessment Tools		
Phonological Awareness (PA)	109	Click on the Assessment Tools tab, select Assessment Materials, then type "Rhyme and Beginning Sounds."
Additional Resources		
Letter–Sound Knowledge	111	Click on the Additional Resources tab, then type "Word Study in Spanish in the Letter Name–Alphabetic Stage."

chapter 5

Word Study for Beginners in the Letter Name–Alphabetic Stage

The letter name–alphabetic stage of literacy development is a period of beginnings. Students begin to read and write in a conventional way. That is, they begin to learn words and actually read text, and their writing becomes readable to themselves and others. However, this period of literacy development needs careful scaffolding because students know how to read and write only a small number of words. The chosen reading materials and activities should provide rich contextual support. In word study, the earliest sorts are pictures; later, students work with words in families and words known by sight. In the following discussion of reading and writing development and instruction, we look closely at the support teachers provide and the way word knowledge develops during this stage. However, before we examine this stage of word knowledge and provide guidelines for word study instruction, let us visit the first grade classroom of Mr. Richard Perez.

During the first weeks of school, Mr. Perez observed his first graders as they participated in reading and writing activities and he used the inventory described in Chapter 2 to collect samples of their spelling for analysis. Like most first grade teachers, Mr. Perez has a range of ability in his classroom, so he manages three instructional groups for reading and word study and uses students' spellings as a guide to plan phonics instruction. Some days he uses part of small-group time for teacher-directed word study.

Cynthia is a typical student in the early letter name–alphabetic group who writes slowly, often needing help sounding out a word and still confusing some consonants such as *y* and *w* and *d* and *t* as shown in Table 5.1. The results of her writing efforts are limited primarily to consonants with few vowels. Cynthia has memorized jingles such as "Five Little Monkeys Jumping on the Bed," but sometimes gets off track when she tries to point to the words as she reads.

Deciding to take a step back with this group, Mr. Perez plans a review of beginning sounds. Each Monday he introduces a set of four initial consonants, such as *b, m, r,* and *s.* After modeling the sort and practicing it in the group, he gives each student a handout of pictures to be cut apart for individual sorting practice, as shown in Figure 5.1(A). The next day the students sort the pictures again and Mr. Perez observes how quickly and accurately they work. On subsequent days of the week during seatwork time or center time, the students draw and label

Table 5.1 Spellings of Three First-Graders

WORD	CYNTHIA	TONY	MARIA
fan	FN	fan	fan
pet	PD	pat	pet
dig	DK	dkg	deg
wait	YAT	wat	wat
sled	SD	sd	sad
stick	SK	sek	stik
shine	CIN	sin	shin

pictures beginning with those sounds, paste and label pictures, and do word hunts (follow-up routines described in Chapter 3).

Each day when Mr. Perez meets with Cynthia's group, they read chart stories, jingles, and books with predictable texts. To help the students in this group develop a sight vocabulary, Mr. Perez started a **word bank** for each child. To create this word bank, he wrote words the students could quickly identify on small cards for their collections. The students add new words several times a week and review their words on their own or with classroom volunteers.

Tony is part of a large group in the middle letter name–alphabetic stage who has beginning and ending consonants under good control but shows little accuracy when spelling digraphs and blends, as shown in Table 5.1. He is using but confusing vowels in some words. Tony points to the words as he reads "Five Little Monkeys" and immediately self-corrects on the rare occasion he gets off track on words with more than one syllable, such as *jumping* and *mama*.

Mr. Perez decides to introduce the digraphs *sh, ch, th,* and *wh* with picture sorts and then begins the study of mixed-vowel word families such as *an, in,* and *un*. He knows that Tony and the other students in that group can read words such as *cat, can,* and *man* and that these words serve as the basis for the study of other words in the same family. Mr. Perez takes 10 to 15 minutes in group time to introduce new word families. The children then receive their own set of words, shown in Figure 5.1(B), to cut apart for sorting. They work alone and with partners to practice the sort, writing and illustrating the words, and then play follow-up games.

Maria represents a third group of students in the late letter name–alphabet stage who correctly spell single consonants, as well as many digraphs and blends, as shown in Table 5.1. This group also uses some short vowels accurately. Maria can read some leveled books independently and is quickly accumulating a large sight vocabulary simply from doing lots of reading.

Mr. Perez reviews different-vowel word families for several weeks, making an effort to include words with digraphs and blends, but he soon discovers that word families are too easy and decides to move to the study of short vowels in nonrhyming words. Each Monday he introduces a collection of words that can be sorted by short vowels into three or four groups. This group also receives a handout of words, as shown in Figure 5.1(C), to cut apart and use for sorting. They learn to work in pairs for buddy sorts, writing sorts, word hunts, and games on other days of the week.

FIGURE 5.1 Word Study Handouts for Letter Name–Alphabetic Spellers in Three Different Instructional Groups

A. Beginning Consonant Sort

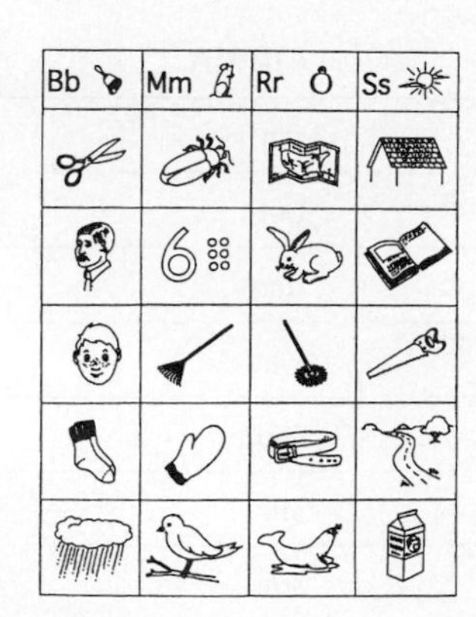

B. Word Family Sort

can	pin	sun
run	fan	tan
man	bun	fun
fin	ran	van
pan	win	plan
chin	grin	than
skin	thin	

C. Short Vowel Sort

pig	cup	*oddball*
zip	bit	but
big	jug	pin
tub	rip	will
him	cut	rub
hum	win	fun
six	nut	run
put	did	gum

Literacy Development of Students in the Letter Name–Alphabetic Stage

Many components of the literacy diet described for the emergent stage continue to develop during the letter name–alphabetic stage. Vocabulary, oral language, and concepts will grow throughout all the stages described in this book, but phonological awareness and concept of word in text will reach maturity. At the beginning of this stage children may only segment and represent the most salient beginning and final consonant sounds, demonstrating only partial phonemic awareness. By the end of the stage they have full phonemic awareness and are able to isolate the elusive vowels and to pull apart the tightly meshed blends. As they learn to segment these sounds they will also learn the letter correspondences that represent them, including initial and final consonants, digraphs, blends, and short vowels. A new component becomes critical during the letter name–alphabetic stage—acquiring a vocabulary of **sight words** than can be recognized automatically in any context. It is this fast and ever-growing word recognition that fuels fluency and comprehension.

PDToolkit for Words Their Way™

Go to PDToolkit for *Words Their Way*, click on the Videos tab, then type "Assessment in the Letter Name–Alphabetic Stage" and watch Ms. Kiernan demonstrate how she conducts word study with first-graders.

Reading

During the letter name–alphabetic stage, children will transition from dependence on simple, **predictable** reading materials that they read with support from shared reading and their memory for language to less predictable beginning reading materials. With less predictable materials readers must rely on an expanding sight vocabulary and the ability to figure out unfamiliar words using a variety of decoding strategies. This transition in reading material should be accompanied by word study instruction that continues to develop the alphabetic principle and letter–sound correspondences.

CONCEPT OF WORD IN TEXT. Students who are in the letter name–alphabetic stage of spelling have acquired a **concept of word**—the ability to track or fingerpoint read a memorized text without getting off track on a two-syllable word. There are two levels of concept of word in text: rudimentary and full (Bear & Barone, 1998; Flanigan, 2006, 2007; Morris, 1981; Morris, Bloodgood, Lomax, & Perney, 2003).

Students with a rudimentary concept of word are able to point and track to the words of a memorized text using their knowledge of consonants as clues to word boundaries. However, they get off track with two-syllable words, and when they are asked to find words in what they read, they are slow and hesitant. They may return to the beginning of the sentence or line to get a running start with memory as a support to read and locate the requested word. Students with a rudimentary concept of word are able to learn a few sight words from familiar stories and short dictations that they have reread several times. In word study, students with a rudimentary concept of word are in the early part of the letter name–alphabetic stage; they need to review beginning consonants and then study blends and digraphs along with same-vowel word families. With a rudimentary concept of word, students' sight vocabulary grows slowly, so most word study is done with picture sorting.

Students with a full concept of word can fingerpoint read accurately, and if they get off track they can quickly correct themselves without starting all over. When asked to find words in the text, they are able to identify them immediately or nearly immediately. They acquire many sight words after several rereadings of familiar text. Students with a full concept of word are ready to study different-vowel word families and then examine individual short vowels and the consonant-vowel-consonant pattern (CVC) for short vowels, including short vowel words containing beginning and ending consonant blends. With an expanding sight word vocabulary, sorts rely more on words than pictures to support word identification.

SIGHT WORD LEARNING. We define **sight word**s as any words that are stored completely enough in memory to be recognized automatically and consistently in and out of context. A large store of sight words makes it possible to read fluently and to devote attention to comprehension rather than to figuring out unknown words. It also provides a corpus of known words from which students can discover generalizations about how words work. However, beginning readers do not recognize many words by sight and what they remember about words may be incomplete. As **partial alphabetic** readers (Ehri, 1997), they know something about consonants, but they lack the vowel knowledge needed to sound out words or easily store words in memory. In a familiar rhyming book like *Five Little Monkeys Jumping on the Bed* by Eileen Christelow, they can point to the words using their memory for the rhyming pattern and their knowledge of beginning sounds /f/, /l/, /m/, /j/, and /b/. The word *monkeys* might be recognized out of context by virtue of several letters in the word (*m-k* or *m-y* perhaps). In another context, however, these partial phonetic cues alone will not suffice. *Monkeys* might be confused with *Mike* or *many*.

The term *sight words* is often confused with **high-frequency words,** which are the most commonly occurring words in print, like *was, the, can, these,* and so on. A list of Fry's top 300 high-frequency words can be found in Appendix E on page 363. It is important to understand that though a reader's store of sight words will include many high-frequency words, it is not limited to them. Any word can be a sight word.

Another common misunderstanding about sight words is that they are phonetically irregular words children cannot sound out and therefore must be learned in a different way, as unanalyzed wholes or "by sight." Although there are some high-frequency words that lack dependable letter–sound correspondences (*of* = /ŭv/ and *was* = /wŭz/), most words are more regular than not, especially in the consonant features that are most likely to be partially understood. For example, the high-frequency word *from* is 75 percent regular; only the *o* in the middle is irregular. There is no evidence that readers learn these words in a different way but, like all word learning at this stage, repetition in and out of context helps.

READING FLUENCY. All beginning readers read slowly, except when they are reading well-memorized texts, and they are often described as word-by-word readers (Bear, 1989, 1991b). They do not have enough sight words to permit fluent reading and their reading rates may be painfully slow. For example, a beginning reader may read at fewer than 50 words per minute. Although fluency is an important goal of learning to read, we find the current focus on getting beginning readers to "read fast" a disturbing trend. Chall called the first stage of reading the "glued to print" stage (1983). Beginning readers need to pay careful attention to the words on the page if they are going to store words fully in memory to build their sight vocabularies.

Most beginning readers point to words when they read, and they read aloud to themselves. This helps them to keep their place and to buy processing time. While they hold the words they have just read in memory, they read the next word, giving them time to fit the words together into a phrase. If you visit a first grade classroom during "sustained silent reading" (SSR) or during "drop everything and read" (DEAR), you are likely to hear a steady hum of voices. Finger pointing, dysfluency, and reading aloud to oneself are natural reading behaviors to expect in beginning readers.

Writing

There is a similar pattern of dysfluency in beginning writing because students often write words slowly, sound by sound (Bear, 1991a). In the previous, emergent stage of development, writers are often unable to later read what they have written because they lack or have limited letter-to-sound correspondences. Students in the letter name–alphabetic stage can usually read what they write depending on how completely they spell, and their writing is generally readable to anyone who understands the logic of their letter name strategy.

A first-grader shares her thoughts about winter in the example shown in Figure 5.2. Ellie represents most beginning and ending single consonants as in her spelling of LK for *like* and WR for *wear* but the blend in *snow*, spelled SO, is incomplete. Many vowels are missing, although she does include some that "say their name" as in MAK for *make* and SO for *snow*. She substitutes *a* for short *i* in *mittens* and *i* for short *o* in *hot*. Notice how she uses the letter *h* to represent the *ch* digraph in *chocolate* (spelled HIKLT) because the name of the letter (*aitch*) has the sound she is trying to represent. Correctly spelled words like *Mom* and *the* are probably sight words.

FIGURE 5.2 Ellie Writes about Winter

I LK WNT. I MAK
a SOMN in the SO
I WR MATS. Mom
Mask Me hit hikIt

I like winter. I make a snowman in the snow. I wear mittens. Mom makes me hot chocolate.

Teachers of letter name students should continue to model writing for a variety of purposes while using print referencing to develop concepts about print as described in Chapter 4. Interactive writing and recording students' individual or group dictations are fertile opportunities for print referencing as well as drawing students' attention to sound and letter correspondences. Students also need to write for themselves and can begin to take part in the writing process, moving from rough drafts to final products. Journal writing, written responses to reading, predictions about reading, and other individual written responses provide authentic reasons to learn about letters and sounds as students are encouraged to "spell as best they can."

Writing in the letter name–alphabetic stage can take many forms, including the following:

- Word study–based sentences in which they "write for sounds" (e.g., Chad loves chocolate chips)
- Story-based sentences (e.g., Run, run, run as fast as you can!)
- Personal sentences (e.g., I am going to be a witch for Halloween)

In the early phases of the letter name–alphabetic stage, teachers may sometimes "dictate" sentences for students to write. This removes the burden of trying to remember what they were trying to write so students can concentrate on writing for sounds. Students should also be composing their own sentences and writing for authentic purposes—letters to friends, narrating a personally meaningful event, and so on. Asking students to simply copy sentences is of little value. It is the hard work of transcribing speech into print that exercises phonemic awareness and students' growing understanding of the orthography.

Children's invented spellings should be valued at this stage so that they can write about the topics that are important to them. At the same time, teachers can begin to hold students accountable for what they have learned in word study by gently urging them to listen for additional sounds in words. Although students cannot be expected to edit for the correct spellings of all the words they use in their writing, they should be prompted to use what they have learned in word study when they write. Editing strategies should be modeled in the context of interactive writing or when teachers take dictations.

Vocabulary Learning

Beginning readers' vocabularies continue to grow with oral language interactions, and the quality and quantity of vocabulary growth is dependent on the richness and frequency of verbal interactions with peers and adults. It is very important for teachers to be mindful and systematic about teaching students new words in the early childhood years as a way to close the tremendous oral vocabulary gap that exists between children who come from literate homes and those who do not (Beimiller, 2005). Merely mentioning the meanings of words or doing lots of reading is not enough to enhance the vocabulary learning of those students who need it the most (Beck et al., 2002). Observations of kindergarten and first grade classrooms reveal that the current focus on teaching phonics in high-risk settings has resulted in measurable progress in decoding skills, but without attention to vocabulary these students will still be at risk in later grades (Juel, Biancarosa, Coker, & Deffes, 2003).

There are many ways teachers of young children can enhance vocabulary development. Read-alouds continue to provide a rich source of new vocabulary as well as complex sentence structures. Several words from a read-aloud can be highlighted and discussed throughout the week. Interactive read-alouds, "turn and talk," retellings, dramatizations of stories, and other suggestions from Chapter 4 continue to play an important role in stimulating oral language and encouraging the use of new vocabulary. In this chapter, we describe creative dramatics, "think, pair, share," and anchored word instruction (Juel et al., 2003) in the activity section. The following descriptions highlight additional vocabulary strategies.

SOPHISTICATED SYNONYMS. Opportunities exist throughout the day for teachers to model sophisticated words for familiar concepts as a way to promote vocabulary growth. Lane and Allen (2010) describe how a kindergarten teacher began the year by asking the "weather watcher" to report to the group using terms such as *sunny*, *cloudy*, or *warm*. However, as the teacher introduced new terms over several months, the appointed "meteorologist" was expected to *observe* the weather *conditions* and report their *forecast* with terms such as *brisk*, *frigid*, or *overcast*. Lane and Allen suggest that teachers look for, gradually teach, and consistently use synonyms for the common language of everyday routines. Students can *distribute*, *replenish*, *dispense*, or *allocate* materials. During group discussions *participants* are encouraged to *contribute*, *articulate*, *verbalize*, and *elaborate* their ideas. The class can be asked to *queue up adjacent* to or *parallel* to the wall and *proceed* in an *orderly* fashion. Students are complimented for being *amiable*, *agreeable*, *courteous*, *proficient*, *gracious*, and *considerate*. Rather than "dumbing down" our language to children, we should consciously elevate our language and provide appropriate explanations, repeated exposure, and opportunities for children to use that same language.

ENRICH SIMPLE TEXT. Most beginning readers and writers are not able to grow their meaning vocabularies through their own reading because the simple predictable texts used for reading instruction rarely include words whose meanings they do not know. However, teachers can infuse more vocabulary as they discuss the story and illustrations using alternative words. For example, *The Cat Sat on the Mat* by Brian Wildsmith is written with very simple, predictable language. However, the cat experiences a range of emotions, from *contented* to *uneasy* to *agitated* to *furious*, as more and more animals gather on the mat. Part of the discussion of this book should focus on how the cat feels, offering the opportunity to introduce many synonyms for *happy*, *sad*, and *mad*—the words children are likely to suggest. Discussing illustrations will especially benefit English learners who will be relying on them to understand much of the story. You might even look up some of the synonyms in their home language. *Content* and *furious* turn out to be *contento* and *furioso* in Spanish! The study of **cognates** (words descended from the same ancestral root) will be addressed more in later chapters but it can begin in the early stages as well.

for **English Learners**

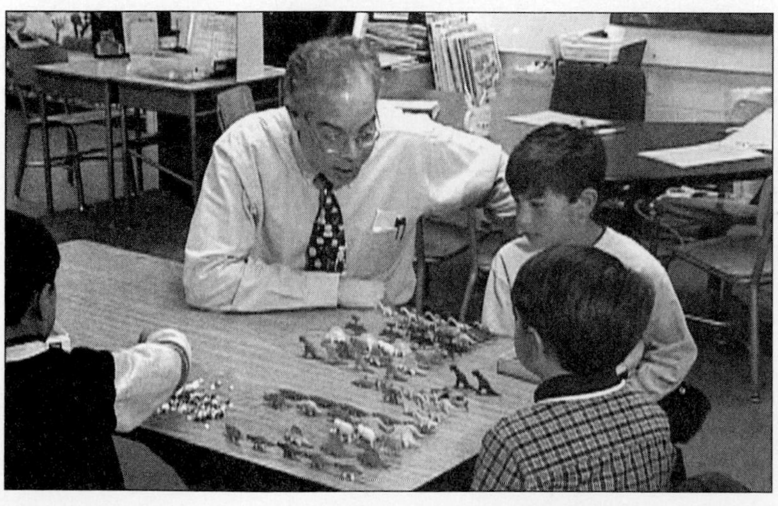

CONCEPT SORTS. Pictures and known words are used in concept sorts to expand children's vocabulary and to encourage rich verbal interactions. For example, letter name–alphabetic spellers can read about and discuss concepts related to weather and sort pictures of mittens, sandals, sunscreen, jackets, and galoshes in addition to known printed words related to weather, such as *sun*, *rain*, *coat*, and *snow*. Teachers should model and use the language of comparison/contrast: "bigger than, smaller than, not as large as," and so forth. This explicit attention to language helps children "unpack" what they tacitly know about the concepts underlying the labels and becomes part of their own discussions about words and concepts. Concept sorts for English learners are particularly worthwhile because pictures can be sorted into categories without needing to know the English terms. At the same time English-speaking partners can supply unknown words and in the process of talking about the sort new vocabulary is exercised. Ideas for some concept sorts are included in the activity section.

PDToolkit for Words Their Way™

Go to PDToolkit for *Words Their Way*, click on the Sorts and Games tab, then select Concept Sorts to find four prepared picture sorts: Work and Play, Clothes and Body Parts, Creatures, and Transportation.

Orthographic Development in the Letter Name–Alphabetic Stage

Students in the letter name–alphabetic stage provide a wonderful example of how learners construct knowledge in an attempt to make sense of the world of print. Without knowing much about orthography, students carefully analyze the sound system more vigorously than do adults, and they make surprisingly fine distinctions about the ways sounds and words are formed in the mouth. They match the phonemes they can segment to the letter names of the alphabet in ways that may seem curious and random to the uninformed adult.

Letter Names

Letters have both sounds and names and students in the letter name–alphabetic stage use their knowledge about the names of the letters in the alphabet to spell phonetically or alphabetically. For example, students in the early part of this stage are likely to spell the word *jeep* as GP, selecting *g* as the first letter because of its name ("gee") and *p* for the final letter because its letter name ("pee") offers a clear clue to the sound it represents. According to letter name logic, there is no need to add the vowel because it is already part of the letter name for *g*. Sometimes early letter name–alphabetic spellers do include vowels, especially when they spell long vowels that "say their name." For example, students might spell *jeep* as GEP. This phenomenon accounts for the reason the stage is called *letter name–alphabetic*. Spellers in this group operate in the first layer of English—the alphabetic layer. They understand that words can be segmented into sounds and that letters of the alphabet must be matched to these sounds in a systematic fashion.

Some letter names do not cue students to the sounds they represent. For example, the letter name for *w* is "double u" and the name for *h* is "aitch." Neither offers a clue to the sound it represents. However, the name for *h* does end with the /ch/ sound and when you say the name of the letter *y* you can feel your lips moving to make the shape of the /w/ sound. Consequently, early letter name–alphabetic spellers may spell *witch* as YH. Read through the letter names in Table 5.2 to see what they offer students in terms of sound matches. Most

Table 5.2 Names of the Letters of the Alphabet

A ay	H aitch	O oh	V vee
B bee	I ie	P pee	W doubleyoo
C see	J jay	Q kyoo	X ecks
D dee	K kay	R are	Y wie
E ee	L el	S es	Z zee
F ef	M em	T tee	
G gee	N en	U yoo	

consonants do offer a clue to the sound they represent either at the beginning ("bee") or the end ("ef") of the letter name.

During the early part of the letter name–alphabetic stage, when students have only partial phonemic awareness, spelling efforts may be limited to the most prominent sounds in syllables, usually the beginning and ending consonants. As phonemic awareness improves by the middle part of this stage, students' spellings gradually include a vowel in each stressed syllable, and they spell short vowels by matching the way they articulate the letter names of the vowels (discussed more later in the chapter). By the end of the letter name–alphabetic stage, students have learned how to spell many words with short vowels correctly and with full phonemic awareness they also spell blends. Table 5.3 summarizes characteristics of the letter name–alphabetic stage.

How Consonant Sounds Are Articulated in the Mouth

Knowing something about phonetics (the science of sounds) will help us understand and appreciate what young spellers are doing as they attempt to represent sounds with letters.

Table 5.3 Characteristics of Letter Name–Alphabetic Spelling

	WHAT STUDENTS DO CORRECTLY	WHAT STUDENTS USE BUT CONFUSE	WHAT IS ABSENT
Early Letter Name–Alphabetic B, BD for *bed* S, SP for *ship* YN for *when* L, LP for *lump* FT for *float* G, J, GF, JF, GV for *drive*	Partial phonological awareness Represent prominent sounds, usually beginning consonants Directionality Use most letters of the alphabet Partial spelling of consonant blends and digraphs Spell some known sight words correctly: *the, is*	Letter name–sound matches Consonants based on manner and point of articulation (*j/dr, b/p*) Concept of word is rudimentary, gets off track on two-syllable words Spaces between words	Vowels Complete blends and digraphs
Middle Letter Name–Alphabetic BAD for *bed* SEP or SHEP for *ship* LOP for *lump* FOT for *float* GRIV for *drive*	Developing phonological awareness All of the above plus: Spell beginning and ending consonants Spell frequently occurring short vowel words: *cat, dog* Concept of word is fully developed	Short vowels by point of articulation Consonant blends and digraphs	Silent letters Preconsonantal nasals
Late Letter Name–Alphabetic *bed* *ship* *lump* STEK for *stick* FLOT for *float* DRIV for *drive* BAKR for *baker*	Full phonological awareness All of the above plus: Spell many short vowels and most consonant blends and digraphs Spell frequently occurring long vowel words: *like, come*	Some short vowels still confused Substitutions of common short vowels for ambiguous vowels: COT for *caught* Preconsonantal nasals Affricate blends (*dr, tr*)	Most long vowel markers or silent vowels Vowels in unstressed syllables

When they spell, letter name–alphabetic students rely not only on what they hear in the letter names, but also on how the letters are articulated, or formed in the mouth. For example, when students try to spell the *dr* in *drive,* they are misled in their spelling by the similarity between *dr* and *jr,* and they may spell *drive* as JRV. Say "drive" and "jrive." Do they sound and feel alike? Linguists call these sounds **affricates,** which are formed by forcing air through a small closure at the roof of the mouth to create a feeling of friction (*friction, affricatives*—see the meaning connection?). English has several other letters and letter combinations that create the affricate sound and these are often substituted for each other: *j, g, ch, dr, tr;* and the letter name for *h* (aitch). Try saying "jip, chip, trip, drip" several times to feel the similarity and help you understand why young spellers confuse these affricates.

The voiced and unvoiced consonant pairs discussed in Chapter 4 and listed in Table 4.2 account for other confusions experienced by letter name–alphabetic spellers. They may spell *brave* as BRAF or *oven* as OFN. Both *v* and *f* are articulated exactly the same, but one is **voiced** and the other is **unvoiced.** When phonemes are voiced, the vocal cords vibrate. You can feel this if you place your fingers on your larynx as you say the words *van* and *fan.* One implication for instruction is that students in the letter name–alphabetic stage benefit from saying the words aloud as they are sorting so that they can feel the sound differences. Another implication is that initial teaching of these sounds should avoid contrasting voiced and unvoiced pairs: *b/p, d/t, g/k, z/s, v/f,* and *j/ch* (Purcell, 2002). Only when most consonant sounds are mastered should children focus attention on these finer distinctions. This is especially true for English learners, who may not have one of the contrasting sounds in their primary languages.

Vowels in the Letter Name–Alphabetic Stage

Vowels pose special problems for letter name–alphabetic spellers, who rely on the names of letters and how sounds feel in the mouth. Try saying the word *lip.* You can feel the initial consonant as your tongue curls up toward your palate and you can feel the final consonant as it explodes past your lips, but did you feel the **vowel?** Unlike the consonants—articulated by tongue, teeth, lips, and palate—the vowels are determined by more subtle variations in the shape of the mouth.

Vowels are elusive but central to every syllable humans speak. Try to say the sound for a consonant such as *b.* What vowels did you attach to the *b?* If you said the letter name ("bee"), then you have used the long *e* vowel. If you said the sound associated with *b* ("buh"), you attached the **schwa** sound (/ə/)—"uh." Now try to say a /b/ sound without a vowel. Try to whisper *b* and cut your breath short in a whisper. The whisper is as close as you come to separating the vowel from the consonant sound. There are some consonants that can be elongated without a vowel; these are the **continuant sounds**: /f/, /l/, /m/, /n/, /r/, /s/, /v/, and /z/. Consonant sounds that cannot be held like these are known as **stop consonants** (*b, d, g, k, p, t*).

Studies in acoustical phonetics have demonstrated that vowels are like musical tones, and without the music of the vowel, the consonants become just noise—clicks and snaps and nothing like speech. Because vowels are so closely wedded to the consonants around them, spellers in the early letter name–alphabetic stage have difficulty separating vowels from consonants. It is as if the consonant were the proverbial squeaky wheel; at first, the consonants seem to demand more attention than the vowel and are more easily examined.

The difference in the medial vowel sounds can be described linguistically as **tense** and **lax.** The vocal cords are tense when producing the **long** *a* sound (*ate*), but relax a bit in producing the **short** *a* sound (*at*). The vowels we call "long" are no longer in duration than short vowels; the terms are holdovers from Classical Latin. Although these terms may not be the most accurate terms linguistically, they are more common than *tense* and *lax* and teachers understand each other when they are used. The simplest way to talk about vowels is probably the best. Descriptions like "in the middle" may suffice to draw students' attention to the vowels at first, but students have no trouble learning *long vowel* and *short vowel* and such terms make word study discussions easier.

FIGURE 5.3 Vowels in the Mouth

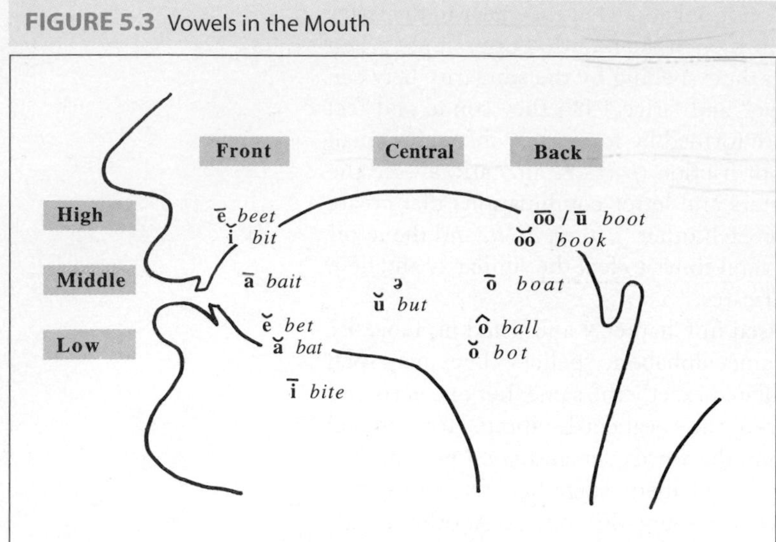

HOW VOWELS ARE ARTICULATED IN THE MOUTH. Over the course of the letter name–alphabetic stage, students become adept at fully segmenting words into phonemes, including the medial vowel, and they use the alphabetic principle to represent each sound with a letter. Long vowels say their letter name, so the letter choices are obvious. Students spell *line* as LIN, *rain* as RAN, and *boat* as BOT. Perhaps what is most interesting about the letter name–alphabetic stage is the way students spell the short vowels. They turn to the names of the letters, but find no clear letter–sound matches for the short vowel sounds. For example, there is no letter name that says the short *i* sound in *bit* or the "uh" sound in *cup*. Very early letter name–alphabetic spellers might use *f* ("ef") or *s* ("ess") for short *e*, but they seldom do. Instead, spellers throughout the letter name–alphabetic stage use their knowledge of the alphabet to find the letter name closest to the place of **articulation** of the short vowel sound they are trying to write.

You may have never analyzed sounds at this level, so let's take a moment to consider the vowels and where and how sounds are made in the vocal tract. In Figure 5.3, the vowels are placed to mimic the general area where speakers can feel their place of articulation. Vowels are subtly differentiated by the shape of the mouth, the openness of the jaw, and the position of the tongue while the word is being said. They are all voiced because it is impossible to articulate a vowel sound without vibrating the vocal cords. Compare the vowels in this figure by saying the following words in sequence several times and trying to identify where the vowel sound is produced:

beet	bit	bait	bet
bat	bite	but	bot
ball	boat	book	boot

Do you feel how the production of the vowels moves from high in the front of the oral cavity (*beet*) to low in the oral cavity (*bite*) to the back of the oral cavity (*bot*), down the front, back, and up (*boot*)? Contrast the rounded vowel in *boot* with the way your lips feel when you say the high front vowel sounds in *beet* or *bit*.

The way a word is pronounced may vary by dialect. For example, many people say *caught* and *cot* the same way. Some rhyme *roof* with *hoof* while others rhyme *roof* with *poof*. Teachers must be aware of dialectical differences when students sort and talk about words. Although these differences do not interfere with word study and learning to spell, an awareness of these differences enhances word study. Everyone speaks a dialect, but we all learn to read and write the same orthography.

A LETTER NAME STRATEGY TO SPELL SHORT VOWELS. Students in the letter name–alphabetic stage use their knowledge of letter names and the feel of the vowels as they are produced in the vocal tract to spell *bet* as BAT. Without being consciously aware that they are doing this, letter name–alphabetic spellers spell short vowels with the letter name closest in articulation to that short vowel. There are five letter names from which to choose: *a*, *e*, *i*, *o*, and *u*. How would an alphabetic speller spell the word *bed?* What letter name is closest to the short *e* sound in *bet?* Try saying *bet/beet* and *bet/bait* to compare how the short vowel sounds and the long vowels or letter names feel in your mouth. Repeat the pairs several times and pay attention to how the mouth is shaped. The short *e* sound is closer in place of articula-

tion to the long *a* or letter name for *a* than it is to the letter name for *e*. Students might spell *ship* as SHEP for a similar reason: The short *i* sound is closer in place of articulation to the letter name for *e* than the letter name for *i*. (If you look back at Figure 5.3, you will see how short *i* and long *e* are both high front vowels, whereas the long *i* is a low front vowel.) Short *a* poses little problem for spellers because the letter name for *a* is already close in place of articulation. This is a good reason to teach it first. However, because short *e* is close to short *a*, these pairs are not good contrasts for first introducing short vowels.

Table 5.4 Letter Substitutions for Short Vowels

SPELLING ATTEMPT	LOGICAL VOWEL SUBSTITUTION
BAT for *bat*	None, short *a* is close to *a*
BAT for *bet*	*a* for short *e*
BET for *bit*	*e* for short *i*
PIT for *pot*	*i* for short *o*
POT for *put*	*o* for short *u*

The wondrous aspect of these letter name substitutions for short vowels is that they are so predictable. Read (1975) found that nearly all students go through a period of time when they substitute the short vowels with other letter names closest in articulation. Table 5.4 will help you remember how the letter names of vowels are substituted for the short vowel sounds beginning readers try to spell.

Through word study, students in the letter name–alphabetic stage learn to spell short vowel words correctly. They see that short vowels follow a specific pattern, a consonant-vowel-consonant (CVC) pattern. Regardless of how many consonant letters are on either side of the single vowel (*cat*, *clap*, *clack*, or *strap*), one vowel letter in the middle signals the short vowel sound. The CVC pattern is introduced in the late letter name–alphabetic stage and is contrasted with long vowel patterns in the within word pattern stage.

As they mature and learn more sight words, students face the ambiguities of homographs, words that are spelled the same but pronounced differently, words like *wind* (noun) and *wind* (verb), for example. Sometimes students in the letter name–alphabetic stage inadvertently create their own homographs in their invented spelling; they may spell *bent*, *bet*, *bat*, and *bait* the same way: BAT. Only memory for the word they intended to write will disambiguate the invented spelling BAT, and once they know how to spell the real word *bat*, that memory may cause a conflict. How could BAT also be *bent*, *bet*, or *bait?* The burden of so many homographs is a catalyst for students to change, a good problem. Letter name–alphabetic spellers are also readers, and when they reread their own spelling of *bait* as BAT, a word that they know spells something else, they experience disequilibrium (Bissex, 1980). This forces them to find other ways to spell a word like *bait*, perhaps as BATE. When students are able to spell basic short vowel patterns and also begin to experiment with long vowel patterns, they have entered the next spelling stage: the within word pattern.

Other Orthographic Features

In addition to short vowels, students work through four other features during the letter name–alphabetic stage: (1) consonant digraphs, (2) consonant blends, (3) preconsonantal nasals, and (4) influences on the vowel from certain surrounding consonants.

CONSONANT DIGRAPHS AND BLENDS. Letter name–alphabetic spellers take some time to learn the consonants known as digraphs and blends. A **digraph** is two letters that represent a single sound. The word *digraph* ends with a digraph, the *ph* that stands for the single sound of /f/. Digraphs are generally easier than blends and can be taught right along with other beginning consonants because they only require segmenting and attending to a single **phoneme.** The commonly recognized digraphs studied in this stage have an *h* as the second letter of the pair. Digraphs include the bold letters in **th**in, fi**sh,** ea**ch,** **wh**en, **ph**one. They can come at the beginnings or ends of words.

A consonant **blend** is slightly different. A blend is a spelling unit (sometimes called a *consonant cluster*) of two or three consonants that retain their identity when pronounced. The word *blend* contains two blends: *bl* and *nd*. Each of the sounds in a blend can still be heard, but they are tightly bound and not easily segmented into individual phonemes, which makes blends difficult for students to spell accurately. This is why the *t* in the *st* blend may be omitted in *stick*, as in the spellings SEK or SEC. In English, blends can occur at the beginnings or ends of syllables, as shown by the bold letters in the following words: **bl**ack, **cl**ap, **tr**ap, ju**st**, li**sp**, ma**sk**.

PRECONSONANTAL NASALS. Some final blends are especially difficult, deserving special mention. Nasals that come right before a final consonant, such as the *n* in *pink*, are known as **preconsonantal nasals.** The nasal sounds associated with *m*, *n*, and *ng* are made by air passing through the nasal cavity in the mouth. The *ng* pair is sometimes considered a digraph but we group it with preconsonantal nasals, as this is the best place to study it. Try saying *bad*, *ban*, and then *band* as you pay attention to the final sounds. You cannot feel the *n* in *band* because it passes out through the nose on the way to the *d*, but it is definitely there! Preconsonantal nasals are often omitted during the letter name–alphabetic stage (*jump* may be spelled JOP and *pink* may be spelled PEK). When students begin to spell words with preconsonantal nasals correctly, they are usually at the end of the letter name–alphabetic stage, having achieved full phonemic awareness.

CONSONANT INFLUENCES ON THE VOWEL. The letters *r*, *w*, and *l* influence the vowel sounds they follow. For example, the vowel sounds in words like *bar*, *ball*, and *saw* are not the same as the short vowel sounds in *bat* and *fast*. They cannot be called short *a*, yet all of these words have the CVC pattern. The consonant sounds /r/ and /l/ are known in linguistics as **liquids** because they roll around in the mouth and have vowel-like qualities. Both can change the pronunciation of the vowel they follow. These spellings are often known as ***r*-influenced** (or *r*-controlled) and *l*-influenced (or *l*-controlled). The *w* also has an effect on vowels that follow it in words such as *want*, *was*, *wash*, *word*, and *war*.

It can be difficult to spell *r*-influenced vowels by sound alone. For example, *fur*, *her*, and *sir* have the same vowel sound yet are spelled three different ways. The *r*-influenced vowels that follow a CVC pattern (*car*, *for*) are examined during the late letter name–alphabetic stage and can be compared with short vowels in word sorts. Students might also contrast consonant blends with an *r* (*fr*, *tr*, *gr*) and *r*-influenced vowels (e.g., *from/form*, *grill/girl*, *tarp/trap*) as a way to compare exactly where the *r* falls. Because the *r* rolls around like liquid in the mouth, these contrasts are difficult.

Word Study Instruction for the Letter Name–Alphabetic Stage

This section discusses the sequence of word study, presents ways to build a sight word vocabulary and use word banks, and offers some tips for how to lead group sorting activities.

Sequence and Pacing of Word Study

Initially, students use beginning consonants in their writing, so this is the place to begin word study in the early letter name–alphabetic stage. As their ability to segment phonemes becomes more complete, they begin to use but confuse short vowels and consonant blends in the middle to late letter name stage. This is the time to study those features. Table 5.5 summarizes the sequence of word study in this stage.

EARLY, MIDDLE, OR LATE. Placing students in the early, middle, or late parts of this stage using the spelling inventory depends primarily on how well they spell short vowels. If students do not attempt vowels, they would be in the early part of the stage. If they use but confuse

Table 5.5 Pacing and Sequence Guide for Letter Name–Alphabetic Spellers

	SLOW INTRODUCTORY PACE		MODERATE PACE		ADVANCED PACE OR REVIEW	
Early Letter Name–Alphabetic						
Initial Sound Sorts	*Beginning consonants* b/m/r/s t/g/n/p c/h/f/d l/k/j/w y/z/v	 w/y g/j p/b d/t	Contrast easily confused consonants w/y/g/j b/p d/t others as needed		Review initial sounds only as needed	
Same-Vowel Word Families	at/an ap/ag op/ot/og	et/eg/en ug/ut/un ip/ig/ill	at/an/ap op/ot/og et/eg/en	ug/ut/un ip/ig/ill	at/an/ap op/ot/og et/eg/en	ug/ut/un ip/ig/ill
Digraphs	c/h/ch s/h/sh h/sh/ch	t/th/h ch/sh/th wh/sh/ch/th	sh/ch/h th/wh wh/sh/ch/th		wh/sh/ch/th	
Blends	st/s/t sp/s/p sc/sn/sw st/sp/sk/sm p/l/pl bl/b/l	pl/bl/gl/sl cr/cl/fl/fr bl/br/gr/gl pr/tr/dr k/wh/qu/tw	st/sp/sk/sm sc/sn/sw/sl cr/cl/fl/fr	bl/br/gr/gl pr/tr/dr	tr/dr/gr others as needed	
Middle Letter Name–Alphabetic						
Mixed-Vowel Word Families	at/ot/it an/un/in am/im/um ad/ed/ab/ob	ag/eg/ig/og/ug ill/ell/all ick/ack/ock/uck ish/ash/ush	at/ot/it/ut an/un/in ag/eg/ig/og/ug ill/ell/all ick/ack/ock/uck ish/ash/ush		ag/eg/ig/og/ug ill/ell/all ick/ack/ock/uck ish/ash/ush	
Picture Sorts for Short Vowels	a/o e/o i/u e/i/o/u Add known words		a/o i/u e/i/o/u Add known words			
Late Letter Name–Alphabetic						
Short Vowels in CVC Words	a/o i/u e/o	e/i e/i/o/u	a/o i/u e/i/o/u		a/e/i/o/u	
Short Vowels with Blends and Digraphs	Ex: **dr**op **tr**ip di**sh**		Ex: **dr**ag da**sh** **sl**ed		Ex: **dr**ill **tr**a**sh** **fr**e**sh**	
Preconsonantal Nasals	an/ant in/ing ug/ung ing/ang/ung	ink/ank/unk amp/ump end/ent/ant	ing/ang/ung ink/ank/unk	amp/ump nd/nt/nk	ng/mp	nt/nd/nk
***R*-Influenced**	a/ar o/or		a/ar o/or		ar/or	

Go to PDToolkit for *Words Their Way,* click on the Assessment Tools tab, then type "Primary Spelling Inventory."

vowels, perhaps getting one or two correct on an inventory, they would be in the middle of the stage. If they spell half or more of the short vowels on an inventory, they would be in the late letter name–alphabetic stage. If students are spelling most short vowels as well as most digraphs and blends, they are ready to move to the study of long vowels in the within word pattern stage, in which short vowels will be reviewed as long vowels are introduced. Table 5.3 will help you identify whether students are in the early, middle, or late part of the stage.

PACING. Although there is a predictable pattern of development, the exact sequence and pace will not be precisely the same for every student because they progress at different rates. However, there is no time to waste. Teachers must set as fast a pace as possible during the letter name–alphabetic stage because success in beginning reading depends on learning the basic phonics elements that are covered in this stage. Pacing should be tied to ongoing assessment to determine whether instruction is effective. Progress monitoring for this stage is discussed on pages 172 and 173.

SEQUENCE. Although converging evidence from research (NRP, 2000) has established that children need systematic phonics instruction, there is disagreement about the nature of that instruction and the exact sequence. Our recommended sequence, outlined in Table 5.5, is based on research in children's spellings over several decades, which has revealed the order in which phonics features are typically mastered. This is one reason we call this book *Words Their Way*™. Consonants are taught first and vowels are placed later in the sequence when students have developed full phonemic awareness.

Until children have acquired some sight words, pictures are used as the basis for sorting by sounds through an analytic phonics approach, which begins with whole words and asks students to break them into letters and sounds that can be compared and examined. Synthetic phonics has a different sequence. Children are taught vowel sounds (usually short vowels) along with consonants in isolation and then expected to sound out words as they learn to read text that is often controlled by how decodable it is based on the phonics features children have been taught. Although children do learn to sound out words in this stage, this is not the starting point for the phonics instruction we recommend. In the whole-to-part model we propose, children learn to read big books, poems, and jingles first and then focus on letter–sound correspondences by analyzing words. We believe this analytic approach to phonics represents an easier and more engaging entry into the world of reading, but teachers can be assured that all the phonics features are covered in a systematic way.

Reading Instruction

Beginning reading should focus on solidifying a concept of word in text so that students can begin to amass a sight word vocabulary as quickly as possible. Acquiring sight words can be thought of as establishing an orthographic lexicon, a mental dictionary of known written words organized by spelling patterns. Sight words are best acquired by reading and rereading familiar texts and by analyzing those known words out of context, in word study. Through rereading children see the same words over and over again and thereby increase the number of words they can recognize automatically.

The more words students can recognize automatically, the greater the opportunity for making generalizations across words in their word sorts. The result is a general increase in word knowledge. But what students know about particular words during the letter name–alphabetic stage may only be partial. For example, as they read, early letter name–alphabetic spellers may substitute *leopard* for *lion* in a story about big cats at the zoo. From such errors, it appears that they are attending to beginning letters for cues. This is also evident in the way they spell during this time. *Lion* might be spelled as LN. Ehri (1997) has described these readers as "partial alphabetic," because their letter–sound knowledge is not automatic or complete and they use only partial letter–sound cues—usually consonant cues—to identify and spell words. Partial information about the alphabetic code is not enough to ensure fast and accurate word recognition. Instead, letter name–alphabetic spellers need support to make reading happen.

SUPPORT READING. Without a large sight vocabulary beginning readers cannot read very much without some kind of support. Support can come from two sources: the text and the teacher. Predictable text has repetitive patterns, rhyme, and simple language that make it memorable when students have recited or sung it, or just read or heard it, many times. Texts are also easy to read when the words are about an event experienced first-hand by the students, as in individual and group dictations created using the language experience approach (LEA) described in the last chapter (also see Activity 5.7). Support from the teacher comes from shared reading strategies such as reading the text aloud and then encouraging students to read in unison (**choral reading**) or immediately after the teacher reads (**echo reading**). Or the teacher may provide a book introduction (Clay, 1991) that uses the language of the text and anticipates difficult words and concepts.

for Words Their Way™

Go to PDToolkit for *Words Their Way,* click on the Videos tab, then type "Whole Class Reading and Picture Sort of Beginning Consonants," where you will see Mrs. Smith lead her students in a choral reading of *Oh, A-Hunting We Will Go.*

A tension lies between these two forms of support. The more predictable a text is, the less support is needed from the teacher. Conversely, the less support provided from recurring elements of text, the more scaffolding is required from the teacher. Because early letter name–alphabetic spellers require support when they read, we often call these beginners "support readers." As students develop a sight vocabulary, they need less support from either teacher or text and they benefit from reading text that is not so predictable.

SIGHT WORD LEARNING. Acquiring a **sight vocabulary** is critical to becoming a fluent reader, but progress will be slow during the early letter name–alphabetic period and students will need repeated exposures to words to fully store them in memory. Taking words first encountered in context and examining them out of context makes a difference in how well students learn those words (Ehri & Wilce, 1980) and how many words they learn over time (Johnston, 1998, 2000). Support reading provides a context for sight word learning; using word banks and personal readers (described below) enhances this learning. Words that have concrete referents (e.g., nouns and adjectives like *moon* or *green*) or that are easily visualized (e.g., action verbs like *run*) are easier to learn than abstract prepositions, articles, or adverbs (such as *from* or *when*), which have no meaning by themselves. Students can be actively involved in the process of determining which words they want to learn through the use of word banks.

Word Banks. **Word banks** are collections of known words gathered from the texts that students have been reading and rereading (Stauffer, 1980). The words are lifted out of context and written on small cards and collected over time. These words are reviewed regularly, and words that have been forgotten are matched back to their counterparts in context or discarded. Sometimes we are asked why students need to review words they already know. The answer is they do not know them the same way more mature readers do; they know them only partially and tentatively. Letter name–alphabetic students may confuse *ran* and *run, stop* and *ship, lost* and *little.* They may read *gingerbread* correctly every time because it is the only long word they know that starts with *g,* but when you ask them to spell it (GNRBRD) you get a better idea of what they really know about the word.

Regular review of word bank words encourages students to look more thoroughly at words and to note individual letter–sound correspondences. As they study initial sounds through picture sorts, students can be asked to find words in their word banks that start with those same sounds. This will help them make connections between the pictures they sort and the words they read. Later in the letter name–alphabetic stage, the word bank becomes a source of known words to be used in word sorts. It is crucial that students work with known words because it is easier to look across known words for similarities and differences in sounds and letters. If students must labor to pronounce the words before analyzing their orthographic features in word study, this added burden will impede their ability to generalize relationships to other words.

The words in a word bank come from many sources that students read and reread: predictable books, preprimer readers, leveled books, poems, and individual and group dictations. By using words from familiar readings and cross-numbering the stories and rhymes to the word cards, students can be encouraged to return to the primary source to find a forgotten word and to match the word bank card to its counterpart in print. More guidelines for word

FIGURE 5.4 Personal Reader with Word Bank

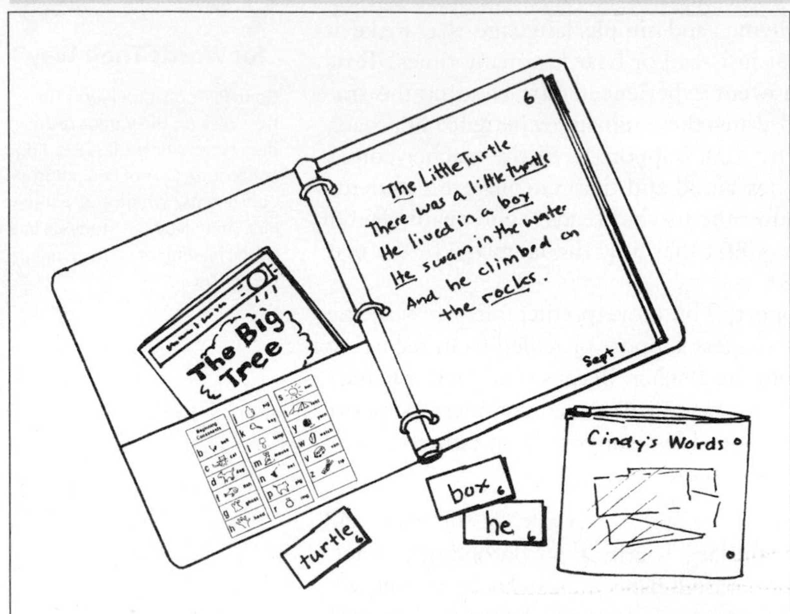

banks and other sight word activities can be found in the activity section at the end of this chapter.

Word banks take extra work but are well worth the effort, particularly for students in the beginning of this stage who are not making good progress in reading. Word banks promote sight word development and growing word knowledge. They are also motivating for students because they offer tangible evidence of their growing word knowledge (Johnston, 1998). When the word bank contains between 150 and 200 words and the student is at the end of the letter name–alphabetic stage, the word bank can be discontinued. If teachers find it overwhelming to manage individual word banks, an alternative is to create a collective version that students in a reading group share.

for Words Their Way™

Go to PDToolkit for *Words Their Way,* click on the Videos tab, then type "Weekly Schedules and Activities in the Letter Name–Alphabetic Stage." Watch how Ms. Kiernan has her first-graders read in their personal readers and go on word hunts.

Personal Readers. Copies of familiar rhymes and jingles, group or individual dictations, or selected passages from books that students have read can be collected in a **personal reader** (Bear, Caserta-Henry, & Venner, 2004). See Figure 5.4. Students are enormously proud of their personal readers and they reread the selections in their personal readers many times before taking them home to read some more. The stories in the personal readers are numbered, and the date they are introduced is recorded. Personal readers are an ideal place for students to collect words for their word banks. They can simply underline the words they know best and these words can then be transferred to small cards. A number can be written on each word card that matches the numbered stories.

In Figure 5.4, the student's word bank is a plastic bag that can be stored in the personal reader. You can also see that little leveled books fit inside the front pocket. In addition, a reduced soundboard (see Appendix B) of consonant sounds is included for a student reference in word study and writing. The personal reader also contains a page that lists the words in the student's word bank.

The Study of Consonant Sounds

Word study with students in the early letter name–alphabetic stage begins with picture sorts to focus students' attention on consonant sounds or beginning phonemes in words. Consonant sounds include single consonants as well as digraphs, blends, and preconsonantal nasals. Picture sorts help students continue to develop the phonemic awareness they will need to segment the two sounds in consonant blends. Phonemic awareness combined with letter knowledge lays the basis for understanding the alphabetic nature of English spelling.

Pictures for sorts can be found in Appendix C and prepared sorts can be found on the website and in the other books in the *Words Their Way*™ series. Chapter 3 identified follow-up activities such as draw and label or cut and paste, and many of the games described for beginning consonants in Chapter 4 can be easily adapted for this stage. There are also games on the website ready to print and use.

for Words Their Way™

Go to PDToolkit for *Words Their Way,* click on the Sorts and Games tab, then type "Beginning Consonant Picture Sorts."

INITIAL CONSONANTS. Children in this stage should have the phonemic awareness to isolate and attend to initial consonant sounds, but they may not be sure of the corresponding letters used to represent those sounds, so a review of initial consonants is in order. Figure 5.5 is an example of a sort that started with pictures and then included sight words from the students' word banks. Picture sorts with initially occurring short vowels can also be included here as a way to introduce those letter–sound correspondences. Pages 112 and 113 in Chapter 4 offer suggestions for how to plan and carry out picture sorts for initial sounds and the activity section has games for further practice.

Mr. Perez, whom we met at the beginning of this chapter, was wise in deciding to take a step back to firm up Cynthia's understandings of consonants. Many students benefit from a fast-paced review of consonants at the beginning of first grade to clear up lingering confusions or to secure tentative letter–sound matches. There is no particular order to the sequence of beginning sounds, but starting with frequently occurring initial consonants in which the contrasts or differences are clear both visually and phonologically is recommended. Many teachers have found the following sequence to be effective for a review.

1. *b m r s*
2. *t g n p*
3. *c h f d*
4. *l k j w*
5. *y z v*

Some students may only have a few lingering confusions with certain letter sounds based on letter name confusions (*y* and *w*, for example) or voiced and unvoiced pairs (*b* and *p*, for example). They will benefit from sorts designed to address these specific confusions. English learners might also need sorts that address the confusions that arise because of sounds that are missing or different in their native language.

A few ending consonants might be introduced and studied with picture sorts, but once students have developed enough phonemic awareness to attend to final sounds, most of them can easily use their knowledge of letter–sound matches to spell those final consonants as well. Some students may have a few remaining confusions even when they are in control of most consonant matches, but do not hesitate to move on if they are beginning to represent vowels in their invented spellings. Beginning consonants are reviewed and ending consonants are targeted in same-vowel word families. English learners whose native language does not have many ending consonants may need more sorts with final consonant sounds.

for **English Learners**

After students know their consonant sounds, they are ready to learn about consonant digraphs and blends. The goal is to not only master letter–sound correspondences but also to help students see these two-letter combinations as single orthographic units in the CVC pattern. Digraphs are introduced before blends because there is only one phoneme to segment and attend to, but most children are ready to study both at about the same time.

DIGRAPHS. The consonants digraphs to be studied in the letter name stage are *ch, sh, th,* and *wh*. There are several things to keep in mind when setting up picture sorting contrasts for digraphs. First, consider the confusions students show in their spelling attempts. Some students substitute *j* for *ch* as they spell words like *chin* as JN or they may confuse the letter name of *h* (aitch) with *ch* and spell *chin* as HN. These affricate confusions suggest that a good sort to study *ch* might include pictures that start with *ch*, *j*, and *h*. *Th* might be compared to single *t*, *sh* to single *s*, and *ch* to single *c*. Note, however, that it would be difficult to sort pictures by *w* and *wh* because many words beginning with *wh* do not have a distinctive sound. (Which witch was which?) Compare *wh* to *th*, *sh*, and *ch* in a culminating digraph sort. Add known words to picture sorts as shown in Figure 5.5. A suggested sequence and possible contrasts for the study of digraphs can be found in Table 5.5. Digraphs are revisited in the study of word families and short vowels in both initial and final positions.

Go to PDToolkit for *Words Their Way,* click on the Sorts and Games tab, then type "Beginning Digraph Picture Sorts" or "Beginning Blends Picture Sorts."

BLENDS. Beginning consonant blends can be grouped as follows:

- *s*-blends: *sc, sk, sl, sn, sm, sp, st, sw*
- *l*-blends: *bl, cl, fl, gl, pl, sl*
- *r*-blends: *br, cr, dr, fr, gr, pr, tr*
- Blends with /w/: *qu, tw*

FIGURE 5.5 Initial Consonant Picture and Word Sort

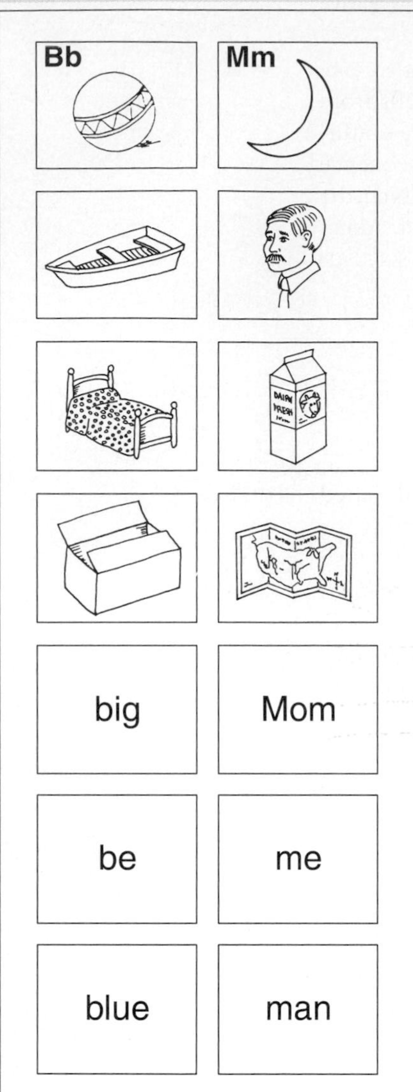

The easiest group to learn seems to be the *s*-blends, because *s* is a continuant that can be held (*sssss*). Blends with the "slippery" *l* or *r* are the hardest because some are confused with affricatives such as *j*. In *qu*, the *u* is acting as a consonant representing the /w/ sound. Three-letter blends (*spr*, *str*, *squ*, *thr*, *shr*) are less common and not studied until the within word pattern stage.

The study of initial consonant blends begins with picture sorts that contrast a single initial consonant with its blend because this is the problem students show us when they spell *sled* as SED. For example, pictures that begin with *st* may be contrasted with pictures that begin with *s* for spellers such as Tony who spell *stick* as SEK. After studying several blends in this fashion, it is best to pick up the pace and introduce other blends in groups. Suggested contrasts are listed in Table 5.5. Once students catch on to how blends work and learn to segment and blend the individual sounds in a consonant blend, they may move quickly through a sequence of study or even skip some contrasts altogether. Known words can be added to picture sorts if they begin with the same consonant blend. The procedures and routines for the study of digraphs and blends are the same as for other beginning sound sorts described in Chapter 4.

Students in the early part of the letter name–alphabetic stage are not expected to acquire great fluency or accuracy in spelling and sorting consonant blends and digraphs because they will be revisited throughout the stage in the study of word families and short vowels. Research (Johnston, 2003) shows that blends, digraphs, and short vowels all begin to appear in children's spellings about the same time, so there should be some interplay among these features in the instructional sequence, as shown in Table 5.5. Consonant blends and digraphs that create an affricate sound (*trip*, *drip*, *chip*) will have to be revisited throughout this stage because their sounds are so similar and take longer to master.

Final consonant blends (*last*, *lisp*, *task*, *left*, *kept*, *felt*, *shelf*, and *help*) are not studied with pictures due to a lack of examples, but should be included toward the end of the stage in the study of short vowel words. Other ending blends that include an *r*, like *rd*, *rt*, and *rp*, are studied with *r*-influenced vowels.

Preconsonantal nasals, a particular type of final blend that includes *mp*, *nt*, *nd*, and *nk*, are also studied at the end of the letter name stage. We add the digraph *ng* as well, which may be studied in word families, as there are many words spelled with *ang*, *ing*, *ong*, or *ung*. Appendix E has lists of words by families that include words with preconsonantal nasals among them. Many children find this feature particularly difficult and will need explicit routines for making words with and without the nasal, changing *rag* into *rang* or *hug* into *hung*, for example. The building, blending, and extending exercises described in Activity 5.19 can be adapted for this.

The Study of Short Vowels

Once letter name–alphabetic spellers have a solid, if not complete, mastery of beginning and ending consonant sounds, they are ready for the study of medial short vowels. Full phonemic awareness is needed to isolate the elusive vowel but if vowels are still missing or used only occasionally in students' spellings, start the study of vowels with word families as Mr. Perez did with his middle group. Once students are using (though still confusing) short vowels consistently, they can be asked to compare short vowels in word sorts that examine the CVC pattern across a variety of vowels, as Mr Perez did with his highest group. Lists of words spelled with short vowels can be found in Appendix D. These lists can be used to create handouts similar to those used by Mr. Perez in Figure 5.1(C). Appendix D also has suggested sorts, and prepared games and more sorts are on the website and in *Words Their Way™: Word Sorts for Letter Name–Alphabetic Spellers.*

WORD FAMILIES. Word families, which are sometimes called **phonograms,** consist of groups of rhyming words such as *cat, mat, sat,* and *bat* that are spelled similarly. They offer an easy and appealing way to introduce the issue of vowels early on in this stage. Students are supported in their first efforts to analyze the vowel because the vowel and the ending letter(s) are presented as a chunk or pattern called a **rime** (i.e., the *at* in *cat* and *mat*). What comes before the vowel is the **onset.** Examples of onset-rime breaks are *m-an, bl-and, m-at,* and *th-at.* Dividing words into onsets and rimes is easier and more natural for students than dividing them into individual phonemes (Goswami, 2008; Treiman, 1985).

PDToolkit for Words Their Way™

Go to PDToolkit for *Words Their Way,* click on the Sorts and Games tab, click Letter Name–Alphabetic Stage, then type "Word Family Sorts" for ready-to-use sorts.

The study of word families makes sense for several other reasons. First, 37 rimes can be used to generate 500 different words that students encounter in primary reading materials (Wylie & Durrell, 1970). In addition, these same rimes will be familiar chunks in thousands of multisyllabic words; the *an* chunk can be found in *canyon, fantastic,* and *incandescent.* Second, vowel sounds are more stable within families than across families (Adams, 1990; Wylie & Durrell, 1970). For example, the word *dog* is often presented as a short *o* word in phonics programs, but in some regions of the United States, it is pronounced more like *dawg.* If you say it that way, then you probably pronounce *fog* as *fawg, frog* as *frawg,* and *log* as *lawg.* In the study of word families, the actual pronunciation of the short vowel does not matter; it is the *og* chunk that is examined and compared.

Knowing that students in the early letter name stage have trouble isolating and attending to the medial vowel, it is a good idea to compare word families that share the same vowel before contrasting different vowels. This supports students' first efforts to read and spell those words. What they really must attend to are the beginning and ending consonants in order to sort and spell the words. The study of same-vowel word families serves to review those features. In sorting words like *mat* and *man,* for example, students must attend to the final consonant more than any other phoneme. Nevertheless, the phonological awareness of the rime unit (e.g., *-at, -an*) lays the foundation for future vowel study as students begin to look inside the word for common features.

There is no particular order to the study of word families, but starting with short *a* families (*at, an, ad, ap, ack*) seems to be a good choice because these words abound in early reading materials, and students are likely to already know several words from these families by sight. In addition, short *a* is the least likely short vowel to be confused when students try to make matches based on letter names and place of articulation. Compare other same-vowel word families in a similar way (*in, it, ip* or *ot, op, og,* etc.).

Move quickly, however, to comparing words that have different vowels. The difference between *top, tip,* and *tap* lies in the medial vowel, and it is through such contrasts that students are forced to attend to the vowel sound itself and look carefully at the vowel in the middle of a word. Students in the middle letter name stage should be ready to study mixed-vowel word families. Words with blends and digraphs should be included after they have been studied with picture sorts. For example, the *ag* family can be expanded to include *flag, brag, drag, shag,* and *snag.*

Table 5.5 suggests contrasts and a sequence for the study of word families under three possible pacing guides. However, it is offered only as a model from which to plan your own course of study. Consider the words that your students know as sight words and the kinds of words they encounter in their reading. If you are reading a story with lots of short *u* words, then study a few short *u* families.

Introducing Word Families with Pictures. Apply the following procedure when introducing a word family sort with pictures (see Figure 5.6).

FIGURE 5.6 Same-Vowel Word Family Sort with Pictures

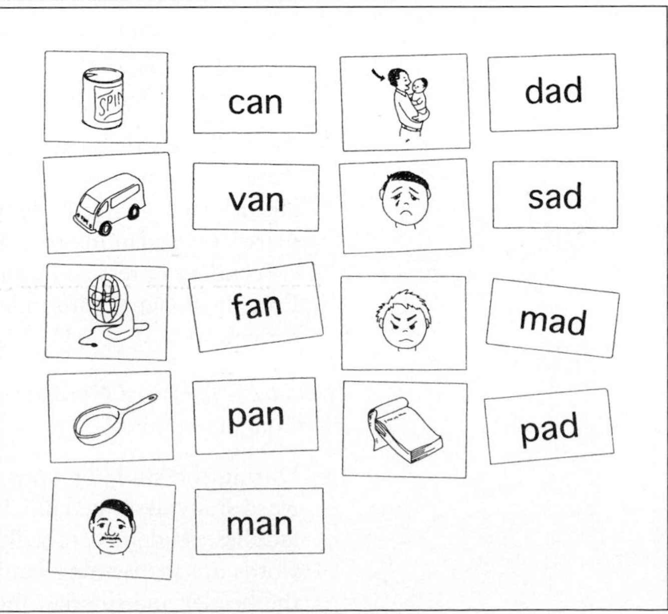

for Words Their Way™

Go to PDToolkit for *Words Their Way,* click on the Videos tab, then type "Word Study Intervention in the Letter Name–Alphabetic Stage." Watch Ms. Kiernan's intervention group learn about word families.

1. Start with just the pictures for a rhyming sort. (See the list of rhyming short vowel pictures at the beginning of Appendix C.) Put down pictures as headers for each column (*can* and *dad*) and then pick up another picture: "*Van.* Does *van* rhyme with *can* or *dad?* I will put it under the *can.*" Model several and then have students help you finish the sort. Name all the pictures in each column and talk about how they rhyme.
2. Now lay out the word cards. Name a header such as *can* and say, "Who can find the word *can?* What letters would you look for at the beginning and end?" Repeat for *dad,* and then ask students to find the word for each picture. After all the words are sorted and matched to the pictures, read down each column. Ask the students how the words are alike. Children should note that they all end with the same two letters. Explain that they are in the same family (the *an* family or *ad* family) and they all rhyme.
3. Remove the words and shuffle them. Give them out to the students to match to the pictures again. Read each column and then remove the pictures to see whether the students can use just the initial sound and the rime to read each word in the column.
4. Give students their own set of pictures and words to sort for seatwork. Follow up with other word family activities such as Build, Blend, and Extend, described in Activity 5.19.

Introducing Mixed-Vowel Word Families with Words. Here is an example of a teacher-directed sort featuring *ig, ag,* and *og.* Students should already know how to read several words in each family.

1. Begin by laying down a known word as a header for each family. Choose words you are sure the students can read, such as *big, dog,* and *bag.* Explain that the rest of the words are to be sorted under one of the headers.
2. Pick up another word such as *frog* and say, "I am going to put this word under *dog* because it ends in *o* and *g.*" Then read the words: "Listen: *dog, frog.*" Continue to model one or two words in each category, always sorting first and then reading down, starting with the header.
3. Ask students to sort the next word. They should sort first and then read from the top of each column to help them identify the new word. They are not expected to sound the word out first and then sort. Instead, their sense of rhyme will support them as they read the new word by simply changing the first sound of a word they already know. The final sort might look like the following:

big	dog	bag
dig	frog	wag
pig	hog	rag
wig	fog	flag
	log	tag

4. After all the words have been sorted, lead a discussion to focus students' attention on the common features (sounds and letters) in each word: "How are the words in each column alike?" After giving students a chance to discuss what they notice about the words, summarize by explaining that the words in each column are in the same family because of the two ending letters and sounds that rhyme.
5. Provide students with individual sorts. Conclude as in the previous sort with follow-up activities.

Guidelines for Word Families. As you implement the study of word families keep the following thoughts in mind:

- During the study of word families, it is appropriate to modify one of the principles of word study described in Chapter 3: *Use words students can read.* When working with word families, students probably cannot read *all* the words initially. However, because the words are in rhyming families, students are supported in reading the words as long as the header and the first few words are familiar. Students sort visually by the spelling of the rime first and then read unknown words by blending different onsets with the rime of the header.

- *Include words with digraphs and blends once they have been introduced.* The study of the *ack* family can grow to be quite large when you include *black, clack, track, shack, quack, stack, snack,* and *crack.* Lists of words and pictures for sorts can be found in the Appendixes.
- *Supply supplemental reading materials that feature word families.* With the publication of research on onsets and rimes and renewed interest in word families, there has been a flood of reading materials for students that feature a particular family or short vowel. Some of these little books are engaging and well written, offering students support in the form of patterned or rhyming text. Such books can be used as a starting point or as a follow-up for word study, and students can use them to go on word hunts for additional words that follow the same phonics feature. However, choose these books carefully. Text featuring sentences such as "The tan man ran the van" make reading into an exercise in word calling. Although some phonics readers are better than others, they should never constitute the sole reading materials used at this level.
- *Plan follow-up activities.* There are lots of activities and games to use in connection with the study of word families. Follow-ups to sorting include re-sorting, blind sorts, and writing sorts, as described in Chapter 3. Board games designed to study beginning sounds can be adapted to word families. Activities like Build, Blend, and Extend; Sound Wheels; Flip Charts; and the Show Me game are favorites and are included in the activities to follow. From this point on, students are expected to spell the words they sort correctly and you can administer short spelling tests to assess their mastery. **Word study notebooks** can be used to record writing sorts and the results of word hunts or brainstorming sessions.
- *Set a fast pace.* The study of word families can take a long time if you feel compelled to study every family in a thorough fashion, but this should not be the case. See Table 5.5 for ideas about how to modify the pace. Although students may still make errors in spelling short vowels, many quickly pick up the notion that words that sound alike probably share similar rimes and are spelled alike. They will also be able to use this knowledge to figure out new words by analogy; for example, noting the *and* in *stand,* they quickly decode it.

THE STUDY OF SHORT VOWELS IN THE CVC PATTERN. Once students are spelling perhaps approximately half of the short vowel words correctly on a spelling inventory and working with mixed-vowel word families easily and accurately, they are ready for the study of short vowels in nonrhyming words outside of word families. This study will ask them to look at words in a new way, not as two units with various rimes (*m-ad, fl-ag, tr-ack*), but as three units with the same CVC pattern (*m-a-d, fl-a-g, tr-a-ck*), one vowel surrounded by consonants. This ability to see words as patterns is the key feature of the next stage, the within word pattern. Over the course of studying the short vowels, students come to see that CVC is the basic pattern for all short vowels across variations that include VC (e.g., *at*), CCVC (e.g., *flat*), CVCC (e.g., *fast*), and CCVCC (e.g., *blast*).

Go to PDToolkit for *Words Their Way,* click on the Videos tab, then type "Sorting Short *e, i, o,* and *u* in Easy CVC Words." Watch as the students in Ms. Kiernan's middle group study vowels.

Word Sorting to Compare Two or More Short Vowels. Following is the basic procedure for a teacher-directed short vowel sort.

1. Make a collection of word cards to model the sort on a tabletop, pocket chart, or overhead projector.
2. Begin by laying down a known word as a key word for each vowel. Read each word and isolate the vowel: "Here is the word *cap.* Listen: *cap, ap,* /ă/. *Cap* has the short *a* sound in the middle. We will listen for other words that have the same vowel sound in the middle." Repeat for each category.
3. Pick up a new word such as *fast* and say, "I am going to put this word under *cap.* Listen: *ca-a-ap, f-a-a-ast.* They have the same vowel sound in the middle." Continue to model one or two words in each category, reading each new word and comparing it to the key word. Hold up an oddball like *for* or *was.* Ask students if they hear the same vowel sound in the middle. Model how to place it in the oddball category because it does not have the same vowel sound. Ask your students to help finish the sort. They should read each word

and then sort it. Once the words are sorted, read down each column to check and discuss how the words are alike in sound and spelling. If they cannot read a word put it aside to revisit later.

4. The final sort might look something like the following:

cap	**pig**	**hot**	**oddball**
fast	ship	stop	for
camp	fish	lock	ball
trap	hill	shop	
sack	flip	block	

5. After all the words have been sorted, discuss the common features: "How are the words in each column alike? How are the oddballs different?" Help students identify the CVC pattern by labeling the units in *cap, pig,* and *hot.* Point out that *hill* and *trap* are also CVC words because *ll* and *tr* are consonant units on each side of the single vowel. At this point revisit any unknown words. The students can be asked to put each in the correct column and sound it out.
6. Reread the words in each column and then lead the students in sorting a second time. Any mistakes should be left until the end and checked by reading down the columns.
7. Students should be given their own set of words to sort at their seats, with partners, or for homework.
8. Because it is easy to sort the words visually by attending to the vowel letters, the blind sort described in Chapter 3 is particularly important as a follow-up activity. Model this first in a small group and then let partners work together. One partner reads each word aloud while the other partner indicates where it goes without seeing the word.

If students are still making errors in the spelling of digraphs and blends, which is likely, include words with those features in the short vowel sorts. At this time, they have many more sight words that contain beginning and ending consonant digraphs and blends. You might even plan a two-way sort as shown below—first by vowel sounds and second by digraphs or blends. This encourages flexibility in word analysis, a desirable trait (Sharp et al., 2008).

First Sort by Vowel

a	*i*	*u*
trap	trick	drug
crack	drill	crumb
drag	trim	truck
crash	drip	drum
track	crib	crush

Second Sort by Blends

tr	*dr*	*cr*
trap	drag	crack
track	drip	crash
trick	drum	crush
trim	drill	crumb
truck	drug	crib

Guidelines for Short Vowels. As you implement the study of short vowels in CVC words, here are some things to keep in mind:

- When beginning the study of short vowels, plan contrasts that are fairly distinct from each other. We recommend that students compare short *a* to short *i* or short *o*. Do not compare short *a* to short *e* or short *e* to short *i*, as those are the very sounds students are most likely to confuse.
- Most sorting for short vowels will be done with printed words, but you can use pictures to focus students' attention on the vowel sounds. You should also use pictures for column headers such as the sound board for vowels on page 328 in Appendix B. Pictures for sorting can be found in Appendix C. Consider what words your students already know from familiar texts and word banks as you select words for sorts.

Go to PDToolkit for *Words Their Way,* click on the Sorts and Games tab, then type "Short Vowel Sorts with CVC Words." Look for ready-to-use sorts with pictures and words for short vowels.

- During the study of short vowels is a good time to establish the **oddball,** or miscellaneous category, to accommodate variations in dialect and spelling. Some students may hear a short *o* in *lost,* but others will hear a sound closer to "aw." Some students hear a different vowel in *pin* and *pen,* but others consider them homophones. Rather than forcing students to doubt their own ear, the oddball category offers an alternative and acknowledges that people do not all speak quite the same way nor does spelling always match pronunciation. Good words to use for oddballs in this stage are high-frequency words students may already know as sight words, such as *for, put, was,* and *what. Was* will be odd in a short *a* sort despite its CVC spelling because it doesn't have the short *a* sound. *Put* will be odd in a short *u* sort because it doesn't have the same sound as *cut, sun,* or *drum.* Other examples can be found in the word lists in Appendix E, in which the top 200 high-frequency words, as determined by Fry (1980), are marked with asterisks.
- Plan word hunts and other follow-ups. It will be fairly easy to find words with short vowels in just about any beginning reading material because they are, by their nature, so common in English. Students should be encouraged to look for two-syllable words with a CVC syllable such as *funny* or *kitten* to add to lists.
- Pacing is important. Be prepared to spend some time on short vowels, as they pose special problems for young spellers and can persist as problems beyond first grade. Start with simple three-letter words that include many of the words studied in word families (i.e., *bag, can, pat*) but then move to the use of more complex words with blends and digraphs at the beginning and end (i.e., *brag, than, path*). However, short vowels will be reviewed when they are compared to long vowels in the next stage, so do not expect 100 percent accuracy. Once students begin using but confusing vowel markers (e.g., RANE for *rain*) you may want to move on to the study of long vowel patterns.

***R*-INFLUENCED VOWELS.** Words like *car* and *for* look as though they follow the CVC pattern, but they do not have the short sounds of *a* or *o*. Instead the vowel sounds are subsumed by the *r* that follows and are known as *r-influenced vowels* (or *r-controlled vowels*). Do not expect children to segment a vowel sound separately from the *r* but instead teach *ar* and *or* as patterns or chunks. Because words spelled with *ar* and *or* are common in beginning reading materials, it is worthwhile to spend some time with them. The *r*-influenced vowels form a major subcategory of vowels that will need to be examined closely during the next stage. Following is a special sort that compares the *r*-influenced sounds with short vowels. Read down each column so you can hear the difference.

Short *a*	*ar*	Short *o*	*or*	***Oddballs***
clap	car	fox	for	word
jam	star	shop	sort	work
black	park	pond	born	
sand	yard	spot	fort	
camp	jar	trot	horn	

This chapter has presented many examples of teacher-directed sorts or closed sorts. The teacher selects the words and leads a group sorting activity accompanied by a discussion of the features of interest. Teacher-directed sorts are recommended when you introduce a new feature such as word families or short vowels. Offer explicit explanations when introducing a new feature but gradually release responsibility to students, who can sort independently as long as they can read the words. Open sorts, as described in Chapter 3, ask students to establish their own categories and offer the teacher diagnostic information that will help to determine how much students understand about the orthography.

Assess and Monitor Progress in the Letter Name–Alphabetic Stage

It is critical that teachers monitor student progress in attaining a firm concept of word (COW) in text and the fundamental phonics/spelling features that support the automatic recognition of a basic reading vocabulary, or sight words. Without these fundamental attainments, students will not progress in reading. Assess regularly to determine whether students need more practice or are ready to move on.

ASSESS AND MONITOR PROGRESS IN CONCEPT OF WORD. Students in the letter name–alphabetic stage move from a rudimentary to a *firm* concept of word in text. Without a firm concept of word in text, students' sight word development will be delayed. Chapter 4 presented a detailed assessment for monitoring COW and the same procedures are appropriate in this stage, with one addition. Not only should children be pointing accurately to words in familiar text without getting off track on two-syllable words, but by the letter name–alphabetic stage, they should also be learning some words to add to their sight vocabularies (although not expected to learn all the words). The ultimate litmus of a firm concept of word in text is students' ability to recognize some words seen previously in context when shown in isolation, in a randomized list. So to the assessment procedures we described in Chapter 4 we add a procedure for assessing word recognition in isolation. See the website for a step-by-step procedure.

PDToolkit for Words Their Way™

Go to PDToolkit for *Words Their Way,* click on the Videos tab, then revisit "Sorting Short *e, i,o,* and *u* with Initial Blends" to see Ms. Kiernan assess students' knowledge in small groups by asking them to explain their sorting.

ASSESS AND MONITOR PROGRESS IN PHONEMIC AWARENESS, PHONICS, AND SPELLING. Phonemic awareness, phonics, and spelling are all highly related. Thus, frequent spelling assessments scored by features are an easy way to monitor student progress. The spelling feature inventories described in Chapter 2 can be administered several times a year to track progress. As shown in Table 5.6, Zack began the year as an early letter name speller, often omitting vowels and blends, which suggests that his phonemic awareness was only partial. By January, he was in the middle letter name stage, including a vowel in each word and spelling many vowels, blends, and digraphs correctly. He had full phonemic awareness, fully segmenting each word into sounds. By May, his correct spelling of short vowels as well as his use of silent *e* showed that he was transitioning into the within word pattern stage. Zack made solid progress over the course of the year in phonemic awareness, phonics, and spelling.

Ongoing assessment can be as simple as observing how quickly and accurately students sort pictures or you can have students paste the pictures they have sorted into categories and label them. Weekly assessment in the middle to late part of this stage may involve a brief spelling test of five to ten words. In addition we provide a series of spell checks on the website for letter name–alphabetic spellers. We recommend that you use these as a pretest before introducing a feature, and after spending a month or so on a feature you can use them as a posttest. Progress monitoring or goal-setting forms are also available.

ASSESS AND MONITOR PROGRESS IN SIGHT WORD DEVELOPMENT. Once students achieve a firm concept of word in text, they must keep reading and rereading and continue to analyze the letter–sound correspondences within words to develop an automatic reading vocabulary. Frequent assessment of students' word recognition in isolation should provide the feedback you need to determine whether or not to back up or move forward in reading levels, spelling features, or pedagogical support. If students are not progressing, make sure they are being given texts that they can read successfully.

PDToolkit for Words Their Way™

Go to PDToolkit for *Words Their Way,* click on the Assessment Tools tab, then type "Goal-Setting/Progress Monitoring Charts."

The easiest way to monitor progress in sight word development is to keep track of the number of words in students' word banks. The number should grow steadily across the early mid to late letter name–alphabetic phase when students are given regular opportunities to select and review words. You will know that a student is developing a solid sight word vocabulary when his or her word bank exceeds 200 known words.

Table 5.6 Zack's Spelling Progress across the First Grade Year

	SEPTEMBER	FEBRUARY	MAY
fan	✓	✓	✓
pet	PAT	✓	✓
dig	DK	deg	✓
rob	✓	✓	✓
hope	HOP	hop	✓
wait	YAT	wat	wate
gum	GM	✓	✓
sled	SLD	slad	✓
stick	STK	stik	✓
shine	SIN	shin	✓
dream	GREM	drem	dreme
blade	BAD	blad	✓
coach	KOH	coh	coche
fright	FRIT	frit	frite

You can also note progress in sight word development as students are able to read increasingly difficult levels of reading materials with less support in the form of shared reading. By the middle to late letter name–alphabetic stage less predictable reading materials require young readers to attend to the print more carefully and rely more on word recognition and less on memory of the language. Running records can be used to monitor word recognition accuracy in context (Clay, 2009).

Teachers must constantly assess and adjust their instruction to match the individual needs of their students. The responsibility is on us as teachers to make sure our students are progressing. We are the first responders!

Word Study with English Learners in the Letter Name–Alphabetic Stage

for **English Learners**

Letter name spellers who are also English learners contrast the sounds in their primary languages as they learn the sounds of English. In general, most other languages do not have as many single consonants or blends as we do in English. English learners may need more time to practice these sounds because they will have to learn how to hear and pronounce the sounds, segment the sounds, and learn the letter correspondences. In Table 5.7 you can see the sounds that these students may omit or mispronounce.

Spanish-speaking students, for example, may confuse words that begin with *d* and *th*, pronouncing *dog* with a *th* sound, more like "thog." *Jump* may be pronounced "chump." It will be important to create sorts that make these comparisons clear (*d* and *th* or *j* and *ch*) once

Table 5.7 Consonant Confusions for English Learners

SOUND	POTENTIAL CONFUSION
b	The voiced *b* is confused with the unvoiced *p* and is difficult in final position.
c	Is often confused with hard *g*. Many languages do not have a hard *c*.
d	Is confused with /th/ in Spanish, so *dog* may be pronounced /thŏg/.
f	Is confused with *v*, especially in Arabic. In Japanese it is confused with /h/.
g	The hard *g* sound may be confused with *k* by speakers of Arabic, French, or Swahili.
h	Is silent in Spanish and in Chinese it sounds more like /kh/ as in *loch*.
j	May be confused with *h* in Spanish and may also be pronounced /ch/.
k	May be confused with hard *g* by Spanish speakers.
l	May be confused with *r*. Final *l* may be especially difficult.
m	May be dropped at the ends of words.
n	Is difficult for speakers of Chinese, especially at the ends of words. May be confused with *l*.
p	Is easily confused with its voiced mate *b*.
r	Is rolled in Spanish and may be spelled with *w*. It is confused with *l* in many Asian languages.
s	Is difficult to perceive in final position.
sh	Is a sound that does not exist in many languages and is confused with *ch*, *g*, and *j*.
s-blends	Blends in Spanish such as *st*, *sk*, and *sp* are separate syllables that begin with *e* as in *es-pañol*.
t	Is confused with the voiced sound of *d* by Spanish speakers and not pronounced at the ends of words.
v	May be confused with *b* in Spanish and Korean. It does not exist in many languages.
w	Is a letter that does not exist in many languages and may be confused with *v*.
y	May sound more like /ch/ in Spanish.
z	May be confused with *s* and not voiced in Spanish.

the other beginning sounds are established. Refer to *Words Their Way™ with English Learners*, *Words Their Way™: Emergent Sorts for Spanish-Speaking English Learners*, and *Words Their Way™: Letter Name–Alphabetic Sorts for Spanish-Speaking English Learners* (Helman et al., 2012) for additional sorts to help students learn these distinctions.

It is common for students to omit the ending consonant sounds in words like *hard*, which may be spelled HAR, or *test*, which may be spelled TES, so final consonant picture sorts may be needed. Only a handful of consonants occur in the final position in Spanish (*d*, *n*, *l*, *r*, *s*, *z*), so sorting words by rhyme or word families like *bag*, *rag*, *tag* can be more of a challenge for English learners. Contrasts in which the vowel and the final consonant differ (*at*, *op*, *un*) are a better starting place. In Spanish, the *s*-blends work differently. In many Spanish words the *sp* blend is split between two syllables. The *s* is given a vowel (*es*) and *p* starts the second syllable, as in *Es-pañol.*

Still, there are many consonants shared by Spanish and English (*b*, *d*, *f*, *g*, *k*, *l*, *m*, *n*, *p*, *r*, *s*, *t*, *w*, *y*), and Spanish-speaking students can begin the study of consonants with these. Spanish picture sorts can be found for Spanish learners on the website under both the Emergent and Letter Name categories. Teachers should talk explicitly about the different sounds in English and Spanish and acknowledge students' confusion as logical. Because students might not be able to name the pictures, you might pair them with an English-speaking partner who can supply the English names.

As with consonants, other languages do not have as many vowel sounds as we do in English. Spanish has only one short vowel sound (short *o*), and it is spelled with the letter *a* as in *gracias*. Expect students to substitute vowels in their own language that are close in point of articulation for these short English vowels when they say and spell English words. Short *e* may be pronounced like long *a* (*pet* as PAIT), short *i* like long *e* (*tip* as TEEP), and short *a* and short *u* like short *o* (*cat* and *cut* as *cot*) (Helman et al., 2012). See Chapter 6 for more information about vowel confusions for students learning English.

PDToolkit for Words Their Way™

Go to PDToolkit for *Words Their Way*, click on the Additional Resources Tab, then type "Word Study in Spanish" for a selection of sorts.

WORD STUDY *Routines and Management*

The letter name–alphabetic stage easily spans kindergarten through second grade. A handful of students in third grade and even a few students in the upper elementary grades will still need to work on the features that characterize this stage. English learners of any age can be in this stage. It may be tempting to rush through, but word study in the letter name–alphabetic stage helps to build a solid foundation for the study of long vowels and other vowel patterns in the next stage.

A balanced literacy program will include Read To, Read With, Write With, Word Study, and Talk With activities (RRWWT). During *read to* time, teachers read aloud literature that offers exposure to new vocabulary and literary language. During *read with* time, students will meet in large groups for shared reading and small groups for instructional-level reading. Teachers model how to compose ideas and spell words as they *write with* children, who will, in turn, write for themselves. *Word study* includes direct instruction in letter–sound correspondences or phonics. Finally, a comprehensive program provides students with ample opportunities to *talk with* teachers and peers about the books and experiences they have shared. Whole-group read-alouds continue to be the best place to focus on vocabulary but teachers should look for other opportunities throughout the day to highlight new vocabulary words. Concept sorts can be developed for science, social studies, and math.

To differentiate instruction small groups are needed. In first grade classrooms teachers like Mr. Perez often find that reading groups and word study groups are virtually the same. Word sorts can be introduced as part of the reading group on Monday. Students practice the sorts across the week for seatwork and in centers with partners or individually once they have learned the routines. Other teachers have a separate word study time, meeting with small groups initially to introduce a sort, but then expecting follow-up routines to be done independently or with partners.

Word study during the letter name–alphabetic stage begins with picture sorts for initial sounds and ends with word sorts for short vowels in nonrhyming words. During this transition, there are a variety of routines and generic activities to help students explore features of study in depth (see Chapter 3). Betty Lee's schedule is particularly appropriate in the early letter name–alphabetic stage for students who are doing picture sorts and keeping their materials in two-pocket folders. Later in the stage when students are sorting words, other routines that involve writing sorts in word study notebooks are more effective. Table 5.8 summarizes routines for this stage. Games and activities are described in detail in the section that follows.

Pacing is an important issue. There are many blends and many word families and if every one were studied for a week, it could take many months. You might want to create two- or three-day cycles. For example, you might introduce two word families on Monday, another two on Wednesday, and then combine them for several days. Be ready to pick up the pace by

Table 5.8 Sample Weekly Schedules for Word Study in the Letter Name–Alphabetic Stage

	PICTURE SORTING	WORD SORTING
Day 1	Small-group sort: Demonstrate, sort and check, reflect	Small-group sort: Demonstrate, sort and check, reflect
Day 2	Seatwork or center: Repeat the sort, check	Seatwork or center: Repeat the sort, check, write the sort in word study notebook
Day 3	Seatwork: Repeat the sort, draw and label	Seatwork, Partner work: Blind sort, writing sort, word study notebook extensions
Day 4	Small group or seatwork: Repeat the sort, word or picture hunts in magazines, ABC books, and familiar texts	Seatwork: Repeat the sort Small group: Word hunt in familiar texts
Day 5	Assessment and games, paste and label pictures used for sorting during the week	Assessment and games
	Homework: Students take pictures home to sort again and hunt for more pictures that begin with the sound	Homework throughout the week: Repeat the sort, blind sort, writing sort, word hunts

combining a number of blends or families into one sort (up to four or five) or by omitting some features. Only your own observations can dictate the particular pace appropriate for your students. Table 5.5 offers three pacing guides that you may use to identify shortcuts for achieving students or more in-depth study for struggling students.

RESOURCES FOR IMPLEMENTING WORD STUDY *in Your Classroom*

Several sources of materials are available to help you implement word study with students in the letter name–alphabetic stage.

1. The pictures in Appendix C and word lists in Appendix E, as well as suggested sorts in Appendix D, are available for use with the templates in Appendix F to create your own picture sorts.
2. Prepared sorts, spell checks, and games are available on the website. With the Create Your Own feature you can drag words and pictures from prepared sorts into a variety of game board templates.
3. *Words Their Way™: Word Sorts for Letter Name–Alphabetic Spellers* provides a complete curriculum of sorts beginning with a review of initial consonants, picture sorts for blends and digraphs, word family sorts, and short vowel sorts. Spell checks are supplied for each of the eight units.
4. *Words Their Way™: Letter Name–Alphabetic Sorts for Spanish-Speaking English Learners* provides different contrasts and additional practice.

ACTIVITIES FOR THE LETTER NAME–ALPHABETIC STAGE

In this section, specific activities for students in the letter name–alphabetic stage have been organized into the following categories.

1. Vocabulary activities
2. Phonemic awareness activities
3. Development and use of personal readers and word banks
4. Study of initial consonant sounds
5. Study of word families
6. Study of short vowels

Some of the games and activities are adaptable, using a variety of features at different stages. These are indicated by the Adaptable for Other Stages symbol.

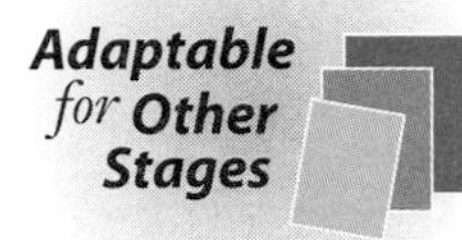

Vocabulary Activities

5.1 Anchored Vocabulary Instruction

Printing out words on cards that will be the focus of vocabulary instruction during a read-aloud is a way to "anchor" the meaning of the word to its sounds and spelling (Juel et al., 2003). These vocabulary cards will also serve as a reminder to review the words over time and in different contexts.

MATERIALS Children's books you will read aloud and a supply of 2-by-6-inch (or larger) cards. Print words neatly with markers.

PROCEDURES

1. Preview a book that you plan to read aloud and select a few words whose meanings may not be known to all of your students. Focus on words that are important to the meaning of the story but are also words that are likely to come up again in other stories. Juel et al. provide the example of *pond*, *mill*, and *haystack* from *Rosie's Walk* (by P. Hutchins) as words urban children would probably not know. Write the words you select on cards in neat block letters.
2. Prior to reading the story introduce the words. You might begin by asking students if they can supply a definition and then back that up with your own. At times you might model using a picture dictionary to look up the meaning of a word. If a concrete word like *haystack* is in the story, show a picture of a haystack. You can supply your own picture, photo, or bring in concrete objects. Even a quick sketch can help and might be added to the card. Always try to use "kid-friendly" definitions with accessible language. For example, a new word like *community* may be defined as a "neighborhood" or *vacant* as "empty." As children develop decoding skills you might begin by asking children to figure a word out before telling them. Students in the late letter name stage, for example, would probably be able to read *mill* but might not know exactly what a mill is.
3. To help anchor the word in memory point to the word as you say it slowly, stretching out the sounds as you touch the letters, and then have the students repeat it with you. You might point out the beginning or ending sound, the length and number of phonemes or syllables, or other letter–sound characteristics of the word, depending on what your students might need. For example, children whose home language is Spanish might have a hard time with double *l*s at the end of a word like *mill*, because that combination (*ll*) has a different letter–sound correspondence in Spanish. You could point out the double *l*s in

mill and have the children say it with you, emphasizing the final sound. Students are not expected to learn these as reading vocabulary, but Juel's research has shown that seeing the words can help students remember them as meaning vocabulary.

4. When you come to the word during the read-aloud, hold up the card and briefly draw attention to it to remind students of its meaning and letter–sound properties. Ask someone to point to the word on the book page.
5. After reading, go through the word cards once more and ask students to say each word, define it, and perhaps use the word in a sentence that also recalls events in the story. For example, you might hold up *pond* and say, "Who can tell me where the fox got all wet? Yes, he fell in the pond." Ask questions that use the words, such as "Would you rather land in a pond or in a haystack? Tell me why."
6. New word cards can be added to a growing set to be reviewed over time. Keep them handy to pull out when you have a few minutes to spare and go through them. It is this continued exposure that will assure that the words are retained over time. If children use the words or notice the anchored words in new contexts, make it a cause for great celebration. You can be deliberate in selecting new read-alouds with these same words, such as *The Little Red Hen*, in which the hen takes grain to the mill, or *The Small Small Pond* by Denise Fleming.

5.2 Think, Pair, Share

In Chapter 4 we described "turn and talk" (Activity 4.3) as a way to give more children the opportunity to engage in oral language and use new vocabulary. Instead of calling on one child to talk, all children are asked to talk with a partner. "Turn and talk" can be used with all ages but "think, pair, share" is a variation that provides more "think time" and ends with the opportunity to share ideas in the larger group. Both activities give less verbal children and English learners a chance to articulate their ideas in a less threatening situation.

PROCEDURES

1. *Think.* During a read-aloud or discussion, instead of raising hands to answer questions, make predictions, share experiences, define words, or use words in sentences, everyone is asked to think of their own response for a few moments.
2. *Pair.* Students then turn and talk to a partner or discuss in small groups. Partners or groups might be assigned in advance and stay together for a week or more. Students can also count off to form groups. The pairs or groups should be observed to make sure all children are participating.
3. *Share.* After everyone has had a chance to talk the teacher may call on individuals or groups to report back to the larger group. By listening in on the groups the teacher might identify ideas or examples that seem particularly worthwhile.

5.3 Books and Concept Sorts

Books make great beginnings for concept sorts. As an example to get you started, *Gregory the Terrible Eater* by Marjorie Sharmat tells the story of a young goat who wants to eat real food while his parents constantly urge him to eat "junk food." In this case, the goats' favorite foods really are junk from the local dump: tires, tin cans, old rags, and so on.

MATERIALS You will need a copy of the book to read aloud. Collect real objects or pictures of items suggested by the story, for example, fruits, vegetables, newspaper, shoelaces, spaghetti, and pieces of clothing.

PROCEDURES

1. After enjoying this story together, the children can be introduced to a concept sort. Gather the children on the rug, around a large table or pocket chart, and challenge them to group the items by the things Gregory likes and the things he dislikes. Encourage them

to talk about the items in complete sentences such as "Carrots are real food that Gregory likes."

2. After deciding where everything should go, ask the students to describe how the things in that category are alike. Decide on a key word or descriptive phrase that will label each category. *Real food* and *junk food* are obvious choices, but your children might be more inventive. As you print the selected key words on cards, model writing for the children. Say each word slowly and talk about the sounds you hear in the words and the letters you need to spell them. Each child in the group might also be given a card and asked to label one of the individual items using invented spelling.
3. Plan time for individual sorting. Keep the items and key word cards available so that children will be free to redo the sort on their own or with a partner at another time, perhaps during free time or center time. Encourage them to talk as they sort.
4. Draw-and-label or cut-and-paste activities should follow the sorting. This may be done as a group activity, in which case a section of a bulletin board or a large sheet of paper is divided into two sections and labeled with the key words. If children work independently, each child can be given a sheet of paper folded into two sections. The children might be asked to draw items or they might be given a collection of magazines or catalogs to search for pictures to cut out and paste into the correct category (seed catalogs are great for fruits and vegetables). Again, they can be encouraged to use invented spelling to label the pictures.

EXTENSIONS *Gregory the Terrible Eater* serves as an excellent introduction to the study of healthy eating. The same pictures the children have drawn or cut out can serve as the beginning pictures for categories such as meats, grains, fruits and vegetables, and dairy products.

VARIATIONS Other books can also serve as the starting point for concept sorts of many kinds, as in the following suggestions.

- *Noisy Nora* by Rosemary Wells. Sort pictures that suggest noisy activities or objects with pictures that suggest quiet activities or objects.
- *Town Mouse, Country Mouse* by Jan Brett and various authors. Sort pictures of things you would see in the country and things you would see in the city.
- *Alexander and the Wind-Up Mouse* by Leo Lionni. Sort pictures of real animals and toys or imaginary animals.
- *Amos and Boris* by William Steig. Sort pictures of things that Amos would see on the land and things that Boris would see in the ocean.

5.4 Thematic Unit on Animals as a Starting Point for Concept Sorts

Teachers of young children often organize their curriculum into thematic units of study. Such units frequently lend themselves to concept sorts, which will review and extend the understandings central to the goals of the unit. The study of animals particularly lends itself to concept sorts and can be used as a way of introducing a unit.

Go to PDToolkit for *Words Their Way,* click on the Sorts and Games tab, then type "Creatures."

MATERIALS Plastic animals or animal pictures.

PROCEDURES Lay out the collection of animals and ask students to think of ways that they can be grouped together. Such an open sort will result in many different categories based on attributes of color, number of legs, fur or feather coat, and so on. A lively discussion will arise as students discover that some animals can go in unexpected categories.

The direction you eventually want this activity to go will depend on the goal of your unit. If you are studying animal habitats, then you will eventually guide the children to sorting the animals by the places they live. If you are studying classes of animals, then the students must eventually learn to sort them into mammals, fish, amphibians, and birds. If you are focusing on the food chain, your categories may be carnivores, herbivores, and omnivores.

5.5 Creative Dramatics

Creative dramatics is a way to encourage students' self-expression as well as vocabulary development. Students enjoy reciting what they hear and appreciate the rhythm of language as they act out memorable scenes from familiar stories. In creative dramatics props are not necessary but add to the fun. For example, after hearing the story *Caps for Sale* (by E. Slobodkina) students walk around the room singing, "Caps for sale, caps for sale, Red and white and blue and green, The finest caps you've ever seen." Students can also act out the part of the story when the monkeys steal the caps from the peddler after he falls asleep under a tree and then mimic the peddler with "Chi, chi, chi, chi."

MATERIALS Any children's picture book can work, as can classic folk tales. There are compilations that have brief stories ready to read to children with scenes to dramatize.

- Johnson, A. P. (1998). How to use creative dramatics in the classroom. *Childhood Education*, *75*(1), 2–6.
- Siks, G. B. (1958). *Creative dramatics: An art for children.* New York: Harper & Row.
- Siks, G. B. (1977). *Drama with children.* New York: Harper & Row.
- Ward, W. (1952). *Stories to dramatize.* Anchorage, Kentucky: The Children's Theatre Press.

FIGURE 5.7 Caps for Sale

Caps for sale
Caps for sale
Red and white and blue and green
The finest caps you have ever seen.

Caps for sale
Caps for sale
Red and white and blue and green
The finest caps you have ever seen.

𝍸 𝍸 𝍸 𝍸

PROCEDURES

1. After listening to a story, ask students to select a character and think about how that particular character acts, like crawling on all fours and roaring like a lion as in *Leo the Lion* or stirring a pot of food after hearing a version of *Stone Soup.*
2. Reread a short scene and have three or four students act out the scene with its movement and a few of its lines.
3. Ask students who were watching to comment on what they liked and how they might improve the next time.
4. Have another three or four students try the same scene.

EXTENSIONS Prepare copies of key lines from the scene in 26-point text that students place in their personal readers to reread, as in Figure 5.7. Note in the figure how the student has underlined words for her word bank and also how she has recorded her rereadings with tick marks. Students draw pictures of the scene they have dramatized and bring the stories they have written to the group to dramatize a scene.

Phonemic Awareness

Phonemic awareness continues to develop from partial to full across the letter name–alphabetic stage. Sorting pictures and words for sounds—first for single consonants, then for blends, followed by onset and rime in word families, and finally all the sounds in short vowel sorts—exercises students' developing phonemic awareness. Routines such as interactive writing and morning message, described in Activities 4.39 and 4.40 in the last chapter, should continue in this stage, providing the opportunity for teachers to model phonemic segmentation. Children will get this same practice as they write with invented spelling for many different purposes. For this reason we do not suggest many separate phonemic awareness activities here. However, children who need extra help developing full phonemic awareness will benefit from the following activity using sound boxes.

5.6 Beginning-Middle-End: Find Phonemes in Sound Boxes

Originally developed by Elkonin (1973), sound boxes serve as a concrete way to demonstrate how words are made of smaller pieces of sound (called *phonemes*). The following variation was developed by Erica Fulmer, a reading specialist, who created a song she and her children sang as they tried to find the location of each sound in the word.

FIGURE 5.8 Sound Boxes

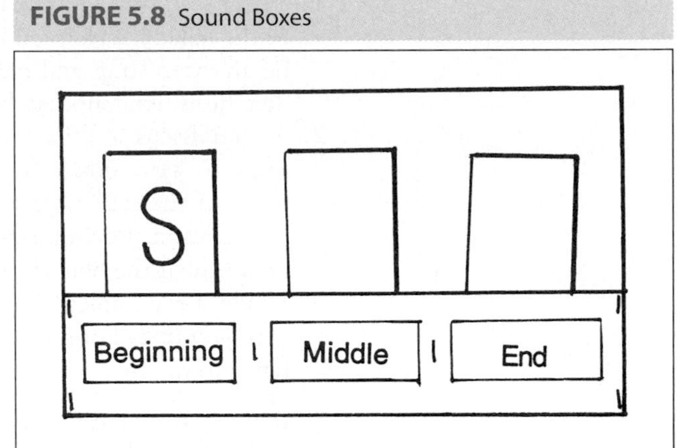

MATERIALS You will need large letter cards and a three-pocket holder such as the one shown in Figure 5.8.

PROCEDURES

1. Place the letters needed to spell a three-letter word in the pocket backwards so the children cannot see the letters. Announce the word, such as *sun*. Choose words from a familiar book, poem, or dictation when possible. Words that start with continuant sounds such as /m/, /s/, or /f/ work well because they can be said slowly.
2. Sing the song to the tune of "Are You Sleeping, Brother John?"

   Beginning, middle, end; beginning, middle, end.
   Where is the sound? Where is the sound?
   Where's the ssss in sun? Where's the ssss in sun?
   Let's find out. Let's find out.

3. Children take turns coming forward to pick the position and check by turning the letter card.

Development and Use of Personal Readers and Word Banks

Personal readers are collections of dictations and other short pieces of text that serve many purposes, helping students develop a concept of word and concepts about print as well as a sight vocabulary. Word banks take words out of context for close study and enhance sight word learning.

5.7 Collecting Individual Dictations and Group Experience Stories

Recording students' individual or group dictations as they talk about personal or group experiences is a key feature of the language experience approach, or LEA (Stauffer, 1980). The text created makes especially good reading material for beginning readers because it is inherently familiar and easy to remember. It is ideal to have every student in a group contribute a sentence, but dictations need to be kept to a reasonable length to be sure beginning readers will be able to read them back. This activity is described in Chapter 4 on pages 114 and 115. Here we offer a more detailed description of using group dictations across a four-day sequence. This can be accomplished in fewer days with smaller groups.

MATERIALS You will need chart paper, an overhead projector, a computer, or another way to record dictation so that students can observe you write. You will also need to make copies of the dictation for each student.

PROCEDURES

Day 1. Share an experience and collect dictations.

1. Select a stimulus (a box turtle, autumn leaves, parts of a flashlight) or experience (a trip to the bakery, a classroom visitor, the first snowfall) to talk about with students. It should be an interesting and memorable experience that encourages discussion. For individual dictations, students can be prompted to just tell about a personal experience.
2. After a discussion that stimulates ideas and vocabulary, ask each student to tell you something to write down. Say each word as you write it and invite the group to help decide some of the letters or spellings you need. Talk about conventions such as capitals and punctuation. Reread each sentence and make any changes the speaker requests. Decide on a title at the end as a kind of summary of the ideas.
3. When it is complete, read the entire dictation. Reread it again as the students read along with you in a choral reading fashion. Then, have them repeat after you, sentence by sentence in the manner of echo reading, as you point to each word.

Before day 2, make a copy of the dictation for each student in the group. Computers make it easy to create these copies. Select a font that has the type of letters easily recognized by young readers (Geneva or Comic Sans MS work well) and enlarge it as much as possible. It is also easy to make copies by writing neatly in your best manuscript handwriting. These copies will go into each student's personal reader and should be numbered.

Day 2. Reread dictations and underline known words.

1. Choral read the dictation again and encourage the students to follow along on their own copies, pointing to words as they read. Individual students can be called on to read a sentence.
2. Once students can read the dictation successfully, they are invited to underline known words for their word bank. Point to the underlined words randomly to make sure they know the words they underline. Students might make an illustration to go with the dictation.

Day 3. Choral read and harvest known words.
Students can work together or individually to read the dictation again. Make word cards for underlined words that are recognized accurately and quickly.

Day 4 and On. Choral read and review new word cards.

1. Students continue to reread their dictations, review the words in their word banks, and complete their pictures. A new dictation or story cycle is begun when students can read the previous dictation with good accuracy and modest fluency.
2. In an intervention program staffed by a specialist or volunteers, students might have personal readers (see page 164) that they take with them back and forth from the tutoring sessions to their classrooms. Students also take the personal readers home, where they reread the stories, review their word banks, and sort words and pictures (Bear et al., 2004; Johnston, Invernizzi, Juel, & Lewis-Wagner, 2009).
3. Bilingual entries in the personal readers are particularly useful during the early part of the letter name–alphabetic stage (Helman et al., 2012). These bilingual stories are written in both the first and second languages. Initially dictations are just one or two sentences long. A school aide or parent can help with the translations.

for **English Learners**

5.8 Support Reading with Rhymes and Pattern Stories

Rhymes and jingles and predictable patterned texts make good reading materials because they provide support for beginning readers and can then be used to harvest known words for word banks. (See Activity 4.41 for a complete guide to the whole-to-part lesson plan and supporting activities.)

MATERIALS Find a rhyme, jingle, song, or predictable story that students will find memorable and readable. You can focus on one major pattern or verse, such as the refrain in *The Gingerbread Man*. Find a big book or make a chart or overhead of the text for group work, and make copies of the rhymes and patterns for students' personal readers.

PROCEDURES

Day 1. Introduce and read the text.

1. Talk about the title and cover and look at the pictures (if applicable) with the students.
2. Read the rhyme or story while fingerpointing the text. Read fluently and with expression, but not too fast. Stop periodically to discuss and enjoy the story.
3. Reread the text and invite students to choral or echo read the entire text if it is short; or read parts of the text.
4. Decide which parts of the text will be compiled for personal readers. Type the text onto a single page that can be duplicated for each student. Number and date this entry.

Days 2, 3, and 4. Reread the rhyme or story and harvest words for word banks. The same procedures described in Activity 5.7 for dictations can be done as follow-ups for rhymes and predictable text. Sentences from the text can also be written on sentence strips, and the students can work to rebuild the text in a pocket chart as described in Activities 4.41 and 4.42. In Figure 5.7 on page 180, you see a sample of a rhyme adapted from the story *Caps for Sale* (by E. Slobodkina). Kari has underlined a number of words to harvest for her word bank. In addition, Kari has made a tick mark each time she reread the rhyme.

5.9 Harvesting Words for Word Banks

Students need to have a stock of sight words that they can read with ease. These can be harvested from books, familiar rhymes, or dictations and stored in a word bank to be reviewed over time. Many of the words will be high-frequency words (*will, this, want*), whereas others will be words that interest the reader (*dinosaur, chocolate, birthday*). These longer concrete nouns may be more memorable to the child than the high-frequency words. Although word bank words are traditionally chosen by the students, teachers can also encourage them to include those high-frequency words that young readers need to learn, or words containing the spelling features being examined during word study. The following activities help students develop and maintain a word bank.

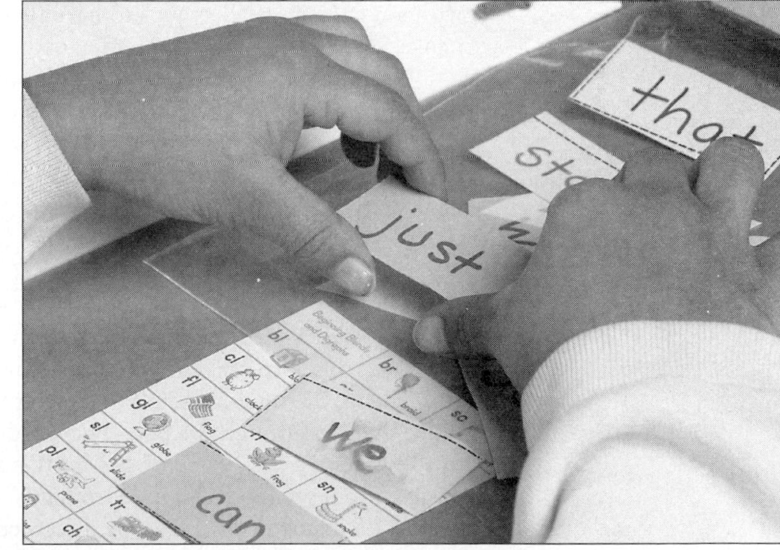

MATERIALS You will need copies of personal readers, dictations, familiar books, and so on. Prepare a collection of blank word cards. Tagboard and index cards can be cut to a size that is large enough to hold easily, yet small enough so that students can work with them on a desktop when sorting (4 by 1.5 inches is about right). Teachers can also create a sheet of words for a particular story or poem read by a group of students. These sheets can be reproduced and cut apart and the words can then be quickly handed out as students identify them.

Students will need to store their words in envelopes, plastic bags, small margarine containers, or small cans. Plastic and metal index card file boxes work well—words can be sorted with dividers. You can start with plastic bags for the first 50 words and then move to a box.

PROCEDURES The following are good sources to harvest words for the word bank.

1. *From personal readers.* If students have an individual copy of dictations, jingles, parts of stories, and so on, they can simply be asked to underline the words they know. Many students will be tempted to underline every word, but over time they will begin to understand the procedure and realize they need to be selective and underline only words they really know. Suggesting that they scan through the text backwards can help some students find known words more accurately. A teacher, assistant, or classroom volunteer points to the underlined words in a random fashion to check whether the student can indeed name the word quickly (without rereading the sentence in which it occurs). Known words are then written on word cards. Having an adult write the word will ensure that it is neat and accurate. The student can be asked to spell it aloud as the adult writes. On each card write the number of the page in the personal reader. This will make it possible for the students to go back and use context clues to name the word if they forget it. The students can be asked to write their initials on the back of each card in case words get mixed up during word bank activities.
2. *From familiar books.* Students can also collect sight words independently from books they have read. Some of the words from the book can be put on word cards that are stored in a library pocket in the back of the book. After reading the text, students are taught to read through the words in the pocket to see which ones they know at sight. Students write the words they know onto their own cards and place them in their word banks. Unknown words can be matched back to their counterparts in the text.
3. *From any text.* The easiest procedure for harvesting words is to simply ask the students to point to words in a book or from a chart that they would like to put in their word bank. After several words have been written on cards, the teacher or helper can hold them up to check for recognition.

Go to PDToolkit for *Words Their Way*, click on the Videos tab, then type "Weekly Schedules and Activities in the Letter Name–Alphabetic Stage." Watch the children in the first grade read in personal readers as a seatwork activity.

VARIATIONS To ensure that unknown words do not enter students' word banks, a **short-term word bank** can be developed for words that students recognize from the latest stories and dictations stored inside their personal readers (see Figure 5.4). Periodically, teachers work with students in small groups to have them read through the words in their short-term word banks. Words they know from memory go into the permanent word bank.

Create a group word bank that can be used instead of or in addition to individual word banks. The group agrees on the words to add (with some gentle prodding by the teacher to add high-frequency words that will show up in other stories) and the words can be reviewed in the group but also made available for individuals or partners to use in the remaining word bank activities in this section.

5.10 The Grand Sort with Word Bank Words

Reviewing the word bank regularly is important to secure those words in memory as sight words. In this sort, students simply go through their word cards, saying the words they know and putting them in one pile and placing the unknown words to the side. The students try to move quickly through the pile. The words that students put in the "I know" pile can be used in subsequent sorts. Students can do this sort under the teacher's supervision, with a partner or classroom volunteer, or independently.

The unknown words can be discarded, but this can be a touchy point for some students who are hesitant to throw away words. There is no harm in letting a few temporarily unknown words remain, but working with a lot of unknown words makes students' work hesitant, prone to errors, and frustrating. Students in the early letter name–alphabetic stage do not have the word knowledge they need to sound out unknown words, so the teacher should show them how to figure out an unknown word by using context. Referring to the number on the card, the students return to their personal reader to find the word and figure it out. Because this procedure can be time-consuming, it is important that only a small percentage of words in a word bank are unknown.

5.11 Reviewing Word Bank Words

There are other ways to review and work with words in the word bank.

1. *Pickup.* Lay out a collection of five to ten words face-up. Words that the student does not know or frequently confuses are good candidates. Someone calls out the words randomly for the student to find and pick up. This simple activity requires the student to use at least partial alphabetic cues to find the words, but does not require him or her to sound out the word.
2. *I Am Thinking Of.* This activity is similar to Pickup, but the student is given clues instead of words: "I am thinking of a word that rhymes with *pet*" or "I am thinking of a word that starts like *play*."
3. *Concentration.* Make a second set of words and play this classic game as described in Activity 4.15. Work with ten sets of words at a time so that the activity moves quickly.
4. *Word Hunts.* Students look through their word banks for words that have a particular feature, for example, words that start with *t*, words that end in *m*, or words that have an *o* in them.
5. *Concept Sorts.* Students look through their word banks for words that fit given semantic categories—for example, words that name animals, words that name people, color words, or things in a house.
6. *Alphabetize Words.* Make and laminate a large alphabet strip up to six feet long. Students place their words under the beginning letter. Pictures can be sorted by beginning sounds as well.

5.12 Read It, Find It

This simple and fun game for two players reinforces the identification of words.

Adaptable *for* Other Stages

MATERIALS You will need 30 pennies, or as many pennies as there are words on the game board. Prepare a game board by writing words onto a 5-by-6-inch grid or a path game board found in Appendix F. Prepare a set of word cards that have the same words as those on the board and place them face-down. It is okay if some words repeat. Words can be taken from word banks or from previous word sorts.

PROCEDURES

1. One player flips a penny for heads or tails position. Each player chooses 15 pennies. One student will be heads and turn all his or her pennies to the heads side. The other will be tails and turn the pennies to the tails side.
2. The player who did not flip will begin by taking a card from the pile and reading it. The player then finds the word on the board and covers it with a penny. If the player cannot read the word or reads it incorrectly, he or she cannot cover the word. The game proceeds as each player draws one card per turn.
3. The first player to cover 15 words, using up all his or her pennies, is the winner.

Study of Initial Consonant Sounds

A number of activities or games in Chapter 4 are appropriate for students in the letter name–alphabetic stage who are working to master single consonants, digraphs, and blends: Soundline (4.32), Letter Spin for Sounds (4.33), Sort Objects by Sounds (4.34), and Initial Consonant Follow-the-Path Game (4.35). Concentration is another adaptable game. Any two pictures that begin with the same sound(s) make a match that can be claimed.

5.13 Sound Boards

MATERIALS Sound boards are references for letter–sound features (beginning consonants, digraphs and blends, and vowels). Examples can be found in Appendix B. They provide a key word and picture for each letter–sound match, helping students internalize the associations.

FIGURE 5.9 Expanding a Word Family Using a Sound Board

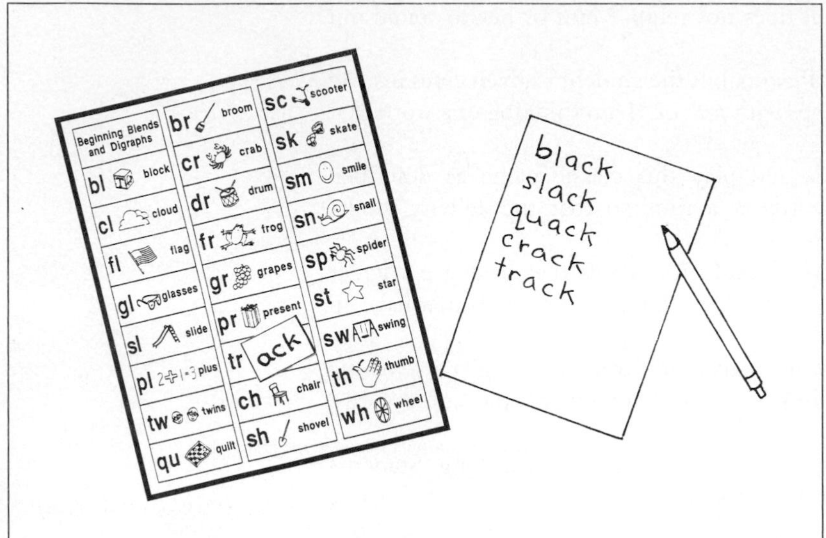

PROCEDURES Place a copy of the sound boards at the front of students' writing folders or personal readers. These boards make it easy for students to find letters to stand for the sounds they want to use. Reduced copies of relevant sound boards can be taped to students' desks. Teachers often post charts of various letter–sound features. Recently, the new technology of chart printers has made it possible to take the individual sound boards and enlarge them to poster size. Add a little color and display them in a prominent place for reference. A sound board can be kept in students' word study folders (see Figure 3.19) to serve as a record of progress. Students can lightly color the letters they have studied. Sound boards can be used to generate more words to add to a word family. The rime of the family is written on a small card and slid down beside the beginning sounds. In Figure 5.9, the word family *ack* has been expanded by adding many different blends and digraphs.

Adaptable for Other Stages

5.14 Word Hunts

Word hunts are conducted several different ways and at different times in the letter name–alphabetic stage: independently, with a partner, or in small groups.

In the early letter name–alphabetic stage, students hunt for pictures that correspond to beginning sounds. Pictures can be cut from magazines or catalogs and pasted onto individual papers, group charts, or into alphabet scrapbooks. When hunting for pictures, it helps if the teacher, aide, or student helper rips out pages on which there are pictures that contain the feature being hunted. Students can be asked to label the pictures they find by spelling as best they can. Students can also hunt for pictures in alphabet books and record their findings as drawings.

Students can hunt for words that begin with the particular initial consonants, blends, or digraphs they are studying. They should look for words they know in familiar reading materials such as their personal readers or by going through their own word banks.

Students can hunt for words or pictures that sound like the short vowels they are studying. Note that hunting for additional word family words can be challenging for certain families unless you have books that have been specially written to contain a lot.

Word hunts can be made into a game in which teams of two or three students hunt for words in a given time period. Students read the words to the teacher or group.

Go to PDToolkit for *Words Their Way*, click on the Sorts and Games tab, then type "Bingo." Click on the Create Your Own button to select words or pictures for your game.

5.15 Initial Sound Bingo

In this version of Bingo, students discriminate among the initial sounds. This is another activity that can be adapted to single consonant, blends, digraphs, and word families.

MATERIALS Make Bingo cards with 9 or 16 squares. In each square, write a letter(s) that features the sounds students have been studying in sorts. Figure 5.10 shows a game prepared to review the *s*-blends. You also need Bingo markers and picture cards to match sounds. Use the Create Your Own feature on the website and drag and drop pictures or words to make Bingo boards.

PROCEDURES Work with small groups of two to four students. Each student gets a Bingo card and markers. Students take turns drawing a card from the stack and calling out the picture name. Students place a marker on the corresponding square. Play continues until someone gets Bingo or the board is filled.

FIGURE 5.10 Blend Bingo Boards

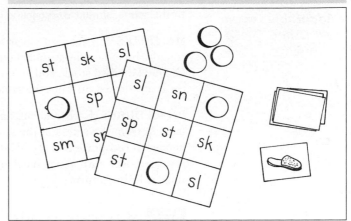

5.16 Gruff Drops Troll at Bridge

This is a special version of the basic follow-the-path game described in Activity 4.35 that reinforces *r*-blends. Easter Heatley developed this after reading Paul Galdone's *The Three Billy Goats Gruff*, which was part of a class study of books about monsters. Many of the books yielded a great crop of consonant-plus-*r* words such as *growl*, *groan*, and *fright*.

Go to PDToolkit for *Words Their Way*, click on the Sorts and Games tab, then type "Gruff Drops Troll at Bridge."

MATERIALS Prepare a game path filled in with *r*-blend letters as shown in Figure 5.11 (or whatever features you want to review). Add some artwork to create a theme. You will also need markers and pictures. Follow-the-path templates and directions for preparing the boards can be found in Appendix F.

PROCEDURES Each player selects a marker. Students turn over picture cards and move the marker to the correct space. In this game, the winner drops the troll from the bridge by turning up a picture that begins with *dr* (for *drop*) or *tr* (for *troll*) for the last space.

FIGURE 5.11 Game Board for Gruff Drops Troll at Bridge

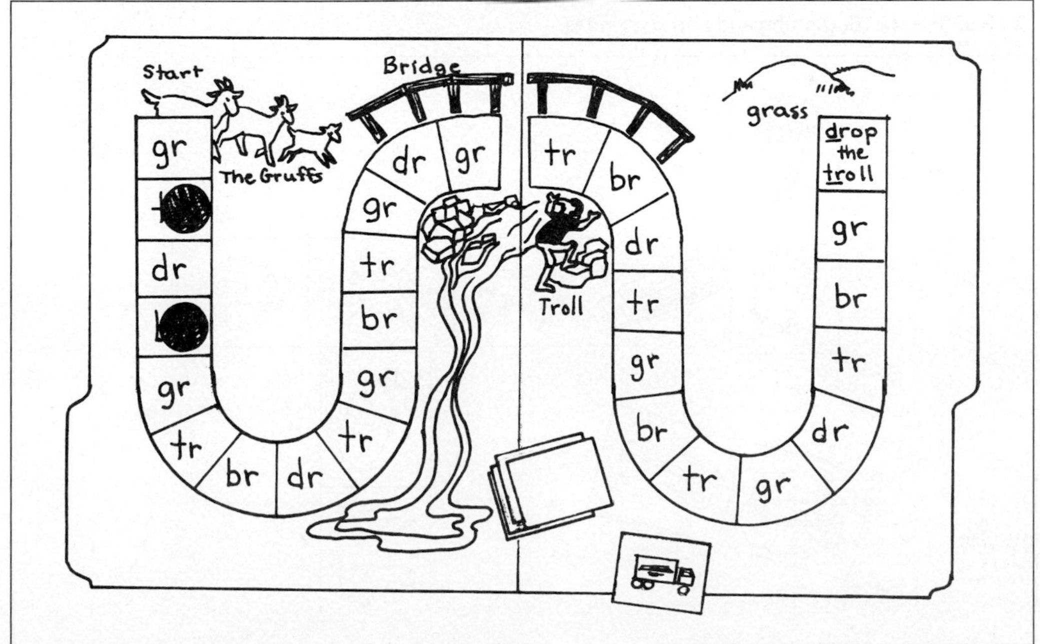

5.17 Match!

In this game, similar to the game of Slap Jack, students look for matches in beginning sounds.

MATERIALS Create a set of cards that feature pictures with four to eight different beginning sounds. Include at least four pictures for each sound. Pictures can be copied from Appendix C, glued on card stock, and laminated. This can also be played with word families. When two cards are turned up from the same family they make a match.

PROCEDURES Each student has half the deck of pictures. Students turn a picture card face-up from their deck at the same time. If the pictures begin with the same sound, the first person to recognize and say "Match!" gets the pair. If the pictures do not match, another set is turned over until a match occurs. There can be penalties for calling out "Match" carelessly, such as losing a turn.

5.18 Beginning and End Dominoes

This activity is a picture sort to match initial and final consonant sounds (e.g., *lamp* matches *pig*).

MATERIALS Pictures for these matches can be found in Appendix C. Divide a 2-by-4-inch card in half and paste a picture from each of the following pairs on each side.

ghost/tub	book/leg	gate/pin	nine/goat	ten/log
dishes/map	pie/bed	desk/mop	pig/nut	tent/bed
rain/dog	goat/zip	pin/sit	tie/mad	door/pear
two/hat	toes/road	doll/rock	key/lips	seal/boat
pen/bug	gas/sun	net/belt	tail/sink	kite/jeep

PROCEDURES Students draw a set of five pairs and try to match the pairs in a single array as in the traditional game of dominoes. They then take turns drawing an additional card to add to the array. See Figure 5.12.

VARIATIONS Students compete to make the longest string they can with a collection of pictures.

FIGURE 5.12 Beginning and End Dominoes

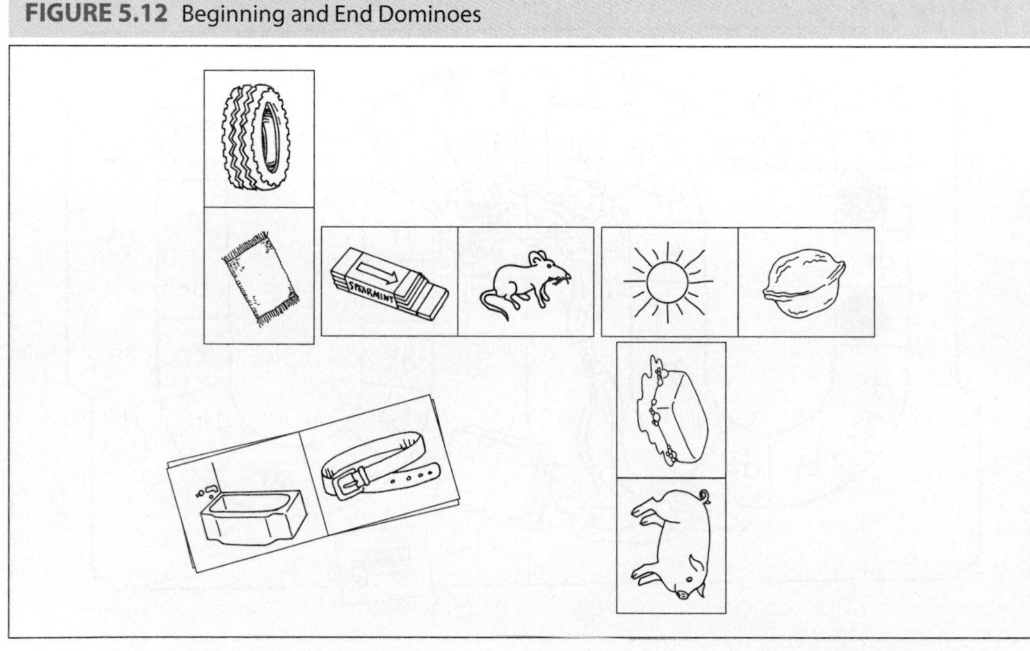

Study of Word Families

Once students begin the study of word families, they are expected to read and spell the words they sort. Many word games can be adapted as follow-up activities for word sorting. Some activities are especially designed to enhance students' understandings of how families work.

5.19 Build, Blend, and Extend

FIGURE 5.13 Build, Blend, and Extend Cards

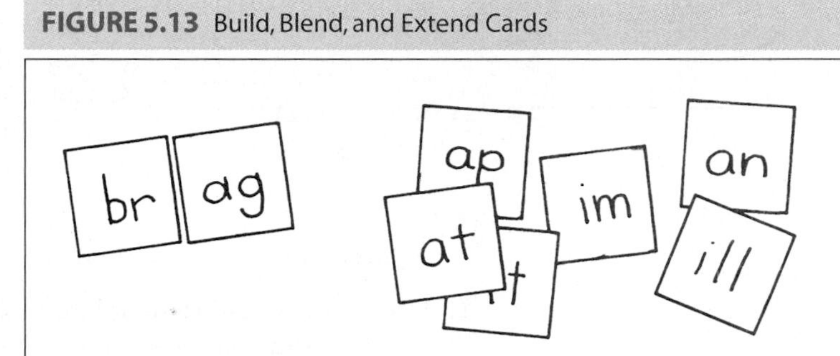

This series of teacher-led activities is designed to reinforce phoneme segmentation, phoneme blending, and the use of analogy as a spelling strategy ("If I can spell *cat*, then I can spell *fat*") as students work with onsets and rimes. This should follow sorting lessons in which students have worked with a collection of word families.

MATERIALS Prepare a set of cards to be used in a pocket chart. Write the targeted onsets and rimes on these cards, keeping the letters of the rime together. For the *at* family, you would have cards with *at, b, c, f, h, m, p, r,* and *s*. As students study digraphs and blends, those can be added as well, such as *th, ch,* and *fl*. See Figure 5.13.

PROCEDURES

1. *Building*. This procedure reinforces the spelling of word families. The teacher should model how to make a word in the family by putting up two cards, such as *m* and *at*. Then students are asked what letter would be needed to make the word *sat*. The teacher would model how to replace the *m* in *mat* with the *s* to make the new word. Students could then be invited to build additional words called by the teacher by substituting beginning letters.
2. *Blending*. This activity reinforces the reading of word families. It is similar to building except that the teacher starts with a word the students all know, such as *cat*, and then substitutes a different beginning letter. The teacher models how to blend the new onset with the familiar rime to read the word: "*Mmmmmm, aaaaaaat, mat.* The new word is *mat*." Students are then asked to use the two parts of the onset and rime to sound out the word just as the teacher has modeled.
3. *Extending*. During the extending part of this activity, the teacher selects words that are not included in the sort to demonstrate to students that they can read and spell many more words once they know how to spell several words in a family. This is a time when you might demonstrate using unusual words like *vat* or challenging words with digraphs and blends such as *chat, flat,* or *scat*.

VARIATIONS

1. Students can work with small cards at their seats as the teacher leads the activity.
2. Add more digraphs and blends as they are studied. There will be many words you can make with families such as *ack* and *ick*.
3. For the study of short vowels and the CVC pattern, the vowel is separated from the rime (*at* is cut apart into *a* and *t*).
4. After working with the cards, students can be asked to write the words on paper, small whiteboards, or chalkboards.

for Words Their Way™

Go to PDToolkit for *Words Their Way*, click on the Sorts and Games tab, then type "Word Wheels and Flip Charts," "Show Me," or "Letter Slide" for ready-to-use word family games.

5.20 Word Family Wheels and Flip Charts

Wheels and flip charts are fun for students to play with independently or with partners. The wheels and flip charts are used to reinforce blending the onset with the rime to read words in word families they have sorted.

FIGURE 5.14 Word Family Wheel and Flip Chart

MATERIALS To make word family wheels, follow these three steps.

1. Cut two six-inch circles from tagboard. Cut a wedge from one circle, as shown in Figure 5.14, and write the vowel and ending consonants or rime to the right of it. Make a round hole in the center.
2. On the second tagboard circle, write beginning sounds that form words with that family. For example, the *op* family can be formed with *b, c, h, l, m, p, s, t, ch, sh, cl,* and *st.* Space the letters evenly around the outside edge so that only one at a time will show through the "window" wedge.
3. Cut a slit in the middle of the second circle. Put the circle with the wedge on top of the other circle. Push a brass fastener through the round hole and the slit. Flatten the fastener, making sure the top circle can turn.

To make flip charts, the steps are as follows.

1. Use a piece of tagboard or lightweight cardboard for the base of the flip book. Write the family or rime on the right half of the base.
2. Cut pages that are half the width of the base piece and staple to the left side of the base. Write beginning sounds or onsets on each one. Students can draw a picture on the backside of the pages to illustrate the word.

5.21 Show Me

This activity is a favorite with teachers who are teaching word families and short vowels.

MATERIALS Make each student an individual three-pocket folder to hold letter cards. To make the folder, cut paper into approximately 7-by-5-inch rectangles. Fold up a one-inch section along the seven-inch side and then fold the whole thing into overlapping thirds. Staple at the edges to make three pockets (see Figure 5.15). Cut additional paper into 1.5-by-4-inch cards to make 14 for each student. Print letters on the top half of each card, making sure the entire letter is visible when inserted in the pocket. A useful assortment of letters for this activity includes the five short vowels and *b, d, f, g, m, n, p, r,* and *t.* Too many consonants can be hard to manage.

FIGURE 5.15 Show Me Game

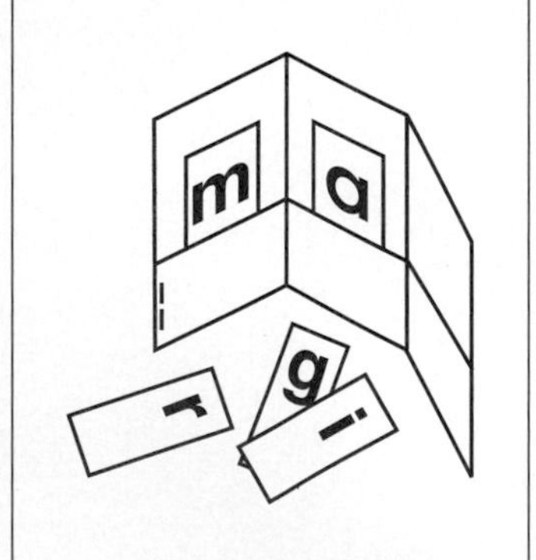

PROCEDURES Each student gets a folder and an assortment of letter cards. When the teacher or designated caller names a word, the students put the necessary letters in the spaces and fold up their pockets. When "Show me" is announced, everyone opens his or her pocket folder at once for the teacher to see. The emphasis is on practice, not competition, but points for accuracy could be kept if desired.

VARIATIONS Start with words having the same families, such as *bad, sad,* or *mad,* in which the students focus primarily on changing the initial consonants. Move on to a different family and different vowels. For example, you could follow this sequence: *mad, mat, hat, hot, pot, pet.* Add cards with digraphs or blends to spell words such as *sh-i-p* or *f-a-st.*

5.22 Word Maker

Students match blends and digraphs with word families to make words.

MATERIALS Create a collection of cards that have onsets on half (single consonants, blends, and digraphs) and common short vowel rimes on the other, such as *at, an, it, ig,* and so on. For students in the later letter name–alphabetic stage, include rimes with ending blends, digraphs, and preconsonantal nasals, such as *ish, ang, ast, amp,* and *all.*

PROCEDURES

1. Each student begins by drawing five cards from the deck. With the five cards face-up, each student tries to create words as shown in Figure 5.13.
2. Once the students have made one or two words from their first five cards, they begin taking turns drawing cards from the deck. Every time they make a word, they can draw two more cards. If they cannot make a word, they draw one card.
3. Play continues until all the letter cards are used up. The player with the most words is the winner.

VARIATIONS Students can work independently with the word maker cards to generate and record as many words as possible.

5.23 Roll the Dice

This game for two to four players reinforces word families.

MATERIALS You need a cube on which to write four contrasting word families, (e.g., *an*, *ap*, *ag*, and *at*). One side is labeled "Lose a Turn," and another is labeled "Roll Again" (see Figure 5.16). You will also need a blackboard or paper for recording words.

FIGURE 5.16 Cube for Roll the Dice Game

PROCEDURES The first player rolls the die. If it lands on a word family, the student must come up with a word for that family and record it on the chalkboard or paper. Students keep their own lists and can use a word only once, although someone else may have used it. If a player is stumped or lands on Lose a Turn, the die is passed to the next person. If the student lands on Roll Again, he or she takes another turn. The person who records the most words at the end of the allotted time wins.

VARIATIONS Play with two teams for a relay. Each team has its own die and a recorder. The first person of each team rolls the die and quickly calls out an appropriate word. The recorder writes the word on the board. The player hands the die to the next player and play goes quickly to the end of the line. With this variation you would not need to use Lose a Turn or Roll Again sides, so six word families are needed. This game can also be used with blends, digraphs, and vowel patterns.

5.24 Rhyming Families

This is a variation of the follow-the-path game used to reinforce word families.

MATERIALS Prepare a game board as shown in Figure 5.17. (You can do this with the Create Your Own feature on the website.) You will also need a single die or a spinner, pieces to move around the board, pencils, and paper for each player. Directions for making game boards and spinners as well as game board templates are in Appendix F. Write a word from each word family you have been studying in each space on the board. You can also write in special directions such as Roll Again, Go Back Two Spaces, and Write Two Words.

PROCEDURES The object is to make new words to rhyme with words on the game board that differ from the other players' words.

1. Spin to determine who goes first. The first player spins and moves the number of places indicated on the spinner. The player reads the word in the space where he or she lands. All players write a rhyming word by changing initial letter(s). Players number their words as they go. Play continues until someone reaches the end of the path.
2. Beginning with the player who reaches the end first, each player reads the first word on his or her list. Players who have a word that is different from anyone else's gets to circle that word. Continue until all words have been compared.
3. Each circle is worth one point; the player who reaches the end first receives two extra points. The student with the most points wins the game.

FIGURE 5.17 Game Board for Word Families

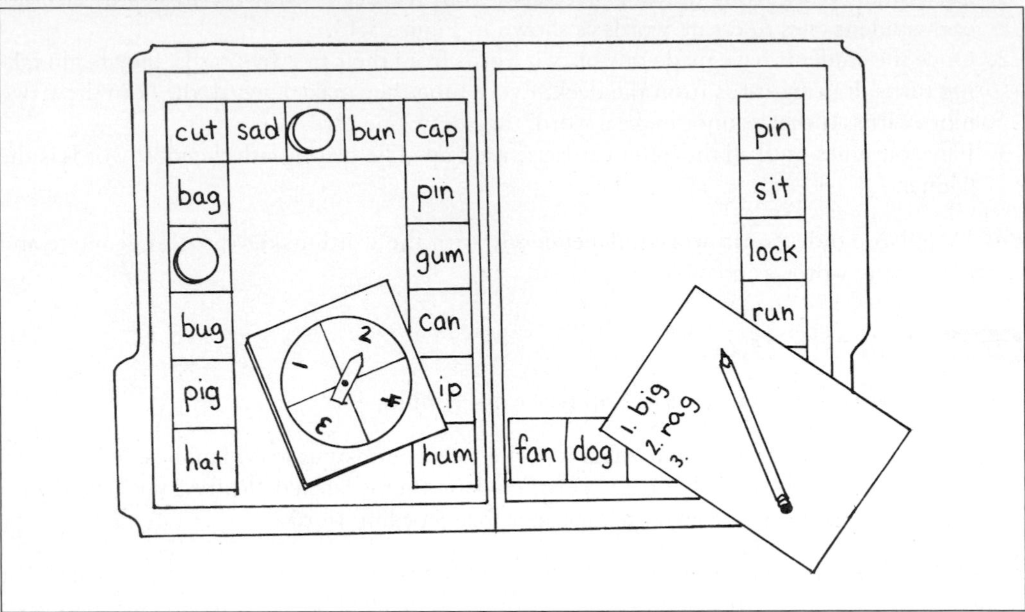

VARIATIONS Label each space on the game board with the rime of a family you have studied (*at, an, ad, ack*). Use no more than five different rimes and repeat them around the path. Prepare a set of cards that have pictures corresponding to the families. Students move around the board by selecting a picture and moving to the space it matches. For example, a student who has a picture of a hat would move to the next space with *at* written on it.

Go to PDToolkit for *Words Their Way*, click on the Sorts and Games tab, then type "Go Fish" and download the ready-to-print version.

5.25 Go Fish

This version of the classic game can be used as a review of word families.

MATERIALS Create a deck of 32 cards with four words from eight different word families written on them (e.g., *that, bat, fat,* and *hat*). Write each word at the top left of the card so that the words are visible when held in the hand, as shown in Figure 5.18.

PROCEDURES

1. Five cards are dealt to each player and the remainder are placed in the middle as a draw pile.
2. The first player asks any other player for a match to a card in his or her hand: "Give me all your words that rhyme with *hat*." If the player receives a matching card, he or she may put the pair down and ask for another card. If the other player does not have the card requested, he or she tells the first player to "Go fish," which means that the first player must draw a card from the "fish pond." The first player's turn is over when he or she can no longer make a match.
3. Play continues around the circle until one player runs out of cards. Points can be awarded to the first person to go out and to the person who has the most matching cards.

FIGURE 5.18 Playing Cards for Go Fish

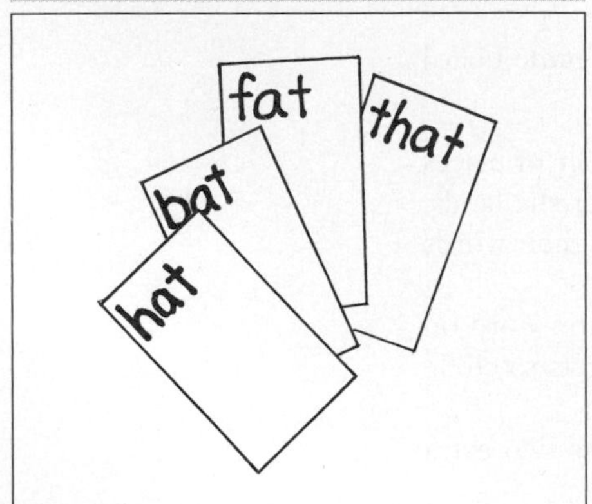

VARIATIONS Go Fish can be adapted for beginning sounds and blends using pictures, or it can be used with vowel patterns.

Study of Short Vowels

After short vowels have been explored through word sorts and weekly routines, games can provide additional practice.

5.26 Hopping Frog Game

This game, created by Janet Bloodgood for two to four players, reviews the five short vowels.

MATERIALS Create a game board like the one shown in Figure 5.19. Cut green circle lily pads for each space and write CVC words students have used in word sorts on each one (e.g., *pin, get, hot, bad, leg, run, bug, wish*). You will need four frog markers. The spinner is marked into five sections, with a vowel in each one. Pictures can be added to cue the sound: *a*, apple; *e*, ten; *i*, fish; *o*, frog; *u*, sun. See Appendix F for directions on how to make a spinner.

PROCEDURES Each student selects a frog marker. Players take turns spinning and moving their markers to the first word that matches the vowel sound on which they land (e.g., *e, get*). They then pronounce this word and must say another word with the same vowel sound to stay on that space. The next player then spins and plays. The first player who can finish the course and hop a frog off the board wins.

Go to PDToolkit for *Words Their Way*, click on the Sorts and Games tab, then type "Frog Marker and Hopping Frog."

FIGURE 5.19 Frog Marker and Hopping Frog Game

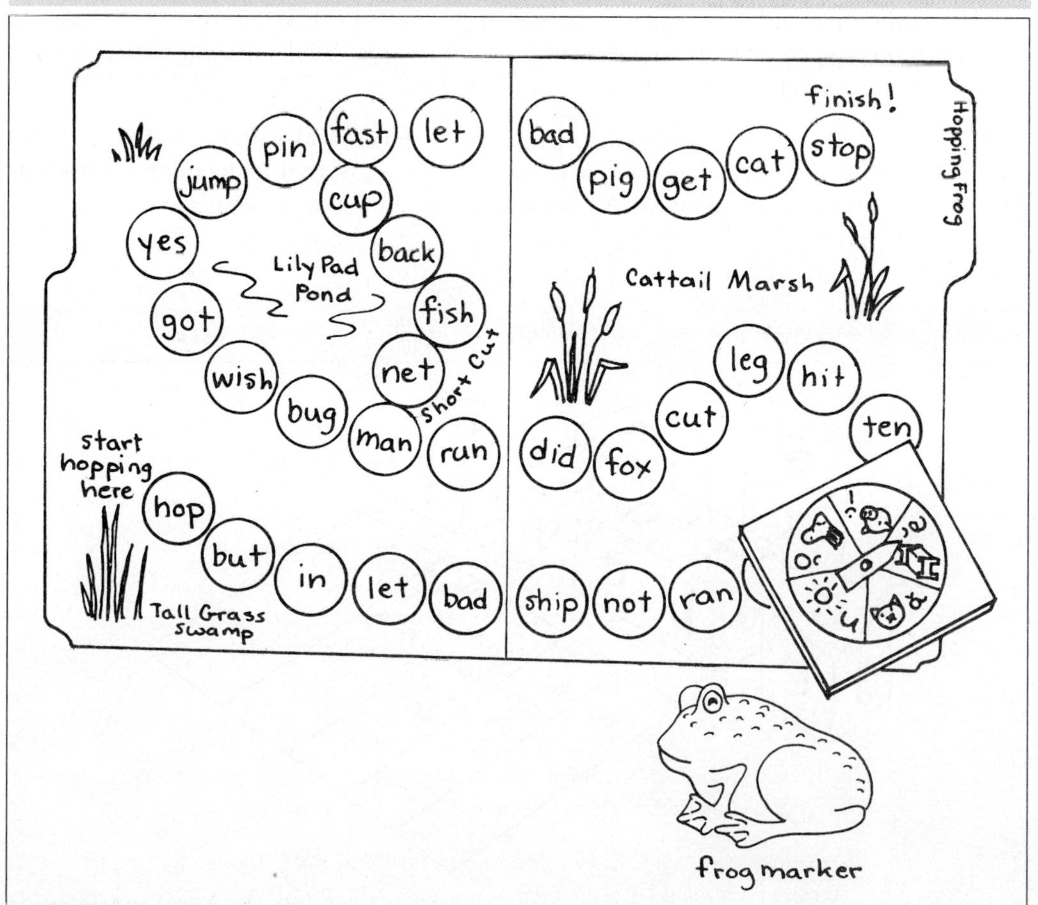

VARIATIONS Label the spaces with *a, e, i, o,* or *u.* Make a collection of short vowel pictures on tagboard using the short vowel pictures in Appendix C. It is important that the pictures do not show through the card. On several additional cards write commands such as Skip a Turn, Go Back Two Spaces, and Move Ahead Three Spaces. The players move around the board by turning over a picture and moving their playing piece to the next free space on the board that has the corresponding short vowel.

5.27 Making-Words-with-Cubes Game

Adaptable for Other Stages

Short vowel words are built with letter cubes in this game. It can be used for other vowels as well.

MATERIALS Letter cubes that can be found in many games (Boggle and Perquackery) are needed. Playing pieces can also be made from blank wooden cubes. Write all the vowels on one cube to be sure that a vowel always lands face up. (The sixth side can be a star that indicates that the player can select the vowel.) Put a variety of consonants on five or six other cubes. (Pairs like *qu* and *ck* might be written together.) The students need a sand clock or timer, paper and pencil, and a record sheet such as the one shown in Figure 5.20.

PROCEDURES

1. In pairs, students take turns being the player and the recorder. The recorder writes the words made by the player.
2. A player shakes the cubes, spills them out onto the table, and then starts the timer. Whatever letters land face-up must be used to make words. The word maker moves the cubes to create words and spells them to the recorder. The cubes can then be moved around to make more words. Errors should be ignored at this point. Write the words in columns by the number of letters in the words.
3. When the time ends, the students review the words and check for accuracy. Words are then scored by counting the total number of letters used. Students soon realize that the bigger the words they make, the greater their score.

VARIATIONS Students in the within word pattern stage should work with two vowel cubes. On a second cube, write vowel markers such as *e* (put two or three), *a, i,* and *o.* By this time, students may be able to use multiplication to total the letters (e.g., 4 three-letter words is 12).

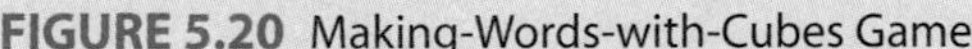

FIGURE 5.20 Making-Words-with-Cubes Game

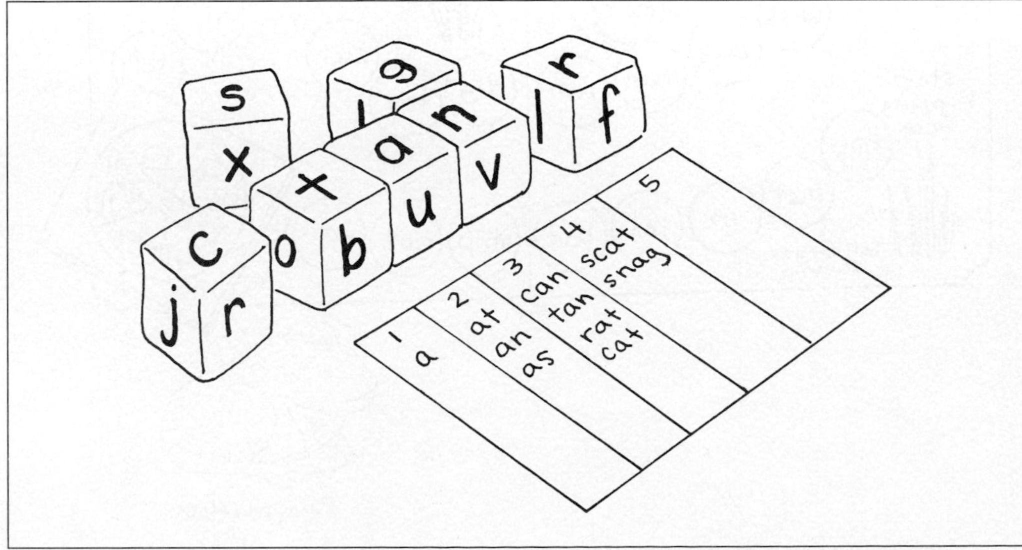

5.28 Follow-the-Pictures Spelling Game

This variation of the basic follow-the-path game works as a follow-up to word sorts for short vowel words.

MATERIALS The easiest way to make this game is to use the Create Your Own feature on the website. Select pictures from the short vowel picture sorts to drag into one of the follow-the-path game templates. Use two, three, four, or five short vowels. You will also need playing pieces to move along the path and a spinner or single die. In some spaces you can write Roll Again, Go Back Two Spaces, and other directives. Include an answer card on which all the words are written in the same order they are pasted on the board to settle any arguments about spelling.

for Words Their Way™

Go to PDToolkit for *Words Their Way,* click on the Sorts and Games tab, then select Letter Name–Alphabetic Stage and Games to access a variety of game boards. Click the Create Your Own button to select words or pictures you would like to use with your game.

PROCEDURES Students take turns spinning for a number. Before they can move to the space indicated by the spinner, they must correctly spell the word pictured. If they cannot spell the word, they must stay where they are for that turn. The student who reaches the end first is the winner.

VARIATIONS Any pictures can be pasted on the game board. Long vowel pictures can be used for students in the within word pattern stage.

5.29 Slide-a-Word

Students can be asked to list and then read all the CVC words they are able to generate using the slider created by Jeradi Cohen (Figure 5.21). As different short vowels are studied, the central vowel letter can be changed.

FIGURE 5.21 Slider for Slide-a-Word

MATERIALS Supplies include tagboard or poster board, ruler, marker, single-edge razor blade, and scissors. Cut a piece of tagboard or poster board into 8.5-by-2.5-inch strips. Using the razor, cut a pair of horizontal slits on each end 1.5 inches apart. Write a vowel in the center. Cut two 12-by-1.5-inch strips for each slider. Thread them through the slits at each end and print a variety of consonants, blends, or digraphs in the spaces as they appear through the slits. Turn the strips over and print additional beginning and ending sounds on the back.

PROCEDURES Students slide the strips to generate as many words as they can, listing each word as they find it.

5.30 Put in an *m* or *n*: Preconsonantal Nasals

The difference between *rag* and *rang* is real but it is subtle, so these contrasts can help learners understand how the preconsonantal nasals work.

MATERIALS Create word pairs like the ones listed below on word cards.

rag	rang	rig	ring	sag	sang	tag	tang
cap	camp	rap	ramp	trap	tramp	bag	bang
dig	ding	pup	pump	hag	hang	lip	limp
rug	rung	gag	gang	bet	bent	wig	wing
sprig	spring	pin	ping	hug	hung	lap	lamp
swig	swing						

PROCEDURES Three or four students can play. All the word cards are shuffled and dealt. Players look for pairs (i.e., *rag/rang*) in their hands and lay them down before play begins. Students then take turns laying down a word from their hand. The student who has the match to the pair takes the card, matches it to the word in his or her hand, and adds the two cards to his or her pile. The student with the most cards is the winner.

MEDIA GUIDE *Word Study for Beginners in the Letter Name–Alphabetic Stage*

SECTION	PAGE	GO TO PDTOOLKIT FOR *WORDS THEIR WAY*™
Videos		
Literacy Development of Students in the Letter Name–Alphabetic Stage	151	Click on the Videos tab, then type "Assessment in the Letter Name–Alphabetic Stage."
Reading Instruction	163	Click on the Videos tab, then type "Whole Class Reading and Picture Sort."
Reading Instruction	164	Click on the Videos tab, then type "Weekly Schedules and Activities in the Letter Name–Alphabetic Stage."
The Study of Short Vowels	167	Click on the Videos tab, then type "Word Study Interventions in the Letter Name–Alphabetic Stage."
The Study of Short Vowels	169	Click on the Videos tab, then type "Sorting Short *e, i, o,* and *u* with Initial Blends."
Assess and Monitor Progress in the Letter Name–Alphabetic Stage	172	Click on the Videos tab, then revisit "Sorting Short *e, i, o,* and *u* with Initial Blends."
Activities for the Letter Name–Alphabetic Stage	184	Click on the Videos tab, then type "Weekly Schedules and Activities in the Letter Name–Alphabetic Stage."
Sorts and Games		
Vocabulary Learning	155	Click on the Sorts and Games tab, then select Concept Sorts to find four prepared sorts: Work and Play, Clothes and Body Parts, Creatures, and Transportation.
The Study of Consonant Sounds	164	Click on the Sorts and Games tab, then type "Beginning Consonant Pictures."
The Study of Consonant Sounds	165	Click on the Sorts and Games tab, then type "Beginning Digraph Picture Sorts" or "Beginning Blend Sorts."
The Study of Short Vowels	167	Click on the Sorts and Games tab, select Letter Name–Alphabetic Stage, then type "Word Family Sorts" for ready-to-use sorts.
The Study of Short Vowels	170	Click on the Sorts and Games tab, then type "Short Vowel Sorts with CVC Words."
Activities for the Letter Name–Alphabetic Stage	179	Click on the Sorts and Games tab, then type "Creatures."
Activities for the Letter Name–Alphabetic Stage	186	Click on the Sorts and Games tab, then type "Bingo." Click on the Create Your Own button to select words for your game.
Activities for the Letter Name–Alphabetic Stage	187	Click on the Sorts and Games tab, then type "Gruff Drops Troll at Bridge."

SECTION	PAGE	GO TO PDTOOLKIT FOR *WORDS THEIR WAY*™
Activities for the Letter Name–Alphabetic Stage	190	Click on the Sorts and Games tab, then type "Word Wheels and Flip Charts," "Show Me," or "Letter Slide" for ready-to-use word family games.
Activities for the Letter Name–Alphabetic Stage	192	Click on the Sorts and Games tab, then type "Go Fish" for a ready-to-print version.
Activities for the Letter Name–Alphabetic Stage	193	Click on the Sorts and Games tab, then type "Frog Marker and Hopping Frog."
Activities for the Letter Name–Alphabetic Stage	195	Click on the Sorts and Games tab, then select Games to access a variety of game boards to practice beginning sounds or vowel sounds.
Additional Resources		
Word Study with English Learners in the Letter Name–Alphabetic Stage	175	Click on the Additional Resources tab, then type "Word Study in Spanish" for a selection of sorts.

c h a p t e r

6

Word Study for Transitional Learners in the Within Word Pattern Stage

Orthographic development and word study instruction during the within word pattern spelling stage helps students build on their knowledge of the sound layer of English orthography and explore the pattern layer. Before we discuss development, let us visit the classroom of Ms. Watanabe, a second grade teacher who is working with a group of eight students in the early part of this stage of development.

On Monday morning, after meeting briefly with a reading group to share responses to *Fox and His Friends* by James Marshall, Ms. Watanabe takes time to introduce a word sort to this group. She has prepared a word study sheet like the one in Figure 6.1 as well as a collection of the words written on index cards that she will use to model the sort in a pocket chart. The students have already studied the common long *a* patterns (CVCe in *cake,* CVV in *say,* and CVVC in *chain*), and this sort will introduce long *e* patterns.

Ms. Watanabe begins by saying, "Let's read these words together." As each of the words is read, Ms. Watanabe places it randomly at the bottom of her pocket chart. There is some discussion of the homograph *read* when Jason points out that it can be read two ways. They agree for now to pronounce it as "reed." She then asks, "What do you notice about these words?"

"They all have *e*s in them," explains Troy.

"Yes, but do they all have the same sound in the middle?" Ms. Watanabe asks. She puts up pictures of a web and a queen as keys to the sounds they are to listen for: "We'll place all the words with short *e* under this picture of a web. We'll put words with the long *e* sound under this picture of a queen. Let's place words that do not fit either under the oddball column." She places a blank word card on the right side of the pocket chart to make a third column. "Let's try a few. Jean, show us how you would figure out where to put this word."

Jean places the word *bed* underneath the picture of the web while she says, "Web. Bed."

"Fine, Jean. Why did you put *bed* under the web?"

"Because they sound alike in the middle. They both say 'eh' in the middle."

"Right. They have the short *e* sound. David, where would this word go?" Ms. Watanabe hands David the word *team.* David takes the word card and talks himself through the task: "Team, web. Team, queen. *Team* has a long *e* sound." He places the word *team* underneath the picture of the queen.

Further into the sort, students decide that *been* does not fit under either picture and should go in the oddball column. After all the words have been sorted, Ms. Watanabe and the students check each category by reading the words from top to bottom. Then Ms. Watanabe poses the next important question: "How are the words in each column alike?"

David notes that the words under the picture of the web all have one *e.* Jean points out that the words in the second column all have two vowels. This leads to the next question: "Do you see some words in the second column that look alike or are spelled alike?" Ms. Watanabe invites Tomas to come up, and he quickly pulls out all the words spelled with *ee* and puts them in a new column, leaving the words spelled with *ea.* Once more Ms. Watanabe asks the students

FIGURE 6.1 Long *e* and Short *e* Word Study Sheet

[web picture]	[queen picture]	Long E Short E Sort 1
web	queen	team
seat	bed	seen
yes	jeep	read
meal	tree	leg
treat	bell	sheep
jet	cream	seed
eat	been	feel

FIGURE 6.2 Long *e* and Short *e* Pattern Sort

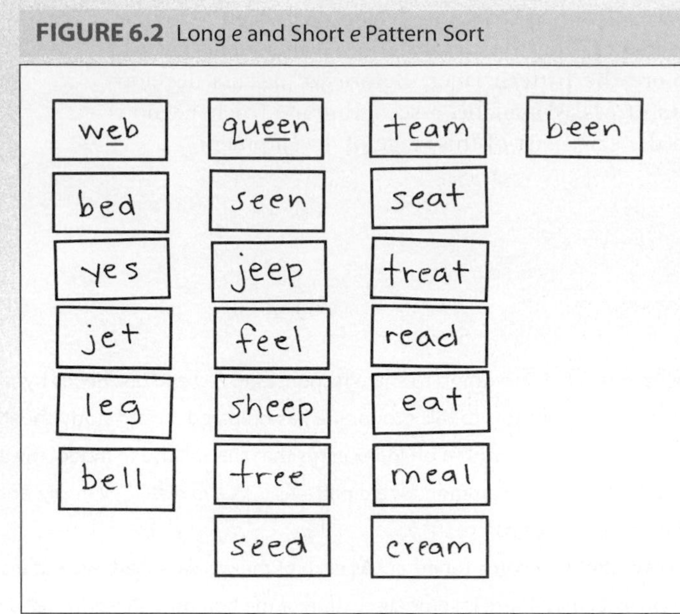

how the words in each column are alike. She helps them come to the conclusion that short *e* is spelled with a single *e* whereas long *e* is spelled with two vowels—either *ee* or *ea*. After underlining the patterns in *web, queen,* and *team* as headers, she removes the rest of the word cards. She mixes up the words and passes them out to the students. They then take turns coming up to sort their words. The final sort is shown in Figure 6.2.

Ms. Watanabe ends this lesson by giving each student a copy of the word study sheet in Figure 6.1. The students return to their seats, cut apart the words, and sort them independently while Ms. Watanabe checks in with another group. Later, Ms. Watanabe moves among the students and asks them, "Why did you put these words together?" This prompt gets students to reflect again on the categories.

To close this word study activity, students store their word cards in plastic bags. The next day they will sort again when they convene in their group, and Ms. Watanabe will watch to see how accurately and easily they sort this second day. Later they will write the sort in their word study notebooks, work with partners to do a blind sort and a writing sort, and go on a word hunt for more words that have the same vowel sounds and patterns.

Literacy Development of Students in the Within Word Pattern Stage

The within word pattern stage is a transitional stage of literacy development between the beginning stage when students' reading and writing are quite labored and the intermediate stage when students can read and write a variety of genres more fluently. We think of transitional readers as the "Wright brothers" of reading: They have taken flight but have limited elevation in their reading, and it does not take much to bring them down to frustration level or to cause them to be less fluent in their reading. Teachers may find transitional students in the middle-to-late part of first grade, but transitional students are found mostly in second, third, and early fourth grade classrooms. You will also find struggling readers in middle and high school who are in this stage (Flanigan, Hayes, Templeton, Bear, Invernizzi, & Johnston, 2011).

Reading in the Within Word Pattern Stage

Transitional readers read most single-syllable words accurately when they read at their instructional level, and they also read many two- and three-syllable words when there is enough contextual support. During this stage, students move from the **full alphabetic phase** to the **consolidated alphabetic phase** (Ehri, 2000b), in which they begin to recognize patterns and chunks to analyze unfamiliar words. Instead of processing a word like *chest* as four or five letters to match to sounds (*ch-e-s-t*), they process it as two chunks (*ch-est*). This enables them to decode and store words more readily and their sight word vocabulary grows quickly. This, in turn, enables them to read in phrases and with greater expression. Most of the finger-pointing characteristics of the beginning stage drop away, and transitional readers approach oral reading rates of 100 words per minute (Bear, 1992; Bear & Cathey, 1989). All of these factors account for the increasing fluency of the transitional reader compared to the dysfluent, word-by-word reading in the beginning stage of literacy.

Students are generally reading orally at the beginning of the transitional period, but by the end they can manage substantial periods of silent reading during Drop Everything and Read (DEAR) or Sustained Silent Reading (SSR). They can be assigned to read independently without the teacher's support and this makes it possible to use reading group time to share reactions to a selection. Transitional readers can discuss what they read in greater depth than they did as beginning readers, partly because what they read is longer and more complex.

Books for transitional readers cover a wide range of levels, from late first/early second through early fourth grade materials. In the early part of this stage, transitional readers read and reread familiar text from several sources: basal readers (or *core* reading programs), picture books, and favorite poems. They can read beginning chapter books such as the Frog and Toad books (by A. Lobel) and Henry and Mudge books (by C. Rylant). By the end of this stage, students' reading includes easy chapter books such as The Time Warp Trio series (by J. Scieska), the Encyclopedia Brown series (by D. Sobol), or the Magic Tree House series (by M. P. Osbourne). Transitional readers also explore different genres, and informational text becomes more accessible. For example, they read informational books from the Let's Find Out and I Can Read series and magazines such as *Ranger Rick*.

Lots of experience in reading is crucial during this stage. Students should read for at least 30 minutes each day in **instructional-** and **independent-level** materials. They need this practice to propel them into the next stage; otherwise, they will stagnate as readers and writers. Repeated and timed repeated readings (Samuels, 1979), reader's theater, and poetry readings are good ways to promote fluent, expressive reading, which is an important goal during this stage (Rasinski, 2010). However, fluent, expressive reading relies on automatic word recognition and extensive word knowledge (Bear, 1989). Simply trying to increase reading rates without building the underlying word knowledge is a shortsighted goal.

Writing in the Within Word Pattern Stage

Just like reading, writing also becomes more fluent during this period of development because students know how to automatically spell many words. The physical act of writing is performed with greater speed and less conscious attention (Bear, 1991a; Nagy, Berninger, Abbott, Vaughan, & Vermeulen, 2003). This added fluency gives transitional writers more time to concentrate on ideas, which may account for the greater sophistication in the way transitional writers express their ideas. Cognitively, they compose with a better sense of the reader's background knowledge and with a greater complexity in the story line or informational piece.

Excerpts of Katrina's two-and-a-half-page single-spaced story about a squirrel named Nuts (see Figure 6.3) show how much students know about written language and spelling in the later part of the within word pattern stage. Katrina, a second grader, has a rich language base and she writes with a strong voice. In terms of orthographic knowledge, Katrina spells most long vowel patterns and *r*-influenced words correctly (*woke*, *search*). But this knowledge is not stable, as seen in her later spelling of *searches* as SERCHES and her overgeneralizing patterns (BREAKFEAST for *breakfast* and HOWL for *whole*). Later in the story, Katrina spelled *thought* as TOOUGHT but then went back and wrote in an *h*. She also confuses homophones (*there*/*their*). Katrina is a late within word pattern speller who would be appropriately

FIGURE 6.3 Katrina's Squirrel Story

Twelve year old Chistine was glad it was
Fially Satarday alltow she loved school
Epspshelly math she loved taking her pet
Squrrle Nuts to the park even more.

(Nuts runs away and)

Christine orginizes a search. She
looked evrywhere. Christine climbd
a tree Nuts wasnt there.

(Nuts returns and the next day)

Christine and Nuts woke up
they went down stairs and there
breakfeast was ready it was
all difrent kinds of pancake
animals.

(Later)

Christine thought
Nuts ran away but he
didn't because Nuts went
tawa difrent park. Christine
serches the howl park.

(The story ends with Christine)

niting a sweter for Nuts
the colors where red, white
and blue.

placed in a word study group in which students were studying diphthongs and ambiguous vowels.

Vocabulary Learning

Estimates vary, but children can, on average, add 10 to 15 new words a week to their oral vocabularies (Biemiller, 2005). During the transitional stage of literacy teachers need to take an active and deliberate role in making sure this vocabulary growth happens for all children. Teachers can make words interesting in many ways and in so doing help their students become "wordsmiths"—kids who are curious about words, their sounds, their meanings, their usage. This type of attitude toward words raises students' **word consciousness** or word awareness, which is a critical aspect of vocabulary growth (Blachowicz & Fisher, 2009; Lubliner & Scott, 2008; Scott, Skobel, & Wells, 2008; Stahl & Nagy, 2006).

Keep in mind that vocabulary instruction should not be confused with spelling or phonics instruction. When we refer to vocabulary we are referring to *meaning*. We have observed that sometimes teachers assign spelling words in elementary classrooms that are really vocabulary words (for example, *butterfly, chrysalis, antenna*). Although students in the within word pattern stage can read and learn the meanings of many multisyllabic words (*glimmer, strategy, gesture*), they should not be expected to spell those words. This difference reflects the slant of development in word learning during the elementary years; the words students may read and study for meaning are more complex than those they study in spelling.

Teachers should use sophisticated language in daily interactions with students (see Chapter 5) and develop the habit of commenting on and making observations about words throughout the day. We next describe how read-alouds, word sorts, and concept sorts provide opportunities to discuss new words and focus on multiple meanings. Students in this stage should start to use a dictionary as a reference tool and can also begin the study of common prefixes.

READ-ALOUDS. Good children's literature continues to be the best starting place for vocabulary learning and is a much richer source than television or adult daily conversation (Hayes

& Ahrens, 1988). Picture books and chapter books are replete with new and rich vocabulary that is wrapped in complex sentences. Context is the key to unpacking the meanings of new words from read-alouds, and with guidance from teachers, students can develop the skill of using context to learn the meanings of new words. During and after listening to books read aloud students should be encouraged to talk about what they have heard. Using the "think, pair, share" strategy described in Activity 5.2 is a good way to maximize the opportunity for everyone to use oral language.

In learning new vocabulary during this stage, students benefit from repeated exposure to words and from seeing the words in print as they hear them (Beck et al., 2002; Rosenthal & Ehri, 2008). It is helpful to record the words on charts and in webs, post them for all to see, and refer to them as a reminder to use them in conversation throughout the day. It takes many exposures, over several weeks, in multiple contexts to learn a new word, so teachers should be deliberate in using new words and encouraging students to use new words. Refer back to the last chapter for anchored vocabulary instruction in Activity 5.1 (Juel et al., 2003).

WORD SORTS AND VOCABULARY. Always take the time to read through words in a sort to be sure students know the meanings of the words. Most of the words will be familiar ones, unless students are English learners, but there are still opportunities to explore the meaning layer of English, most specifically in the case of homophones and homonyms. Students will encounter many **homophones** during this stage; these words that sound the same but are spelled differently provide rich fodder for vocabulary development. Why is *thrown*, the verb, spelled with an *ow?* Because the vowel-consonant-*e* pattern is already taken for the noun *throne*—the chair occupied by kings and queens. The spelling pattern reflects the different meaning! We share with students that "we spell these words differently *because they mean different things!*" This insight provides a fun and interesting approach to both spelling and vocabulary instruction.

Creating an ongoing collection such as a Homophone Pear/Pair Tree can be a whole-class activity in second or third grade classrooms that goes on all year long. When a homophone pair is discovered it is written on a pear shape and added to the branches of a tree posted on a bulletin board. This encourages students to always be on the lookout for homophones in their reading. Students in the transitional stage will truly become wordsmiths as they collect hundreds of homophones, such as the ones on page 372 in Appendix E. Usually there is one homophone in a pair that is familiar (*bear*) whereas the other one (*bare*) is what Beck and colleagues (2002) would call a "Tier 2" word. These are words that have high utility in multiple contexts and are part of the *core academic* vocabulary that students need to acquire throughout the school years (Templeton, Bear, Invernizzi, & Johnston, 2010). Students can better remember the spelling of a homophone, and often expand their vocabulary at the same time, by thinking about the *meaning* of the homophone whenever they read and write it. As teachers, we can never *rest* until we *wrest* every ounce of meaning from word study!

English is rich in words that are spelled the same but have multiple meanings (*park* the car or play in the *park*). These are known as **homonyms** or *polysemous* words. Look for these words in word sorts and take the time to explore the multiple meanings through discussion, illustration, and examples in sentences. Consider a simple homonym like *block*, which is something you build with, something you run around in the neighborhood, something you might do during a soccer game, and a portion of time. There are also polysemous words and phrases that share meaning in their origin, like the *bed* for sleeping and a place for a stream or the two meanings of *head*—a part of the body or the chief of an organization. Native speakers and English learners alike will benefit from some time spent attending to the many meanings of words. Be sure to point out how context helps to determine which meaning should be taken into account.

Once single-syllable words are read easily, including homophone pairs like *meat/meet*, *rows/rose*, and *threw/through*, however, by the middle of this stage, two-syllable polysemous words come to the fore. The word *temple* is an example of a word that students in the within word pattern can read but are not studying in spelling. They are busy making the meaning connections from context: There is the *temple* that is the side of the head, and there is the *temple* as a place of worship and a sacred place.

CONCEPT SORTS. The study of nonfiction and subjects such as math, science, and social studies will expose children to new concepts and new vocabulary. Concept sorts are a powerful way to actively explore vocabulary. In Activity 6.17 we describe a concept sort with math terms related to addition (*plus, combine, increase*) and subtraction (*take away, difference, decrease*) and also offer other examples for different areas of study. To prepare concept sorts, teachers preview the vocabulary in textbooks or other curricular materials and create sorts of the key terms. Students and teacher can also work together to brainstorm words on a particular topic (e.g., words related to outer space, government words, or key vocabulary words from other content areas) that can then be sorted into categories.

Many teachers conduct concept sorts at the beginning of a unit of study as an informal assessment of background knowledge. Begin by going over the words to be sure students can read them and have some familiarity with the meanings of the words (they will develop deeper understanding with repeated exposure). Students sort the words as an **open sort** either individually or with a partner. In this way teachers see what students know about a topic and obtain a sense of the difficulty of the reading. Similarly, at the end of a unit of study, teachers ask students to complete the sort again and to add related words. These sorts at the end of a unit of study show what students have learned.

DICTIONARIES. By the within word pattern stage students can begin using dictionaries on a regular basis to check word meanings. This does not mean they should be assigned to look up ten definitions to fulfill a seatwork or homework requirement—a strategy sure to make students dislike dictionaries. Instead, the dictionary should be used as a resource during reading groups, class discussions, word study lessons, and content area study to seek information about a word that presents a puzzle. What does *vent* mean in the sentence "He had to vent when he got outside with his friends." Which definition fits the context?

Constantly model how you use a dictionary and show children how they are organized. Once children have some skill in using alphabetical order and guide words, take turns assigning a child each day to be the dictionary "meister" responsible for looking up any word that the class is curious about. During word study time each child in the group might be asked to look up one word and be ready to report what he or she found out about it, particularly the multiple meanings of words like *block, drive,* or *fudge.* Children's dictionaries are most appropriate for second to fourth grade, in which most within word pattern spellers fall. Modern dictionaries such as the *Merriam-Webster Children's Dictionary* published by DK are visual feasts that invite children to browse. Children can learn to use online dictionaries at this stage also.

A popular dictionary game titled How Many Turns is a way for students to pick up fluency in scanning through a dictionary. The game is straightforward: Students are asked to find a word and whoever can find it in the fewest number of turns win. Begin with words spelled with initial letters like *d, p, s,* or *t.* As students gather confidence, refine with requests for them to find words that begin with two or three consonant letters (e.g., *sp, st, str*).

SIMPLE PREFIXES AND SUFFIXES. A systematic and extensive exploration of prefixes and suffixes occurs in the next stage—**syllables and affixes.** However, students can be taught simple affixes as meaning vocabulary beginning in second grade when most students are developmentally in the within word pattern stage of spelling. These prefixes and suffixes are now included at the primary level in the Common Core State Standards adopted by 48 of the 50 states, as well as the District of Columbia and two territories (2010). Understanding how these simple affixes combine with base words lays the foundation for more extensive exploration in word formation processes later on. Words with these affixes are explored first as vocabulary words students encounter in their reading and are not treated as spelling words until students know how to spell the base words on which they are built.

The most common prefixes in the English language are *un-* (meaning "not"), *re-* ("again"), *in-* ("not"), and *dis-* ("not"); these four prefixes account for about 58 percent of all prefixes in the language (White, Sowell, & Yanagihara, 1989). The prefixes that most states have mandated for study in grade 2 are *un-* and *re-*. These can be explored as vocabulary words, beginning with simple base words such as *do* and discussing what happens when *un-* and *re-* are added to *do*. Several states mandate that the suffixes *-ly*, *-ful*, and *-y* and the comparatives *-er/-est* be taught in grade 2. Using frequently occurring and easily understood words, walk children through a discussion of, for example, *small/smaller/smallest* versus *tall/taller/tallest*. Beginning with the word *care*, talk about being *careful* and watching over a baby brother or sister *carefully*. Appendix E has lists of words with prefixes and suffixes.

Orthographic Development in the Within Word Pattern Stage

Students in the within word pattern stage use but confuse vowel patterns (Invernizzi, Abouzeid, & Gill, 1994). They no longer spell *boat* sound by sound to produce BOT but as BOTE, BOWT, BOOT, or even *boat* as they experiment with the possible patterns for the long *o* sound. When spellers begin including silent letters, they are ripe for instruction in long vowel patterns. In Eduardo's early within word pattern writing in Figure 6.4, we can see that he knows a good deal about short vowel patterns, spelling *with*, *pick*, *on*, *it*, and *up* correctly and *blanket* as BLANCKET. But Eduardo is also experimenting with long vowel patterns, as in PLAED for *played* and TOOTHE for *tooth*.

FIGURE 6.4 Eduardo's Tooth Story

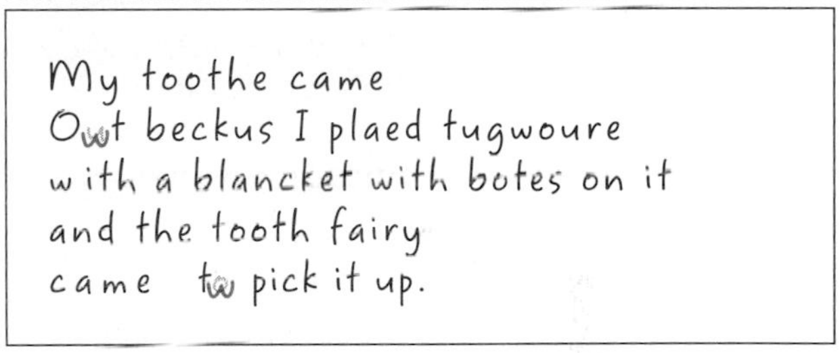

My toothe came
Owt beckus I plaed tugwoure
with a blancket with botes on it
and the tooth fairy
came tw pick it up.

The orthographic development of students across the within word pattern stage is summarized in Table 6.1. By the time students reach the within word pattern stage, their **phonemic awareness** is well developed. Short vowels, blends, and digraphs are nearly mastered and should only require some review. Students can isolate the vowel sounds in the middles of words, but learning the variety of ways those vowel sounds can be spelled challenges within word pattern spellers, which accounts for the name selected to label this stage.

The Pattern Principle

Students in this stage explore the **pattern layer** of English spelling. This requires a higher degree of abstract thinking because they face two tasks at once. They must not only isolate the phonemes to determine the sounds they need to represent but must also choose from a variety of patterns that represent the same phoneme, which usually involve silent letters as part of the vowel spelling (*cute, through suit*) or special consonant patterns (***lodge, itch***). There are several reasons why the same phoneme may be spelled with different patterns.

- *How words are spelled may depend on their histories and origins.* English has been enriched with the addition of vocabulary from many different languages over hundreds of years and in the process has imported diverse vowel sounds and spelling patterns as well. In addition, certain patterns represent sounds that have changed over the centuries. For example, *igh* as in *knight* was once a sound quite different from long *i* (the word was pronounced *k-n-ict* in early Middle English) but over time pronunciation tends toward simplification

Table 6.1 Characteristics of Within Word Pattern Spelling

	WHAT STUDENTS DO CORRECTLY	WHAT STUDENTS USE BUT CONFUSE	WHAT IS ABSENT
Early Within Word Pattern *ship, when, jump* ROBE *for rob* FLOTE *for float* TRANE *for train* BRITE *for bright*	Consonants, blends, digraphs Preconsonantal nasals Short vowels in CVC words *r*-Influenced CVC words: *car, for, her* Spell known sight words	Silent letters in long vowel patterns *-k, -ck,* and *-ke* endings: SMOCK *for smoke,* PEKE *for peak* Substitutions of short vowels for ambiguous vowels: COT for *caught*	Vowels in unaccented syllables: FLOWR for *flower* Consonant doubling: SHOPING *for shopping* *e*-Drop: DRIVEING for *driving*
Middle Within Word Pattern *float, train* FRITE *for fright* TABUL *for table*	All of the above plus: Common long vowel patterns (CVCe, CVVC) *-k, -ck,* and *-ke* endings	Less common and ambiguous vowel patterns *-ed* and other common inflections: MARCHT for *marched,* BATID for *batted*	Consonant doubling *e*-Drop
Late Within Word Pattern *bright* SPOYLE *for spoil* CHOOD *for chewed* SURVING *for serving*	All of the above plus: Long vowel patterns in one-syllable words *r*-Influenced vowel patterns	Ambiguous vowels Complex consonant units: SWICH for *switch,* SMUGE for *smudge* Vowels in unaccented syllables: COLER for *color*	Consonant doubling Changing *y* to *i:* CAREES *for carries*

whereas spelling tends to stay the same. Therefore, one vowel sound may be spelled many different ways (Vallins, 1954).

- *How sounds are spelled may depend on their position within a word.* Comparing words such as *say* and *rain* reveals that, in single-syllable words, long *a* is usually spelled *ay* at the end of a word (but rarely in the middle) and often *ai* in the middle (but never at the end). Similarly *oy, ew,* and *ow* are patterns that usually occur at the ends of words whereas *oi, ui,* or *ou* rarely occur at the end.
- *How sounds are spelled may depend on other sounds next to them.* Words such as *ridge* and *cage* reveal that the /j/ sound is usually spelled *dge* when it follows a short vowel and *ge* when it follows a long vowel.
- *How words are spelled may depend on the meaning of the word.* Although the long vowel sound in /pān/ may be spelled *a*-consonant-*e* or *ai,* the appropriate spelling is determined by *meaning.* Are you writing about the glass in a window or extreme discomfort? The meaning carries with it a consistent spelling: The glass in a window will always be spelled *pane* and the extreme discomfort will always be spelled *pain.* The /sāl/ on a boat will always be spelled *sail;* the /sāl/ where products are sold will always be spelled *sale.* For homophones like these, we hang our memory for spelling on a meaning hook.

The Complexities of English Vowels

The study of vowel patterns characterizes much of the word study during the within word pattern stage. Short vowels pose a problem for letter name–alphabetic spellers because they do not match a letter name. However, once students have learned to associate the five common short vowel sounds with *a*, *e*, *i*, *o*, and *u*, the relationship is usually one letter to one sound. In contrast, the mastery of other vowels is challenging due to the following factors.

1. There are many more vowel sounds than there are letters to represent them. Each designated vowel, including *y*, is pressed into service to represent more than one sound. Listen to the sound of *a* in these words: *hat, car, war, saw, father, play.* To spell such a variety of sounds, vowels are often paired (for example, the *ai* as a long *a* in *rain* or *au* for the sound in *caught*), or a second vowel or consonant is used to mark or signal a particular sound. The silent *e* in *came*, the *y* in *play*, and the *w* in *saw* are examples of silent **vowel markers.**
2. Not only are there more vowel sounds than vowels, most of those sounds are spelled a number of different ways, as indicated in Table 6.2. However, some spelling patterns are far more likely to occur than others. For example, there are more instances of the *a*-consonant-*e* pattern (VCe) for the long *a* sound in the middle of a syllable than for any of the other patterns. It is important to know that there just aren't that many words in which long *a* is spelled *ea* as in *great*.
3. In addition to short and long vowels, there are many more vowel sounds, all of which are spelled with a variety of patterns. These include *r*-influenced vowels (*car, sir, earn*), **diphthongs** (*brown, cloud, boil, toy*), and other **ambiguous vowels** that are neither long nor short (*caught, chalk, straw, thought*). These vowel patterns involve either a second vowel, or the vowel is influenced by a letter that has some vowel-like qualities. The letters *l*, *r*, and *w* are examples of consonants that influence the sound of the vowel (*bald, bird, crowd*). These additional vowel patterns are also shown in Table 6.2.
4. English is a language of multiple dialects, and the differences among dialects are very noticeable in the pronunciations of vowels. In some regions of the United States, the long *i* sound in a word like *pie* is really more of a vowel glide or diphthong as in *pi-e*. *House* may be pronounced more like *hoose* in some areas, and *roof* may sound like *ruff.* Sometimes the final *r* in *r*-controlled vowels is dropped, as in Boston where you "pahk the cah" (park the car). In other regions, a final *r* is added to words as in the "hollers" (hollows) of southwest Virginia. Such regional dialects add color and interest to the language, but teachers may

for Words Their Way™

Go to PDToolkit for *Words Their Way,* click on the Videos tab, then type "Classroom Organization in the Within Word Pattern Stage." Ms. Flores discusses the patterns her students are examining in the within word pattern stage of spelling.

Table 6.2 Vowel Patterns

LONG VOWEL PATTERNS		CONSONANT-INFLUENCED VOWELS	DIPHTHONGS AND AMBIGUOUS VOWELS
Common long *a* patterns:	*a-e* (*cave*), *ai* (*rain*), *ay* (*play*)	*r*-Influenced vowels	o͞o (*moon*) and o͝o (*book*)
Less common:	*ei* (*eight*), *ey* (*prey*)	*a* with *r*: *ar* (*car*), *are* (*care*), *air* (*fair*)	*oy* (*boy*), *oi* (*boil*)
Common long *e* patterns:	*ee* (*green*), *ea* (*team*), *e* (*me*)		*ow* (*brown*), *ou* (*cloud*)
Less common:	*ie* (*chief*), *e-e* (*theme*)	*o* with *r*: *or* (*for*), *ore* (*store*), *our* (*pour*), *oar* (*board*)	*aw* (*crawl*), *au* (*caught*)
Common long *i* patterns:	*i-e* (*tribe*), *igh* (*sight*), *y* (*fly*)		*al* (*tall*), *o* (*dog*)
Less common:	*i* followed by *nd* or *ld* (*mind, child*)	*e* with *r*: *er* (*her*), *eer* (*deer*), *ear* (*dear*), *ear* (*learn*)	
Common long *o* patterns:	*o-e* (*home*), *oa* (*float*), *ow* (*grow*)	*i* with *r*: *ir* (*shirt*), *ire* (*fire*)	
Less common:	*o* followed by two consonants (*cold, most, jolt*)	*u* with *r*: *ur* (*burn*), *ure* (*cure*)	
Common long *u* patterns:	*u-e* (*flute*), *oo* (*moon*), *ew* (*blew*)	A *w* influences vowels that follow: *wa* (*wash, warn*), *wo* (*won, word*)	
Less common:	*ue* (*blue*), *ui* (*suit*)	An *l* influences the *a* as heard in *al* (*tall, talk*).	

be worried about how speakers of such dialects will learn to spell if they cannot pronounce words "correctly." Rest assured that these students will learn to associate certain letter patterns with their own pronunciations and will also, over time, learn the sound patterns of Standard American English (Cantrell, 2001). The value of word sorting over more inflexible phonics programs is that students can sort according to their own pronunciations, and a miscellaneous or oddball column can be used for variant pronunciations.

5. Many words in English do not match even one of the patterns listed in Table 6.2. These words have sometimes been called exceptions to the rule. We prefer to put them in the miscellaneous or **oddball** category. During word study in the within word pattern stage, the oddball category will get a lot of use. Sometimes these words are true exceptions, as with *was*, *build*, and *been;* at other times they are not exceptions, but rather part of a little known category. Examples of these words are *dance*, *prince*, and *fence*, which, because of the final *e*, may look like they should have long vowel patterns. But in these words the *e* is there to signal or mark the "soft" /s/ sound of *c* (consider the alternative: *danc*, *princ*, and *fenc*). Such exceptions should not be ignored, and in fact, a few such words should be deliberately included in the sorts you plan. They become memorable as deviations from the common patterns and therefore spelled correctly.
6. English vowels pose special challenges for English learners because English has so many more vowel sounds than most languages. This will be discussed in more depth later.

Despite the complexity of vowel spellings, by the end of the within word pattern stage, students who have experienced a systematic word study approach have a good understanding of vowel patterns in one-syllable words. This knowledge is prerequisite to the examination of the way syllables are joined during the next stage of development, the syllables and affixes stage. For example, when students understand the patterns in words like *bet* and *beat*, they are ready to understand why *betting* has two *t*s and *beating* has only one.

The Influence of Consonants on Vowels

In English, vowel patterns often consist of two vowels, one of which signals or marks a particular sound for the other vowel. Common examples are the silent *e* in words such as *bake* and *green;* however, consonants are also vowel markers, such as the *gh* in *night* and *sigh*, which signals the long *i* sound. Students who have come to associate the CVC pattern with short vowels may be puzzled when presented with *saw*, *joy*, *hall*, or *car*. In those words, *w*, *y*, and *l* are no longer acting as consonants but are taking on vowel-like qualities. The consonant sound of *l* is lost in a word like *talk* but it is part of the vowel sound, which is neither long nor short. The *r* retains its identity as a consonant in *car*, but the preceding vowel has a sound quite different from short *a*. When *w* precedes *a*, *ar*, and *or* the vowel takes on a different sound as in *wand*, *war*, and *word*. These words may look like they are exceptions, but they are, in fact, simply additional patterns that are very regular. This is why it is so important to learn patterns that relate to sound and meaning at this stage rather than rules. The influence of *r* is particularly common and deserves further discussion.

THE *R*-INFLUENCED VOWELS. As our friend Neva Viise says, "*R* is a robber!" The presence of an *r* following a vowel robs the sound from the vowel before it. The terms ***r*-influenced** or ***r*-controlled** both refer to this situation. The influence of *r* causes some words with different vowel spellings to become homophones (*fir/fur*) and makes vowel sounds spelled with *er*, *ir*, and *ur* indistinguishable in many cases (*herd*, *bird*, *curd*). Even long vowel sounds before the robber *r* are pronounced differently than the same vowels preceding other consonants (*pair* versus *pain*).

The *r*-blends are sometimes confused with *r*-influenced vowels as in the spelling of *girl* as GRIL or *bird* as BRID. The *r*-influenced vowel sorts draw students' attention to the location of the *r* and to the subtle difference in sound that location creates. Word study of *r*-influenced words can begin with activities that contrast initial consonant *r* blends (*grill*, *bring*) with *r*-influenced vowels (*girl*, *bird*).

Triple Blends, Silent Initial Consonants, and Other Complex Consonants

There are several other consonant issues that pose challenges for within word pattern spellers who already know basic beginning and ending consonant blends and digraphs. For example, three-letter blends and digraphs often require further study: *spr* (*spring*), *thr* (*throw*), *squ* (*square*), *scr* (*scream*), *shr* (*shred*), *sch* (*school*), *spl* (*splash*), and *str* (*string*). Because words that contain these triplets have a variety of vowel patterns, they are specifically studied toward the end of the stage but can be included in sorts throughout the stage when appropriate. There are also several silent consonants to study that occur in one-syllable words: *kn* (*knife*), *wr* (*wrong*), and *gn* (*gnaw*).

What is of special interest in this stage are other characteristics of consonants that are related to vowel sounds. Based on Venesky's (1970) work, Henderson (1990) called these **complex consonant patterns.** For example, students in the within word pattern stage can examine words that end in *ck* (*kick*), *tch* (*catch*), and *dge* (*ledge*). Contrasting these pairs will enable students to make interesting discoveries. Say the following word pairs and listen to the vowel sounds.

tack	take	fetch	peach	fudge	huge
lick	like	notch	roach	badge	cage
rack	rake	patch	poach	ledge	siege
smock	smoke	sketch	reach	ridge	page

Notice that *ck* (*tack*), *tch* (*fetch*), and *dge* (*fudge*) patterns are associated with short vowel sounds, whereas *ke* (*take*), *ch* (*peach*), and *ge* (*huge*) are associated with long vowel sounds.

The consonants *g* and *c* have two sounds that are determined by the vowel that follows them. When *g* and *c* are followed by *a*, *o*, and *u*, they have a "hard" sound, as in *gate* and *cake*. When they are followed by *i*, *e*, or *y*, they have a "soft" sound (/s/ or /j/) as in *ginger* or *cent*. (*C* is more regular than *g* because the *g* is hard in many words like *girl* and *gill*.) In a similar fashion, words ending in *ce* (*dance*), *ge* (*edge*), *ve* (*leave*), and *se* (*sense*) have a silent *e* associated with the consonant rather than the vowel. These patterns illustrate the understanding that how sounds are spelled very often depends on other sounds next to them.

Homophones, Homographs, and Other Features

Recall the three layers of English orthography. In this stage, students continue to rely on sound while learning patterns, but they are also beginning to scratch the meaning layer. A group of third-graders observed that *weight* and *height* had three things in common: They were both spelled with an *ei*, they both made a vowel sound that was unexpected, and they both had to do with measurement. Sound, pattern, and meaning are emphasized in the study of homophones (*meat* and *meet*), homographs (*tear:* I *tear* the sheet into rags with a *tear* in my eye), and many irregular verbs (*deal:* I *deal* the cards after you *dealt* them on the previous hand).

Homophones will inevitably turn up in the study of vowel patterns and can be included in the word sorts you plan even at the beginning of this stage, but an intensive look at homophones at the end of this stage is also recommended. At this point, students know most of the vowel patterns and are ready to focus on the meanings of the words. Students enjoy creating lists of homophones (*bear/bare*, *Mary/marry/merry*) and homographs (*wind* up string/listen to the *wind*). The different spellings of homophones may seem capricious, but they reflect their historical origins and may even make reading easier and meaning clearer (cf., Taft, 1991; Templeton, 1992). Contrast the sentence pairs below:

The weigh Peat cot the bare was knot fare.	We rowed around the lake.
The way Pete caught the bear was not fair.	We rode around the lake.

Pairs of homographs and homophones sometimes differ grammatically as well as semantically. For example, when discussing the homophones *read* and *red*, it makes sense to talk about the past tense of the verb *to read* and the color word *red.* Many irregular or "strong" verbs also present an opportunity to explore the interaction of sound, pattern, and meaning. Many of these verbs differ by vowel sounds (*drink/drank*) and spelling patterns (*pay/paid*) or both (*sweep, swept*).

The study of contractions also presents a new series of features to examine that are rooted in the pattern and meaning layers of the orthography. We examine meaning in contractions, for example, when we compare *its* and *it's* or *we're* and *were.*

Word Study Instruction for the Within Word Pattern Stage

Carefully planned word sorts are a systematic way to guide students' mastery of the complexities of vowel and consonant patterns in the within word pattern stage. Principles previously outlined in Chapter 2 apply to this stage:

- *Students should be able to read the words before sorting.* Be sensitive to the difficulty of words in the sort and make sure students can read the majority of them easily. Words starting with consonant blends, like ***bl**ame* or ***fr**ame*, are harder than words starting with single consonants like ***c**ame* or ***n**ame* even though they share the same CVCe spelling pattern. Likewise, words that contain triple blends or complex consonants (***scr**eam*, ***squ**eek*, ***thr**oat*, *lo**dge**, hi**tch***) are harder to analyze and spell than two-letter blends (***st**eam*, ***sl**eek*, etc.). These features are studied near the end of the stage once students have mastered the many different vowel patterns needed to spell the words.
- *Choose sorts that match students' development and represent what they use but confuse.* A spelling inventory will give you a good idea of what students know and what they are ready to learn. However, it is also important to look in your students' own writing and reading materials for words to include in sorts. The words students can already read and spell are still useful when they are looking for patterns across words to form generalizations.
- *Avoid teaching rules—instead, have students find reliable patterns.* It has been a common practice to teach students rules about silent *e* and jingles like "when two vowels go walking the first one does the talking," but rules are less reliable than the patterns themselves. For example, the rule about two vowels works for *oa* and *ai* in *boat* and *rain*, but not for *oy* or *oi* in *boy* or *join*, yet *oy* and *oi* are very regular spelling patterns (Johnston, 2001). We prefer to talk about patterns rather than rules and the time to talk about these is when students have already observed and understand the pattern. Remember that rules are useful mnemonics for something already understood; they are not teaching tools.

PDToolkit
for Words Their Way™

Go to PDToolkit for *Words Their Way,* click on the Sorts and Games tab, then select Within Word Pattern stage for ready-made sorts and games.

- *Sort by sound and pattern.* Plan sorts that first ask students to contrast vowels by how they *sound.* Long vowels should be first introduced by comparing them to their corresponding short vowel sounds, as Ms. Watanabe did in the vignette at the beginning of this chapter. The *r*-influenced vowels (such as the *ar* in *car*) can be compared with the short CVC patterns (such as short *a* in *cash* or *trap*). Sound sorts are important because sound is the first clue that spellers use and because certain patterns go with certain vowel sounds. Long and short vowel pictures can be used for sound sorts, but most of these sound sorts are done with words at this stage. After sorting by sound, sort by sight—look for the visual orthographic spelling patterns used to spell each sound category.

Go to PDToolkit for *Words Their Way,* click on the Assessment Tools tab, then type "Goal-Setting/Progress Monitoring Charts."

- *Don't hide exceptions.* Include two or three oddball words in sorts when appropriate. For example, a long *o* sort could include *love* and *some*, which look as though they fit the

CVCe pattern but whose vowel sounds are not long. However, don't overdo it. Too many oddballs placed in a sort can make it difficult for students to find the pattern. The best oddballs are high-frequency words like *done* or *come* that students already know how to read or less common patterns that will be studied later, like *most* or *mind*. High-frequency words (both regular and irregular) are listed in Appendix E and marked with asterisks in the word lists. Help students see, however, that even the "oddballs" are *mostly* correct in terms of sound–spelling correspondences. In *most* and *mind*, for example, the consonant spellings are consistent—it is the "oddball" vowel sound to which they should attend because most vowel sounds in a CVCC pattern are short. Students enjoy the challenge of finding the oddballs in a sort and the oddballs often serve as the real test of whether students are sorting carefully.

The Word Study Lesson Plan in the Within Word Pattern Stage

Word sorts often begin as a teacher-directed activity and then offer individual practice throughout the week. Most sorts will follow the standard format presented in Chapter 3 and reviewed here.

for **English Learners**

1. *Demonstrate the sort.* When starting a sort, go over the words with students to be sure they are able to read them, and talk briefly about the meanings of unfamiliar words or multiple meanings of polysemous words like *park* or *block*. If there are more than a few words whose meanings students do not know, which is often the case for English learners, continue to talk about the meanings of the words throughout the week. After going over the words, you might ask a simple open-ended question to begin the sort, such as "What do you notice about these words?"

   As described in Chapter 3, there are many ways to introduce a sort. In a **teacher-directed** or **closed sort,** set up the categories with **key pictures** or **key words,** as Ms. Watanabe did with short *e* and long *e*. Other teachers like the key words to be established as part of the group discussion with students, then highlighted. Teacher-directed closed sorts are helpful when students are new to sorting or when they start the study of a new feature. Once students understand the process, use **open sorts** to require more analytic thinking and encourage discovery. Students look for their own categories and are asked to explain why they sorted the way they did. After sorting, lead a discussion to focus students' attention on the distinguishing features: "How are the words in this column alike?"

2. *Sort and check.* After a group sort, it is important for students to work independently or with partners using their own sets of words. Some teachers create reusable sorts in manila folders with the key words or pictures at the top and the words stored in a plastic bag inside the folder. Figure 6.5 shows a student isolating the long *e* sound in *leaf* before placing it in the column with the picture of the feet at the top. Saying the words aloud and comparing them in this way is a necessary strategy when students begin a sort. After sorting, encourage students to check their words by saying all the words aloud in each column to make sure they all fit. When errors are made, offer gentle hints such as "One word in this column does not sound (or look) right. Can you find it?"

FIGURE 6.5 Long Vowel Sorts: Student Sorts by Sound

3. *Reflect: Declare, compare, and contrast.* "Why did you sort the way you did?" Asking this question to start the reflection part of a lesson is designed to get students to tell what they have learned. You might ask students to turn and talk to a partner as a good first step. If students do not come up with the insights needed to understand the feature, be ready to model your own thinking and the language students need to talk about words. You might say for example, "When I look at all the words in this column, I notice that the vowel sound is long and the pattern is consonant-vowel-vowel-consonant." A sort is successful when students sort accurately and quickly and can discuss why they sorted as they did. If students seem just to mimic other students, you can ask them to say it another way, or ask, "What else did you notice about the words we sorted?"
4. *Extend: Students work independently across the week.* Word study is extended beyond the small-group sessions through activities students complete at their seats, in word study notebooks, at a word study center, or at home. **Blind sorts** that involve students sorting words by sound as a partner reads them aloud are particularly recommended at this stage because students must not only distinguish the sound of the vowel but also associate it with a visual orthographic pattern. Games provide enjoyable practice in reading the words and thinking about their patterns. Many games are described in the activities section at the end of this chapter or can be adapted from games in the previous chapter.

for Words Their Way™

Go to PDToolkit for *Words Their Way,* click on the Videos tab, then type "Short *a* and Long *a*." Watch as Ms. Flores conducts a lesson using the CVC, CVCe, CVV, and CVVC patterns.

The three examples of introductory lessons that follow can serve as models for most of the sorts used in this stage.

Picture Sorts to Contrast Long and Short Vowels

Students in the early part of the within word pattern stage who may still have problems distinguishing between spoken short and long vowel sounds benefit from a picture sort. Picture sorts develop phonemic awareness and focus attention on the sound without the support of the printed word. They might be used for just one day and then followed up with word sorts.

1. Select 10 to 14 pictures for one short vowel and its corresponding long vowel from the picture sets that come with this book. These can be arranged in a template that students can later sort on their own or pasted on index cards for a group sort. Prepare headers such as "Short e" and "Long e" and decide on a picture that will be a key word. *Bed* and *feet* are good headers used in many sorts and can be found on a sound board in Appendix B.
2. Set up the headers and explain to the students that they will be listening to the vowel sound in the middle of each word that names the pictures. Some words have the short *e* sound as in *bed*. (Isolate the vowel by peeling off the initial consonant and then the final consonant: *bed, ed, e*). Some words will have the long *e* sound as in *feet* (*feet, eet, ee*).
3. Model several pictures: "Here is a sheep. Listen to the vowel: *sh-eeeee-p*. Will I put that under *bed* or *feet?* Yes, *sheep* has the long vowel sound in the middle just like *feet. F-eeee-t, sh-eeee-p;* they both have the *eeeee* sound in the middle."
4. Students should sort the remaining pictures. Then check the sort by naming the pictures in each column and ask the students why they sorted as they did.
5. Give the students their own set of pictures to sort and observe to see how accurately they sort. *Do not expect students to spell these words* because they have not been working with the printed forms.

Teacher-Directed Two-Step Sort for Long Vowels

One basic procedure is a two-step sort that begins with sound and moves to pattern. The example that follows is similar to the sort done by Ms. Watanabe but contrasts short *a* and long *a* sounds and patterns. This teacher-directed sort starts with one set of words that everyone uses, after which students use their own sets at their seats.

1. Use a prepared sort or words from the list in Appendix E, selecting about seven short *a* words, seven long *a* words that are spelled with the CVVC pattern (*rain, pail*), and seven with the CVCe pattern (*cake, tape*). Include one or two oddballs that do not fit the expected sound or pattern (*was* or *said*, for example). Short *a* and long *a* pictures (e.g., *cat* and *cake*) may be used as sound headers. Prepare word cards or write the words randomly on a word study handout template for students to cut apart for independent sorting. Prepared sorts can be found on the website.

2. Introduce the sort by reading the words together and talking about any whose meaning may be unclear. If there are homophones like *tale* and *tail*, talk about what each means. Invite students to make observations about the words: "What do you notice?"

3. Introduce the cat and cake key words for the sound sort. Say, "Listen to the vowel sound in the middle of *cat*. What vowel sound do you hear? *Cat* has a short *a*." Repeat with *cake*. Then model how to sort a few words by the sound of the vowel in the middle and then ask the students to help you finish the sort. Warn them that there are a few oddballs with neither a short nor long vowel sound and challenge students to be on the lookout for them. As they are identified, set the oddballs off to the side. Read all the words in each column to check them and verify that they all have the same sound.

Go to PDToolkit for *Words Their Way*, click on the Sorts and Games tab, then type "Long Vowel Sorts."

4. After discussing the two sound categories, ask students to look for patterns in the long *a* column and separate them into two subcategories. Talk about how the words in each column have different spelling patterns and why the oddballs do not fit. Point out that the words with a silent *e* fit the CVCe pattern: a consonant, a vowel, another consonant, and the silent *e*. Repeat for the CVVC pattern and contrast with the CVC words in the short vowel category. Decide on key words for new headers from among the word cards and underline them or add labels for CVC, CVCe, and CVVC.

5. Keep the headers in place and scramble the words to sort a second time. Do not make any corrections until the end. Check each column by reading the words and review how the words in each column are alike by sound and by pattern. If a mistake has been made, ask the students to find it. Talk about why the oddballs don't fit and review the homophones once more. The final categories will look something like the following sort.

CVC	CVCe	CVVC	
cat	*cake*	*rain*	was
gas	game	tail	said
back	lake	chain	
has	cape	paint	
camp	tale	pain	
tack	trade	train	

6. Students need their own sheet of words to cut apart and sort. Remind students to scribble on the back or draw three stripes in a color they can recognize if a word card is lost. Some teachers ask students to quickly initial each word card instead. Identify the headers and ask students to sort under teacher observation. After sorting, check and reflect and then ask students to shuffle the words and store them for activities on subsequent days.

Open Sorts

After students are familiar with listening for vowel sounds and looking for the patterns, they can be challenged by open-ended sorts such as the following. The open sort starts with everyone sorting their own set of words. Remind them to mark the back with an assigned color or initial so the words don't get mixed up.

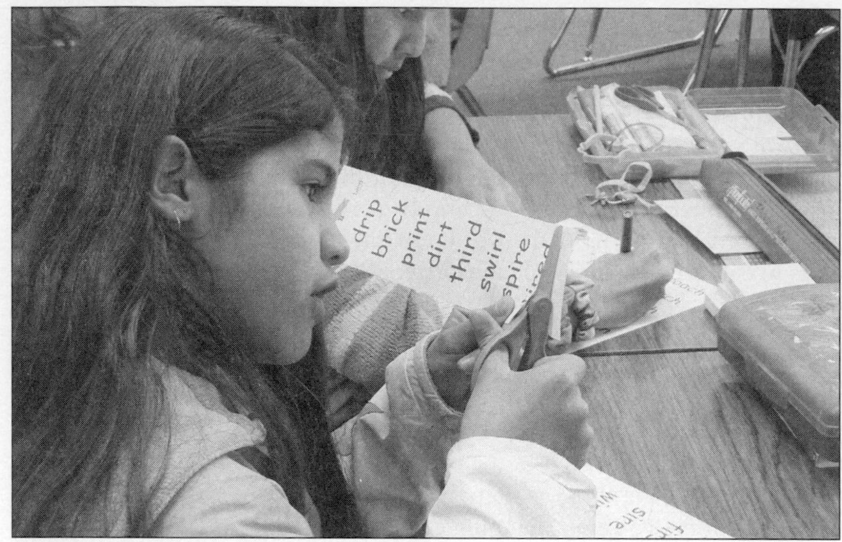

1. Use a prepared sort or select about 20 words that are spelled with *ir* (*bird*), *ire* (*fire*), or *ier* (*drier*). Look for words that your students should already know how to read. You may also include one or two oddballs that have the same sound but not the same spelling pattern or vice versa (*fur* and *their*, for example). Write the words randomly on a word study handout template for students to cut apart.

2. Introduce the sort by reading the words together and talking about any whose meaning may be unclear. Then ask, "Can you figure out how to sort these words?" Invite students to make observations, discover the categories, and find the oddballs. Call on different students to describe the rationale for their sorts. Accept all reasonable categories but come to an agreement about whether to sort by sounds or patterns or both.

3. Agree on key words and underline them to use as headers. Then ask all the students to sort the same way. The categories will look something like the following sort. Discuss the categories and oddballs with open-ended questions such as "What do you notice about the words in each column?" Ask students to identify the homophones (*fir and fur*) and define or use them in sentences.

bird		**fire**	**drier**	
fir	swirl	wire	pliers	fur
first	chirp	tire	flier	their
dirt	skirt	hire	crier	
third	twirl			
birth	stir			
shirt	firm			

4. Ask the students to scramble their words and sort a second time. Shuffle and store the words for sorting activities on subsequent days.

Sequence and Pacing of Word Study in the Within Word Pattern Stage

The sequence of word study in the within word pattern transitional stage begins by taking a step back with a review of short vowel sounds as they are compared with long vowel sounds in CVCe words. Then the focus shifts to other common and less common long vowel patterns and *r*-influenced vowel patterns. Ambiguous vowels and complex consonant patterns are studied toward the end of the stage.

PDToolkit for Words Their Way™

Go to PDToolkit for *Words Their Way*, click on the Assessment Tools tab, then type "Primary Spelling Inventory" or "Elementary Spelling Inventory."

EARLY, MIDDLE, OR LATE PLACEMENT. Identifying whether students are in the early, middle, or late part of the stage (see Table 6.1) will help you target where in the sequence of features to begin word study instruction. After administering a spelling inventory, consider your students' scores in the different categories of vowels.

Early. In the early within word pattern stage, students know blends and digraphs and spell most short vowels correctly. They are often experimenting with silent letters that mark long vowels. The final silent *e* is the most common pattern and the most likely to turn up first. might be used but confused when spelling short vowels (*job* as JOBE) or long vowel patt (FLOTE for *float*). If students spell fewer than two of the CVCe long vowels correctly are probably in the early part of the stage.

Middle. By the middle of this stage, students are spelling the vowels with the CVCe pa correctly but still making errors on the less common long vowel patterns as well as other vowels such as *r*-influenced vowels and ambiguous vowels.

Late. By the end of this stage, students will have mastered the long vowel patterns but will be making a few errors in the other vowels—*r*-influenced and ambiguous. They may also be missing some of the complex consonants studied in the late within word pattern stage.

PACING. Table 6.3 suggests contrasts and a sequence of word study under three possible pacing guides in the early, middle, and late part of this stage. Pacing can be adjusted by adding more categories to a single sort (up to four or five) or by dropping back to fewer categories when students exhibit confusion. Because there is a lot to cover in this stage, two years is not too long to address the range of features for students of average achievement.

Pacing will depend on several factors: **developmental level**, grade level, and rate of progress. For early within word pattern spellers in late first or early second grade, an introductory pace is recommended. Start with some picture sorts to focus attention on the different short and long vowel sounds and then study the common CVCe pattern across four long vowels (long *e* is not studied because the CVCe pattern is rare in one-syllable words). During this introductory pace, students may be using word study notebooks for the first time and learning new sorting routines.

If you teach students beyond the primary grades who are still in the early part of this stage, there is a greater sense of urgency to catch them up with peers. The moderate pace is a good place to start, but monitor progress through observation and assessments to determine whether to go faster or slower. The first few vowels may take more time than those studied later. Students in the middle within word pattern stage might benefit from the fast pace outlined in the last column: a quick review of long vowels before going on to *r*-influenced and ambiguous vowels.

Many teachers are expected to use their school district's adopted phonics or spelling program and/or their district's core reading program. Although these published programs may follow a developmental sequence similar to the one in Table 6.3, they often set a pace that is too fast for low-achieving spellers and do not supply enough practice to master the features. To differentiate instruction at students' developmental levels, you must monitor progress and adjust the lessons by adding extra sorts for students who need a slower pace or skip some sorts to increase the pace when possible.

Keep in mind that the study of vowel patterns in single-syllable words lays a critical foundation for the study of two-syllable words in the next stage and cannot be shortchanged. Perhaps 25 percent of the adult population in the United States is stunted at this point of literacy proficiency. Even community college and university students who are poor spellers would benefit from beginning their word study with a review of vowel sounds and their spelling patterns (Massengill, 2006). It is important to take a step back and conduct word study activities that help them cement their knowledge of vowel patterns in single-syllable words to get a running start as they study two-syllable words. For many of these students, the fast pace in the third column of Table 6.3 may be appropriate.

The Study of High-Frequency Words

A number of spelling programs feature high-frequency or high-utility words. The authors of these programs argue that spelling instruction should focus on a small core of words students need the most, words such as *said, because, there, they're, friend,* and *again.* Unfortunately, this narrow view of word study ignores the relationship between reading and spelling

Table 6.3 Pacing and Sequence Guide for Within Word Pattern

SLOW INTRODUCTORY PACE	MODERATE PACE	ADVANCED PACE OR REVIEW
Use easy words with few blends or digraphs. Less common patterns may be oddballs.	Use oddballs and some words with blends and digraphs.	Use more words spelled with blends and digraphs, odd-balls, and less common patterns.
Early Within Word Pattern—Common and Less Common Long Vowels		
Long and short vowels in picture and word sorts Short *a, a-e* Short *i, i-e* Short *o, o-e* Short *u, u-e* Combine all CVC vs. CVCe Final *-k, -ck, -ke* Short *a, a-e, ai* Short *o, o-e, oa* Short *u, u-e, oo, ui* Short *e, ee, ea* Review CVVC across all vowels Short *a, a-e, ai, ay* Short *o, o-e, oa, ow* Short *u, u-e, ew, ue* Short *i, i-e, igh, y* VCC in *il, in, ol ,os*	Short *a, a-e* Short *i, i-e* Short *o, o-e* Short *u, u-e* Combine all CVC vs. CVCe Final *-k, -ck, -ke* *a-e, ai, ay* *o-e, oa, ow* *u-e, ui, oo, ew* *e, ee, ea* *i-e, igh, y* Review CVVC across vowels VCC in *ol, il, in*	*a-e, ai, ay* *ai, ay, ei, ey* *o-e, oa, ow* *u-e, ui, oo, ew* *ee, ea, ie* *i-e, igh, y* VCC in *ol, os, il, in*
Middle Within Word Pattern—*r*-Influenced Vowels		
Short *a, o, ar, or* Short *i, e, u ir, er, ur* *r*-Blends, *ar, ir, or* *a-e, are, air* *er, ere, eer, ear* *i-e, ire, ier* *o-e, oar, ore , oor* *ur, ure, ur-e, ea* *or, ur, ir* *w+or, w+ar*	*ar, are, air* *er, ear, eer* *ir, ire, ier* *or, ore, oar, w+or* *ur, ure, ur-e* *ar, or, w+ar, w+or*	*ar, are, air, w+ar* *er, ear, eer* *ir, ire, ier* *or, ore, oar, w+or* *ur, ure, ur-e*
Late Within Word Pattern—Diphthongs and Other Ambiguous Vowels		
Long *o, oi, oy* *oo* (*boot, book*) Short *o, ou, ow* *oi, oy, ou, ow* Short *a, al, aw* *al, au, aw* Review *ow, ew, aw*	*oi, oy* *aw, au* *wa, al, ou* *ou, ow*	*oi, oy, ou, ow* *al, au, aw, w+a*

Table 6.3 Continued

SLOW INTRODUCTORY PACE	MODERATE PACE	ADVANCED PACE OR REVIEW
Complex Consonants		
kn, wr, gn	*kn, wr, gn*	*shr, thr, str, squ*
sh, shr, th, thr	*thr, shr, squ*	Hard/soft *g* and *c*
scr, str, spr	*scr, str, spr, spl*	*dge, ge, tch, ch*
spl, squ	Hard/soft *g* and *c*	
Hard/soft *c* and *g*	*dge, ge*	
dge, ge	*ch, tch*	
ch, tch	*ce, se, ve, ze*	
ce, se, ve, ge		
Miscellaneous		
Contractions	Contractions	
Plurals	Plurals	
Homophones	Homophones	
Irregular vowels		

and reduces spelling to a matter of brute memorization. It offers students no opportunity to form generalizations that can extend to the reading and spelling of thousands of unstudied words.

Many high-frequency words do not follow common spelling patterns but can be included in within word pattern sorts as oddballs. For example, the word *said* is usually examined with other words that have the *ai* pattern, such as *paid, faint,* and *wait.* It becomes memorable because it stands alone in contrast to the many words that work as the pattern would suggest. It is also likely to be spelled correctly by most students because they have seen it so often when they read. Note that most of the top 200 most frequently occurring words (Dolch, 1942; Fry, 1980; Zeno, Ivens, Millard, & Duvvuri, 1996) are covered by the end of the within word pattern stage.

Some words in English, however, persist as problems for young writers. There are also some words students need to write frequently in the lower grades that are not included in the weekly lessons designed to meet their developmental needs. An example is the word *because*, which occurs often in the writings of first-graders. Many teachers will accept students' inventions for such words (BECUZ, BECALZ, BECAWS), but some teachers grow tired and concerned about such errors, especially beyond the primary grades. Although we feel confident that such errors will be worked out over time with developmentally paced instruction, there are sometimes good reasons to address them sooner.

Some teachers study about five high-frequency words a week as part of word wall activities (Cunningham, 2008). An alternative is to have a weeklong unit of high-frequency words several times a year. In either case, studying high-frequency words should not replace the developmental study of words by features, but rather should supplement such study. The words chosen should be few in number and consist of highly functional words seen in your students' own writing. They should also not be too far in advance of your students' developmental levels. Words that students need for short periods of time such as *Thanksgiving, leprechaun,* and *tyrannosaurus* can simply be posted for easy reference and are not appropriate spelling words for students who are still learning to spell one-syllable words.

Go to PDToolkit for *Words Their Way,* click on the Videos tab, then type "Weekly Schedules and Activities in the Within Word Pattern Stage, Part I." Watch students in Ms. Flores's second grade classroom record high-frequency words in personal dictionaries.

The following guidelines will help when planning the study of high-frequency words:

1. Select 6 to 10 words for one week of each nine-week period for a total of 24 to 40 words a year. (Short weeks of two to three days might be good for these.) A list developed in a second grade class might include *know, friend, again, our, went, would,* and *once.* Students can take part in this selection by choosing words they have difficulty spelling or by choosing words from the teacher's master list. A cumulative list of these words in alphabetical order should be posted in the room for reference, with the understanding that students are expected to spell those words correctly in all their written work once they have been studied. Individual student copies of these words in alphabetical order can also be created and added to as words accumulate. Students may place the individual lists in their writing workshop folders or in a section of their word study notebooks.

2. Develop routines such as the following to help students examine and study the words carefully.

   - *Introduction and discussion.* As the teacher writes the words on the board, the students copy them on their own paper in a column. (Be sure that everyone copies correctly!) The teacher should then lead a discussion about each word. "What part of this word might be hard to remember and why?" (For the word *friend,* the discussion would focus on the fact that it has a silent *i.*) "What might help you remember how to spell this word?" (Students might note that it ends with *end.*)
   - *Self-corrected test method.* After each word has been written and discussed, students should fold their paper over so that the list is covered. The teacher calls the words aloud while the students write them again. The students then check their own work by unfolding the paper to compare what they copied to what they spelled. Any words spelled incorrectly should be rewritten. The self-corrected text method to support memorization has been well researched (Horn, 1954; Templeton & Morris, 2000).
   - *Self-study method.* The self-study method is a long-standing activity that appears in most published spelling books. This process can be used independently after students are taught the steps: (1) Look at the word and say it; (2) cover the word; (3) write the word; (4) check the word; and (5) write the word again if it is spelled incorrectly.
   - *Practice test.* The words are called aloud. Students spell each word and then immediately check it by looking at the chart posted in the room. Students become familiar with using the chart as a reference and can call the words to each other in pairs or small groups, or the teacher may lead the practice test.
   - *Final test.* The chart is covered and students spell the words as they are called aloud. Because the number of words is kept low, the chance of 100 percent success is high. Once students have been tested they are responsible for those words from then on. The teacher will undoubtedly need to remind students often to reread a piece of written work to check for the posted words in the editing stage. Students will have about eight weeks to work at getting any problematic words under control; any word that continues to be a problem can reappear on the next list.

for Words Their Way™

Go to PDToolkit for *Words Their Way,* click on the Videos tab, then type "Weekly Schedules and Activities in the Within Word Pattern Stage, Part II." Watch as Ms. Flores meets with each group for a spelling test of the words from their sorts.

Assess and Monitor Progress in the Within Word Pattern Stage

By the end of second grade, most students should be well into the middle of the within word pattern stage or beyond. Students who are not should be getting carefully planned systematic word study in supplemental interventions. There are several ways to monitor progress of students in the within word pattern stage.

Weekly Spelling Tests

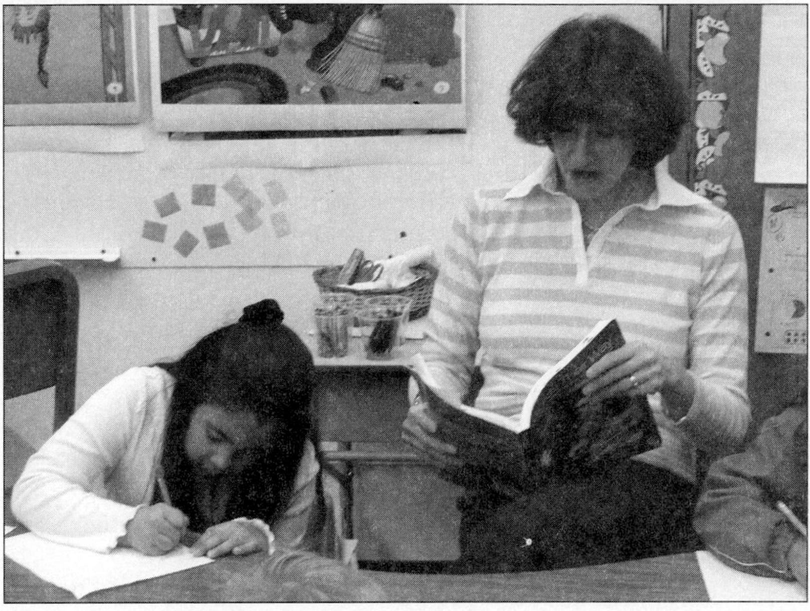

In this stage we recommend weekly spelling tests as a way to both monitor progress and to make students accountable for their learning. Select ten words from the sort and call them out in a traditional way. Many teachers also call out one or two transfer words, words that fit the features but that were not included in the sort. Students might be prompted to use analogy by saying something like "If you know how to spell *rain*, then you can spell *stain*." When students are appropriately placed they should score 90 to 100 percent on these weekly assessments. If they do not, you should reconsider the placement or pacing of instruction. Also consider whether students are getting enough practice with the words across a week. We also recommend designing your weekly spelling test as a **blind writing sort,** having students sort the words as they write them. This will reward the kind of thinking about sound, pattern, and meaning that is the whole point of word study. Give one point for the correct spelling and a second point for the correct grouping.

Unit Assessments and Goal Setting

Teachers often observe that students study for weekly tests and then forget the words when they need them for real writing (Gill & Scharer, 1996; Graham, Morphy, Harris, Fink-Chorzempa, Saddler, Moran, & Mason, 2008; Schlagal, 2007). For this reason, we recommend periodic unit spell checks to determine whether the words and features are being retained over time. Spell checks have been developed for each of the major units of study and can be found on the website and in *Words Their Way™: Word Sorts for Within Word Pattern Spellers.* Teachers can easily create their own spell checks to use every three to six weeks by selecting words from the word sorts to assess retention of studied words and perhaps adding additional transfer words to see whether students can apply their growing knowledge of sounds and patterns to unstudied words. Use these spell checks to monitor progress and fine-tune your instructional pacing. Depending on results, you may find you need to drop back to a slower pace or conversely ratchet up to a quicker pace, as suggested in Table 6.3.

Students in the within word pattern stage can be involved in setting their own goals using the forms described in Chapter 2. This is especially beneficial for students who struggle with spelling and need to see their own progress.

PDToolkit
for Words Their Way™

Go to PDToolkit for *Words Their Way,* click on the Videos tab, then type "Professional Development with 2nd Grade Teachers." Listen as the teachers meet with their literacy leader, Ms. Simeral, to discuss instruction and students' progress.

Word Study with English Learners in the Within Word Pattern Stage

When planning word study with English learners it is important to know something about their native languages and what literacy experiences they have had. Students who are literate in their first language may spell the sounds they hear in English with the letter–sound correspondences they know from their first language, or if the sounds do not exist they will substitute close approximations. Knowing something about students' native languages and writing systems is helpful so teachers can guide comparisons and understand the difficulties English learners face.

Teaching Vowels to English Learners

for **English Learners**

As hard as vowels are for English-speaking children, they can be truly challenging for English learners because many vowel sounds in English do not exist in other languages (Bear, Templeton, Helman, & Baren, 2003; Helman, 2004). Let's use Spanish as an example because it is the second most commonly spoken language in the United States. Unlike English, the vowels of Spanish have only one sound for each letter. Some of the correspondences are the same as English, but others are different. For example, *o* and *u* represent long *o* and long *u* as in *uno*. However *i* represents the long *e* sound as in *amigo* or *si* and *e* represents a sound that is close to long *a* as in *tres* /trās/. The letter *a* is the only vowel in Spanish that is close to a short vowel sound in English: "ah" (/ŏ/) as in *la*. Table 6.4 shows some of the spelling errors students who are literate in Spanish might make, such as spelling *job* as JAB.

Vowel pairs do occur in Spanish but no vowel is truly silent as they often are in English. The combination *ai*—pronounced "ah-ee"—is close to English long *i*. In vowel combinations such as *uo* ("oo-oh") or *ei* ("ay-ee"), both vowels are pronounced although one is often weaker than the other. The diphthong *oy* or *oi* ("oh-ee") is pronounced the same in Spanish and English.

For students who have learned to spell in Spanish there will be some predictable confusions such as using *e* for long *a*, as in LEK for *lake* or *ai* for long *i* as in NAIT for *night*. See Table 6.4 for more examples. In addition, students literate in Spanish expect each vowel sound to be represented. What English speakers think of as a single long vowel is actually sometimes pronounced as a diphthong as in "pi-e" (*pie*) or "lay-eek" (*lake*)—depending on one's dialect. Spanish speakers may be more sensitive to subtle vowel sounds and overanalyze them, spelling *float* as FLOUT—"floh-oot" (Helman et al., 2012).

Other Romance languages, such as French, also represent long *a* with *e* (*tres*) and long *e* with *i* (*merci*). Four to five hundred years ago English strayed from the original continental pronunciation of vowels and has, over time, changed or dropped the pronunciation of one vowel in combinations such as *ai*, *oa*, *ea*, or *ui*, so that the second vowel is now silent.

Table 6.4 Vowels in Spanish and Predictable Spelling Errors

LETTERS	COMPARABLE SOUND IN SPANISH	SPANISH EXAMPLES	POSSIBLE SPELLING ERRORS IN ENGLISH
a	/ŏ/ "ah"	*papa, madre, casa*	*job* as JAB
e	/ā/ "ay"	*tres*	*lake* as LEK or LEIK
i	/ē/ "ee"	*si, mi, amigo*	*reach* as RICH
ai	/ī/ "eye"	*aire*	*night* as NAIT
o	/ō/ "oh"	*uno, loco*	*float* as FLOT or FLOUT
u	/ū/ "oo" (never "yoo")	*uno, tu, mucho*	*tune* as TUN

Source: Adapted from *Words Their Way™ with English Learners: Word Study for Phonics, Vocabulary, and Spelling Instruction* (2nd ed.), by Lori Helman, Donald R. Bear, Shane Templeton, Marcie Invernizzi, and Francine Johnston. Boston: Pearson/Allyn & Bacon.

Strategies for Teaching and Assessing English for English Learners

Some English learners are able to memorize many words, but their strategies for spelling unknown words often indicate that their orthographic knowledge could be deeper. For example, a student memorized the spelling of *rain* but continued to spell unknown long *a* words with an *e* (*train* as TREN), using the Spanish spelling of the long *a* sound as in Table 6.4. When it seems that students' spelling of sight words is ahead of their more conceptually based orthographic knowledge, use a moderate or introductory pace when following the sequence of word study in Table 6.3. The spelling errors in uncorrected writing and spelling inventories described in Chapter 2 help us understand what word knowledge English learners bring to the task of reading and writing English.

Go to PDToolkit for *Words Their Way*, click on the Assessment Tools tab, then type "Spanish Spelling Inventory."

There may be times when you want to assess students' spelling development in their primary languages. There is a Spanish inventory on the website and inventories for Spanish, Chinese, and Korean are available in *Words Their Way™ with English Learners*. These inventories will help you find out what students know about their own written language. The more literate students are in their first language, the more information there is to transfer to learning to read in English (Proctor, August, Carlo, & Snow, 2006).

Word sorting lessons are an explicit way to draw English learners' attention to both the similarities and differences between languages in terms of sounds and spelling as well as helping to build vocabulary. The following suggestions can enhance the effectiveness of your word study with English learners:

- Be prepared to understand and talk about differences in sounds and spelling between languages whenever possible. You can gather information about many of the languages you are likely to encounter in your classroom from searching online resources.
- Reduce the number of words in a sort so students will not be overwhelmed with too many new vocabulary words.
- Pair words and pictures when possible. Long and short vowel pictures are included in the pictures that come with this book; more images can be downloaded from the Internet (e.g., Google images).
- Discuss the meanings of the words in the introductory lesson and throughout the week as needed. Act out words when appropriate and supply photographs or drawings to develop meaning.
- Students can illustrate words in their word study notebooks or add a small drawing or definition to the back of the word cards to remind them of meaning. See Figure 6.6.
- Spend extra time reading the words in columns aloud as students check their sorts.
- Pair English learners with native English speakers who can supply pronunciations of the words in partner sorts.
- Model careful pronunciation but do not be overly concerned if English learners do not master the correct pronunciations.

Go to PDToolkit for *Words Their Way*, click on the Videos tab, then type "Short *a* and Long *a*" to see English learners as they discuss the meanings and pronunciations of words before sorting.

For further information on these recommendations, refer to *Words Their Way™ with English Learners*.

FIGURE 6.6 Simple Drawings Help English Learners Associate Meaning with Spelling

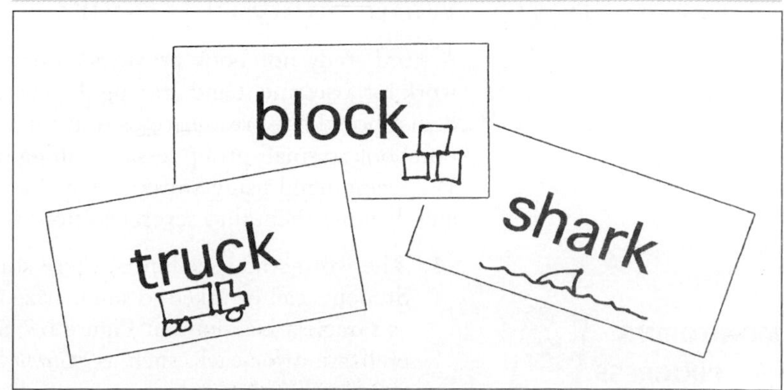

The Influence of Dialects

Some students, including many English learners, speak with dialects in which the pronunciations of long vowels are quite different from standard pronunciations. However, Cantrell (2001) found that Appalachian students' pronunciations of long vowels changed as a result of word study; the more they read in English, the more "standardized" their speech became. Eventually, students with other dialects and first languages acquire a literate register that reflects their expanded knowledge about English spelling, pronunciation, academic vocabulary, and characteristics of texts.

Teachers need to accept variations in pronunciation due to individual and regional dialectical differences. This means that some students will sort words by sound a little differently than the teacher or other classmates, but there is no harm in this. Let students sort by sound in ways that make sense to them, and observe what students do differently but consistently. After focusing on sounds in sorts, students turn to the patterns of the words. The goal is for students to associate patterns with their own pronunciations.

Occasionally, disputes arise among the students about whether words are oddballs. Some students may pronounce *again* with a long *a*, whereas most say it with a short *i*. *Poem* has a long *o* to some students and an *oi* sound to others. Some people pronounce *bear* and *bar* as homophones. Teachers should treat these dialectical contrasts as variations, not as issues of right or wrong. You will find that the fourth grade social studies curriculum in many parts of the United States is a great place to discuss dialects as students study the diverse groups that have settled in their state.

WORD STUDY *Routines and Management*

Go to PDToolkit for *Words Their Way*, click on the Videos tab, then type "Weekly Schedules and Activities in the Within Word Pattern Stage, Part I." Watch Ms. Flores walk students through the weekly schedule for word study.

The within word pattern stage easily spans a number of grade levels, usually from first to fourth grades and beyond that for struggling readers. A typical third grade class will have students in the middle and late within word pattern stage as well as students in the next stage, syllables and affixes. Differentiation occurs when students meet in small groups in which sorts are introduced and discussed under the guidance of the teacher. However, after that, everyone can engage in the same weekly routines described in Chapter 3 (blind sorts, writing sorts, word hunts, speed sorts, homework). Figure 3.20 (p. 79) shows a two-week schedule for students in the within word pattern stage and Figure 3.22 (p. 80) offers some variations on these. Once students learn the schedule and the routines they can work independently, with partners, or in small groups on most days of the week, freeing the teacher to meet with instructional-level reading groups. As in the letter name–alphabetic stage, teachers find that their reading groups are usually the same as their word study groups.

Vocabulary instruction is usually not differentiated unless it involves words from the weekly sort or words that turn up in reading groups. Instead, vocabulary instruction usually takes place in whole-groups settings, during read-alouds and content area instruction.

Word Study Notebooks in the Within Word Pattern Stage

A word study notebook provides an organizational structure and documentation of student work for assessment and grading. It is used across the week for a number of activities and students should have ready access to it throughout the day. Students can be asked to bring their notebook to small-group sessions, along with reading materials and response journals or logs. We recommend using sturdy stitched composition notebooks with a hard marbleized cover and dividing them into several sections set off with a tab or Post-it note:

1. The word study section is where students record their weekly sort and other activities. Students can be asked to summarize what they learn from their sorts in their own words, as Graciela has done in Figure 6.7 She has numbered each column and written a generalization for each, such as "*Climb* is the same as *bind*, *wind*, and *hind*." These written reflections help teachers assess students' progress.

FIGURE 6.7 A Page from Graciela's Word Study Notebook

Graciela
10/22

I that say his name

shine	climb	sky	right	wind
bite		try	slight	find
slide		my	sigh	blind
slime	2	3	night	hind
spine				
1			4	
				5

1. This word Say i by the e at the end.
2. Climb is the same as bind, wind, and hind.
3. a i tarn's into an y.
4. The i is with gh we can not hear it.
5. This word all got an i-n-d.

2. The vocabulary section of the word study notebook is where students will record words from their reading or from content area instruction. When reading *Stuart Little*, for example, some students might be encouraged to make lists of boat terms (*rigging, bow, stern*) or weather-related words (*squall, breeze, mist*). These words can be shared and then combined and sorted into semantic categories, or added, where possible, to the spelling sorts (e.g., *breeze* could be added to a long *e* category of *ee* patterns). Students might create a science web on pandas, make a list of concepts related to immigration, or compare and contrast geometric terms.
3. A third section might be an ongoing list of homophones, homographs, and polysemous (multiple meaning) words, with sentences or pictures to illustrate the different meanings of the words.

Word Hunts

To help students see the connection between word study and reading, ask them to go through what they have recently read to find words that fit the particular sound or pattern they are studying. The common vowel patterns will turn up frequently in most reading materials, but you may also find decodable text or **phonics readers** that focus on a particular pattern useful for word hunts. Although word sorts are usually limited to one-syllable words in this stage, two- and three-syllable words are welcome additions in a word hunt (e.g., *ai* in *rainbow* or *painted*). Such words often extend generalizations into more difficult vocabulary as well as offer opportunities for applying knowledge of vowel patterns to the decoding of longer words in texts. The results of word hunts can be recorded on charts and/or in word study notebooks. In addition, students should be challenged to always be on the lookout for new words that they might add to earlier sorts. In this way, sounds and patterns are constantly revisited.

FIGURE 6.8 Word Study Homework Checklist

Word Study at Home Name ____________________________

Check off the activities you complete and return this to your teacher.

_____ Sort the words into the same categories you did in school.

_____ Write the words into categories.

_____ Blind sort with someone at home.

_____ Write the words into categories as someone calls them aloud.

_____ Hunt for more words that fit the categories and write them here:

Parent's Signature __________________

Homework

In Figure 3.24 in Chapter 3, there is a letter for parents describing homework routines for each day of the week. These routines are especially appropriate for within word pattern spellers for whom homework will provide much needed extra practice. A checklist such as the one in Figure 6.8 can be sent home with an extra copy of the words for the week. Everything can go into an envelope or plastic zip bag. Students might be allowed to choose two or three activities and more options can be added to the checklist occasionally, such as using a small number of words in sentences.

Resources and Games

A search of the World Wide Web provides a variety of related free or for-purchase materials that teachers can use in the classroom or students can access at home. (Search "word study," "phonics," or the actual feature you want to study.) Spellingcity.com allows you to type in your own word lists for a variety of games and the BBC offers game-oriented software. Another site for resources is maintained by Sadlier-Oxford.

RESOURCES FOR IMPLEMENTING WORD STUDY *in Your Classroom*

There are a number of materials available to help you implement word study with students in the within word pattern stage.

- Word lists in Appendix E, as well as suggested sorts in Appendix D can be used with the template on page 398 to create your own sorts.
- Prepared sorts, spell checks, and games are available on the website. With the Create Your Own feature you can make your own variations of sorts and games by selecting pictures and words to add to templates.
- *Words Their Way™: Word Sorts for Within Word Pattern Spellers* provides a complete curriculum of 50 sorts divided into ten units. The spell checks that are supplied for each unit can be used for pretesting to better identify what students are ready to study and for posttesting to monitor progress.

ACTIVITIES FOR THE WITHIN WORD PATTERN STAGE

In this section, games and other activities extend and reinforce students' understandings after they have sorted the words multiple times and reflected on the sounds and patterns. Many games from the previous chapter—particularly the ones marked with the Adaptable for Other Stages logo—can be utilized with the features covered in this stage.

6.1 Word-O or Word Operations

This is an activity students can complete in their word study notebooks. It is especially appropriate for the within word pattern stage because it shows students how analogy can help them spell.

PROCEDURES Students are given a word (such as *cart*) and then asked to add, drop, or change one or two letters at a time to create a new word. Typically consonants, blends, and digraphs are exchanged at the beginning (*part, chart, smart*) or the end (*card*), but vowels can also be exchanged (*green, groan, grain*). Model this activity and show students how to use sound boards as in Appendix B for ideas. Challenge students to see how many words they can form. Here is an example:

space pace place lace race trace track rack crack clack lack slack sack Mack mask ask task bask base vase case cast last lass glass grass brass brash trash crash cash

PDToolkit for Words Their Way™

Go to PDToolkit for *Words Their Way,* click on the Sorts and Games tab, then select Within Word Pattern and Games, where you will find many ready-to-use games and templates. Click the Create Your Own button if you would like to choose word cards to use with the games.

6.2 Train Station Game

This board game created by Janet Bloodgood is used to emphasize automaticity with common long vowels.

MATERIALS Use a basic follow-the-path board found in Appendix F, decorated as in Figure 6.9. Write in words that have been studied in word sorts as well as additional words that share

FIGURE 6.9 Train Station Game: Long Vowel Patterns

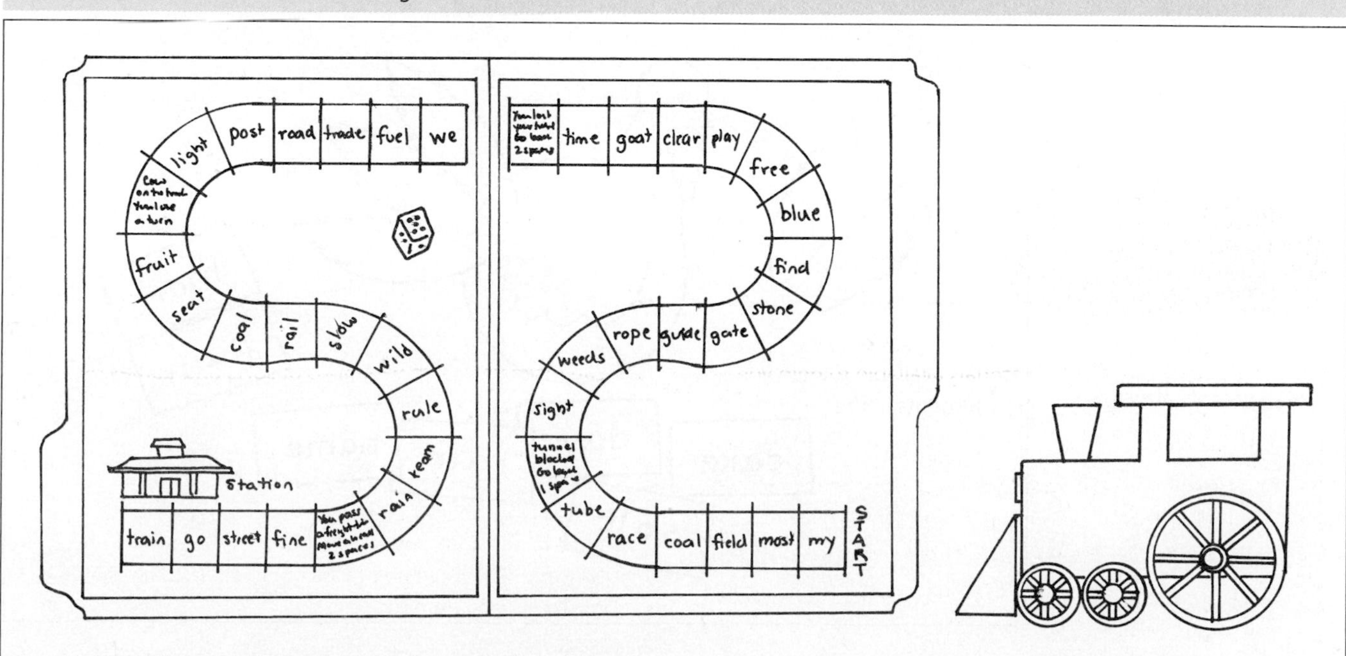

Go to PDToolkit for *Words Their Way*, click on the Sorts and Games tab, then select Within Word Pattern Stage and Games, where you will find many ready-to-use games and templates. Click the Create Your Own button if you would like to choose word cards to use with the games.

the same feature. Incorporate four special squares into the game board: (1) Cow on the track. Lose 1 turn. (2) You pass a freight train. Move ahead 2 spaces. (3) Tunnel blocked. Go back 1 space. (4) You lost your ticket. Go back 2 spaces.

PROCEDURES This game can be played with up to four students. Each child selects a game piece. The first child then spins or rolls the die and moves the appropriate number of spaces. Players pronounce the word they land on and identify the vowel. If students have studied the long vowel patterns within each long vowel, they can be asked to say the pattern. For example, "*Nail* is a long *a* with a CVVC pattern." In addition, the child must say another word containing the same vowel sound to stay on that space. Play continues in this fashion until someone reaches the station.

VARIATIONS Divide a spinner into five sections and label each with a vowel. Students move to the next word with the vowel sound they spin.

6.3 Turkey Feathers

In this game created by Marilyn Edwards, two players compare patterns across a single long vowel.

MATERIALS You will need two paper or cardboard turkeys without tail feathers, as in Figure 6.10; 10 construction paper feathers; and at least 20 word cards representing the long vowel studied (e.g., for long *a: a-e, ai,* and *ay*).

PROCEDURES

1. One player shuffles and deals five cards and five feathers to each player. The remaining cards are placed face-down for the draw pile.
2. Each player puts down pairs that match by pattern. For example, *cake/lane* would be a pair, but *pain/lane* would not. Each time a pair is laid down, the player puts one feather on his or her turkey.

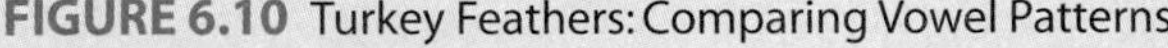

FIGURE 6.10 Turkey Feathers: Comparing Vowel Patterns

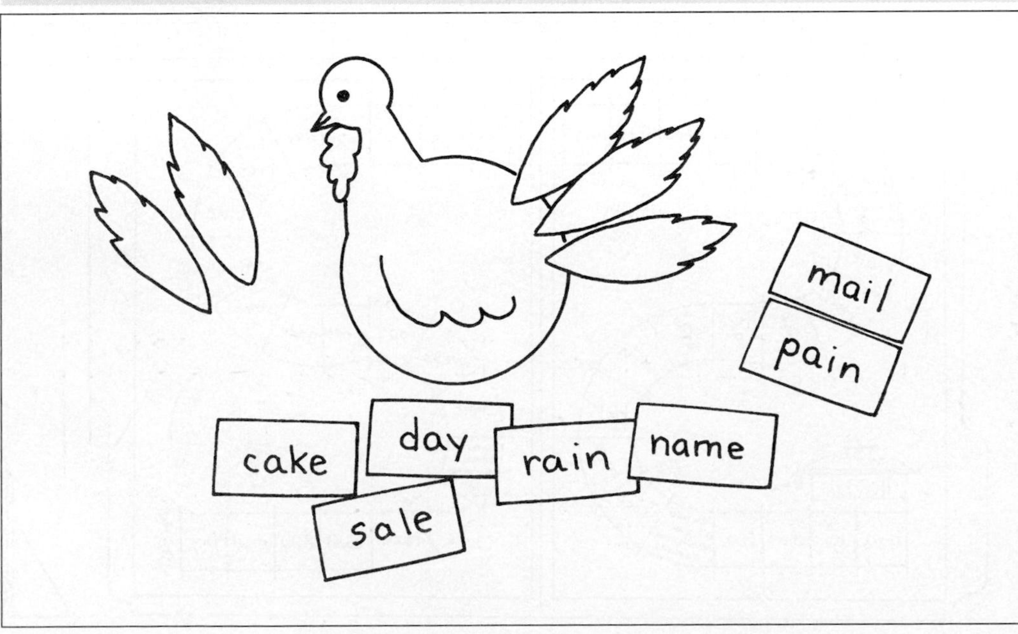

3. The dealer goes first, saying a word from his or her hand, and asks if the second player has a card with the same pattern.
4. If the second player has a matching pattern, the first player gets the card and lays down the pair and a feather; if not, the first player draws a card. If the player draws a card that matches any word in his or her hand, the pair can be discarded, and a feather is earned. The next player proceeds in the same manner.
5. The player using all five feathers first wins. If a player uses all the cards before earning five feathers, the player must draw a card before the other player's turn.

6.4 The Racetrack Game

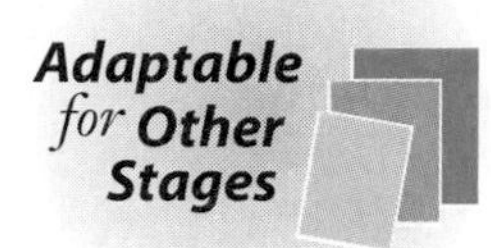

Darrell Morris (1982) developed this game, which has become a classic. It can be used for any vowel pattern and serves as a good review of the many patterns for the different vowels.

MATERIALS This game, for two to four players, is played on an oval race track divided into 20 to 30 spaces. It can be found in Appendix F and on the website. A sample game board appears in Figure 6.11. Different words following particular patterns are written into each space, except for a star drawn in two spaces. For example, *night, light, tie, kite, like, my, fly, wish,* and *dig* could be used on a game designed to practice patterns for long and short *i*. Prepare a collection of 40 to 50 cards that share the same patterns. A number spinner or a single die is used to move players around the track.

Go to PDToolkit for *Words Their Way,* click on the Sorts and Games tab, then type "Racetrack Game." Click the Create Your Own button to select words or pictures you would like to use with your game.

PROCEDURES

1. Shuffle the word cards and deal six to each player. Turn the rest face-down to become the deck. Playing pieces are moved according to the number on the spinner or die.
2. When players land on a space, they read the word and then look for words in their hands that have the same pattern. For example, players who lands on *night* may pull *sign* and

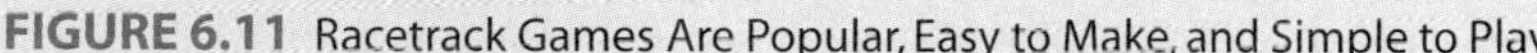
FIGURE 6.11 Racetrack Games Are Popular, Easy to Make, and Simple to Play

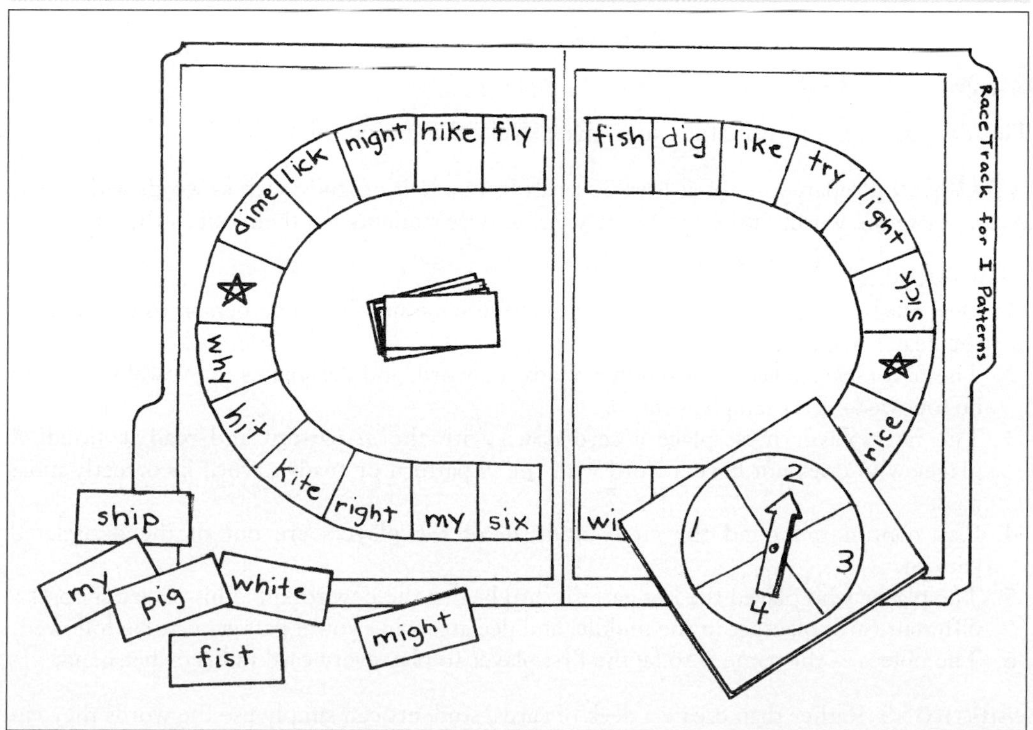

right to put in their point pile. If they move to a space with a star, they dispose of any oddballs they might have (such as *give*) or choose their own pattern.

3. Any cards played are replaced by drawing from the deck. A player who has no match for the pattern must draw a card anyway.
4. The game is over when there are no more cards to play. The winner is the player who has put down the most word cards.

6.5 The Spelling Game

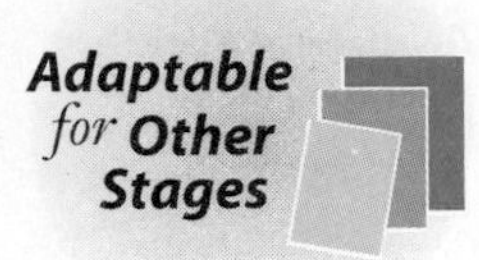

This game for two to four players can be used for any feature and is easily changed from week to week by simply replacing the word cards.

MATERIALS Use a follow-the-path game board, but leave the spaces blank except for several spaces where you may write directions such as Go Back 3 Spaces, Lose a Turn, and Go Ahead 2 Spaces. Add playing pieces and a spinner or die. Students use their own collections of words for the week.

PROCEDURES

1. Students each roll or spin. Whoever has the highest number will start and play proceeds clockwise.
2. The second player draws from the face-down stack of word cards. The player says the word to the first player, who must spell the word aloud. If players spell correctly, they can spin or roll to move around the path. Players who misspell the word cannot move.
3. The winner is the first one to get to the end of the path by landing on the space.

VARIATIONS This game can be used with word families, short vowels, and multisyllabic words, as well as the many one-syllable words explored in the within word pattern stage. Students in Nicole Doner's class created a game for strong verbs (e.g. *sleep*, *slept*, *draw*, *drew*, *came*, *come*). In this adaptation players drew a card with a verb and had to name the related verb and spell it on a dry erase board before claiming their space.

6.6 "I'm Out"

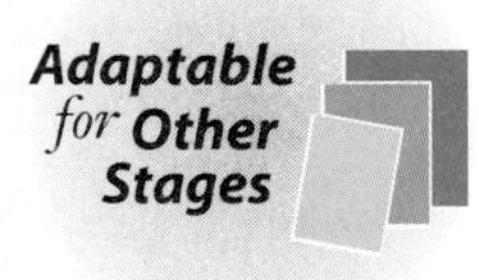

This card game is a favorite for two to five players; three is optimal.

MATERIALS Prepare a set of at least 30 cards from a unit of study such as words with *a*, *a-e*, *ay*, *ai*. Write the words at the top for easy visibility as students fan them out in their hands.

PROCEDURES

1. Deal all the cards so that each player gets the same number. The person to the right of the dealer begins.
2. The first player places a card down, reads the word, and designates the vowel pattern to be followed—for example, *rain–ai*.
3. The next player must place a card down with the *ai* pattern and read it aloud. A player who does not have a word with the *ai* pattern or reads a word incorrectly must pass.
4. Play continues around the circle until all of the players are out of the designated pattern.
5. The player who played the last pattern card begins the new round. This player chooses a different card, places it in the middle, and declares what vowel pattern is to be followed.
6. The object of the game is to be the first player to play every card in his or her hand.

VARIATIONS Rather than create a deck of cards, students can simply use the words they cut out for sorting. Combine two sets and deal them all out.

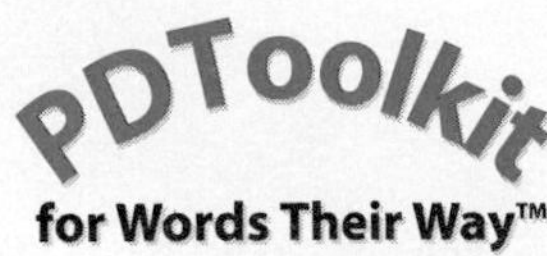

Go to PDToolkit for *Words Their Way*, click on the Sorts and Games tab, then select Within Word Pattern Stage and Games to choose a ready-made game or template. Next, click the Create Your Own button to select words or pictures you would like to use with your game.

6.7 Vowel Spin

Players spin for a feature (vowel sounds or vowel pattern) and remove pictures or words from their game boards that match the feature.

Adaptable for Other Stages

MATERIALS Make game boards divided like Tic-Tac-Toe as shown in Figure 6.12. The game can be played without the board by simply laying out the word cards in a three-by-three array. Make 30 or more word cards or picture cards that correspond to the feature students have been studying. You will also need a spinner divided into three to six sections and labeled with the vowel sounds or patterns to be practiced. You can find directions for making a spinner in Appendix F.

PROCEDURES

1. Put the cards in a deck face-down. Players draw nine cards and turn them face-up on their boards or in a three-by-three array.
2. The first player spins and removes the picture or word cards that fit the sound or pattern indicated by the spinner. The cards go into the player's point pile. That same player draws enough cards from the deck to replace the gaps on the playing board before play moves to the next player.
3. Play continues until a player is out of cards and there are no more to be drawn as replacements. The player who has the most cards in his or her point pile wins.

VARIATIONS Players prepare boards as described, but turn a winning card face-down as in a tic-tac-toe game instead of removing it. The winner is the first player to turn down three in a row. Blackout is a longer version of Tic-Tac-Toe. Players must turn over all their cards to win. A large die (one-inch square) can be made instead of a spinner. Use sticky dots to label the sides with the different features.

FIGURE 6.12 Vowel Spin Game: Finding Words to Match the Spinner

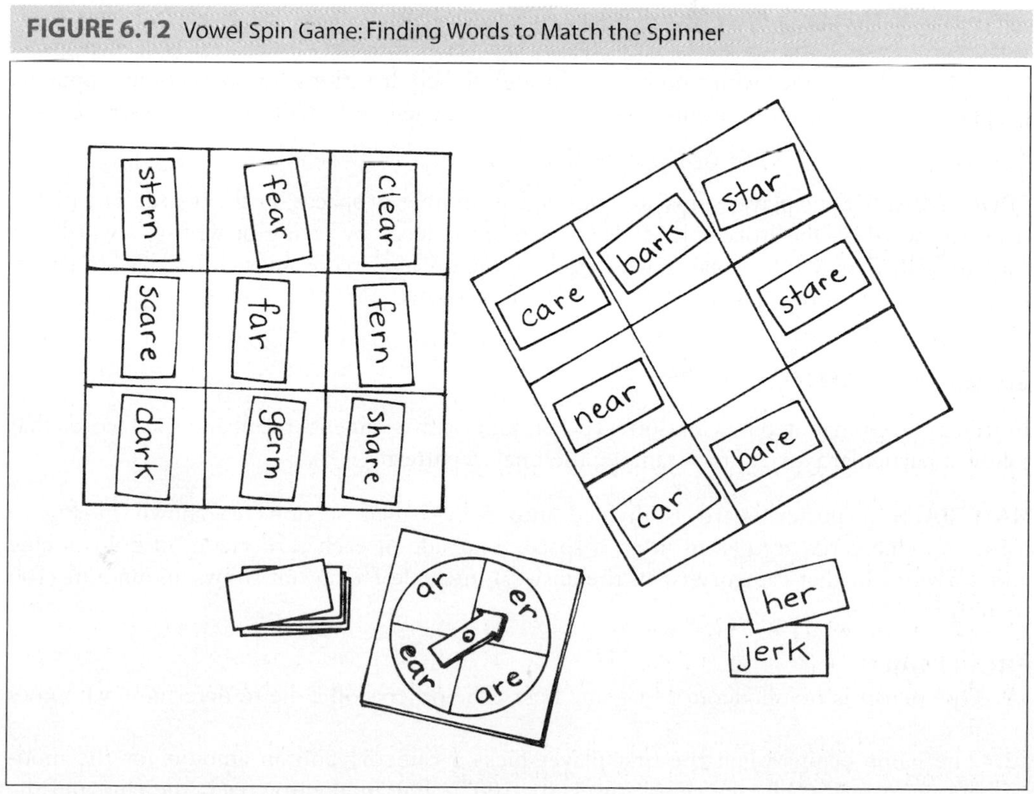

FIGURE 6.13 Board Game for *Sheep in a Jeep*

6.8 Sheep in a Jeep Game

Students should be familiar with *Sheep in a Jeep* (by N. Shaw, illustrated by M. Apple). In this game, created by Allison Dwier-Seldon, players examine the *ee* and *ea* patterns.

MATERIALS Prepare a game board using a follow-the-path template as shown in Figure 6.13. Write long *e* words from the book as well as other words with the same patterns in each space. You will need a spinner with numbers 1 through 4 (see directions for spinners in Appendix F), playing pieces to move around the board, and a pencil and small piece of paper for each player.

PROCEDURES One player spins and moves that number of spaces on the board. The player reads the word on the space and "adds a sheep to the jeep" by saying or writing a word that rhymes with that word. A player who reads the word incorrectly must move back a space. Players alternate turns. The first player to the finish wins.

6.9 Jeopardy Game

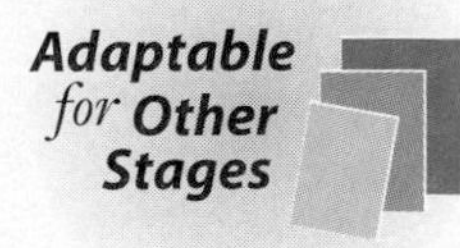

In this game contributed by Charlotte Tucker, four or five students recall and spell words that follow a particular pattern, for example, the final *ch* pattern.

MATERIALS A poster board is divided into 5-by-5-inch sections as shown in Figure 6.14, and clue cards are placed in each space. The side of each card facing in holds a clue about a word in that category (with the answer); the side facing out shows an amount (100 to 400).

PROCEDURES

1. One player is the moderator or game host. The others roll a die to determine who goes first.
2. The game begins when the first player picks a category and an amount for the moderator to read ("I'll take short vowels for 100"). The moderator reads the clue and the

FIGURE 6.14 Word Jeopardy Game

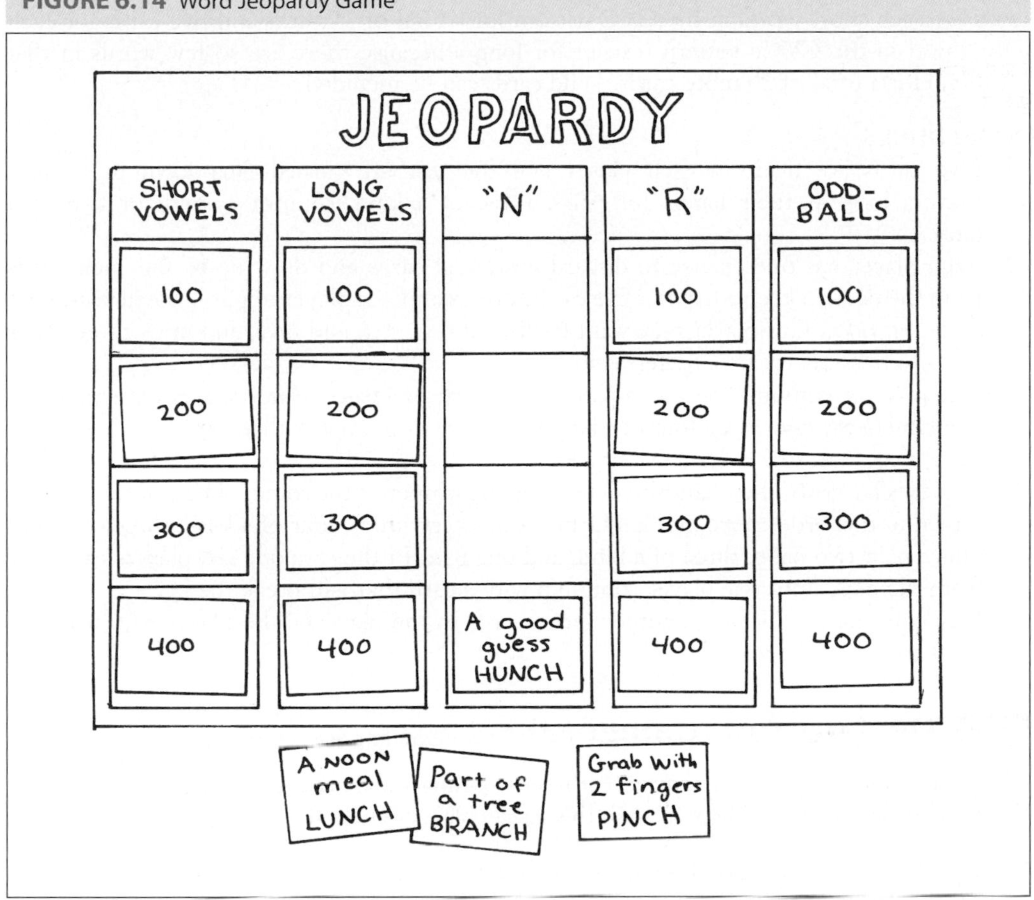

player must respond by phrasing a question and spelling the word, as in the following example.

Moderator: When struck, it produces fire.
Player: What is a match? *M-a-t-c-h.*

3. If the answer is correct, the player receives the card and chooses another clue. (A player can only have two consecutive turns.) If the player misses, the player to the left may answer.
4. The game continues until all the clue cards are read and won or left unanswered. Players add their points, and the one with the highest amount wins.

The following words could be used for a game reviewing *ch* and *tch*.

R	N	Short Vowels	Long Vowels	Oddballs
march	bench	stitch	beach	much
perch	lunch	watch	teach	such
porch	branch	sketch	roach	rich
torch	pinch	witch	coach	which

6.10 Vowel Poker Card Game

Up to four students practice grouping short and long vowel words by pattern. Thanks to Fran de Maio, who suggested this game.

MATERIALS A deck of 35 to 45 cards is needed. A good starting combination might be five cards for each short vowel in the CVC pattern for a total of 25 cards and five cards for each long vowel in the CVCe pattern (except for long *e* because there are so few words in that category) for a total of 20 more cards. Wild cards can be included.

PROCEDURES

1. Five cards are dealt to each player and the rest are turned face-down in a deck. Players look in their hands for pairs, three of a kind, four of a kind, or five of a kind.
2. Each player has one chance to discard unwanted cards and draw up to four new cards from the deck to keep a hand of five cards. For example, a player might be dealt *bone, rope, that, wet, rake*. This player may want to discard *that, wet*, and *rake*, and draw three other cards to possibly create a better hand.
3. The possible combinations are a pair (*that, camp*); two pairs (*that, camp, bone, rope*); three of a kind (*bone, rope, rode*); four of a kind (*bone, rope, rode, smoke*); three of a kind plus a pair (*bone, rope, rode, hat, rat*); or five of a kind.
4. Students lay down their hands to determine the winner of the round. The winner is determined in this order: Five of a kind (this beats everything), four of a kind, three of a kind plus a pair, two pairs, three of a kind, and one pair. In the case of a tie, players can draw from the deck until one player comes up with a card that will break the tie.
5. Play continues by dealing another set of cards to the players. The player who wins the most rounds is the victor.

6.11 Declare Your Category!

This card game for two to five players (three is optimal) works best with students who have had some experience playing games. In this game, players guess the first player's category.

MATERIALS Create a deck of 45 word cards with a variety of vowels and vowel patterns. Make at least four cards with any one pattern.

PROCEDURES

1. Seven cards are dealt to each player and the remainder are placed face-down in a deck. Players lay out their seven cards face-up.
2. The first player turns up a key card from the deck (*home*, for example) and looks for a word in his or her hand to match in some way. It might have the same sound and/or spelling pattern (either *o-e* or VCe). *Soap, bone*, or *gave* might be matched to *home*, for example. The match is laid down for all to see and the player announces, "Guess my category." Play moves to the next person, who must search his or her hand for a similar match. Players can pass when they wish. The player who started the category keeps the sorting strategy a secret. Play keeps going until the last player to put a card down declares the category.
3. If the person who set up the category does not think the next player has put down an acceptable card, he or she can send a card back and give that player another chance. Mistakes are discussed at the end of each round.
4. The player who plays the last card has to declare the category to win and keep all the cards. If the player is wrong, the previous player gets a chance to declare the category.
5. At the end of each round, students are dealt enough cards to get them back to seven. The winner of the round turns up a card from the pile and makes up the next category.
6. Play continues until the deck is empty. The player with the most cards wins.

VARIATIONS Add wild cards to the pile to change categories in midstream. The person who establishes a new category must guess the original category correctly. This player becomes the new judge: "Your category was by words with long *o* and the silent *e*. I am putting down my wild card and laying down *loan*. Guess my category." The rules of the game can be expanded to include semantic (e.g., types of birds) and grammatical (e.g., nouns) categories.

6.12 Word Study Pursuit

Adaptable *for* Other Stages

This game for four players was adapted from Trivial Pursuit by Rita Loyacono. It is easy to create variations of this game for different features.

MATERIALS You will need poster board, construction paper in four different colors, four envelopes, a die or spinner, and game piece markers. To construct the game board, glue 1½-inch squares of construction paper in four colors onto the poster board, alternating colors and making a trail from start to finish around the outside edge of the game board. Write words from a unit of study on cards cut from the same four colors and store them in envelopes marked by the corresponding color.

PROCEDURES

1. Players determine the order of play by spinning or tossing the die. The winner chooses a color and goes first; each player in turn selects a color.
2. Each player takes the packet of word cards corresponding to his or her color and calls one of these words out when another player lands on that color. Players landing on their own colors take another turn. A student landing on a space already occupied by another card must sort by pattern as well, placing a word that sounds alike and looks alike on top of the word or to the side if it sounds alike but does not look the same.

   For example, suppose Adam spins a 5 and lands on a green square. The person with the green packet calls out the word *dream*. Adam spells the word correctly, and the card is placed face-up on the square. Bonita takes a turn and also lands on the green square. After successfully spelling *queen*, she must decide if it is to be placed on top of the first word (follows the same pattern) or beside it (is a different pattern). She decides that *dream* and *queen* have the same long *e* sound but different patterns. In this way, students spell the words as well as sort them by pattern.
3. Players who misspell the word must go back one square and try a word from that color—provided it is not their own color (in which case they move back two squares). If players are unable to spell that word, they remain where they are and lose one turn. If players are unable to sort the word properly, they must move back one space (if it is not their color; if so, they move back two spaces), but do not lose a turn. The first player to get to the finish square is the winner and will be referee the next time.

VARIATIONS Because neither the game board nor the envelopes are marked, the board can be changed for any word patterns that are being studied. Having several sets of the game allows different groups of four students to play the same game while practicing different patterns.

6.13 Word Study Uno

This game is a version of the popular card game for three to four players created by Rita Loyacono.

MATERIALS Create a set of at least 27 word cards by writing words in the upper left corners of tagboard rectangles or blank cards. Include the patterns that you have been studying. For example, if students are studying long *o* patterns, create word cards that have *o-e*, *oa*, and *ow* combinations. Also create four wild cards and two of each of the following cards:

Skip *o-e*	Draw 2 *o-e*
Skip *ow*	Draw 2 *ow*
Skip *oa*	Draw 2 *oa*

PROCEDURES

1. Deal five cards to each player. The remaining cards are placed in a deck face-down and the top card is turned face-up to start the discard pile.
2. Players take turns playing cards that match the pattern of the face-up card or play one of the special cards (Skip, Draw 2, Wild). For example, if the beginning card is *boat*, the first player could put down *soap*, *road*, or *goat* or play a special card. The Skip card indicates that the next player loses a turn. The Draw 2 card forces the next player to pick two cards from the pile without playing any cards.
3. Skip and Draw 2 cards indicate the next pattern that must be played. When a Wild card is played, the player can select the category. A player who cannot put down a card must draw from the pile, and if the draw matches the pattern of the face-up card, it can be played.
4. A player who has only one card remaining must yell, "Uno." If the player forgets, another player can tell the player with one card to draw another card.
5. The first player to run out of cards wins the game.

6.14 Homophone Win, Lose, or Draw

Four or more students work in teams to draw and guess each other's words in a game that resembles charades. A list of homophones can be found in Appendix E. Barry Mahanes based this game on the television show.

PROCEDURES

1. Write homophone pairs on cards and shuffle.
2. Students divide into two equal teams, and one player from each team is selected as the artist for that round. The artist must draw a picture representing a given homophone, which requires understanding a homophone's spelling and meaning.
3. A card is pulled from the deck and shown simultaneously to the artists for both teams. As the artists draw, their teammates call out possible answers. When the correct word is offered, the artist calls on that team to spell both words in the pair.
4. A point is awarded to the team that provides the correct information first. The artist then chooses the next artist and play proceeds in the same fashion.

PDToolkit for Words Their Way™

Go to PDToolkit for *Words Their Way*, click on the Sorts and Games tab, then select Within Word Pattern Stage and Games to select a ready-to-use game or template. Next, click the Create Your Own button and choose words you would like to use with your games.

6.15 Homophone Rummy

This activity is suitable for two to six students. The object of the game is to get the most homophone pairs.

FIGURE 6.15 Homophone Rummy

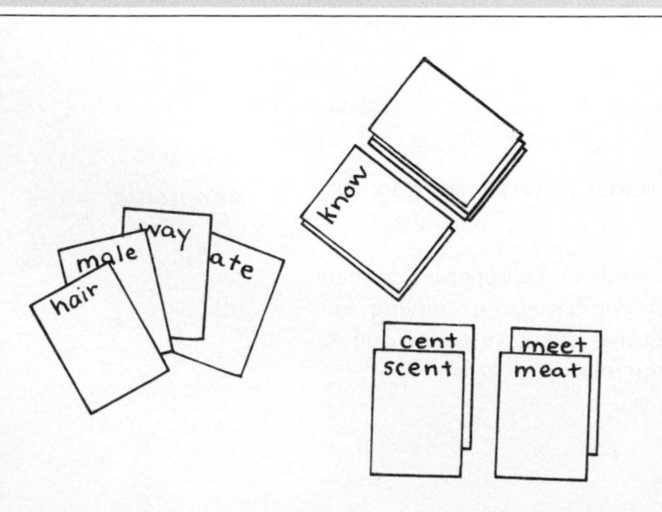

MATERIALS Prepare several decks of homophone pairs (52 cards, 26 pairs). A list of homophones can be found in Appendix E. Select words with which your students have some familiarity. Write the words in the upper left corner of the cards as shown in Figure 6.15.

PROCEDURES

1. Players are dealt seven cards and begin the game by checking their hands for already existing pairs. Pairs can be laid down in front of the player, who must give the meaning for each word or use it in a sentence that makes the meaning clear.
2. The remainder of the deck is placed in a central location and the first card is turned face-up beside it to form a discard pile.
3. The person on the left of the dealer goes first. Each player draws from either the deck or the discard pile. Any new pairs are laid down and defined. The

player must then discard one card to end the turn. *Note:* If a card is taken from the discard pile, all the cards below are also taken and the top card must be used to make a pair.

4. A player can be challenged by someone else disagreeing with the definitions. The person who challenges looks up the words in the dictionary. Whoever is right gets to keep the pair.
5. The game is over when one player has no cards left. That person yells, "Rummy!" Then the pairs are counted up to determine the winner.

6.16 Hink Pinks

Hink Pinks is a traditional language game that involves a riddle answered by a pair of rhyming words—for example, "What do you call a chubby kitty or an obese feline? (*fat cat*). What do you call an angry father? (*mad dad*). What do you call a plastic pond? (*fake lake*)." Hinky Pinky usually demands two-syllable rhymes: What is a bloody tale? (*gory story*), whereas Hinkety Pinkety requires three-syllable answers: What is the White House? (*presidents' residence*). You can find lots more examples by searching online. Visual hink pinks are featured in the book *One Sun: A Book of Terse Verse*, by Bruce McMillan (1990).

FIGURE 6.16 Hink Pinks

1. Share examples of hink pinks and discuss the structure of the language or read *One Sun* with your students and talk about the riddles and photographs.
2. Brainstorm objects and possible adjectives that rhyme—for example, *pink/sink*, *bear/lair*, *sled/bed*. When students understand the concept, have them work in small groups or individually to think of their own hink pinks.
3. Challenge students to draw a picture to illustrate their hink pink (see Figure 6.16) or to write a riddle. These can be exchanged with a friend.

Vocabulary Activities

6.17 Concept Sort for Math

Concept sorts are an excellent way for students to work with vocabulary related to units of study. In this example students categorize terms related to addition and subtraction that they are likely to encounter in word problems.

MATERIALS Prepare a set of word cards with the terms to sort on the front and sample word problems on the back using the terms—for example, *take away*/If I have three books and you *take away* two how many will I have? If you want students to work with these terms individually use a blank template and write the terms in the boxes in random order. Set off the headers in bold or underline.

PROCEDURES

1. Remind students that there are many words that mean the same thing as "add" and "subtract" and that these words will show up in written word problems.
2. Set up the headers Add and Subtract. Introduce each new term in a simple problem sentence. "*Lost*. I had 10 pencils and I *lost* three so how many do I have left?" Or "*Difference*. What is the *difference* between six goals and three goals? Do I add or subtract to get the answer?"
3. Continue to sort all the terms. The final sort will look something like the following set of lists. Then put the words in a center to sort independently or give students their own sheets to cut apart and sort.

4. Challenge students to write their own word problems using the terms.

add +		**subtract –**	
and	plus	minus	difference
in all	more	take away	leave/left
combine	sum	lost	less
increase	join	decrease	delete
together		fewer	reduce

VARIATIONS Terms for multiplication and division can be added. Many content area terms and concepts can be sorted in a similar manner. Simply write words into a template or onto cards, draw a simple figure, or use an online search engine to find pictures you can download (e.g., Google images). Use both a picture and word when appropriate.

FIGURE 6.17 Sorting Words by Part of Speech

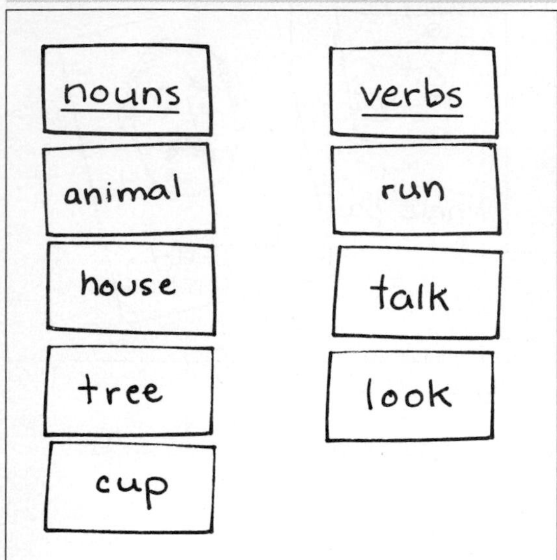

- Geometric shapes: right triangle, equilateral triangle
- Open and closed figures
- Objects that will or will not be attracted to a magnet
- Food groups: protein, fruits, vegetables
- Parts of speech: nouns, verbs, adjectives, adverbs (See Figure 6.17)
- Animals by carnivores, herbivores, or omnivores; mammals, birds, reptiles, and amphibians
- Things we can recycle and things we cannot
- States of matter: solids, liquids, and gas
- Simple machines: lever, pulley, wedge, inclined plane, wheel, screw
- Fact and opinion statements
- Habitats and the plants and animals that live there.
- Equivalent fractions
- Objects you would or would not see used by settlers or Native Americans of the Old West.

6.18 Semantic Brainstorms

This small-group activity focuses on the meanings of the words and serves as a great activity for content studies.

PROCEDURES

1. Choose a topic related to an area of study. Start with easy, familiar topics such as sports and locations (as well as countries, animal life, clothes, furniture, or modes of transportation).
2. Students brainstorm related words and then record them. Using chart paper is a good way to record these sorts.
3. Students share their findings and see whether they can come up with subcategories from their brainstorming. Categories can be circled by color or written over into columns.

VARIATIONS Look in magazines, newspapers, and catalogs. Circle words that express feelings, color words, people's names, or parts of speech. Organizing software (e.g., Inspiration) can be used to record these brainstorms in a chart form. Additional software, such as VISIO software for drawing graphics, can be used in the same way. You can record student responses within circles and rectangles using the drawing toolbar in PowerPoint software.

FIGURE 6.18 Honey Bee Semantic Sort

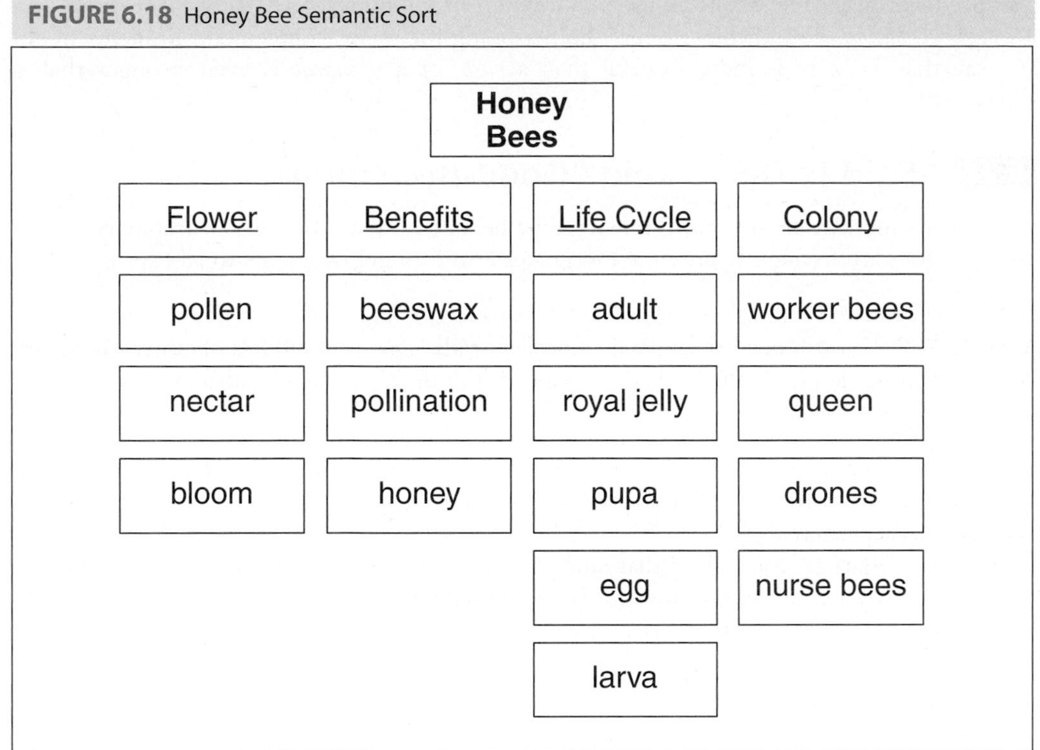

6.19 Semantic Sorts

Students work with content-related words to compare and contrast. In Figure 6.18 terms related to bees have been sorted into categories.

PROCEDURES

1. Look through a chapter or unit in a textbook and make a list of the key terms. Often they are listed at the end of a unit. Make word cards for the words.
2. Students sort the words in an open sort, establishing their own categories. Start with easy and familiar topics.
3. The sorts are copied into word study notebooks in a separate section for that content area.

6.20 Shades of Meaning

This small-group activity focuses on the nuances of meaning among words in the same semantic category. It is a particularly useful activity for nurturing word consciousness in writing as well as reading. The focus of this activity is on the discussion. There is no right or wrong answer.

PROCEDURES

1. Choose a vocabulary word that is essential to understanding a particular book or topic of study. For example, you might choose the word *stampede* from Scieszka's *The Good, the Bad, and the Goofy,* because this term describes so much of the action in this book.
2. Come up with other words that are similar to a stampede (noun): a *charge, rush, flight, mad dash,* and so on. Students can also contribute words.

3. Students place the words along a continuum of strength (*move, rush, flight, mad dash, charge, stampede*) and then discuss the reasoning for their arrangement. Students might say that a *charge* is more forceful than a *rush*, or a *stampede* is even stronger than a *charge*.

6.21 "Said Is Dead" and "Good-Bye Good"

As students increase their writing fluency they benefit from a more vivid vocabulary. These two activities are frequently presented in grades 2 to 6 to help students to add spice to their writing.

MATERIALS You will need chart paper, a projector, thesauri, and models of either exemplary or tired writing. Some teachers use chart paper cut in the shape of a headstone.

PROCEDURES

1. Begin with a piece of literature and project the writing for all to see. Look through the selection for words that are used for overworked language—in this activity, either the verb *said* or the adjective *good.*
2. Begin a chart of vocabulary that students may consider for their own writing. Post it where students can refer to it or insert additional terms.
3. Students can refer to a thesaurus for related words.

   A brief list of words developed by students to replace *said* might include the following:

stated	declared	laughed	ordered
remarked	screamed	blurted	yelled
exclaimed	cried	boasted	requested
chuckled	explained	asked	muttered
chortled	scolded	argued	whispered

   Another list to replace *good* might include the following:

fantastic	awesome	wonderful	fantastic	superb
cool	joyful	fabulous	super	excellent
nice	terrific	perfect	fine	pleasant
marvelous	enjoyable	great	honorable	compassionate
beautiful	exciting	lovely	solid	considerate

VARIATIONS Another way to approach this activity is to share a writing sample in which *said* or *good* are overused. Have students brainstorm words that are more descriptive. These choices become the beginning of a chart to display options for students to consider in their own writing. There are many sites online that have word lists to browse. Simply search by "synonyms for said" or "synonyms for good."

MEDIA GUIDE *Word Study for Transitional Learners in the Within Word Pattern Stage*

SECTION	PAGE	GO TO PDTOOLKIT FOR *WORDS THEIR WAY*™
Videos		
The Complexities of English Vowels	207	Click on the Videos tab, then type "Classroom Organization in the Within Word Pattern Stage."
The Word Study Lesson Plan in the Within Word Pattern Stage	212	Click on the Videos tab, then type "Small Group Sorting in the Within Word Short *a* and Long *a*."
The Study of High-Frequency Words	217	Click on the Videos tab, then type "Weekly Schedules and Activities in the Within Word Pattern Stage, Part I."
Assess and Monitor Progress in the Within Word Pattern Stage	218	Click on the Videos tab, then type "Weekly Schedules and Activities in the Within Word Pattern Stage, Part II."
Unit Assessments and Goal Setting	219	Click on the Videos tab, then type "Professional Development with 2nd Grade Teachers."
Strategies for Teaching and Assessing English for English Learners	221	Click on the Videos tab, then type "Small Group Sorting in the Within Word Short *a* and Long *a*."
Word Study Routines and Management	222	Click on the Videos tab, then type "Weekly Schedules and Activities in the Within Word Pattern Stage, Part I."
Sorts and Games		
Word Study Instruction for the Within Word Pattern Stage	210	Click on the Sorts and Games tab, then select Within Word Pattern Stage for ready-made sorts and games.
Teacher-Directed Two-Step Sort for Long Vowels	213	Click on the Sorts and Games tab, then type "Long Vowel Sorts."
Activities for the Within Word Pattern Stage	226	Click on the Sorts and Games tab, then select Within Word Pattern Stage, where you will find ready-to-use games. Click the Create Your Own button to create your own materials.
Activities for the Within Word Pattern Stage	227	Click on the Sorts and Games tab, then type "Racetrack Game." Click the Create Your Own button to select words or pictures you would like to use with your game.
Activities for the Within Word Pattern Stage	228	Click on the Sorts and Games tab, then selects Games and choose a template. Click the Create Your Own button, then choose the words you would like to use for sorts or card games.
Activities for the Within Word Pattern Stage	234	Click on the Sorts and Games tab, then select Games and choose a template. Click the Create Your Own button, then choose the words you would like to use for sorts or card games.
Assessment Tools		
Strategies for Teaching and Assessing English for English Learners	221	Click on the Assessment Tools tab, then type "Spanish Spelling Inventory."

chapter 7

Word Study for Intermediate Readers and Writers: The Syllables and Affixes Stage

Beginning in second and third grade for some students, and in fourth grade for most, cognitive and language growth supports movement into the syllables and affixes stage of word knowledge. Although students have been reading, and even writing, words of more than one syllable for some time, it is during this stage that they systematically study the generalizations that govern how syllables are joined and how **affixes** (both **prefixes** such as *re-* or *un-* and **suffixes** such as *-ing* or *-ly*) affect the spelling, meaning, and use of base words.

Many teachers find that there is much about English **orthography** at this stage that is new to them as well as to their students. Your own curiosity about words and a willingness to dig deeper into the way words work will enable you to learn right along with your students. This chapter and supporting material will help you facilitate students' word explorations to help them discover the patterns of sound, spelling, and meaning that link thousands of words. This knowledge will help them read, write, and spell much more effectively.

Before we talk in detail about the features of study in this stage, let's visit Sharon Lee's fourth grade classroom in midyear. Ms. Lee has a range of abilities in her classroom that are evident in both reading levels and spelling inventory results. She has a large group of 14 students who fall into the syllables and affixes stage, 4 students who remain in the within word pattern stage, and 5 students who are in derivational relations. She makes time to meet with each group several times a week for systematic word study while the other groups work independently. In the following vignette, Ms. Lee calls for the attention of the large syllables and affixes group at the front of the room for a 20-minute lesson while the rest of the students find comfortable places to read and discuss in the "Book Club" format (Raphael, Pardo, Highfield, & McMahon, 1997). The syllables and affixes students are studying the final **unaccented syllable** *ar/er/or* that poses a challenge for spellers because it is pronounced the same, /ər/, across the different spellings.

In preparation for a directed spelling thinking activity (Zutell, 1996), Ms. Lee begins her word study unit for this week by asking her students to spell three words: *dollar, faster,* and *actor.* She then calls on several students to tell how they spelled each word as she writes their answers on an overhead transparency, encouraging a variety of answers. The results include *doller, dollor, dollar, faster, acter, actor.* Ms. Lee then "thinks aloud": "Hmmm . . . This is very interesting. We agree on how to spell the first syllable of each word, but we don't always agree about how to spell the final syllable. What makes this part hard?" Jason volunteers that the words sound the same at the end. "Do the rest of you agree?" Ms. Lee asks. "Let's say each word and listen carefully. Do they sound alike? Let's find out if this is true for other words as well."

Ms. Lee has made a transparency of the weekly word sort and cut it apart to sort on the overhead projector. She discusses *blister* and *mayor* with the students to make sure they are clear on each word's meaning and then reviews the meanings of *lunar* and *solar* from their recent study of space. Next she asks, "How might we sort these words?" Sara suggests that they sort by the last two letters. "Let's do that," Ms. Lee responds, "and as we sort them, let's say them aloud and listen for the sound in the last syllable."

Ms. Lee removes all the words except *dollar, faster,* and *actor,* which she underlines to use as key words for the sort. She then places each word in turn on the overhead and calls on a student to read it and tell her where to put it. The final sort is shown in Figure 7.1. After reading the words in each column, Ms. Lee asks the students, "What have we found out about these words?" Several students offer ideas, and Ms. Lee summarizes by saying, "When we hear /ər/, the sound will not help us spell it, so we will have to concentrate on remembering whether it is spelled *er, or,* or *ar.*"

FIGURE 7.1 Final *ar/er/or* Word Sort

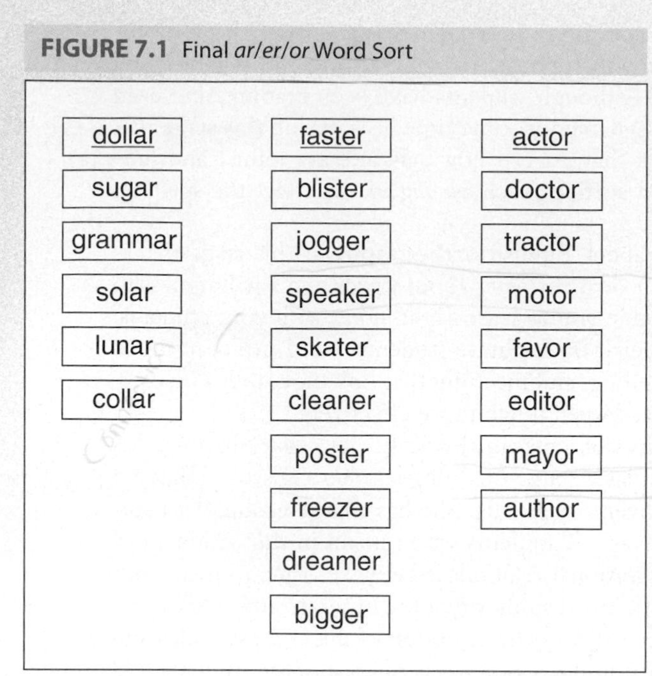

dollar
sugar
grammar
solar
lunar
collar
faster
blister
jogger
speaker
skater
cleaner
poster
freezer
dreamer
bigger
actor
doctor
tractor
motor
favor
editor
mayor
author

Ms. Lee hands out copies of the word sort and goes over the students' word study assignments for the week. Students are expected to cut apart and sort the words independently and then write the word sort in their word study notebooks. While they do that, Ms. Lee will meet with another group for word study. On other days they will work independently by sorting again with a buddy, sorting at home, and hunting for additional words in trade books. On Friday, Ms. Lee will give them a spelling test, but she will also call the group together to compile a large class list of the words they were able to find in their word hunts. This will be used to introduce the following week's lesson, in which students will be helped to discover that *er* is the most common way to spell the final sound, that it is always used to spell comparative adjectives (*faster, smaller, longer*), and that *er* and *or* are often used to spell agents or people who do things (*teacher, worker, author, sailor*).

Ms. Lee's lesson promotes two key ideas of this stage. (1) It demonstrates to students how much they already know about spelling a particular word—spelling is not an all-or-none affair. Usually they will get most of the word correct, and teachers need to remind and reassure students about this. (2) It demonstrates to students what they need to focus on when they look at a word. Because they already know most of the word, they need to attend to the part that is still challenging.

Literacy Development of Students in the Syllables and Affixes Stage

Students in the syllables and affixes stage of word knowledge are what Henderson (1990) called *intermediate readers*—students who are not yet mature or advanced readers. Henderson noted the wide divergence of reading skill during this stage of development, spanning, on average, six grade levels, from grade 3 to grade 8. The range of reading skill within this stage makes it imperative to revisit many of the orthographic concepts underlying syllables and affixes in light of a more complex reading vocabulary.

Reading

The intermediate and middle school years are a time of expanding reading interests and fine-tuning of reading strategies. Students will be expected to read textbooks and other informational text as classroom instruction shifts to a greater emphasis on content area subjects.

In previous developmental stages, the challenges posed by reading stem mostly from children's ability to identify words as they read about familiar topics. At the intermediate level however, background knowledge and vocabulary become critical elements in comprehension as students explore new genres and topics. Developing word knowledge lets students read more fluently, which in turn allows them to exercise and expand their increasing level of cognitive and language sophistication.

During the syllables and affixes stage, students will learn to look at words in a new way, not as single-syllable units with CVC, CVVC, or other vowel patterns, but as two or more syllabic or morphemic units. This **structural analysis** is a more sophisticated decoding strategy than the phonics instruction typically offered in the primary grades using consonants, blends, digraphs, and vowel patterns—elements that students master in Ehri's full alphabetic phase (1997). In the syllables and affixes stage students are in Ehri's **consolidated alphabetic phase** in which they use larger chunks to decode, spell, and store words in memory as sight words. For example, a word like *unhappy* can be analyzed as three syllabic chunks (*un-hap-py*) or two **morphemic** chunks (*un-happy*). Word study in the syllables and affixes stage helps students learn where these syllable and morphemic breaks occur in words so that they can use the appropriate chunks to read, spell, and determine the meanings of polysyllabic words.

Students in the intermediate stage read with greater fluency than in the previous stage. They have many words stored in memory for automatic retrieval and they are learning how to use syllabic and morphemic chunks to quickly and accurately figure out unfamiliar words. This ease of word identification and attention to punctuation help them read with phrasing and expression. By the end of this stage we can expect oral reading rates of up to 140 words per minute (Hasbrouck & Tindal, 1992) and faster silent reading rates approaching 200 words per minute (Morris, 2008).

Writing

Intermediate writers become increasingly confident and fluent in their writing and are able to work on longer pieces over many days. The ability to spell the vast majority of the words they need for writing allows them to focus more attention on the meaning they are trying to convey. You are likely to hear "voice" in their writing and they are more aware of their audience. Intermediate writers can be expected to revise their written work and to edit it for accuracy of spelling and punctuation.

Lexi's essay on the changes she would make to the Lincoln Middle School cafeteria exudes middle school bravado (see Figure 7.2). She touches on all things cool: sound systems, student choice, hamburgers and fries, and celebrities—all of which are sure to bring her the recognition she craves as "manager of the year." Lexi, a sixth-grader, is in the later part of the syllables and affixes stage. She spells *manager* correctly and incorrectly

FIGURE 7.2 Lexi's Middle School Essay

If I could be the managar of the
cafeteria at Lincoln Middle School
I would make some awsome changes.
The instalation of a sound system
would be my first decesion. The
kids could rotate bringing there own
chocie of musick. Then I would make
radacle changes in the menu like
we'd have hamburgers and fries
and no rootine school menues. Then
I'd send an invatation to Miley
Cyrus to join us for lunch. If
she acepts I'd get the Best Manager
of the Year Award!

(MANAGAR) in the same essay and uses but confuses the unaccented final syllables of other words like *radical* (RADACLE) and *music* (MUSICK). Vowel patterns in accented syllables are still not firm (AWSOME for *awesome*), and she is still uncertain about the double consonants within base words containing an affix (INSTALATION for *installation*). Once these syllable and affix issues are firmed up, Lexi will be poised to study the spelling–meaning connections of the next stage of development—derivational relations. At that time she will discover that the reason DECESION is spelled with an *i* instead of an *e* is because it comes from the word *decide*.

Vocabulary

In this stage students' own reading becomes the primary source of new vocabulary as they encounter within texts more and more words whose meanings they do not know. This is especially true in the content areas such as science and social studies beyond third grade as students read information books and textbooks. However, learning words from context cannot be left to chance; teachers need to take an active role in making sure that students' vocabularies are growing steadily. We have learned much in recent years about the importance of teaching vocabulary directly to students at all levels. This is particularly important as we guide students' understanding of both core academic and content-specific academic vocabulary (Farstrup & Samuels, 2008; Hiebert, 2005; Pearson, Hiebert, & Kamil, 2007; Zweirs, 2008). Remember that your own enthusiasm and curiosity about words is likely to enhance students' **word consciousness** (Blachowicz & Fisher, 2009; Lubliner & Scott, 2008; Scott, Skobel, & Wells, 2008; Stahl & Nagy, 2006). Look for books about language to read to your students such as *Miss Alaineous: A Vocabulary Disaster* by Debra Frasier (2007), *The Boy Who Loved Words* by Roni Schotter (2006), and *Frindle* by Andrew Clements (1998).

You will notice that authors of many textbooks try to provide a rich context to support new vocabulary and often highlight important new terms for the reader. Although students need to learn about bolded terms, they also need to learn the strategy of breaking words into parts (prefixes, suffixes, and base words) so that they can grow confidently and competently into independent word learners. This strategy depends critically on the students' knowledge of word structure. Adams (1990) best emphasized this importance:

> Learning from context is a very, very important component of vocabulary acquisition. But this means of learning is available only to the extent that children bother to process the spelling—the orthographic structure—of the unknown words they encounter. Where they skip over an unknown word without attending to it, and often readers do, no learning can occur. (p. 150)

MORPHEMIC ANALYSIS. One of your most important responsibilities for word study instruction at this stage is to engage students in examining how important word elements—prefixes, suffixes, and **base words**—combine; this **morphemic analysis** is a powerful tool for vocabulary development and figuring out unfamiliar words during reading. You can show students directly how to apply this knowledge by modeling the following strategy for analyzing unfamiliar words that they cannot identify in their reading.

1. Examine the word for meaningful parts—base word, prefixes, or suffixes.
    - If there is a prefix or a suffix, take it off so you can find the base.
    - Look at the base to see if you know it or if you can think of a related word (a word that has the same base).
    - Reassemble the word, thinking about the meaning contributed by the base, the suffix, and then the prefix. This should give you a more specific idea of what the word is.
2. Try out the meaning in the sentence; check if it makes sense in the context of the sentence and the larger context of the text that is being read.

3. If the word still does not make sense and is critical to the meaning of the overall passage, look it up in the dictionary.
4. Record the new word on a chart or in a word study notebook to be reviewed over time.

Let us take a look at how Ms. Lee models this process for students, beginning with a familiar word and then extending the lesson to an unfamiliar word.

"I've underlined one of the words in this sentence: *They had to redo the programs after they were printed with a spelling error.* What does *redo* mean? Yes, Chloe?"

"When you have to do something over again?"

"Okay! So you already had done something once, right?

"Now, let's cover up this first part that we call a prefix [covers *re*]. What word do we have? Right—*do,* this is a base word. Now, let's look at these words."

Ms. Lee writes the words *join, tell,* and *write* on the board; then she writes the prefix *re-* in front of each base word as she pronounces the new word. "When we join the prefix *re-* to each base word, what happens? Right! We are going to be doing these things again—we can *rejoin* a group, *retell* a story, *rewrite* a paper." She then asks the students what they think the prefix *re-* means. After a brief discussion, she asks a student to look up the prefix in the dictionary to check their definitions.

Ms. Lee's next step is to model this strategy with a word she is fairly certain the students do not yet know. She shows the following sentence on the overhead:

> As they got closer to the front of the line, her friends had to reassure Hannah that the Big Thunder roller coaster ride was safe.

"Okay," Ms. Lee proceeds, "I've underlined this word [pointing to *reassure*]. Any ideas what this word is?" Most students shake their heads; Kaitlyn squinches up her face as she slowly pronounces "REE–sure." "Good try, Kaitlyn," Ms. Lee responds. "You're trying to pronounce it, but it doesn't sound like a word we've heard before. What about the beginning of the word, though? Could that be the prefix we've just been thinking about?"

This prompt works for the students and they start trying to pronounce the base, *assure,* without the prefix *re-*. "Right," Ms. Lee encourages. "You've taken off the prefix, *re-*, and are trying to figure out the base word. Any ideas?" Though a couple of students are pronouncing *assure* correctly, they are uncertain about its meaning.

Ms. Lee continues: "Well, we know that, whatever *assure* means, the prefix *re-* means it's being done again! Let's look back at the sentence. Do you think Hannah can't wait to go on the roller coaster—or is she beginning to be worried?" After some discussion with the students, Ms. Lee talks about the base word, *assure,* and explains that Hannah's friends had probably already talked with her about how safe the roller coaster was, that there had never been any accidents, and had helped Hannah to feel more confident—*assured* her—that Big Thunder was safe. (Most students are nodding their heads now, saying things such as "Oh, yeah, I've heard that word before.") As Hannah and her friends got closer to actually going on the roller coaster, however, they had to assure her again—*re*assure her. Students are then asked to check the dictionary definition to confirm the meaning of the word (to remove doubts or fears).

Ms. Lee summarizes: "Most of the time, by looking carefully at a word you don't know—looking for any prefixes, suffixes, and thinking about the base—you can get pretty close to the actual meaning of the word. Then ask yourself if this meaning makes sense in the sentence and text that you're reading."

It is critical to model and reinforce this strategic approach to analyzing unfamiliar words in text. Students need plenty of opportunities to try it out under your guidance (Baumann, Edwards, Font, Tereshinksi, Kame'enui, & Olejnik, 2003). Encourage your students to talk about their ideas as they apply the process so that you can encourage, facilitate, and redirect as necessary. Morphemic analysis will become one of the most effective means of developing and extending students' vocabulary knowledge. It is also important, however, to model what to do when the process does not yield an appropriate meaning for the unfamiliar word—analyzing *repel* into *re* + *pel* will not be of much help—and then the dictionary might be consulted.

DICTIONARIES. It is important to have unabridged dictionaries and online dictionaries available in the classroom as well as dictionaries that are published for intermediate students; for example, the *American Heritage Children's Dictionary* (grades 4–6) and the *American Heritage Student's Dictionary* (grades 5–9) are very helpful at this stage. Attractive in format, they present definitions, word histories, and usage information in student-friendly language.

A dictionary offers opportunities for determining the precise meaning of a word students need to know in their reading as well as for understanding a word deeply. For example, based on Robyn Montana Turner's biography of Faith Ringgold, Ms. Lee focuses on the word *enhancing* in the sentence "Faith Ringgold decided to use cloth frames as a way of enhancing her art." Pronouncing the word does not seem to help because it is not in the students' speaking/listening vocabularies and breaking the word into parts does not help. Ms. Lee talks about the context in which the word occurs; it may narrow the possibilities somewhat, but possible meanings suggested by the context might include, for example, "protecting" or "showing." This is definitely a situation in which the dictionary will be of use and strategies for looking words up should be modeled.

Ms. Lee underlines the word *enhancing* and explains that, to check the meaning of this word in the dictionary, they would need to look up the base word, *enhance*. Reminding the students that they may need to watch out for changes in spelling when they are trying to figure out the base word for an unfamiliar word, she notes that the *e* is dropped when the *-ing* is added. Looking up a base word also helps to highlight the spelling of other forms of the word.

The students find that the dictionary definition for *enhance* is "to make greater, as in value, beauty, or reputation." Ms. Lee has the students return to the sentence in the text and discuss which of these features they believe Faith Ringgold had in mind when she decided to use cloth frames. The students agree that, in the context of the sentence and the overall text, Faith Ringgold probably wanted to make her quilts more "beautiful."

Dictionaries can also provide helpful information about the history of a word and make explicit the interrelationships among words in the same meaning "families." A discussion of dictionary entries illustrates how one word's entry can include information about words related in spelling and meaning—the entry for *enhance*, for example, also includes *enhancement*. Sections labeled "Usage Notes," "Synonyms," and "Word History" provide important information about the appropriateness of particular words and subtle but important differences among their meanings. Some entries contain stories that explain spellings and deepen understanding of important terms.

WORD SORTS AND VOCABULARY. The word sorts you use to teach spelling generalizations are likely to contain words whose meanings should also be explored, perhaps briefly, as Ms. Lee did with *blister* and *mayor*. Part of your introductory routine might be for a student to look up a word and be ready to report to the group its meaning or multiple meanings. This is a good way to encourage regular dictionary use for an authentic reason. Keep dictionaries handy for students, but avoid assigning students to look up long lists of words and remember the limitations of dictionaries. Sometimes you can offer a better definition than the dictionary because you know what your students are likely to understand. Follow-up word study notebook routines might include illustrating words or using them in sentences to highlight their meanings. Students might also select several words each week to look up in the dictionary and then record definitions or other information (parts of speech, origins, etc.) in notebooks.

TEACHING CONTENT VOCABULARY. A quarter century of research has supported particular approaches to learning new words and/or challenging concepts. Not surprisingly, these approaches engage students' prior knowledge and get them talking with the teacher and with one another about the meanings and associations of words.

How do teachers select new vocabulary words? In addition to the words that emerge from narrative reading and writing, words from specific content areas become increasingly important as students move through the grades. You will find these words in your district and state standards and the curricula for the different content areas—social studies, science, math, and so forth. If there is a required textbook for a particular content area, it will usually reflect the important concepts and the words that represent those concepts.

Once words have been selected, the following steps should be followed in the context of engaging activities.

1. Activate background knowledge. Find out what students already know about the concept, and remind them of related concepts they have already learned.
2. Explain the concept and its relationship to other concepts.
3. Use graphic organizers, charts, or diagrams as needed to portray relationships among concepts.
4. Discuss examples and non-examples.

A number of graphic organizer formats developed over the years have proven very effective in facilitating the types of engagements with new and/or difficult concepts that lead to understanding and deeper knowledge (Blachowicz & Fisher, 2009; Diamond & Gutlohn, 2006, Robb, 1999; Stahl & Nagy, 2006; Templeton et al., 2010). One key to the effectiveness of graphic organizers is their visual presentation of the relationships among target vocabulary and related concepts. Two examples that can be found in the activity section of this chapter are semantic maps and concept or word maps. It is critical to emphasize how important discussion is in the context of using graphic organizers in the classroom. As Stahl and Nagy (2006) observe, "The graphs and procedures are no more than structures to explain to students what particular words mean. It is the explanation, the talk, that is important" (p. 96).

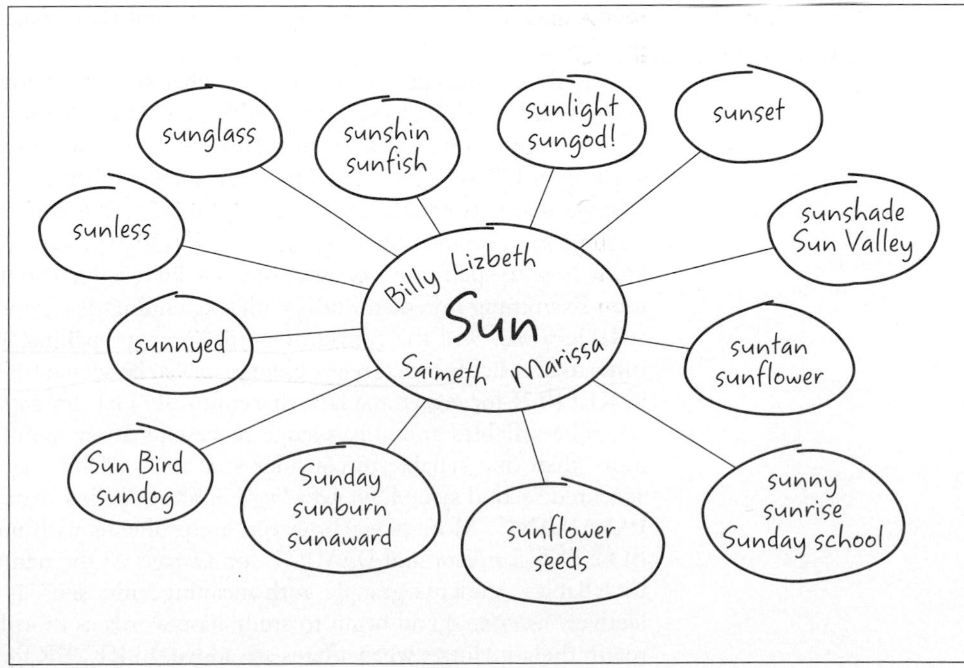

It is important to remember that most reading vocabulary encountered in content areas is developmentally ahead of spelling vocabulary. Two-syllable words like *mantle*, *pressure*, *pumice*, and *lava* might be added to sorts featuring syllable patterns and accent, but other words (e.g., *teutonic*, *bacteria*) would not be appropriate spelling words for students

FIGURE 7.3 Concept Sort

Sort 1

Figures	
planes	*solids*
circle	cube
square	cone
rectangle	prism
triangle	pyramid
rhombus	sphere
	cylinder

Sort 2

Solids	
flat surface	*curved surface*
cube	sphere
rectangular prism	cone
triangular prism	cylinder
rectangular pyramid	
triangular pyramid	

in the syllables and affixes stage. Words with complex Greek and Latin word parts are studied in the next stage, derivational relations.

CONCEPT SORTS AND CONTENT LEARNING. With the growing focus on content area instruction in the intermediate grades (*Common Core State Standards*, 2010) will come many opportunities to use concept sorts as described in earlier chapters. In order for new vocabulary to "stick," students need multiple exposures to those words in multiple contexts (Beck et al., 2002). Concept sorts provide that exposure but also help students form relationships between words and their ideas.

Figure 7.3 presents a concept sort developed by a fourth grade math teacher to introduce the exploration of planes and solids. The students were given a list of figures and asked to work with a partner to discuss what they understood about the terms and to sort them into one of the two categories: planes and solids. Then the students were asked to come together as a whole class to share. In this fashion, understandings and misunderstandings were brought to the fore and the teacher got a good sense of the level and depth of students' background knowledge of these terms.

The math teacher introduced a second sort of solid figures later in the unit to fine-tune students' understanding. At the end of the unit, concept sorts such as these were used to review or assess the vocabulary.

Orthographic Development in the Syllables and Affixes Stage

In previous chapters, systematic word study has been limited to vowel and consonant patterns within single-syllable words to build a foundation for the polysyllabic words of intermediate word study in much the same way that basic math facts build a foundation for long division. Once students have this foundation, they are ready to begin the study of polysyllabic words. As shown in Lexi's writing sample in Figure 7.2, students in this stage spell most words correctly, making their writing quite readable, but they continue to make more advanced spellings errors.

Table 7.1 provides a summary of what students know, what they use but confuse, and what is still missing in the early, middle, and late syllables and affixes stage. In the early part of this stage you may still see lingering confusions with **ambiguous vowel** patterns as in the spelling of CRALL for *crawl.* However, for the most part students know how to spell single-syllable words correctly and are ready to study the conventions involved in the addition of endings such as *-ing*. Spellings such as SHOPING and AMAZZING show us that students know how to spell the *-ing* suffix but lack knowledge about the doubling rule where syllables join. Examining inflected words with *-ing* endings is a good introduction to the study of two-syllable words and the conventions that govern spelling where syllables meet—the **syllable juncture.** Syllable juncture problems can also be seen in the used but confused doubled letters in KEPPER for *keeper* and lack thereof in BOTEL for *bottle.*

The syllables and affixes stage represents a new point in word analysis because there is more than one syllable to consider and each syllable may present a spelling problem. The accented second syllable in *parading* might be spelled with a variant long vowel pattern, as in PARAIDING. More likely, however, are problems with unaccented final syllables evident in BOTTEL for *bottle* and DAMIGE for *damage.* As the name of the stage suggests, in addition to syllables, students grapple with meaning units such as prefixes and suffixes (known collectively as *affixes*) and begin to study base words as morphemes or meaning units that must retain their spellings when affixes are added. In KEPER for *keeper*, the student may be relying

Table 7.1 Characteristics of Syllables and Affixes Spelling

	WHAT STUDENTS DO CORRECTLY	WHAT STUDENTS USE BUT CONFUSE	WHAT IS ABSENT
Early Syllables and Affixes CRALL for *crawl* SHOPING *for shopping* AMAZZING for *amazing* BOTEL for *bottle* KEPER or KEPPER *for keeper*	Blends, digraphs, short vowels Vowel patterns in one-syllable words Complex consonant units in one-syllable words Spell known sight words correctly	Ambiguous vowels Consonant doubling and *e*-drop Syllable juncture: open- and closed-syllable patterns	Few things are completely missing Occasional deletion of reduced syllables: DIFFRENT for *different* Doubled consonant for absorbed prefixes
Middle Syllables and Affixes SELLER for *cellar* DAMIGE for *damage* PERAIDING for *parading*	All of the above plus: Doubling and *e*-drop with inflectional endings Syllable juncture: open- and closed-syllable patterns	Vowel patterns in accented syllables Unaccented final syllables	Doubled consonant for absorbed prefixes
Late Syllables and Affixes *parading* *cattle, cellar* CONFEDENT for *confident*	All of the above plus: Vowel patterns in accented syllables Unaccented final syllables	Some suffixes and prefixes: ATTENSION for *attention,* PERTEND for *pretend* Reduced vowels in unaccented syllables	Doubled consonant for absorbed prefixes

on sound rather than knowledge of the word *keep*. In the sections that follow we describe the major features for instruction in the syllables and affixes stage.

Base Words and Inflectional Endings/Suffixes

One category of suffixes, known as **inflectional endings,** includes *-s*, *-ed*, and *-ing*. These suffixes change the number and tense of the base word but do not change its meaning or part of speech. Although inflectional endings have been used in oral language since the preschool years, studying them in spelling will introduce students to base words and suffixes as well as the rules that govern spelling changes.

Probably the most common suffix students learn to use is the plural, adding *-s* even when the sound it represents varies, as in *cats* (/s/) and *dogs* (/z/). However, plurals deserve to be addressed systematically to cover additional issues.

1. Add *-es* when words end in *ch*, *sh*, *ss*, *s*, and *x*. When *-es* is added to a word, students can usually "hear" the difference because it adds another syllable to the word (*dish* becomes *dish-es*, unlike *spoons*).
2. Change the *y* at the end of a word to *i* before adding *-es* when the word ends in a consonant + *y* (*baby* to *babies*) but not when it ends in a vowel + *y* (*monkeys*).
3. Words may change spelling and pronunciation in the plural form. Some words with final *f* or *fe* change the *f* to *v* and add *es* (*wife* to *wives*, *wolf* to *wolves*). Other words take a new form (*goose* to *geese* and *mouse* to *mice*). And some words remain the same (*fish*, *sheep*, *deer*).

One of the major challenges students face when adding *-ed* or *-ing* is whether to double the final letter of the base word. The basic doubling rule is that when a suffix beginning with

FIGURE 7.4 Adding Inflectional Endings to Base Words

Sort 1

resting	jogging
reading	running
feeding	shopping
walking	winning
sleeping	planning
jumping	skipping
waiting	sobbing
smelling	hugging
dressing	snapping

Sort 2

CVVC	CVCC	CVC
reading	resting	jogging
feeding	walking	running
sleeping	jumping	shopping
waiting	smelling	winning
raining	dressing	planning
		skipping
		sobbing
		snapping

a vowel is added to a base word containing a single vowel followed by a single consonant (i.e., *shop*), double the final consonant (i.e., *shopping, shopped*). This can be simplified as the one–one–one rule: one syllable, one vowel, one consonant—double. There are a handful of exceptions such as words that end with *x* and *w*, which never double (*taxing, showed*), but the doubling rule is certainly worth learning and has implications for syllable juncture, as described shortly. It does take time, however, for students to develop a firm understanding of it.

Rather than teaching rules, we suggest a series of word sorts that will allow children to discover the many principles at work. In Sort 1 of Figure 7.4, the students first sort by words that double and those that do not and are asked to underline the base word. In Sort 2 of Figure 7.4, sorting by the vowel pattern in the base word helps students discover that there are two conditions when the ending is simply added (CVVC words like *read* and CVCC words like *rest*) whereas only CVC words need to double. This will help clear up the confusion of *smelling* and *dressing*, words that students may initially place in the doubled column.

Table 7.2 summarizes the conditions that govern the addition of inflectional endings. The rules can get quite complicated, but when planning instruction, begin with the most common in the early syllables and affixes stage (numbers 1–5) and expect to reinforce these throughout the intermediate grades and even beyond in the case of two- and three-syllable words (where rules apply only if the final syllable is accented). Remember that it will take time for children to master these generalizations, and they should know the spellings of the base words before they are asked to think about how to add suffixes.

Compound Words

When students explore **compound words,** they can develop several types of understandings. First, they learn how words can combine in different ways to form new words (*sunlight, lightweight*). This is an introduction to the combinatorial features of English words in building vocabulary. Second, the study of compound words lays the foundation for explicit attention to syllables: very often, compound words comprise two smaller words, each of which is a single syllable. Third, students reinforce their knowledge of the spellings of many high-frequency, high-utility words in English that are compound words (*someone, anything*). Look at Activity 7.4 on page 263 for specific ideas such as illustrating words and brainstorming words that share the same base.

Table 7.2 **Changes to Base Words When Adding Inflectional Endings or Other Suffixes That Start with a Vowel**

BASE WORDS	+ *ING*	+ *ED* (OR *ER*)	+ *S*
1. CVVC, CVCC Ex: *look, walk*	No change Ex: *looking, walking*	No change Ex: *looked, walker*	No change Ex: *looks, walks*
2. CVC* Ex: *bat*	Double final letter Ex: *batting*	Double final letter Ex: *batted, batter*	No change Ex: *bats*
3. CVCe Ex: *skate*	Drop final *e* Ex: *skating*	Drop final -*e* Ex: *skated, skater*	No change Ex: *skates*
4. Words that end in a consonant + *y* Ex: *cry*	No change Ex: *crying*	Change *y* to *i* Ex: *cried, crier*	Change *y* to *i* and add *es* Ex: *cries*
5. Words that end in a vowel + *y* Ex: *play*	No change Ex: *playing*	No change Ex: *played, player*	No change Ex: *plays*
6. Two-syllable words accented on second syllable Ex: *admit, invite, apply, destroy*	Follow rules for 1–5 Ex: *admitting, inviting, applying, destroying*	Follow rules for 1–5 Ex: *admitted, invited, applied, destroyed, destroyer*	Follow rules for 1–5 Ex: *admits, invites, applies, destroys*
7. Words that end in a *c* Ex: *mimic*	Add a *k* Ex: *mimicking*	Add a *k* Ex: *mimicked*	No change Ex: *mimics*

*Words ending in *x* and *w* do not double (e.g., *boxed, chewed*). Words that end in *ck* avoid having to double a final *k* (*blocked, blocking*). Words that end in *ve* avoid having to double a final *v* (*loved, loving*).

Open and Closed Syllables and Syllable Patterns

Why is *Tigger,* the name of the tiger from *Winnie the Pooh,* spelled with two *g*s? How do you pronounce *Caddie Woodlawn?* Answering these questions depends on whether you are dealing with an open or a closed syllable. **Open syllables** (CV) end with a long vowel sound: ***ti**ger,* ***Ka**ty,* ***rea**son.* **Closed syllables** (CVC) contain a short vowel sound that is usually "closed" by two consonants: ***Tig**ger,* ***Cad**die,* ***rack**et.*

Students are first introduced to the basics of open and closed syllables when they examine what happens when *-ed* and *-ing* are added to short and long vowel pattern words. If they are writing about how a rabbit moves along the ground (*hopping*) and do not double the *p,* they will wind up with an entirely different meaning (*hoping*). Consider the following examples, in which doubling the consonant keeps the short vowel sound in *rid* and *grip:*

rid + ing = ***ridding*** *ride + ing =* ***riding***
grip + ed = ***gripped*** *gripe + ed =* ***griped***

As Henderson (1985) explained, "The core principle of syllable juncture is that of doubling consonants to mark the short English vowel" (p. 65). Students learn that when they are uncertain about whether to double the consonants at the juncture of syllables, they should say the word and listen to the vowel sounds. If they hear a long vowel sound, the syllable is open and will not end with a consonant (*hu-man*). If they hear a short vowel sound, the odds are likely that the syllable is closed with an extra consonant (*mam-mal*). Knowledge about whether

Table 7.3 Syllable Juncture Patterns

LABEL	TYPE	EXAMPLES
VCCV	Closed	*skipping, button, rubber* (doublets) *chapter, window, garden* (two different consonants)
V/CV	Open	*lazy, coma, beacon, bacon*
VC/V	Closed	*river, robin, cover, planet*
VCCCV	Closed	*laughter, pilgrim, instant, complain*
VV	Open	*create, riot, liar*

to double develops first through examining base words plus inflectional suffixes and is later applied *within* base words: Because the vowel in the first syllable of *Tigger* is short, the *g* is doubled; because the vowel in the first syllable of *tiger* is long, the *g* is not doubled.

Another way of describing what goes on where syllables meet is through **syllable juncture patterns,** as shown in Table 7.3. For example, ***hopping***, ***Tigger***, and ***stripping*** illustrate the VCCV syllable juncture pattern; ***hoping***, ***tiger***, and ***striping*** illustrate the VCV syllable juncture pattern. The first two syllable patterns, the open V/CV pattern and the closed VC/CV pattern, are the most frequent. The third pattern, the closed VC/V pattern, with only a single consonant at the juncture after a short vowel (*nev-er*; *pan-ic*) occurs less frequently. The fourth pattern, the closed VCCCV pattern, includes words that have a consonant digraph or blend at the syllable juncture (*ath-lete*, *hun-dred*). In the VV pattern, each vowel contributes a sound; the word is usually divided after the first long vowel sound (*cre-ate*, *li-on*) so it is another example of an open syllable.

PDToolkit for Words Their Way™

Go to PDToolkit for *Words Their Way*, click on the Videos tab, then type "Syllable Juncture in VCV and VVCV Patterns, Day 1" and watch as Ms. Bruskotter meets with a small group of students to introduce a lesson on open and closed syllables.

Figure 7.5 shows a two-step sort that can be used to introduce syllable juncture patterns. You might begin by sorting three to four words into each column in a Guess My Category activity. Start asking students to help you sort the rest of the words as shown in Sort 1. After sorting, ask the students how the words in each column are alike. Probe by asking them if anyone noticed the vowel sounds and where the words were "divided" when you pronounced them. After completing this first sort, the words in the second column could be sorted further by those that have different consonants at the juncture and those that have the same, as shown in Sort 2.

FIGURE 7.5 Introducing Syllable Juncture Patterns

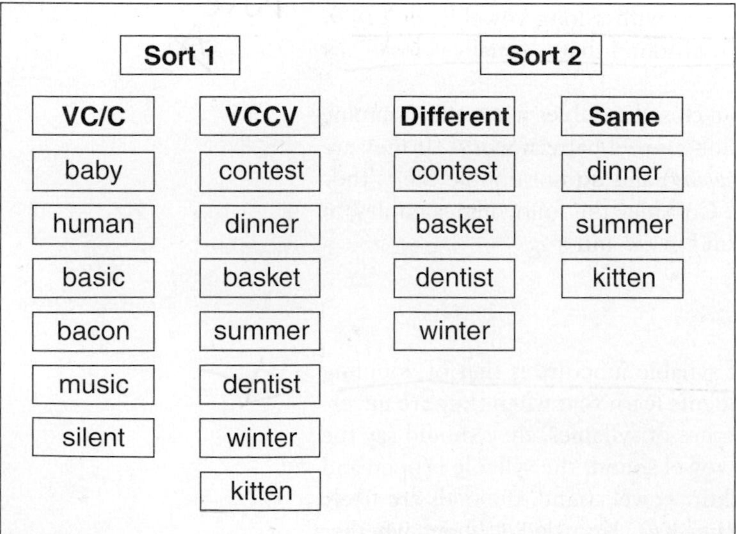

Review Vowel Patterns in Two-Syllable Words

Vowels can be reexamined in two-syllable words as a way to review those patterns and extend students' understanding of how those patterns work in polysyllabic words. For example, look at the familiar long *a* patterns in the sort in Figure 7.6. Students in the syllables and affixes stage learn to listen for the stressed syllable and see the familiar vowel patterns (*ai*, *ay*, and *a-e*) they learned in the previous developmental stage, the within word pattern.

There are a number of vowel patterns within single-syllable and polysyllabic words that are not sorted out until the intermediate grades. These are often called **ambiguous vowels** because they represent a range of sounds and spellings. For example, the vowel sound is the same in *cause*, *lawn*, and *false*, but is spelled three different ways. The *ou* spelling pattern has four different sounds in *shout*, *touch*, *through*, and *thought*. These variations are often cited as examples of the irregularity of English spelling, but word sorting allows students to see that they nevertheless represent categories like other vowel patterns (Johnston, 2001).

By paying attention to the position of ambiguous vowels, students can often determine which spelling pattern occurs most often. For example, *aw* and *oy* usually occur at the ends of words or syllables (*straw*, *boycott*), whereas *au* and *oi* are found within syllables (*fault*, *voice*). If these patterns persist as problems into the syllables and affixes stage, then it is appropriate to take a step back and spend a little more time with these vowels in one-syllable words. They also can be examined, with other vowel patterns, in two-syllable words like *mouthful*, *counter*, and *lousy* versus *coward*, *chowder*, and *brownie*.

FIGURE 7.6 Common Long *a* Spellings in Two-Syllable Words

maintain	dismay	debate
raisin	crayon	bracelet
dainty	decay	parade
trainer	layer	mistake
sailor	today	escape

Accent or Stress

In most words of two or more syllables, one syllable is emphasized, **stressed,** or **accented** more than the others. Some dictionaries use apostrophes to show which syllables are stressed; others boldface the stressed syllable. Teach your students both systems. Determining the stressed syllable can be a challenge for teachers and students, but starting with a sort of students' names is a good way to introduce the concept. When we pronounce a familiar name, where do we put the most emphasis? Which syllable seems to "sound louder" than the others? Molly's name is pronounced "***moll** ee*," not "*mo* ***lee***." We say "***jen** ifer*," not "*je* ***ni** fer*" or "*jenni* ***fer***." One way to test for accent is to hold the back of your hand lightly under your chin as you say a two-syllable word such as *a-round*. Your jaw probably drops more for the accented syllable.

Now try this with certain homographs—words that are spelled alike but whose meanings and parts of speech change with a shift in accent:

> Would you pre**sent** the **pres**ent to the guest of honor?
> It is a good idea to re**cord** your expenses so you have a **rec**ord of them.
> The landfill might re**fuse** the **ref**use.

Thinking about accent as it works with names and then with certain homographs should help solidify the idea of stress or accent.

When examining words of more than one syllable, knowing about accent helps students identify what they know about the spelling of a polysyllabic word and what they do not know, that is, what they will need to pay particular attention to. For example, when students pronounce the word *market*, they realize they know the spelling of the accented syllable (*mar*), yet may be uncertain about the vowel spelling in the *final unaccented syllable* (*ket* or *kit?*). When students grasp the concept of an accented syllable, therefore, they also learn about the other side of this concept, the unaccented syllable. The unaccented syllable is the one in which the spelling of the vowel is not clearly long or short, so students will need to pay close attention to it. The sound in this syllable is often represented by the **schwa** sound—the upside down *e* in a dictionary pronunciation key (ə). By the middle of the syllables and affixes stage, word study can focus on these unaccented final syllables.

> /ər/ as in *sup**er***, *act**or***, and *sug**ar***
> /əl/ as in *ang**le***, *ang**el***, *met**al***, *civ**il***, and *fert**ile***
> /ən/ as in *sudd**en***, *hum**an***, *bas**in***, *apr**on***, and *capt**ain***
> /chər/, /yər/, and /zhər/ as in *lec**ture***, *fig**ure***, and *trea**sure***
> /ĭj/ as in *vill**age*** and *dam**age***
> /ē/ as in mon**ey**, cook**ie**, and stor**y**

When sorting these words, you will find there is often no tidy generalization that governs the spelling and students may have to simply commit many of these words to memory.

However, sometimes the part of speech is related to the ending. For example, verbs and adjectives tend to end in *-en* (*waken, golden*) whereas nouns end in *-on* (*prison, dragon*). Comparative adjectives are always spelled with *-er* as in *smarter, faster,* and *taller.* What is probably most useful for students to discover is that some spellings are simply more common than others. For example, there are over 1,000 words than end in *-le* but only about 200 that end in *-el.* The ending *-er* is much more common than *-ar* or *-or.* An excellent follow-up to sorting these words is creating class lists that will give students insight into their frequencies. Then they might use a "best guess" strategy when spelling an unfamiliar word.

Identifying the vowel in unaccented syllables is one of the biggest challenges we all face as spellers. As our colleague Tom Gill explains to students, "You can't trust sound when your voice goes down." However, as we have discussed briefly and shall see further in the next chapter, the spelling of the schwa in the unaccented syllable can sometimes be explained in terms of parts of speech or meaning. At this stage, for example, you may introduce and begin to discuss how the "spelling–meaning connection" may explain some of these spellings. The *-el* ending in *angel,* for example, also occurs in the related word *angelic;* the *-al* in *metal* also occurs in the related word *metallic;* and the *-an* in *human* also occurs in *humanity.* The stressed syllables in these related words often provide a clue to the spellings of unstressed syllables, as well as expanding students' vocabularies.

Further Exploration of Consonants

Consonants continue to be revisited in more difficult words during this stage. Consider words like *circus* or *garbage,* in which *c* and *g* represent two different sounds. (They might be spelled phonetically as /sər-kəs/ and /gär-bĭj/.) Generalizations about the spelling of hard and soft *g* and *c* reveal an underlying logic. As in one-syllable words, the sounds of *g* and *c* depend on the vowel that follows (*a, o,* and *u* follow the hard sound, whereas *e, i,* and *y* follow the soft sound), which results in some interesting spellings. Why is there a silent *u* in *tongue?* Without it, the *g* would become soft (/tənj/). The sound of /k/ can be spelled with *ck* (*shamrock*), *c* (*magic*), *x* (*index*), and *qu* (*antique*), and many words contain silent consonants such as *t* (*moisten*), *h* (*honest*), *k* (*knuckle*), *gh* (*daughter*), and *h* (*rhythm*). The study of silent consonants foreshadows the in-depth study of spelling–meaning connections explored in the next stage, derivational relations, in which silent letters like the *t* in *moisten* can be explained by its connection to *moist.*

Base Words and Simple Derivational Affixes

While students are spending time examining and consolidating their word knowledge at the level of the syllable, part of their focus will naturally include attention to base words and simple **derivational affixes** (both prefixes and suffixes). Unlike inflectional suffixes that do not significantly affect the bases to which they are attached, derivational affixes affect their bases—their meanings and often their grammatical functions in a sentence.

The terms *base word* and *root word* are often used interchangeably. We prefer to use *base word* when referring to words that stand on their own after all prefixes and suffixes have been removed (*govern* in *government; agree* in *disagreement*). Base words such as these are also known as **free morphemes.** We use the term *word root* to refer to a word part that remains after all prefixes and suffixes have been removed but is *not* itself a word that can stand alone (*vis* in *visible* and *spec* in *spectator*). These **roots,** also called **bound morphemes,** usually come from Greek or Latin; they will be studied extensively in the next stage.

Teachers lay the groundwork for this study during the within word pattern stage when they talk about simple prefixes and suffixes in reading vocabulary. At the syllables and affixes stage, students' understanding of how prefixes and suffixes combine with base words and word roots to create new words is vital. This understanding can help students analyze unknown words they encounter in their reading and leads to a rich expansion and elaboration of their vocabularies.

The sort in Figure 7.7 is one way to introduce prefixes and base words in a systematic way. The teacher might begin by inviting the students to do an open sort. Many students will probably sort by the prefix, but don't begin by discussing what the words and prefixes mean. Students should be encouraged to first develop their own hypotheses about the meanings of the prefixes as they consider the list of words. Then they share their conclusions with the group and the teacher for feedback. Using the words in sentences, such as "I must *obey* my parents because if I *disobey* I can get in trouble," helps to focus on the shifts in meaning. The **generative** aspect of combining prefixes and bases can be explored by constructing different words through combining and recombining prefix and base word cards or tiles in various ways: *dis-*, *re-*, *un-* can be combined with *able* and *order* to produce *disable*, *disorder*, *reorder*, and *unable*.

FIGURE 7.7 Simple Prefix Sort

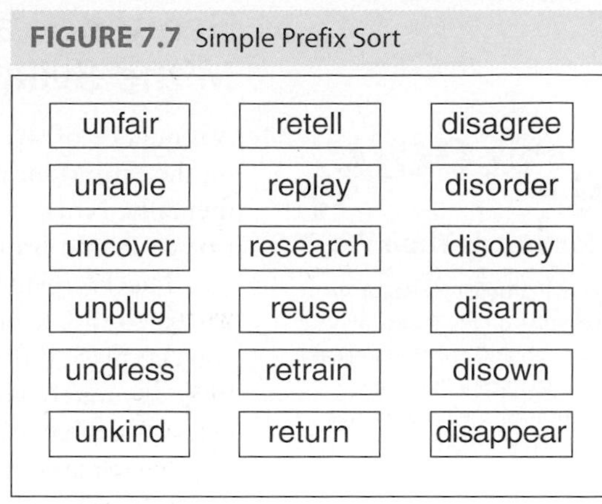

unfair
retell
disagree
unable
replay
disorder
uncover
research
disobey
unplug
reuse
disarm
undress
retrain
disown
unkind
return
disappear

Suffixes can also be introduced through sorts in which students make discoveries about how the derivational suffixes affect the meanings of known words as well as parts of speech. For example, adding *-y* to the noun *guilt* produces the adjective *guilty*; adding *-ly* produces the adverb *guiltily*. Some derivational suffixes to study in this stage for both vocabulary and spelling include the following:

-er as in *quicker* and *-est* as in *quickest* (denotes a comparison of some type)
-er as in *farmer* and *-or* as in *professor* (both denote "agents or someone or something who does something"; words of Latin origin use the *-or* spelling)
-y, *-ly*, *-ful*, *-less*, and *-ness* (these suffixes generally change the meaning and part of speech, creating adjectives, adverbs, and nouns)

Students will need to revisit the rules that govern *e*-drop and doubling as they add suffixes to base words. *Brave* becomes *bravely* with no change, but when adding *-er* to *flat* to make *flatter*, the doubling rule applies. In addition, *y* must be changed to *i* before adding suffixes (*silly* to *sillier*, *silliest*, *silliness*).

Word Study Instruction for the Syllables and Affixes Stage

Too often spelling instruction at the intermediate level and above has lacked systematic attention to generalizations. Without a good understanding of the features that require instruction at this level, teachers in the upper grades often give students lists of spelling words from content areas that are really vocabulary words. Such words lack any common spelling features and may not be developmentally appropriate.

We hope you have come to understand from this chapter that systematic word study targeted to meet student needs can advance students' spelling knowledge, their vocabularies, and their strategies for figuring out unknown words in reading. At the intermediate and middle grades, the following principles should guide instruction:

- Students should be actively involved in the exploration of words; they are then more likely to develop a positive attitude toward word learning and a curiosity about words.
- Students' prior knowledge should be engaged; this is especially important if they are learning specialized vocabulary in different disciplines or content areas.
- Students should have many exposures to words in meaningful contexts, both in and out of connected text.
- Students need systematic instruction of structural elements and how these elements combine; elements include syllables, affixes, and the effects of affixes on the base words to which they are attached.

Sequence and Pacing of Word Study in the Syllables and Affixes Stage

Go to PDToolkit for *Words Their Way,* click on the Assessment Tools tab, and select Assessment Materials. Scroll through the inventories, spell checks, and goal-setting charts.

A sequence of word study during this stage is presented in Table 7.4. This sequence touches on the important patterns and features to consider and is based on what students do developmentally. Normally achieving students in the intermediate grades will typically take at least two years and probably more to progress through this stage.

The Elementary Spelling Inventory (ESI) or the Upper-Level Spelling Inventory (USI) described in Chapter 2 will help you collect information about students' spelling errors so that you can place them appropriately for word study in this stage. Spell checks can also be used to more accurately identify what features students are ready to study. Use Table 7.1 (see p. 249) to determine what features they are using but confusing to plan instruction. If in doubt about where to place students, remember it is best to take a step back and study earlier features that students may not fully understand even if they are spelling many words with those features correctly.

We recommend that you do not rush students in the elementary grades through the syllables and affixes stage and into the derivational relations stage because they may not be ready for the more advanced vocabulary used in the word sorts. On the other hand, students in the middle grades who are still in the syllables and affixes stage should be moved along at a steady pace and might skip the late features because they are covered again in early derivational relations. Students in the middle grades and high school who are in this stage may need the extra support suggested in *Words Their Way™ with Struggling Readers: Word Study for Reading, Vocabulary and Spelling Instruction, Grades 4–12* (Flanigan, Hayes, Templeton, Beer, Invernizzi, & Johnston, 2011).

EARLY. Students early in this stage will know how to spell the vowel patterns in most single-syllable words but will make errors when adding inflectional endings as in SHOPING for *shopping* and CARRYES for *carries.* They are ready to explore the "double, drop, or nothing" principles that govern the place where base word and inflection meet.

MIDDLE. Students squarely in the middle of the stage will usually add inflectional endings correctly but will make mistakes with syllable junctures within words and with unaccented final syllables as in RIPPIN for *ripen* and BOTEL for *bottle.* They are ready to extend their understanding of doubling to syllable junctures within words as they study open and closed syllables. Vowel patterns students learned in the within word pattern stage are reviewed within the accented syllable. After studying accented syllables, students in the middle of the syllables and affixes stage look at the final unstressed syllable and two-syllable homophones and homographs. Some unusual consonant sounds and spellings are also examined.

LATE. Students who can spell most words correctly in the syllables and affixes categories on the inventory are transitioning into the derivational relations stage. They study simple prefixes and derivational suffixes that change the meanings of familiar base words in straightforward ways (*rebuild, dislike*). This serves as an introduction to the **spelling–meaning connection** that is the focus in the derivational relations stage. For a faster pace, students in the middle grades or high school might skip this introduction and go to the sorts recommended for early derivational relations in which they review these affixes in more advanced words (*reconsider, discourage*).

Assess and Monitor Progress in the Syllables and Affixes Stage

There is a lesser sense of urgency than earlier stages for students in the elementary grades who have reached the syllables and affixes stage because they have mastered much of what is typically considered "phonics" (consonants, blends, digraphs, and vowels) and they can spell most single-syllable and high-frequency words. However students still have much to master

Table 7.4 Sequence of Word Study: Syllables and Affixes

PATTERNS AND FEATURES	EXAMPLES
Early	
Plural endings -*s* and -*es*	*books/dishes*
Unusual plurals	*goose/geese, knife/knives, fish, sheep*
Inflectional endings:	
Sort by sound of -*ed* suffix	*walked* /t/, *wagged* /d/, *shouted* /əd/
Doubling	*stopping, stopped* (CVC)
e-Drop	*skating, skated* (CVCe)
No change	*walking, walked* (CVCC) and *nailing, nailed* (CVVC)
Change final *y* to *i* and add -*ed* or -*s*	*cried* (*y* after a consonant), *plays* (*y* after a vowel)
Compound words	*pancake, sidewalk*
Middle	
Open and closed syllables:	
VCCV doublet at juncture	***butto****n*, *h****appy***
VCCV different consonants at juncture	*w****indow****, **siste**r*
V/CV open with long vowel	*b****aco****n, **lazy***
VC/V closed with short vowel	***rive****r, c****ame****l*
VCCCV blend or digraph at juncture	***pilgri****m, t****angle***
V/V	*g****ia****nt, d****ie****t*
Vowel patterns in accented syllables:	
Common vowel patterns in accented syllable	***lone****ly, t****oa****ster,* ***ow****ner*
Less common and ambiguous vowels in accented syllables	*f****ou****ntain, p****ow****der, l****au****ndry,* ***aw****ful, m****ar****ble, prep****are****, rep****air****, n****ar****row*
Final unaccented syllables:	
/ər/	*begg****ar****/barb****er****/act****or***
/ən/	*capt****ain****/hum****an****/fright****en****/bas****in****/apr****on***
/əl/	*ang****el****/ab****le****/centr****al****/civ****il****/fert****ile***
/chər/ and /zhər/	*cult****ure****/mea****sure****/tea****cher***
Spelling /j/	*bad****g****er/ma****j****or/villa****ge***
Two-syllable homophones	*pedal/petal/peddle*
Two-syllable homographs	***reb****el/re****bel***
Special consonants in two-syllable words	hard and soft *g* and *c*
	silent consonants (***w****ritten,* ***k****nuckle, r****h****ythm*)
	ph (*dol****ph****in*), *gh* (*lau****gh****ter, dau****gh****ter*)
	qu (***qu****estion, anti****que***)
Late	
Simple prefixes and base words	*un-* (not–***un****lock*), *re-* (again–***re****make*), *dis-* (opposite–***dis****miss*), *in-** (not–***in****decent*), *non-* (not–***non****fiction*), *mis-* (wrong–***mis****fire*), *pre-* (before–***pre****view*), *ex-* (out–***ex****clude*), *uni-* (one–***uni****cycle*), *bi-* (two–***bi****cycle*), *tri-* (three–***tri****cycle*)
Simple suffixes	-*y* (*adjective*–like, tending, toward: *jump****y***), -*ly* (*adverb*–like: *glad****ly***), -*er*, -*est* (comparatives), -*ful* (full: *grace****ful***), -*less* (without: *penni****less***), -*ness* (condition: *happi****ness***)

*There are other meanings for *in-*, but this is the most frequent and occurs more often in words at this level of reading.

FIGURE 7.8 Error Reflections

Word	*Error*	*What went wrong*
guide	giude	I reversed the u and i. The u keeps the g from taking the soft j sound before an i.
iceberg	iceberge	Don't need an e on the end of this word because the sound is hard g, not the soft j sound.

in terms of spelling and knowing how to tackle unfamiliar multisyllabic words they encounter in reading. In addition, the study of generative vocabulary using base words, roots, and affixes is a world waiting to be explored. Students at this stage can be involved in their own progress monitoring, which, as they track their progress over time, can be very motivating.

Weekly Assessments and Spell Checks

Weekly spelling tests and unit assessments have been described in Chapter 6 as a means by which teachers can monitor student progress. You might call out ten of their sorting words each week but also include some words that assess transfer of a feature (i.e., more words to which *-ing* or *-ed* must be added) or words from a previous week's sort to send the message that students are not just responsible for the set of words they sorted that week. When students make errors on these assessments, you can ask them to go back to their word study notebooks to review the generalizations they explored and then to analyze their errors in an attempt to determine why they misspelled. Figure 7.8 shows two examples from a lesson on hard and soft *g*.

Goal Setting and Monitoring Progress

for Words Their Way™

Go to PDToolkit for *Words Their Way,* click on the Assessment Tools tab, and type "Goal-Setting/Progress Monitoring Charts."

To assess retention over time simply prepare an assessment that samples words from previous lessons or use the unit spell checks on the website or in *Words Their Way™: Word Sorts for Syllables and Affixes Spellers*. Word study notebooks can be reviewed once a week and graded. In addition, the student contract (see Figure 3.17 on page 77) and grading form (see Figure 3.23 on page 82) are helpful to monitor progress. Results from these assessments can then be used to determine whether students have met the goals in the goal-setting charts available on the website.

In Figure 7.9 there is an example of the goal-setting chart for early syllables and affixes. We recommend that you meet with students individually to go over the spelling inventory you used to assess them initially and to identify where to begin the study of features listed on the chart. When students score 90 to 100 percent on weekly tests and 80 to 100 percent on unit spell checks, that feature can be considered "mastered." If students do not meet these goals you should consider whether they were appropriately placed for instruction or whether they got adequate practice each week with the words. Reteaching may be necessary using different sets of words or you may want to increase the number of times students sort their words during the week.

Word Study with English Learners in the Syllables and Affixes Stage

for **English Learners**

English learners in the syllables and affixes stage have mastered many of the basic phonics and spelling generalizations of English and are ready to study the more advanced features of this

FIGURE 7.9 Goal-Setting Chart

SYLLABLE AND AFFIXES MONITORING CHART

Name ______________________________ Teacher _______________ Date _______________

Goals for Early Syllables and Affixes

18.	Spell inflected endings (*ed, ing, s*)	Double _____ e-drop _____ Nothing _____ Change *y* to *i* _____ *es* _____
Criterion Met		Spell Check 18
19.	Spell syllable juncture patterns	VCV _____ VCCV _____ VCV _____ VCCCV _____ VV _____
Criterion Met		Spell Check 19

Goals for Middle Syllables and Affixes

20.	Spell long vowel patterns in accented syllables	*a-e/ai/ay* _____ *e-e/ea/ee* _____ *i-e/igh* _____ *o-e/oa/ow* _____ *oo/u-e/ew* _____
Criterion Met		Spell Check 20

stage. However, many of the words used in sorts at this stage may be new vocabulary. For this reason, it is especially important to make word study a language-learning event. Words that are featured due to spelling issues should be defined and used in conversational speech as a part of every lesson. The suggestions offered in Chapter 6 to support English learners remain applicable in this stage as well. (See also Helman, Bear, Templeton, Invernizzi, & Johnston, 2012.)

There will be many features in the syllables and affixes stage that may present some conceptual difficulty for English learners. Verb forms may be constructed differently in the native language, particularly inflected verbs. In Spanish, for example, the corresponding equivalent to the English *-ing* is often an infinitive used as an abstract noun (e.g., *To sleep is good for you*). As a result, English learners may have difficulty understanding English sentences that use the *-ing* form as the subject of the sentence (e.g., *Sleeping is good for you*) or perceiving the pronunciation of *-ing* or *-ed* at the ends of English words (Swan & Smith, 2001).

Plurals may also be formed differently in the native language. Perceiving and producing the pronunciations of *-s* or *-es* at the end of a word may require explicit attention. Learning the small subset of English nouns, verbs, and adjectives that involve unusual internal spelling–sound changes (*knife/knives, leave/left, child/children*) may not be as simple as it seems. Comparatives may also be constructed differently. Instead of being signaled by spelling changes or different words altogether, comparatives may be signaled by changes in accent.

The compounding and generative aspects of English may not occur in the native language. Compound words like *outsmart* or *windfall* may seem quite strange to English learners, especially when they are metaphoric (*headstrong*) rather than literal (*sundown*). Similarly, the common use of affixes and base words in English to generate new words may be rare in other languages. The explicit study of these features will be important in helping English learners not only learn the spellings and meanings of words but also understand *why* words work they way they do in English.

for Words Their Way™

Go to PDToolkit for *Words Their Way,* click on the Additional Resources tab, then type "Sorts and Games for Spanish-Speaking Students."

PDToolkit

for Words Their Way™

Go to PDToolkit for *Words Their Way,* click on the Videos tab, then type "Classroom Organization in the Syllables and Affixes Stage" and listen to the students in Ms. Bruskotter's class brainstorm a set of expectations for when they work together.

WORD STUDY *Routines and Management*

At the intermediate and middle grade levels, word study should occur intentionally as well as spontaneously. It should continue to be systematic as teachers identify stages of development and features students need to study, but it should also be serendipitous, taking place whenever the teacher sees an opportunity to draw students' attention to words that arise in reading, writing, and content areas. Word study instruction takes place all day long across all subject areas.

Word Study Lesson Plans and Weekly Routines

The basic word study lesson plans described in detail in Chapters 3 and 6 are recommended for this stage as well. Teacher-directed sorts are a good way to introduce new features but open sorts will involve students in more active thinking. Teachers are often skeptical about using word sorts with older students, but experience proves the value of sorts at this level. Even adults who are poor spellers enjoy and benefit from hands-on sorting activities (Massengill, 2006). Use the following basic routines for sorts:

1. Model or have students sort under your direction and lead them in a discussion of the generalizations revealed by the sort as Ms. Lee did at the beginning of this chapter. At this point you should also discuss word meanings before or after sorting.
2. Students sort their own set of words and check their sorts. Sorting the weekly words, not once but eight times or more, is the most valuable routine for students and should be at the heart of systematic developmental word study.
3. Oral and written reflections encourage students to clarify and summarize their understandings.
4. Extension activities across the week reinforce and broaden students' understandings. Activities include homework and working with partners in blind sorts, writing sorts, and timed sorts as described in Chapter 3. Games and other activities are another way to engage students in further exploration and review of the features they are learning in their sorts.

Organizing instructional-level groups for word study is a challenge but will best serve the needs of students, especially those who might be below grade level. The key to finding time for meeting with small groups is establishing routines. When students learn weekly word study routines, they become responsible for completing much of their work independently (both in class and at home) or with partners, and this leaves teachers free to work with other small groups. Other tips for organization can be found in Chapter 3.

Word Study Notebooks

The use of **word study notebooks** in this stage continues to be an easy way to help students and teachers manage the routines and organization of word study (see Chapters 3 and 6). With the increased emphasis on vocabulary learning you may want to have your students divide their word study notebooks into two sections. In Tamara Barnen's class the first section is titled "Word Study" and contains the assigned sorts. This section includes weekly records of sorts, word hunts, lists generated in small groups, written reflections of sorts, timed sorts, and writing sorts. The second section is called "Looking into Language" and contains lists of words related to themes and units, words categorized by parts of speech, and semantic webs of content area studies. Other teachers add a section called a "Personal Dictionary," in which students record words they frequently need to use in writing. Because these notebooks will be used constantly, we recommend stiff-backed, stitched composition books.

for Words Their Way™

Go to PDToolkit for *Words Their Way,* click on the Videos tab, then type "Vocabulary Study of Prefixes and Suffixes, Day 1." Watch Ms. Bruskotter lead a whole-class vocabulary sort on the interactive whiteboard.

RESOURCES FOR IMPLEMENTING WORD STUDY *in Your Classroom*

A sample of prepared sorts can be found on the website and in Appendix D. These resources offer sample sorts and lists of words for other sorts or to modify the suggested sorts.

Words Their Way Word™: Sorts for Syllables and Affixes Spellers (Johnston, Invernizzi, Bear, & Templeton, 2009) has 56 prepared sorts divided into eight units of study with spell checks. The spell checks can be used to better identify what students are ready to study and also for pre- and posttesting to monitor progress.

Word lists in Appendix E

In addition to basic word sorting routines, you may want to develop a list of additional word study notebook activities from which students select when they work independently or for homework. Some of these may be more appropriate at times than others, and some can be done to review previous lessons.

- Find words that have base words and underline the base word.
- Break words into syllables and underline the accented syllables.
- Make appropriate words on your lists plural or add *-ing* or *-ed.*
- Circle or underline any prefixes or suffixes you find in the words on your list.
- Add a prefix and/or suffix, when possible, to words on your list.
- Select five words and use them in sentences or illustrate them.
- Sort your words by parts of speech or subject areas and record your sort.
- Go for speed. Sort your words three times and record your times.
- Select five words to look up in the dictionary. Record the multiple meanings you find for each word.

Guidelines for Creating Sorts in the Syllables and Affixes Stage

In earlier stages teachers were urged to exercise caution when selecting words for sorts to be sure students could read the words. However, it is likely that intermediate grade students in the syllables and affixes stage can read words whose meanings elude them. It is important to consider the semantic difficulty of the words as much as the spelling challenge when selecting words and features to study at this stage. For example, the old saying "*i* before *e* except after *c* or when sounded like *a* as in *neighbor* and *weigh*" is worthwhile to teach, but many of the words that follow the saying may not be in the speaking vocabulary of elementary students (*conceive*, *perceive*, *conceited*, *receipt*). It is fine to select a few words whose meanings students might not know, or words that they only know tenuously, but do not overburden sorts with these words.

Go to PDToolkit for *Words Their Way*, click on the Sorts and Games tab, select Syllables and Affixes Stage, then click on Word Sorts. You can also click the Create Your Own button to develop your own sorts.

ACTIVITIES FOR THE SYLLABLES AND AFFIXES STAGE

This section outlines activities and games for readers and writers in the syllables and affixes stage. The activities and games are designed to reinforce the word study introduced first in sorting activities.

There are many games described in previous chapters that are adaptable for use with the features studied in this stage.

1. The Spelling Game (6.5) can be used with any feature, as it involves asking a player to spell a word before moving on the board. The word cards from any sort can be used as the playing cards for the game.
2. Go Fish (5.25), The Racetrack Game (6.4), "I'm Out" (6.6), Jeopardy (6.9), Declare Your Category (6.11), Word Study Uno (6.13), and Homophone Rummy (6.15) work well with the many features that have three or more categories: syllable patterns, vowel patterns in stressed syllables, unaccented final syllables, silent consonants, hard and soft *g* and *c*, prefixes, suffixes, and so on.

7.1 Semantic Maps

Semantic maps provide an excellent way to activate students' background knowledge on a topic by asking them to brainstorm words related to a topic. This can give the teacher an idea of how much students already know. After or during the brainstorming the terms are organized into categories using a graphic map such as the one in Figure 7.10. The map can remain posted throughout a unit and new terms can be added. "Animals" is used as an example here.

PROCEDURES

1. To kick off a unit on animals, the teacher simply writes the word *animals* on the board and then asks students what words or ideas they associate with animals. She writes these words on a chart; afterward, she adds a few additional terms that were not mentioned but are important terms in the unit.
2. Next the teacher talks with the students about different ways in which these words may be categorized, and then she arranges the words, with students' input, along the appropriate "leg" (category) of the map. This may lead students to think of more terms. As they talk and read further, they will be growing their understanding of the new terms and their relationships to more familiar words and concepts. Students might be asked to make their own copy of the map as a follow-up activity and add to it over time.
3. These maps should be kept up throughout the unit of study, prominently displayed, and students may add terms to them as they move through the unit. Students may also decide that a particular term belongs to a different category, and if they can justify it, then the term may be moved to the new category.

7.2 Concept Mapping

Concept or word maps focus on a specific term and visually represent its place in a conceptual hierarchy using guided questions. In Figure 7.11, the word *colony* is the focus. When the teacher first presents the map, the ovals are blank except for the headings: What is it? What is it like? What are some examples? What are some non-examples? As each question is discussed, the teacher fills in ideas offered by students.

7.3 Vocabulary Jeopardy

Students enjoy playing the familiar Jeopardy game after brainstorming terms related to a unit of study.

MATERIALS Create vocabulary cards for a unit of study. Start with the vocabulary students generate on their own, followed by a scan through texts and materials. Determine four to five categories such as "What Comes Out of a Volcano" with terms such as *pumice*, *sulfur*, *ash*, *lava*, and *molten rock*. With these cards, students make a Jeopardy game. (A sample game board can be found in Activity 6.9.) Students write items on cards that relate to facts and concepts

FIGURE 7.10 Semantic Map for Animals Unit

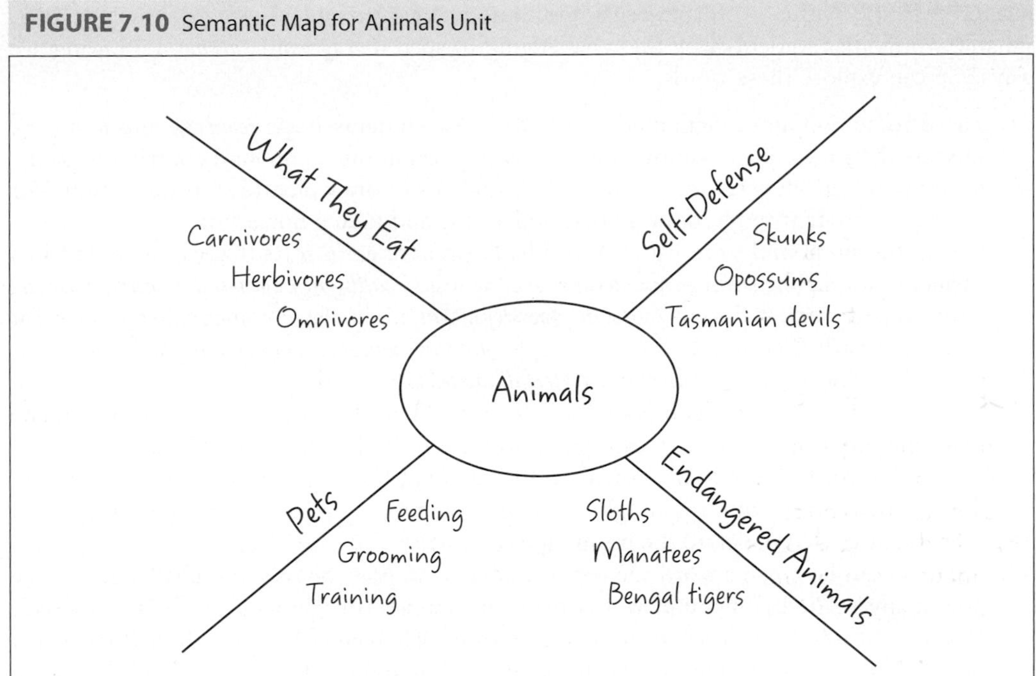

studied. Correct responses are written on the back side. For example, *Material that comes out of a volcano* could take responses that include *What is ash?* or *What is molten rock?*

Teams of students play the game as a whole-class vocabulary review of the unit.

7.4 Compound Word Activities

When examining compound words, consider the difficulty of the base words that make them up. *Cupcake* and *outfit* are made up of two words that have common one-syllable patterns

FIGURE 7.11 Concept or Word Map: *Colony*

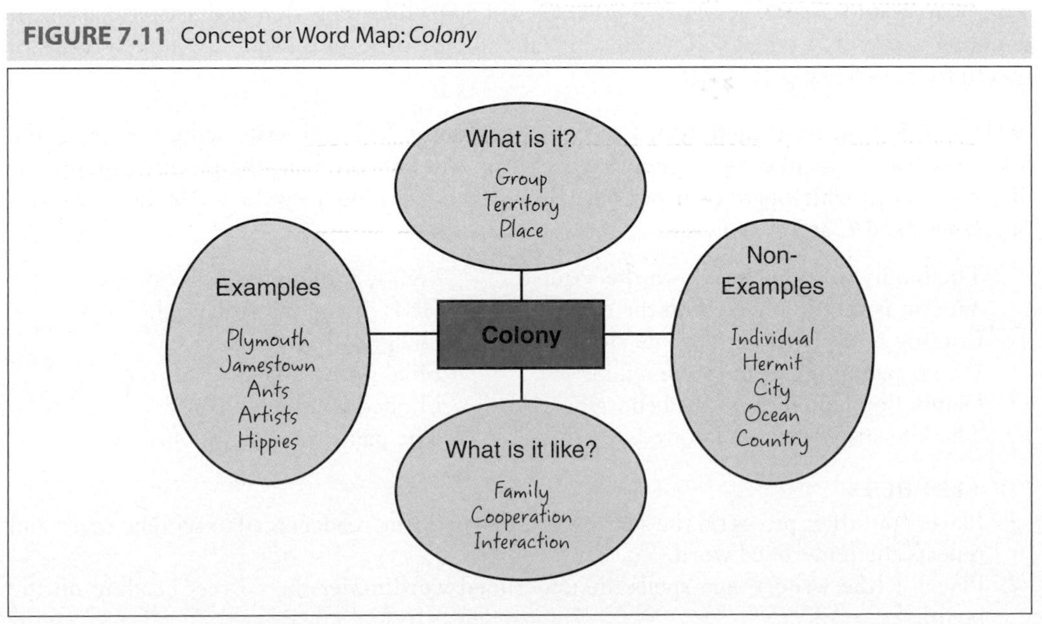

mastered in the within word pattern stage, but *cheeseburger* and *grandparent* include two-syllable words that students may find challenging to spell (*burger* and *parent*). Following are ways you can explore these words.

1. Share some common compound words with the students (e.g., *cookbook* and *bedroom*). Discuss their meanings, pointing out how each word in the compound contributes to the meaning of the whole word. You might ask students to draw pictures for illustration. For example, a student might draw a horse and a shoe and then a horseshoe.
2. Using the compound word list in Appendix E, prepare word sorts that can be sorted in a variety of ways. The sort can focus on shared words (***head**light*, ***head**band*, ***head**ache*, ***head**phones* versus ***foot**ball*, ***foot**hill*, ***foot**print*, ***foot**step*). You might also conduct concept sorts, for example, words that have to do with people (*anyone*, *someone*, *somebody*, *anybody*) or things we find outdoors (*sunlight*, *airplane*, *waterfall*, *airport*).
3. Have students cut a set of compound words apart. Then challenge them to create as many new compound words as they can. Some words will be legitimate words (*mailbox*); others will be words that do not formally exist but could (*bookbox*). Have students share and discuss their words. Students might then write sentences using these pseudo-words and draw pictures that illustrate the meaning of each.
4. Students can be given a word such as *fire*, *man*, *head*, *book*, or *rain* and challenged to see how many related compound words they can brainstorm (*fireplace*, *firefighter*, *cookbook*, *bookmark*, *rainbow*, *raincoat*). Teams compete to see who can come up with the longest list in a variation of Scattergories. Let the team with the longest list read it aloud. Everyone crosses out any word that another team has also thought of. Only words that no other team thinks of earn points. Repeat until every team has had a chance to read the words remaining on their list. Remember that each part of the word must stand alone as a free morpheme.
5. More advanced students at this stage may be challenged to sort compound words according to their underlying structure (Bravo, Hiebert, & Pearson, 2005)—for example, noun + noun (*headlight*, *wasteland*); noun + verb (*windswept*, *handshake*); adjective + noun (*anyplace*, *hardwood*).
6. Create a yearlong class collection of compound words on a chart or in word study notebooks. This collection can include hyphenated words (*good-bye*, *show-off*, *push-up*, etc.).

7.5 Double Scoop

Go to PDToolkit for *Words Their Way*, click on the Sorts and Games tab, then type "Double Scoop" for a ready-to-use version of this game.

This board game created by Marilyn Edwards will help children review and master consonant doubling and *e*-drop when adding inflectional endings. It is appropriate for small groups of two to four students.

MATERIALS Prepare a game board as shown in Figure 7.12 and write sentences, as in the following list, on small cards to go into a deck. You will also need playing pieces, a spinner or die, and a small whiteboard or paper on a clipboard for writing answers under the categories of *e-Drop*, *Double*, and *No Change*.

The bunny was hopping down the road.
The cat is sunning herself on the chair.
Brittany shopped at her favorite store.
We go swimming in the summer.
Danny flopped down on his bed.
The kite string became knotted.

I enjoy trading baseball cards.
He is diving into the pool.
She glided across the ice.
I like riding bikes.
I hoped you would come.
The paint was flaking off.

PROCEDURES

1. Players put their pieces on the sun to start. Player 2 (the reader) reads a sentence card and repeats the underlined word.
2. Player 1 (the writer) then spells the underlined word under the correct heading on the board.

FIGURE 7.12 Double Scoop Game Board

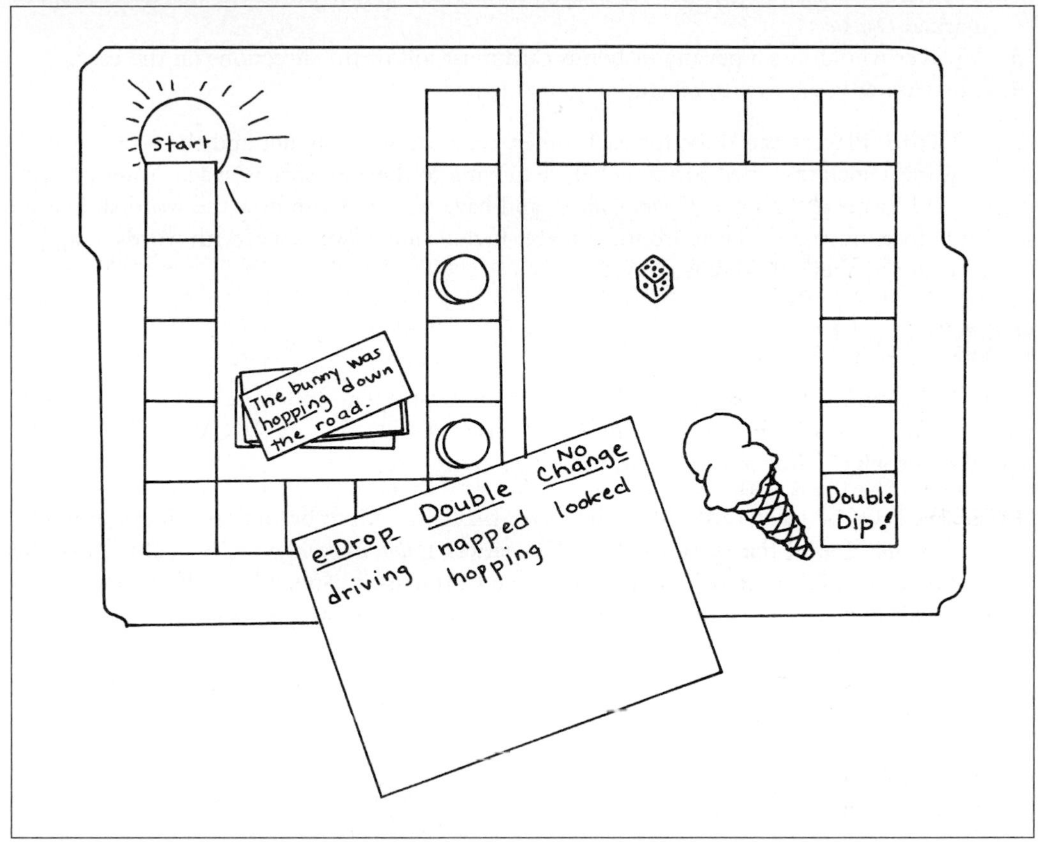

3. Player 2 checks player 1's answer by comparing it with the sentence card. If it is correct, player 1 spins and moves that number of spaces on the playing board.
4. Play then moves to the next student who must spell and sort the underlined word given by the next player. If there are only two players, they simply switch roles.
5. The first player to reach the double scoop of ice cream wins.

7.6 Freddy, the Hopping, Diving, Jumping Frog

In this board game for two to four players, students review generalizations for adding *-ing*.

MATERIALS Create a game board using one or more of the follow-the-path templates in Appendix F or by arranging green circles in a path to represent lily pads much like the game board for the Hopping Frog game in Activity 5.26 of Chapter 5. On each space, write either *Double*, *e-Drop*, or *Nothing*. Prepare playing cards by writing a variety of words with *-ing* added until there is an equal number for each rule (i.e., *hopping, diving, jumping*). Use words that students have been sorting and add more words from the syllables and affixes word lists in Appendix D. You can also add penalty or bonus cards such as the following:

You have the strongest legs. Jump ahead to the next lily pad.
You are the fastest swimmer. Skip 2 spaces.
Your croaking made me lose sleep. Move back 2 spaces.
You ate too many flies. Move back 2 spaces.

Go to PDToolkit for *Words Their Way,* click on the Videos tab, then type "Weekly Schedules and Activities in the Syllables and Affixes Stage" to see students in Ms. Bruskotter's class play word study games like Freddy, the Hopping, Diving, Jumping Frog and Double Scoop.

PROCEDURES

1. Place playing cards face-down and put playing pieces on the starting space.

2. Each player draws a card, reads the card aloud, and moves to the closest space that matches. For example, if the card says *hopping*, the player moves to the nearest space marked *Double*.
3. A player who draws a penalty or bonus card must follow the directions on the card.
4. The winner is the first to reach the home lily pad.

VARIATIONS Players can draw for each other, read the word aloud, and the player whose turn it is must spell the word correctly before moving to the appropriate space. You can write uninflected forms on cards (*hop, jump, dive*), and have players write how the word should be spelled before moving to the appropriate place. Include an answer sheet with words in alphabetical order to check if there is disagreement.

7.7 Slap Jack

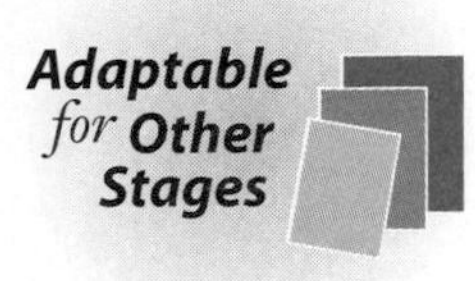

This card game for two people may be used to contrast open- and closed-syllable words as represented by any of the syllable spelling patterns (V/CV vs. VCCV; V/CV vs. VC/V). The object of the game is for one player to win all 52 cards.

MATERIALS On 52 small cards, write the words that you want to be contrasted. For example, 26 words would follow the open-syllable VCV pattern (*pilot, human*) and 26 would follow the closed-syllable VCCV pattern (*funny, basket*). See word lists in Appendix E. Write the words on both ends of the cards so that neither player has to read the words upside down.

PROCEDURES

1. The cards are dealt one at a time until the deck is gone. Players keep their cards face-down in a pile in front of them.
2. Each player turns a card face-up in a common pile at the same time. When two words with either open syllables or closed syllables are turned up together, the first player to slap the pile takes all the cards in the common pile and adds them at the bottom of his or her pile.
3. Turning cards and slapping must be done with the same hand.
4. A player who slaps the common pile when there are not two open- or closed-syllable words must give both cards to the other player.
5. Play continues until one player has all the cards. If time runs out, the winner is the player with the most cards.

VARIATIONS Additional syllable juncture patterns may be added to the deck—for example, closed-syllable VCV (*cabin, water*) and VV (*riot, diet*). Word cards could be prepared for any feature that has two or three categories, such as inflected forms with *-ed* that players would slap when both words represent *e*-drop, double, or no change.

7.8 Double Crazy Eights

This activity for two to three players is based on the traditional card game Crazy Eights and works well to review vowel patterns, syllable juncture, and accented syllables. The object of the game is to get rid of all the cards in your hand.

MATERIALS Prepare 40 or more word cards comprising four suits and four Crazy Eight cards designated by the numeral 8. In this example words with long *a* are used: *rainbow, painter, raisin, complain, remain, explain, trainer, daisy, exclaim, regain, refrain, waiter, crayon, mayor, maybe, decay, today, payment, player, prayer, delay, hooray, dismay, replay, grateful, bracelet, mistake, parade, amaze, basement, escape, vibrate, baseball, insane, replace, neighbor, weightless, freighter, eighteen, eighty.*

PROCEDURES

1. The dealer gives each player eight cards. The remaining cards become the draw pile. The dealer turns the top card of the draw pile over and places it beside the deck. This card becomes the starter card and is the first card in the discard pile.

2. The player to the left of the dealer begins by placing a card that matches the starter card onto the discard pile. Matches may be made in three ways:
   - By pattern: **cray**on/hoo**ray** or wa**i**ter/compl**ai**n
   - By stress: first syllable **train**er/**pray**er or second syllable de**cay**/com**plain**
   - By unaccented syllable: dais**y**/eight**y** or pay**ment**/base**ment**
3. With a Crazy Eight card, the player can change the suit to anything the player chooses.
4. If the player does not have a match, he or she must draw from the draw pile until one is found.
5. If all the cards in the draw pile are used up, reserve the top card from the discard pile, shuffle the rest of the cards, and place them face-down on the table as the new draw pile.
6. Play continues until one player has discarded all cards.

VARIATIONS This game can be adapted simply by making up a new deck using words that focus on another spelling feature. Remember that the deck must have four suits and allow for matching by at least two different elements.

7.9 Pair Them Up

In this version of Memory or Concentration, students match up unusual plurals.

Adaptable for Other Stages

MATERIALS Create 11 sets of cards using word pairs such as the following: *wife/wives, leaf/leaves, life/lives, wolf/wolves, knife/knives, man/men, woman/women, mouse/mice, goose/geese, tooth/teeth, child/children.* Make one card each of *fish, sheep,* and *deer.*

PROCEDURES

1. Shuffle the cards and lay them all out face-down in a 5 × 5 array.
2. Each player turns over two cards at a time. If the cards make a match, the player keeps them and turns over two more.
3. If *fish, sheep,* or *deer* are turned over, there is no match and the player automatically gets to keep the card and go again.

VARIATIONS Create a similar game for two-syllable homophones (*berry, bury*) or for irregular past-tense pairs: *sleep/slept, slide/slid, shine/shone, freeze/froze, say/said, think/thought,* and so on.

7.10 The Apple and the Bushel

The purpose of this board game created by Charlotte Tucker is to give students added practice in differentiating between *-le* and *-el* endings.

MATERIALS Prepare the Apple and Bushel game board (see Figure 7.13) and word cards with words that end in *-el* and *-le* (*bushel, angel, apple, angle*).

PROCEDURES

1. Players draw for each other and read the word aloud.
2. Players must spell the word orally or in writing correctly and then move the marker to the nearest *-le* or *-el* ending that spells the word.
3. The game continues until one player reaches the bushel. (*Note:* To get in the bushel, an *-el* word must be drawn. A player who draws an *-le* word must move backward and continue playing from that space.)

VARIATION Add words that end with *-il* (*pencil*) and *-al* (*pedal*).

FIGURE 7.13 Apple and Bushel Game Board

7.11 Prefix Spin

This game for two to four players reinforces the idea that prefixes and base words can be combined in different ways. Let students play this after they have sorted words with the featured prefixes.

MATERIALS Make a spinner using the directions in Appendix F. Divide the spinner into six sections and write each of these prefixes in a section: *mis-*, *pre-*, *un-*, *dis-*, and *re-* (use *re-* twice because it can be used in twice as many words as the others). Prepare a deck of 24 cards with the following base words written on them: *judge*, *match*, *take*, *wrap*, *set*, *test*, *view*, *charge*, *pay*, *able*, *like*, *form*, *count*, *place*, *use*, *order*, *cover*, and *pack* (you can duplicate the last six to enlarge the deck; each can combine with three of the prefixes, for example, *misplace*, *replace*, and *displace*). Include paper and pencil for each player to record their matches. You may also want to include a list of allowable words to solve disputes. Matches include the following:

> miscount, misjudge, mismatch, misplace, mistake, misuse, prejudge, preset, pretest, preview, preform preorder, prepay, recount, rematch, replace, retake, reuse, reset, retest, review, recharge, reform, reorder, repay, recover, repack, rewrap, unable, uncover, unlike, unpack, unwrap, discount, displace, discharge, disorder, disable, discover, dislike, disuse

PROCEDURES

1. Turn the base word cards face-down in a deck in the center of the playing area. Turn one card up at a time.
2. The first player spins for a prefix (such as *un-*). If the prefix can be added to the base word to form a real word (such as *unwrap*), the player takes the card and records the whole word on paper.
3. If the first player spins a prefix that cannot be added (such as *mis-*), the next player spins and hopes to land on a prefix that will work with the base word. This continues until someone can form a word.

4. A new base word is turned up for the next player and the game continues.
5. The winner is the player who has the most base word cards at the end of the game.

VARIATIONS

1. Two spinners could be used with suffixes written on the second one, such as *-s*, *-ed*, *-ing*, and *-able*. A bonus point could be assigned when a player can use both the prefix and suffix with a base word, as in *replaceable* or *discovering*.
2. Make two sets of cards with the base words and pass out four words to each player that are laid out face-up. Each player spins and tries to match the prefix with one of the words he or she has. A word that is successfully matched can be turned over in a point pile and another card drawn so the player always has four cards for possible matches. This works well with prefixes that might not be as common as the original five.

7.12 Word Study Pursuit

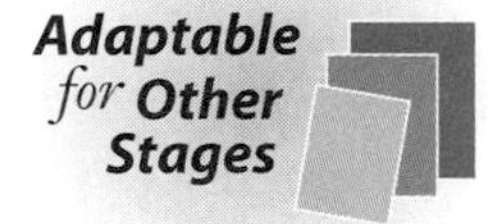

This game for four players was adapted from Trivial Pursuit by Rita Loyacono. Students who know that game will quickly learn this one. It is easy to create variations of this game for different features.

MATERIALS You will need poster board, construction paper in four different colors, four envelopes, a die or spinner, and game piece markers. To construct the game board, glue 1½-inch squares of construction paper in four colors onto the poster board, alternating colors and making a trail from start to finish around the outside edge of the entire game board. Write words from a unit of study on cards cut from the same four colors and store them in envelopes marked by the corresponding color.

PROCEDURES

1. Players determine the order of play by spinning or tossing the die. The winner chooses a color and goes first; each player in turn selects a color.
2. Players take the packet of word cards corresponding to their colors and use these to call out a word when another player lands on their respective color. If players land on their own color, they may take another turn. A student who lands on a space where there is already another card must sort by common features, placing a word that sounds alike or looks alike on top of the word or to the side if there is no common feature.

   For example, suppose Adam spins a 5 and lands on a green square. The person with the green packet calls out the word *carpet*. Adam spells the word correctly, and the card is placed face-up next to Adam. Bonita takes a turn and lands on the same green square. After successfully spelling her word—*service*—she must decide if it is to be placed on top of the first word or beside it. *Carpet* and *service* have different *r*-influenced vowels but both are accented on the first syllable. In this way, students spell the words as well as sort them by common features.
3. Players who misspell the word must go back one square and try a word from that color, providing it is not their own color (in which case they move back two squares). If players are unable to spell that word, they remain where they are and lose one turn. If players are unable to sort the word properly, they must move back one space (if it is not their color; if so, they move back two spaces), but do not lose a turn. The first player to get to the finish square is the winner and will be referee the next time.

VARIATIONS Because neither the game board nor the envelopes are marked, the board can be changed for any features that are being studied. Having several sets of the game allows different groups of four students to play the same game while practicing different words.

7.13 Homophone Solitaire

Building on the traditional game of Solitaire, this simple card game requires flexible thinking and versatile attention to words. Word cards are matched by homophone, syllable pattern, or whether the homophonic spelling change is in the stressed or unstressed syllable. The object of the game is to end up with all the words in one pile.

MATERIALS You will need 52 word cards using two-syllable homophones. The cards are composed of two suits: (a) homophones in the stressed syllable and (b) homophones in the unstressed syllable. There are 13 pairs of matching homophones from each suit. (See the homophone list in Appendix E.)

PROCEDURES

1. Shuffle the deck; then turn one card over at a time. Say the word, observe the pattern, and place the card down, face-up.
2. Turn over the next card. Place it on top of the previous card if it matches by any of the following three features:
   - Exact homophone (e.g., *alter/altar*).
   - Syllable pattern: VCCV doublet (e.g., *mussel* could be placed on *lesson*); VCCV different (e.g., *canvas* could be placed on *incite*); open V/CV (e.g., *miner* could be placed on *rumor*); closed VC/V (e.g., *baron* could be placed on *profit*).
   - Spelling change in the stressed or unstressed syllable. For example, suppose *sender* was the last card played; the homophone for *sender* is *cinder*—the spelling change in the *sender/cinder* homophone pair occurs in the stressed syllable. If a student is holding the card *morning*, she could place it on *sender* because the homophone for *morning* is *mourning*, which also has the spelling change in the stressed syllable. Alternately, if the student is holding the card *presents*, he could play it on *miner* because the homophone for *presents* is *presence* and the homophone for *miner* is *minor*—the spelling change occurs in the *un*stressed syllables.
3. If there is no match, place the card to the right of the last card played.
4. Continue play in this way, placing cards with no matches to the right of the last card played. Stacks may be picked up and consolidated at any time. The top card played on a stack determines the movement.
5. Players may move back no more than four stacks for play.
6. Play continues until the entire deck is played. Then shuffle and play again!

MEDIA GUIDE *Word Study for Intermediate Readers and Writers: The Syllables and Affixes Stage*

SECTION	PAGE	GO TO PDTOOLKIT FOR *WORDS THEIR WAY*™
Videos		
Open and Closed Syllables and Syllable Patterns	252	Click on the Videos tab, then type "Syllable Juncture in VCV and VVCV Patterns, Day 1."
Word Study Routines and Management	260	Click on the Videos tab, then type "Classroom Organization in the Syllables and Affixes Stage."
Word Study Notebooks	260	Click on the Videos tab, then type "Vocabulary Study of Prefixes and Suffixes, Day 1."
Activities for the Syllables and Affixes Stage	265	Click on the Videos tab, then type "Weekly Schedules and Activities in the Syllables and Affixes Stage."
Sorts and Games		
Guidelines for Creating Sorts in the Syllables and Affixes Stage	261	Click on the Sorts and Games tab, select Syllables and Affixes Stage, then click on Word Sorts.
Assessment Tools		
Sequence and Pacing of Word Study in the Syllables and Affixes Stage	256	Click on the Assessment Tools tab, select Assessment Materials, and scroll through the inventories, spell checks, and goal-setting charts.
Goal Setting and Monitoring Progress	258	Click on the Assessment Tools tab, then type "Goal-Setting/Progress Monitoring Charts."
Additional Resources		
Word Study with English Learners in the Syllables and Affixes Stage	259	Click on the Additional Resources tab, then type "Word Study in Spanish" and choose an applicable sort.

chapter 8

Word Study for Advanced Readers and Writers: The Derivational Relations Stage

The term **derivational relations** is used to describe the type of word knowledge that more advanced readers and writers possess. The term emphasizes how spelling and vocabulary knowledge at this stage grow primarily through processes of *derivation*—from a single base word or word root, a number of related words are derived through the addition of prefixes and suffixes. Students begin to explore these processes at the syllables and affixes stage, but their understanding expands and becomes much more elaborate at the derivational relations stage. In contrast to the syllables and affixes stage, exploration of words at the derivational relations stage draws on more extensive experience in reading and writing. There is reciprocity between growth in vocabulary and spelling knowledge and the amount of reading and writing in which students are engaged (e.g., Berninger, Abbott, Nagy, & Carlisle, 2009; Cunningham & Stanovich, 2003; Mahony, Singson, & Mann, 2000; Smith, 1998). The word sorts in which students are engaged at this level, together with their exploration of words more generally, have more to do with *vocabulary* development than simply spelling development.

We will visit the sixth and seventh grade classrooms of Jorge Ramirez and Kelly Rubero several times in this chapter. Here Mr. Ramirez illustrates how a teacher can guide students to understand how thinking about the base word and its meaning can be a clue to spelling a word.

Writing the misspelled word COMPISITION on the board, Mr. Ramirez begins: "I'd like to point something out to you: Words that are related in meaning are often related in spelling as well. For example [pointing to COMPISITION], everything is correct in this word except for the letter *i* in the second syllable. However, there's a word that is related in spelling and meaning that actually provides a clue to the correct spelling. Any ideas what this word might be?"

No one responds. Mr. Ramirez continues. "Well, let's look at this word [writes *compose* directly above COMPISITION]. Are *compose* and *composition* related in meaning? Yes, they are! Can you hear the long *o* sound in *compose?* You know how to spell this sound, and because *compose* and *composition* are related in meaning, the *o* in *compose* is the clue to the spelling of what we call the schwa sound in *composition.*

"Keeping this fact in mind can help you spell a word you may not be sure of, like *composition.* Why? Because schwas don't give you any clue to the spelling—they can be spelled with any of the vowel letters. You've got a powerful strategy you can use, though: By thinking of a related word, like *compose,* you can get a clue.

"Let's try another one. Here's a misspelling I've seen a lot." He writes OPPISITION on the board. "Is there a word that is related in meaning and spelling that can give you a clue about how to spell the schwa sound?" He points to the *i* in the second syllable of OPPISITION.

There are a few seconds of silence before a student tentatively responds, "*Oppose?*"

"Could be! Let's check it out." He writes *oppose* directly above OPPISITION. "We can clearly hear the sound that *o* in the second syllable of *oppose* stands for, and sure enough, *opposition* comes from *oppose*—they're similar in meaning—so Darci is right! *Oppose* gives us the clue for remembering the spelling of *opposition.* Remember: Words that are related in meaning are often related in spelling as well. So by thinking of a word that is related to one you're trying to spell, you will often discover a helpful clue to the spelling."

Development of Students in the Derivational Relations Stage

Students in the derivational relations stage will be found in upper elementary, middle school, high school, and into adulthood. Students at this level are fairly competent spellers, so the errors they make are "high level," requiring a more advanced foundation of spelling and vocabulary. However, misspellings such as INDITEMENT, ALLEDGED, IRELEVANT, and ACCOMODATE do occur among highly skilled and accomplished readers and writers. (Indeed, the persistence of such misspellings leads many adults to lament that, though they are good readers, they are "terrible" spellers!) Exploring the logic underlying correct spellings of these words not only helps individuals learn and remember the correct spelling but, more importantly, leads to a deeper understanding and appreciation of how words work. This understanding and appreciation leads in turn to the growth and differentiation of concepts—to vocabulary development.

Reading

The type of word knowledge that underlies advanced reading and writing includes an ever-expanding conceptual foundation and the addition of words that represent these concepts. Advanced readers are able to explore the Greek and Latin word elements that are the important **morphemes** out of which thousands of words are constructed. Linguists refer to this process as **generative** and estimate that 60 to 80 percent of English vocabulary is generated through the combination of roots, prefixes, and suffixes (Nagy & Anderson, 1984). Over 90 percent of science and technology vocabulary is generated through this process (Green, 2008). Students who understand this generative process will be in position to analyze and understand the unfamiliar content-specific academic vocabulary they will encounter in the reading materials of middle school and high school. Reading is the primary means by which students gain access to these words; the words simply do not occur with nearly as great a frequency in oral language.

During reading, this additional layer of word knowledge makes it possible to add a morphological layer to the perception of polysyllabic words. In addition to the syllabic chunks that intermediate readers (syllables and affixes) pick up in such words, the advanced reader (derivational relations) picks up **morphemic** chunks as well (Taft, 2003; Templeton, 1992). For example, an intermediate reader attempting to read the word *morphology* would most likely analyze it syllable by syllable, picking up the letter sequences *mor-pho-lo-gy*. The advanced reader would most likely use **morphemic analysis,** picking up on the letter sequences *morph-ology*, which cross syllable boundaries.

Writing

Proficient writers have the potential to exercise fully the forms and functions—structures and purposes—of different genres. Together with their expanding vocabularies, this knowledge of form and function helps to inform their voice or stance in their writing, which in turn guides their word choice when they write and revise. This understanding and sensitivity is often evidenced in their informal writing as well, such as in journals. Figure 8.1 presents an excerpt from a sixth-grader's response journal; her literature response group has been reading Scott O'Dell's *Island of the Blue Dolphins*. Her writing shows literary insights ("Every once in a while, the book gives you hints about things that will happen . . .") and a humorous stance ("Sometimes this book is Eerrie with a capital E").

Vocabulary Learning

Growth in core academic as well as content-specific vocabulary accelerates dramatically at the derivational relations stage. Students' general and content-specific knowledge grows through wide reading and study in specific content domains, and this leads to significant vocabulary and conceptual growth—which in turn leads to further growth in knowledge. It is important to note the distinction between *word-specific* and *generative* vocabulary instruction at this stage: There are very effective activities for teaching a deep understanding of the concepts that specific words represent—which has been the traditional objective of vocabulary instruction (Beck, McKeown, & Kucan, 2002, 2008). It is equally important, however, to teach *about* words (Bowers & Kirby, 2010; Nagy, 2007; Templeton et al., 2010)—the morphological or generative processes by which meaningful word parts combine. Although students are introduced to the base word/word root distinction during the syllables and affixes stage, their understanding of the generative features of Greek and Latin affixes and roots really takes off during the derivational relations stage.

FIGURE 8.1 Sixth-Grader's Response Journal—*Island of the Blue Dophins*

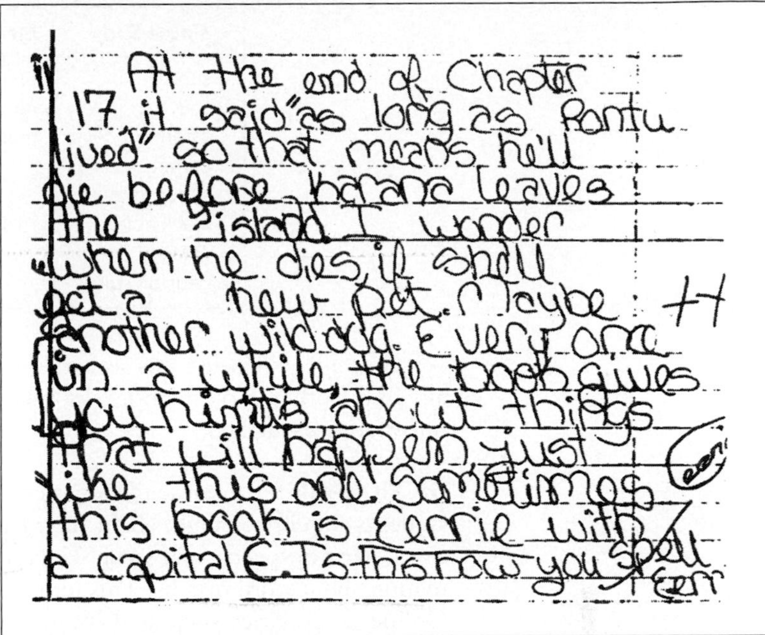

Source: From S. Templeton. *Children's Literacy Text,* 1st ed. Copyright © 1995 Wadsworth, a part of Cengage Learning, Inc. Reproduced by permission. www.cengage.com/permissions

Flanigan et al. (2011) note that developing students' generative understanding is like the old saying "Give someone a fish, they can eat for a day. Teach them to fish, they can eat for a lifetime." Word-specific instruction gives our students the fish; generative instruction teaches them *how* to fish. For this reason, most of our emphasis in this chapter is on generative instruction—giving students the keys to fully unlock the meaning code in the structure of English words.

Word sorts continue to provide a very effective context in which meaning and structure may be explored. We will examine the relationships between spelling and meaning in some depth, because these relationships are generative and apply to most words in the English language. Word sorts, however, also help students remember the spellings and meanings of specific words.

CONCEPT SORTS. An excellent framework for developing word-specific knowledge as well as relationships among the concepts that the words represent, **concept sorts** help to activate background knowledge and generate interest in and questions about the topic. Based on the students' level of background knowledge, concept sorts may be closed or open, depending on whether categories are defined. Usually, the words to be sorted are the key vocabulary and important related words for a topic of study. For example, the following vocabulary terms are for a science unit focusing on "Heavenly Bodies" (Templeton et al., 2010):

planet star sun moon asteroid comet meteorite meteoroid nebula
white dwarf supernova black hole neutron star galaxy

The teacher has selected words the students will know *(planet, star, moon, sun)* as well as some of the new words for the unit *(asteroid, neutron star, white dwarf)*. Because the students have a fair degree of background knowledge about "space" and astronomy, the teacher asks them to work with a partner to see how many different ways they can think of to sort the words or concepts, producing the following possibilities:

- In or out of our solar system
- Single bodies or members of a group
- Generating light or reflecting light

The following is one possible Single Body/Member of a Group concept sort.

Single Body	*Member of a Group*	*Not Sure*
sun	planet	meteoroid
star	moon	nebula
asteroid	meteorite	white dwarf
comet		
supernova		
black hole		
galaxy		
neutron star		

As students discuss this sort, the words and concepts in one category may be moved to any of the other two categories. In the process, more background information is engaged and uncertainties clarified.

DICTIONARIES. Because dictionaries will get a lot of use in the derivational relations stage, students should be taught about their features, such as pronunciation guides, multiple definitions, parts of speech, and so on. Have at least one dictionary in the classroom that has information about word origins. This information is usually in brackets at the end of a main entry. Online dictionaries such as dictionary.com, yourdictionary.com, and onelook.com are also useful. The following materials should always be readily available to students:

- Intermediate and collegiate dictionaries; enough copies for six to eight students to work in a small group
- Thesaurus collection: enough for six to eight students in small-group work
- Several word history (etymological) dictionaries and root books (see next section)

for Words Their Way™

Go to PDToolkit for *Words Their Way,* click on the Videos tab, then type "Vocabulary with Root Tree (*tract*), Day 1." Notice how Ms. Rubero uses etymology resources during word study.

WORD ORIGINS. Exploring the origins of words and the processes of word creation provides a powerful knowledge base for learning spelling and vocabulary, as well as for facilitating more effective reading and writing. **Etymology,** the study of word origins (from the Greek *etumon,* meaning "true sense of a word"), may develop into a lifelong fascination for many students. As you engage students in examining word roots and affixes, you are laying the groundwork for more focused exploration of etymology.

Students develop a real sense of how words work at this level as well as a general sense of how words can move through history. Kelly Rubero often reminds her students of the depth of their insights as they engage in this type of exploration during word study. Using a resource such as Shipley's *Origins of English Words* (1984), the class can explore the derivations of words. These explorations invariably bring a wealth of additional words and relationships to students' attention. For example, the entry for *peter,* the original Indo-European root for "father," explains how the Romans created the name of the god *Jupiter* from the Greeks' *Zeus + peter.* Although all students benefit from these types of investigations, more verbally advanced students in the intermediate grades often become true "word nerds" once they are initiated.

Although many times the spelling of a word may appear odd, an understanding of its origin can provide the most powerful key to remembering the spelling. Knowing that so many words have come from mythology, literature, and historical events and figures provides important background knowledge for students' reading in the various content areas. The books and websites listed in the Resource Connections: Resources for Word Study box (p. 277) also help in this regard. To stimulate students' curiosity about word origins you might read aloud excerpts from such books when you have a few extra minutes.

Another way to add interest to the study of word origins is to talk about words we have imported from other countries. A significant number of words have recently come into American English from other contemporary languages, primarily Spanish (*quesadilla, chili con carne*) but some from French (*bistro, a la carte*) and Italian (*al fresco, cappuccino*) as well. As you have probably inferred, most such words initially turn up on our menus. Given enough time, however, such "borrowed" words or "loanwords" become so familiar they don't strike us as foreign: *algebra* and

RESOURCE CONNECTIONS

Resources for Word Study

Greek and Latin Elements

Ayers, D. M. (1986). *English words from Latin and Greek elements* (2nd ed., revised by Thomas Worthen). Tucson: The University of Arizona Press.

Crutchfield, R. (1997). *English vocabulary quick reference: A comprehensive dictionary arranged by word roots.* Leesburg, VA: LexaDyne.

Danner, H., & Noel, R. (2004). *Discover it! A better vocabulary the better way* (2nd ed.). Occoquan, VA: Imprimis Books.

Fine, E. H. (2004). Illustrated by K. Donner. *Cryptomania: Teleporting into Greek and Latin with the cryptokids.* Berkeley, CA: Tricycle Press.

Fry, E. (2004). *The vocabulary teacher's book of lists.* San Francisco: Jossey Bass.

Kennedy, J. (1996). *Word stems: A dictionary.* New York: Soho Press.

Moore, B., & Moore, M. (1997). *NTC's dictionary of Latin and Greek origins: A comprehensive guide to the classical origins of English words.* Chicago: NTC Publishing Group.

Rasinski, T., Padak, N., Newton, R., & Newton, E. (2008). *Greek and Latin roots: Keys to building vocabulary.* Huntington Beach, CA: Shell Education.

Word Origins

Asimov, I. (1961). *Words from the myths.* Boston: Houghton Mifflin. (The most readable and interesting resource of this kind, available on any website that sells out of print books. Two of our favorites are http://daedalusbooks.com and http://alibris.com.)

Ayto, J. (1993). *Dictionary of word origins.* New York: Arcade. (Accessible for some students in the intermediate grades and most in the middle and secondary grades.)

D'Aulaire, I., & D'Aulaire, E. (1980). *D'Aulaires' book of Greek myths.* New York: Doubleday. (Of interest to third-graders and up; upper intermediate reading level.)

Fisher, L. (1984). *The Olympians: Great gods and goddesses of ancient Greece.* New York: Holiday House. (Of interest to third-graders and up; third grade reading level.)

Gates, D. (1983). *Two queens of heaven: Aphrodite and Demeter.* New York: Puffin. (Of interest to fourth-graders and up; upper intermediate reading level.)

Jones, C. F. (1999). Illustrated by J. O'Brian. *Eat your words: A fascinating look at the language of food.* New York: Delacorte Press.

Merriam-Webster new book of word histories. (1995). Springfield, MA: Merriam-Webster. (Of interest to most middle grade and secondary students.)

Robinson, S. (1989). *Origins* (Volume 1: *Bringing words to life;* Volume 2: *The word families*). New York: Teachers and Writers Collaborative. (Fascinating explorations for elementary students of selected Indo-European roots. These two volumes are still available on the "Publications" link of the Teachers and Writers Collaborative website at www.twc.org.)

Shipley, J. (2001). *The origins of English words.* Baltimore: Johns Hopkins University Press. (For teachers who are truly dedicated wordsmiths, Shipley's book is the ultimate source. A delightful read!)

algorithm from Arabic, *adventure* and *marine* from French, *husband* and *window* from Scandinavian, *canyon* and *ranch* from Spanish, *tomato* and *chocolate* from Native American languages. A popular classroom activity is to post a large world map on the wall and display words according to their country of origin. For example, where would you post the word *segue?*

ONLINE RESOURCES. The number of vocabulary- and word-themed websites seems to be increasing exponentially. Some of our favorites are listed in Resource Connections: Web Resources about Words (p. 278). One in particular, Visual Thesaurus, offers significant potential for students' explorations. Users type in a word, and the word is then presented in a "Thinkmap" web that visually displays the meaning relationships shared by the target word or concept and other terms. Clicking on any word in the web reveals definitions and examples in context, as well as a new web of relationships. Figure 8.2 shows the thinkmap for the word *tranquil.* Clicking on the node above *tranquil* reveals the definition as it applies to individuals; clicking on the lower node describes *tranquil* in relation to a body of water. Figure 8.3 displays

RESOURCE CONNECTIONS

▶ Web Resources about Words

www.onelook.com A comprehensive dictionary website. Most of the major, well-respected dictionaries are available. Onelook.com also has excellent search capabilities that allow you to search for words that contain specific roots and affixes, spelling patterns, words as they occur in specific phrases, and words that relate to a particular concept.

www.americancorpus.org The Corpus of American English (Davies, 2008) is an invaluable online resource for locating related words in English. It requires that you register, but registration is free. It may be used to search for the occurrence of words in different contexts—for example, spoken language, magazines, fiction, and academic texts.

www.etymonline.com Very useful for exploring word histories, this site includes much of the etymological information you would find in the Oxford English Dictionary.

http://dictionary.reference.com/languages This site accesses the Kernerman English Multilingual Dictionary, which provides, for any word in English, words in a number of other languages that have the same or similar meaning. It is an excellent resource for finding cognates.

www.wordsmith.org You may subscribe for free and receive a new word in your inbox every day. Words follow a theme each week, and the categories of words discussed in this chapter—for example, eponyms—will be represented.

www.verbivore.com/rllink.htm An especially good site for wordplay, with innumerable links to excellent and informative language and word sites.

www.visualthesaurus.com One of the most comprehensive interactive sites on the Web. There is an annual subscription fee, but the benefits are more than worth the modest price.

www.visuwords.com Similar in format to visualthesaurus.com, this site offers a more abbreviated web display. One significant feature is that, at the time of this writing, the site is free.

Source: Adapted from Templeton et al., 2010.

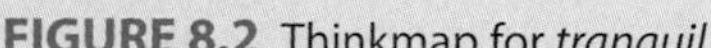

FIGURE 8.2 Thinkmap for *tranquil*

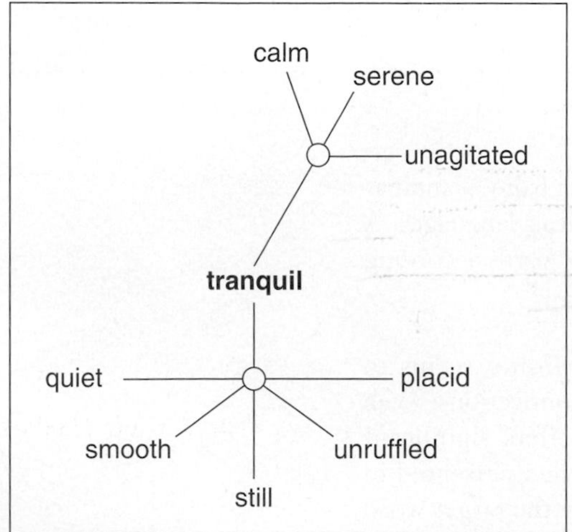

Source: Image from the Visual Thesaurus, http://www.visualthesaurus.com. Copyright © 2011 Thinkmap, Inc. All rights reserved.

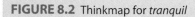

FIGURE 8.3 Thinkmap for *lithosphere*

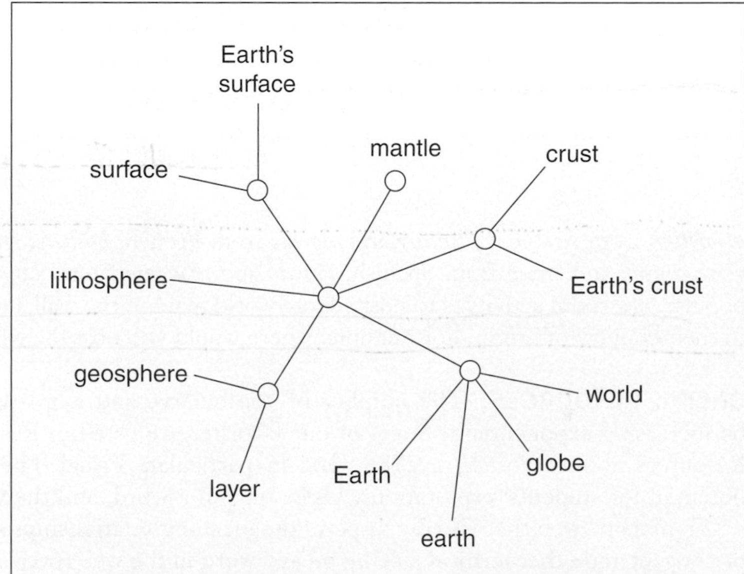

Source: Image from the Visual Thesaurus, http://www.visualthesaurus.com. Copyright © 2011 Thinkmap, Inc. All rights reserved.

▶ Resources for Word-Specific Vocabulary Activities

Beck, I., McKeown, M., & Kucan, L. (2002). *Bringing words to life.* New York: Guilford.

Beck, I., McKeown, M., & Kucan, L. (2008). *Creating robust vocabulary: Frequently asked questions.* New York: Guilford.

Blachowicz, C., & Fisher, P. (2009). *Teaching vocabulary in all classrooms* (4th ed.). Boston: Allyn & Bacon.

Diamond, L., & Gutlohn, L. (2007). *Vocabulary handbook.* Baltimore: Paul Brookes.

Flanigan, K., Hayes, L., Templeton, S., Bear, D. R., Invernizzi, M., & Johnston, F. (2011). *Words their way with struggling readers: Word study for reading, vocabulary, and spelling instruction, grades 4–12.* Boston: Pearson/Allyn & Bacon.

Nilsen, A. J., & Nilsen, D. L. F. (2004). *Vocabulary plus high school and up: A source-based approach.* Boston: Allyn & Bacon.

Stahl, S., & Nagy, W. (2006). *Teaching word meanings.* Mahwah, NJ: Erlbaum.

Templeton, S., Bear, D. R., Invernizzi, M., & Johnston, F. (2010). *Vocabulary their way: Word study with middle and secondary students.* Boston: Pearson/Allyn & Bacon.

the thinkmap for *lithosphere*, an important term in a science unit on the four earth systems. Exploring the different nodes and the word or conceptual relationships they reveal provides students a framework for exploring in breadth and depth an understanding of the lithosphere and its relationship to the other three earth systems, as well as their characteristics and functions. Another very helpful resource in the Visual Thesaurus website is the "Vocabgrabber," an excellent tool for assisting you to analyze the type, frequency, and relevance of the vocabulary in any text you wish to use with your students.

We must offer a cautionary note about any website that we recommend. Powerful tools though they are, they do not of course know your students. *How* you use them and the information they provide will ultimately rest on your own judgment. For example, though "Vocabgrabber" will generate lists of important vocabulary words, *which* words you include rests on your judgment and knowledge of your students.

Additional ideas about word-specific activities for derivational relations students may be found in Resource Connections: Resources for Word-Specific Activities.

Orthographic Development in the Derivational Relations Stage

Table 8.1 (p. 280) summarizes some of the characteristics of spellers in this stage. At first glance, misspellings at the derivational relations stage appear similar in type to those at the syllables and affixes stage: Errors occur at the **syllable juncture** and with the vowel in unaccented or unstressed syllables. In contrast to the two-syllable words in which these errors occur at the syllables and affixes stage, however, derivational relations errors occur primarily in words of three or more syllables.

The Upper-Level Spelling Inventory (USI) is useful for collecting spelling errors for analysis. Specific spelling errors characteristic of this stage fall into three main categories.

1. Polysyllabic words often have **unstressed** syllables in which the vowel is reduced to the **schwa** sound, as in the second syllable of *opposition*. Remembering the root from which this word is derived (*oppose*) will often help the speller choose the correct vowel.
2. Several suffixes have different spellings despite similar pronunciations. For example, the *-tion* in *opposition* is easily confused with *-ian* (*clinician*) and *-sion* (*tension*), which sound the same.

Go to PDToolkit for *Words Their Way*, click on the Assessment Tools tab, then type "Upper Spelling Inventory." You can use the Assessment Application to enter scores electronically.

Table 8.1 Characteristics of Derivational Relations Spelling

	WHAT STUDENTS DO CORRECTLY	WHAT STUDENTS USE BUT CONFUSE	WHAT IS ABSENT
Early Derivational Relations *trapped, humor, sailor* CONFUDENSE for *confidence* OPISISION for *opposition*	Spell most words correctly Vowel patterns in accented syllables Doubling and *e*-drop at syllable juncture	Unstressed vowels in derivationally related pairs—CONFUDENT Some suffixes and prefixes—INCISSIVE Other spelling–meaning connections—CRITISIZE/*critic*	*Note:* No features are completely absent
Middle Derivational Relations CLOROFIL for *chlorophyll*	All of the above plus: Common Latin suffixes and prefixes Spelling constancy of most bases and word roots	Some Greek letter–sound relationships—EMFASIZE *for emphasize* Greek and Latin elements	
Late Derivational Relations COMOTION for *commotion* DOMINENCE for *dominance*	All of the above	Absorbed prefixes—SUCESSION, ILITERATE Advanced Latin suffixes—DEPENDANCE	

3. Other errors occur in the feature known as an **absorbed** or **assimilated prefix.** The prefix in *opposition* originally comes from *ob*, but because the word root starts with the letter *p* (*pos*), the spelling has changed to reflect an easier pronunciation. (Try pronouncing *ob-position*—it's awkward to move rapidly from a /b/ to a /p/ sound.)

The Spelling–Meaning Connection

The **spelling–meaning connection** is another way of referring to the generative understanding of words—the significant role that **morphology** plays in the spelling system. As we begin to explore spelling–meaning relationships, we help students become explicitly aware of this principle as it applies in English: Words that are related in meaning are often related in spelling as well, despite changes in sound (Chomsky, 1970; Templeton, 1983, 1992, 2004). As Mr. Ramirez pointed out to his students, this in turn supports a powerful spelling strategy. If you are unsure how to spell a word, try to think of a word that is similar in meaning and structure that you *do* know how to spell. This consistency presents an excellent opportunity to integrate spelling and vocabulary instruction.

The awareness that there are logical spelling–meaning connections that apply to most words in the English language results in far more productive and reassuring word learning than the traditional one-word-at-a-time approach—demonstrating the "teach someone *how* to fish" aphorism here as well. For example, *paradigmatic* will be better learned, understood, and retained when related to *paradigm*, as well as providing a helpful clue to remembering the silent *g* in *paradigm;* in the same way, *mnemonic* can be related to *amnesia* and *amnesty*, all of which have to do with memory.

AFFIXES. The spelling–meaning connection is first explored in the study of affixes in the syllables and affixes stage and is reviewed in derivational relations with more advanced vocabulary and additional affixes. Figure 8.4 presents the most frequently occurring prefixes and suffixes.

FIGURE 8.4 Sequence of Word Study

AFFIXES: PREFIX AND SUFFIX STUDY

Review and explore affixes introduced during the syllables and affixes stage (*in-, un-, dis-, mis-, re-, ex-, pre- ,-er, -est, -ful, -ness,–less, -ly*) in more advanced vocabulary.

Additional Suffixes and Prefixes

-er/-or/-an/-ist	people who do or believe	defender, creator, guardian, specialist
-ary/-ory/-ery	having to do with (whatever it is affixed to)	stationary, victory, machinery
-al/-ic	relating to, characterized by	fictional, magnetic

inter-	between	*counter-*	opposing	*fore-*	before	*sub-*	under
intra-	within	*anti-*	against	*post-*	after	*quadr-*	four
super-	over, greater	*ex-*	out, former	*pro-*	in front of, forward	*pent-*	five

CONSONANT AND VOWEL ALTERNATIONS

A number of suffixes affect the pronunciations of bases to which they are attached. These are examined in the context of consonant and vowel alternations.

Consonant Alternations

silent/sounded	*sign/signal, condemn/condemnation, soften/soft*
/t/ to /sh/	*connect/connection, select/selection*
/k/ to /sh/	*music/musician, magic/magician*
/k/ to /s/	*critic/criticize, political/politicize*
/s/ to /sh/	*prejudice/prejudicial, office/official*

Vowel Alternations

Long to short	*crime/criminal, ignite/ignition, humane/ humanity*
Long to schwa	*compete/competition, define/definition, gene/genetic*
Schwa to short	*local/locality, legal/legality, metal/metallic*

Predictable Spelling Changes in Consonants and Vowels

/t/ to /sh/	*permit/permission, transmit/transmission*	/sh/ to /s/	*ferocious/ferocity, precocious/precocity*
/t/ to /s/	*silent/silence, absent/absence*	Long to short	*vain/vanity, receive/reception, retain/retention*
/d/ to /zh/	*explode/explosion, decide/decision*	Long to schwa	*explain/explanation, exclaim/exclamation*

GREEK AND LATIN WORD ELEMENTS

Start with Greek number prefixes *mono-* (one), *bi-* (two), *tri-* (three), and move to the Greek roots *tele-* (far, distant), *therm-* (heat), *photo-* (light), and *astr-* (star). (See lists in Appendix E.)

Move to frequent Latin roots with the aim of gaining a working understanding of a few frequently occurring roots with relatively concrete and constant meanings: *tract* (draw, pull), *spect* (look), *port* (carry), *dict* (say), *rupt* (break), and *scrib* (write). (See lists in Appendix E.)

Greek Suffixes

Suffix	**Meaning**
-crat/-cracy	rule: *democracy*—rule by the *demos*, people
-ism/-ist	belief in; one who believes: *communism/communist, capitalism/capitalist*
-logy/-logist	science of; scientist: *geology*—science of the earth, studying the earth; *geologist*—one who studies the earth
-pathy/-path	feeling emotion, suffer/disease; *sympathy*—feeling with; *apathetic*—no feeling; *sociopath*—someone with a personality disorder
-phobia	abnormal fear: *claustrophobia*—fear of being closed in or shut in (*claus*)

ADVANCED SUFFIX STUDY

1. *-able/-ible*	*respectable, favorable* versus *visible, audible*
2. *-ant/-ance* *-ent/-ence*	*fragrant/fragrance, dominant/dominance* *dependent/dependence, florescent/florescence*
3. Consonant doubling and accent	*occurred, permitted* versus *traveled, benefited*

ABSORBED PREFIXES

1. Prefix + base word	*in + mobile = immobile; ad + count = account*
2. Prefix + word root	*ad + cept = accept, in + mune = immune*

ADDING *-ION* TO WORDS. The suffix pronounced "shun" can be spelled several ways, as in *protection, invasion, admission,* and *musician.* This suffix also affects the base word in interesting ways. It sometimes may cause a final consonant sound to alternate (as in *detect/detection,* in which the /t/ becomes /sh/) or a vowel to alternate (as in *decide/decision*). Hundreds of words in English end with this suffix, which means "act, process, or the result of an act or process." In the case of *-ian* it means "person": *clinician, dietician.* Usually a verb is changed to a noun with the addition of *-ion,* as in *elect* to *election* or *create* to *creation.* The generalizations that govern changes in spelling when this suffix is added are rather complex but can be addressed early in the derivational relations stage because there are so many familiar words to examine.

In order to spell the /shən/ suffix, the ending of the base word must be considered. The following list provides a summary of the generalizations about this suffix and the order in which they can be introduced.

1. Base words that end in *-ct* or *-ss* just add *-ion* (*traction, expression*).
2. Base words that end in *-ic* add *-ian* (*magician*).
3. Base words that end in *-te* drop the *e* and add *-ion* (*translation*).
4. Base words that end in *-ce* drop the *e* and add a *-tion* (*reduce/reduction*).
5. Base words that end in *-de* and *-it* drop those letters and add *-sion* or *-ssion* (*decide/decision, admit/admission*).
6. Sometimes *-ation* is added to the base word, which causes little trouble for spellers because it can be heard (*transport/transportation*).

FIGURE 8.5 Word Sort to Explore *-ion* Ending

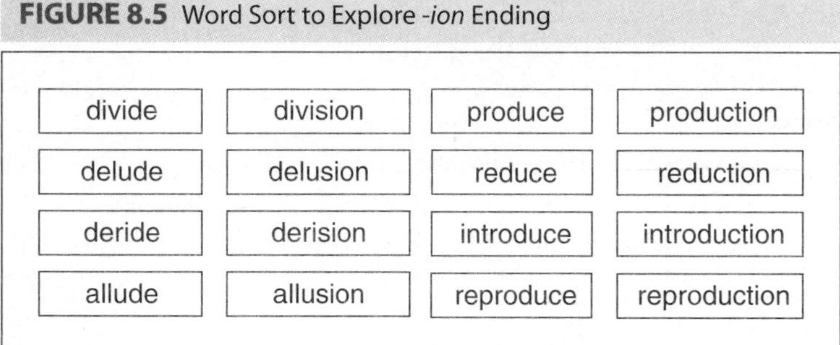

divide	division	produce	production
delude	delusion	reduce	reduction
deride	derision	introduce	introduction
allude	allusion	reproduce	reproduction

In Figure 8.5, students first pair the base word (the verb) with its derivative (the noun) and then group the pairs by the spelling patterns to determine the generalization. Students should also look for the type of vowel or consonant alternations that have occurred.

Sound Alternation

An excellent way to explore the spelling–meaning connection is to examine more directly how the sound of vowels and consonants change or alternate in related words. Despite these changes in sounds, the spelling often remains the same to preserve the meaning connection.

CONSONANT ALTERNATION. Consonants that are silent in one word are sometimes "sounded" in a related word, as in the words *sign, signal,* and *signature.* This phenomenon is known as **consonant alternation.** A very common type of consonant alternation happens when the suffix *-ion* is added to words. Listen how the sound of the *t* in *prevent* changes in *prevention.* The *t* now has the /sh/ sound. Other examples include /s/ to /sh/ in *compress* to *compression* and /k/ to /sh/ in *magic* to *magician.* We begin the examination of consonant alternation with silent/sounded pairs such as ***bomb/bombard, crumb/crumble, muscle/muscular, hasten/haste, soften/soft.*** As students move through the grades, they will encounter more words that follow this pattern, thereby expanding their vocabularies: *column/columnist, solemn/solemnity, assign/assignation.* Rather than trying simply to remember the spelling of one silent consonant in one word, students learn the following strategy: To remember the spelling of a word with a silent consonant, try to think of a word related in spelling and meaning. You may get a clue from the consonant that is sounded.

VOWEL ALTERNATION. In the pair *revise/revision,* the long *i* in the base word (*revise*) changes to a short *i* in the derived word (*revision*). **Vowel alternation** occurs in many related words in which the spelling of the vowels remains the same despite an alternation or change in the sound represented by the spelling. These alternations occur as affixes are added and the accented syllables change (e.g., *im pose' / im po si' tion*). Students benefit most from the study of vowel alternation patterns when these patterns are presented in a logical sequence. Begin with the study of related words containing simple vowel alternations that change from long to short vowel sounds as suffixes are added, as in *n**a**ture* to *n**a**tural*, *s**a**ne* to *s**a**nity*, and *div**i**ne* to *div**i**nity*.

Next, students may explore in depth the spelling of the schwa, or least accented vowel sound. As affixes are added to words, the accented syllables change—*re side'* to *res' **i** dent*—and this reduction in stress influences the sound of the vowel. Note the long-to-schwa alternation in *res**i**de* to *res**i**dent*, *opp**o**se* to *opp**o**sition*, and *inv**i**te* to *inv**i**tation*. In many words, the vowel is reduced from the short sound to the schwa: *all**e**ge* to *all**e**gation*, *exc**e**l* to *exc**e**llent*, *hab**i**tual* to *hab**i**t*.

Help your students notice that very often *multiple* alternations are occurring in a group of related words. This insight might lead to an investigation of how many vowel and consonant alternations students can find within a group of words, such as the following:

ferocious	ferocity
diplomatic	diplomacy
specific	specificity
pugnacious	pugnacity

In *ferocious* and *ferocity*, for example, there is a long-to-short *o* vowel alternation and a /sh/-/s/ consonant alternation.

The spelling–meaning connection explored through consonant and vowel alternations plays a very important role in fine-tuning spelling knowledge and in expanding students' vocabularies. Once students understand how the principle operates in known words, we show them how it applies in unknown words. For example, let us say a student understands but misspells the word *solemn* as SOLEM in his writing. You would then show him the related word *solemnity*. In so doing, you have the opportunity to address two important objectives. First, the reason for the so-called silent *n* in *solemn* becomes clear—the word is related to *solemnity*, in which the *n* is pronounced. Second, because students already know the meaning of *solemn*, they are able to understand the meaning of the new but related word *solemnity*. You have just used the spelling system, in other words, to expand this student's vocabulary.

Greek and Latin Elements

Word root is the term that we use to introduce the concept of Greek and Latin word parts. Word roots, in contrast to **base words,** usually cannot stand alone after all affixes have been removed—for example, *chron* ("time") in *chronology* and *struc* ("build") in *restructure*. The study of Greek and Latin word roots offers an incredibly rich terrain to explore and should begin in the upper elementary and middle grades and extend throughout high school and beyond. Choosing which roots to study may depend on the number of words that will be at least partially familiar to your students. You may also select roots on the basis of content areas of study. If you are studying forms of government, for example, words like *democracy*, *monarchy*, and *plutocracy* suggest an examination of the common roots.

It is important to note that, over the years, educators and linguists have used different terms to refer to these elements and to make distinctions between roots of Greek or Latin origin (Dale, O'Rourke, & Bamman, 1971; Henry, 2003; Moats, 2000; Templeton, 1996). For example, roots of Greek origin are often labeled "combining forms" and those of Latin origin simply "roots." This is to distinguish the flexibility of Greek elements from Latin elements. Greek roots such as *photo* and *graph* may combine in different places in words—at the beginning, middle, or end (*tele**photo***, ***graph**ic*, ***photograph***). Latin roots, on the other hand, tend to stay in one place, with prefixes and suffixes attached (***cred**ible*, ***cred**ence*, *in**cred**ible*). After students understand these word parts and how they work, it may be helpful—as well as interesting—to point out this distinction between Greek and Latin roots. As with so much of word study, we need to know the various terms and usages but must use them judiciously and

Go to PDToolkit for *Words Their Way*, click on the Videos tab, then type "Vocabulary with Root Tree (*tract*), Day 2" and watch how Ms. Rubero uses an interactive whiteboard in a discussion of the word root *tract*.

consistently with our students so as not to overwhelm them with labels when they are first learning a concept.

In the following lesson, Jorge Ramirez shows his students how Latin word roots function within words. He begins by passing out a sheet of words and asks students for ideas about how to sort them. The students quickly discover that the words contain similar word parts—*struct* and *fract*. Mr. Ramirez writes the key words *fracture* and *construct* and then writes the rest into categories as students call them out.

Mr. Ramirez points out *fracture* and *fraction* on the board. "We know what these two words are and what they mean. What happens when you *fracture* your arm?"

Students respond, "You break it."

"What do you do when you divide something into *fractions?"* Mr. Ramirez elicits from the students that you break whole numbers down into fractions.

"Good! Now, both words *fracture* and *fraction* have *fract* in them. Is *fract* a word?"

Students respond, "No."

"It's a very important part of the words *fracture* and *fraction,* however. We call *fract* a *word root. Fract* comes from a word in Latin that means 'to break.' Remember our discussion about the history of English and how so many words and word parts in English come from the Greek and Latin languages? *Fract* lives on in the words *fracture* and *fraction.* Word roots are everywhere! Let's look at these words."

Mr. Ramirez points to the words under *construct: construction, structure.* "What's the same in these three words?"

Students point out *struct.*

"Good! You've found the word root! Now, let's think about what this word root might mean. Think about what happens when construction workers construct a building or structure." Students engage in a brief discussion in which the meaning "to build" emerges. "Right! *Construct* means 'to build something,' and *structure* is another term we often use to refer to a building or something that has been built."

Next, Mr. Ramirez points to the word *instruct* and asks the students how the meaning of "build" might apply to the word. Through discussion, students come to the realization that *instruct* refers to how learning or knowledge is "built."

Mr. Ramirez assigns his students the task over the next few days of finding more words with the *fract* and *struct* roots. Students brainstorm, use the class dictionary, and consult an online dictionary to develop a long list of words including ***fract****ious,* ***fract****als, in****fract****ion, re****fract****ion, super****struct****ure, recon****struct****ion, un****struct****ured, de****struct****ion, inde****struct****ible, ob****struct****ion,* and *in****struct****ional.* Students record the words they find in the word study section of their vocabulary notebooks and come together to compare their findings.

Word roots nestle within a word and are the meaningful anchor to which prefixes and suffixes may attach. Roots also follow the basic spelling–meaning premise that words with similar meanings are usually spelled similarly. It is important to point out to students that spelling *visually* represents the meanings of these elements and preserves the meaning relationships among words that at first may appear quite different. The consistent spelling of word roots is their best clue to identifying them and examining how they function within words (***insp****ect,* ***spect****ator; pre****dict****,* ***indict***). Occasionally, the spelling of the roots may change—both *vid* (in ***vid****eo* and ***evid****ent*) and *vis* (in ***vis****ible* and ***televis****ion*) come from the Latin word *videre,* meaning "to see." Students may already have noted some of these variations in their exploration of spelling–meaning relationships. For example, you might ask them to think about how *receive* and *reception* are related in meaning. Students can now examine these words while attending to the meaning of the root within the related words (*ceiv* and *cep* both mean "take"). It also helps that these changes are usually predictable (see next section).

At the derivational relations stage, exploration of Greek and Latin elements begins with those that occur with greatest frequency in the language and are most transparent in the words in which they occur. They should be sequenced according to the abstractness of their meanings, from concrete to more abstract. For example, the Greek roots *therm* (heat) and *photo* (light) and the Latin roots *spect* (to look), *rupt* (to break, burst), and *dict* (to speak, say) are introduced and explored early in the sequence. The way in which other roots function within words is often not as transparent, however, so those roots are explored later—for example, the Latin roots *fer* (to carry) in *defer* and *spir* (to breathe) in *inspiration*. Figure 8.4 lists the roots that are first studied. More Greek and Latin roots can be found in Appendix E.

Predictable Spelling Changes in Vowels and Consonants

After students have systematically explored some word roots and their derivational relatives that share the same spelling, they can begin to examine related words in which both the sound *and* the spelling change. This change is predictable or occurs regularly in families. For example, the spelling change of the long *a* in *explain* from *ai* to a reduced *a* in the derived word *explanation* is not the only word in which this type of change occurs; it also occurs in *exclaim/exclamation* and *proclaim/proclamation;* a similar change from long to short *e* occurs in *receive/reception* and *deceive/deception*. Students learn that, if the base word has the *ai* or *ei* spelling, the derived word's spelling is simply *a* or *e*. Students are ready to examine these words because they understand the spelling–meaning patterns presented earlier. As noted in the previous section, they also are learning that these spelling changes occur within word roots.

Students first do a sort in which each base word is paired with its derivative and then sort the word pairs according to the specific spelling change that occurs. The following sort illustrates this feature.

rec**ei**ve/rec**e**ption	excl**ai**m/excl**a**mation	det**ai**n/det**e**ntion
conc**ei**ve/conc**e**ption	procl**ai**m/procl**a**mation	ret**ai**n/ret**e**ntion
dec**ei**ve/dec**e**ption	recl**ai**m/recl**a**mation	
perc**ei**ve/perc**e**ption	accl**ai**m/accl**a**mation	

Advanced Suffix Study

A handful of suffixes present occasional challenges even for advanced readers and writers. The adjective-forming suffix *-able/-ible* seems to be a classic for misspelling. However, there is a generalization that usually helps determine whether this suffix is spelled *-able* or *-ible*. Consider the sort below and look for the root or base word from which each word is derived.

dependable	credible
profitable	audible
agreeable	edible
predictable	visible

A fairly powerful generalization emerges: If the suffix is attached to a base word that can stand alone (*depend*), it is usually spelled *-able;* if it is attached to a word root (*cred*), it is usually spelled *-ible*. Base words that end in *e* will usually drop the *e* and add *-able* (*desire/desirable*);

however, soft *c* or *g* endings may be followed by *-ible* as in *reducible* and sometimes a final *e* is retained to keep the soft sound, as in *noticeable* and *manageable*.

The connection between the suffixes *-ant/-ance* and *-ent/-ence* can also be understood when pairs are examined: *brilliant/brilliance*, *confident/confidence*. Sound is no clue, but if you know the spelling of a word that ends in one of these suffixes, that word is a clue to the spelling of the suffix in the related word (Templeton, 1980). At this level, most individuals know how to spell one of the words in such pairs correctly; making this spelling–meaning relationship explicit is extremely helpful for the learner.

Whether consonants are doubled when **inflectional endings** are added in words like *committed* and *benefited* is revisited in the derivational relations stage with words of more than one syllable. Jorge Ramirez provides a collection of words that double and words that don't and challenges his students to figure out why.

"Okay, we've got a few words here to sort. What do you notice about these words? That's right, they all end in *-ed*. What do you notice about the base words?" He and his students discuss the fact that in some cases the final consonant has been doubled before adding *-ed,* and in others it has stayed the same. He has them sort the words into two columns by those features:

excelled	edited
occurred	limited
submitted	orbited
referred	conquered

Mr. Ramirez asks the students to work in pairs to talk about what they see and hear when they contrast the words in both columns. He encourages them to read the base words in each column several times. If no one brings up "accent" as a possible explanation, he asks them to listen as he reads the base words in each column, emphasizing the accented syllable: *ex**cel**, oc**cur**, sub**mit**, re**fer***. Then he reads ***ed**it, **lim**it, **or**bit, **con**quer.*

"I get it, I get it!" yells Silvio. "The accent is on a different syllable! When it is on the last syllable you have to double!"

Silvio understands the generalization toward which Mr. Ramirez is working: If the last syllable of the base word is accented, double the final consonant before adding *-ed* (and *-ing* as well). If the last syllable is not accented, then do not double the final consonant.

Mr. Ramirez follows up the sort by pointing out the following bit of history:

"Remember when Daire brought in the British copy of *Harry Potter and the Goblet of Fire* that her grandma bought for her in England and we noticed how the spelling of some of the words was different than in American English? For example, there were a lot of doubled consonants that we don't have—*benefited* had two *t*s at the end. Actually, in just about every situation where we in the United States do not double the final consonant, people in other English-speaking countries do. Do you know who we can blame for making it so that Americans have to think about whether or not to double? Would you believe it was Noah Webster? Yes! The man who brought us our dictionary!

"Actually, what Webster wanted to do was make English spoken and written in the United States different in many ways from English spoken in Britain. When he did this, our country wasn't getting along too well with Britain—after all, we had fought a war to become independent not long before! So in his dictionary of American English—the first of its kind—Webster decided to change many spellings. One of the most obvious ways was to take out the *u* in words such as *honour* and *behaviour.*" Mr. Ramirez writes these words on the board. "He also switched the *re* in words such as *theatre* and *centre.*" He writes these on the board.

When students notice exceptions to this principle—when they see the spelling *travelled* or *benefitted,* for example—ask them to check the dictionary. Though they will see the correct spelling they will also see the alternative spelling listed, perhaps with the label *Brit* because final consonants like *l* are more likely to be doubled in British English whether they are accented or not.

Assimilated Prefixes

Prefixes are first studied in the syllables and affixes stage and then throughout the derivational relations stage. Prefixes are often obvious visual and meaning units that are easy to see and understand, as in *unlikely* or *inaccurate*. However, there is a group of prefixes that are somewhat disguised, as in the word *illegal.* The only clue to the prefix is the doubled letters. Known as **absorbed** or **assimilated** prefixes, their spellings may pose a significant challenge for students because they depend on considerable prior knowledge about other basic spelling–meaning patterns, processes of adding prefixes to base words, and simple Greek and Latin roots. Most adults are unaware of this feature but it can resolve many spelling dilemmas—such as how to spell *accommodate,* the most frequently misspelled word in the English language.

The following sort might be used to explore the idea of absorbed prefixes. The words are first presented in a random list and students are asked to discuss their meanings. The students are likely to conclude that they all seem to mean "not" or "the opposite of." When asked how they might sort the words, the following categories emerge:

ineffective	illiterate	immature	irregular	impossible
inorganic	illegal	immobile	irrational	impatient
inactive	illogical	immortal	irrelevant	improper
infinite	illegible	immodest		

The students could then be asked what they notice about the base words in each column. You might suggest they try saying "inmobile" or "inrelevant." It is of course possible to pronounce them, but definitely awkward—we have to stress the prefix in order to do so (in most words the accent does not fall on the prefix). And changing from the *n* to the *m* in *immobile* is cumbersome. At this point, some should realize that the particular spelling of the prefix *in-* often depends on the first letter of the base word, taking on the same spelling (i.e., being "absorbed"). In fact, if they go to the dictionary to look up the prefixes or the words, they will be referred back to the original prefix *in-*. Jorge Ramirez describes the process for his students.

In discussing the prefix sort, Mr. Ramirez poses the question, "If all these prefixes mean the same thing why do we spell it so many different ways?" The students notice that the spelling seems to be related to the baseword; *il-* is used before words starting with *l* and *ir-* before words starting with *r*. "Good observations," he responds. "Let's take the word *immobile.* A long time ago, someone combined the prefix *in-* with the word *mobile* to create a new word that meant 'not mobile.' Now, try pronouncing the word like it was pronounced when it first came into existence: ***in**mobile.* Does that feel kind of weird? Does your tongue kind of get stuck on the beginning of *mobile*? Mine sure does! Over time it became easier for people to leave out the /n/ sound when pronouncing the word. The sound of the *n* became 'absorbed' into the /m/ sound at the beginning of the base word *mobile.* Before long, the spelling of the *n* changed to indicate this change in pronunciation—but it's important to remember that this letter didn't disappear. They knew it was necessary to keep the two letters in the prefix to indicate that it was still a prefix. If the last letter of the prefix had been dropped, then the meaning of the prefix would have been lost."

Primarily Latin in origin, absorbed or assimilated prefixes are widespread in English. An extensive list of assimilated prefixes can be found in Appendix E. Although the prefix *ad-* is the most common, it is also the most abstract, so explore others first. By the way, *accommodate* has two assimilated prefixes: The *d* in the prefix *ad-* is absorbed into the first letter sound of the second prefix *con-*, and the *n* in *con-* is absorbed into the first letter sound of the word root *modate.*

for Words Their Way™

Go to PDToolkit for *Words Their Way,* click on the Videos tab, then type "Prefix Assimilation (*com-*), Day 1" to see Ms. Rubero guiding her students in a discussion.

Word Study Instruction for the Derivational Relations Stage

The principles for instruction listed for intermediate readers and writers also guide our instruction at the advanced level. As at the intermediate level, word study for advanced readers emphasizes active exploration of words and the application of word knowledge to spelling, vocabulary development, and the analysis of unknown words encountered in reading. We can initiate word study for advanced readers by observing, "You know, when you first learned to read you had to learn how spelling stands for sounds. Now you're going to be learning how spelling stands for meaning."

Sequence and Pacing

Figure 8.4 on page 281 presents a general sequence for word study in the derivational relations stage. Just as at the syllables and affixes stage, decisions about what features to teach are often restricted by the difficulty of the word meanings rather than any problems with reading or spelling the words. Assimilated prefixes, for example, are examined later because many of the words that contain them will not occur with much frequency in the reading materials or be in the speaking vocabularies of most upper elementary students (for example, *immunity* or *innumerable*). Although some new vocabulary words can be included in every sort at this level, there should still be a good number of familiar words from which students can begin to make generalizations, moving from the known to the unknown.

Placement of students in the derivational relations stage is not simply a matter of the difficulty of the spelling features, as it is in earlier stages. It often depends on students' grade level. For example, students in the upper elementary grades would be ready for the study of a root like *spec* in words such as *inspect* and *spectator* but would find words like *circumspect* and *retrospective* difficult to understand and unlikely to show up in their grade-level reading materials. At the same time, those words would be very useful words for high school students to examine and learn. Table 8.1 on page 280 presents the spelling characteristics across the early, middle, and late derivational relations stage.

An important caution: You may wish to confirm that students who seem to be at the derivational stage based on the Elementary Spelling Inventory (ESI) are indeed at that level. Administering the Upper-Level Spelling Inventory will provide that additional information.

EARLY/MIDDLE. Students in the early stage of derivational relations have mastered most syllable juncture conventions, including the spellings of most prefixes and suffixes and what happens when they are affixed to bases. They are working through the juncture conventions that govern the spelling of the frequent suffix *-ion* (*-tion*, *-sion*, *-ssion*). Occasionally a common prefix may be misspelled, such as *permission* spelled PURMISSION by analogy with words such as *purchase* or *destroy* spelled DISTROY because of the pronunciation of the first syllable and the frequency of the prefix *dis-*. Students in the early phase are also still learning how meaning is a clue to spelling unstressed vowels, such as not realizing that IMPASITION (*imposition*) is explained by the related word *impose*. By the middle phase, the spellings of prefixes and most suffixes is fairly locked in, as are the spellings of most bases and roots across morphologically related words (*compete/competi**tive**/competi**tion***).

LATE. You may find that a few students in the upper elementary grades are in the late derivational relations stage, but most will not reach this stage until at least middle school and high school. Learners at this phase are able to spell most new academic vocabulary words correctly when first encountering them. They use but confuse assimilated prefixes, however, as well as the suffixes *-able/-ible*, *-ant/-ent*, and *-ance/-ence*. As we have noted, this phase is not an "end" to development but rather part of a never-ending, fascinating journey.

Assess and Monitor Progress in the Derivational Relations Stage

MONITORING PROGRESS

By definition, students in the derivational relations stage are becoming very good spellers. As we have emphasized in this chapter, word study for these students is focused primarily on the generative aspects of morphology and how the structure of words is usually the key to their meanings. Assessment, therefore, should address more than just spelling. When you do assess with a focus on spelling, you needn't call out all the words in a sort, but rather only 10 or 15. Every few weeks, administer a cumulative review consisting of selected words representing different elements and patterns. There are several ways to assess.

- Ask students to spell the words studied that week. This will work well for endings such as *-ion*, *-ible/-able*, and *-ence/-ance*, in which sound is not a clue.

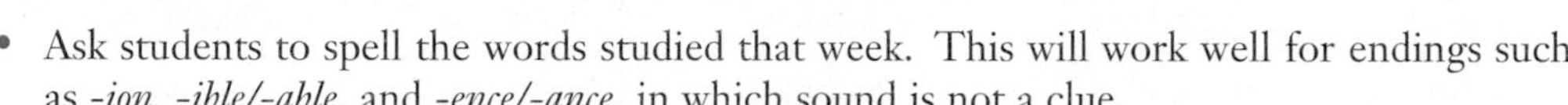

- Ask students to both spell and define words. Definitions should be in their own words.
- Give students a base word and ask them to add suffixes, such as adding *-er* to words like *strange* (*stranger*), *noisy* (*noisier*), and *clean* (*cleaner*). Use words that they have not sorted to test for generalizations.
- Ask students to generate words given a prefix, suffix, or root. For example, the root *mal* should yield words like *malignant*, *dismal*, *malice*, and *malfunction*.
- Ask students to generate a related word in which a consonant or vowel sound is heard. For example, there is a silent letter in *moisten*. Write a related word in which you can hear the sound of the letter (*moist*).
- Ask students to match elements to meaning, such as matching *post-* and *pre-* to the meanings "before" and "after."
- Ask students to spell a word and then underline a prefix, suffix, or root and also define the element, such as *fracture* means "*break*."
- Provide a sentence and ask students to supply or select the target word, as in the following: He loved to learn *magic* tricks and wanted to become a ______________.

As in the syllables and affixes stage, students at this stage can be involved in monitoring their own progress. There is less urgency in this stage because word study for derivational relations is typically spread out over the middle school and high school years and beyond—literally for the rest of their lives. Think about the word sorts you do with students at this level as supporting their vocabulary knowledge, both word-specific and generative. Unlike earlier developmental stages, sorts at this level need not be one-week affairs. Rather, they often stretch across two and sometimes three weeks.

for Words Their Way™

Go to PDToolkit for *Words Their Way*, click on the Assessment Tools tab, and type "Goal Setting/Progress Monitoring Charts."

As at all stages, vocabulary notebooks may be reviewed and graded—usually every two to three weeks is sufficient for derivational spellers. Teachers attend to the range of words collected during word hunts for particular patterns, the types of open sorts that are recorded, and how well new words have been collected and described (see p. 292).

Word Study with English Learners in the Derivational Relations Stage

English learners have the potential to be *more* sensitive to words than monolingual speakers simply because they must be more analytical—of their home language as well as of English—in order to negotiate the nature of spelling–sound–meaning relationships (Templeton, 2010). The study of **cognates** seems particularly fruitful at the derivational relations stage and can also benefit native English speakers who might be learning Spanish, French, or German as a foreign language. Cognates are words in different languages that share similar structures and similar meanings because they share similar origins.

for **English Learners**

Many words in English are derived from Latin; this is true for other languages as well. You can see the spelling–meaning connection in *mater* (Latin), *madre* (Spanish), *mere* (French), *mutter* (German), and *mother* (English). Attention to cognates helps both English learners and native speakers of English see morphological similarities between their native language and their to-be-learned language. Just as with our word sorts in English, sorting English and Spanish cognates offers opportunities for examining spelling–meaning relationships and grammatical features. For example, students may be guided to notice the common suffixes and their spellings that key different parts of speech (Nash, 1997):

	Nouns	*Adjectives*	*Verbs*	*Adverbs*
English	alphabet	alphabetic	alphabetize	alphabetically
Spanish	alfabeto	alfabético	alfabetizar	alfabéticamente
English	favor	favorable	favor	favorably
Spanish	favor	favorable	favorecer	favorablemente

Opportunities for attention to cognates abound in specific content areas such as science (Bravo, Hiebert, & Pearson, 2005), math, and social studies (Templeton, 2010). In science or math, for example, students may match and discuss what they notice about the following cognates:

polygon	quadrilateral	hexagon	pentagon	triangle
polígono	cuadrilatero	hexágono	pentágono	triángulo

Word roots also offer a very rich terrain for exploring cognates in other languages: *nocturno* and *extensor* in Spanish have very similar meanings to *nocturnal* and *extensive* in English. Make it a point to look for cognates as you study the different Latin roots—*port* shows up in Spanish *importar* and *exportar* and means the same thing as in *export* and *import*. You may want to initiate a chart in your classroom of cognates as students discover them. While most cognates across languages have the same or similar meanings, it is also important to be aware of potential "false friends." For example, the Spanish word *suburbio* looks a lot like the English word *suburbia*, or *suburbs*, but the Spanish word *suburbio* refers to the slums (Swan & Smith, 2001). Likewise, the Spanish word *éxito* doesn't correlate with *exit* at all, but means "success."

WORD STUDY *Routines and Management*

There are three basic points to keep in mind regarding students' word study at this level (Templeton, 1989, 1992):

1. Words and word elements selected for study should be *generative*, which means that, when possible, we teach about words in "meaning families." This highlights the awareness that particular patterns of relationships can be extended or generalized to other words. For example, an awareness of the long-to-short vowel alternation pattern that was introduced during the syllables and affixes stage with words such as *please* and *pleasant* can generalize to words such as *compete/competitive*.
2. The words that we initially select for exploration by our students should be based on how obvious their relationship is. For example, we will teach clearly related words such as *represent/misrepresent* before teaching about words that are less clearly related, such as *expose/exposition*.
3. There should be a balance of teacher-directed instruction with students' exploration and discussion.

Teacher-Directed Word Study Instruction

Word study should take place all day long and in all content areas as teachers pause to examine words, talk about unusual spellings (*pneumonia*), search for clues to meaning in the word and in context, and look up and discuss words in the dictionary. But, as in other stages, students in the derivational relations stage still need in-depth systematic attention to features at their developmental level. We emphasize the importance of word study at this developmental level for middle and secondary students, especially if these students have not experienced this type of systematic word study in school prior to this time.

Teachers who use the Upper-Level Spelling Inventory available in the Assessment Database on the website will be better able to identify the spelling–meaning "landscape" that their students will be exploring. Because meaning is so important in attending to these patterns, students will examine words that they are already spelling correctly. Typically there is a plateau effect with upper-level assessments, which suggests that students in homogeneous classes may all benefit from similar instruction. Small group differentiated instruction is less important if students are all advanced readers and spellers.

Routines

The routines and word study notebook activities appropriate for earlier stages need to be carefully considered at this stage. The categorization of words through sorting is still a powerful learning activity; however, some teachers rely more on writing words into categories than on cutting out words and sorting them physically. Blind sorts still work well when spelling is an issue (as in *-able* and *-ible* sorts or when working with the /shən/ ending) but will not pose much of a challenge when the sort features prefixes and roots.

Go to PDToolkit for *Words Their Way,* click on the Videos tab, then type "Vocabulary with Root Tree (*tract*), Day 2." After brainstorming and sorting, Mrs. Rubero's students look through www.onelook.com for words with the *tract* root.

Word hunts should extend over longer periods of time because the words and features at this level are less common, especially in literary texts. They are more likely to occur in textbooks. However, brainstorming additional words (word hunts in the head) sometimes works well and dictionaries can become a place for word hunts. Students can be taught to search online dictionaries by using an asterisk before and/or after the word part to get a list of words (e.g., **cian* will give you words that end with *-cian; *hydr** will yield the hundreds of words that contain this root).

Ongoing classroom displays of words provide continual review as words turn up in reading and class discussions; these can be added to categories started weeks before. As students explore word histories, they may be shown how to reference and read the entries in unabridged dictionaries, and most important, in the resources available for such exploration (see Resource Connections: Resources for Word Study, p. 277).

The *meanings of words* are a critical focus throughout the derivational relations stage. Include routines that focus on meanings. For example, students can be asked to use the dictionary to look up and record definitions and word origins of selected words (but not 20 at a time, however). They can be asked to use words in sentences to demonstrate their understanding of meaning, but invite them also to try illustrations or cartoons. These visual representations can be powerful mnemonics, as shown in Figure 8.6. Having students work cooperatively and letting them share their sentences or drawings can also be engaging.

Games are still a valuable way to review words not only for a test, but also over time. At this level students can create many games themselves based on popular games like Concentration,

FIGURE 8.6 Illustrating Word Relationships

Rummy, War, Slap Jack, Uno, Trivial Pursuit, and Jeopardy. Give them blank game board templates from Appendix F or card stock for playing cards and they can do the rest. In the process of creating games they will remember the words and come to understand the feature better.

At this stage, exploration of a particular group of words and the spelling–meaning patterns they represent offer a number of paths to explore. For this reason, some teachers adopt a two-week schedule that includes a word study contract such as the one in Figure 3.17 on page 77. Students are given a collection of 20 to 40 words and complete a selection of routines independently in school or for homework. Testing is done every two weeks and often includes an assessment of mastery of meaning as well as of spelling. Students are asked, for example, to explain the meaning of a prefix, root, or particular words.

Word study notebooks are an integral part of students' word learning at this stage (Gill & Bear, 1989; Templeton et al., 2010). They are used, for example, to record word sorts and add words to the sorts after going on word hunts. To begin, divide the notebooks into three sections:

1. *Word Study.* A weekly record of sorts, reflections, and homework. This is also the section to record words that consistently present spelling challenges. Thinking of related words is one way to help clarify spellings.
2. *Looking into Language.* Records of whole-group word study of related words, concept sorts, interesting word collections, investigations, and theme study words.
3. *New and Interesting Words.* Words students encounter in their reading that really grab them (much as "golden lines" do in their reading) are *golden words* (Templeton et al., 2010). These are often new words, perhaps difficult words. Teach the following steps to facilitate older students in collecting "golden words":

   - *Collect the word.* While reading, mark words that really "grab" you or that you find difficult. When you are through reading or studying, go back to these words. Read around each word, and think about its possible meaning.
   - *Record the word and sentence.* Write the word, followed by the sentence in which it was used, the page number, and an abbreviation for the title of the book. (At times the sentence will be too long. Write enough of it to give a clue to meaning.) Think about the word's meaning.
   - *Look at word parts and think about their meanings.* Look at the different parts of the word—prefixes, suffixes, and base word or root word. Think about the meanings of the affixes and the base or root.
   - *Record related words.* Think of other words that are like this word, and write them underneath the part of the word that is similar.
   - *Use the dictionary.* Look the word up in the dictionary, read the various definitions, and in a few words record the meaning (the one that applies to the word in the book you are reading) in your notebook or on a card. Look for similar words (both in form and meaning) above and below the target word and list them as well. Look at the origin of the word, and add it to your entry if it is interesting.
   - *Review the words.*

A realistic goal is to collect five to ten words a week. These words may be brought up in class and shared, as in the following example:

- Collect the word: *orthography.*
- Record the word and sentence: "English *orthography* is not crazy, and it carries the history of the word with it." p. 22, *Sounds of Language.*

- Look at word parts and think about their meanings: *ortho/graph* (may have something to do with writing).
- Record possible related words: *orthodontist, orthodox, graphics, orthographer.*
- Study the word in the dictionary, and record interesting information: "A method of representing the sounds of a language by letters; spelling." Origin: *ortho*—"correct;" *graph*—"something written."

Vocabulary Their Way™ by Templeton, Bear, Invernizzi, and Johnston (2010) provides background and a wealth of instructional support for students at this level. You should find this resource especially helpful for derivational level students at the intermediate grades, extending the types of activities and instruction presented in this chapter. In addition, you may find that it will extend your own knowledge base as well and provide you with the confidence to explore words more deeply with your students.

Preparing Sorts in the Derivational Relations Stage

There are a number of word sorts in Appendix D and on the website that are appropriate for more advanced derivational relations students. Additional words can be found in the lists in Appendixes D and E, which will suggest other sorts as well. These resources present avenues of word study that will be engaging and rewarding for students who are verbally advanced. Students should already be able to spell and define at least half of the words. With more advanced students, a larger proportion of the words included in sorts may be unfamiliar, but the students usually are able to infer the meanings because these words share similar meaning elements with the known words.

This type of exploration and curiosity about words will become part of students' learning repertories when it is consistently modeled by their teachers. Indeed, it is more a mindset

for Words Their Way™

Go to PDToolkit for *Words Their Way,* click on the Sorts and Games tab, then select the "Derivational Relations Stage" to find ready-to-use sorts. Or you can click on the Create Your Own button to develop your own sorts.

RESOURCES FOR IMPLEMENTING WORD STUDY *in Your Classroom*

A sample of prepared sorts can be found on the website and in Appendix D. These resources offer sample sorts and lists of words for other sorts or to modify the sorts that are suggested.

Words Their Way™: Word Sorts for Derivational Relations Spellers (Templeton, Johnston, Bear, & Invernizzi, 2009) has 60 prepared sorts divided into nine units of study with assessments. Although these assessments mainly tap spelling knowledge, they often bring out morphological or vocabulary knowledge as well (e.g., matching prefixes with their meanings).

Vocabulary Their Way™ (Templeton, Bear, Invernizzi, & Johnston, 2010) offers guided walk-throughs in the appendixes that address the concrete-to-abstract spelling–meaning continuum and Greek/Latin roots. These are particularly useful for teachers working with middle grade and secondary students.

than a strategy per se. Students become lifelong wordsmiths and almost automatically wonder about the relationships among words in general and about a particular word specifically; for example, does the similarity in spelling between ***applaud/plaudit*** and ***mordant/morsel*** capture underlying meaning relationships? (Yes!) When you share this type of awareness and curiosity, you nourish the continual growth of vocabulary and conceptual networks.

ACTIVITIES FOR THE DERIVATIONAL RELATIONS STAGE

The following routines, activities, and games are designed for students in the derivational relations stage. Games described in other chapters can also be adapted for features studied in this stage.

8.1 Stressbusters

The purpose of this board game is to practice identifying the accented or stressed syllable in a given word. Students can play the game in pairs after they have been introduced to the idea of accent and know how to determine it. Brenda Reibel contributed this game.

MATERIALS Create a Stressbusters game board with a template from Appendix F or using circles as shown in Figure 8.7. Prepare game cards with familiar two- and three-syllable words.

FIGURE 8.7 Stressbusters Game Board

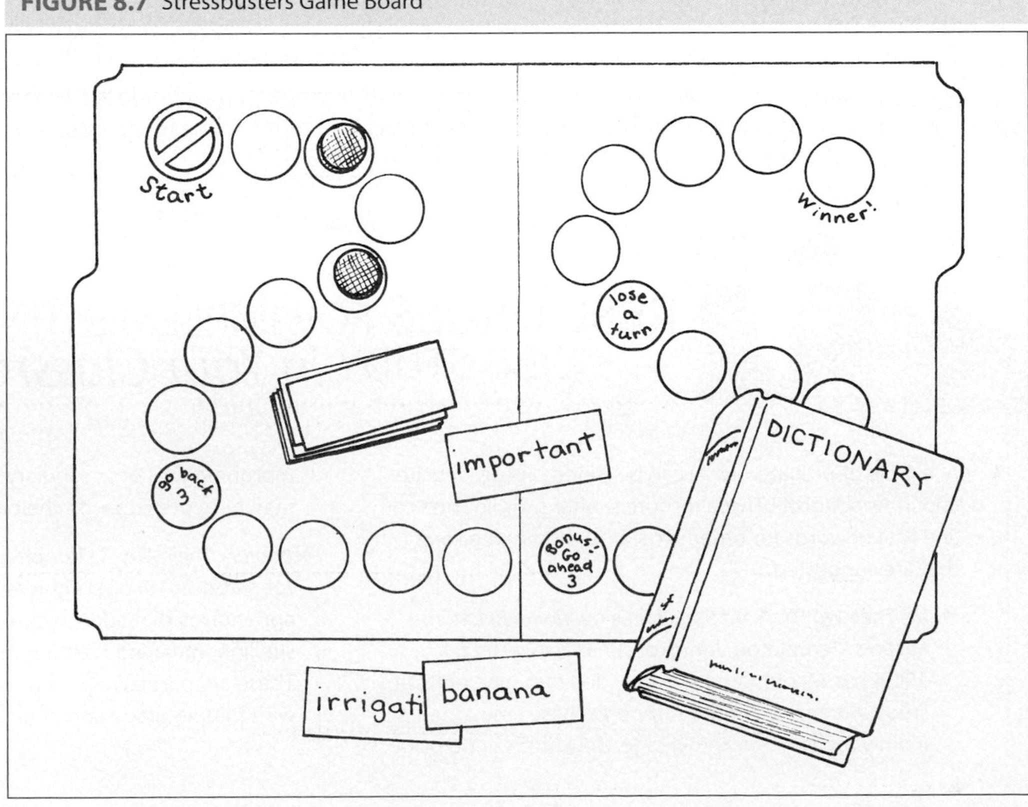

(You might start with names of students in the class.) You will also need playing pieces and a dictionary (to verify placement of stress or accent).

PROCEDURES

1. As students correctly identify the placement of stress, they will do the following: If the accent falls in the beginning syllable, the player moves one space; if the accent falls in the second syllable, the player moves two spaces; if the accent is on the third syllable, the player moves three spaces.
2. The game continues until one player reaches the finish circle.
3. Players may challenge the acceptability of accent answers by looking the word up in the dictionary to determine the accented syllable. If correct, the challenger gets to move his or her game piece forward one, two, or three places, depending on where the accent falls. If the player is correct and the challenger is wrong, the challenger must move back. If the challenger thinks the word is accented on the second syllable and is incorrect, he or she must move back two spaces; if the challenger thinks the accent is on the third syllable and is incorrect, he or she moves back three spaces.

   Words that are accented on the third syllable are also accented on the first syllable. These words may be challenged. If a player moves one space for the word *constitution*, for example, not realizing it is also accented on the third syllable, then the other player could challenge.

8.2 You Teach the Word

Students need to learn many vocabulary words for content areas. One way to handle these is to assign one word to each student, who then becomes responsible for teaching that word to the rest of the class. Ask each student to create a small poster to add to a class word wall, such as the one in Figure 8.8, that includes a definition, a synonym and/or antonym, an etymology, a sentence, or an illustration. Students can share their posters but can also be encouraged to think of creative ways to help each other learn the word, such as by acting it out. For more advanced students, see the "Word Museum" project in Templeton et al. (2010).

FIGURE 8.8 Poster for Laissez Faire

laissez faire
/lay-zay fair/
definition: noninterference, lack of government intervention
origin: French laisser - to let + faire - to do
example: The teacher had a laissez faire attitude about chewing gum in school.

8.3 We Think (with *-tion/-sion*)

This activity will involve students in small groups or two teams of two each, examining words to determine clues for spelling the *-tion* or *-sion* suffixes. For most students at this stage, the activity offers a good opportunity to reflect explicitly on the conditions that govern how this suffix is spelled.

MATERIALS Each team or group needs a sheet divided into two columns. The left column is labeled "We Think" and the right column is labeled "Because."

PROCEDURES

1. Each team gets a stack of cards to sort (e.g., *act, action, separate, separation, express, expression*) that contain several categories and three to four words in each category. The same words are in each stack; to keep word cards for each team separate, one stack is printed in black letters and the other in red.

2. Each team first pairs up the base words and derived words and then sorts them into categories.
3. After looking closely at the words sorted, each team individually fills out their "We Think" sheets with generalities they notice for words taking the *-tion* or *-sion* endings.
4. After the teams have filled out their "We Think" sheets and supported their generalized rules under the "Because" section, the teams have a meeting of the minds to compare findings.

VARIATIONS This activity will work with other base words, word roots, and derivatives. An excellent activity contrasts *-ian* with *-ion* (*electrician, clinician, magician* vs. *adoption, prevention, digestion*) (Nunes & Bryant, 2006). As noted above, *-ian* denotes "person," whereas *-ion* does not.

8.4 Words That Grow from Base Words and Word Roots

FIGURE 8.9 Word Tree: Words That Grow from Base Words and Roots

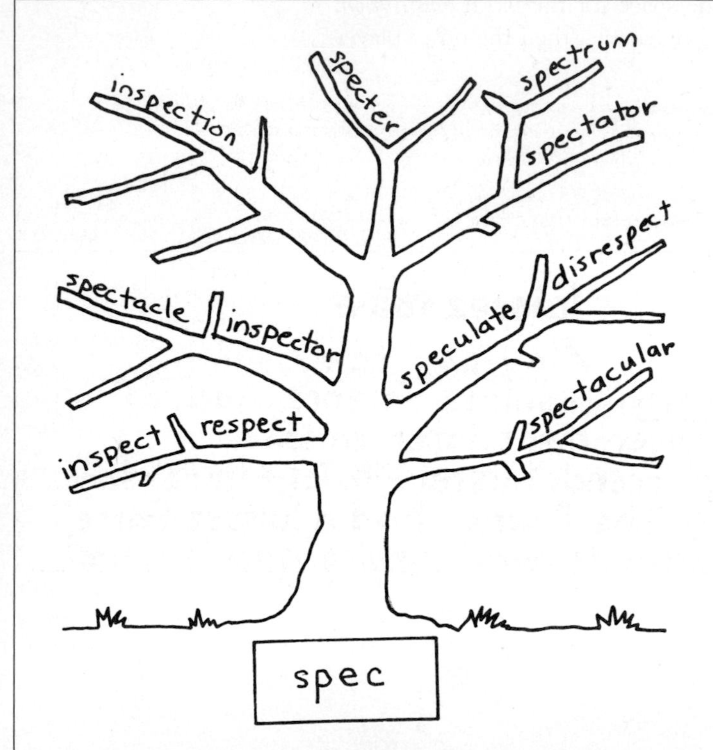

In this whole-class or small-group activity, students see directly how words "grow." It builds on and extends the understanding, begun during the syllables and affixes stage, of how word elements combine.

MATERIALS You will need a drawing of a tree (see Figure 8.9).

PROCEDURES

1. Decide on a base word or a word root to highlight. Begin with more frequently occurring ones; over time, move to less frequently occurring roots.
2. Write the base word or word root at the bottom of the tree, and think of as many forms as possible.
3. Write the different forms on individual branches.
4. Display the word tree in the classroom for several days and encourage students to think of, find, and record more derived words. At the end of the week wipe them off and begin again with the introduction of a new base or word root.

VARIATIONS After making the words, students may use them individually in sentences and/or discuss their meanings. Confirm with the dictionary.

8.5 Latin Jeopardy

At least three students are needed for this game (a host and scorekeeper as well as two players), but lots more can play as well. The whole class can be divided into two teams.

MATERIALS Create a grid with five columns and six rows. Insert headers to indicate the categories. Make a clue card by writing the points on one side and the answer on the other. During the game, turn over the square that is requested so the answer can be read. An alternative for a large group is to make a transparency or interactive whiteboard version of the Latin Root Jeopardy and Double Latin Root Jeopardy boards shown in Figures 8.10 and 8.11. If

PDToolkit for Words Their Way™

Go to PDToolkit for *Words Their Way,* click on the Sorts and Games tab, then type "Latin Root Jeopardy" for a ready-to-use version of this game.

FIGURE 8.10 Latin Root Jeopardy Board

LATIN ROOT JEOPARDY				
SPECT (to look)	FORM (shape)	PORT (to carry)	TRACT (draw or pull)	DICT (to say, speak)
100 One who watches; an onlooker	100 One "form" or style of clothing such as is worn by nurses	100 Goods brought into a country from another country to be sold	100 Adjective: having power to attract; alluring; inviting	100 A book containing the words of a language explained
200 The prospect of good to come; anticipation	200 One who does not conform	200 One who carries burdens for hire	200 A powerful motor vehicle for pulling farm machinery, heavy loads	200 A speaking against, a denial
300 To regard with suspicion and mistrust	300 To form or make anew; to reclaim	300 To remove from one place to another	300 The power to grip or hold to a surface while moving, without slipping	300 A blessing often at the end of a worship service
400 Verb: to esteem Noun: regard, deference Literally: to look again	400 To change into another substance, change of form	400 To give an account of	400 An agreement: literally, to draw together	400 An order proclaimed by an authority
500 Looking around, watchful, prudent	500 Disfigurement, spoiling the shape	500 A case for carrying loose papers	500 To take apart from the rest, to deduct	500 To charge with a crime

you're using a transparency, cover the clues with sticky notes. You will be able to construct a similar framework for your digital display.

PROCEDURES The game consists of two rounds: Jeopardy and Double Jeopardy.

1. The game is modeled after the *Jeopardy* television game. The clue is in the form of an answer and players must phrase their response in the form of a question:

   Answer clue: Coming from the Latin root *tract*, it means "a machine for pulling heavy loads."
   Question response: What is *tractor?*

2. Determine who will go first. The player will select the first category and point value. The host uncovers the clue and reads it aloud.
3. The first player responding correctly adds the point amount of the question to his or her total or gets to keep the card that was turned over. He or she then chooses the next category and point amount. An incorrect answer means that the points are subtracted.
4. The winner is the one with the most points.

FIGURE 8.11 Latin Root Double Jeopardy Board

LATIN ROOT DOUBLE JEOPARDY				
CRED (to believe)	DUCT (to lead)	FER (to bear, carry)	PRESS (to press)	SPIR (to breathe)
200 A system of doing business by trusting that a person will pay at a later date for goods or services	200 A person who directs the performance of a choir or an orchestra	200 (Plants) able to bear fruit; (Animals) able or likely to conceive young	200 A printing machine	200 An immaterial intelligent being
400 A set of beliefs or principles	400 To train the mind and abilities of	400 To carry again; to submit to another for opinion	400 Verb: to utter; Noun: any fast conveyance	400 To breathe out: to die
600 Unbelievable	600 To enroll as a member of a military service	600 To convey to another place, passed from one place to another	600 To press against, to burden, to overpower	600 To breathe through; to emit through the pores of the skin
800 Verb, prefix meaning "not"; word means to damage the good reputation of	800 The formal presentation of one person to another	800 Endurance of pain; distress	800 State of being "pressed down" or saddened	800 To breathe into; to instruct by divine influence
1000 An adjective, prefix *ac,* word means officially recognized	1000 An artificial channel carrying water across country	1000 Cone bearing, as the fir tree	1000 To put down, to prevent circulation	1000 To plot; to band together for an evil purpose

"Questions" for Latin Root Jeopardy

	spect	*form*	*port*	*tract*	*dict*
100	spectator	uniform	import	attractive	dictionary
200	expectation	nonconformist	porter	tractor	contradiction
300	suspect	reform	transport	traction	benediction
400	respect	transform	report	contract	edict
500	circumspect	deformity	portfolio	subtract	indict

"Questions" for Double Latin Root Jeopardy

	cred	*duct*	*fer*	*press*	*spir*
200	credit	conductor	fertile	press	spirit
400	creed	educate	refer	express	expire
600	incredible	induct	transfer	oppress	perspire
800	discredit	introduction	suffering	depression	inspire
1000	accredited	aqueduct	coniferous	suppress	conspire

VARIATIONS

1. A round of Final Jeopardy can be added if you wish. When it is time for the Final Jeopardy question, players see the category, but not the answer. They then decide how many of their points they will risk. When they see the answer, they have 30 seconds to write the question. If they are correct, they add the number of points they risked to their total; if incorrect, that number of points is subtracted from their total.
2. Play can alternate from one player to the next or from one team to the next rather than being based on who shouts out the response first. If one player misses, the other team gets a chance to respond. If they are correct, they also get another turn.
3. Daily Doubles may be included, if desired. (The number of points for an answer is doubled and, if correct, added to the player's score; if incorrect, the doubled number of points is subtracted from the player's score.)
4. Develop a Vocabulary Jeopardy to accompany a unit of study. Generate vocabulary cards from a unit of study that fit into four or five categories (for example, "Food Groups" or "Habitats"). Write questions that relate to facts and concepts studied on cards. Teams of students play the game as a whole-class vocabulary review of the unit.

FIGURE 8.12 Word Shuffle Cards

8.6 Word Part Shuffle

Word Part Shuffle is a noncompetitive word building activity (Moloney, 2008). A group of students receives a stack of cards consisting of a majority of the most generative prefixes, suffixes, and bases/word roots (see Figure 8.12). The group first creates a number of words that may be found in a standard dictionary. Then the group coins a new word, using as many of the cards as they can. They create a definition for the new word and then share with other groups. Kara Moloney has created a deck of these cards with color-coded margins indicating prefix, suffix, or base/root, available at http://verbumnosvocat.com.

PDToolkit for Words Their Way™

Go to PDToolkit for *Words Their Way,* click on the Sorts and Games tab, then type "Word Part Shuffle Cards."

8.7 Quartet

Many games can be played with a deck of word cards made into suits of four. This game is much like Go Fish, except the object is to collect and lay down a suit of four cards (or a quartet).

MATERIALS Create 10 to 12 suits of four cards composed of words that share a common root—for example, *biology, biography, biome, antibiotic.* Write the words at the top left so the words can be read when they are held in the hand.

PROCEDURES

1. Each player is dealt seven cards; the rest are put in a deck. Each player looks through his or her cards for words in the same suit.
2. The first player turns to the next and asks for a particular root: "Give me any cards with the *bio* root." If the player's hand has any cards with the root asked for, the player must give them up and the first player gets to go again. If the player does not have any matches, he or she responds, "Draw one" and the first player draws from the deck.
3. Play proceeds in a clockwise fashion. When a player has a complete suit of four cards, he or she may lay them down. The player who has the most suits at the end—when someone runs out of cards—is the winner.

8.8 It's All Greek to Us

In this card game, the deck is composed of words derived from Greek roots. Three to five players may participate, one of whom will serve as game master and hold and read definition cards.

MATERIALS Using the list of Greek roots and derived words in Appendix E, prepare ten definition cards that consist of a root and definition such as *derm*—"skin." For each root, create four or more word cards (*epidermis, dermatology, taxidermist, hypodermic, pachyderm*). Write these words at the top so they can be seen when held in the hand.

PROCEDURES

1. The game master shuffles the word cards, deals ten cards per player, and places the remaining word cards face-down.
2. The game master reads a definition card and lays it down face-up. All players who are holding a card that matches the definition read it and place it below the corresponding Greek root. If no player can respond to the definition, the game master places the definition card on the bottom of his or her cards for rereading later in the game.
3. To begin the next round, a new definition card is laid down.
4. The player who discards all ten word cards first is the winner and becomes the next game master.

8.9 Brainburst

In this game, players compete to brainstorm as many words as they can that are derived from the same root. Only unique words will earn points.

MATERIALS Write different roots on cards such as *graph, phon, scope, aud, dict, port, tract, struct, spect*—roots that have a wide variety of possible derivations. Each team or player needs a pencil and sheet of paper. A timer is needed, as well as a standard dictionary (condensed dictionaries may not have enough words).

PROCEDURES

1. Select one card and announce the root. Set the timer for two to three minutes. Each player or team tries to think of as many words as possible derived from that root.
2. When the timer goes off, players draw a line under their last words and count the number they have.
3. The player with the longest list reads the list aloud. If another player has the same word, it is crossed off of everyone's list. Any words that are not on another list are checked.
4. Each player in turn reads aloud any words that no one else has called to determine if he or she has a unique word. Disputes should be settled with the help of a dictionary.
5. The player or team with the most unique words is the winner of the round.

VARIATIONS This game can also be played with prefixes (*ex-, sub-, pre-, post-*, etc.) and suffixes (*-ible, -able, -ant, -ent*, etc.).

8.10 Joined at the Roots

This concept sort is an effective extension of students' exploration of Latin and Greek word roots. It is appropriate for individuals, partners, or small groups.

MATERIALS You will need a word sort board, word cards, and vocabulary notebook.

PROCEDURES

1. The teacher begins by modeling how to place words with appropriate roots under a particular category—for example, "Speaking and Writing," "Building/Construction,"

"Thinking and Feeling," and "Movement." The teacher then involves the students in the categorization.

2. Once students have grasped how this categorization scheme works, they can work in small groups or in pairs. Each group or pair will take a different category and sort words whose roots justify their membership in that category.
3. Lists can be written in vocabulary notebooks and brought back to the larger group to share and discuss. (*Note:* Several of the words to be sorted may be placed under different categories.) Following are some examples of categories and a few illustrative words.

Speaking and Writing	***Building/ Construction***	***Thinking and Feeling***	***Government***	***Movement***	***Travel***
autobiography	technology	philanthropy	economy	synchrony	astronaut
photograph	construct	philosophy	demagogue	fracture	exodus
catalogue	tractor	attraction	politics		
emphasis					

8.11 Root Webs

Root webs like the one in Figure 8.13 are a graphic way to represent the links among words derived from a common root.

PROCEDURES

1. Choose a set of common roots, such as *photo-*, *geo-*, *aqua-*, and *astro-*.
2. The teacher should first model as students complete their own webs in their vocabulary notebooks. Once students understand how to create the root webs, they can do them independently or in small groups.
3. Brainstorm related words. Students should use dictionaries to locate roots, verify their meanings, find their origins, and search for related words.
4. Honor all suggestions. Eliminate words that do not fit the meaning of a root. Lead students to examine parts and meaning.

FIGURE 8.13 "Root Web" in Student's Vocabulary Notebook

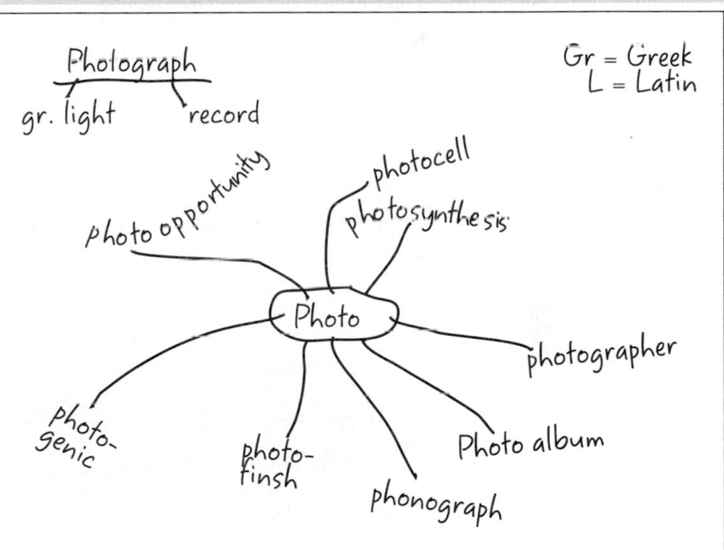

VARIATION A progressive root web (Templeton et al., 2010) provides the context for a more systematic walk-through of how words are generated from a common word root. Figure 8.14 is an example of a completed progressive web for the root *ject*, meaning "throw." The teacher first walks through each addition of an affix on one strand of the web, writing the derived word and discussing its meaning with the students. Students may be invited to come up to complete the other strands, discussing the meaning of each derived word with the class. This model can then be used with other roots by students who work in pairs or small groups.

8.12 Identifying the Meanings of Word Roots

Given a series of words that share the same root, students analyze the words to determine the meaning of the root. Each group of three words can be finished with one of the words provided. For example, in item 1 of the first grouping, students would look for which of the three words—*introspection*, *interrupt*, or *distract*—contains the same root as *spectator*, *inspect*, and *prospector*

FIGURE 8.14 Progressive Root Web

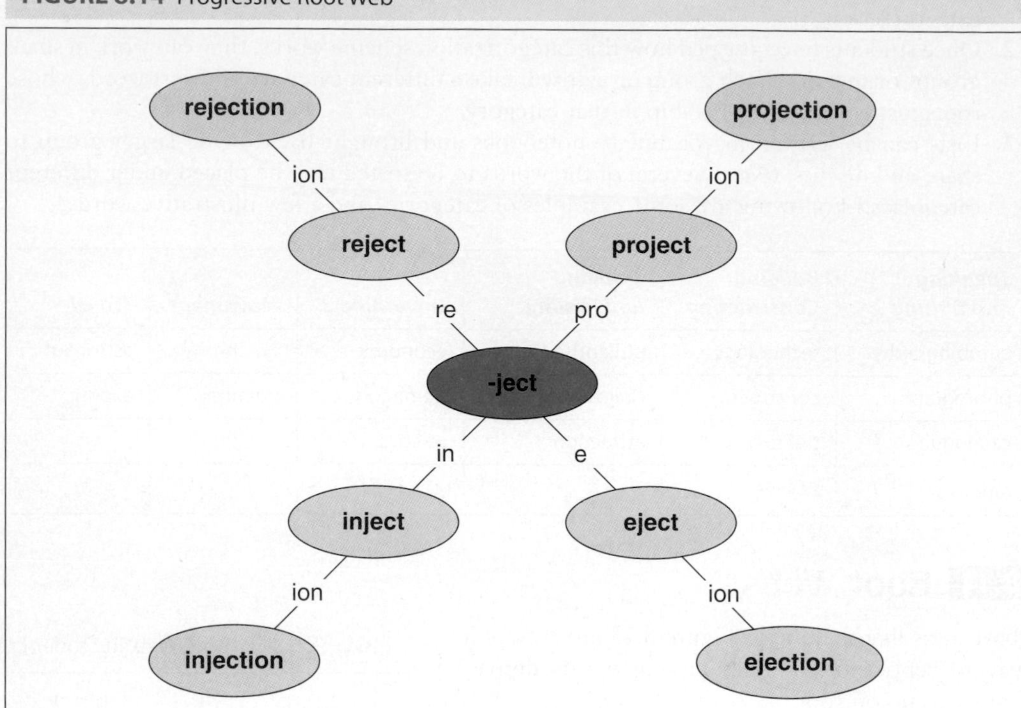

(*introspection*). In the sentence that follows this, they would then write what they believe the root *spect* means. In the next sentence, they would decide which of the remaining words—*interrupt* or *distract*—contains the same root as *corrupt*, *disrupt*, and *eruption*—and so on. This is an excellent activity for students to work on in pairs.

introspection interrupt distract

1. spectator, inspect, prospector, __________

   The root *spect* means __________. (look, count, divide)

2. corrupt, disrupt, eruption, __________

   The root *rupt* means __________. (speak, break, fall)

3. tractor, attract, extract, __________

   The root *tract* means __________. (place, look, pull)

audience refract contradict

1. audible, auditory, audio, __________

   The root *aud* means __________. (throw, hear, touch)

2. fraction, fracture, infraction, __________

   The root *fract* means __________. (stretch, eat, break)

3. dictate, diction, predict, __________

   The root *dict* means __________. (say, touch, fight)

dermatologist nominative invaluable

1. nominate, nominal, nominee, __________

   The root *nom* means __________. (write, figure, name)

2. value, valor, devalue, __________

   The root *val* means __________. (money, to be strong/to be worth, truth)

3. hypodermic, epidermis, dermatology, __________

   The root *derm* means __________. (skin, medicine, platform)

VARIATIONS Following this format, groups of students can construct their own exercises and then swap with other groups. Appendix E has additional roots.

8.13 Combining Roots and Affixes

In a matrix such as the one in Figure 8.15, students indicate with an X words that can be made by combining the prefix and the root. Then they write the words below. A variation is to indicate with a "?" words that do not exist in English, but could. Students may write these words in a special section of their vocabulary notebooks, creating a definition and using each in a sentence. When students are uncertain about whether a word is an actual word in English, they may check it in the dictionary.

FIGURE 8.15 Matrix of Roots and Prefixes

	duce/duc/duct	port	spect	dict	tract
in/im		x			
trans					
ex					
pre					
		import			

8.14 From Spanish to English— A Dictionary Word Hunt

The purpose of this activity is to expand students' vocabularies through discovering relations among *cognates.*

for **English Learners**

PROCEDURES

1. Look through a Spanish–English dictionary to find words in Spanish that remind you of words in English. Briefly note the definition or synonym (see Nash, 1997).
2. With an English dictionary, find words that share the same root or affix. Write these related words in your vocabulary notebook.
3. Record findings in the vocabulary notebook and create a class chart.

Following are sample entries on a class chart of cognates that one group of students collected in this activity.

Spanish (Translation)	*English Relations*	*Spanish Relations*
presumir (boast)	presume, presumption, presumptuous	presunción, presumido
extenso (extensive)	extend, extension	extensivo, extender
nocturno (nightly)	nocturnal, nocturne	noche, noctámbulo
polvo (powder)	pulverize (from Latin *pulvis,* meaning "dust")	polvillo, polvorear

8.15 The Synonym/Antonym Continuum

This activity encourages students to think about the subtle differences between word meanings as they work with antonyms and synonyms.

MATERIALS Think of opposites like *hot/cold, brave/frightened, old/young, lazy/energetic*, and so on. Use a thesaurus to find synonyms for each word in the pair and write them on cards or in a list.

PROCEDURES Have students arrange the words along a continuum. At the ends of the continuum will be the antonyms (words that are most opposite in meaning). Next to each of these words students will decide where to place synonyms (words that are closest to the meaning of the opposite words) and so on until all words have been used.

For example, the words *balmy, frigid, chilly, boiling, frozen, tepid, hot, cool*, and *warm* could be arranged this way:

frigid frozen chilly cool tepid balmy warm hot

Students might first work individually and then compare their continua with one another. They should discuss differences and provide rationales for why they arranged particular words the way they did. The dictionary will be the final judge of any disagreements. Encourage students to add other words like *sweltering, steamy, balmy*, and so on by brainstorming or using a thesaurus or dictionary. Give students a word pair of opposites and send them to a thesaurus to create a list of words. They can then order them as above or present them to another team to order.

8.16 Semantic Webs

Semantic webs are graphic aids that may be used to (a) fine-tune students' understanding of words and concepts in the same semantic "family" and (b) expand students' vocabularies by presenting new terms. The example in Figure 8.16 elaborates and expands the concepts associated with *trip*. All the words except *excursion* should be familiar to the students.

PROCEDURES

1. When introducing semantic webs, present a completed web. Later, students will help you create them.
2. Have students discuss their understandings of the familiar words (as with the synonym/antonym activity, this discussion requires them to make finer distinctions among the

FIGURE 8.16 Semantic Web

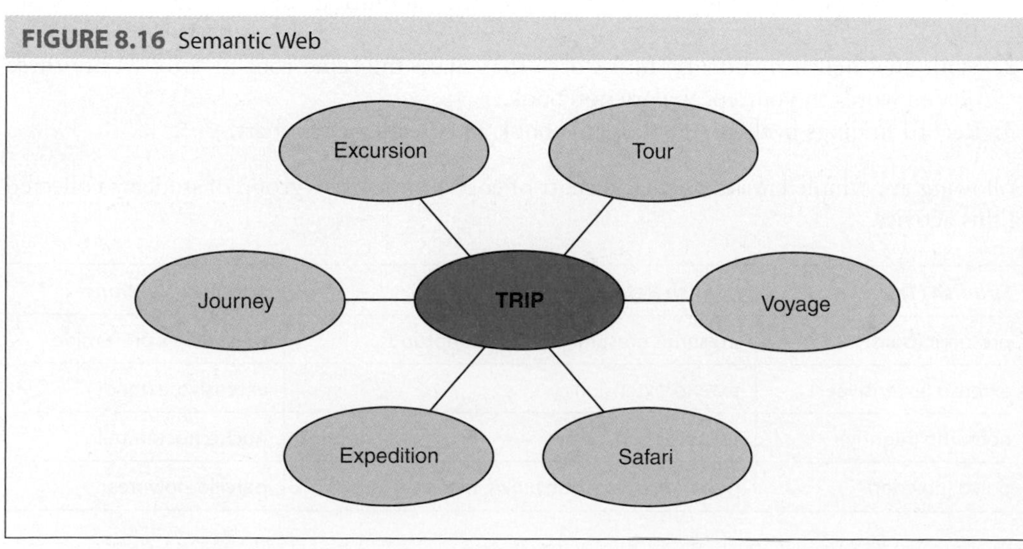

concepts). As they discuss meanings, encourage them to use the words in sentences. As always, the dictionary can resolve uncertainties.

3. Ask students if they have heard or seen the unfamiliar word (*excursion*) before. Discuss its possible meanings. Check the dictionary.
4. Ask students if they can think of any other words that could be added to the web.

VARIATIONS When students are used to this format, involve them in generating a web. Present your "core" word or concept, and then have students brainstorm other words that occur to them. You may then add one or two of your own words that will extend students' vocabularies.

8.17 Semantic Feature Analysis

This analysis (Anders & Bos, 1986) engages students in the examination of words and definitions in relation to each other.

PROCEDURES

1. Write the words to be examined down the left margin of a matrix. (In this example, the words are *prefix, base word, affix, suffix,* and *word root.*) Then write the features of these words across the top. When you introduce this activity to students, list these features yourself. Later, after students understand how the analysis works, they can be involved in suggesting the features that will be listed.
2. Discuss the matrix with the whole class or with small groups. Students will mark each cell with one of the following symbols: a plus sign (+) indicates a definite relationship between the word and a feature; a minus sign (–) shows the word does not have that feature; and a question mark (?) says that students feel they need more information before responding.
3. After students complete the matrix, point out (1) they now *really* know how much they know about each word, and (2) they also know what they still need to find out (Templeton, 1997).

Figure 8.17 illustrates a semantic feature analysis completed by a group of sixth grade students under the teacher's guidance to clarify the meanings of word study terms.

8.18 Which Suffix?

This activity is an excellent follow-up to previous work with base words, word roots, and suffixes. It is appropriate for individuals, buddies, or small groups. The suffixes included are *-tion/-sion, -ible/-able, -ence/-ance,* and *-ary/-ery.*

MATERIALS You will need a word sort board, word cards, and a vocabulary notebook.

FIGURE 8.17 Semantic Feature Analysis

	Cannot Stand Alone	Comes Before a Base Word or Root Word	Usually Comes from Greek or Latin	Can Stand Alone	Comes After Base Word or Word Root
Prefix	+	+	+	–	–
Base word	–	–	?	+	–
Affix	+	?	+	–	?
Suffix	+	–	+	–	+
Word root	+	–	+	–	–

PROCEDURES

1. The teacher decides how many suffix pairs to place at the top of the word sort board. (Note that several of the words to be sorted may be placed under different suffixes, for example, *permit: permissible, permission.*) Each card has the base word written on one side and the same word with allowable suffixes on the other side.
2. The teacher mixes up the word cards and places the deck with base words face-up. The students in turn choose the top card and decide in which suffix category it belongs.
3. After all the cards are placed, the students record in their vocabulary notebooks what they think is the correct spelling of the word.
4. After recording all the words, students turn the cards over to self-check the correct spelling.

VARIATIONS Students can work as buddies to explore a particular suffix "team" (e.g., *-tion* and *-sion*) to see what generalization(s) may underlie the use of a suffix.

8.19 Defiance or Patience?

The game Defiance (if using the *ant/ance/ancy* family) or Patience (if using the *ent/ence/ency* family) is for three to five players. The object of the game is to make as many groups of two, three, or four cards of the same derivation as they can and to also be the first to run out of cards.

MATERIALS Using words from the lists in Appendix E, create a deck of 52 cards with suits of two, three, or four words (e.g., *attend, attendance*, and *attendant* is a set of three, and *radiate, radiant, radiance*, and *radiancy* for a set of four). Write each word across the top of a card, and your deck is prepared.

PROCEDURES

1. Each player is dealt five cards from the deck. The player to the left of the dealer begins the game. The player may first lay down any existing groups of two, three, or four held in hand. This player then may ask any other player for a card of a certain derivation in his or her own hand: "Matthew, give me all of your *resistance*." (This could result in gaining *resistance, resistant, resistancy*, or *resist.*)
2. If a player does not have cards with the feature being sought, he or she responds, "Be Defiant" or "Be Patient," depending on which game is being played.
3. At this point, the asking player must draw another card from the deck. If the card is of the same family being sought, the player may lay down the match and continue asking other players for cards. If the card is not of the correct derivational group, play passes to the person on the left and continues around the circle in the same manner. If the drawn card makes a match in the asking player's hand but was not in the group being sought, he or she must hold the pair in hand until his or her turn comes up again. Of course, this means there is a risk of another player taking the pair before the next turn.
4. Play ends when one of the students runs out of cards. The player with the most points wins.
5. Players may play on other people's card groups, laying related cards down in front of themselves, not in front of the player who made the original match.
6. Scoring is as follows.

Singles played on other people's matches	1 point
Pairs	2 points
Triples	6 points
Groups of four	10 points
First player to run out of cards	10 points

VARIATIONS

1. Play a version called Defy My Patience that mixes sets of words from both lists to create an *ent/ant* deck.
2. Challenge My Patience or Defy My Challenge: In this version, during scoring, before everyone throws down his or her hand, students should secretly write additional words that have not been played for groups they have laid down. Before hands are revealed, these lists should be shared and an additional point added to the player's score for each related word he or she wrote. Any player who doubts the authenticity of a word claimed by an opponent may challenge the word. The challenger loses a point if the word is valid or gains a point if it is not. The player, likewise, counts the word if it is valid or loses a point if the challenger proves him or her wrong.
3. Students should be encouraged to develop their own derivational families to be added to this game or another feature to be substituted for the *ant/ent* contrast.

8.20 Assimile

This game created by Telia Blackard can be played by two to six players.

Go to PDToolkit for *Words Their Way*, click on the Sorts and Games tab, then type "Assimile" for a ready-to-use version of this game.

MATERIALS The game board is modeled after a Monopoly board (see Figure 8.18). You will also need dice, game playing pieces, a deck of prefixes that can be assimilated (*ad-*, *sub-*, *in-*, *ex-*, *com-*, *ob-*), a deck of base words that can take assimilated prefixes (e.g., base words such as *company* [*accompany*] or *mortal* [*immortal*]), and a set of chance cards. The chance cards are similar to the base word cards but should be written on cards of a different color. Players will need a sheet of paper and pencil or pen to use in spelling words.

PROCEDURES This game is modeled after Monopoly.

1. Place base words face-down around the board, one in each space. A particular prefix is chosen as the focus and placed face-up in the center of the board. Chance cards are also placed in the middle.
2. Players roll the dice to see who goes first. The player with the highest number rolls again and moves that number of spaces on the board.

FIGURE 8.18 Assimile Game Board

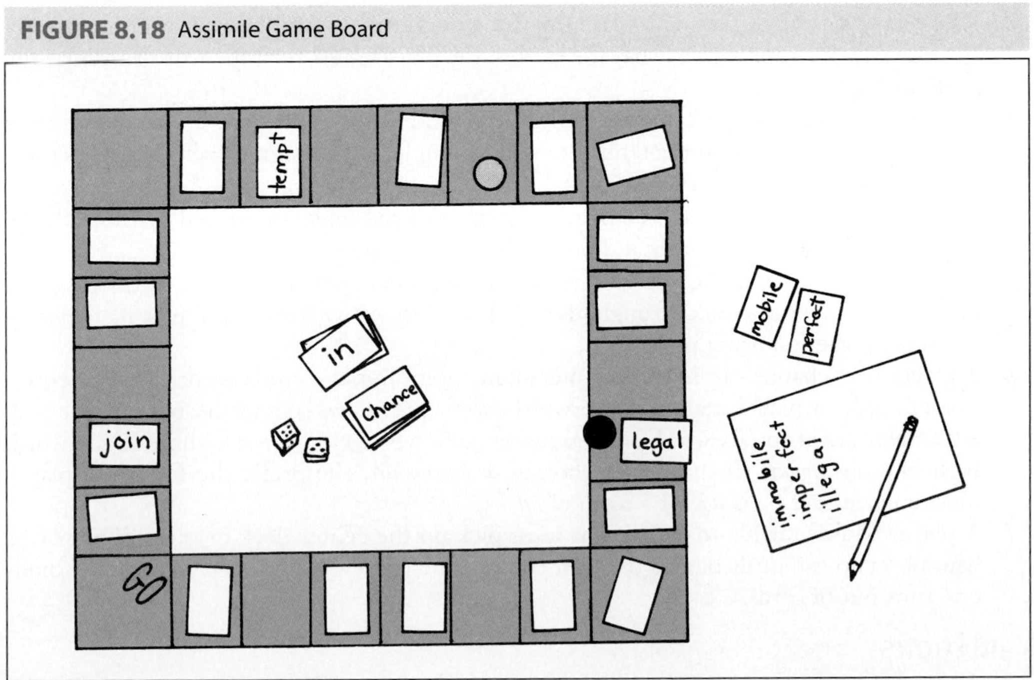

3. After landing on a particular space, the player turns up a word card and must determine whether this word can be assimilated to the prefix in the center of the board. If the card can be made into a word, the player attempts to both say the word and correctly spell it. A player who is able to correctly spell the word gets to keep the card. If the word cannot be assimilated, it is kept on the board face-up (this word will not be played again). However, if the word can be assimilated but the player misspells the word, the card is turned back over to be played later in the game.
4. A player who is unable to come up with a word (for whatever reason) forfeits a turn, and play moves to the next player.
5. When a player passes "Go" or lands on a card that is face-up, he or she can draw from the chance pile. Chance cards provide players a chance to think of their own assimilated prefix word using the base word on the card and any assimilated prefix.
6. The game is over when all cards that can be played are played. The winner is the player with the most correctly spelled words.

VARIATIONS A separate set of Community Chest cards using all of the original assimilated prefixes can be placed in the middle of the board, from which players can draw after each round of turns. This ensures that all prefixes are studied. (Community Chest cards will have the prefixes *ad-*, *in-*, *com-*, *ob-*, *sub-*, *ex-*, *per-*, and *dis-*.) With this method, the word cards that cannot be played with one particular prefix are turned back over until they are able to be played.

8.21 Rolling Prefixes

Players must be familiar with all types of assimilated prefixes to play this card game.

MATERIALS Create a deck of 32 word cards of assimilated prefixes (eight sets of four). Each group of four should consist of a mixed sort from each of the seven sets of assimilated prefixes: *ad-*, *in-*, *com-*, *ob-*, *sub-*, *ex-*, and *dis-*. One set will have to be a "wild set" (words with the aforementioned prefixes).

PROCEDURES

1. Each player is dealt eight cards—three cards to each player on the first round, two cards to each player on the second round, and three cards to each player on the third round.
2. The player on the dealer's left starts the game by putting a card face-up in the center of the table. It does not matter what the card is; the player must read the word and state the prefix.
3. The next player to the left and the others that follow attempt to play a card of the same suit as the first one put on the table ("suit" meaning having the same prefix). Players must read their word and state the prefix.
4. If everybody follows suit, the cards in the center of the table are picked up after all the players have added their cards and put to the side. No one scores.
5. The game continues in the same fashion until someone is unable to follow suit. When this occurs, the player can look through his or her hand for a "wild card" and play it, changing the suit for the following players.
6. A player may change suit in this manner at any point in the game if he or she so chooses. For example, a player may play the word *collide* (prefix *com-*), and the next player may either play a *com-* prefix word (such as *concoct*) or a word with *com* elsewhere in the word, such as *accommodate*. If the player chooses *accommodate*, the prefix the following player must concentrate on is *ad-* or a form of *ad-*.
7. A player who is unable to follow suit must pick up the center deck of cards. The player who picks up the cards begins the next round. The game continues this way until someone runs out of cards.

VARIATIONS

- At first, players may not wish to state the original prefix of the words.

- Multiple decks of assimilated prefixes can be made, allowing for variation.
- Instead of ending the game after one person runs out of cards, the game can continue by the winner of the first round receiving one point for each card that the other players hold in their hands at the end of the round.

8.22 Eponyms: Places, Things, Actions

Eponyms are words that refer to places, things, and actions that have been named after an individual (from Greek *epi-* for "after" + *noma* for "name"). Students' interest in word origins is often sparked by finding out where such words originate. As these words are discovered, they can be recorded in the "Looking into Language" section of the vocabulary notebook and/or displayed on a bulletin board.

Following is a sampler of common eponyms.

bloomers	Amelia Bloomer, an American feminist in the late nineteenth century
boycott	Charles Boycott, whose servants and staff refused to work for him because he would not lower rents
diesel	Rudolph Diesel, a German engineer who invented an alternative engine to the slow-moving steam engine
Ferris wheel	G.W.C. Ferris, designer of this exciting new ride for the 1893 World's Fair in Chicago
guillotine	Joseph Guillotin, a French physician and the inventor of the device
leotard	Jules Leotard, a French circus performer who designed his own trapeze costume
magnolia	Pierre Magnol, French botanist
pasteurize	Louis Pasteur, who developed the process whereby bacteria are killed in food and drink
sandwich	John Montagu, the Earl of Sandwich, who requested a new type of meal
sax	Antoine Joseph Sax, Belgian instrument maker, designer and builder of the first saxophone

The following resources include lists and information about eponyms:

Freeman, M. S. (1997). *A new dictionary of eponyms.* New York: Oxford University Press.
Marciano, J. (2009). *Anonyponymous: The forgotten people behind everyday words.* New York: Bloomsbury.
Terban, M. *Guppies in tuxedos: Funny eponyms.* New York: Clarion.

MEDIA GUIDE *Word Study for Advanced Readers and Writers: The Derivational Relations Stage*

SECTION	PAGE	GO TO PDTOOLKIT FOR *WORDS THEIR WAY*™
Videos		
Vocabulary Learning	276	Click on the Videos tab, then type "Vocabulary with Root Tree (*tract*), Day 1."
Greek and Latin Elements	283	Click on the Videos tab, then type "Vocabulary with Root Tree (*tract*), Day 2."
Assimilated Prefixes	287	Click on the Videos tab, then type "Prefix Assimilation (*com-*), Day 1."
Routines	291	Click on the Videos tab, then type "Vocabulary with Root Tree (*tract*), Day 2."
Sorts and Games		
Activities for the Derivational Relations Stage	296	Click on the Sorts and Games tab, then type "Latin Root Jeopardy" for a ready-to-use version of this game.
Activities for the Derivational Relations Stage	299	Click on the Sorts and Games tab, then type "Word Part Shuffle Cards."
Activities for the Derivational Relations Stage	307	Click on the Sorts and Games tab, then type "Assimile" for a ready-to-use version of this game.
Assessment Tools		
Orthographic Development in the Derivational Relations Stage	279	Click on the Assessment Tools tab, then type "Upper Spelling Inventory Feature Guide."
Assess and Monitor Progress in the Derivational Relations Stage	289	Click on the Assessment Tools tab, then type "Goal-Setting/ Progress Monitoring Charts."

APPENDIXES

This section of the text contains seven segments, or Appendixes. Appendix A provides the materials you will need for assessments. (Printable versions of these materials are also on the website along with other assessments described in Chapter 2). Other Appendixes contain pictures, sample sorts, word lists, and templates that you can use to create your own word study activities.

Appendix A Assessment Materials

Qualitative Spelling Checklist

Student ______________________ Observer ______________________

Use this checklist to analyze students' uncorrected writing and to locate their appropriate stages of spelling development. There are three gradations within each stage—early, middle, and late. Words in parentheses are examples.

The spaces for dates at the top of the checklist are used to follow students' progress. Check when certain features are observed in students' spelling. When a feature is always present check "Yes." The last place where you check "Often" corresponds to the student's stage of spelling development.

Dates: ________ ________ ________

EMERGENT STAGE			
Early			
• Does the child scribble on the page?	Yes ____	Often ____	No ____
• Are letter-like forms arranged linearly?	Yes ____	Often ____	No ____
Middle			
• Are there random letters and numbers used in pretend writing? (4BT for *ship*)	Yes ____	Often ____	No ____
Late			
• Are key sounds used in syllabic writing? (/s/ or /p/ for *ship*)	Yes ____	Often ____	No ____
LETTER NAME–ALPHABETIC			
Early			
• Are salient sounds represented? (BD for *bed*)	Yes ____	Often ____	No ____
• Are blends and digraphs represented partially? (SP for *ship*)	Yes ____	Often ____	No ____
Middle			
• Are there logical vowel substitutions with a letter name strategy? (FLOT for *float*, BAD for *bed*)	Yes ____	Often ____	No ____
Late			
• Are some consonant digraphs and blends spelled correctly? (***sh**ip*, ***wh**en*, ***fl**oat*)	Yes ____	Often ____	No ____
• Are short vowels spelled correctly? (*b**e**d*, *sh**i**p*, *wh**e**n*, *l**u**mp*)	Yes ____	Often ____	No ____
• Is the *m* or *n* included in front of other consonants? (*lu**m**p*, *sta**n**d*)	Yes ____	Often ____	No ____
WITHIN WORD PATTERN			
Early			
• Are long vowels in single-syllable words used but confused? (FLOTE for *float*, TRANE for *train*)	Yes ____	Often ____	No ____
• Are the most common consonant digraphs and blends spelled correctly? (***sl**ed*, ***dr**eam*, ***fr**ight*)	Yes ____	Often ____	No ____
Middle			
• Are common vowel words spelled correctly, but some long vowel spelling and other vowel patterns used but confused? (DRIEV for *drive*)	Yes ____	Often ____	No ____
Late			
• Are complex consonants spelled correctly? (*spe**ck***, *swi**tch***, *smu**dge***)	Yes ____	Often ____	No ____
• Are most other vowel patterns spelled correctly? (*sp**oil***, *ch**ew**ed*, *s**er**ving*)	Yes ____	Often ____	No ____
SYLLABLES & AFFIXES			
Early			
• Are inflectional endings added correctly to CVVC and CVCC words? (*rain**ing***, *walk**ed***)	Yes ____	Often ____	No ____
Middle			
• Are inflectional endings added correctly to base words? (*chew**ed***, *march**ed***, *show**er***)	Yes ____	Often ____	No ____
• Are junctures between syllables spelled correctly? (*ca**tt**le*, *ce**ll**ar*, *ca**rr**ies*, *bo**tt**le*)	Yes ____	Often ____	No ____
Late			
• Are unaccented final syllables spelled correctly? (*bott**le***, *fortun**ate***, *civil**ize***)	Yes ____	Often ____	No ____
• Are prefixes and suffixes spelled correctly? (*fav**or***, *rip**en***, *cell**ar***, *color**ful***)	Yes ____	Often ____	No ____
DERIVATIONAL RELATIONS			
Early			
• Are most polysyllabic words spelled correctly? (*fortunate*, *confident*)	Yes ____	Often ____	No ____
Middle			
• Are unaccented vowels in derived words spelled correctly? (*confident*, *civilize*, *category*)	Yes ____	Often ____	No ____
Late			
• Are assimilated prefixes spelled correctly? (*illiterate*, *correspond*, *succeed*)	Yes ____	Often ____	No ____

General Directions for Administering the *Words Their Way* Inventories

Students should not study the words in advance of testing. Assure students that they will not be graded on this activity, and that they will be helping you plan for their needs. Following is a possible introduction to the assessment.

> *I am going to ask you to spell some words. Spell them the best you can. Some of the words may be easy to spell; some may be difficult. When you do not know how to spell a word, spell it the best you can.*

Ask students to number their paper (or prepare a numbered paper for kindergarten or early first grade). Call each word aloud and repeat it. Say each word naturally, without emphasizing phonemes or syllables. Use it in a sentence, if necessary, to be sure students know the exact word. Sample sentences are provided along with the words. After administering the inventory, use a Feature Guide, Class Composite Form, and, if desired, a Spelling-by-Stage Classroom Organization Chart to complete your assessment. Error Guide forms for the Primary and Elementary Inventories are available at PDToolkit for *Words Their Way*. The online assessment application will help complete the feature guide and create a class composite automatically.

Scoring the Inventory Using the Feature Guides

1. To score by hand, make a copy of the appropriate Feature Guide (PSI p. 316, ESI p. 320, USI p. 323) for each student. Draw a line under the last word used if you called fewer than the total number and adjust the possible total points at the bottom of each feature column.
2. Score the words by checking off the features spelled correctly that are listed in the cells to the right of each word. For example, if a student spells *bed* as BAD, he gets a check in the initial *b* cell and the final *d* cell, but not for the short vowel. Write in the vowel used (*a*, in this case), but do not give any points for it. If a student spells *train* as TRANE, she gets a check in the initial *tr* cell and the final *n* cell, but not for the long vowel pattern. Write in the vowel pattern used (*a–e* in this case), but do not give any points for it. Put a check in the "Correct" column if the word is spelled correctly. Do not count reversed letters as errors but note them in the cells. If unnecessary letters are added, give the speller credit for what is correct (e.g., if *bed* is spelled BEDE, the student still gets credit for representing the consonants and short vowel), but do not check "Correct" spelling.
3. Add the number of checks under each feature and across each word, double-checking the total score recorded in the last cell. Modify the ratios in the last row depending on the number of words called aloud.

Interpreting the Results of the Spelling Inventory

1. Look down each feature column to determine instructional needs. Students who miss only one (or two, if the features sample 8 to 10 words) can go on to other features. Students who miss two or three need some review work; students who miss more than three need careful instruction on this feature. If a student did not get any points for a feature, earlier features need to be studied first.
2. To determine a stage of development, note where students first make two or more errors under the stages listed in the shaded box at the top of the Feature Guide. Circle this stage.
3. Raw scores or total number correct can also be used as a guide to calling the stage. Refer to the chart on page 34.

Using the Classroom Composite and Spelling-by-Stage Classroom Organization Chart

1. Staple each Feature Guide to the student's spelling paper and arrange the papers in rank order from highest to lowest total points or use raw scores.
2. List students' names in this rank order in the left column of the appropriate Classroom Composite (PSI p. 317, ESI p. 321, USI p. 325) and transfer each student's feature scores from the bottom row of the individual Feature Guides to the Classroom Composite. If you do not call out the total list, adjust the numbers on the Possible Points row of the Classroom Composite.
3. Highlight cells where students make two or more errors on a particular feature to get a sense of your students' needs and to form groups for instruction.
4. Many teachers find it easier to form groups using the Spelling-by-Stage Classroom Organization Chart (p. 318). List each student under the appropriate spelling stage (the stage circled on the Feature Guide) and determine instructional groups.

The electronic assessment tool on the website will automate many of these steps for you.

Note: See Chapter 2 for more detailed directions on choosing, administering, scoring, and interpreting the inventories, as well as using them to form instructional groups.

Primary Spelling Inventory (PSI)

The Primary Spelling Inventory (PSI) is used in kindergarten through third grade. The 26 words are ordered by difficulty to sample features of the letter name–alphabetic to within word pattern stages. Call out enough words so that you have at least five or six misspelled words to analyze. For kindergarten or other emergent readers, you may only need to call out the first five words. In late kindergarten and early first grade classrooms, call out at least 15 words so that you sample digraphs and blends; use the entire list for late first, second, and third grades. If any students spell more than 22 words correctly, you may want to use the Elementary Spelling Inventory.

1. fan	I could use a fan on a hot day. *fan*
2. pet	I have a pet cat who likes to play. *pet*
3. dig	He will dig a hole in the sand. *dig*
4. rob	A raccoon will rob a bird's nest for eggs. *rob*
5. hope	I hope you will do well on this test. *hope*
6. wait	You will need to wait for the letter. *wait*
7. gum	I stepped on some bubble gum. *gum*
8. sled	The dog sled was pulled by huskies. *sled*
9. stick	I used a stick to poke in the hole. *stick*
10. shine	He rubbed the coin to make it shine. *shine*
11. dream	I had a funny dream last night. *dream*
12. blade	The blade of the knife was very sharp. *blade*
13. coach	The coach called the team off the field. *coach*
14. fright	She was a fright in her Halloween costume. *fright*
15. chewed	The dog chewed on the bone until it was gone. *chewed*
16. crawl	You will get dirty if you crawl under the bed. *crawl*
17. wishes	In fairy tales wishes often come true. *wishes*
18. thorn	The thorn from the rosebush stuck me. *thorn*
19. shouted	They shouted at the barking dog. *shouted*
20. spoil	The food will spoil if it sits out too long. *spoil*
21. growl	The dog will growl if you bother him. *growl*
22. third	I was the third person in line. *third*
23. camped	We camped down by the river last weekend. *camped*
24. tries	He tries hard every day to finish his work. *tries*
25. clapping	The audience was clapping after the program. *clapping*
26. riding	They are riding their bikes to the park today. *riding*

Words Their Way Primary Spelling Inventory Feature Guide

Student's Name ______________ Teacher ______________ Grade ________ Date ________

Words Spelled Correctly: _____ / 26 *Feature Points:* _____ / 56 *Total:* _____ / 82 *Spelling Stage:* ______________

SPELLING STAGES →	EMERGENT LATE		LETTER NAME–ALPHABETIC EARLY	MIDDLE	LATE	WITHIN WORD PATTERN EARLY	MIDDLE	LATE / SYLLABLES AND AFFIXES EARLY		
Features →	**Consonants Initial**	**Consonants Final**	**Short Vowels**	**Digraphs**	**Blends**	**Common Long Vowels**	**Other Vowels**	**Inflected Endings**	**Feature Points**	**Words Spelled Correctly**
1. fan	f	n	a							
2. pet	p	t	e							
3. dig	d	g	i							
4. rob	r	b	o							
5. hope	h	p				o-e				
6. wait	w	t				ai				
7. gum	g	m	u							
8. sled			e		sl					
9. stick			i		st					
10. shine				sh		i-e				
11. dream					dr	ea				
12. blade					bl	a-e				
13. coach				ch		oa				
14. fright					fr	igh				
15. chewed				ch			ew	-ed		
16. crawl					cr		aw			
17. wishes				sh				-es		
18. thorn				th			or			
19. shouted				sh			ou	-ed		
20. spoil							oi			
21. growl							ow			
22. third				th			ir			
23. camped								-ed		
24. tries					tr			-ies		
25. clapping								-pping		
26. riding								-ding		
Totals	/ 7	/ 7	/ 7	/ 7	/ 7	/ 7	/ 7	/ 7	/ 56	/ 26

Words Their Way Primary Spelling Inventory Classroom Composite

Teacher ______________ School ______________ Grade ________ Date ________

SPELLING STAGES →	EMERGENT LATE		LETTER NAME–ALPHABETIC EARLY	MIDDLE	LATE	WITHIN WORD PATTERN EARLY	MIDDLE	LATE	SYLLABLES AND AFFIXES EARLY	
Students' ↓ Names	Consonants Initial	Final	Short Vowels	Digraphs	Blends	Common Long Vowels	Other Vowels	Inflected Endings	Correct Spelling	Total Rank Order
Possible Points	**7**	**7**	**7**	**7**	**7**	**7**	**7**	**7**	**26**	**82**
1.										
2.										
3.										
4.										
5.										
6.										
7.										
8.										
9.										
10.										
11.										
12.										
13.										
14.										
15.										
16.										
17.										
18.										
19.										
20.										
21.										
22.										
23.										
24.										
25.										
26.										
Highlight for instruction*										

*Highlight students who miss more than 1 on a particular feature; they will benefit from more instruction in that area.

Spelling-by-Stage Classroom Organization Chart

SPELLING STAGES →	EMERGENT			LETTER NAME–ALPHABETIC			WITHIN WORD PATTERN			SYLLABLES AND AFFIXES			DERIVATIONAL RELATIONS		
	EARLY	MIDDLE	LATE	EARLY	MIDDLE	LATE	EARLY	MIDDLE	LATE	EARLY	MIDDLE	LATE	EARLY	MIDDLE	LATE
CHAPTERS IN *WORDS THEIR WAY*	CHAPTER 4			CHAPTER 5			CHAPTER 6			CHAPTER 7			CHAPTER 8		

Elementary Spelling Inventory (ESI)

The Elementary Spelling Inventory (ESI) covers more stages than the PSI. It can be offered as early as first grade, particularly if a school system wants to use the same inventory across the elementary grades. The 25 words are ordered by difficulty to sample features of the letter name–alphabetic to derivational relations stages. Call out enough words so that you have at least five or six misspelled words to analyze. If any students spell more than 20 words correctly, use the Upper-Level Spelling Inventory.

1. bed	I hopped out of bed this morning. *bed*
2. ship	The ship sailed around the island. *ship*
3. when	When will you come back? *when*
4. lump	He had a lump on his head after he fell. *lump*
5. float	I can float on the water with my new raft. *float*
6. train	I rode the train to the next town. *train*
7. place	I found a new place to put my books. *place*
8. drive	I learned to drive a car. *drive*
9. bright	The light is very bright. *bright*
10. shopping	She went shopping for new shoes. *shopping*
11. spoil	The food will spoil if it is not kept cool. *spoil*
12. serving	The restaurant is serving dinner tonight. *serving*
13. chewed	The dog chewed up my favorite sweater yesterday. *chewed*
14. carries	She carries apples in her basket. *carries*
15. marched	We marched in the parade. *marched*
16. shower	The shower in the bathroom was very hot. *shower*
17. bottle	The bottle broke into pieces on the tile floor. *bottle*
18. favor	He did his brother a favor by taking out the trash. *favor*
19. ripen	The fruit will ripen over the next few days. *ripen*
20. cellar	I went down to the cellar for the can of paint. *cellar*
21. pleasure	It was a pleasure to listen to the choir sing. *pleasure*
22. fortunate	It was fortunate that the driver had snow tires. *fortunate*
23. confident	I am confident that we can win the game. *confident*
24. civilize	They wanted to civilize the forest people. *civilize*
25. opposition	The coach said the opposition would be tough. *opposition*

Words Their Way Elementary Spelling Inventory Feature Guide

Student's Name ______________________ Teacher ______________________ Grade __________ Date __________

Words Spelled Correctly: _____ */ 25* *Feature Points:* _____ */ 62* *Total:* _____ */ 87* *Spelling Stage:* ______________________

SPELLING STAGES →	EMERGENT LATE	LETTER NAME–ALPHABETIC EARLY	MIDDLE	LATE	WITHIN WORD PATTERN EARLY	MIDDLE	LATE	SYLLABLES AND AFFIXES EARLY	MIDDLE	LATE	DERIVATIONAL RELATIONS EARLY	MIDDLE		
Features →	Consonants Initial	Consonants Final	Short Vowels	Digraphs	Blends	Common Long Vowels	Other Vowels	Inflected Endings	Syllable Junctures	Unaccented Final Syllables	Harder Suffixes	Bases or Roots	Feature Points	Words Spelled Correctly
1. bed	b	d	e											
2. ship		p	i	sh										
3. when			e	wh										
4. lump	l		u		mp									
5. float		t			fl	oa								
6. train		n			tr	ai								
7. place					pl	a-e								
8. drive		v			dr	i-e								
9. bright					br	igh								
10. shopping			o	sh				pping						
11. spoil					sp		oi							
12. serving							er	ving						
13. chewed				ch			ew	ed						
14. carries							ar	ies	rr					
15. marched				ch			ar	ed						
16. shower				sh			ow			er				
17. bottle									tt	le				
18. favor									v	or				
19. ripen									p	en				
20. cellar									ll	ar				
21. pleasure											ure	pleas		
22. fortunate							or				ate	fortun		
23. confident											ent	confid		
24. civilize											ize	civil		
25. opposition											tion	pos		
Totals		/ 7	/ 5	/ 6	/ 7	/ 5	/ 7	/ 5	/ 5	/ 5	/ 5	/ 5	/ 62	/ 25

Words Their Way Elementary Spelling Inventory Classroom Composite

Teacher ______________________ School ______________________ Grade ____________ Date ____________

SPELLING STAGES →	EMERGENT LATE	LETTER NAME–ALPHABETIC EARLY	MIDDLE	LATE	WITHIN WORD PATTERN EARLY	MIDDLE	LATE	SYLLABLES AND AFFIXES EARLY	MIDDLE	LATE	DERIVATIONAL RELATIONS EARLY	MIDDLE		
↓ Students' Names		Consonants	Short Vowels	Digraphs	Blends	Common Long Vowels	Other Vowels	Inflected Endings	Syllable Junctures	Unaccented Final Syllables	Harder Suffixes	Bases or Roots	Correct Spelling	Total Rank Order
Possible Points		7	5	6	7	5	7	5	5	5	5	5	25	87
1.														
2.														
3.														
4.														
5.														
6.														
7.														
8.														
9.														
10.														
11.														
12.														
13.														
14.														
15.														
16.														
17.														
18.														
19.														
20.														
21.														
22.														
23.														
24.														
25.														
26.														
Highlight for instruction*														

*Highlight students who miss more than 1 on a particular feature; they will benefit from more instruction in that area.

Upper-Level Spelling Inventory (USI)

The Upper-Level Spelling Inventory (USI) can be used in upper elementary, middle, high school, and postsecondary classrooms. The 31 words are ordered by difficulty to sample features of the within word pattern to derivational relations spelling stages. With normally achieving students, you can administer the entire list, but you may stop when students misspell more than eight words and are experiencing noticeable frustration. If any students misspell five of the first eight words, use the ESI to more accurately identify within word pattern features that need instruction.

1. switch — We can switch television channels with a remote control. *switch*
2. smudge — There was a smudge on the mirror from her fingertips. *smudge*
3. trapped — He was trapped in the elevator when the electricity went off. *trapped*
4. scrape — The fall caused her to scrape her knee. *scrape*
5. knotted — The knotted rope would not come undone. *knotted*
6. shaving — He didn't start shaving with a razor until 11th grade. *shaving*
7. squirt — Don't let the ketchup squirt out of the bottle too fast. *squirt*
8. pounce — My cat likes to pounce on her toy mouse. *pounce*
9. scratches — We had to paint over the scratches on the car. *scratches*
10. crater — The crater of the volcano was filled with bubbling lava. *crater*
11. sailor — When he was young, he wanted to go to sea as a sailor. *sailor*
12. village — My Granddad lived in a small seaside village. *village*
13. disloyal — Traitors are disloyal to their country. *disloyal*
14. tunnel — The rockslide closed the tunnel through the mountain. *tunnel*
15. humor — You need a sense of humor to understand his jokes. *humor*
16. confidence — With each winning game, the team's confidence grew. *confidence*
17. fortunate — The driver was fortunate to have snow tires on that winter day. *fortunate*
18. visible — The singer on the stage was visible to everyone. *visible*
19. circumference — The length of the equator is equal to the circumference of the earth. *circumference*
20. civilization — We studied the ancient Mayan civilization last year. *civilization*
21. monarchy — A monarchy is headed by a king or a queen. *monarchy*
22. dominance — The dominance of the Yankees baseball team lasted for several years. *dominance*
23. correspond — Many students correspond through e-mail. *correspond*
24. illiterate — It is hard to get a job if you are illiterate. *illiterate*
25. emphasize — I want to emphasize the importance of trying your best. *emphasize*
26. opposition — The coach said the opposition would give us a tough game. *opposition*
27. chlorine — My eyes were burning from the chlorine in the swimming pool. *chlorine*
28. commotion — The audience heard the commotion backstage. *commotion*
29. medicinal — Cough drops are to be taken for medicinal purposes only. *medicinal*
30. irresponsible — It is irresponsible not to wear a seat belt. *irresponsible*
31. succession — The firecrackers went off in rapid succession. *succession*

Words Their Way Upper-Level Spelling Inventory Feature Guide

Student's Name ____________________ Teacher ____________________ Grade __________ Date __________

Words Spelled Correctly: _____ / 31 *Feature Points:* _____ / 68 *Total:* _____ / 99 *Spelling Stage:* ____________________

SPELLING STAGES →	WITHIN WORD PATTERN (EARLY, MIDDLE, LATE)			SYLLABLES AND AFFIXES (EARLY, MIDDLE, LATE)			DERIVATIONAL RELATIONS (EARLY, MIDDLE, LATE)				
Features →	**Blends and Digraphs**	**Vowels**	**Complex Consonants**	**Inflected Endings and Syllable Juncture**	**Unaccented Final Syllables**	**Affixes**	**Reduced Vowels in Unaccented Syllables**	**Greek and Latin Elements**	**Assimilated Prefixes**	**Feature Points**	**Words Spelled Correctly**
1. switch	sw	i	tch								
2. smudge	sm	u	dge								
3. trapped	tr			pped							
4. scrape		a-e	scr								
5. knotted		o	kn	tted							
6. shaving	sh			ving							
7. squirt		ir	squ								
8. pounce		ou	ce								
9. scratches		a	tch	es							
10. crater	cr			t	er						
11. sailor		ai			or						
12. village				ll	age						
13. disloyal		oy			al	dis					
14. tunnel				nn	el						
15. humor				m	or						
16. confidence						con	fid				
17. fortunate					ate			fortun			
18. visible						ible		vis			
19. circumference						ence		circum			
20. civilization							liz	civil			
Subtotals	/ 5	/ 9	/ 7	/ 8	/ 7	/ 4	/ 2	/ 4	/ 0	/ 46	/ 20

Words Their Way Upper-Level Spelling Inventory Feature Guide (Continued)

Student's Name ______________ Teacher ______________ Grade ________ Date ________

Words Spelled Correctly: _____ / 31 *Feature Points:* _____ / 68 *Total:* _____ / 99 *Spelling Stage:* ______________

SPELLING STAGES →	**WITHIN WORD PATTERN** EARLY MIDDLE		LATE	**SYLLABLES AND AFFIXES** EARLY	MIDDLE	LATE	**DERIVATIONAL RELATIONS** EARLY	MIDDLE	LATE		
Features →	**Blends and Digraphs**	**Vowels**	**Complex Consonants**	**Inflected Endings and Syllable Juncture**	**Unaccented Final Syllables**	**Affixes**	**Reduced Vowels in Unaccented Syllables**	**Greek and Latin Elements**	**Assimilated Prefixes**	**Feature Points**	**Words Spelled Correctly**
21. monarchy								arch			
22. dominance						ance	min				
23. correspond							res		rr		
24. illiterate					ate				ll		
25. emphasize						size	pha				
26. opposition							pos		pp		
27. chlorine						ine		chlor			
28. commotion						tion			mm		
29. medicinal					al			medic			
30. irresponsible						ible	res		rr		
31. succession						sion			cc		
Subtotals	/ 0	/ 0	/ 0	/ 0	/ 2	/ 6	/ 5	/ 3	/ 6	/ 22	/ 11
Totals	/ 5	/ 9	/ 7	/ 8	/ 9	/ 10	/ 7	/ 7	/ 6	/ 68	/ 31

Words Their Way Upper-Level Spelling Inventory Classroom Composite

Teacher ______________ School ______________ Grade ________ Date ________

SPELLING STAGES →	WITHIN WORD PATTERN: EARLY	MIDDLE	LATE	SYLLABLES AND AFFIXES: EARLY	MIDDLE	LATE	DERIVATIONAL RELATIONS: EARLY	MIDDLE	LATE		
Students' ↓ Names	Blends and Digraphs	Vowels	Complex Consonants	Inflected Endings and Syllable Juncture	Unaccented Final Syllables	Affixes	Reduced Vowels in Unaccented Syllables	Greek and Latin Elements	Assimilated Prefixes	Correct Spelling	Total Rank Order
Possible Points	**5**	**9**	**7**	**8**	**9**	**10**	**7**	**7**	**6**	**31**	**99**
1.											
2.											
3.											
4.											
5.											
6.											
7.											
8.											
9.											
10.											
11.											
12.											
13.											
14.											
15.											
16.											
17.											
18.											
19.											
20.											
21.											
22.											
23.											
24.											
25.											
26.											
27.											
Highlight for instruction*											

*Highlight students who miss more than 1 on a particular feature if the total is between 5 and 8. Highlight those who miss more than 2 if the total is between 9 and 10.

Appendix B Sound Boards

Sound Board for Beginning Consonants and Digraphs

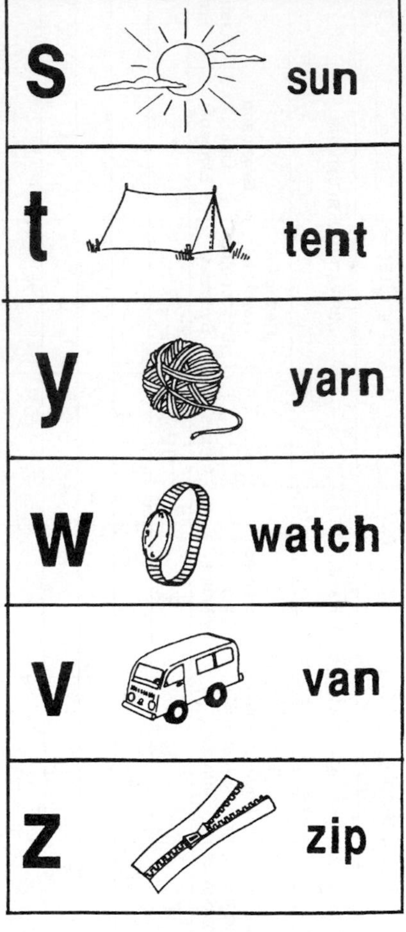

Beginning Digraphs

Sound Board for Beginning Blends

Beginning Blends	br  broom	sc  scooter
bl  block	cr  crab	sk  skate
cl  cloud	dr  drum	sm  smile
fl  flag	fr  frog	sn  snail
gl  glasses	gr  grapes	sp  spider
sl  slide	pr  present	st  star
pl 2+1=3 plus	tr  tree	sw  swing
tw  twins	qu  quilt	

Sound Board for Long and Short Vowels

Short Vowels		
a cat		
e bed		
i pig		
o sock		
u cup		

Long Vowels	
a cake	a tray
	a rain
e feet	e leaf
i kite	i light
o bone	o soap
u tube	

Appendix C Pictures for Sorts and Games

The pictures that follow can be employed in a number of ways. For example, they can be used like clip art to create picture sorts. Suggested contrasts for picture sorts can be found in Chapters 4 and 5 or you can create your own. Simply make copies of the pictures you need (combining two, three, or four sounds) and glue them randomly onto a template such as the one on page 397. You will probably want to enlarge the pictures about 50 percent. You can insert labels from the sound board boxes as headers. You may also want to make a complete set of pictures for modeling, small-group work, or centers. Pictures can be glued or copied to card stock and perhaps colored and laminated for durability. Pictures can be used for games and other activities as well.

Pictures are grouped by beginning consonants, digraphs, blends, short vowels, and long vowels. The following list will help you find pictures for rhyme sorts, word families, additional short vowels, and long vowels. The pictures in bold type are in either the short or long vowel picture section while the others can be found by their beginning sounds.

Long Vowel Picture Rhymes

tape	**game**	**soap**	**beach**	deer	**slide**	fire	
cape	**frame**	**rope**	**peach**	spear	**bride**	tire	
vine	**bone**	**toad**	pear	**moon**	**seal**	**cube**	**bead**
nine	**cone**	**road**	chair	spoon	**heal**	**tube**	**read**
suit	gate	**snake**	**glue**	jeep	school	**peas**	
fruit	plate	**cake**	**shoe**	sheep	stool	**cheese**	
flute	skate	**rake**	zoo	sleep	spool	**keys**	
		lake		sweep			
hive	**rose**	**coat**	**three**	**hay**	**cane**	**pie**	**whale**
five	**nose**	**boat**	**bee**	**pay**	**rain**	**tie**	**tail**
dive	**toes**	**goat**	**knee**	pray	**chain**	**fly**	**mail**
drive	hose	**float**	tree	tray	plane	cry	snail
		note	key	play	train	fry	sail
							pail
							nail
							scale

Note: More long vowel pictures can be found among initial sounds: paint, vase, shave, blade, flame, grapes, braid, leaf, leash, steam, seal, key, wheel, sleeve, teeth, queen, dream, bike, dice, dime, kite, pipe, smile, prize, climb, price, globe, snow, comb, ghost, smoke, toast, flute

Short Vowel Picture Rhymes

glass	lamp	four	bus	trunk	duck	switch	mitten
grass	stamp	door	plus	skunk	truck	witch	kitten
vest	**wig**	car	**leg**	**cut**	**sun**		
chest	**pig**	jar	egg	**hut**	**bun**		
nest	**dig**	star	peg	**nut**	**run**		
wall	**box**	hook	**pup**	jump			
saw	**fox**	book	**cup**	stump			
claw	socks						
hen	**bed**	kick	**gum**	dog	**pot**	**fin**	**net**
men	**sled**	stick	drum	log	**dot**	**pin**	**jet**
ten	shed	chick	plum	jog	**hot**	chin	**pet**
pen	bread	brick	thumb	frog	**cot**	twin	vet
bag	**can**	**cat**	king	**sock**	**shell**		
rag	**man**	**bat**	ring	**rock**	**bell**		
wag	**fan**	**hat**	wing	**lock**	**well**		
flag	pan	mat	sting	**clock**	smell		
tag	van	bat	swing	block			
cap	**mop**	**zip**	**jack**	**mug**	**pill**		
map	**hop**	**lip**	**sack**	**bug**	**hill**		
nap	**top**	**rip**	**pack**	**jug**	**mill**		
trap	**pop**	ship	shack	**tug**	spill		
clap	chop	whip	quack	**rug**	drill		
snap	shop	skip	track	plug	grill		
	stop	clip	crack				
		drip					
		flip					

Note: Bolded words may be found in vowel pictures. More short vowel pictures can be found among initial sounds: gas, ham, mask, match, glass, crab, sad, trash, desk, check, belt, web, dress, fish, six, bridge, swim, crib, flip, kiss, kit, twin, cup, gum, tub, brush

Initial Consonants

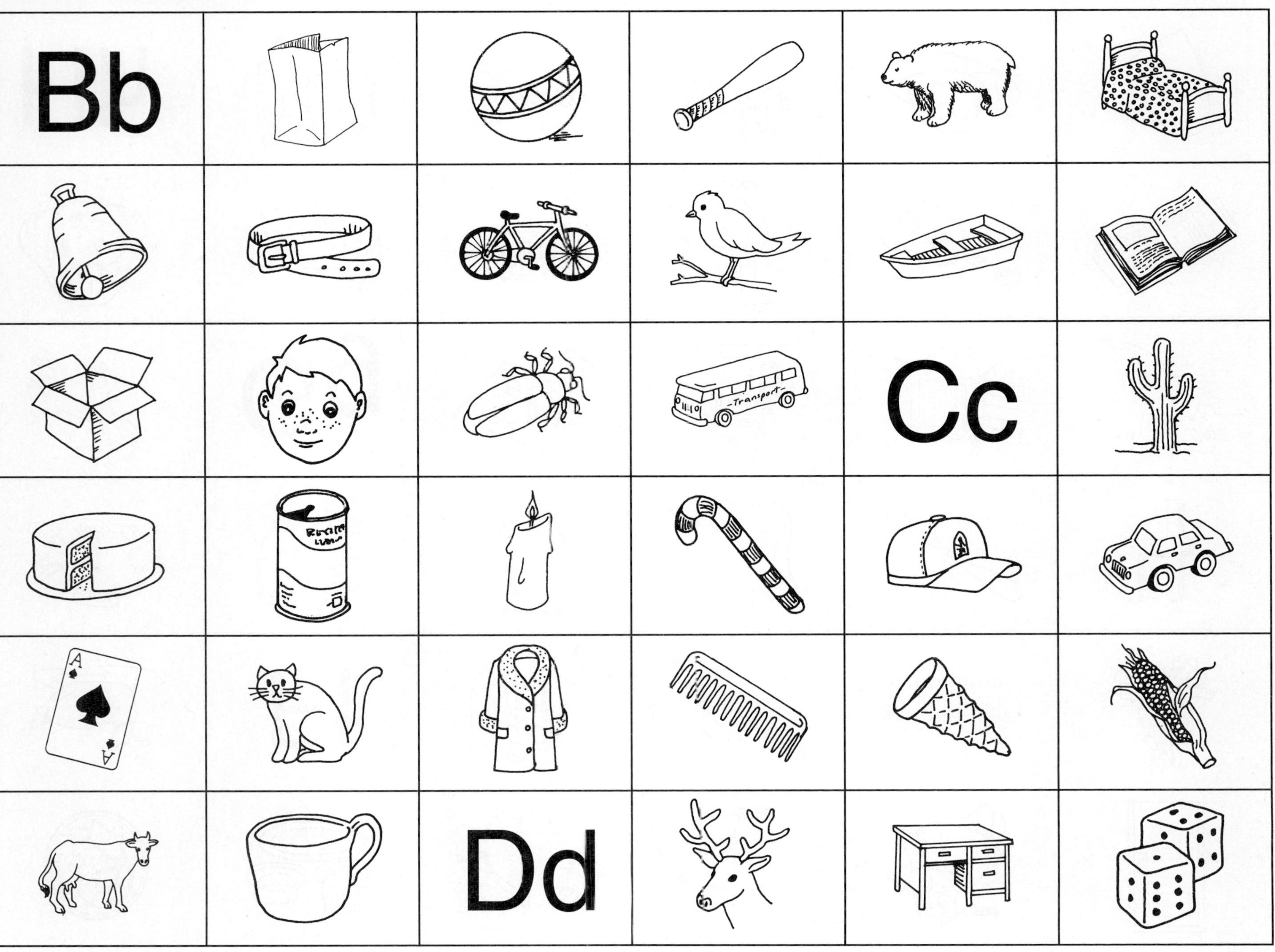

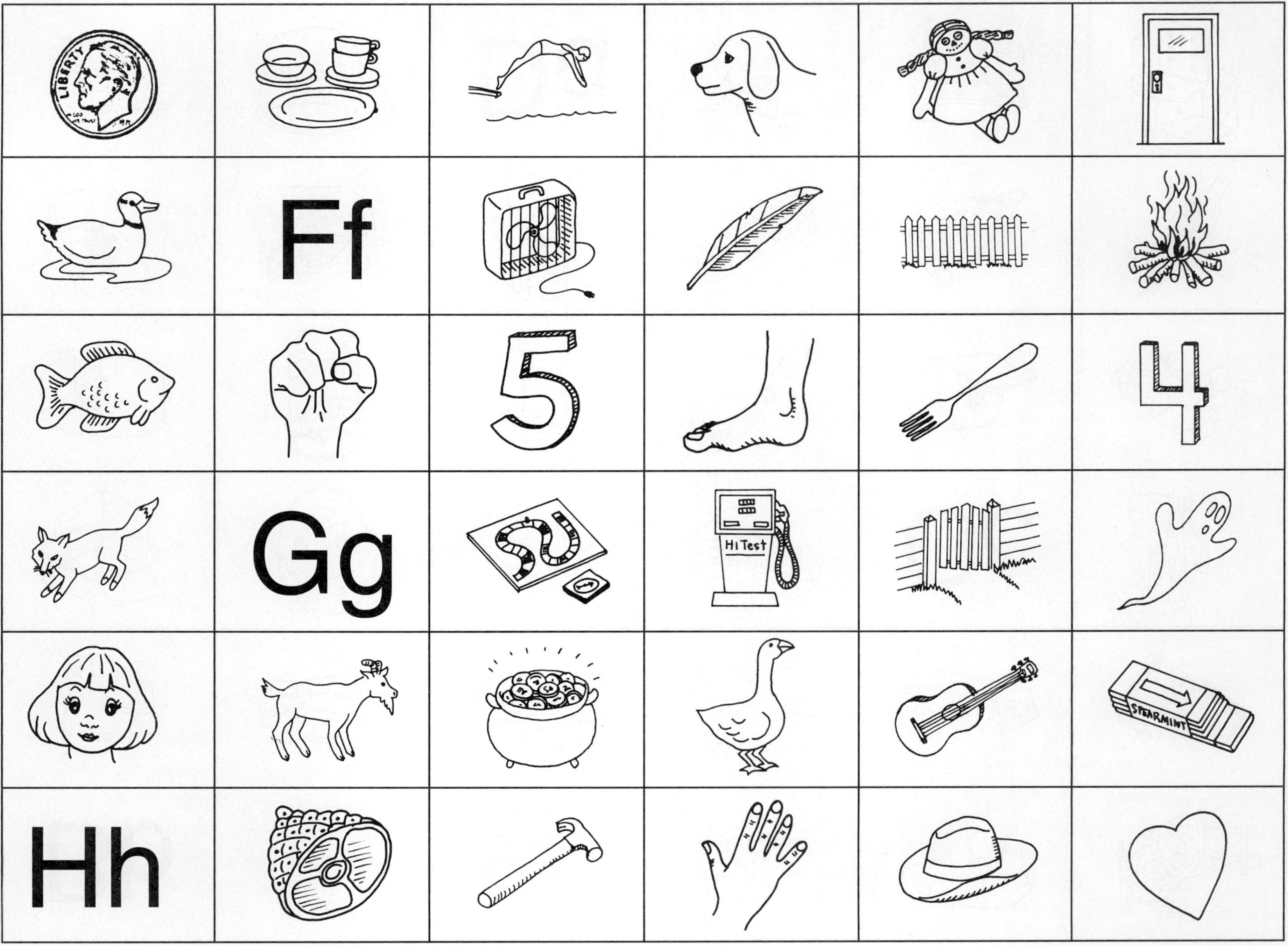
LIBERTY
Ff
5
4
Gg
Hi Test
SPEARMINT
Hh

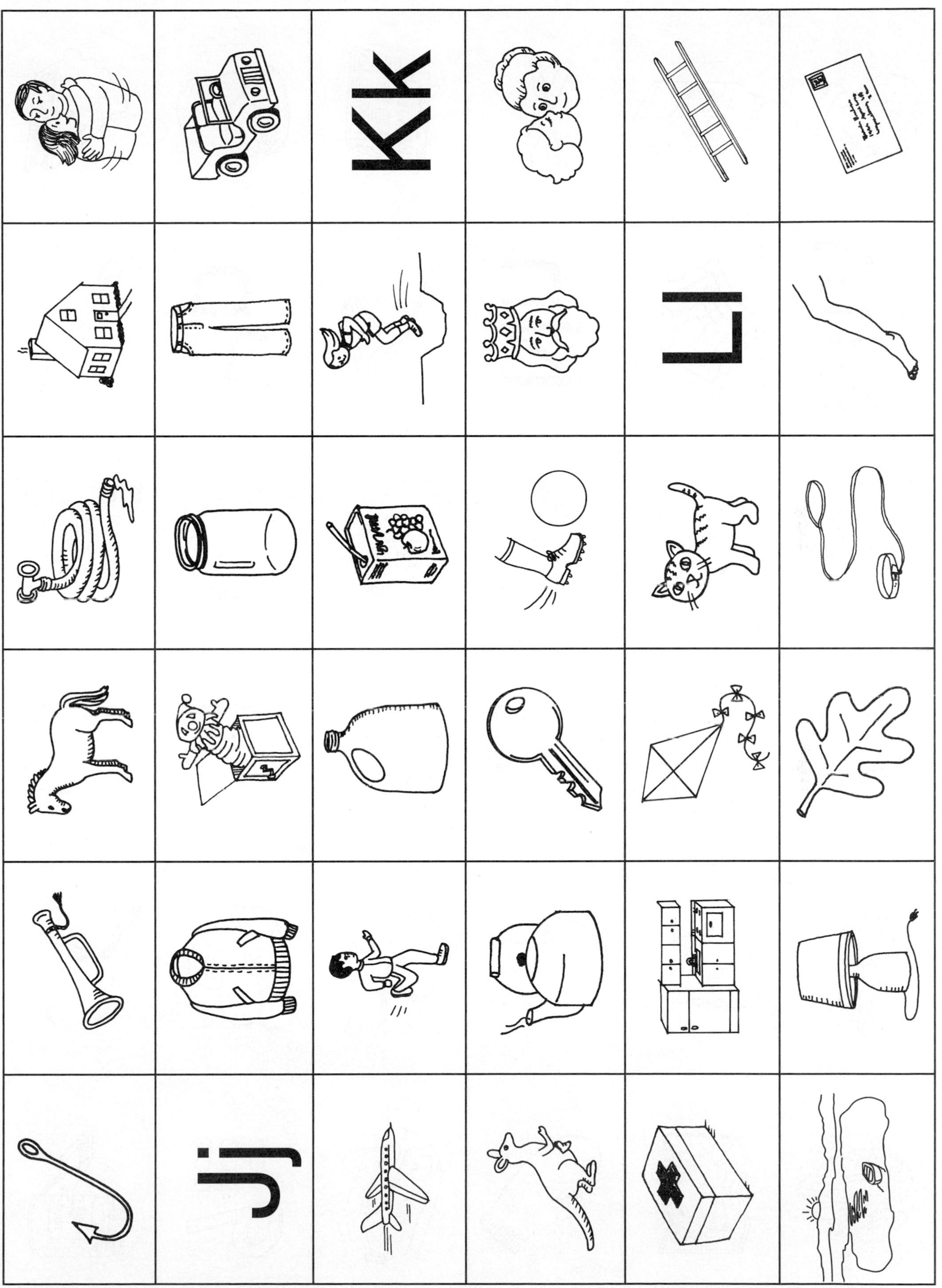
Kk
Ll
Jj

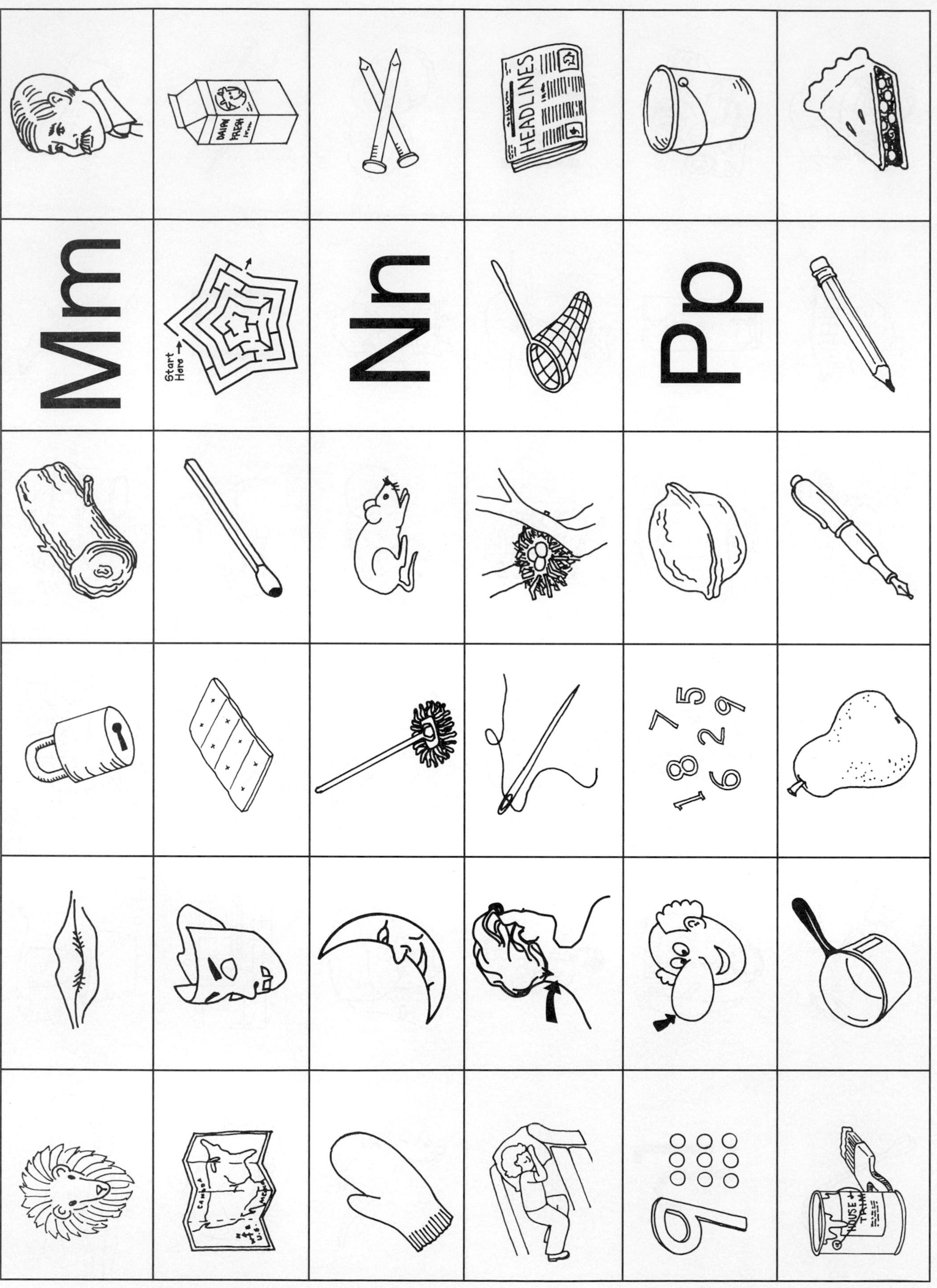
HEADLINES
Mm
Start Here
Nn
Pp
7 5
2 9
8
1 6
9

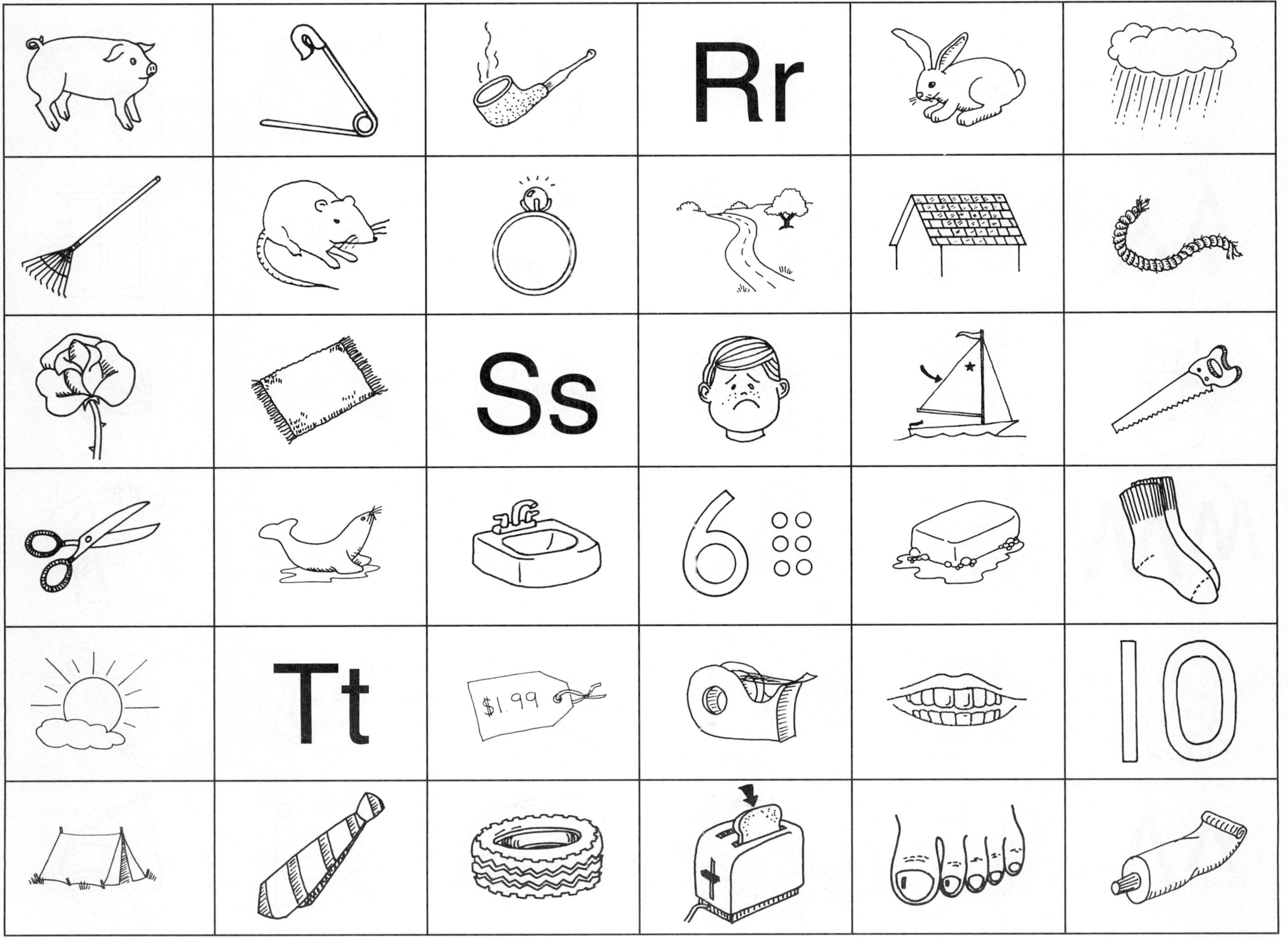
Rr
Ss
Tt
$1.99

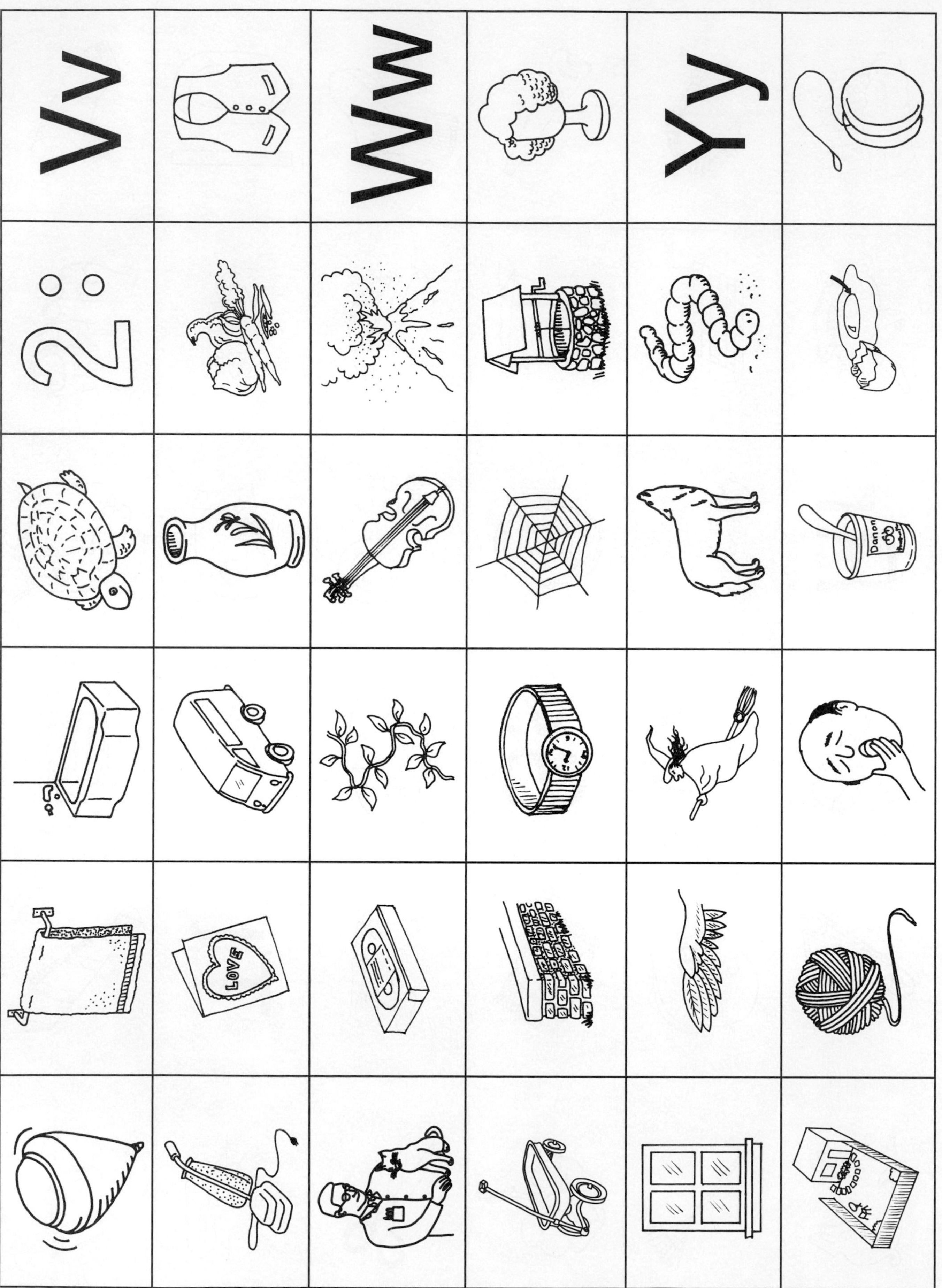
Vv
Ww
Yy
LOVE
Danon

Initial Digraphs

ch					
					sh
th					
13			wh		

Initial Blends

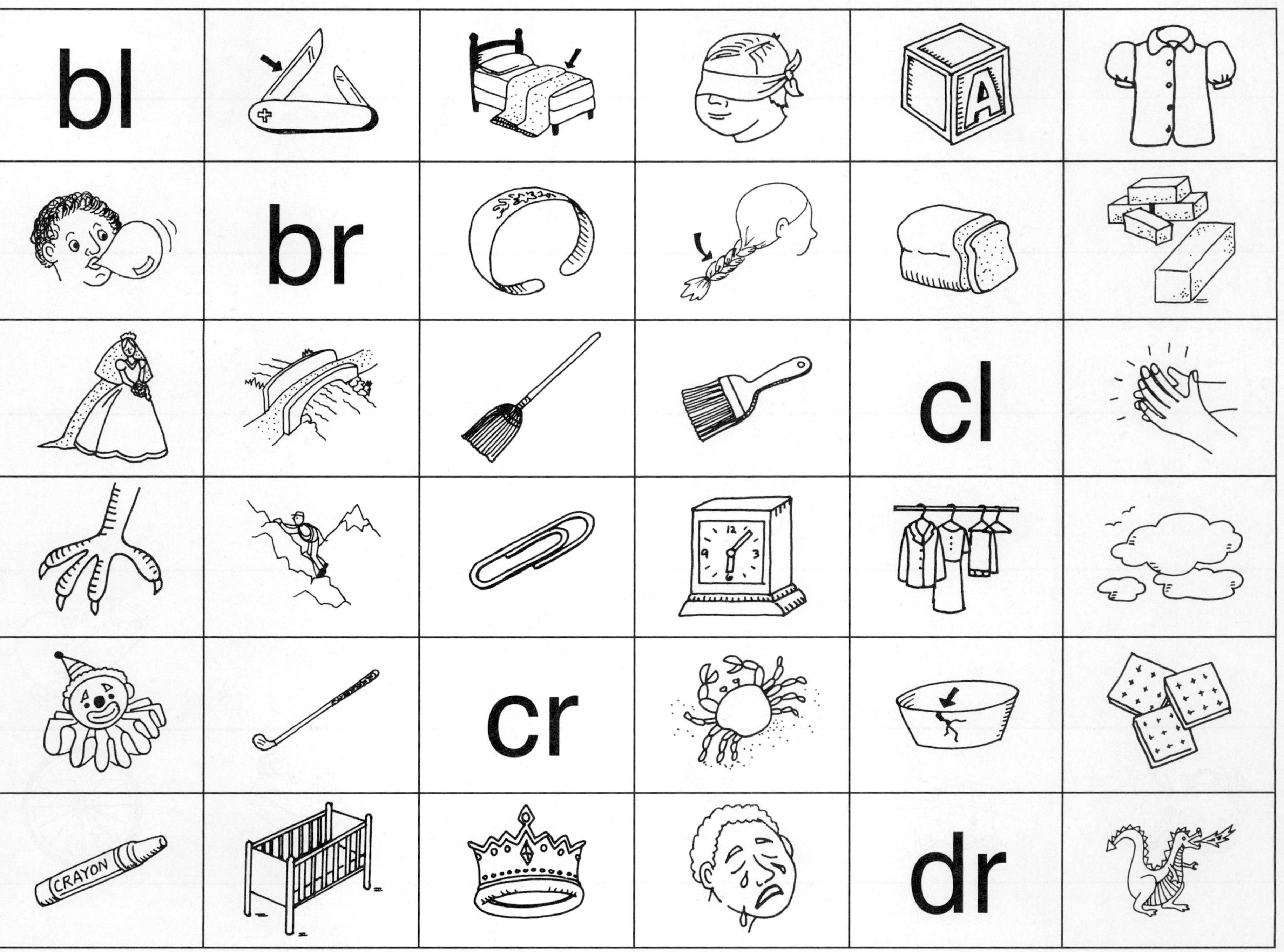

fl
Dental Care
fr
gl
gr

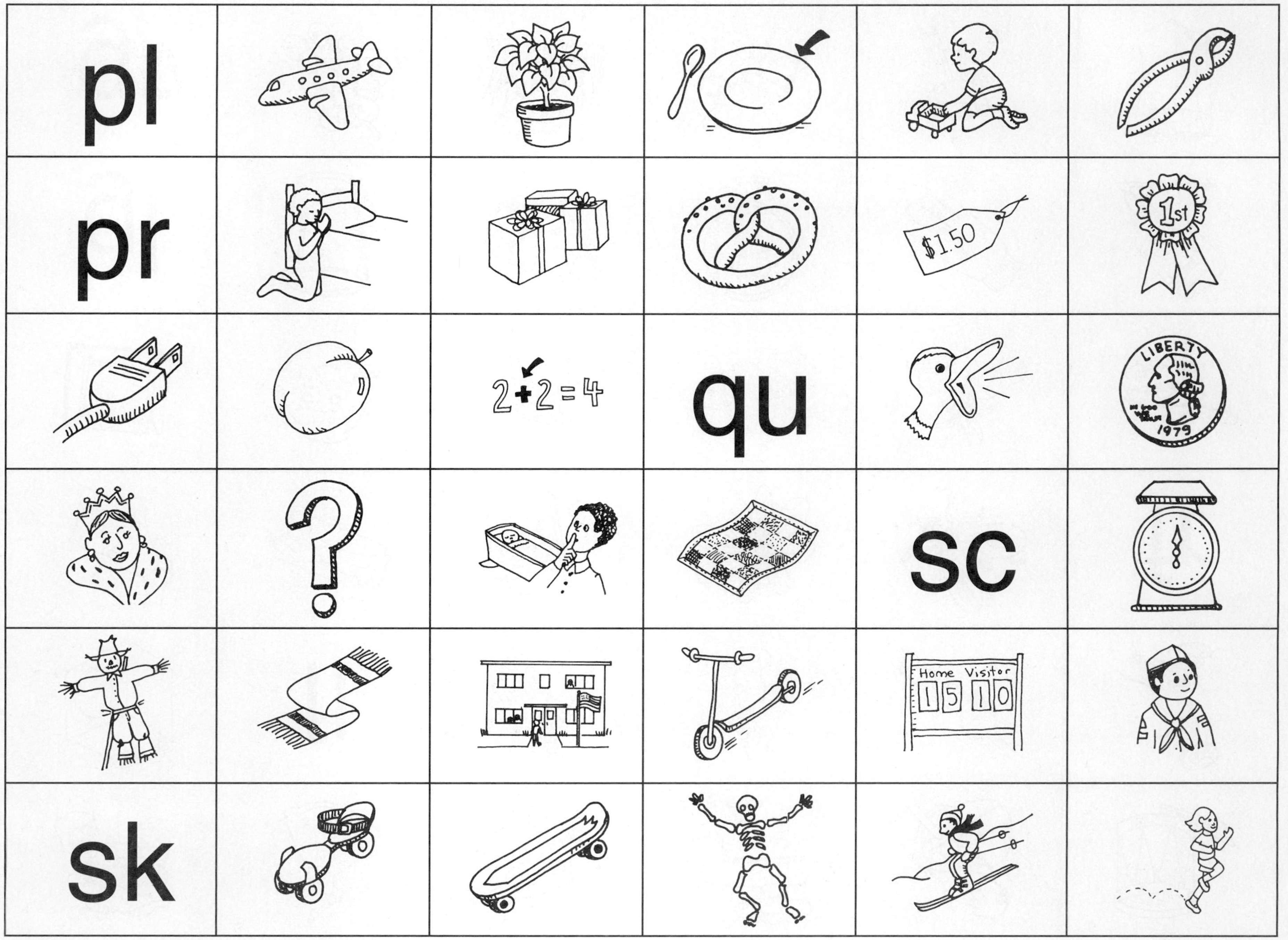

pl
pr
$1.50
1st
2+2=4
qu
LIBERTY
1979
sc
Home Visitor
15 10
sk

sl
sm
sn
sp
sw

st
25¢
STOP
tr
tw
12
20

Initial Short Vowel Sounds

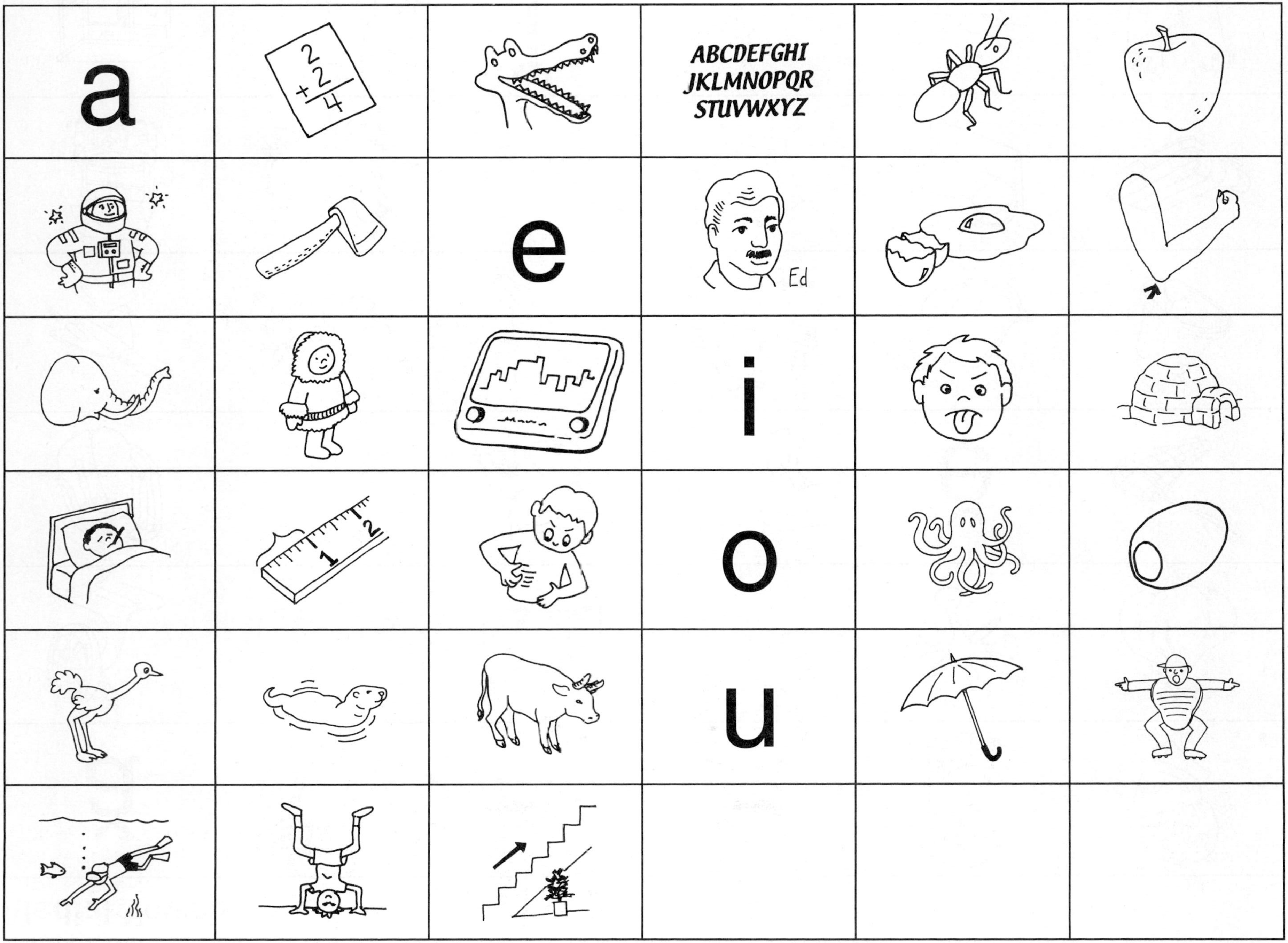

a	2 + 2 = 4		ABCDEFGHI JKLMNOPQR STUVWXYZ		
		e	Ed		
			i		
	1 2		o		
			u		

Medial Vowels

ĕ

ĭ

ă

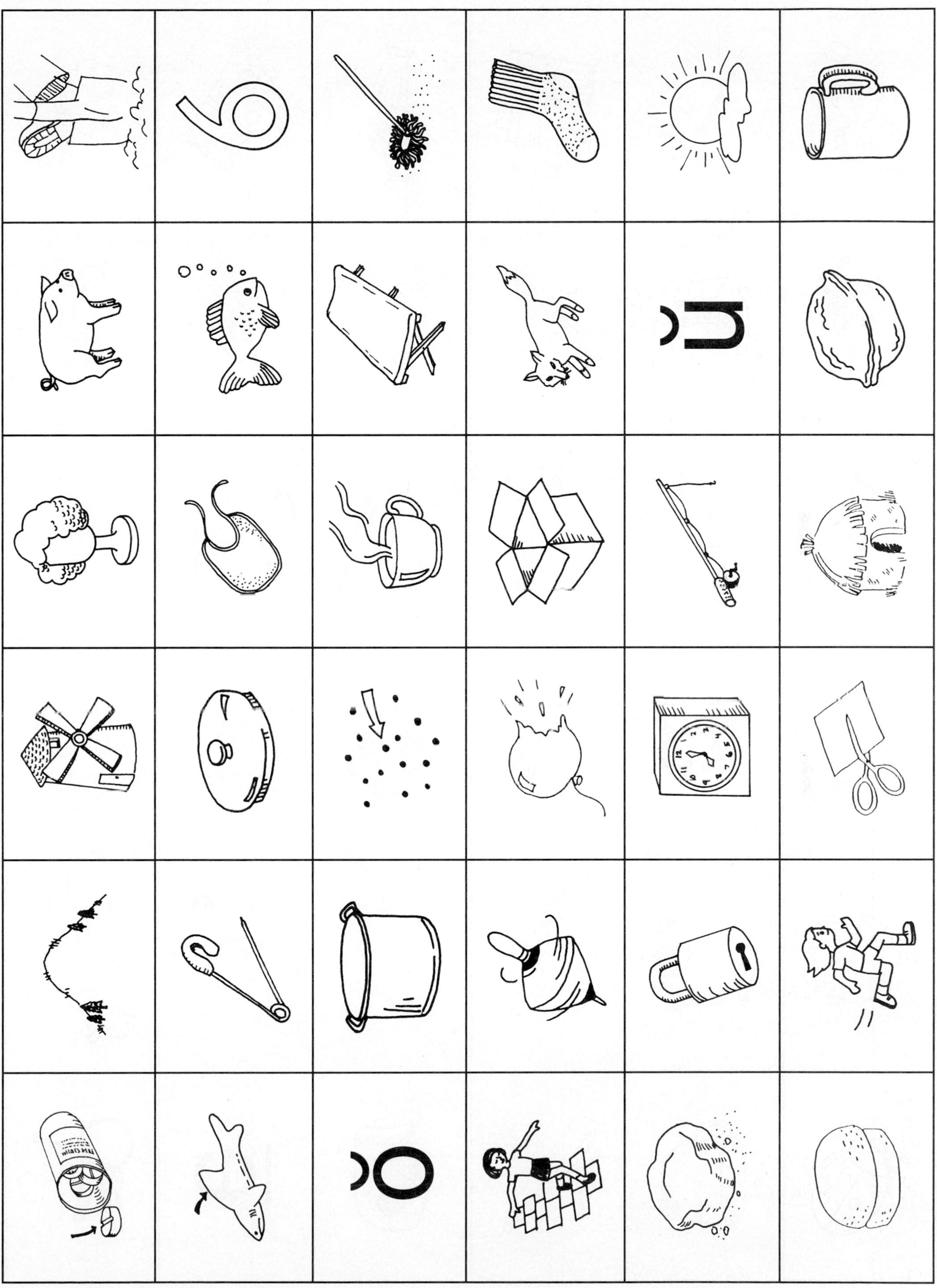

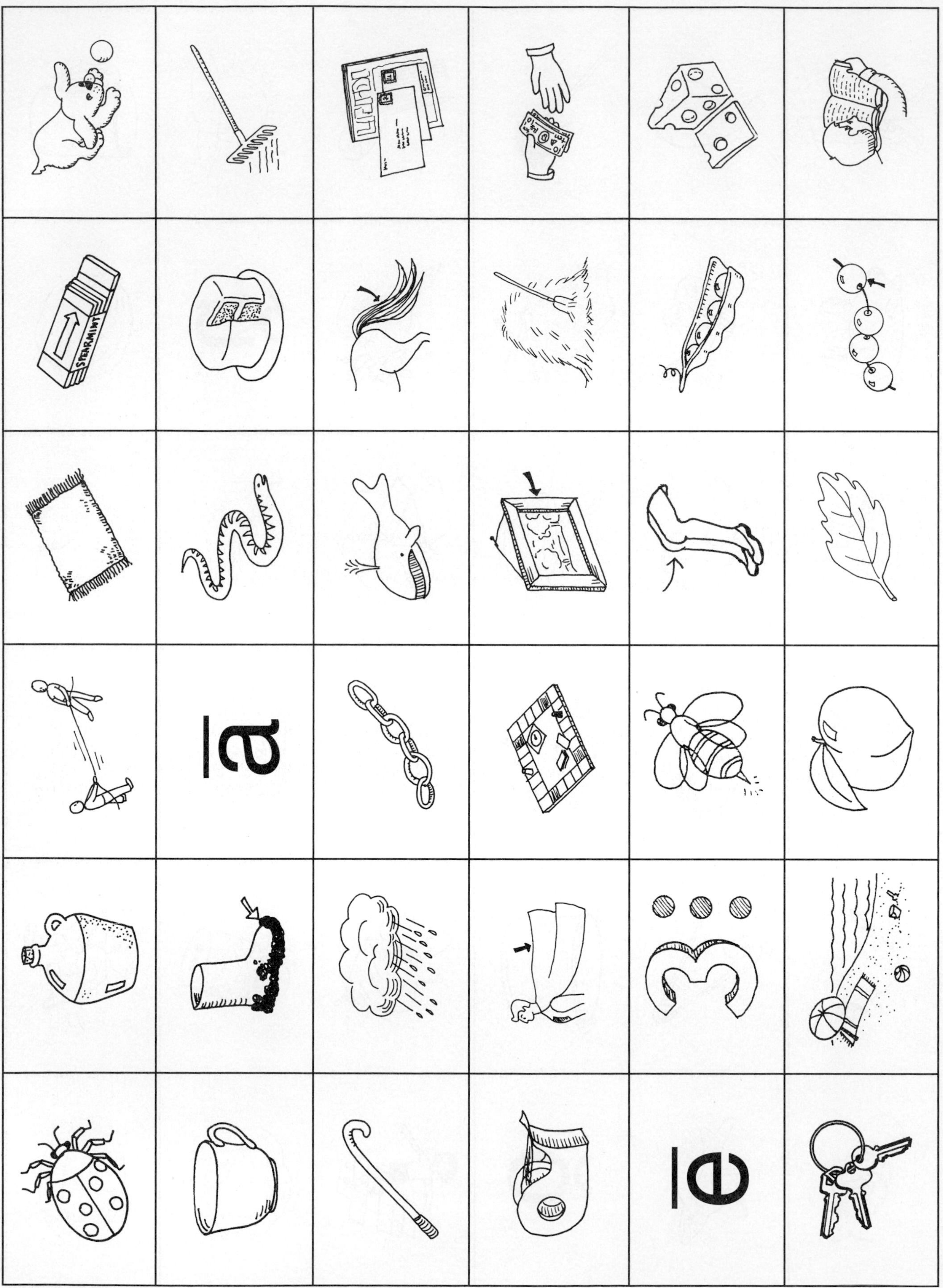
SPEARMINT

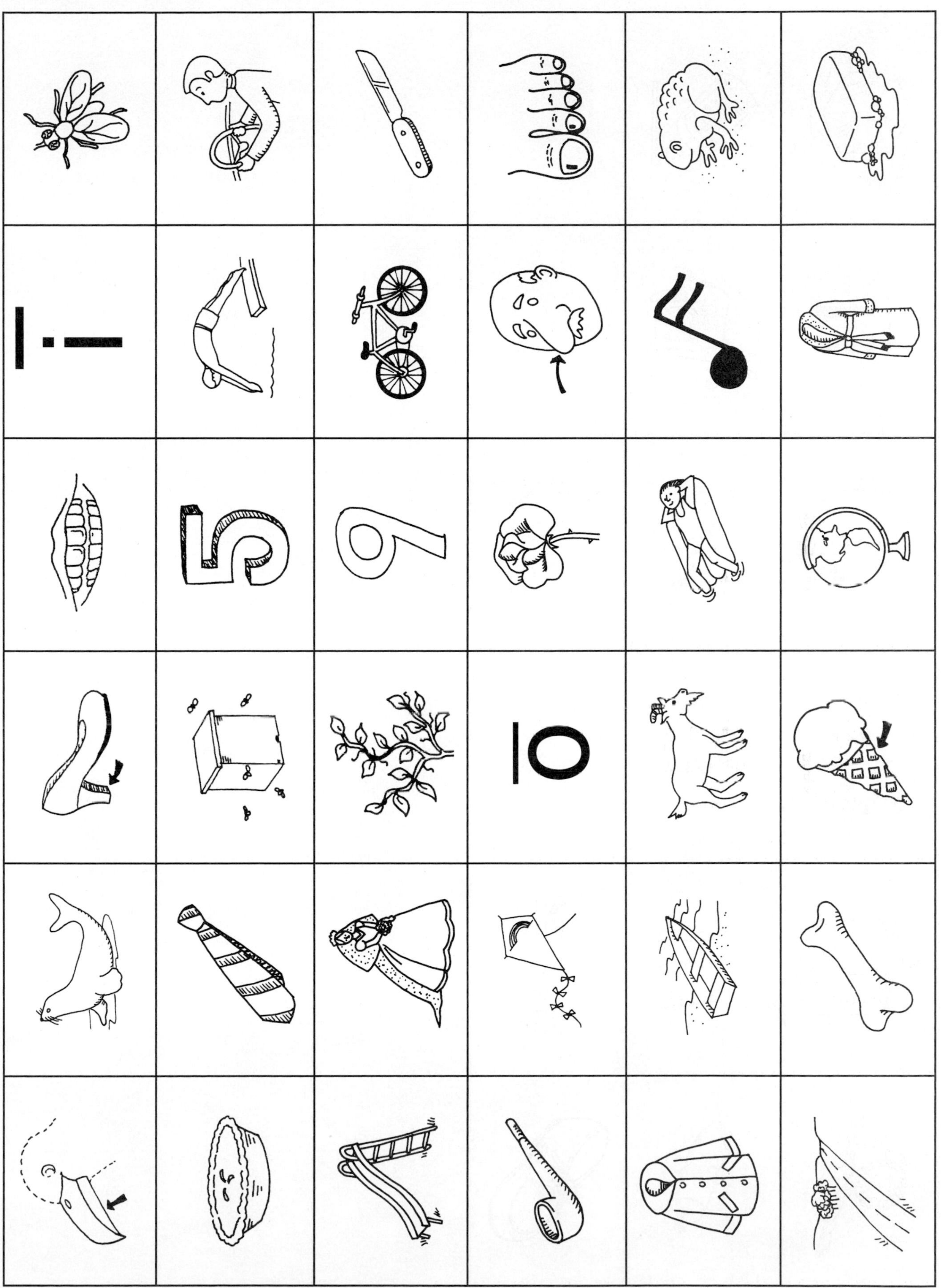

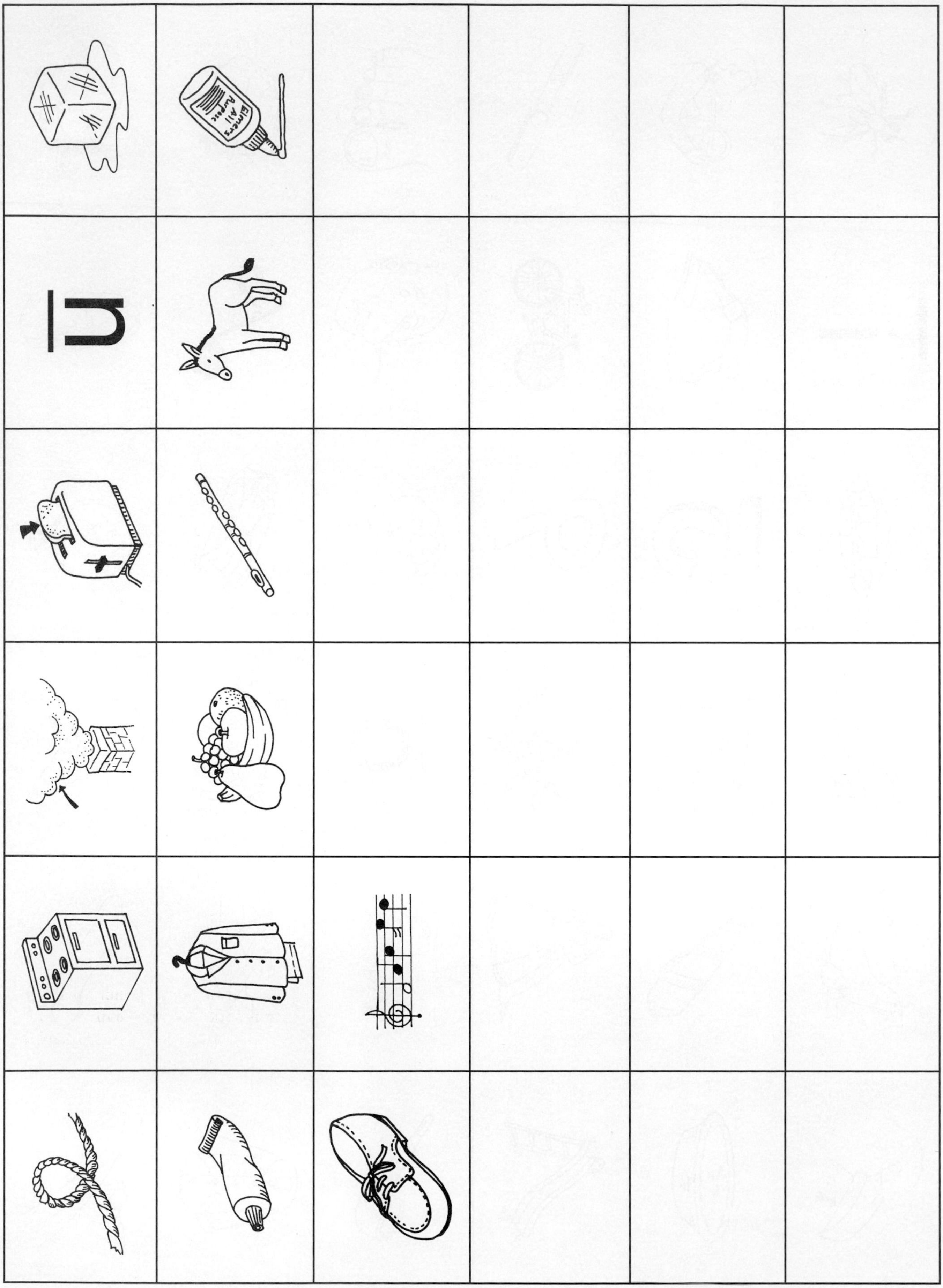

Appendix D Sample Word Sorts by Spelling Stage

The sample word sorts on the following pages are arranged sequentially by spelling stage. Prepare word sorts for your students by writing the words on a template such as the one on page 398. Be sure to write the words on the template randomly so students can make their own discoveries as they sort. Several points need to be made considering the use of these sorts.

- These sorts are not intended to be a sequence for all students. Chapter 2 will help you match your students to the stages of spelling. There are additional suggestions in each instructional chapter about the pacing and sequencing of word study for each stage. Choose appropriate sorts from among those presented here.
- This is not an exhaustive list of sorts, but it does give you a starting point for creating your own. You can adapt these sorts by adding, deleting, or substituting words that are more appropriate for your students. Word lists are provided in Appendix E.

Letter Name–Alphabetic Sorts

Letter name–alphabetic spellers will also need to study initial consonants, digraphs, blends, and short vowels with picture sorts. Use the pictures in the previous section to create these sorts and refer to Table 5.5 for a scope and sequence.

Same Short Vowel Word Families

1. Short *a*

cat	man
bat	can
sat	pan
fat	ran
mat	fan
rat	van
hat	tan

2. More Short *a*'s

sad	cap	bag
mad	tap	rag
dad	map	wag
had	nap	tag
pad	lap	flag
	rap	

3. Short *i*

sit	big
bit	wig
hit	pig
fit	dig
kit	fig
quit	

4. More Short *i*'s

pin	pill	rip	sick
win	will	lip	pick
fin	fill	hip	lick
thin	hill	zip	kick
chin	mill	dip	tick
	bill		chick
	kill		

5. Short *o*

not	hop
got	pop
hot	mop
lot	cop
pot	stop
dot	shop
shot	

6. More Short *o*'s

job	lock	dog
rob	rock	log
cob	sock	frog
mob	dock	fog
blob	clock	jog
sob	block	

7. Short *e*

pet	ten	bed	bell
net	hen	red	tell
met	pen	fed	well
set	men	led	fell
jet	then	sled	shell
bet	when		
get			

8. Short *u*

cut	tub	bug	fun	duck
nut	rub	rug	bun	luck
hut	cub	dug	run	suck
but	club	jug	sun	truck
shut		hug	gun	tuck
		tug		

Mixed Short Vowel Word Families

9. Short *a, i, u*

man	pin	fun
can	win	run
fan	fin	sun
ran	thin	bun
than	grin	gun
plan	chin	
van	skin	

10. Short *a, i, o, u*

cat	sit	not	cut
mat	fit	hot	mut
hat	hit	got	nut
sat	kit	pot	but
rat	bit	rot	hut
that	pit	cot	shut
	quit	dot	

11. Short *a, i, e*

bag	big	pill	bell
rag	wig	will	sell
wag	pig	hill	tell
flag	jig	fill	well
tag	dig	bill	fell
snag	fig	spill	shell
		drill	smell

12. Families with *ck*

back	sick	lock	duck	neck
sack	lick	rock	suck	peck
tack	pick	sock	tuck	deck
jack	tick	dock	truck	speck
pack	kick	clock		
black	chick	block		

13. Preconsonantal Nasals

camp	jump	band	sink
lamp	dump	hand	pink
ramp	hump	sand	think
stamp	stump	land	wink
damp	lump	stand	drink

14. Families Ending in *sh*

mash	fish	mush
cash	dish	hush
trash	wish	rush
rash	swish	gush
dash		brush
crash		
flash		

Short Vowels in CVC Words

15. Short *a* and Short *o*

cat	not	*
bag	job	was
mad	top	for
pan	fox	
pat	got	
cab	top	
jam	not	

16. Short *e* and Short *u*

pet	but	*
bell	sun	put
red	cup	push
yes	mud	
let	cut	
ten	hug	
beg	duck	
	gum	

17. Short *a*, Short *i*, and Short *o*

hat	big	pop
fan	six	rock
cab	lip	box
tax	did	mom
bat	dig	stop
back	zip	lock
	will	hop
	win	hot

18. All Short Vowels

can	let	hit	sock	hug
that	fed	fish	mop	luck
lap	met	fill	dot	run
last	web	six	box	bus
sack	fell	this	rob	pup
	wet	sick		bun
		wig		rug

19. Short Vowels with Digraphs

that	ship	when
chat	chill	check
than	whip	shed
shall	this	shell
shack	whiz	then
chap	chip	them
wham	thin	
	thick	

20. Two-Step Sort with Blends and Short Vowels

a. Initial consonant and blends

rack	tack	dug	trick	drum
rag	tag	dip	track	drill
rash	tap	duck	trash	drag
rug	tick		trap	drug
rip			trip	drip
			truck	

b. Short vowels

tack	tick	truck
tap	trip	drum
trash	drill	dug
drag	dip	rug
rack	rip	duck
rag	trick	drug
rash	drip	
trap		

21. Two-Step Sort with Blends and Short Vowels

a. Blends

cram	slip	spill
crab	slid	spin
crash	slap	spot
crib	clock	snap
brag	blob	
brat	flag	
grip	flop	
	flock	

b. Vowels

crab	clip	trot
cram	slid	drop
brag	spill	spot
brat	grip	flop
slap	slip	clock
crash	spin	blob
flag	crib	flock
snap	twig	

22. Two Step Sort with Preconsonantal Nasals

a. Preconsonantal Nasals

sang	camp	pant	pink	sand
king	lamp	plant	think	land
sing	stamp	print	junk	
swing	limp	hunt	trunk	
sting	jump	want		
sung	bump			

b. Short Vowels

sang	king	jump	*
camp	limp	sung	want
sand	print	bump	
lamp	pink	junk	
pant	sing	hunt	
land	think	trunk	
plant	swing	skunk	
stamp	sting		

**Note:* Oddballs are marked with asterisks.

Within Word Pattern Sorts

23. Short/Long *a*

hat	name	*
jack	date	have
ask	race	what
slap	plane	
fast	cape	
lamp	page	
flag	same	
pass	safe	
path	gave	
glad	gate	

24. Short/Long *a*

cap	lake	rain
last	wave	wait
plan	late	nail
sat	tape	gain
flat	bake	fail
tax	base	pail
	shade	plain
	made	sail
	maze	
	sale	

25. Long *a* Patterns

same	mail	day	*
whale	pain	say	said
flake	train	play	have
grape	paid	may	
stage	brain	pay	
grade	snail	stay	
chase	chain	clay	
shave	tail		
tale	waist		
waste			

26. Short/Long *e*

well	week	she
step	peel	he
west	weed	we
men	peek	me
bed	speed	
help	keep	
belt	pee	

27. Short/Long *e*

best	green	mean	*
left	wheel	team	been
neck	sheet	deal	head
bell	need	reach	
bled	bleed	beach	
yet	teeth	steam	
	creep	clean	
	speed	bean	

28. Short/Long *e*

mess	head	neat
rest	dead	meal
bell	deaf	speak
kept	breath	meat
nest	death	treat
shell	dread	sneak
vest	bread	heat

29. Short/Long *i*

dish	hike	*
chip	ride	give
king	ripe	live
whip	nice	
twin	white	
miss	dime	
pink	fine	
rich	life	

30. Short/Long *i*

clip	mine	try	*
win	price	fly	eye
trick	spine	shy	buy
gift	lime	why	bye
list	wife	sky	
mitt	vine	dry	
thick	five		
swim			

31. Short/Long *o*

lock	home	*
odd	slope	move
crop	note	gone
shot	hose	some
clock	vote	
shock	joke	
knob	smoke	
slot	hope	
	choke	

32. Long *o* Patterns

rope	road	blow	*
woke	boat	grow	now
close	soap	know	cow
stone	soak	slow	
bone	moan	throw	
phone	loaf	snow	
broke	coach	low	
hole	load	bow	
vote	toast	flow	

33. Short/Long *u*

bun	June	blue	*
fuss	cute	glue	truth
luck	rule	clue	
lump	tube	due	
trust	tune	true	
plum	huge		
crust	cube		

34. Long *u* Patterns

rude	fruit	new	*
crude	suit	chew	fuel
flute	juice	drew	build
mule	bruise	knew	
fume	cruise	stew	
chute		few	
dune		dew	
use		brew	

35. Less Common Long *a*

hay	prey	eight	break
tray	they	weigh	great
stray	obey	vein	steak
pray	hey	veil	
sway		freight	
play		sleigh	
		neigh	

36. *R*-influenced *a*

car	care	chair	*
star	share	pair	bear
bark	bare	hair	
card	mare	air	
far	rare		
dark	scare		
arm	hare		
start			

37. Less Common Long *e*

greed	chief	these	*
speech	field	scene	vein
greet	brief	theme	friend
creek	grief	eve	seize
fleet	shriek		
geese	piece		
cheese	thief		
	niece		

38. *r*-Influenced *e*

her	near	cheer	bear	*
fern	clear	deer	pear	heart
germ	dear	sneer	wear	
jerk	year	queer	swear	
herb	spear	peer		
herd	beard			
perch				

39. Long *i* Patterns

kite	might	mind
bride	night	wild
write	right	kind
spice	bright	blind
hide	light	find
wipe	tight	child
mice	sight	mild
		grind

40. *r*-Blends/ *r*-Influenced *i*

grin	third	hire
bring	shirt	tire
drip	dirt	fire
grill	bird	wire
trick	skirt	tired
drink	girl	
brick		
crib		

41. Ambiguous/Long *o*

soft	roll	ghost	*
moth	cold	most	son
cost	stroll	host	from
cross	mold	post	
cloth	scold		
lost	fold		
toss	told		
frost	folk		
long			

42. *r*-Influenced *o*

for	more	door	*
born	store	poor	your
short	chore	floor	
porch	tore		
storm	shore		
north	score		
fort	wore		
torch	swore		

**Note:* Oddballs are marked with asterisks.

43. Other Long *u*

gloom	new	who
bloom	grew	to
roost	crew	too
smooth	flew	two
scoop	blew	
school	stew	
mood	dew	
pool	knew	

44. *r*-Influenced *u*

hurt	cure	heard
turn	pure	learn
church	sure	earn
burst	lure	pearl
curl		yearn
purr		earth
purse		search

45. *r*-Blends/Vowels

grill	girl
trap	tarp
crush	curl
fry	first
price	purse
track	dark
brag	bark
drip	dirt
frog	fort

46. *r*-Influenced Vowels

car	her	for
shark	first	short
farm	bird	corn
hard	burn	horn
card	word	scorn
yard	worm	torn
scar	world	
march	dirt	
	jerk	

47. *ck, k, ke*

lick	leak	like
lack	seek	lake
tack	soak	take
snack	sleek	snake
stuck	weak	stake
stick	week	strike
whack	croak	wake

48. CVCe Sorts across Vowels

cave	drive	drove	huge
crane	while	those	fume
taste	smile	throne	prune
stage	twice	phone	chute
trade	crime	wrote	flute
waste	guide	quote	mule

50. CVVC across Vowels

road	team	rain	*
boast	stream	strain	board
coach	sweet	claim	great
groan	queen	waist	
throat	peach	faith	
toast	thief	praise	
roast	peace	strain	
		trail	

Ambiguous Vowels and Complex Consonants

50. Diphthongs

toy	coin	town	sound
boy	foil	clown	mouth
joy	boil	brown	scout
	spoil	gown	round
	noise	frown	couch
	point	howl	loud

51. More Diphthongs

row	owl	out
snow	growl	found
blown	drown	shout
flown	crown	cloud
grown	plow	south
thrown	fowl	foul
	prowl	doubt

52. Ambiguous Vowels

salt	hawk	fault	*
bald	draw	caught	fought
chalk	lawn	cause	ought
stall	raw	taught	
false	crawl	sauce	
small	claw	haul	
walk	paw	pause	

53. Words Spelled with *w*

watch	war	wrap
swamp	warn	wreck
swan	warm	write
wand	dwarf	wrist
swat	swarm	wren
wash	wart	wrong
wobble	worn	wriggle
wasp	Warble	wrestle

54. Complex Consonants

scram	straight	shrank	square
scrape	strange	shrink	squawk
scratch	stretch	shred	squint
screech	strict	shrunk	squash
screw	string	shriek	squeeze
screen	strong	shrimp	squirt
scrap			

55. *tch* and *ch*

catch	reach	*
witch	coach	rich
patch	peach	such
fetch	roach	
hutch	screech	
itch	beach	
switch	pouch	
ditch		
latch		

56. *dge* and *ge*

badge	page
ridge	stage
edge	huge
fudge	rage
bridge	cage
judge	
hedge	
lodge	

57. Hard and Soft *c* and *g* across Vowels

cave	coat	cute	cent	cyst
camp	coast	cup	cell	gym
cast	cost	cue	cease	
gave	gold	gum	gem	
gain	golf	gush	germ	
gasp	goof			

58. *ce, ge, ve, se*

dance	charge	glove	cheese
chance	large	give	please
prince	wedge	curve	tease
fence	dodge	shove	loose
since	ridge	live	choose
voice	edge	above	
juice	change	have	

Concept Sorts

59. What Lives in Water?

Yes	No
frog	toad
fish	lizard
whale	zebra
sea turtle	tortoise
clam	elephant
crab	horse

60. Edible Plants

Grain	Fruit	Vegetable
wheat	apples	carrots
oats	peaches	beans
rice	berries	lettuce
rye	pears	cucumber
barley	bananas	cabbage
	oranges	beets

61. Animal Attributes

Fish	Bird	Mammal
scale	feather	hair
eggs	eggs	born alive
gills	lungs	lungs
heart	heart	heart
no legs	two legs	legs
fins	wings	

62. States

East	West	North	South
Virginia	California	Maine	Florida
North Carolina	Nevada	Vermont	Mississippi
Maryland	Utah	New York	Texas
Delaware	Arizona		Alabama

63. Geometry Terms

Shapes	Lines	Measurements
triangle	ray	perimeter
rhombus	angle	degrees
square	line	diameter
rectangle	right angle	circumference
parallelogram	obtuse angle	area
isosceles triangle		radius

Syllables and Affixes Sorts

Inflected Endings (*ed* and *ing*), Consonant Doubling, and Plurals

64. Sort for Sound of *ed*

trapped	waited	played
mixed	dotted	mailed
stopped	patted	boiled
chased	treated	raised
cracked	traded	tried
walked	ended	filled
asked	handed	seemed
jumped	needed	yelled

65. Plural Words (*s* and *es*)

cows	boxes	buses	dishes
chicks	mixes	glasses	benches
farms	axes	dresses	watches
fences	foxes	passes	lashes
gates		gases	churches
horses		guesses	ashes
			brushes

66. Plurals with *y*

babies	plays
carries	monkeys
ponies	boys
bodies	trays
pennies	donkeys
worries	enjoys
daddies	turkeys
berries	valleys
parties	

67. Base Words + *ed* and *ing*

jump	jumped	jumping
hike	hiked	hiking
dress	dressed	dressing
wait	waited	waiting
stop	stopped	stopping
pass	passed	passing
live	lived	living
wag	wagged	wagging

68. Adding *ing* (double and *e*-drop)

batting	baking
shopping	skating
bragging	biting
hopping	hoping
humming	sliding
begging	waving
skipping	moving
swimming	caring

69. Adding *ed* (double, nothing)

slipped	picked	traded
grabbed	called	baked
stopped	tracked	wasted
wagged	peeled	liked
tripped	watched	stared
knotted	cheered	waved
rubbed	talked	skated
whizzed	dreamed	tasted

70. Adding *ing* (double, *e*-drop, nothing)

				*
trimming	diving	pushing	floating	
running	riding	jumping	raining	mixing
popping	sliding	finding	sleeping	taxing
dragging	driving	kicking	boating	
wagging	wasting	wanting	waiting	
quitting	whining	munching	cheering	

71. Past Tense Verbs

kneel	knelt	chase	chased
teach	taught	mix	mixed
bring	brought	walk	walked
deal	dealt	bake	baked
sweep	swept	shop	shopped
send	sent		
think	thought		
lend	lent		
drink	drank		

Syllable Juncture Sorts, Open and Closed Syllables (VCCV, VCV)

72. Compound Words

landfill	downtown	backyard	homework
homeland	downstairs	backbone	homemade
wasteland	lowdown	backpack	hometown
landlord	downcast	backward	homeroom
landslide	downfall	bareback	homesick
landscape	downpour	flashback	
landmark	breakdown	piggyback	
mainland	countdown	paperback	

73. VCCV at Juncture (same/different)

button	market
sunny	garden
yellow	signal
happy	member
happen	basket
sitting	center
fellow	plastic
matter	tablet

74. Syllable Juncture (VCCV, open VCV)

tablet	baby
napkin	human
happen	music
winter	fever
foggy	silent
tennis	duty
sudden	writer
fossil	rival

75. VCV Open and Closed

		*
meter	petal	water
human	rapid	busy
secret	punish	
paper	magic	
lazy	shiver	
even	comet	
major	river	
climate	clever	
crater	proper	
clover	liquid	
bacon		

76. Closed VCCV/Open VCV

funny	picture	pilot
summer	expert	navy
pretty	until	nature
dollar	forget	music
butter	napkin	spoken
gossip	canyon	frozen
letter	sister	spider
pattern	army	student
	number	

77. Closed/Open with Endings

sadden	dusting	sliding
chipped	rented	shining
matted	helping	named
scarred	sifted	scaring
winner	faster	rider
biggest	longest	tamest
running	walker	moping

78. VCC/CV, VC/CCV, and V/V

			*
athlete	pilgrim	create	cruel
pumpkin	control	poet	
English	complete	riot	
kingdom	children	trial	
mushroom	monster	lion	
halfway	kitchen	diet	
	hundred		

Unaccented Syllable Sorts

79. *le* and *el*

		*
fable	camel	pencil
angle	angel	journal
little	model	
rattle	gravel	
settle	motel	
cattle	bushel	
nibble	level	
turtle	pretzel	
table	travel	
middle		

80. *er, ar, or*

bigger	burglar	doctor
freezer	grammar	favor
dreamer	collar	author
faster	dollar	editor
blister	lunar	tractor
jogger	solar	motor
speaker		mayor
skater		
smaller		

81. *er, ar, or*

Comparatives	Agents	Things
sweeter	worker	cellar
thinner	teacher	meter
smarter	waiter	river
slower	voter	pillar
younger	actor	anchor
gentler	beggar	vapor
steeper	barber	trailer
cheaper	skater	flower

82. Final *en/on/in/ain*

broken	dragon	cousin	mountain
hidden	weapon	cabin	captain
heaven	apron	napkin	fountain
chosen	ribbon	pumpkin	curtain
children	gallon		certain
eleven	cotton		

83. Unaccented First Syllables

again	decide	beyond
away	design	begin
another	defend	between
aloud	debate	behave
agree	depend	before
afraid		beside
awoke		

84. /j/ Sound

carriage	budget	magic
voyage	agent	engine
message	angel	region
postage	gorgeous	fragile
village	danger	margin
storage	legend	logic
sausage	pigeon	
savage	dungeon	
courage	gadget	

85. Changing *y* to *i*

cry	cries	cried
hurry	hurries	hurried
party	parties	partied
empty	empties	emptied
baby	babies	babied
reply	replies	replied
supply	supplies	supplied
carry	carries	carried
fry	fries	fried

86. *y* Words by Part of Speech

Long *i*	Long *e*		
Verb	Noun	Adjective	Adverb
try	celery	happy	happily
certify	candy	pretty	correctly
apply	gypsy	guilty	clearly
occupy	quarry	angry	safely
rely	country	silly	horribly
	cemetery		hourly
	category		certainly
	copy		sensibly

Sorts to Explore Stress

87. Stress in Homographs

re'cord n.	re cord' v.
protest n.	protest v.
conduct n.	conduct v.
subject n.	subject v.
extract n.	extract v.
permit n.	permit v.
insert n.	insert v.
desert n.	desert v.
rebel n.	rebel v.
combat n.	combat v.
conflict n.	conflict v.

88. Long *u* in Stressed Syllable

bu' gle	a muse'
future	compute
ruby	confuse
rumor	reduce
tulip	perfume
tuna	pollute
tutor	salute
super	excuse
pupil	abuse
ruler	include

Revisiting Vowel Patterns in Longer Words

89. Patterns for Long *a*

debate	explain	layer
mistake	dainty	dismay
amaze	trainer	payment
parade	complain	crayons
engage	acquaint	hooray
bracelet	raisin	decay
estate	refrain	betray
escape	painter	

90. Patterns for Long *u* and *o*

rooster	useful	toaster	suppose
cartoon	refuse	oatmeal	decode
scooter	amuse	approach	remote
balloon	reduce	loafer	erode
noodle	conclude	rowboat	tadpole
	pollute	goalie	lonesome
	perfume		explode

91. Patterns for Long *e* and *i*

needle	reason	polite	highway	*
succeed	eager	decide	lightning	sweater
fifteen	increase	advice	delight	believe
thirteen	defeat	invite	tonight	
canteen	season	surprise	resign	
steeple	conceal	survive		

92. Diphthongs in Multisyllable Words

moisture	joyful
appoint	boycott
poison	royal
turquoise	soybean
moisten	oyster
pointless	voyage
broiler	annoy
embroider	enjoy
rejoice	destroy
noisy	employ
avoid	
pointed	

93. More Diphthongs

county	flower	*
council	allow	double
lousy	brownie	
fountain	vowel	
mountain	shower	
scoundrel	towel	
counter	tower	
around	chowder	
bounty	coward	
mouthful	drowsy	
	powder	
	power	

94. Spelling the *er* Sound in Stressed and Unstressed Syllables

cer'tain	re verse'	sur prise'	lan'tern
person	observe	perhaps	concert
thirsty	alert	survive	modern
service	prefer	surround	western
hurry	emerge		govern
turkey			

95. Words with *ure* and *er* *(ture, sure, cher)*

capture	measure	archer	*
creature	treasure	butcher	injure
fracture	pleasure	preacher	failure
mixture	closure	stretcher	
pasture	leisure	teacher	
texture		rancher	
future			
nature			

Affixes

96. Prefixes

unfair	retell	disagree
unable	replay	disappear
uncover	retrain	disgrace
unkind	return	disarm
undress	reuse	disorder
unplug	research	disobey
unequal	regain	disable
uneven	reword	displaced
unpack	rebuild	disloyal
unusual	remodel	dishonest

97. More Prefixes

preschool	explode	misspell
preview	exceed	mistreat
prevent	expose	misplace
preheat	explore	misuse
prefix	exile	misbehave
prepare	expand	mistake
predict	exclaim	

98. Number Prefixes

unicycle	bicycle	tricycle
unison	biweekly	trilogy
unicorn	bisect	triangle
unique	bilingual	tripod
uniform	biplane	triple
universe	bifocals	trio
		triplets

99. Suffixes

sunny	slowly	happily
rainy	quickly	angrily
foggy	sadly	nosily
guilty	calmly	busily
bossy	bravely	drily
dirty	hardly	daintily
messy	strangely	gaily
wordy	weakly	greedily

100. More Suffixes

darkness	harmless	colorful
kindness	fearless	faithful
illness	homeless	dreadful
weakness	restless	thankful
freshness	ageless	thoughtful
hardness	mindless	painful
blindness	helpless	

Derivational Relations Sorts

Adding Suffixes

101. Adding *-ion*

ct + -ion		*ss + -ion*	
act	action	express	expression
distinct	distinction	impress	impression
select	selection	process	procession
extinct	extinction	depress	depression
predict	prediction	success	succession
subtract	subtraction	profess	profession
contract	contraction	discuss	discussion
affect	affection		

102. *e*-Drop + *-ion*

te + -ion		*ce + -ion*		*se + -ion*	
educate	education	induce	induction	expulse	expulsion
congratulate	congratulation	introduce	introduction	convulse	convulsion
create	creation	produce	production	repulse	repulsion
decorate	decoration	deduce	deduction		
generate	generation	reproduce	reproduction		
imitate	imitation	reduce	reduction		
fascinate	fascination				
complicate	complication				
separate	separation				

103. *-sion* and Spelling Changes

t to *s* + *-sion*		*de*-drop, + *-sion*	
commit	commission	explode	explosion
transmit	transmission	collide	collision
permit	permission	conclude	conclusion
emit	emission	persuade	persuasion
omit	omission	erode	erosion
regret	regression	delude	delusion
remit	remission	include	inclusion
		divide	division
		intrude	intrusion

104. *e*-Drop + *-ation* or *-ition*

e-drop + *-ation*		*e*-drop + *ition*	
admire	admiration	compose	composition
determine	determination	define	definition
explore	exploration	dispose	disposition
combine	combination	oppose	opposition
declare	declaration	expose	exposition
inspire	inspiration	decompose	decomposition
organize	organization		
examine	examination		
perspire	perspiration		

105. *-ible* and *-able*

base + *-able*	root + *-ible*
dependable	audible
expendable	edible
breakable	visible
agreeable	feasible
predictable	terrible
remarkable	possible
readable	legible
profitable	plausible
perishable	horrible
punishable	tangible
laughable	credible

106. *-able* after *e*

e-drop	soft *ce/ge*	hard *c/g*
presumable	changeable	navigable
desirable	manageable	amicable
usable	peaceable	despicable
lovable	serviceable	impeccable
deplorable	noticeable	applicable
comparable		
excusable		

107. Assimilated Prefix Sort

com-	*ad-*	*in-*
compound	adverse	inactive
conform	affair	irresponsible
colleague	affront	immature
compact	assemble	irrational
context	affirm	immortal
correlate	arrange	illogical
constrain	acclaim	innumerable
	admit	illegal

Vowel Alternations

108. Vowel Alternations in Related Pairs

Long *a* to Short *a*	Long *a* to Schwa
cave/cavity	major/majority
humane/humanity	narrate/narrative
nation/national	relate/relative
volcano/volcanic	famous/infamous
grave/gravity	able/ability
nature/natural	native/nativity
insane/insanity	educate/educable
flame/flammable	proclaim/proclamation
profane/profanity	stable/stability

109. Vowel Alternations in Related Pairs

Long *e* to Short *e*	Long *e* to Schwa
serene/serenity	compete/competition
brief/brevity	repeat/repetition
proceed/procession	remedial/remedy
recede/recession	
succeed/succession	
conceive/conception	
receive/reception	

110. Vowel Alternations in Related Pairs

Long *i* to Short *i*	Long *i* to Schwa
resign/resignation	invite/invitation
sign/signal	define/definition
divine/divinity	reside/resident
divide/division	recite/recitation
revise/revision	deprive/deprivation
deride/derision	admire/admiration
criticize/criticism	inspire/inspiration
arise/arisen	preside/president

112. Vowel Alternations in Related Pairs

Long to Short	Long to Schwa	Schwa to Short
induce/induction	compose/composition	metal/metallic
seduce/seduction	propose/proposition	brutal/brutality
reduce/reduction	impose/imposition	local/locality
produce/production	expose/exposition	spiritual/spirituality
telescope/telescopic	harmonious/harmony	vital/vitality
microscope/microscopic	compete/competition	fatal/fatality
prescribe/prescription	serene/serenity	total/totality
		final/finality
		original/originality

Sorting by Roots

112. Latin Stems (contrast 3 or 4 at a time)

judge	traction	suspect	visual	formulate	credit	portable	dictate
adjudicate	contract	spectator	visionary	uniform	incredible	porter	contradict
judgment	attract	inspect	vision	reform	discredit	reporter	prediction
judicial	intractable	respect	vista	transform	creed	portfolio	verdict
prejudice	subtraction	spectacular	visible	deformed	credulous	export	dictionary
judicious	tractor	inspector	revise	nonconformist	accredit	import	dictator
prejudicial	contraction	spectacles	television				diction
judiciary	protractor	disrespect	supervise				
	distraction	expectation					
		circumspect					

conduct	fertile	pressure	respiration
induct	refer	express	spirit
educate	transfer	depression	expire
introduction	suffer	suppress	perspire
produce	conifer	impression	inspiration
reduce	conference	oppressive	conspire
induction			

113. Greek Roots

autograph	telegram
automatic	telepathy
autobiography	telegraph
autonomy	televise
automobile	telephone
autonomous	teleconference

114. Greek and Latin Science Vocabulary Sort

astro	astronomer, astronaut, astrology, astrolabe
bio	biology, biome, biosphere, biotic
chlor	chlorophyll, chloroplast, chlorine, chlorella
eco	ecology, economy, ecosystem, ecotype
hydro	hydrophobia, hydrology, hydrogen
hypo	hypodermis, hypodermic, hypothermia, hypotension
photo/phos	phosphorescent, photography, telephoto
vor	voracious, omnivore, carnivore

Note: For more Greek and Latin root sorts, see pages 393–395.

Appendix E Word Lists

Creating Your Own Word Sort Sheets

The following lists of words are organized by features students need to study in the letter name–alphabetic through derivational relations stages. Under each feature the words are generally grouped by frequency and complexity. For example, under short *a*, the early part of the list offers words most likely encountered by first graders (*am*, *ran*, *that*). The latter part of the list contains words that may be obscure in meaning and spelled with blends or digraphs (*yam*, *brass*, *tramp*). Fry's 300 instant words are the most frequent words and should be included in beginner sorts.

The following lists include possible exceptions or oddballs that can be added to sorts. Sometimes the oddballs you include will be true exceptions (such as *said* in a sort with long *a* patterns), but other times oddballs may represent a less common spelling pattern, such as *ey* representing long *a* in *prey* and *grey*.

Prepare word sorts to use with your students by writing the selected words on a template such as the one on page 398. We recommend that you enlarge it about 5 to 8 percent before writing in the words neatly. Be sure to insert the words randomly so students can make their own discoveries as they sort. Many people find it easy to create computer-generated word sort sheets using the "table" function in a word processing program. First set the margins all around at .5, and then insert a table that is three columns by six to eight rows. Type in words in each cell, leaving a blank line before and after each word. After typing in all words, "select" the entire table and click on the "center" button. Choose a simple font (Ariel and Geneva work well) and a large font size (26 works well). After creating the sort, save it using a name that defines the features such as "Short Vowels: a, o, e." You can contrast sounds, spelling patterns, word endings, prefixes, root words, and so on. Create a template that you use each time.

Here are some reminders and tips about creating your own word sorts.

1. Create sorts that will help your students form their own generalizations about how words work. Use a collection of 15 to 25 words so that there are plenty of examples to consider.
2. Contrast at least two and up to four features in a sort. There are many sample sorts in Appendix D to give you ideas.

   Examples of sound sorts:
   Contrast short *o* and long *o*.
   Contrast the sound of *ear* in *learn* and in *hear*.
   Contrast the sound of *g* in *guest* and *gym*.

   Examples of pattern sorts:
   Contrast long *o* spelled with *oa*, *o-e*, and *ow*.
   Contrast words that end with *or*, *er*, and *ar*.
   Contrast words that double a consonant before *-ing* with those that do not.

   Examples of meaning sorts:
   Contrast words derived from *spect* and *port*.
   Contrast words with prefixes *sub*, *un*, and *trans*.

   The best sorts are those that combine a sound sort with a pattern sort. For example, a long *o* and short *o* sort can begin with a sound sort and then proceed to sort the long vowels by patterns—CVVC and CVCe.
3. Consider whether you want to underline key words or create headers for the sort. Your decision will depend on the level of support you feel your students need, as described in Chapter 3.
4. In most sorts, include up to three oddballs—words that have the same sound or pattern but are not consistent with the generalization that governs the other words. For example, in a long *o* sort, with words sorted by the *oa*, *o-e*, and *ow* patterns, the exceptions might

include the words *now* and *love* since they look like they would have the long *o* sound but do not. The best oddballs are high-frequency words students already know from reading. These are marked with asterisks under "oddballs" in the word lists in this appendix; a list of Fry's top 300 words follows this introduction.

4. Words in a sort can be made easier or harder in a number of ways.
   - Common words like *hat* or *store* are easier than uncommon words like *vat* or *boar.* It is important to use words students know from their own reading in the letter name–alphabetic and within word pattern stages to make sorts easier. This is less important when you get to syllables and affixes and derivational relations stages in which words sorts can help to extend a student's vocabulary.
   - Add words with blends, digraphs, and complex consonant units (i.e., *ce*, *dge*, or *tch*) to make words harder. *Bat* and *blast* are both CVC words, but *blast* is harder to read and spell.
   - Adding more oddballs to a sort makes the sort harder. Oddballs should never, however, constitute more than about 20 percent of the words in a sort or students might fail to see the generalizations that govern the majority of words. Don't use oddballs children are not likely to know (like *plaid* in a long *a* sort for students early in the within word pattern stage).

300 Instant High-Frequency Words

First Hundred

a
about
after
again
all
an
and
any
are
as
at
be
been
before
boy
but
by
can
come
day
did
do
down
eat
for
from
get
give
go
good
had
has
have
he
her
here
him
his
how
I
if
in
is
it
just
know
like
little
long
make
man
many
me
much
my
new
no
not
of
old
on
one
or
other
our
out
put
said
see
she
so
some
take
that
the
their
them
then
there
they
this
three
to
two
up
us
very
was
we
were
what
when
which
who
will
with
work
would
you
your

Second Hundred

also
am
another
away
back
ball
because
best
better
big
black
book
both
box
bring
call
came
color
could
dear
each
ear
end
far
find
first
five
found
four
friend
girl
got
hand
high
home
house
into
kind
last
leave
left
let
live
look
made
may
men
more
morning
most
mother
must
name
near
never
next
night
only
open
over
own
people
play
please
present
pretty
ran
read
red
right
run
saw
say
school
seem
shall
should
soon
stand
such
sure
tell
than
these
thing
think
too
tree
under
until
upon
use
want
way
where
while
white
wish
why
year

Third Hundred

along
always
anything
around
ask
ate
bed
brown
buy
car
carry
clean
close
clothes
coat
cold
cut
didn't
does
dog
don't
door
dress
early
eight
every
eyes
face
fall
fast
fat
fine
fire
fly
food
full
funny
gave
goes
green
grow
hat
happy
hard
head
hear
help
hold
hope
hot
jump
keep
letter
longer
love
might
money
myself
now
o'clock
off
once
order
pair
part
ride
round
same
sat
second
set
seven
show
sing
sister
sit
six
sleep
small
start
stop
ten
thank
third
those
though
today
took
town
try
turn
walk
warm
wash
water
woman
write
yellow
yes
yesterday

Word Lists

a Families

at	*ad*	*ag*	*an*	*ap*	*ab*	*am*	*all*	*ar*	*art*
at*	had*	bag	man*	cap	cab	am**	all*	bar	cart
cat	bad	rag	than**	lap	dab	dam	ball**	car	dart
bat	dad	sag	ran**	gap	jab	ham	call**	far**	mart
fat	mad	wag	can*	map	nab	ram	tall	jar	part
hat	pad	nag	fan	nap	lab	jam	fall	par	tart
mat	sad	flag	pan	rap	tab	clam	hall	star	start
pat	rad	brag	tan	yap	blab	slam	mall		chart
rat	glad	drag	van	tap	crab	cram	wall		smart
sat	lad	shag	plan	zap	scab	wham	small		
that*		snag	clan	clap	stab	swam	stall		
flat		lag	scan	flap	grab	yam			
brat		tag		slap	slab	gram			
chat				trap					
gnat				chap					
				snap					
				wrap					
				strap					

and	*ang*	*ash*	*ack*	*ank*	*amp*	*ast*	*ant*	*atch*	*ass*
hand**	bang	bash	back**	bank	camp	fast	ant	batch	mass
band	fang	cash	pack	sank	damp	cast	pant	catch	pass
land	hang	dash	jack	tank	lamp	past	chant	hatch	class
sand	sang	gash	rack	yank	ramp	last**	slant	latch	grass
brand	rang	hash	lack	blank	champ	mast	grant	match	brass
grand	clang	mash	sack	plank	clamp	vast	plant	patch	glass
stand**		rash	tack	crank	cramp			snatch	bass
strand		sash	black**	drank	stamp			scratch	
		lash	quack	prank	tramp				
		trash	crack	spank	scamp				
		crash	track	thank					
		smash	shack						
		slash	snack						
		clash	stack						
		flash							

More Short *a* Words

as*	wax	bath	fact	draft	ranch	*Oddballs*	
has*	ask	path	mask	shaft	grasp	want**	saw**
gal	yak	task	bask	craft	plant	what*	laugh
pal	tax	calf	raft	staff	shall**	was*	
gas	math	half	lamb	graph	branch		

*Occurs in first 100 instant words.

**Occurs in second 100 instant words.

e Families

et	*en*	*ed*	*ell*	*eg*	*ess*	*eck*	*est*	*end*	*ent*
get*	men**	red**	tell**	beg	less	deck	best**	end**	bent
let**	den	bed	bell	peg	mess	neck	nest	bend	dent
bet	hen	fed	cell	leg	guess	peck	pest	lend	cent
met	ten	led	fell	keg	bless	wreck	rest	mend	lent
net	pen	wed	jell		dress	speck	test	send	rent
pet	then*	bled	sell		press	check	vest	tend	sent
set	when*	fled	well		stress	fleck	west	blend	tent
wet	wren	sled	shell				chest	spend	vent
vet	Ben	shed	smell				jest	trend	went
fret	Ken	shred	spell				crest		scent
jet			swell				guest		spent
yet			dwell						

More Short *e*

								Spelled ea	
yes	gem	pep	left**	melt	self	etch	clench	read**	death
web	them*	step	kept	pelt	shelf	fetch	drench	head	breath
egg	hem	held	slept	knelt	fresh	sketch	tempt	bread	dread
elm	stem	help	wept		flesh	wretch	tenth	dead	deaf
next**		desk	swept			stretch	debt	lead	wealth
								tread	health
								spread	

Short *i* Families

it	*id*	*ig*	*in*	*ill*	*im*	*ip*	*ick*	*ink*	*int*	*itch*	*ing*
it*	did*	big**	in*	will*	dim	dip	lick	link	mint	itch	king
bit	hid	dig	fin	dill	him*	hip	kick	mink	lint	pitch	ping
fit	lid	fig	pin	fill	Jim	lip	pick	pink	hint	ditch	sing
hit	kid	jig	tin	hill	Kim	nip	sick	sink	print	pitch	ring
lit	bid	pig	din	kill	rim	rip	tick	rink	glint	hitch	wing
pit	rid	rig	win	gill	Tim	sip	slick	wink	flint	witch	thing**
sit	slid	wig	bin	mill	trim	tip	quick	think**		switch	bring**
kit	skid	zig	thin	pill	brim	zip	trick	blink			sling
wit		twig	twin	till	swim	whip	chick	drink			sting
skit			chin	bill	slim	clip	flick	stink			swing
spit			shin	drill	whim	flip	brick	clink			spring
slit			spin	grill	grim	slip	stick	shrink			string
quit			grin	chill	skim	skip	thick				cling
				skill		drip	click				fling
				spill		trip	prick				wring
				still		chip					
				thrill		ship					
				quill		snip					
						strip					

More Short *i*

											Oddballs
if*	his*	mix	mitt	crib	cliff	rich	film	risk	swift	disc	child
is*	this*	six	hiss	fish	stiff	wind	tilt	brisk	inch	sixth	mind
with*	which*	fix	kiss	dish	lift	fist	limp	sift	pinch	fifth	find**
wish**	live**	whiz	milk	swish	gift	inn	limb	shift			climb

Short *o* Families

ot		*ob*	*og*†	*op*	*ock*	*ong*	*oss*
not*	blot	bob	dog	cop	cock	long*	boss
got**	slot	cob	bog	hop	dock	bong	toss
hot	plot	job	fog	pop	lock	gong	moss
jot	shot	rob	hog	mop	mock	song	loss
lot	spot	gob	jog	top	rock	strong	gloss
pot	knot	mob	log	slop	sock	throng	cross
cot	trot	sob	clog	flop	tock		
dot		snob	frog	drop	block		
		blob		shop	clock		
		glob		stop	flock		
		knob		crop	smock		
		throb		plop	shock		
				prop	stock		

More Short *o* Words

					Ambiguous Sounds of o†			*Oddballs*	
box**	rod	prod	fond	notch	on*	lost	moth	of*	for*
ox	sod	odd	bond	romp	off	cost	cloth	won	from*
fox	god	mom	blond	stomp	loft	frost	broth	son	cold
pox	plod	con	gosh	prompt	soft	doll	golf	front	post

u Families

ut	*ub*	*ug*	*um*	*un*	*ud*	*uck*	*ump*	*ung*
but*	cub	bug	bum	run**	bud	buck	bump	sung
cut	hub	dug	gum	fun	mud	duck	jump	rung
gut	rub	hug	hum	gun	stud	luck	dump	hung
hut	tub	jug	sum	bun	thud	suck	hump	lung
nut	club	mug	plum	sun		tuck	lump	swung
rut	grub	rug	slum	spun		yuck	pump	clung
jut	snub	tug	scum	stun		pluck	rump	strung
shut	stub	slug	chum			cluck	plump	slung
strut	scrub	plug	drum			truck	stump	sprung
	shrub	drug	strum			stuck	thump	wrung
		snug					clump	flung
							slump	stung
							grump	

uff	*unk*	*ush*	*ust*	*unch*	*umb*
buff	bunk	gush	must**	bunch	dumb
cuff	hunk	hush	just*	hunch	numb
huff	junk	mush	gust	lunch	crumb
muff	sunk	rush	dust	munch	thumb
ruff	chunk	blush	bust	punch	plumb
puff	drunk	brush	rust	crunch	
fluff	flunk	crush	crust	brunch	
stuff	skunk	flush	trust		
snuff	shrunk	slush			
scuff	stunk				
gruff	slunk				
bluff	trunk				

†These words do not have a short *o* in some dialects, but instead are pronounced as "aw."

More Short *u* Words

					ul‡	*ou* = *u*	*o* = *u*	*o-e* = *u*	*Oddballs*
up*	much*	buzz	gull	hunt	gulp	tough	of*	come*	put*
us*	such**	fuzz	dull	grunt	bulge	rough	does	some*	push
pup	plus	tusk	mutt	stunt	bulk	touch	son	none	bush
cup	thus	dusk	butt	shucks	gulf	young	ton	done	truth
bus	fuss	husk	tuft		sulk		won	love	
					pulse		from*	dove	
							front	glove	

Long *a* Words

CVCe						CVVC			CVV-Open	CVVC
a-e						*ai*			*ay*	*ei*
made**	ate	wake	tame	ape	pane	rain	wait	snail	day	eight
name**	gate	fake	fame	gape	vane	pain	bait	frail	jay	neigh
same	hate	shake	flame	grape	mane	tail	gain	praise	may**	rein
came**	late	brake	blame	drape	slate	nail	vain	trail	play**	weigh
make*	date	flake	lame	trace	scale	mail	main	strait	say**	weight
take*	sale	base	lane	grace	stale	sail	plain	saint	stay	eighth
bake	male	vase	plane	space	gaze	pail	chain	quaint	way**	freight
cake	tale	chase	cane	waste	daze	rail	stain	strain	clay	reign
lake	whale	race	crane	paste	blaze	fail	drain	faith	gray	veil
age	pale	lace	rate	taste	graze	jail	grain	straight	pray	sleigh
cage	fade	place	fate	haste	haze	gain	brain		tray	weigh
page	wade	pace	crate	sake	range	main	aim		slay	beige
face	shade	state	grate	quake	change	train	claim			heir
gave	grade	plate	bathe	drake	strange	aid	ail			vein
save	trade	skate	cave	phase		paid	aide	*Oddballs*	*Oddballs*	
wave	shape	rage	grave	jade	*Oddballs*	maid	raid	said*	they*	*Oddballs*
tape	cape	stage	slave	blade	have*	laid	paint	again*	prey	break
safe	mate				dance	braid	waist	their*	grey	great
					chance				hey	steak

Long *e* Words

CVCe	CVVC									
e-e	*ea*				*ee*					*ie*
eve	read**	beak	east	leave**	see*	deep	tree**	sheep	spree	thief
scene	sea	leak	feast	weave	seem**	beep	flee	sleep	geese	chief
scheme	eat*	weak	least	flea	bee	seep	glee	creep	cheese	grief
theme	beat	peak	clean	peace	feed	jeep	knee	steep	sneeze	brief
these**	seat	lean	steal	please**	feel	keep	free	sweep	breeze	yield
	meat	heal	knead	cease	feet	seek	three*	creek	freeze	field
Open	mean	real	sneak	crease	beet	week	kneel	cheek	sleeve	shield
me*	bean	deal	creak	grease	meet	beef	steel	sleek	screen	niece
he*	seal	meal	steam	squeal	seen	reef	wheel	speech	preen	piece
we*	tea	heap	dream	league	week	deep	speed	teeth		shriek
be*	pea	leap	cream	breathe	peek	eel	bleed	sleet		priest
the*	bead	seam	scream	squeak	wee	heel	greed	greet		grieve
she*	neat	each**	stream		free	reel	breed	sheet		fierce
	team	teach	plead	*Oddballs*	seed	peel	keen	sweet	*Oddballs*	fiend
	beam	beach	knead	head	need	deed	green	fleet	been*	siege
	lead	reach	beast	dead	tree**	weed	queen	street	seize	pier
	ear**	peach	treat	steak	peep	knee			weird	
				great					vein	*Oddballs*
				break					suite	friend**

‡These words have a slightly different *u* sound before the *l*.

Long *i* Words

CVCe

i-e					
like*	five**	while**	wide	white**	tribe
bike	mine	ice	slide	quite	scribe
dime	fine	mice	pride	write	stride
time	nine	nice	tide	spite	stripe
hide	vine	rice	glide	site	strike
ride	shine	mile	wipe	lice	spine
side	drive	file	pipe	spice	whine
line	dive	pile	swipe	slice	prime
live	hive	smile	spike	twice	chime
kite	life	wise	lime	price	fife
size	ripe	rise	crime	guide	knife
bite	hike	wife	pine	prize	thrive

CV open

ie	*y/ye*
lie	my*
pie	by*
tie	why**
die	fly
	cry
Oddballs	sky
buy	try
guy	dry
live**	shy
give*	sly
eye	spry
	dye
	lye
	rye

iCC

igh	
high**	find**
night**	kind**
right**	mind
light	climb
might	child
bright	wild
fight	mild
sigh	blind
tight	grind
flight	hind
fright	sign
sight	bind
slight	wind
thigh	hind
	rind

Long *o* Words

CVCe

o-e			
home**	wove	rove	slope
nose	drove	cove	lope
hole	dome	stove	lone
rope	globe	whole	stroke
robe	cone	sole	throne
note	zone	wrote	quote
hose	role	choke	clothe
hope	stole	broke	
vote	doze	poke	
code	froze	smoke	
mole	pose	yoke	
pole	chose	spoke	
joke	those	tone	
stone	close	shone	
	owe	phone	

CVVC

oa		
boat	foam	float
coat	roam	coach
goat	goal	roach
road	coal	throat
toad	loaf	toast
load	coax	coast
soap	whoa	boast
oat	loan	roast
oak	moan	cloak
soak	groan	croak
whoa	moat	loaves

Oddballs		
one*	love	some*
done	dove	come*
none	glove	move
gone	prove	lose
once	shove	whose
tomb		

Open

o
go*
no*
so*
ho
yo-yo
oe
toe
woe
doe
hoe
foe
Oddballs
to*
do*
who*
two*
shoe
broad
sew

CVV

ow
bow
know*
show
slow
snow
crow
blow
glow
grow
sow
low
tow
flow
own**
flown
throw
thrown
blown
grown
bowl

VCC

oCC	
old*	both**
gold	most**
hold	folk
cold	roll
told	poll
fold	stroll
mold	scroll
sold	post
bold	ghost
scold	host
bolt	comb
colt	
jolt	
volt	

Long *u* Words

CVCe			CVVC	CVV		CVV		
u-e			*ui*	*ue*		*ew*		*Oddballs*[§]
use**	cube	fume	fruit	blue	sue	new*	brew	do*
cute	duke	chute	suit	due	fuel	dew	stew	you*
rude	huge	mute	bruise	clue	cruel	chew	crew	to*
rule	dude	plume	cruise	glue		drew	whew	two*
mule	nude	prune	juice	true		few	screw	build
tune	crude	muse		flue		flew	threw	built
June	dune	spruce		hue		knew	shrewd	guide
tube	flute			cue		grew	strewn	truth
								through
								guilt
								suite

Ambiguous Vowels: *ô* sound

al	*au*	*aw*		*o*		*ough*	*w + a*
tall	caught	saw**	gnaw	on*	loss	cough	was*
wall	taught	paw	thaw	off	cross	ought	want**
mall	pause	law	caw	dog	gloss	fought	wash
talk	sauce	draw	bawl	frog	cloth	bought	wand
walk	fault	claw	awe	log	moth	thought	wasp
calm	haunt	dawn	drawn	fog	broth	brought	watt
palm	launch	lawn	crawl	bog	soft	trough	swap
bald	because**	yawn	shawl	hog	loft		swat
halt	fraud	fawn	sprawl	lost	golf		watch
salt	haul	hawk	squawk	cost	bong		
small	maul	raw	straw	frost	song		*/w/ + a*
stall	jaunt	gawk	scrawl	boss	long*		squash
stalk	gaunt			toss	strong		squat
chalk				moss	throng		squad
waltz	*Oddballs*						
false	aunt						
scald	laugh						

Ambiguous Vowels/Diphthongs (*ou/ow* and *oi/oy*)

ow		*ou*			*oo*	*oo* – $/\bar{u}/$			*oi*	*oy*
how*	drown	out*	house**	*Oddballs*	book**	too**	soon**	school**	coin	boy*
now	frown	our*	about*	could**	look**	zoo	noon	spoon	join	toy
cow	crown	loud	mouse	would*	good*	moo	moon	tooth	oil	joy
down*	crowd	ouch	foul	should**	cook	boot	room	shoot	foil	enjoy
bow	fowl	cloud	mouth	touch	took	root	zoom	smooth	soil	soy
wow	scowl	proud	shout	young	foot	food	boom	roost	boil	ploy
town	prowl	count	pout	cough	wood	mood	loom	proof	coil	
gown	growl	round	scout	tough	hook	tool	bloom	stool	point	
brown	vow	sound	snout	through	shook	cool	gloom	spook	joint	
clown		found**	stout	rough	stood	fool	loop	brood	hoist	
owl		pound	sprout		wool	pool	troop		moist	
howl		mound	pouch		crook	roof	whoop	*Oddballs*	toil	
sow		bound	couch		hood	goof	scoop	two*	broil	
plow		hound	crouch		hoof			blood	voice	
		wound	drought		soot			flood	noise	
		ground	doubt		brook				choice	
					nook					

[§]See also *oo* words.

r-Influenced Vowels

ar		*ar + e*	*are*	*air*	*ear /ee/*	*eer*	*er*	*ear /ə/*	*Oddballs*
far**	dart	carve	care	fair	ear**	deer	her*	heard	very*
car	start	large	bare	hair	near**	cheer	fern	earth	their*
jar	bark	starve	dare	pair	hear	steer	herd	learn	there*
star	shark	barge	share	stair	dear**	queer	jerk	earn	were*
card	lark	charge	stare	flair	year**	jeer	term	search	here*
hard	scar		mare	chair	fear	sneer	germ	pearl	where**
yard	mar	*Oddballs*	flare	lair	tear	peer	stern	yearn	heart
art	barb	are*	glare		clear		herb		bear
part	harp	war	rare		beard		per		wear
cart	sharp	warm	scare		gear		perk		swear
bar	snarl		hare		spear		perch		pear
arm	scarf		snare		shear		clerk		hearth
harm	charm		blare		smear		nerve		
dark	arch		fare				serve		
park	march		square				verse		
spark	smart						swerve		
yarn	chart								

ur	*ir*	*ire*	*or*	*ore*	*our*	*oar*	*w + ar*	*w + or*
burn	girl**	fire	or*	more**	your*	roar	warm	work*
hurt	first**	tire	for*	store	four**	soar	war	word
turn	bird	wire	born	shore	pour	boar	ward	world
curl	dirt	hire	corn	bore	mourn	coarse	wharf	worm
curb	stir	sire	horn	chore	court	hoarse	quart	worth
burst	sir		worn	score	fourth	board	swarm	worse
church	shirt	*ure*	cord	sore	gourd		warp	
churn	skirt	sure**	cork	before*	source	*oor*	wart	
surf	third	cure	pork	wore	course	door	warn	
purr	birth	pure	fort	tore		poor		
burr	firm	lure	short	swore	*Oddballs*	floor		
blur	swirl		nor		our*			
lurch	twirl	*ier*	ford		flour			
lurk	chirp	drier	lord		hour			
spur	squirt	pliers	storm		scour			
hurl	thirst	flier	porch		sour			
blurt	squirm	crier	torch					
curve			force					
			north					
			horse					
			forth					
			scorn					
			chord					
			forge					
			gorge					

Complex Consonants

ch	*tch*	*Cch*		*Hard g*		*Soft g*	*dge*	*Cge*
teach	catch	ranch	arch	frog	guide	huge	edge	range
reach	patch	branch	march	drug	guard	cage	ledge	change
beach	hatch	lunch	starch	twig	guilt	age	hedge	barge
peach	latch	bunch	search	flag	guess	page	wedge	charge
coach	match	munch	perch	shrug	guest	stage	pledge	large
speech	watch	punch	lurch	gave	ghost	rage	badge	forge
couch	ditch	bench	church	game		orange	ridge	gorge
crouch	pitch	clench	birch	gain	*Oddballs*	gem	bridge	surge
pouch	witch	trench	torch	gauge	get*	germ	lodge	bulge
screech	switch	wrench	porch	gone	girl**	gene	dodge	strange
pooch	fetch	drench	scorch	goat	gift	gym	judge	sponge
	sketch	pinch		gold	gear	gyp	budge	plunge
Oddballs	clutch	finch		goose	geese	giant	fudge	hinge
rich	scratch	hunch		goof		gist	smudge	merge
such	stretch	mulch		golf			trudge	lounge
much*	stitch	gulch		gulp			grudge	
which*	twitch	launch		gull				
	blotch			gust				
				gulf				

Hard c	*Soft c*	*ce*	*se /z/*	*se /s/*	*-ze*	*-z*	*-ve*	*Voiceless th*	*Voiced th*
card	cell	rice	wise	cease	size	buzz	love	bath	bathe
cave	cent	face	chose	dense	haze	fizz	dove	cloth	clothe
cast	cease	place	close	false	doze	jazz	shove	booth	soothe
cause	cinch	brace	phase	geese	prize	frizz	glove	loath	loathe
caught	cyst	slice	muse	goose	froze	quiz	have*	teeth	teethe
couch	cite	price	those	loose	graze	quartz	give*	breath	breathe
core		truce	these**	moose	blaze	waltz	move		seethe
coin		trace	prose	mouse	gauze		weave	*Silent w*	
coast		since	cause	nurse	seize		leave	write	*Silent k*
cost		fence	noise	purse	freeze		curve	wrist	know*
coach		peace	pause	sense	sneeze		nerve	wrap	knew
cough		juice	raise	tense	snooze		serve	wrong	knee
curb		niece	tease	rinse	breeze		twelve	wreck	knit
curl		voice	cheese	verse	maize		solve	wring	knock
curve		sauce	please	chase	bronze		prove	who*	knife
cult		once	poise	close	wheeze		sleeve		knight
cuff		hence	browse	blouse	squeeze			*Silent g*	knob
		force	choose	house**				gnaw	knot
		ounce	bruise	pulse				gnome	
		dance	cruise	lapse				gnat	*Silent b*
		chance		worse				gnash	crumb
		prince		hoarse				gnu	comb
		fleece		glimpse					limb
		piece						*Silent h*	thumb
		bounce						ghost	climb
		source						herb	lamb
		choice						honest	doubt
		fierce						rhino	tomb
								rhyme	numb
								hour	

Homophones

be/bee
blue/blew
I/eye/aye
no/know
here/hear
to/too/two
hi/high
new/knew/gnu
see/sea
there/they're/their
bear/bare
by/buy/bye
deer/dear
ate/eight
for/four/fore
our/hour
red/read
lead/led
meat/meet
plane/plain
rode/road/rowed
sail/sale
stare/stair
we'd/weed
we'll/wheel
hole/whole
wear/ware/where
one/won
flower/flour
right/write
your/you're
lye/lie
its/it's
not/knot
gate/gait
jeans/genes
time/thyme
son/sun
hey/hay
made/maid
male/mail
nay/neigh
oh/owe
pail/pale
pair/pear/pare
peek/peak/pique
reed/read/Reid
so/sew/sow
root/route
shone/shown
aid/aide
add/ad
break/brake
cent/sent/scent
flee/flea
creak/creek
die/dye
fair/fare
hair/hare
heard/herd
night/knight
steel/steal
tail/tale
thrown/throne
fir/fur
waist/waste
week/weak
we've/weave
way/weigh
wait/weight
threw/through
vail/veil/vale
aisle/I'll/isle
ball/bawl
beat/beet
bolder/boulder
serial/cereal
cheap/cheep
days/daze
dew/do/due
doe/dough
heel/heal
horse/hoarse
ho/hoe
in/inn
need/knead
lone/loan
we/wee
ring/wring
peddle/petal/pedal
straight/strait
pole/poll
earn/urn
past/passed
sweet/suite
ore/or
rain/reign/rein
role/roll
sole/soul
seller/cellar
shoo/shoe
soar/sore
steak/stake
some/sum
tow/toe
vein/vane/vain
medal/metal/meddle
wrote/rote
forth/fourth
tea/tee
been/bin
board/bored
course/coarse
boy/buoy
Mary/marry/merry
great/grate
seem/seam
knew/new
stair/stare
hour/our
rough/ruff
poor/pour
haul/hall
piece/peace
ant/aunt
flair/flare
mist/missed
mane/main
wail/whale/wale
died/dyed
manor/manner
pier/peer
Ann/an
tacks/tax
cash/cache
rap/wrap
maze/maize
air/heir
bail/bale
ail/ale
prays/praise
base/bass
faint/feint
wade/weighed
wave/waive
knave/nave
whet/wet
sell/cell
bell/belle
bowled/bold
bough/bow
browse/brows
bred/bread
guessed/guest
rest/wrest
beech/beach
real/reel
peel/peal
team/teem
leak/leek
sees/seas
sheer/shear
feet/feat
hymn/him
whit/wit
scents/cents/sense
tents/tense
gilt/guilt
knit/nit
tic/tick
sight/site/cite
rye/wry
style/stile
might/mite
climb/clime
fined/find
side/sighed
tide/tied
vice/vise
awl/all
paws/pause
born/borne
chord/cord
foul/fowl
mall/maul
mourn/morn
rot/wrought
bald/balled

Compound Words by Common Base Words

We have limited the list here to words that have base words across a number of compound words.

aircraft	checkbook	foothold	homesick	snowman	raincoat
airline	cookbook	footlights	homespun	fireman	raindrop
airmail	scrapbook	footnote	homestead	gentleman	rainfall
airplane	textbook	footprint	homework	handyman	rainstorm
airport	buttercup	footstep	horseback	policeman	roadblock
airtight	butterfly	footstool	horsefly	salesman	roadway
anybody	buttermilk	barefoot	horseman	nightfall	roadwork
anymore	butterscotch	tenderfoot	horseplay	nightgown	railroad
anyone	doorbell	grandchildren	horsepower	nightmare	sandbag
anyplace	doorknob	granddaughter	horseshoe	nighttime	sandbar
anything	doorman	grandfather	racehorse	overnight	sandbox
anywhere	doormat	grandmother	sawhorse	outbreak	sandpaper
backboard	doorstep	grandparent	houseboat	outcast	sandpiper
backbone	doorway	grandson	housefly	outcome	sandstone
backfire	backdoor	haircut	housewife	outcry	seacoast
background	outdoor	hairdo	housework	outdated	seafood
backpack	downcast	hairdresser	housetop	outdo	seagull
backward	downhill	hairpin	birdhouse	outdoors	seaman
backyard	download	hairstyle	clubhouse	outfield	seaport
bareback	downpour	handbag	doghouse	outfit	seasick
feedback	downright	handball	greenhouse	outgrow	seashore
flashback	downsize	handbook	townhouse	outlaw	seaside
hatchback	downstairs	handcuffs	landfill	outline	seaweed
paperback	downstream	handmade	landlady	outlook	snowball
piggyback	downtown	handout	landlord	outnumber	snowflake
bathrobe	breakdown	handshake	landmark	outpost	snowman
bathroom	countdown	handspring	landscape	outrage	snowplow
bathtub	sundown	handstand	landslide	outright	snowshoe
birdbath	touchdown	handwriting	dreamland	outside	snowstorm
bedrock	eyeball	backhand	farmland	outsmart	somebody
bedroom	eyebrow	firsthand	homeland	outwit	someone
bedside	eyeglasses	secondhand	highland	blowout	someday
bedspread	eyelash	underhand	wasteland	carryout	somehow
bedtime	eyelid	headache	wonderland	cookout	somewhere
flatbed	eyesight	headband	lifeboat	handout	something
hotbed	eyewitness	headdress	lifeguard	hideout	sometime
sickbed	shuteye	headfirst	lifejacket	workout	underline
waterbed	firearm	headlight	lifelike	lookout	undergo
birthday	firecracker	headline	lifelong	overall	underground
birthmark	firefighter	headlong	lifestyle	overboard	undermine
birthplace	firefly	headmaster	lifetime	overcast	underwater
birthstone	firehouse	headphones	nightlife	overcome	watercolor
childbirth	fireman	headquarters	wildlife	overflow	waterfall
blackberry	fireplace	headstart	lighthouse	overhead	watermelon
blackbird	fireproof	headstrong	lightweight	overlook	waterproof
blackboard	fireside	headway	daylight	overview	saltwater
blackmail	firewood	airhead	flashlight	playground	windfall
blacksmith	fireworks	blockhead	headlight	playhouse	windmill
blacktop	backfire	figurehead	moonlight	playmate	windpipe
bookcase	bonfire	homeland	spotlight	playpen	windshield
bookkeeper	campfire	homemade	sunlight	playroom	windswept
bookmark	football	homemaker	mailman	playwright	downwind
bookworm	foothill	homeroom	doorman	rainbow	headwind

Plurals

ch + es	*sh + es*	*ss + es*	*x + es*	*y + s*	Change *y* to *i* + *es*				*f* to *ves*
arches	bushes	bosses	foxes	plays	flies	babies	daisies	stories	wives
watches	dishes	classes	boxes	stays	fries	berries	guppies	buddies	knives
coaches	flashes	glasses	taxes	trays	cries	bodies	ladies	sixties	leaves
couches	brushes	crosses	axes	donkeys	tries	bunnies	parties		loaves
inches	ashes	guesses	mixes	monkeys	skies	cities	pennies	*Oddballs*	lives
peaches	wishes	kisses		jockeys	spies	copies	ponies	goalies	wolves
notches	crashes	passes	*s + es*	turkeys	dries	counties	supplies	taxies	calves
lunches	leashes	dresses	gases	volleys		fairies	puppies	movies	elves
switches	lashes	guesses	buses	valleys		duties	bullies	cookies	scarves
churches				enjoys		armies	hobbies		selves
branches				obeys		fairies	spies		shelves
benches				decays			skies		

Verbs for Inflected Ending Sorts

VCC		CVVC	*e*-Drop		CVC Words That Double			Don't Double	Irregular Verbs
help	act	need	live**	dance	stop	drip	grab	level	see/saw
jump	add	wait	time	glance	pat	fan	hug	edit	fall/fell
want**	crash	boat	name	hike	sun	flop	jam	enter	feel/felt
ask	crack	shout	bake	hire	top	grin	kid	exit	tell/told
back**	block	cook	care	serve	hop	grip	log	limit	grow/grew
talk	bowl	head	close	score	plan	mop	map	suffer	know/knew
call**	count	meet	love	solve	pot	plod	nap	appear	draw/drew
thank	brush	peek	move	sneeze	shop	rob	nod	complain	blow/blew
laugh	bump	bloom	smile	trace	trip	shrug	pin	explain	throw/threw
trick	burn	cool	use**	trade	bet	sip	dip	repeat	find/found
park	climb	cheer	hate	vote	cap	skin	dim	attend	drink/drank
pick	camp	clear	hope	drape	clap	skip	rub	collect	sink/sank
plant	curl	dream	ice	fade	slip	slam	beg		hear/heard
rock	dash	float	joke	graze	snap	slap	blur	**Double**	break/broke
start	dust	flood	paste	praise	spot	snip	bud	admit	hold/held
bark	farm	fool	phone	scrape	tag	sob	chip	begin	stand/stood
work**	fold	join	prove	shave	thin	strip	chop	commit	build/built
walk	growl	lean	race	shove	trap	wrap	crop	control	ring/rang
yell	hunt	mail	scare	snare	trot	zip	strum	excel	sing/sang
wish**	kick	nail	share	cause	tug	brag	swap	forbid	sweep/swept
guess	land	moan	skate	cease	wag	chug	swat	forget	sleep/slept
turn	learn	scream	stare	pose	drop	hem		omit	keep/kept
smell	nest	pour	taste	quote	drum	jog		permit	drive/drove
track	lick	sail	wave	rove	whiz	mob		rebel	shine/shone
push	lock	trail	carve	blame	flap	plot		refer	feed/fed
miss	melt	zoom			flip	prop			bleed/bled
paint	point				scar	blot	*Oddballs*	***e*-Drop**	lay/laid
wash	print				skim	chat	box**	arrive	pay/paid
wink	quack				slug	scan	fix	escape	say/said
rest	reach				stab	slop	wax	excuse	speak/spoke
					throb		row	nibble	send/sent
							chew	rattle	buy/bought
							sew	refuse	bring/brought
							show	amuse	tear/tore
							snow	ignore	wear/wore
								retire	

Pairs to Contrast

hoping	hopping
taping	tapping
pining	pinning
griping	gripping
striping	stripping
moping	mopping
waging	wagging

Syllable Juncture

VCCV Doublet

pretty**
better**
blizzard
blossom
button
cabbage
copper
cottage
dipper
fellow
foggy
follow
common
funny
happen
mammal
message
office
pattern
sudden
tennis
traffic
tunnel
valley
village
hollow
dessert
butter
hammer
attic
gallon
rabbit
gallop
lesson
banner
kitten
ribbon
mitten
bonnet
bottom
cotton
fossil
gossip
muffin
puppet
yellow

VCCV

after*
under**
number
chapter
pencil
picnic
basket
cactus
canyon
capture
center
window
compass
contest
costume
doctor
picture
plastic
public
problem
reptile
rescue
sentence
seldom
fabric
helmet
husband
lumber
master
napkin
dentist
blanket
tablet
bandit
campus
frantic
magnet
mascot
sandal
pretzel
splendid
kidnap
wisdom
goblet
goblin
tonsil
finger
signal
sister
subject
Sunday
temper
thunder
trumpet
twenty
umpire
walnut
welcome
whimper
winter
wonder
index
insect
injure
elbow
enter
velvet
chimney

VCV Open

over**
open**
baby
writer
basic
even
bacon
chosen
moment
human
pilot
silent
vacant
navy
music
female
robot
crater
climate
duty
famous
fever
final
flavor
humid
labor
legal
local
pirate
private
program
recent
rumor
siren
solar
spiral
crazy
bonus
lazy
paper
secret
hero
zero
spider
tiger
rodent
super
bonus
tulip
sequel

VVCV Open

season
reason
peanut
leader
sneaker
easy
floated
waiter
needed
reading

Oddballs
cousin
water
busy

VCV Closed

never**
present**
cabin
planet
finish
robin
magic
limit
manage
prison
habit
punish
cover
promise
closet
camel
cavern
comet
dozen
finish
habit
honest
level
lever
lizard
modern
oven
palace
timid
panic
rapid
visit
solid
wagon
vanish
topic
travel
study
seven
rigid
polish
legend
banish
gravel
tragic

VV

create
riot
liar
fuel
poem
diary
cruel
trial
diet
neon
lion
poet
giant
chaos
idea
video
meteor
violin
annual
casual
radio
alien
piano
area
mosaic

VCCCV

constant
dolphin
laughter
pilgrim
instant
complain
hundred
monster
orchard
orphan
purchase
complete
athlete
kitchen
children
inspect
pumpkin
English
kingdom
bottle
mumble
sandwich
actress
enchant
congress
ostrich
subtract
pitcher
stretcher
control
mushroom
thimble

a Patterns in Stressed Syllables

Long *a* VCV open Accent in 1st

baby
nation
vapor
skater
lazy
bacon
wafer
raven
famous
fatal
navy
basic
flavor
data
crater
savor
raking
labor
vacant
radar
hazel

Oddballs

any*
many*
water

Long *a* Accent in 1st

rainbow
painter
raisin
railroad
daisy
dainty
sailor
straighten
failure
tailor
waiter
traitor
mailbox
maybe
player
crayon
mayor
payment
prayer
layer
crayfish
bracelet
pavement
basement
baseball
grateful
graceful
safety
statement
wakeful
mayhem
painless
ailment

Oddballs

again*
captain
bargain
postage

Long *a* Accent in 2nd

complain
contain
explain
remain
terrain
exclaim
refrain
campaign
regain
obtain
maintain
decay
dismay
delay
portray
mistake
parade
amaze
replace
dictate
crusade
debate
behave
cascade
escape
disgrace
erase
essay
foray
invade
insane
sustain
betray
evade
disdain

Oddballs

obey
survey

Short *a* in VCCV Accent in 1st

attic
hammer
batter
happen
mammal
valley
cabbage
traffic
pattern
scatter
ballot
daddy
gallop
massive
napkin
basket
fabric
plastic
master
cactus
chapter
canyon
capture
tadpole
ambush
lantern
scamper
canvas
package
tablet
lather

Short *a* in VCW Accent in 1st

wagon
cabin
planet
magic
habit
camel
habit
rapid
panic
panel
palace
cavern
manage
vanish
travel
satin
tragic
falcon
shadow
chapel
facet
radish
tavern
statue

Broad *a* VCV

bravo
father
drama
water
plaza
llama
squalid

Broad *a* in VCCV

swallow
wallet
wallow

***ar* Accent in 1st**

artist
marble
garden
party
carpet
pardon
market
tardy
harvest
parka
charter
larva
garland
parcel
barber
starchy
charter
garlic
margin
hardly
partner
bargain
carbon
farther
jargon
scarlet
parlor
sharpen
sparkle
target
tarnish
harbor
partial
marshal
martyr
carton
darling
varnish

Oddballs

toward
lizard

***air* Accent in 1st**

stairway
fairway
airport
dairy
haircut
fairy
airplane
chairman
prairie

Accent in 2nd

repair
despair
unfair
impair
affair

***arr/are* Accent in 1st**

marry
parrot
narrow
carrot
sparrow
narrate
barrel
carry
parent
careful
barely
barefoot

Accent in 2nd

prepare
compare
beware
aware
declare

e Patterns in Stressed Syllables

Long *e* VCV open Accent in 1st

even
female
fever
zebra
legal
meter
recent
depot
cedar
detour
veto
prefix
tepee
decent
preview
prefix
evil
zenith

VV

neon
create
area
idea
video

Long *e* Accent in 1st

needle
freedom
freezer
breezy
cheetah
steeple
tweezers
beetle
feeble
greedy
sweeten
beaver
eager
easy
easel
season
reason
reader
feature
creature
meaning
eastern
bleachers
cleaner
eager
treaty
neatly
peanut
weasel
greasy
beacon
beagle
eagle
measles

Long *e* Accent in 2nd

succeed
indeed
fifteen
thirteen
canteen
agree
degree
between
proceed
asleep
delete
supreme
trapeze
compete
extreme
stampede
deplete
recede
convene
mislead
disease
increase
defeat
repeat
conceal
ideal
reveal
ordeal
appeal
mislead
obese
esteem
redeem
retreat
ordeal
decree
complete

Oddballs

people
hearty
pretty
cherry
leopard
heifer
neighbor
reindeer

Long *ie* Accent in 1st

briefly
diesel

Accent in 2nd

believe
achieve
retrieve
relief
besiege
apiece
relieve
belief

Long *ei* Accent in 1st

either
ceiling
leisure
seizure
neither

Accent in 2nd

receive
perceive
receipt
deceive
conceive
caffeine

Short *e* in VCCV Accent in 1st

better
letter
fellow
tennis
message
penny
beggar
pencil
dentist
center
helmet
reptile
rescue
seldom
sentence
temper
twenty
welcome
velvet
pesky

Short *e* in VCV Accent in 1st

medal
metal
level
lever
never
debit
denim
lemon
melon
memo
pedal
petal
seven
clever
credit
senate
tenor
epic
relic

Short *ea*

feather
heavy
steady
ready
leather
weather
pleasant
sweater
healthy
weapon
sweaty
heaven
heather
meadow
measure
treasure
breakfast

***er* = *ur* Accent in 1st**

person
perfect
nervous
sermon
serpent
hermit
thermos
kernel
perky
permit
sherbet
gerbil
mermaid
certain
merchant
version
servant
verbal
mercy
verdict

ear* = *ur

early
earnings
earthworm
pearly
earnest
yearning
rehearse
research
earthquake
learner

***eer/ear/ere* Accent in 1st**

eerie
deerskin
cheerful
earache
fearful
earmuff
spearmint
yearbook
dreary
bleary
clearly
nearby
hearsay
teardrop
weary
merely
nearly
clearing
dearest
spearmint

Accent in 2nd

career
appear
overhear
endear
adhere
austere
revere
severe
sincere
interfere

i Patterns in Stressed Syllables

Long *i* VCV open Accent in 1st

pilot
silent
diner
writer
tiger
siren
pirate
private
spiral
biker
spider
visor
minus
rival
bison
item
Friday
sinus
slimy
icy
climax
idol

VV

lion
dial
diet
riot
pliers
diary
vial
triumph
friar
liar
trial
violin
client
science
violet

Oddballs

machine
liter
mirror
pizza
spirit
busy
women

Long *i* Accent in 1st

ninety
driveway
sidewalk
iceberg
lively
mighty
slightly
frighten
lightning
highway
brightly
higher
nightmare
tighten
fighter
highlight
sightsee
blindfold
kindness
climber
wildcat
wildlife

Long *i* Accent in 2nd

polite
surprise
decide
advice
survive
combine
arrive
invite
describe
divide
excite
provide
confide
recline
ignite
despite
oblige
divine
tonight
resign
design
delight
guitar
rewind
unkind
behind
beside
inside
recite
collide
advise
confine

Short *i* in VCCV Accent in 1st

into**
kitten
dipper
slipper
mitten
dinner
silly
skinny
ribbon
pillow
dizzy
chilly
bitter
minnow
blizzard
tissue
mixture
fifty
picnic
picture
chimney
frisky
windy
signal
sister
whimper
finger
winter
kidnap
jigsaw
window
blister
fiction
listen
scissors

Short *i* in VCV Accent in 1st

finish
limit
river
lizard
timid
visit
given
city
sliver
civil
digit
prison
wizard
quiver
figure

***ir* Accent in 1st**

thirty
firmly
dirty
birthday
thirsty
birdbath
circle
circus
stirring
firmly
virtue
stirrup
twirler
skirmish
circuit
irksome
whirlpool
chirping
flirting
squirrel

***ire* Accent in 1st**

tiresome
firefly
direful

Accent in 2nd

require
rehire
attire
inquire
expire
desire
perspire
admire
inspire
entire
acquire
retire

***y* = /i/ Accent in 1st**

typist
dryer
flyer
tyrant
hydrant
bypass
nylon
stylish
rhyming
python
cycle
tryout
cyclone
hybrid
hyphen
stylish
skyline
hygiene
tycoon

Accent in 2nd

defy
July
apply
rely
imply
supply
reply
deny

***y* = /ĭ/ Accent in 1st**

crystal
hymnal
pygmy
rhythm
symbol
system
sylvan
cynic
physics
cymbal

o Patterns in Stressed Syllables

Long *o* VCV open Accent in 1st

robot
pony
chosen
donate
motor
soda
notice
sofa
frozen
local
moment
rodent
grocer
potion
ocean
rotate
hoping
stolen
solar
poem

Long *o* Accent in 1st

lonely
lonesome
hopeful
homework
closely
goalie
loafer
coaster
toaster
coastal
soapy
roadway
owner
bowling
rowboat
snowfall
lower
mower
slowly
towboat
soldier
poster
hostess
postage
smolder
molten
molding
folder
oatmeal

Long *o* Unaccented

yellow
pillow
shadow
mellow
willow
hollow
fellow
sparrow
follow
window

Long *o* Accent in 2nd

alone
explode
erode
awoke
decode
enclose
dispose
suppose
compose
remote
unload
approach
afloat
below
bestow
aglow
disown
enroll
behold
revolt
almost
expose
oppose
console

Long *o* VV

poet
poem
boa
oasis
coerce

Oddball

hotel
only**

Short *o* in VCCV Accent in 1st

foggy
follow
copper
blossom
cottage
common
office
hollow
nozzle
bottle
comma
cotton
hobby
yonder
popcorn
contest
costume
doctor
bonfire
bother
cobweb
conquer
problem
posture
monster
congress
collar
volley
goblin

Oddballs

dolphin
stomach
Europe
sorry

Short *o* in VCV Accent in 1st

robin
closet
comet
promise
honest
modern
solid
topic
volume
body
novel
profit
promise
comic
logic
proper
novice

Short *o* /u/

oven
onion
shovel
monkey
mother
nothing
smother
wander
dozen
stomach

***or* Accent in 1st**

morning**
forty
stormy
story
corner
border
torment
forest
fortress
shortage
torrent
tortoise
portrait
forfeit
shorter
order
normal
northern
forward
corncob
chorus
florist
boring
sporty
hornet
organ
morsel
mortal
orbit
orchard

Accent in 2nd

report
record
perform
inform
afford
reform
absorb
abhor
adorn
distort
endorse

***wor* Accent in 1st**

worker
worry
worthy
worship

war/quar

warning
warden
warrior
wardrobe
quarrel
quarter
reward

***ore/oar/our* Accent in 1st**

boredom
shoreline
scoreless
hoarsely
coarsely
hoarding
sources
fourteen
pouring
mournful
foursome
courtroom

Accent in 2nd

before*
ignore
restore
explore
galore
aboard
ashore
adore

u Patterns in Stressed Syllables

Long *u* VCV open Accent in 1st	Long *u* Accent in 1st	Long *u* Accent in 2nd	Short *u* in VCCV Accent in 1st	Short *u* in VCV Accent in 1st	*ur* Accent in 1st	*ure* Accent in 2nd	VV
super	useful	amuse	supper	punish	sturdy	secure	fuel
music	Tuesday	misuse	button	suburb	purpose	assure	cruel
ruby	juicy	confuse	funny	pumice	further	endure	annual
tuna	chewy	reduce	sudden	study	hurry	impure	casual
truly	dewdrop	conclude	tunnel		purple	mature	usual
pupil	jewel	dilute	puppet		turtle	unsure	dual
rumor	pewter	exclude	buddy		furnish	obscure	duel
human	skewer	include	butter		Thursday	manure	fluent
humid	sewage	pollute	fuzzy		blurry	brochure	duet
future	poodle	excuse	guppy		turkey	unsure	
tutor	rooster	resume	ugly		current	disturb	
tumor	moody	compute	husband		purchase		
futile	doodle	abuse	lumber		burger		
student	noodle	perfume	number		furry		
tuba	scooter	protrude	public		murky		
tulip	toothache	salute	Sunday		mural		
unit	neutral	dispute	thunder		surfer		
ruler	sewer	askew	trumpet		burden		
	feudal	assume	umpire		bureau		
		immune	under**		burrow		
		consume	hundred		curfew		
		accuse	mumble		hurdle		
		intrude	lucky		jury		
		pollute	hungry		murmur		
		review	bucket		turnip		
		cartoon	bundle		burner		
		raccoon	public		gurgle		
		lagoon	custom		burglar		
		shampoo	juggle		curtain		
		balloon	luster		during		
		baboon	publish		further		
		cocoon	suffer		murder		
		maroon	yummy		surplus		
		tattoo		*Oddballs*			
				cougar			
				beauty			
				cousin			

Ambiguous Vowels in Stressed Syllables

Accent in 1st

oy/oi
voyage
loyal
joyful
boycott
royal
soybean
oyster
moisture
poison
noisy
pointed
toilet
ointment

Accent in 2nd

annoy
enjoy
employ
destroy
ahoy
appoint
avoid
exploit
rejoice

Accent in 1st

oo
poodle
foolish
rooster
scooter

Accent in 2nd

balloon
cartoon
shampoo
baboon
caboose
cocoon
harpoon
igloo
platoon
raccoon
typhoon
papoose
maroon
tattoo
lagoon

ow
powder
power
flower
prowler
coward
tower
drowsy
brownie
rowdy
chowder
vowel
dowdy
towel
shower
cowboy
powwow
drowning
trowel

Accent in 2nd

allow

ou
county
counter
thousand
fountain
mountain
council
lousy
scoundrel
bounty
boundary
founder
doubtful
southeast
voucher
cloudy
flounder
trousers

Accent in 2nd

about*
without
around
announce
profound

ou = short u
trouble
double
southern
couple
cousin
touched
younger
youngster
moustache
nervous
famous
country

ou = long u
coupon
toucan
youthful
cougar
crouton
souvenir

Accent in 2nd

routine
acoustics
bouquet

au
saucer
author
August
autumn
laundry
caution
faucet
sausage
auction
haunted
cauldron
gaudy
daughter
jaunty
naughty
slaughter
trauma
pauper
nausea
laundry

Accent in 2nd

because**
exhaust
assault
applause

aw
awful
awkward
lawyer
awesome
awfully
gnawing
gawking
flawless
drawing
jawbone
lawless
tawny
yawning
clawed
brawny
bawdy
gnawed

Oddball
drawer

al
also**
always
almost
halter
salty
balky
balmy
calmly
falter
halting
hallway
waltzing
alter
asphalt
walnut
walrus

Oddballs
laughed
all right
balloon
gallon

Final Unstressed Syllables

al	*il/ile*	*el*	*le*		*et*	*it*
normal	stencil	model	fiddle	scribble	target	profit
central	April	angel	little*	people**	basket	audit
crystal	civil	barrel	able	hurdle	blanket	bandit
cymbal	council	bagel	ample	hustle	bucket	credit
dental	evil	bushel	angle	juggle	budget	digit
fatal	fossil	camel	ankle	jungle	carpet	edit
feudal	gerbil	cancel	apple	kettle	closet	exit
final	lentil	channel	battle	knuckle	comet	habit
focal	nostril	chapel	beagle	maple	cricket	hermit
formal	pencil	diesel	beetle	middle	faucet	limit
global	peril	flannel	bottle	needle	fidget	merit
journal	pupil	funnel	bramble	noodle	gadget	orbit
legal	tonsil	gravel	bridle	noble	hatchet	rabbit
mammal	docile	hazel	bubble	paddle	helmet	spirit
medal	facile	jewel	buckle	pebble	hornet	summit
mental	fertile	kennel	bundle	pickle	jacket	unit
metal	fragile	kernel	bugle	purple	locket	visit
nasal	futile	label	candle	puzzle	magnet	vomit
naval	hostile	level	castle	riddle	midget	
neutral	missile	morsel	cattle	saddle	planet	*-ate*
oval	mobile	nickel	cable	sample	poet	climate
pedal	sterile	novel	chuckle	settle	puppet	private
petal		panel	circle	single	racket	senate
plural		parcel	cradle	steeple	scarlet	pirate
rascal		quarrel	cripple	struggle	secret	chocolate
rival		ravel	cuddle	stumble	skillet	
royal		satchel	cycle	tackle	sonnet	*Oddball*
rural		sequel	dimple	tickle	tablet	biscuit
sandal		shovel	doodle	title	thicket	
scandal		shrivel	double	triple	toilet	
signal		squirrel	eagle	trouble	trumpet	
spiral		swivel	fable	twinkle	velvet	
tidal		tinsel	freckle	turtle	wallet	
total		towel	fumble	waffle	diet	
vandal		travel	gamble	whistle	market	
vital		tunnel	gargle	wrinkle	pocket	
vocal		vessel	gentle	muscle	quiet	
local		vowel	grumble	simple	poet	
coastal			handle	temple	rocket	
		Oddball	idle	wrestle	violet	
		motel	rattle	ripple		
		hotel	rifle	huddle		
			sprinkle	dribble		
			brittle	straddle		
			crinkle	stubble		
			gurgle			
			humble			
			pimple			
			puddle			
			sparkle			

er

other*
under**
better**
never**
over**
mother**
another**
banner
blister
border
clover
cluster
fiber
freezer
liter
litter
lumber
manner
spider
sister
brother
father
lather
poster
printer
shower
timber
toaster
trouser
ladder
counter
crater
cancer
cider
scorcher
ledger
stretcher
pitcher
answer
blender
flower
bother
center
copper
finger
power
powder
proper
quiver
roller
rubber
sander
saucer
scooter
shaver
weather
silver

er
Agents

butcher
robber
swimmer
runner
drummer
jogger
dreamer
dancer
speaker
teacher
skater
marcher
shopper
racer
grocer
barber
peddler
plumber
ranger
usher
voter
catcher
baker

er
Comparatives

bigger
cheaper
cleaner
farther
quicker
slower
younger
older
flatter
plainer
lighter
darker
weaker
stronger
wilder
sweeter
cooler
braver

ar

beggar
burglar
scholar
cellar
cedar
cheddar
collar
cougar
dollar
grammar
hangar
lunar
solar
molar
polar
sugar
nectar
pillar
liar

or

color**
actor
author
doctor
editor
mayor
neighbor
sailor
tailor
traitor
tutor
visitor
donor
armor
error
favor
anchor
rumor
mirror
horror
humor
meteor
motor
razor
scissors
splendor
sponsor
terror
tractor
tremor
vapor
cursor
honor
tumor
harbor

/chər/

culture
capture
creature
denture
feature
fixture
fracture
future
gesture
juncture
lecture
injure
nurture
rapture
sculpture
stature
stricture
texture
tincture
torture
venture
adventure
departure
mixture
moisture
picture
pasture
posture
puncture
nature
furniture
miniature
premature
signature

/shər/

pressure
fissure
reassure

/yər/

failure
manicure
figure

/zhər/

leisure
measure
closure
pleasure
treasure
enclosure
exposure
composure
disclosure

Oddballs

senior
danger

/jər/

conjure
injure
procedure

ain

captain
certain
curtain
fountain
mountain
villain
bargain
chieftain

an

human
organ
orphan
slogan
urban
woman

en Verb

frighten
sharpen
shorten
sweeten
thicken
widen
deafen
flatten
lengthen
open**

en Noun

chicken
children
garden
kitten
mitten
women
heaven
oxygen
siren
linen
eleven

en Adjective

golden
open**
rotten
spoken
sunken
swollen
wooden
broken
hidden
chosen
stolen

in

basin
cabin
cousin
margin
pumpkin
raisin
robin
dolphin
muffin
penguin
satin
napkin

on

apron
button
cannon
common
dragon
wagon
pardon
person
reason
season
salmon
bacon
carton
cotton
gallon
lemon
lesson
prison
poison
ribbon
weapon

/ij/		/is/		/ē/ = ey	/ē/ = ie	/ē/ = y	
voyage	sausage	justice	furnace	chimney	cookie	very*	berry
bandage	cabbage	practice	surface	donkey	movie	pretty**	body
village	rummage	service	palace	turkey	brownie	early	beauty
message	savage	office	necklace	jockey	genie	crazy	drowsy
cottage	passage	crevice	menace	valley	goalie	candy	empty
wreckage	image	notice	grimace	volley	sweetie	daisy	guilty
courage	marriage	novice	terrace	journey	zombie	forty	tidy
storage	manage	bodice		honey	birdie	envy	treaty
luggage	sewage	crisis		money	eerie	worry	carry
damage	language	tennis	*Oddballs*	jersey	bootie	gravy	bossy
postage	package	axis	lettuce	pulley	rookie	sorry	trophy
garbage		basis	porpoise	hockey	pinkie	dizzy	stingy
hostage	*Oddballs*	iris	tortoise	galley	prairie	cherry	bury
storage	knowledge			monkey		funny	easy
shortage	cartridge			alley		happy	story
						hurry	icy

Prefixes and Suffixes

mis-	*pre-*	*re-*	*un-*	*dis-*	*in- "not"*	*non-*
misbehave	precook	rebound	unable	disable	incomplete	nonsense
misconduct	predate	recall	unafraid	disagreeable	incorrect	nonstop
miscount	prefix	recapture	unarmed	disappear	indecent	nonfiction
misdeed	pregame	recharge	unbeaten	disarm	indirect	nonfat
misfit	preheat	reclaim	unbroken	discharge	inexpensive	nonprofit
misgivings	prejudge	recopy	uncertain	disclose	inflexible	nondairy
misguide	premature	recount	unclean	discolor	informal	nonstick
misjudge	prepay	recycle	unclear	discomfort	inhuman	nonviolent
mislay	preschool	reelect	uncommon	discontent	injustice	nonskid
mislead	preset	refill	uncover	discover	insane	nonstandard
mismatch	preteen	refinish	undone	dishonest	invalid	
misplace	pretest	reform	unequal	disinfect	invisible	*de-*
misprint	preview	refresh	unfair	dislike	inept	deflate
misspell	prewash	relearn	unkind	disloyal		defrost
mistake	predict	remind	unlike	disobey	*in- "in" or "into"*	deprive
mistreat	precede	remodel	unlock	disorder	income	decrease
mistrust	prehistoric	renew	unpack	displace	indent	delete
misuse	prepare	reorder	unreal	disregard	indoor	deport
mischief	prevent	repay	unripe	disrespect	inset	detract
	precaution	reprint	unselfish	distaste	insight	deficient
	preschool	research	unstable	distrust	inside	degrading
	prenatal	restore	unsteady	disgrace	inlaid	denounce
	prescribe	retrace	untangle		inmate	depleted
		return	untie		ingrown	deprived
		review	unwrap		inboard	detached
		rewrite	unbutton		inland	deviate
		rebuild	uneven		infield	deodorant
		report	unhappy		inflate	decongestant
		recall	unopened		inhale	dehydrated
		refuel	unheated		insert	desegregated
		reject	unattached		inspect	decaffeinated
		reassure	unplanned		inspire	demerits
		reconsider	unplug		intake	

uni-
unicorn
unicycle
uniform
unify
union
unique
unison
universal
universe

bi-
biceps
bicycle
bifocals
bilingual
binoculars
bisect
biweekly
biannual

tri-
triangle
triple
triceps
triceratops
tricycle
trilogy
trio
trivet
triplets
tripod
triad
trinity
trident
triathlon
trillion

fore-
forearm
forecast
foretell
foresee
foresight
forehand
forehead
foreman
forethought
foreshadow
forepaw
foremost
forefathers

sub-
subset
subtract
subdivide
subgroup
submerge
submarine
submerse
submit
subway
subtotal
subtitle
sublet
subsoil
subject

ex-
expel
express
explore
exceed
excerpt
exclaim
exclude
excrete
exhale
exile
expand
explode
exit
extend
exempt
exhaust

en-
enable
endanger
enact
enclose
encourage
enforce
enjoy
enslave
enlarge
enlist
enrage
enrich
enroll
entrust

-ly
badly
barely
bravely
closely
costly
cruelly
deadly
loudly
proudly
smoothly
kindly
nicely
nightly
safely
friendly
gladly
lonely
nearly
quickly
quietly
slowly
surely
lively

Change *y* to *i*
noisily
lazily
angrily
busily
easily
happily
luckily
daily
gaily
bodily
readily
steadily

-y
breezy
bumpy
chilly
choppy
cloudy
dirty
dusty
easy
floppy
frosty
gloomy
greasy
grouchy
gritty
noisy
rainy
sandy
soapy
snowy
stormy
sweaty
thirsty
windy
dressy
skinny
speedy
floppy
lucky
grubby

-er/-est
blacker/blackest
bigger/biggest
bolder/boldest
braver/bravest
calmer/calmest
closer/closest
cheaper/cheapest
cleaner/cleanest
cooler/coolest
colder/coldest
smaller/smallest
thinner/thinnest
fewer/fewest
finer/finest
hotter/hottest
harder/hardest
sadder/saddest
newer/newest
quicker/quickest
lighter/lightest
louder/loudest
larger/largest
meaner/meanest

Change *y* to *i*
funnier/funniest
noisier/noisiest
prettier/prettiest
dirtier/dirtiest
easier/easiest
juicier/juiciest
lazier/laziest
luckier/luckiest
busier/busiest
crazier/craziest
heavier/heaviest
clumsier/clumsiest

-less
ageless
breathless
careless
ceaseless
endless
helpless
homeless
lawless
painless
powerless
priceless
reckless
spotless
tasteless
useless
fearless
lifeless
speechless
thankless
cloudless
fruitless
jobless
scoreless
sleeveless
pointless
restless
worthless

Change *y* to *i*
penniless
pitiless
merciless

-ful
careful
cheerful
colorful
fearful
graceful
harmful
hopeful
lawful
peaceful
playful
powerful
tasteful
thoughtful
truthful
useful
wasteful
wonderful
youthful
beautiful
armful
dreadful
respectful
faithful
grateful
hateful
helpful
joyful
painful
skillful
thankful
wishful
fretful

-ness
awareness
closeness
coolness
darkness
firmness
goodness
openness
ripeness
sickness
sharpness
stiffness
stillness
thinness
weakness
moistness
vastness
dullness
kindness
dampness
blindness
tenderness
eagerness

Change *y* to *i*
dizziness
emptiness
laziness
readiness
fussiness
happiness
ugliness
clumsiness
liveliness

Special Consonants

Hard g

gadget
gallon
gallop
gamble
garage
gully
golden
gossip
guilty
gorilla
gopher
gather
gutter
guitar
gobble
goggles
gaily
gallery

Oddballs

giggle
geyser
gecko

Soft g

genie
genius
genre
general
gentle
gerbil
gesture
giant
ginger
giraffe
gypsy
gyrate
gently
gender

Hard c

cabin
cafe
cactus
campus
candle
canyon
cavern
carpet
cable
comma
copy
cozy
cocoa
comet
coffee
corner
county
cubic
cuddle
culprit
curtain
custom
concern
concert
cancel
cancer

Soft c

city
cider
civil
cinder
circle
circus
citric
cedar
celery
cement
census
center
cereal
ceiling
certain
cycle
cynic
cymbal
cyclist
cyclone
cylinder
cellar

Final c

attic
music
topic
zodiac
clinic
comic
cynic
toxic
panic
picnic
classic
critic
elastic
exotic
frantic
graphic
hectic
garlic
fabric
frolic
logic
drastic
scenic
basic
plastic
public
traffic
arctic
mystic
skeptic
metric
mimic

que

antique
unique
clique
opaque
critique
physique
mystique
brusque
conquer
boutique

x

relax
complex
index
perplex
reflex
vortex
vertex
prefix
phoenix
annex

ck

attack
gimmick
hammock
ransack
padlock
potluck
hemlock
carsick
haddock

k / ke

namesake
cupcake
earthquake
forsake
keepsake
mistake
pancake
provoke
slowpoke
turnpike
evoke
homework
embark
landmark
network
berserk

ph

trophy
dolphin
orphan
phonics
gopher
nephew
phantom
pheasant
phony
physics
triumph
photo
telephone
alphabet

Silent Letters

wrinkle
wreckage
wriggle
wryly
wrestle
answer

knuckle
knowledge

gnaw
gnarl
gnome
gnostic
gnu

ghetto
ghastly
ghoul

honest
honor
rhombus
rhyme
rhythm
shepherd

solemn
column
autumn
condemn

castle
thistle
whistle
fasten
listen
often*
soften
moisten

daughter
naughty
height
weight
freight
assign
design
resign

Alternations

Silent to Sounded Consonant	*Long to Short*	*Long to Schwa*	*Short to Schwa*
bomb/bombard	cave/cavity	able/ability	metallic/metal
column/columnist	flame/flammable	famous/infamous	academy/academic
soften/soft	grave/gravity	major/majority	malice/malicious
crumb/crumble	nature/natural	native/nativity	periodic/period
debt/debit	athlete/athletic	prepare/preparation	emphatic/emphasis
damn/damnation	please/pleasant	relate/relative	celebrate/celebrity
design/designate	crime/criminal	stable/stability	democratic/democracy
fasten/fast	decide/decision	compete/competition	excel/excellent
hasten/haste	revise/revision	combine/combination	perfection/perfect
hymn/hymnal	wise/wisdom	define/definition	critic/criticize
malign/malignant	know/knowledge	invite/invitation	habit/habitat
moisten/moist	episode/episodic	recite/recitation	mobility/mobile
muscle/muscular	assume/assumption	reside/resident	prohibit/prohibition
resign/resignation	produce/production	compose/composition	geometry/geometric
sign/signal	convene/convention	expose/exposition	
condemn/condemnation	volcano/volcanic	custodian/custody	
	serene/serenity	pose/position	
	ignite/ignition	social/society	
	humane/humanity		
	divide/division		

Adding /shun/ to base words

ct + ion
action
subtraction
distinction
election
prediction
extinction
detection
selection
rejection
reaction
connection
distraction
objection
infection
instruction
protection
conviction
correction
detection
abstraction
inspection
injection
reflection

ss + ion
expression
oppression
possession
profession
confession
compression
obsession
digression
impression
discussion
aggression
depression
procession
recession

c + ian
magician
musician
optician
logician
clinician
diagnostician
electrician
politician
technician

t + ion
assertion
digestion
invention
suggestion
adoption
insertion
congestion
prevention
distortion
exhaustion
eruption
exception
desertion

t + ation
adaptation
temptation
presentation
indentation
plantation
infestation
lamentation
confrontation
expectation

d, de to sion
explosion
decision
division
invasion
conclusion
intrusion
protrusion
allusion
collision
evasion
erosion
seclusion
persuasion
expansion
ascension
suspension
exportation
consultation

e-drop + ion
creation
decoration
generation
imitation
illustration
indication
translation
congratulation
frustration
operation
location
vibration
circulation
pollution
dictation
hesitation
donation
devotion
graduation
migration
navigation
isolation

it to ission
admission
omission
permission
submission
transmission

e-drop + tion
production
introduction
reduction
reproduction
deduction
seduction

be to p + tion
description
prescription
inscription
subscription
transcription

Vowel Alternations with Change in Accent When Adding Suffixes

Schwa to Short with ity

mental/mentality
general/generality
moral/morality
brutal/brutality
central/centrality
eventual/eventuality
personal/personality
neutral/neutrality
original/originality
normal/normality
mental/mentality
formal/formality
equal/equality
vital/vitality
legal/legality
local/locality
hospital/hospitality
personal/personality

Long to Short with cation

apply/application
certify/certification
clarify/clarification
classify/classification
gratify/gratification
imply/implication
notify/notification
purify/purification
modify/modification
unify/unification
simplify/simplification
multiply/multiplication
magnify/magnification
specify/specification
verify/verification
qualify/qualification
identify/identification
justify/justification
beautify/beautification

Long to Schwa with ation

declare/declaration
degrade/degradation
prepare/preparation
admire/admiration
combine/combination
define/definition
deprive/deprivation
derive/derivation
incline/inclination
invite/invitation
recite/recitation
compile/compilation
perspire/perspiration
explore/exploration

Adding the Suffix *able/ible*

Root Word + ible

audible
credible
edible
eligible
feasible
gullible
horrible
invincible
legible
plausible
possible
terrible
visible
indelible
intangible
compatible
combustible
responsible
defensible
divisible
plausible
tangible
accessible

Base Word + able

affordable
agreeable
allowable
avoidable
breakable
comfortable
dependable
expandable
favorable
laughable
payable
preferable
predictable
profitable
punishable
reasonable
refillable
remarkable
respectable
transferable

e-drop + able

achievable
admirable
adorable
advisable
believable
comparable
conceivable
consumable
debatable
deplorable
desirable
disposable
excitable
lovable
notable
pleasurable
recyclable
valuable

ce/ge + able

manageable
enforceable
noticeable
changeable

y to i + able

variable
reliable
pliable
pitiable
justifiable
identifiable
deniable
enviable
remediable

Drop *ate* in Base

tolerable
vegetable
operable
navigable
abominable
negotiable
educable
estimable
irritable
appreciable

Adding *ant/ance/ancy* and *ent/ence/ency*

hesitant/hesitance/hesitancy
abundant/abundance/abundancy
relevant/relevance/relevancy
extravagant/extravagance/extravagancy
malignant/malignance/malignancy
petulant/petulance/petulancy
radiant/radiance/radiancy
brilliant/brilliance/brilliancy
defiant/defiance
reluctant/reluctance
exuberant/exuberance
fragrant/fragrance
instant/instance
elegant/elegance
vigilant/vigilance
resistant/resistance
significant/significance
tolerant/tolerance
observant/observance
resistant/resistance

competent/competence/competency
dependent/dependence/dependency
emergent/emergence/emergency
equivalent/equivalence/equivalency
excellent/excellence/excellency
expedient/expedience/expediency
lenient/lenience/leniency
resident/residence/residency
resilient/resilience/resiliency
convenient/convenience
different/difference
diligent/diligence
evident/evidence
impatient/impatience
independent/independence
patient/patience
innocent/innocence
intelligent/intelligence
obedient/obedience
indulgent/indulgence
violent/violence

Using *ary, ery,* and *ory*

ary	*ery*	*ary with Schwa*	*ery with Schwa*	*ory*	*ory with Schwa*
customary	very	anniversary	artery	allegory	compulsory
fragmentary	cemetery	boundary	bribery	auditory	cursory
extraordinary	stationery	documentary	celery	category	directory
hereditary	confectionery	elementary	discovery	dormitory	memory
imaginary		glossary	gallery	explanatory	satisfactory
legendary		salary	grocery	inventory	theory
literary		summary	machinery	observatory	victory
military		burglary	mystery	territory	history
missionary		diary	nursery	circulatory	memory
necessary		infirmary	scenery	derogatory	accessory
ordinary		auxiliary	surgery	laboratory	compulsory
revolutionary		documentary	drapery	mandatory	victory
secretary		rudimentary	forgery	respiratory	
solitary			misery		
stationary					
temporary					
vocabulary					
primary					
dictionary					

Accent in Polysyllabic Words

First Syllable

anything
somebody
beautiful
families
grandfather
January
libraries
Wednesday
wonderful
populate
acrobat
amateur
cantaloupe
comedy
customer
engineer
evidence
forestry
generator
improvise
iodine
meteorite
navigator
average
aptitude
architect
artery
avalanche
calculator
camera
carpenter
everything
colorful
gasoline
everywhere
hamburger

Second Syllable

December
November
October
September
uncommon
unusual
unwanted
protection
reduction
romantic
unable
providing
vacation
asparagus
attorney
computer
election
endurance
executive
erosion
ignition
judicial
mechanic
banana
department
important
whoever
accountant
agility
amphibian
apprentice
deliver
remember
whenever
tomorrow
abilities
apartment
companion
condition

Third Syllable

constitution
population
planetarium
Sacramento
Tallahassee
understand
imitation
regulation
California
definition
diagnosis
hippopotamus
irrigation
Mississippi
declaration
exclamation

Prefixes

anti "against"

antifreeze
antidote
antitoxin
antibiotic
anticlimactic
antisocial
antigen
antipathy
antiseptic

auto "self"

autograph
automation
autobiography
automobile
autocrat
autonomy
autopsy

circum "around"

circumference
circumvent
circumstance
circumspect
circumscribe
circumlocution
circumnavigate

inter "between"

interact
intercede
interfere
interloper
interchange
interject
interrupt
intercede
intercom
international
interlocking
intermission
international
intermural

intra "within"

intramural
intravenous
intrastate

mal "bad"

malice
malignant
maltreated
malpractice
maladjusted
malnutrition
malcontent
malfunction
malady

peri "around"

perimeter
period
periphery
periscope
peripatetic
periodontal

post "after"

posterior
posterity
posthumous
postpone
postscript
postmortem
postgraduate
postmeridian
postseason
postdated

pro "before," "forward"

proceed
propel
produce
progress
provide
program
projector
protective
proclaim
profess
profile
promotion
prohibit
procreate
propitious
pronounce
promulgate
propensity
proficient
protracted

super "higher"

superpower
supervision
supermarket
supernatural
superman
supersede
supersonic
superstition
superficial
supercilious

trans "across"

transfer
transport
transmit
transplant
translate
translucent
transparent
transform
transient
transcend
transact

Number-Related Prefixes (see also *uni, bi,* and *tri* under "Prefixes and Suffixes" on page 385)

mon, mono	*cent*	*mil*	*oct*	*poly*	*semi*	*multi*
monarchy	centigrade	million	octagon	polygon	semiannual	multitude
monastery	centimeter	millimeter	octopus	polygamy	semicolon	multiply
monogram	centipede	milligram	October	polychrome	semicircle	multicolored
monologue	centennial	millennium	octave	polyhedron	semisolid	multipurpose
monorail	century	millionaire	octahedron	polyglot	semiconscious	multicultural
monotone	percent		octogenarian	polyester	semifinal	multimedia
monotonous	bicentennial	*deca/deci*	octane	polygraph	semiweekly	multiplex
monolith		decade		polymath	semiprecious	multifaceted
monopoly	*sex/hex*	December	*pent*	polymers		multivitamin
monochrome	sextant	decahedron	pentagon	polyp	*quad*	multifarious
monogamy	sextuplets	decagon	pentameter	polytechnic	quadrangle	multiplication
	hexagon	decimal	pentacle		quadrant	
		decathlon			quarter	

Assimilated or Absorbed Prefixes

in ("not")	*il*	*im*		*ir*
inaccurate	illogical	immature	impure	irrational
inefficient	illegal	immaterial	impaired	irreconcilable
inoperable	illiterate	immobile	impartial	irreparable
insecure	illegible	immodest	impossible	irregular
innumerable	illicit	immoderate	impediment	irrelevant
inactive	illustrious	immoral	imperfect	irreplaceable
inappropriate	illegitimate	immortal	impersonal	irresistible
incompetent	illuminate	immovable	improper	irresponsible
indecent		immigrant	impractical	irreversible
		immediate		irradiate
		immerse		irreligious

sub ("under" or "lower")		*suf*	*sup*	*sur*
subversion	subatomic	suffix	supplant	surreal
subterranean	subcommittee	suffuse	suppliant	surrender
suburban	subdivision	suffer	support	surrogate
substitute	submarine	suffice	supposition	surreptitious
substandard	subconscious	sufficient	suppress	
subsidize	subcontractor	suffocate	supplicant	*suc*
subclass	subjugate		supplement	succumb
sublease	subscribe			succeed
subscript	subscription			success
subtract	submarine			succinct
subdue	submit			successive

com ("with" or "together")
common
community
combination
committee
company
comply
compress
compound
companion
compact
complete
comrade
combine

col
collection
collide
collision
collage
collaborate
colleague
collapse
collusion
collate
collateral
colloquial
collect

con
conspire
concert
connect
congress
congestion
congregation
conclude
condense
construct
constellation
connote

cor
correlate
corroborate
correct
correspond
corrupted
corrugated

co
coagulate
coexist
coalition
coauthor
coeducational
cohabit
cohesion
cohort
coincide
cooperate
coordinate

ad ("to" or "toward")
adjacent
adjoining
addicted
adhesive
adjacent
adaptation
additional
adjective
adjust
admire
admission
advocate

at
attend
attune
attract
attach
attack
attain
attention
attempt
attitude
attribute
attrition

ac
accompany
acceptable
access
accident
accommodate
accomplish
accumulate
accelerate
acquisition
acquire
acquisitive

af
affinity
affable
affection
affluence
affiliate
affricative
affirmation

ag
aggregate
aggravate
aggression
aggrieved

al
alliance
alliteration
allowance
allusion
alleviate
allotment

an
annex
annihilate
announce
annul
annotate

ap
approach
approximate
appropriate
apprentice
apprehend
appreciate
application
applause
appetite
appendix
appear
appeal

as
assemble
associate
assimilate
assent
assault
assertion
assessment
assume
assiduous
assistance
assuage
assumption

ar
arrange
arrest
array
arrive
arrogant

dis ("not" or "opposite of" or "apart")
disadvantage
dissatisfied
disillusioned
disaster
disability
disagreeable
disseminate
disappoint
discern
disdain
disarray
disconcerted
discharged
disclaimer
disconsolate
discouraged
disregard
disenchanted
disoriented

dif
difficult
diffusion
different
diffidence

ex ("out or "from")
extract
excavate
exceed
exception
excerpt
excursion
exhale
exile
expansion
expenditure
exclaim
explode
excrete
exhume
extinct
expand
extend
exclude
exhaust
extension
explosion

ef
efface
effect
efferent
efficiency
effrontery
effusive
effort
effront
effluent
effervescent

ec
ecstasy
eccentric
ecclesiastical

ob ("to," "toward," or "against")
oblong
objection
obligation
obliterate
oblivious
obscure
observant
obstruction
obstreperous
obstinate
obscure
oblique
obstacle
obsolete
obnoxious

op
opponent
opposite
opportunity
opposition
oppress

of
offend
offensive
offering
offense
officious

oc
occurrence
occasion
occupation
occupy
occlude

Greek Roots

aer	"air" aerate, aerial, aerobics, aerodynamic, aeronautics, aerosol, aerospace
arch	"rule, chief" monarchy, anarchy, archangel, archbishop, archetype, architect, hierarchy, matriarch, patriarch
aster, astr	"star" aster, asterisk, asteroid, astrology, astronomy, astronaut, astronomical, astrophysics, disaster
bi, bio	"life" biology, biography, autobiography, biopsy, symbiotic, biodegradable, antibiotic, amphibious, biochemistry
centr	"center" center, central, egocentric, ethnocentric, centrifuge, concentric, concentrate, eccentric
chron	"time" chronic, chronicle, chronological, synchronize, anachronism
cosm	"world" cosmic, cosmology, cosmonaut, cosmopolitan, cosmos, microcosm
crat	"rule" democrat, plutocrat, bureaucrat, idiosyncratic, technocrat
crit	"judge" critic, criticize, critique, criterion, diacritical, hypocrite
cycl	"circle" cycle, bicycle, cyclone, tricycle, unicycle, recycle, motorcycle, cyclical, encyclopedia
dem	"people" demagogue, democracy, demographics, endemic, epidemic, epidemiology
derm	"skin" dermatologist, epidermis, hypodermic, pachyderm, taxidermist, dermatitis
geo	"earth" geology, geophysics, geography, geothermal, geocentric, geode
gram	"to write" diagram, program, telegram, anagram, cryptogram, epigram, grammar, monogram
graph	"to write" graph, paragraph, autograph, digraph, graphics, topography, biography, bibliography, calligraphy, choreographer, videographer, ethnography, phonograph, seismograph, lexicographer
homo	"same" homophone, homograph, homosexual, homogeneous
hydra	"water" hydra, hydrant, hydrate, hydrogen, hydraulic, hydroelectric, hydrology, hydroplane, hydroponics, anhydrous, hydrangea, hydrophobia
logo	"word, reason" logic, catalogue, dialogue, prologue, epilogue, monologue
logy	"study" biology, geology, ecology, mythology, pathology, psychology, sociology, theology, genealogy, etymology, technology, zoology
meter	"measure" centimeter, millimeter, diameter, speedometer, thermometer, tachometer, altimeter, barometer, kilometer
micro	"small" microscope, microphone, microwave, micrometer, microbiology, microcomputer, microcosm
ortho	"straight, correct" orthodox, orthodontics, orthography, orthodontists, orthopedic
pan	"all" pandemic, panorama, pandemonium, pantheon, Pan-American
path	"feeling, suffer" sympathy, antipathy, apathetic, empathize, pathogen, pathologist, pathetic, pathos, osteopath
ped	"child" (see Latin *ped* for "foot") pedagogy, pediatrician, pedophile, encyclopedia
phil	"loving" philosophy, philharmonic, bibliophile, Philadelphia, philanderer, philanthropy, philatetic, philter
phobia	"fear" phobia, acrophobia, claustrophobia, xenophobia, arachnophobia, xenophobia
phon	"sound" phonics, phonograph, cacophony, earphone, euphony, homophone, microphone, telephone, xylophone, saxophone, phoneme, symphony
photo	"light" photograph, telephoto, photocopier, photographer, photosynthesis, photocell, photogenic, photon
phys	"nature" physics, physical, physician, physiology, physique, astrophysics, physiognomy, physiotherapy
pol	"city" politics, police, policy, metropolis, acropolis, cosmopolitan, megalopolis, Minneapolis
psych	"spirit, soul" psyche, psychology, psychoanalyst, psychiatry, psychedelic, psychosis, psychosomatic, psychic
scope	"see" microscope, periscope, scope, telescope, stethoscope, gyroscope, horoscope, kaleidoscope, stereoscope
sphere	"ball" sphere, atmosphere, biosphere, hemisphere, ionosphere, stratosphere, troposphere
tech	"build, art, skill" technical, technician, technology, polytechnic
tele	"far" telecast, telegraph, telegram, telescope, television, telethon, teleconference, telepathy
therm	"heat" thermal, geothermal, thermometer, thermonuclear, thermos, thermostat, thermodynamic, exothermic
typ	"to beat, to strike" typewriter, typist, typographical, archetype, daguerreotype, prototype, stereotype, typecast
zo	"animal" zoo, zoology, protozoan, zodiac, zoologist

Latin Stems

aud	"hear" audio, auditorium, audience, audible, audition, inaudible, audiovisual
bene	"well" benefactor, benevolent, beneficial, benefit, benign, benefactress, benediction
cand, chand	"shine" candle, chandelier, incandescent, candelabra, candid, candidate
cap	"head" captain, capital, capitol, capitalize, capitulate, decapitate, per capita, captivity
cide	"cut, kill" incise, incision, concise, circumcise, excise, fungicide, herbicide, pesticide, insecticide, suicide, homicide, genocide

clud, clos, clus	"shut" close, closet, disclose, enclose, foreclose, conclude, exclude, exclusive, preclude, occlude, seclude, seclusion, recluse
cogn	"know" recognize, incognito, cognizant, cognition, recognizance
corp	"body" corpse, corporal, corporation, corpus, corpulent, incorporate, corpuscle
cred	"trust, believe" credit, credible, credentials, incredible, accredited, credulous
dent, dont	"tooth" dentist, dentures, orthodontist, indent
dic, dict	"speak" dictate, diction, dictionary, predict, verdict, benediction, contradict, dedicate, edict, indict, jurisdiction, valedictorian, dictation
doc	"teach" documentary, indoctrinate, doctorate, doctor, docent, docile, doctrine
duc, duct	"lead" abduct, conductor, deduct, aqueduct, duct, educate, educe, induct, introduction, reduce, reproduce, viaduct
equa, equi	"equal" equal, equality, equation, equator, equity, equivalent, equilibrium, equivocate, equidistant, equinox
fac, fec	"do" factory, manufacture, faculty, artifact, benefactor, confection, defect, effect, facile, facilitate, facsimile, affect, affection
fer	"carry" ferry, transfer, prefer, reference, suffer, vociferous, inference, fertile, differ, conifer, conference, circumference
fid	"trust" fidelity, confidant, confidence, diffident, infidelity, perfidy, affidavit, bona fide, confidential
fin	"end" final, finale, finish, infinite, definitive
flex, flect	"bend, curve" flex, flexible, inflexible, deflect, reflection, inflection, circumflex, genuflect
flu	"flow" fluid, fluent, influx, superfluous, affluence, confluence, fluctuate, influence
form	"shape" conform, deform, formal, formality, format, formation, formula, informal, information, malformed, platform, reform, transform, uniform
grac, grat	"thankful" grace, gratuity, gracious, ingrate, congratulate, grateful, gratitude, ingratiate, persona non grata, gratify
grad, gress	"go, step" graduate, gradual, gradient, grade, retrograde, centigrade, degraded, downgrade, digress, aggressive, congress, egress, ingress, progress, regress, transgression
ject	"throw" eject, injection, interject, object, objection, conjecture, abject, dejected, projection, projectile, projector, reject, subjective, trajectory
jud	"judge" judge, judgment, prejudice, judiciary, judicial, adjudge, adjudicate, injudicious
junct	"join" junction, juncture, injunction, conjunction, adjunct, disjunction
langu, lingu	"tongue" language, bilingual, linguistics, linguist, linguine, lingo
lit	"letter" literature, illiterate, literal, literacy, obliterate, alliteration, literary
loc, loq	"speak" elocution, eloquent, loquacious, obloquy, soliloquy, ventriloquist, colloquial, interlocutor
mal	"bad" malady, malignant, maladroit, malaria, malcontent, malicious, malign, maladjusted, malevolent, malfunction, malnourished, malpractice
man	"hand" manual, manufacture, manicure, manuscript, emancipate, manacle, mandate, manipulate, manage, maneuver
mem	"memory, mindful" remember, memory, memorize, memorial, memorandum, memento, memorabilia, commemorate
min	"small" diminish, mince, minimize, minute, minuscule, minus, minor, minnow, minimum
miss, mit	"send" transmission, remission, submission, admit, transmit, remit, submit, omit, mission, missile, demise, emission, admission, commission, emissary, intermission, intermittent, missionary, permission, promise
mob, mot	"move" mobile, motion, motor, remote, automobile, promote, motivate, motel, locomotion, immobile, emotion, demote, commotion
pat	"father" paternal, patrimony, expatriate, patron, patronize
ped	"foot" pedal, pedestal, pedicure, pedigree, biped, centipede, millipede, moped, impede, expedite, orthopedic, pedestrian, quadruped
pens, pend	"hang" appendage, appendix, pending, pendulum, pension, suspended, suspense, compensate, depend, dispense, expend, expensive, pensive, stipend, impending, pendant
port	"carry" porter, portfolio, portage, portable, export, import, rapport, report, support, transport, comportment, deport, important, portmanteau
pos, pon	"put, place" pose, position, positive, a propos, compose, composite, compost, composure, disposable, expose, impose, imposter, opposite, postpone, preposition, proponent, proposition, superimpose, suppose
prim, princ	"first" prime, primate, primer, primeval, primitive, prima donna, primal, primary, primogeniture, primordial, primrose, prince, principal, principality, principle
quir, ques	"ask" inquire, require, acquire, conquer, inquisition, quest, question, questionnaire, request, requisite, requisition
rupt	"break" rupture, abrupt, bankrupt, corrupt, erupt, disrupt, interrupt
sal	"salt" salt, saline, salary, salami, salsa, salad, desalinate

sci	"know" science, conscience, conscious, omniscience, subconscious, conscientious
scrib, script	"write" scribble, script, scripture, subscribe, transcription, ascribe, describe, inscribe, proscribe, postscript, prescription, circumscribe, nondescript, conscription
sect, seg	"cut" bisect, dissect, insect, intersect, section, sector, segment
sent, sens	"feel" sense, sensitive, sensory, sensuous, sentiment, sentimental, assent, consent, consensus, dissent, resent, sensation
sequ, sec	"follow" sequel, sequential, consequence, consecutive, non sequitur, persecute, second, sect, subsequent
son	"sound" sonic, sonnet, sonorous, unison, ultrasonic, assonance, consonant, dissonant, resonate, sonate
spec, spic	"see" spectacle, spectacles, spectacular, specimen, prospect, respect, retrospective, speculate, suspect, suspicion, aspect, auspicious, circumspect, inspector, introspection
spir	"breathe" spirit, respiration, perspire, transpire, inspire, conspire, aspirate, dispirited, antiperspirant
sta, stis	"stand" stable, state, station, stationary, statistic, statue, stature, status, subsist, assist, consistent, desist, insistent, persistent, resist
stru	"build" construct, instruct, destruction, reconstruction, obstruct
tain, ten	"hold" detain, obtain, pertain, retain, sustain, abstain, appertain, contain, entertain, maintain
tang, tact	"touch" tangible, intangible, tangent, contact, tactile
tend, tens	"stretch" distend, tendon, tendril, extend, intend, intensify, attend, contend, portend, superintendent
term	"end" term, terminal, terminate, determine, exterminate, predetermine
terra	"earth" terrain, terrarium, terrace, subterranean, terrestrial, extraterrestrial, Mediterranean, terra cotta, terra firma
tort, torq	"twist" contort, distort, extort, torture, tortuous, torque
tract	"pull" tractor, traction, contract, distract, subtract, retract, attract, protracted, intractable, abstract, detract
vac	"empty" vacant, vacuum, evacuate, vacation, vacuous, vacate
val	"strong, worth" valid, valiant, validate, evaluate, devalue, convalescent, valedictorian, invalid
ven, vent	"come" vent, venture, venue, adventure, avenue, circumvent, convention, event, intervene, invent, prevent, revenue, souvenir, convenient
vers, vert	"turn" revert, vertex, vertigo, convert, divert, vertical, adverse, advertise, anniversary, avert, controversy, conversation, extrovert, introvert, inverse, inverted, perverted, reverse, subvert, traverse, transverse, universe, versatile, versus, vertebra
vid, vis	"see" video, vista, visage, visit, visual, visa, advise, audiovisual, envision, invisible, television, supervise, provision, revision, improvise
voc	"call" vocal, vociferous, evoke, invoke, advocate, avocation, convocation, equivocal, invocation, provoke, revoke, vocabulary, vocation
vol, volv	"roll" revolve, evolve, involve, volume, convoluted, devolve

Appendix F Games and Templates for Sorts

Game Boards

Figures F.1 through F.8 are game board templates that can be used to create some of the games described throughout the book. Note that there are two sides for each game board. When the two sides are placed together, they form a continuous track or path. These games can be adapted for many different features and for many different levels. Here are some general tips on creating the games.

1. The game boards can be photocopied (enlarge slightly) and mounted on manila file folders (colored ones are nice), making them easy to create and store. All the materials needed for the game, such as spinners, word cards, or game markers, can be put in plastic bags or envelopes labeled with the name of the game and stored in the folder. You might mark the flip side of word cards in some way so that lost cards can be returned to the correct game. Rubber stamp figures work well.
2. When mounting a game board in a folder, be sure to leave a slight gap (about an eighth of an inch) between the two sides so that the folder will still fold. If you do not leave this gap, the paper will buckle. Trim the sheets of paper so the two new sides line up neatly, or cut around the path shape and line up the two pieces of the pathway.
3. A variety of objects (buttons, plastic discs, coins, and bottle caps) can be used for game markers or pawns that the children will move around the board. Flat objects store best in the folders or you may just want to put a collection of game markers, dice, and spinners in a box. This box can be stored near the games, and students can take what they need.
4. Add pizazz to games with pictures cut from magazines or old workbooks, stickers, comic characters, clip art, and so on. Rubber stamps, your drawings, or children's drawings can be used to add interest and color. Create catchy themes such as Rabbit Race, Lost in Space, Through the Woods, Mouse Maze, Rainforest Adventure, and so forth.
5. Include directions and correct answers (when appropriate) with the game. They might be stored inside along with playing pieces or glued to the game itself.
6. Label the spaces around the path or track according to the feature you want to reinforce, and laminate for durability. If you want to create open-ended games that can be adapted to a variety of features, laminate the path before you label the spaces. Then you can write in letters or words with a washable overheard pen and change them as needed. Permanent marker can also be used and removed with hairspray or fingernail polish remover.
7. Add interest to the game by labeling some spaces with special directions (if you are using a numbered die or spinner) or add cards with special directions to the deck of words. Directions might offer the students a bonus in the form of an extra turn or there might be a penalty such as lose a turn. These bonus or penalty directions can tie in with your themes. For example, in the Rainforest Adventure the player might forget a lunch and be asked to go back to the starting space. Keep the reading ability of your children in mind as you create these special directions.

Spinners

Many of the word study games described in this book use a game spinner. Figure F.8 provides simple directions for making a spinner.

Templates for Sorts

TEMPLATE FOR PICTURE SORTS

TEMPLATE FOR WORD SORTS

FIGURE F.1 Racetrack and Game Board (left and right)

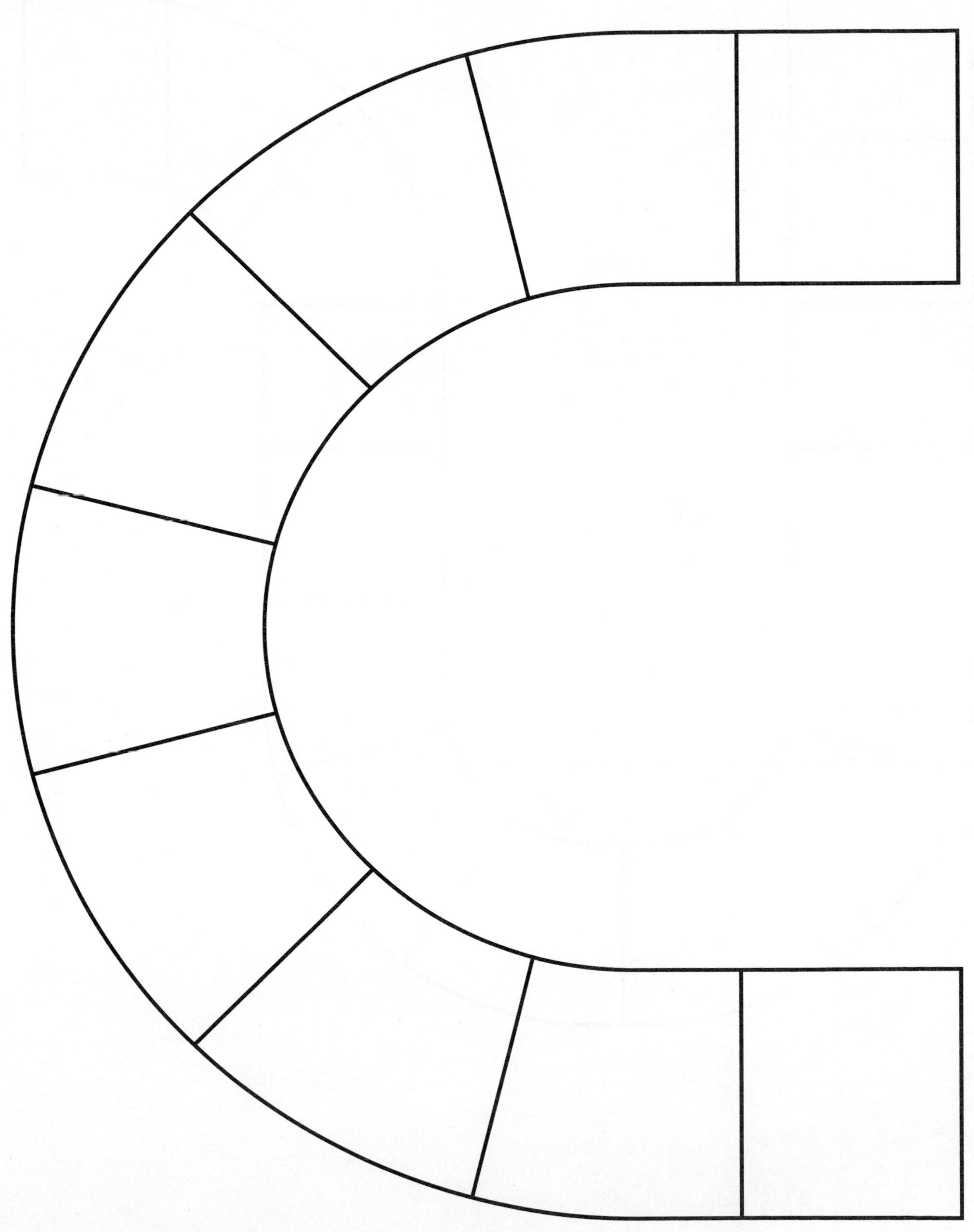

FIGURE F.2 U Game Board (left)

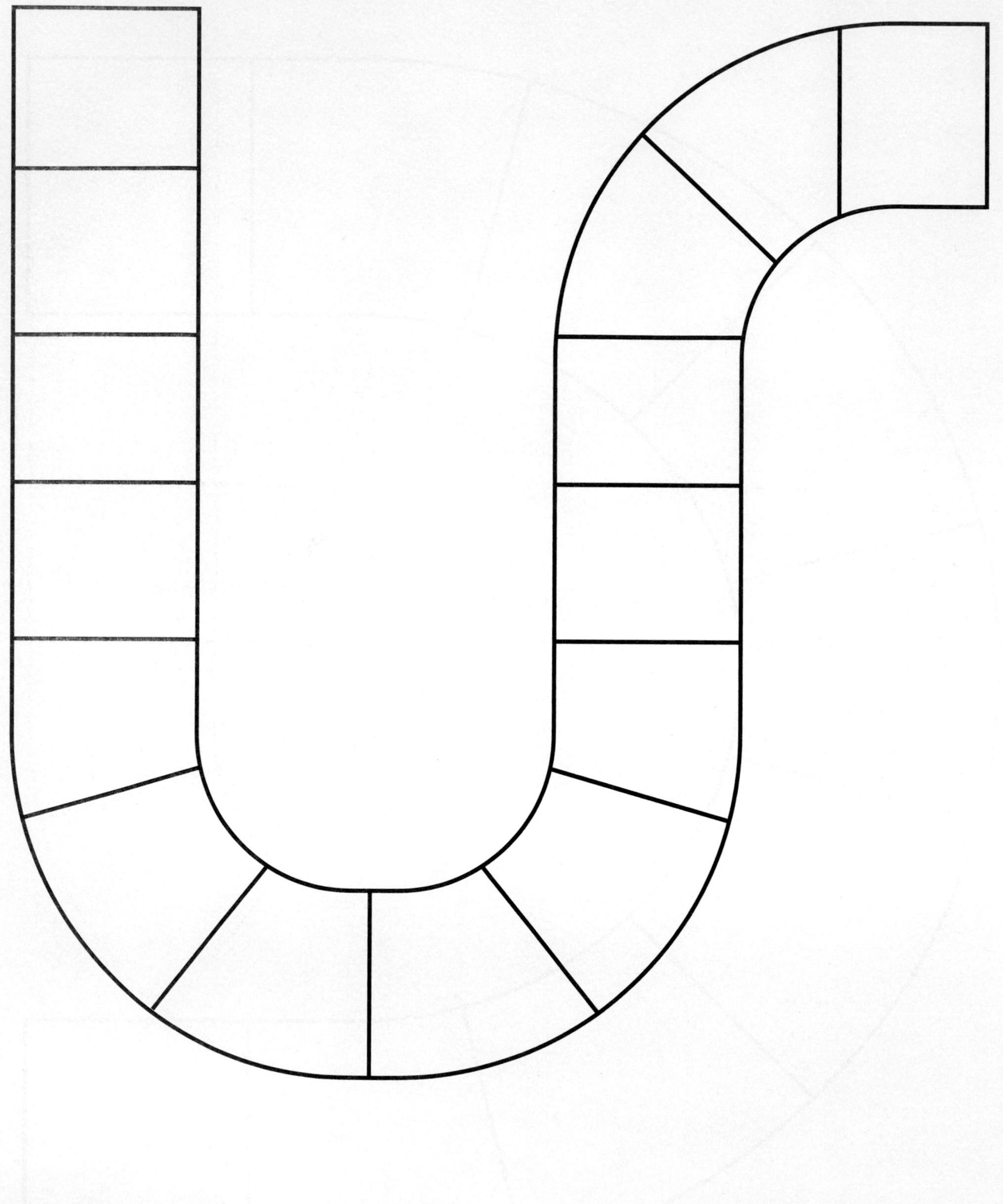

FIGURE F.3 U Game Board (right)

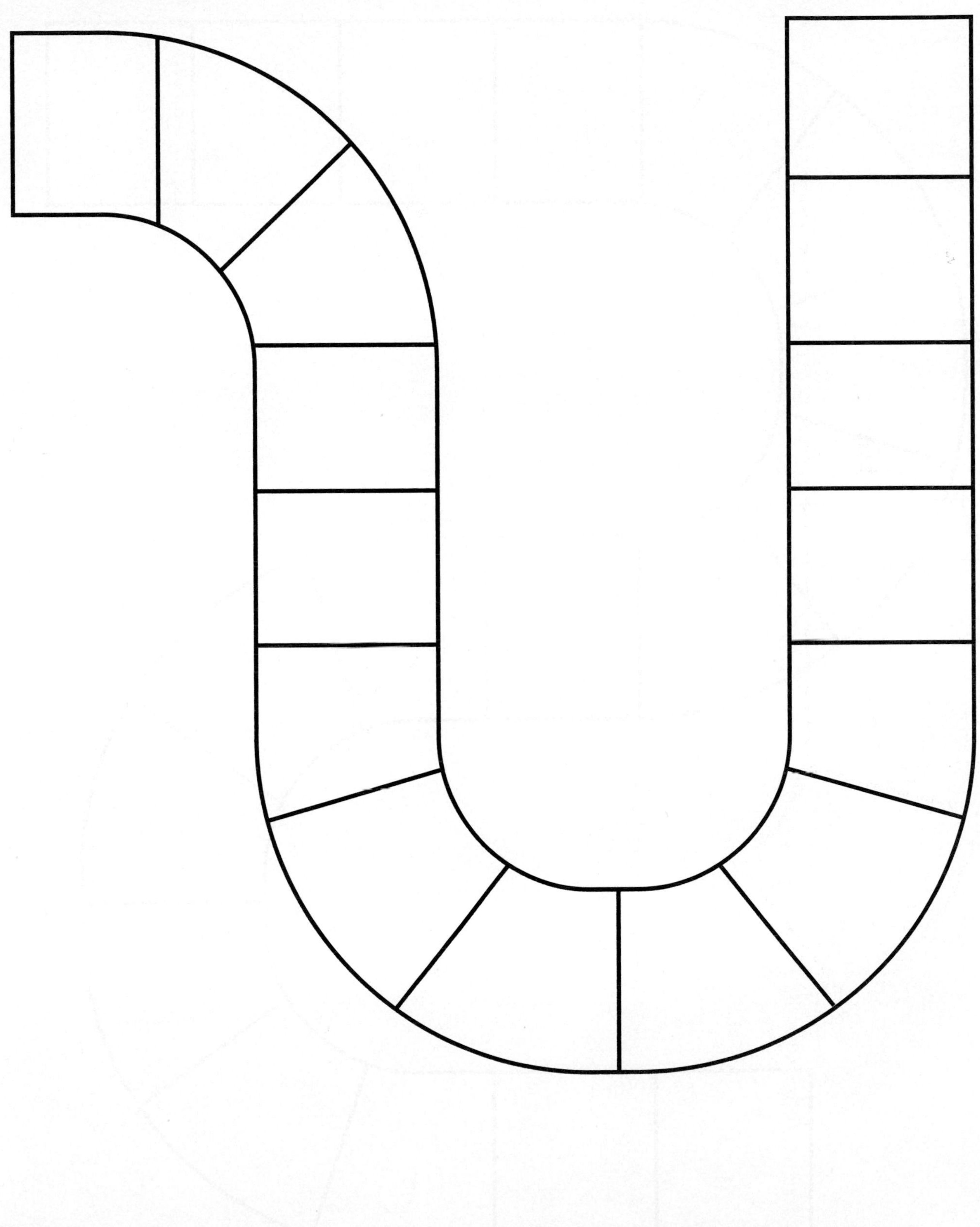

FIGURE F.4 S Game Board (left)

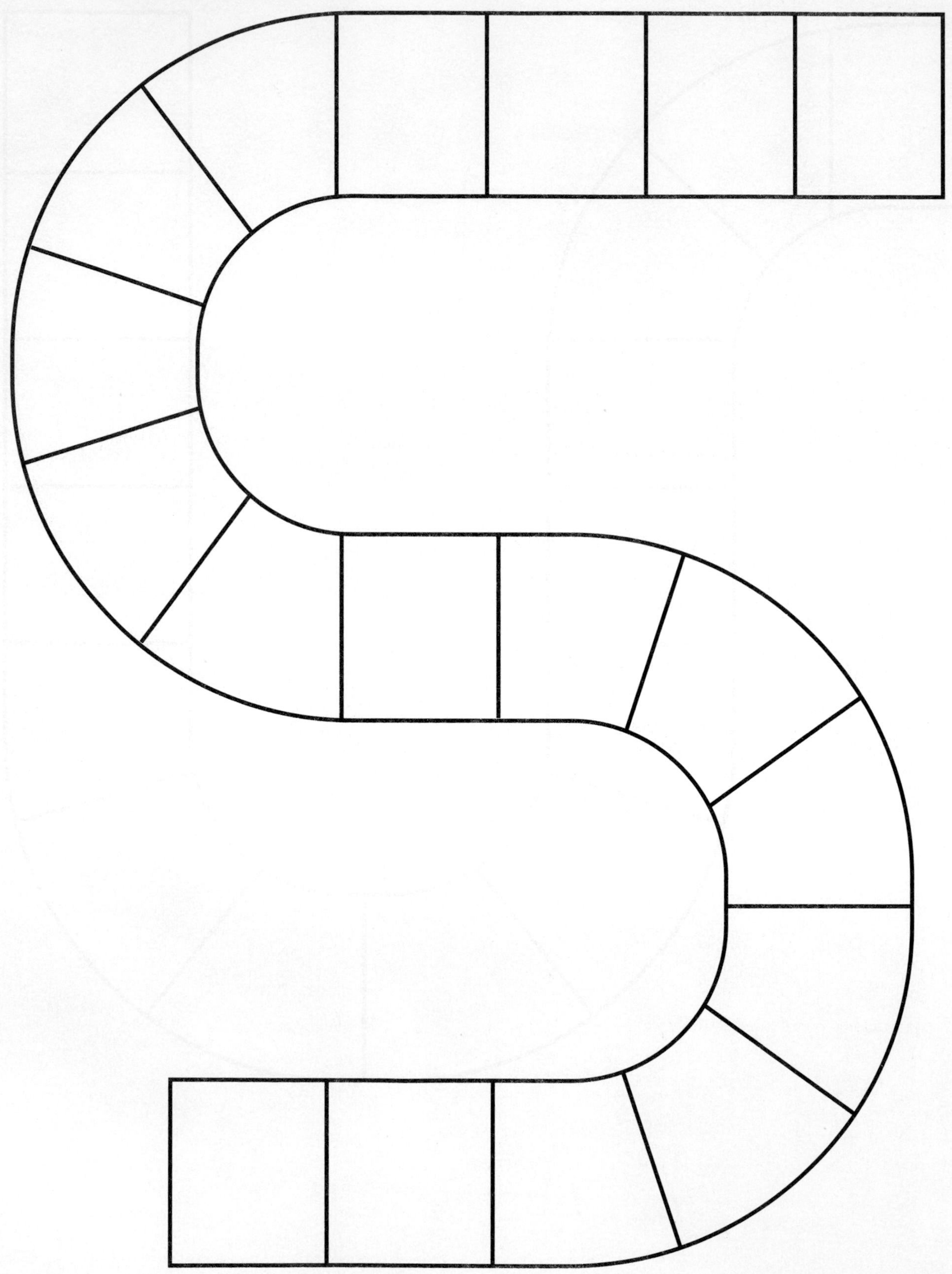

FIGURE F.5 S Game Board (right)

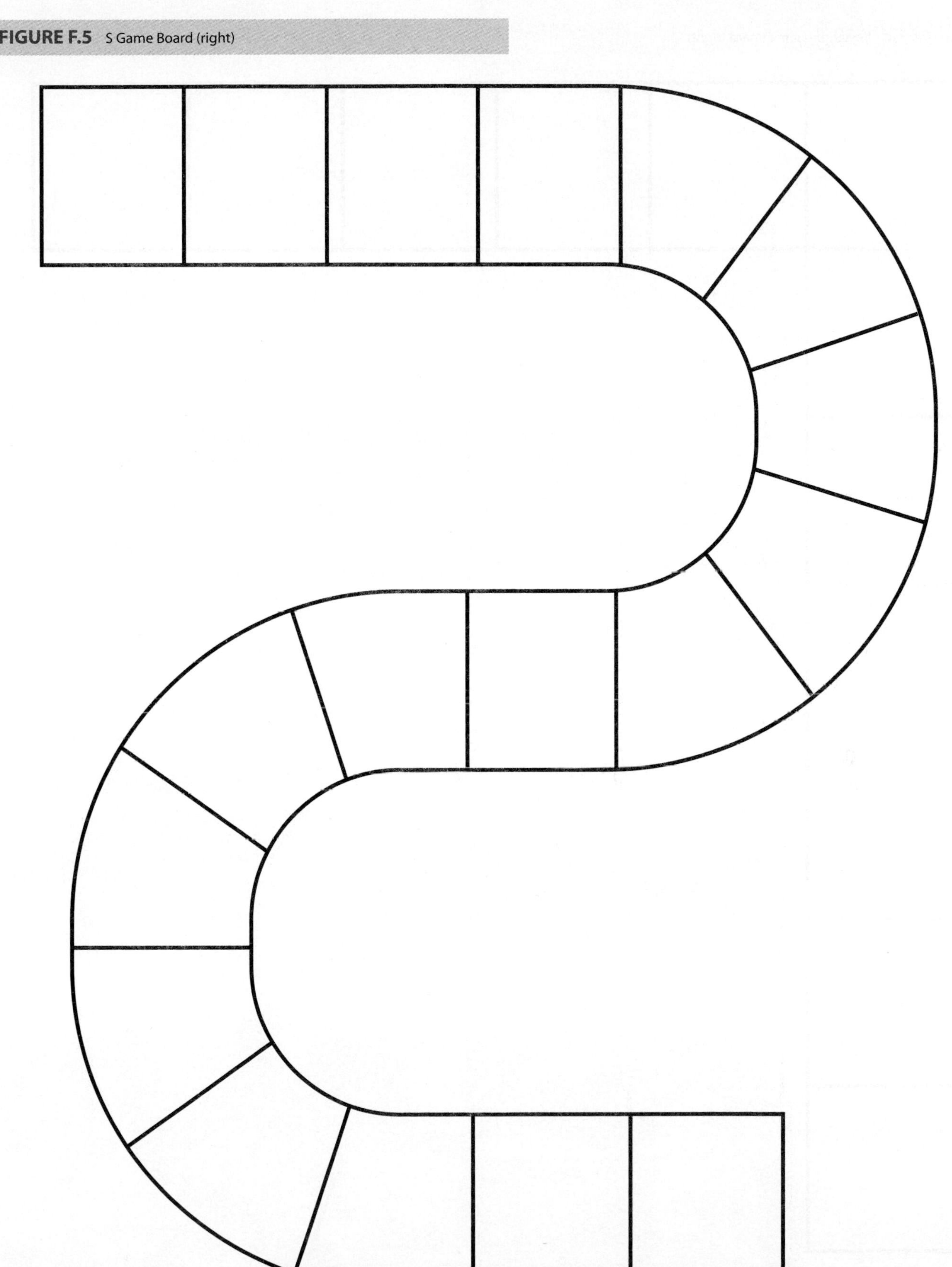

FIGURE F.6 Rectangle Game Board (right)

FIGURE F.7 U Rectangle Board (right)

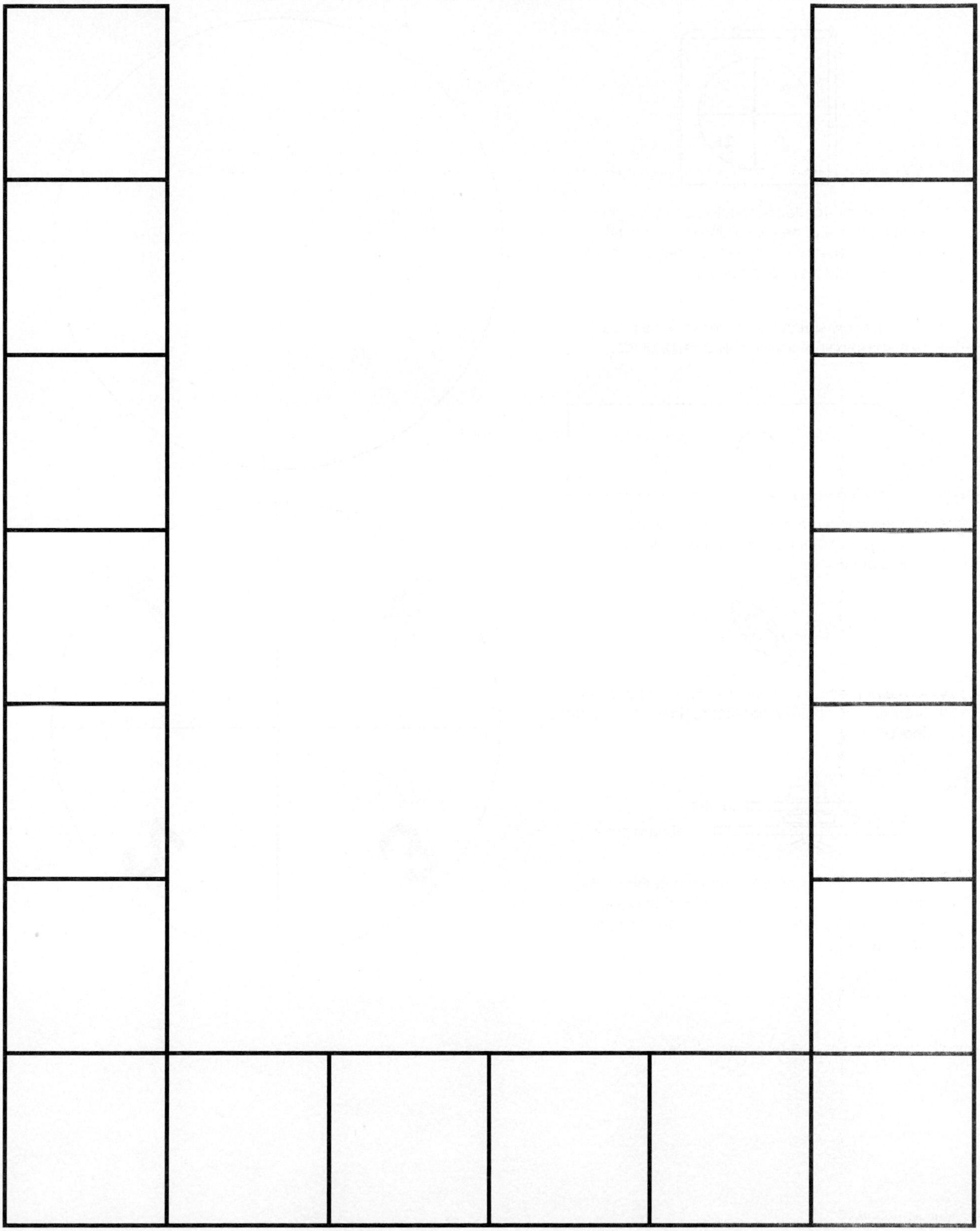

FIGURE F.8 Directions for Making a Game Spinner

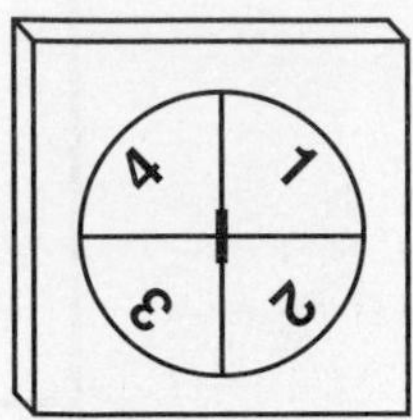

1. Glue a circle (patterns or cutouts to the right) onto a square of heavy cardboard that is no smaller than 4" × 4". Square spinner bases are easier to hold than round bases.

2. Cut a narrow slot in the center with the point of a sharp pair of scissors or a razor blade.

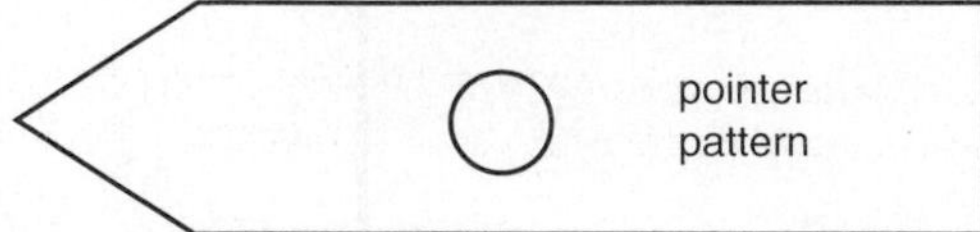

3. Cut the pointer from soft plastic (such as a milk jug) and make a clean round hole with a hole punch.

4. A washer, either a metal one from the hardware store or one cut from cardboard, helps the pointer move freely.

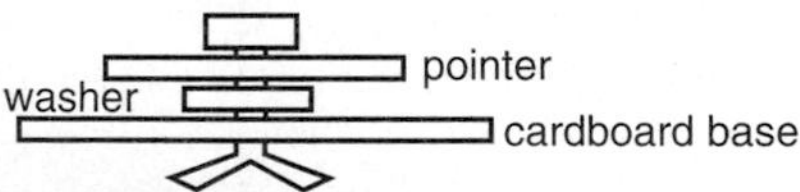

5. Push a paper fastener through the pointer hole, the washer, and the slot in the spinner base. Flatten the legs, leaving space for the pointer to spin easily.

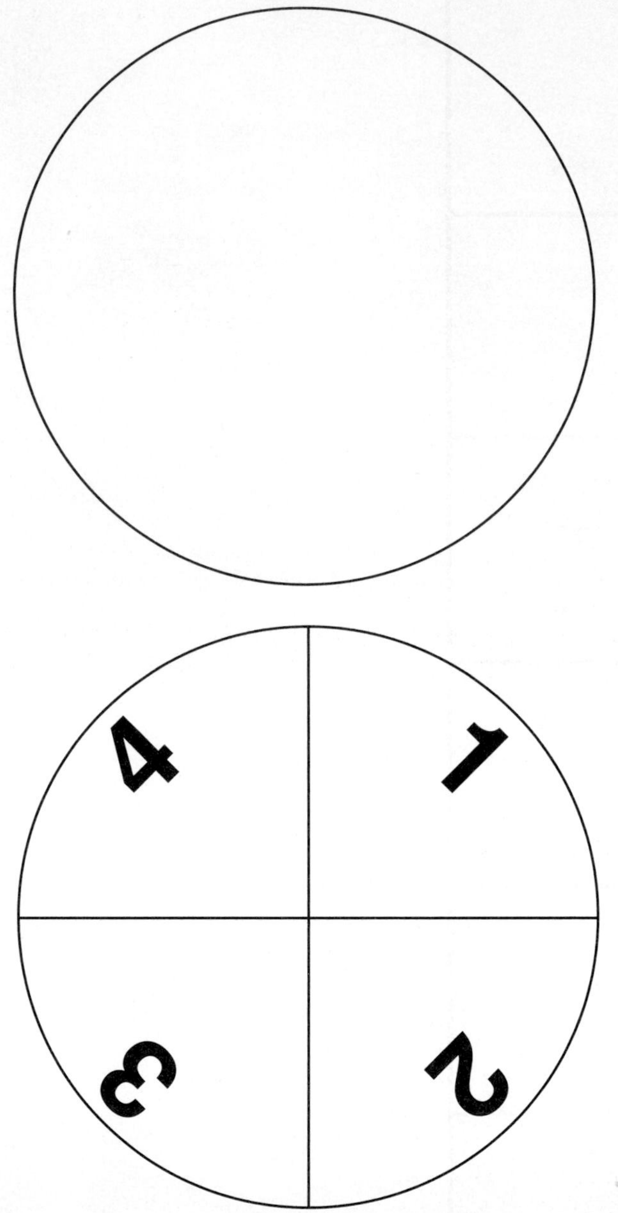

Appendix G Other Resources

Children's Literature

Azarian, M. (1981). *A farmer's alphabet.* Boston: David Godine.

Base, G. (1986). *Animalia.* New York: Harry Abrams.

Blume, J. (1971). *Freckle juice.* New York: Yearling.

Blume, J. (2003). *Superfudge.* New York: Penguin.

Brett, J. (2003). *Town mouse, country mouse.* New York, NY: Putnam.

Bruna, D. (1978). *B is for bear.* New York: Price Stern Sloan.

Cameron, P. (1961). *I can't, said the ant.* New York: Putnam Publishing.

Carle, E. (1974). *My very first book of shapes.* New York: HarperCollins.

Carle, E. (1987). *Have you seen my cat?* Picture Books.

Christelow, E. (1989). *Five little monkeys jumping on the bed.* Boston: Clarion Books.

Cleary, B. (1968). *Ramona the pest.* New York: HarperCollins.

Clements, A. (1996). *Frindle.* New York: Atheneum.

Crews, D. (1995). *Ten black dots.* New York: Harper Trophy.

Dahl, R. (1988). *Fantastic Mr. Fox.* New York: Puffin Books.

Fleming, D. (1993). *In the small small pond.* New York: Henry Holt and Company.

Florian, D. (1987). *A winter day.* New York: Scholastic.

Florian, D. (1990). *A beach day.* New York: Greenwillow.

Frasier, D. (2007). *Miss Alaineus: A vocabulary disaster.* Sandpiper.

Freeman, D. (1968). *Corduroy.* New York: Viking Juvenile Books.

Galdone, P. (1973). *The three billy goats gruff.* New York: Clarion Books.

Galdone, P. (2006). *The little red hen.* Boston: Clarion.

Garten, J. (1994). *The alphabet tale.* New York: Greenwillow.

Guarina, D. (1989). *Is your mama a llama?* Illustrated by Steven Kellogg. New York: Scholastic.

Heller, R. (1993). *Chickens aren't the only ones.* New York: Putnam.

Hoban, T. (1978). *Is it red? Is it yellow? Is it blue?* New York: Greenwillow Books.

Hutchins, P. (2005). *Rosie's walk.* Fullerton, CA: Aladdin.

Langstaff, J. (1974). *Oh, a hunting we will go.* New York: Atheneum.

Lionni, L. (1969). *Alexander and the wind-up mouse.* New York: Pantheon.

Martin, B., & Archambault, J. (1989). *Chicka chicka boom boom.* New York: Simon & Schuster.

Marshall, E., & Marshall, J. (1994). *Fox and his friends.* New York: Puffin Books.

McCloskey, R. (1948). *Blueberries for Sal.* Newk York: Puffin Books.

McGovern, A. (1996). *Stone soup.* New York: Scholastic.

McMillan, B (1990). *One sun: A book of terse verse.* New York: Holiday House.

Milne, A. A. (2009). *Winnie the Pooh.* New York: Dutton Juvenile.

O'Dell, S. (2010). *Island of the blue dolphins.* Sandpiper.

Raffi. (1976). *Singable songs for the very young.* Universal City, CA: Troubadour Records.

Raffi. (1985). *One light, one sun.* Universal City, CA: Troubadour Records.

Rowling, J. K. (2000). *Harry Potter and the goblet of fire.* New York: Scholastic.

Schotter, R. (2006). *The boy who loved words.* New York: Schwartz & Wade.

Scieszka, J. (1992). *The good, the bad, and the goofy.* New York: Viking Press.

Seuss, Dr. (1963). *Dr. Seuss's ABC.* New York: Random House.

Seuss, Dr. (1974). *There's a wocket in my pocket.* New York: Random House.

Sharmat, M. (1980). *Gregory the terrible eater.* New York: Four Winds Press.

Shaw, N. (1986). *Sheep in a jeep.* Boston: Houghton Mifflin.

Slepian, J., & Seidler, A. (1967). *The hungry thing.* New York: Follet.

Slepian, J., & Seidler, A. (1990). *The hungry thing returns.* New York: Scholastic.

Slobodkina, E. (1947). *Caps for sale.* New York: Harper Trophy.

Steig, W. (1978). *Amos and Boris.* New York: Farrar, Straus and Giroux.

The tree (A First Discovery Book). (1992). New York: Cartwheel Books.

Wagener, G. (1991). *Leo the lion.* New York: New York: HarperCollins.

Wallner, J. (1987a). *City mouse–country mouse.* New York: Scholastic.

Wallner, J. (1987b). *The country mouse and the city mouse and two more mouse tales from Aesop.* New York: Scholastic.

Wells, N. (1980). *Noisy Nora.* New York: Dial Press.

White, E. B. (1945). *Stuart Little.* New York: Harper Row.

Wildsmith, B. (1982). *The cat on the mat.* New York: Oxford Press.

Bibliography of Word Study Books

Allen, M. S., & Cunnigham, M. (1999). *Webster's new world rhyming dictionary.* New York: Simon & Schuster.

Asimov, I. (1959). *Words of science, and the history behind them.* Boston: Houghton Mifflin.

Asimov, I. (1962). *Words on the map.* Boston: Houghton Mifflin.

Balmuth, M. (1992). *The roots of phonics: An historical introduction.* Austin, TX: Pro-Ed.

Black, D. C. (1988). *Spoonerisms, sycophants and sops; A celebration of fascinating facts about words.* New York: Harper & Row.

Byson, B. (1990). *The mother tongue: English and how it got that way.* New York: Morrow.

Byson, B. (1994). *Made in America: An informal history of the English language in the United States.* New York: Morrow.

Ciardi, J. (1980). *A browser's dictionary: A compendium of curious expressions and intriguing facts.* New York: Harper & Row.

See pages 118, 128, 132, 133, 141, 277, and 309 for other lists of children's literature and word study books.

Collis, H. (1981). *Colloquial English.* New York: Regents Pub.

Collis, H. (1986). *101 American English idioms.* New York: McGraw Hill.

Crystal, D. (1987). *The Cambridge encyclopedia of language.* New York: Cambridge University Press.

Cummings, D. W. (1988). *American English spelling.* Baltimore: Johns Hopkins University Press.

Editors of the American Heritage Dictionaries. (2008). *Curious George's dictionary.* Boston: Houghton Mifflin Harcourt.

Editors of the American Heritage Dictionaries. (2009). *The American Heritage first dictionary.* Boston: Houghton Mifflin Harcourt.

Folsom, M. (1985). *Easy as pie: A guessing game of sayings.* New York: Clarion.

Franlyn, J. (1987). *Which is witch?* New York: Dorset Press.

Fry, E. B., & Kress, J. E. (2006). *The reading teacher's book of lists* (5th ed.). Jossey-Bass.

Funk, C. E. (1948). *A hog on ice and other curious expressions.* New York: Harper & Row.

Funk, C. E. (1955). *Heavens to Betsy and other curious sayings.* New York: Harper & Row.

Funk, W. (1954). *Word origins and their romantic stories.* New York: Grosset & Dunlap.

Gwynne, F. (1970). *The king who rained.* New York: Simon & Schuster.

Gwynne, F. (1976). *A chocolate moose for dinner.* New York: Simon & Schuster.

Gwynne, F. (1980). *A sixteen hand horse.* New York: Simon & Schuster.

Gwynne, F. (1988). *A little pigeon toad.* New York: Simon & Schuster.

Harrison, J. S. (1987). *Confusion reigns.* New York: St. Martin's Press.

Heacock, P. (1989). *Which word when?* New York: Dell Pub.

Heller, R. (1987). *A cache of jewels and other collective nouns.* New York: Grosset & Dunlap.

Heller, R. (1988). *Kites sail high.* New York: Grosset & Dunlap.

Heller, R. (1989). *Many luscious lollipops: A book about adjectives.* New York: Grosset & Dunlap.

Heller, R. (1990). *Merry-go-round: A book about nouns.* New York: Grosset & Dunlap.

Heller, R. (1991). *Up, up and away: A book about adverbs.* New York: Grosset & Dunlap.

Heller, R. (1995). *Behind the mask: A book about prepositions.* New York: Grosset & Dunlap.

Hoad, T. F. (1986). *The concise Oxford dictionary of English etymology.* New York: Oxford University Press.

Kinsley, C. (1980). *The heroes.* New York: Mayflower.

Kress, J. E. (2002). *The ESL teacher's book of lists.* John Wiley & Sons.

Lewis, N. (1983). *Dictionary of correct spelling.* New York: Harper & Row.

Maestro, G. (1983). *Riddle romp.* New York: Clarion.

Maestro, G. (1984). *What's a frank frank? Easy homograph riddles.* New York: Clarion.

Maestro, G. (1985): *Razzle-dazzle riddles.* New York: Clarion.

Maestro, G. (1986). *What's mite might? Homophone riddles to boost your word power.* New York: Clarion.

Maestro, G. (1989). *Riddle roundup: A wild bunch to beef up your word power.* New York: Clarion.

Merriam-Webster children's dictionary. (2008). New York: DK Publishing.

Nash, R. (1991). *NTC's dictionary of Spanish cognates thematically organized.* Chicago: NTC Publishing Group.

Partridge, E. (1984). *Origins: A short etymological dictionary of modern English.* New York: Greenwich House.

Pei, M. (1965). *The story of language.* Philadelphia: Lippincott.

Presson, L. (1996). *What in the world is a homophone?* Hauppauge, NY: Barron's.

Presson, L. (1997). *A dictionary of homophones.* New York: Barron's.

Randall, B. (1992). *When is a pig a hog? A guide to confoundingly related English words.* New York: Prentice Hall.

Room, A. (1992). *NTC's dictionary of word origins.* Lincolnwood, IL: National Textbook.

Safire, W. (1984). *I stand corrected: More on language.* New York: Avon.

Sarnoff, J., & Ruffins, R. (1981). *Words: A book about word origins of everyday words and phrases.* New York: Charles Scribner's Sons.

Schleifer, R. (1995). *Grow your own vocabulary: By learning the roots of English words.* New York: Random House.

Scragg, D. G. (1974). *A history of English spelling.* Manchester, England: Manchester University Press.

Shipley, J. T. (1967). *Dictionary of word origins.* Lanham, MD: Rowman & Littlefield.

Shipley, J. (2001). *The origins of English words.* Baltimore: Johns Hopkins University Press.

The Oxford English Dictionary on CD-ROM. (1994). Oxford: Oxford University Press.

The American heritage book of English usage: A practical and authoritative guide to contemporary English. (1996). Boston: Houghton Mifflin.

The Scholastic dictionary of synonyms, antonyms, homonyms. (1965). New York: Scholastic.

Terban, M. (1982). *Eight ate: A feast of homonym riddles.* New York: Clarion.

Terban, M. (1983). *In a pickle and other funny idioms.* New York: Clarion.

Terban, M. (1984). *I think I thought and other tricky verbs.* New York: Clarion.

Terban, M. (1986). *Your foot's on my feet! And other tricky nouns.* New York: Clarion.

Terban, M. (1987). *Mad as a wet hen! and other funny idioms.* New York: Clarion.

Terban, M. (1988a). *The dove dove: Funny homograph riddles.* New York: Clarion.

Terban, M. (1988c). *Too hot to hoot: Funny palindrome riddles.* New York: Clarion.

Terban, M. (1991). *Hey, hay! A wagonful of funny homonym riddles.* New York: Clarion.

Terban, M. (1992). *Funny you should ask: How to make up jokes and riddles with wordplay.* New York: Clarion.

Venesky, R. (1970). *The structure of English orthography.* The Hague: Mouton.

Venezky, R. L. (1999). *The American way of spelling: The structure and origins of American English orthography.* New York: Guilford Press.

Webster's dictionary of word origins. (1992). New York: Smithmark.

Weiner, S. (1981). *Handy book of commonly used American idioms.* New York: Regents Pub.

Yopp, H. K., & Yopp, R. E. (2000). *Oo-pples and boo-noo-noos.* Portsmouth, NH: Heineman.

Young, S. (1994). *Scholastic rhyming dictionary.* New York: Scholastic.

Glossary

absorbed (assimilated) prefixes Prefixes in which the spelling and sound of the consonant has been absorbed into the spelling and sound at the beginning of the base or root to which the prefix is affixed (e.g., *ad* + *tract* = *attract*).

accented/stressed syllable The syllable in a word that receives more emphasis when spoken and usually has a clearly pronounced vowel sound. Compare to *unaccented syllable.*

affix Most commonly a suffix or prefix attached to a base word, stem, or root.

affixation The process of attaching a word part, such as a prefix or suffix, to a base word, stem, or root.

affricate A speech sound produced when the breath stream is stopped and released at the point of articulation, usually where the tip of the tongue rubs against the roof of the mouth just behind the teeth, such as when pronouncing the final sound in the word *clutch* or the beginning sound in the word *trip*.

alliteration The occurrence in a phrase or line of speech of two or more words having the same beginning sound.

alphabetic A writing system containing characters or symbols representing individual speech sounds.

alphabetic layer The first layer of word study instruction, focusing on letter–sound correspondences. Old English was phonetically regular to a great extent.

alphabetic principle The concept that letters and letter combinations, are used to represent phonemes in orthography. See also *orthography; phoneme.*

ambiguous vowels A vowel sound represented by a variety of different spelling patterns, or vowel patterns that represent a wide range of sounds (e.g., the *ou* in *cough*, *through*, and *could*).

analytic phonics Word study that divides words into their elemental parts through phonemic, orthographic, and morphological analysis.

articulation How sounds are shaped in the mouth during speech. Some confusions are made in spelling based on similarities in articulation (e.g., *tr* for *dr*).

assimilated prefixes See *absorbed (assimilated) prefixes.*

automaticity Refers to the speed and accuracy of word recognition and spelling. Automaticity is the goal of word study instruction and frees cognitive resources for comprehension.

base word A word to which prefixes and/or suffixes are added. For example, the base word of *unwholesome* is *whole.*

blends A phonics term for an orthographic unit of two or three letters at the beginning or end of words that are blended together. There are *l*-blends such as *bl, cl* and *fl; r*-blends such as *gr, tr,* and *pr; s*-blends such as *pc, scr,* and *squ;* and final blends such as *ft, rd,* and *st.* Every sound represented in a blend is pronounced, if only briefly.

blind sort A picture or word sort done with a partner in which students who are responsible for sorting cannot see the word. They must instead attend to the sounds and sometimes visualize the spelling pattern to determine the category.

blind writing sort A variant of a blind sort in which one student (or teacher) names a word without showing it to another student, who must write it in the correct category under a key word.

bound morphemes Meaning units of language (morphemes) that cannot stand alone as a word. *Respected* has three bound morphemes: *re+spect+ed.* Compare to *free morphemes.*

center time Work completed independently in prepared areas within a classroom.

choral reading Oral reading done in unison with another person or persons.

circle time Group work conducted under the teacher's direction.

classroom composite A classroom profile that organizes children into instructional groups by features to be taught within each stage.

closed sorts Word sorts based on predetermined categories.

closed syllable A syllable that ends with or is "closed" by a consonant sound. In polysyllabic words, a closed syllable contains a short vowel sound that is closed by two consonants (e.g., *rabbit, racket*). Compare to *open syllable.*

cognates Words in different languages derived from the same root.

complex consonant patterns Consonant units occurring at the end of words determined by the preceding vowel sound. For example, a final *tch* follows the short vowel sound in *fetch* and *scotch*, while a final *ch* follows the long-vowel sound in *peach* and *coach.* Other complex consonant patterns include final *ck* (*pack* vs. *peak*) and final *dge* (*badge* vs. *cage*).

compound words Words made up of two smaller words. A compound word may or may not be hyphenated, depending on its part of speech.

concept of word The ability to match spoken words to printed words, as demonstrated by the ability to point to the words of a memorized text while reading.

concepts about print (CAP) Understandings about how books are organized (front to back page turning, titles, illustrations), how print is oriented on the page (top to bottom, left to right), and features of print such as punctuation and capitalization.

concept sorts A categorization task in which pictures, objects, or words are grouped by shared attributes or meanings to develop concepts and vocabulary.

consolidated alphabetic readers/phase Ehri's fourth phase of word recognition, in which readers use patterns, chunks, and other word parts to figure out unfamiliar words.

consonant alternation The process in which the pronunciation of consonants changes in the base or root of derivationally related words while the spelling does not change (e.g., the silent-to-sounded *g* in the words *sign* and *signal;* the /k/ to /sh/ pattern in the words *music* and *musician*).

consonant blend See *blends.*

consonant digraph See *digraph.*

consonants Letters that are not vowels (*a*, *e*, *i*, *o*, and *u*). Whereas vowel sounds are thought of as musical, consonant sounds are known for their noise and the way in which air is constricted as it is stopped and released or forced through the vocal tract, mouth, teeth, and lips.

continuant sound A consonant sound, such as /s/ or /m/, that can be prolonged as long as the breath lasts without distorting the sound quality.

cut and paste activities A variation of picture sorting in which students cut out pictures from magazines or catalogs and paste them into categories.

derivational affixes Affixes added to base words that affect the meaning (sign, **re**sign; break, break**able**) and/or part of speech (beauty, beauti**ful**). Compare to *inflectional endings.*

derivational relations spelling stage The last stage of spelling development, in which spellers learn about derivational relationships preserved in the spelling of words. *Derivational* refers to the process by which new words are created from existing words, chiefly through affixation; and the development of a word from its historical origin. *Derivational constancy* refers to spelling patterns that remain the same despite changes in pronunciation across derived forms. For example, *bomb* retains the *b* from *bombard* because of its historical evolution.

developmental level An individual's stage of spelling development: emergent, letter name–alphabetic, within word pattern, syllables and affixes, or derivational relations.

digraph Two letters that represent one sound. There are consonant digraphs and vowel digraphs, though the term most commonly refers to consonant digraphs. Common consonant digraphs include *sh*, *ch*, *th*, and *wh*. Consonant digraphs at the beginning of words are *onsets.*

diphthong A complex speech sound beginning with one vowel sound and moving to another within the same syllable. The *oy* in *boy* is a diphthong, as is the *ou* in *cloud.*

directionality The left-to-right direction used for reading and writing English.

draw and label activities An extension activity for a picture sort in which students draw pictures of things that begin with the sounds under study. The pictures are drawn in the appropriate categories and labeled with the letter(s) corresponding to that sound.

echo reading Oral reading in which the student echoes or imitates the reading of the teacher or partner. Echo reading is used with very beginning readers as a form of support. Echo reading can also be used to model fluent reading.

emergent A period of literacy development ranging from birth to beginning reading. This period precedes the letter name–alphabetic stage of spelling development.

eponyms Places, things, and actions that are named after an individual.

etymology The study of the origin and historical development of words.

feature analysis More than scoring words right and wrong, feature analyses provide a way of interpreting children's spelling errors by taking into account their knowledge of specific orthographic features such as consonant blends or short vowels. Feature analyses inform teachers what spelling features to teach.

feature guide A tool used to classify students' errors within a hierarchy of orthographic features. Used to score spelling inventories to assess students' knowledge of specific spelling features at their particular stage of spelling development and to plan word study instruction to meet individual needs.

free morphemes Meaning units of language (morphemes) that stand alone as words. (*Workshop* has two free morphemes: *work* and *shop*.) Compare to *bound morphemes.*

frustration level A dysfunctional level of instruction where there is a mismatch between instruction and what an individual is able to grasp. This mismatch precludes learning and often results in frustration.

full alphabetic readers/phase Ehri's third phase of word recognition, in which readers are able to sound out words using letter–sound correspondences or phonics they know.

generative An approach to word study that emphasizes processes that apply to many words, as opposed to an approach that focuses on one word at a time.

headers Words, pictures, or other labels used to designate categories for sorting.

high-frequency words Words that make up roughly 50 percent of any text—those that occur most often (e.g., *the, was, were, is*).

homographs Words that are spelled alike, but have different pronunciations and different meanings (e.g., "*tear* a piece of paper" and "to shed a *tear*"; "*lead* someone along" and "the element *lead*").

homonyms Words that share the same spelling but have different meanings (tell a *yarn*, knit with *yarn*). See *homographs; homophones.*

homophones Words that sound alike, are spelled differently, and have different meanings (e.g., *bear* and *bare*, *pane* and *pain*, and *forth* and *fourth*).

independent level That level of academic engagement in which an individual works independently, without need of instructional support. Independent-level behaviors demonstrate a high degree of accuracy, speed, ease, and fluency.

inflected/inflectional endings Suffixes that change the verb tense (walk**s**, walk**ed**, walk**ing**) or number (dog**s**, box**es**) of a word.

instructional level A level of academic engagement in which instruction is comfortably matched to what an individual is able to grasp. See also *zone of proximal development (ZPD).*

key pictures Pictures placed at the top of each category in a picture sort. Key pictures act as headers for each column and can be used for analogy.

key words Words placed at the top of each category in a word sort. Key words act as headers for each column and can be used for analogy.

kinetic reversal An error of letter order (PTE for *pet*).

language experience approach An approach to the teaching of reading in which students dictate to a teacher, who records their language. Dictated accounts can then be used as familiar reading materials.

lax Lax vowels are commonly known as the short-vowel sound.

letter name–alphabetic spelling stage The second stage of spelling development, in which students represent beginning, middle, and ending sounds of words with phonetically accurate letter choices. Often the selections are based on the sound of the letter name itself, rather than abstract letter–sound associations. The letter name *h* (aitch), for example, produces the /ch/ sound, and is often selected to represent that sound (HEP for *chip*).

liquids The consonant sounds for /r/ and /l/, which, unlike other consonant sounds, do not obstruct air in the mouth. The sounds for /r/ and /l/ are more vowel-like in that they do not involve direct contact between the lips, tongue, and the roof of the mouth as other consonants do. Instead, they " roll around" in the mouth, as if liquid.

long vowels Every vowel (*a, e, i, o,* and *u*) has two sounds, commonly referred to as "long" and "short." The long vowel sound "says its letter name." The vocal cords are tense when producing the long vowel sound. Because of this, the linguistic term for the long vowel sound is *tense.*

meaning layer The third layer of English orthography, including meaning units such as prefixes, suffixes, and word roots. These word elements were acquired primarily during the Renaissance, when English was overlaid with many words of Greek and Latin derivation.

meaning sorts A type of word sort in which the categories are determined by semantic categories or by spelling–meaning connections.

memory reading An accurate recitation of text accompanied by fingerpoint reading.

morphemes Meaning units in the spelling of words, such as the suffix *–ed*, which signals past tense, or the root *graph* in the words *autograph* or *graphite.* See also *bound morphemes; free morphemes.*

morphemic Referring to morphemes.

morphemic analysis The process of analyzing or breaking down a word in terms of its meaning units or morphemes (e.g., *in-struct-or*).

morphology The study of word parts related to syntax and meaning.

nasals A sound such as /m/, /n/, or /ng/ produced when the air is blocked in the oral cavity but escapes through the nose. The first consonants in the words *mom* and *no* represent nasal sounds.

oddballs Words that do not fit the targeted feature in a sort.

onset The initial consonant(s) sound of a single syllable or word. The onset of the word *sun* is /s/. The onset of the word *slide* is /sl/.

open sorts A type of picture or word sort in which the categories for sorting are left open. Students sort pictures or words into groups according to the students' own judgment.

open syllable Syllables that end with a long vowel sound (e.g., *la-bor; sea-son*). Compare to *closed syllable.*

orthography The writing system of a language—specifically, the correct sequence of letters, characters, or symbols.

partial alphabetic readers/phase Ehri's second phase of word recognition, in which children use partial clues, primarily initial consonants to identify words. Also known as selective cue stage.

pattern A letter sequence that functions as a unit to represent a sound (such as *ai* in *rain, pain* and *train*) or a sequence of vowels and consonants, such as the consonant-vowel-consonant (CVC) pattern in a word such as *rag* or at a syllable juncture such as the VCCV pattern in *button.*

pattern layer The second layer or tier of English orthography, in which patterns of letter sequences, rather than individual letters themselves, represent vowel sounds. This layer of information was acquired during the period of English history following the Norman invasion. Many of the vowel patterns of English are of French derivation.

pattern sort A word sort in which students categorize words according to similar spelling patterns.

personal readers Individual books of reading materials for beginning readers. Group experience charts, dictations, rhymes, and short excerpts from books comprise the majority of the reading material.

phoneme The smallest unit of speech that distinguishes one word from another. For example, the *t* of *tug* and the *r* of *rug* are two phonemes.

phoneme segmentation The process of dividing a spoken word into the smallest units of sound within that word. The word *bat* can be divided or segmented into three phonemes: /b/, /ă/, /t/.

phonemic awareness The ability to consciously manipulate individual phonemes in a spoken language. Phonemic awareness is often assessed by the ability to tap, count, or push a penny forward for every sound heard in a word like *cat:* /c/, /ă/, /t/.

phonetic Representing the sounds of speech with a set of distinct symbols (letters), each denoting a single sound. See also *alphabetic principle.*

phonics The systematic relationship between letters and sounds.

phonics readers Beginning reading books written with controlled vocabulary that contain recurring phonics elements.

phonograms Often called *word families*, phonograms end in high-frequency rimes that vary only in the beginning consonant sound to make a word. For example, *back*, *sack*, *black*, and *track* are phonograms with the rime *-ack*.

phonological awareness An awareness of various speech sounds such as syllables, rhyme, and individual phonemes.

picture sort A categorization task in which pictures are sorted into categories of similarity and difference. Pictures may be sorted by sound or by meaning. Pictures cannot be sorted by pattern.

prealphabetic readers/ phase Ehri's first phase of word recognition, in which children use nonalphabetic clues like word length or distinctive print to identify words. Also known as *logographic.*

preconsonantal nasals Nasals that occur before consonants, as in the words *bump* or *sink.* The vowel is nasalized as part of the air escapes through the nose during pronunciation. See also *nasals.*

predictable Text for beginning readers with repetitive language patterns, rhythm and rhyme, and illustrations that make it easy to read and remember.

prefix An affix attached at the beginning of a base word or word root that changes the meaning of the word.

prephonetic Writing that bears no correspondence to speech sounds; literally, "before sound." Prephonetic writing occurs during the emergent stage and typically consists of random scribbles, mock linear writing, or hieroglyphic-looking symbols.

pretend reading A paraphrase or spontaneous retelling told by children as they turn the pages of a familiar story book.

print referencing The practice of referring to features of print such as punctuation, capital letters, directionality, and so forth as a way to teach children concepts about print. See also *concepts about print (CAP).*

prosodic The musical qualities of language, including intonation, expression, stress, and rhythm.

reduced vowel A vowel occurring in an unstressed syllable. See also *schwa.*

rimes A rime unit is composed of the vowel and any following consonants within a syllable. For example, the rime unit in the word *tag* would be *ag.*

***r*-influenced (*r*-controlled) vowels** In English, *r* colors the way the preceding vowel is pronounced. For example, compare the pronunciation of the vowels in *bar* and *bad.* The vowel in *bar* is influenced by the *r.*

root word/roots Words or word parts, often of Latin or Greek origin, they are often combined with other roots to form words such as *telephone* (*tele* and *phone*). See also *stems.*

salient sounds A prominent sound in a word or syllable that stands out because of the way it is made or felt in the mouth, or because of idiosyncratic reasons such as being similar to a sound in one's name.

schwa A vowel sound in English that often occurs in an unstressed syllable, such as the /uh/ sound in the first syllable of the word *above.*

seatwork School work that is completed at the student's own desk. Seat work is usually on a student's independent level and is usually assigned for practice. See also *independent level.*

semiphonetic Writing that demonstrates *some* awareness that letters represent speech sounds. Literally, "part sound." Beginning and/or ending consonant sounds of syllables or words may be represented, but medial vowels are usually omitted (ICDD for *I see Daddy*). Semiphonetic writing occurs at the end of the emergent stage or the very outset of the early letter name–alphabetic stage.

shared reading An activity in which the teacher pre-reads a text and then invites students join in on subsequent readings.

short vowels Every vowel (*a, e, i, o,* and *u*) has two sounds, commonly referred to as "long" and "short." The vocal cords are more relaxed when producing the short vowel sound than the long vowel sound. Because of this, short vowel sounds are often referred to as *lax.* The five short vowels can be heard at the beginning of these words: *apple, Ed, igloo, octopus,* and *umbrella.* Compare to *long vowels.*

sight words/vocabulary Printed words stored in memory by the reader that can be read immediately, "at first sight," without having to use decoding strategies.

sound board Charts used by letter name–alphabetic spellers that contain pictures and letters for the basic sound–symbol correspondences (e.g., the letter *b*, a picture of a bell, and the word *bell*).

sound sort Sorts that ask students to categorize pictures or words by sound as opposed to visual patterns.

speed sorts Pictures or words that are sorted under a timed condition. Students try to beat their own time.

spelling-by-stage classroom organization chart A classroom composite sheet used to place children in a developmental spelling stage and form groups.

spelling inventories Assessments that ask students to spell a series of increasingly difficult words used to determine what features students know or use but confuse, as well as a specific developmental stage of spelling.

spelling–meaning connections Words that are related in meaning often share the same spelling despite changes in pronunciation from one form of the word to the next. The word *sign*, for example, retains the *g* from *signal* even though it is not pronounced, thus "signaling" the meaning connection through the spelling.

static reversal A handwriting error that is the mirror image of the intended letter (*b* for *d* or *p* for *d*).

stop consonants A consonant sound such as /b/ or /t/ that is formed by obstructing air at a given place of articulation; stop consonant sounds cannot be prolonged without distorting the sound.

structural analysis The process of determining the pronunciation and/or meaning of a word by analyzing word parts including syllables, base words, and affixes.

suffix An affix attached at the end of a base word or word root.

syllable juncture The transition from one syllable to the next. Sometimes this transition involves a spelling change such as consonant doubling or dropping the final *-e* before adding *ing*.

syllable juncture patterns The alternating patterns of consonants (C) and vowels (V) at the point where syllables meet. For example, the word *rabbit* follows a VCCV syllable pattern at the point where the syllables meet.

syllables Units of spoken language that consist of a vowel that may be preceded and/or followed by several consonants. Syllables are units of sound and can often be detected by paying attention to movements of the mouth. Syllabic divisions indicated in the dictionary are not always correct because the dictionary will always separate meaning units regardless of how the word is pronounced. For example, the proper syllable division for the word *naming* is *na-ming;* however, the dictionary divides this word as *nam-ing* to preserve the *ing*.

syllables and affixes stage The fourth stage of spelling development, which coincides with intermediate reading. Syllables and affixes spellers learn about the spelling changes that often take place at the point of transition from one syllable to the next. Frequently this transition involves consonant doubling or dropping the final *-e* before adding a suffix.

synchrony Occurring at the same time. In this book, stages of spelling development are described in the context of reading and writing behaviors occurring at the same time.

synthetic phonics Phonics instruction that begins with individual sounds and the blending of sounds to form words.

teacher-directed sorts An explicit word study lesson in which the teacher models and leads students through the sorting process, offers explanations, and facilitates a discussion about the features and the meaning of words.

tense A vowel sound that is commonly known as the long vowel sound. Long vowel sounds are produced by tensing the vocal cords.

tracking The ability to fingerpoint read a text, demonstrating concept of a word.

unaccented/unstressed syllable The syllable in a word that gets little emphasis and may have an indistinct vowel sound such as the first syllable in *about*, the second syllable in *definition*, or the final syllables in *doctor* or *table*. See also *schwa*.

unvoiced A sound that, when produced, does not necessitate the vibration of the vocal cords.

voiced A sound that, when produced, vibrates the vocal cords. The letter sound *d*, for example, vibrates the vocal cords in a way that the letter sound *t* does not. Compare to *unvoiced*.

vowel A speech sound produced by the easy passage of air through a relatively open vocal tract. Vowels form the most central sound of a syllable. In English, vowel sounds are represented by the following letters: *a*, *e*, *i*, *o*, *u*, and sometimes *y*. Compare to *consonants*.

vowel alternation The process in which the pronunciation of vowels changes in the base or root of derivationally related words, while the spelling does not change (e.g., the long-to-short vowel change in the related words *crime* and *criminal;* the long-to-schwa vowel change in the related words *impose* and *imposition*).

vowel digraphs A phonics term for pairs of vowels that represent a single vowel sound (such as *ai* in *rain*, *oa* in *boat*, *ue* in *blue*). Compare to *digraph*.

vowel marker A silent letter used to indicate the sound of the vowel. In English, silent letters are used to form patterns associated with specific vowel sounds. Vowel markers are usually vowels, as the *i* in *drain* or the *a* in *treat*, but they can also be consonants, as the *l* in *told*.

within word pattern spelling stage The third stage of spelling development, which coincides with the transitional period of literacy development. Within word pattern spellers have mastered the basic letter–sound correspondences of written English and they grapple with letter sequences that function as a unit, especially long-vowel patterns. Some of the letters in the unit may have no sound themselves. These silent letters, such as the silent *e* in *snake* or the silent *i* in *drain*, serve as important markers in the pattern.

word A unit of meaning. A word may be a single syllable or a combination of syllables. A word may contain smaller units of meaning within it. In print, a word is separated by white space. In speech, several words may be strung together in a breath group. For this reason, it takes a while for young children to develop a clear concept of word. See also *concept of word.*

word bank A collection of known words harvested from frequently read texts such as little leveled books, dictated stories, basal preprimers, and primers. Word bank words are written on small cards. These words, which students can recognize with ease, are used in word study games and word sorts.

word cards Words written on 2-by-1-inch pieces of cardstock or paper.

word consciousness An attitude of curiosity and attention to words critical for vocabulary development.

word families Phonograms or words that share the same rime. (For example, *fast, past, last,* and *blast* all share the *ast* rime.) In the derivational relations stage, *word families* refers to words that share the same root or origin, as in *spectator, spectacle, inspect,* and *inspector.* See *phonograms; rimes.*

word hunts A word study activity in which students go back to texts they have previously read to hunt for other words that follow the same spelling features examined during the word or picture sort.

word root See *root word/roots.*

word sort A basic word study routine in which students group words into categories. Word sorting involves comparing and contrasting within and across categories. Word sorts are often cued by key words placed at the top of each category.

word study A learner-centered, conceptual approach to instruction in phonics, spelling, word recognition, and vocabulary, based on a developmental model.

word study notebooks Notebooks in which students write their word sorts into columns and add other words that follow similar spelling patterns throughout the week. Word study notebooks may also contain lists of words generated over time, such as new vocabulary, homophones, cognates, and so on.

writing sorts An extension activity in which students write the words they have sorted into categories.

zone of proximal development (ZPD) A term coined by the Russian psychologist Vygotsky, referring to the ripe conditions for learning something new. A person's ZPD is that zone which is neither too hard nor too easy. The term is similar to the concept of *instructional level.*

References

Adams, M. J. (1990). *Beginning to read: Thinking and learning about print.* Cambridge, MA: MIT Press.

Adams, M. J., Foorman, B. R., Lundberg, L., & Beeler, T. (1998). The elusive phoneme: Why phoneme awareness is so important and how to help children develop it. *American Educator, 22,* 18–29.

Allen, R. V. (1976). *Language experiences in communication.* Boston: Houghton-Mifflin.

Allington, R. L. (1983). The reading instruction provided readers of differing abilities. *Elementary School Journal, 83,* 548–559.

Allington, R. L., & Cunningham, P. M. (2006). *Schools that work: Where all children read and write.* (3rd ed.). Boston: Allyn & Bacon.

Anders, P., & Bos, C. (1986). Semantic feature analysis: An interactive strategy for vocabulary development and text comprehension. *Journal of Reading, 29,* 610–616.

Aram, D., & Biron, S. (2004). Intervention programs among low SES Israeli preschoolers. The benefits of joint storybook reading and joint writing to early literacy. *Early Childhood Research Quarterly, 19,* 588–610.

Armbruster, B. B., Lehr, F., & Osborn, J. (2001). *Put reading first: The research building blocks for teaching children to read.* Washington, DC: The Partnership for Reading.

Ball, E. W., & Blachman, B. A. (1988). Phoneme segmentation training: Effect on reading readiness. *Annals of Dyslexia, 38,* 208–225.

Balmuth, M. (1992). *The roots of phonics: A historical introduction.* Austin, TX: Pro-Ed.

Baretta-Lorton, M. L. (1968). *Math their way.* Reading, MA: Addison-Wesley.

Barrentine, S. J. (1996). Engaging with reading through interactive read-alouds. *The Reading Teacher, 50,* 36–42.

Baumann, J. F., Edwards, E. C., Font, G., Tereshinski, C. A., Kame'enui, E. J., & Olejnik, S. (2003). Teaching morphemic and contextual analysis to fifth-grade students. *Reading Research Quarterly, 37*(2), 150–176.

Bear, D. (1982). *Patterns of oral reading across stages of word knowledge.* Unpublished manuscript, University of Virginia, Charlottesville.

Bear, D. (1989). Why beginning reading must be word-by-word. *Visible Language, 23*(4), 353–367.

Bear, D. (1991a). Copying fluency and orthographic development. *Visible Language, 25*(1), 40–53.

Bear, D. (1991b). "Learning to fasten the seat of my union suit without looking around": The synchrony of literacy development. *Theory into Practice, 30*(3), 149–157.

Bear, D. (1992). The prosody of oral reading and stage of word knowledge. In S. Templeton & D. Bear (Eds.), *Development of orthographic knowledge and the foundations of literacy: A memorial Festschrift for Edmund H. Henderson* (pp. 137–186). Hillsdale, NJ: Lawrence Erlbaum.

Bear, D., & Barone, D. (1989). Using children's spellings to group for word study and directed reading in the primary classroom. *Reading Pyschology, 10,* 275–292.

Bear, D., & Barone, D. (1998). *Developing literacy: An integrated approach to assessment and instruction.* Boston: Houghton Mifflin.

Bear, D. R., Caserta-Henry, C., & Venner, D. (2004). *Personal readers and literacy instruction with emergent and beginning readers.* Berkeley, CA: Teaching Resource Center.

Bear, D., & Cathey, S. (1989, November). *Reading fluency in beginning readers and expression in practiced oral reading: Links with word knowledge.* Paper presented at National Reading Conference, Austin, TX.

Bear, D. R., & Helman, L. (2004). Word study for vocabulary development: An ecological perspective on instruction during the early stages of literacy learning. In J. F. Baumann & E. J. Kame'enui (Eds.), *Vocabulary instruction: Research to practice* (pp. 139–158). New York: Guilford Press.

Bear, D., Helman, L., Invernizzi, M., Templeton, S., & Johnston, F. (2007). *Words their way with English learners.* Upper Saddle River, NJ: Merrill/Prentice Hall.

Bear, D. R., Helman, L. A., Templeton, S., Invernizzi, M. A., & Johnston, F. (2007). *Words their way with English learners: Word study for phonics, vocabulary, and spelling instruction.* Columbus, OH: Merrill/Prentice Hall.

Bear, D. R., Helman, L., & Woessner, L. (2009). Word study assessment and instruction with English learners in a second grade classroom: Bending with students' growth. In J. Coppola & E. V. Primas (Eds.), *One classroom, many learners: Best literacy practices for today's multilingual classrooms* (pp. 11–40). Newark, DE: International Reading Association.

Bear, D. R., Invernizzi, M., Johnston, F., & Templeton, S. (2010). *Words their way: Letter and picture sorts for emergent spellers* (2nd ed.). Boston: Allyn & Bacon.

Bear, D. R., & Smith, R. (2009). The literacy development of English learners: What do we know about each student's literacy development? In L. A. Helman (Ed.), *Literacy development and instruction of English learners* (pp. 87–116). New York: Guilford Press.

Bear, D., & Templeton, S. (1998). Explorations in developmental spelling: Foundations for learning and teaching phonics, spelling and vocabulary. *The Reading Teacher, 52,* 222–242.

Bear, D., Templeton, S., Helman, L., & Baren, T. (2003). Orthographic development and learning to read in different languages. In G. Garcia (Ed.), *English learners: Reaching the highest level of English literacy* (pp. 71–95). Newark, DE: International Reading Association.

Bear, D., Templeton, S., & Warner, M. (1991). The development of a qualitative inventory of higher levels of orthographic knowledge. In J. Zutell & S. McCormick (Eds.), *Learner factors/teacher factors: Issues in literacy research and instruction: Fortieth yearbook of the National Reading Conference* (pp. 105–110). Chicago: National Reading Conference.

Bear, D., Truex, P., & Barone, D. (1989). In search of meaningful diagnoses: Spelling-by-stage assessment of literacy proficiency. *Adult Literacy and Basic Education, 13*(3), 165–185.

Beck, I. L., McKeown, M. G., & Kucan, L. (2002). *Bringing words to life: Robust vocabulary instruction.* New York: Guilford Press.

Beck, I., McKeown, M., & Kucan, L. (2008). *Creating robust vocabulary: Frequently asked questions.* New York: Guilford.

Becker, W. C., Dixon, R., & Anderson-Inman, L. (1980). *Morphographic and root word analysis of 26,000 high frequency words.* Eugene, OR: University of Oregon Follow Through Project. (Technical Report 1980-1).

Beers, J. W., & Henderson, E. H. (1977). A study of developing orthographic concepts among first grade children. *Research in the Teaching of English, 11,* 133–148.

Berninger, V. W., Abbott, R. D., Nagy, W., & Carlisle, J. (2009). Growth in phonological, orthographic, and morphological awareness in grades 1 to 6. *Journal of Psycholinguistic Research, 39*(2), 141–163.

Berninger, V. W., Vaughn, K., Abbott, R. D., Brooks, A., Abbott, S. P., Rogan, L., Reed, E., & Graham, S. (1998). Early interventions for spelling problems: Teaching functional spelling units of varying size with a multiple-connections framework. *Journal of Educational Psychology, 90,* 587–605.

Biemiller, A. (1970). The development of the use of graphic and contextual information as children learn to read. *Reading Research Quarterly, 6,* 1, 75–96.

Biemiller, A. (2001). Teaching vocabulary: Early, direct, sequential. *American Educator, 25*(1), 24–28.

Biemiller, A. (2003). Vocabulary: Needed if more children are to read well. *Reading Psychology, 24*(3–4), 323–335.

Biemiller, A. (2004). Teaching vocabulary in the primary grades: Vocabulary instruction needed. In J. F. Baumann & E. J. Kame'enui (Eds.), *Vocabulary instruction: Research to practice* (pp. 28–40). New York: Guilford Press.

Biemiller, A. (2005). Size and sequence in vocabulary development: Implications for choosing words for primary grade vocabulary instruction. In E. H. Hiebert & M. L. Kamil (Eds.), *Teaching and learning vocabulary: Bringing research to practice* (pp. 223–242). Mahwah, NJ: Lawrence Erlbaum.

Biemiller, A., & Boote, C. (2006). An effective method for building vocabulary in primary grades. *Journal of Educational Psychology, 98*(1), 44–62.

Biemiller, A., & Slonim, N. (2001). Estimating root word vocabulary growth in normative and advantaged populations: Evidence for a common sequence of vocabulary acquisition. *Journal of Educational Psychology, 93,* 498–520.

Bissex, G. L. (1980). *Gnys at wrk: A child learns to read and write.* Cambridge, MA: Harvard University Press.

Blachman, B. A. (1994). What we have learned from longitudinal studies of phonological processing and reading, and some unanswered questions: A response to Torgeson, Wagner, and Rashotte. *Journal of Learning Disabilities, 27,* 287–291.

Blachowicz, C., & Fisher, P. J. (2009). *Teaching vocabulary in all classrooms* (4th ed.). Boston: Allyn & Bacon.

Blackwell-Bullock, R., Invernizzi, M., Drake, A. E., & Howell, J. L. (2009). A concept of word in text: An integral literacy skill. *Reading in Virginia, 31,* 30–35.

Bourassa, D. C., & Treiman, R. (2008). Morphological constancy in spelling: A comparison of children with dyslexia and typically developing children. *Dyslexia, 14,* 155–169.

Bowers, P. N., & Kirby, J. R. (2010). Effects of morphological instruction on vocabulary acquisition. *Reading and Writing: An Interdisciplinary Journal, 23*(5), 515–537.

Bravo, M. A., Hiebert, E. H., & Pearson, P. D. (2005). Tapping the linguistic resources of Spanish/English bilinguals: The role of cognates in science. In R. K. Wagner, A. E. Muse, & K. R. Tannenbaum (Eds.), *Vocabulary acquisition: Implications for reading comprehension* (pp. 140–156). New York: Guilford Press.

Brown, K. (2003). What do I say when they get stuck on a word?: Aligning teacher's prompts with student's level of development. *The Reading Teacher, 56,* 720–734.

Bryant, P., Nunes, T., & Bindman, M. (1997). Backward readers' awareness of language: Strengths and weaknesses. *European Journal of Psychology of Education, 12*(4), 357–372.

Button, K., Johnson, M. J., & Furgerson, P. (1996). Interactive writing in a primary classroom. *The Reading Teacher, 49,* 446–454.

Cantrell, R. J. (2001). Exploring the relationship between dialect and spelling for specific vocalic features in Appalachian first-grade children. *Linguistics and Education, 12*(1), 1–23.

Carey, S. (2001). On the very possibility of discontinuities in conceptual development. In E. Dupoux (Ed.), *Language, brain, and cognitive development: Essays in honor of Jacques Mehler* (pp. 303–324). Cambridge, MA: The MIT Press.

Carlisle, J. F. (2000). Awareness of the structure and meaning of morphologically complex words: Impact on reading. *Reading and Writing: An Interdisciplinary Journal, 12,* 169–190.

Carnine, D., Silbert, J., Kame'enui, E. J., & Tarver, S. G. (2009). *Direct instruction reading* (5th ed.). Upper Saddle River, NJ: Prentice Hall.

Cataldo, S., & Ellis, N. (1988). Interactions in the development of spelling, reading, and phonological skills. *Journal of Research in Reading, 11,* 86–109.

Cathey, S. S. (1991). *Emerging concept of word: Exploring young children's abilities to read rhythmic text.* Doctoral dissertation, University of Nevada, Reno, NV, UMI #9220355.

Chall, J. S. (1983). *Stages of reading development.* New York: McGraw-Hill.

Chliounaki, K., & Bryant, P. (2007). How children learn about morphological spelling rules. *Child Development, 78*(4), 1360–1373.

Chomsky, C. (1970). Reading, writing, and phonology. *Harvard Educational Review, 40*(2), 287–309.

Chomsky, C. (1971). Write first read later. *Childhood Education, 47,* 296–299.

Chomsky, N., & Halle, M. (1968). *The sound pattern of English.* New York: Harper & Row.

Clarke, L. K. (1988). Invented versus traditional spelling in first graders' writing: Effects on learning to spell and read. *Research in the Teaching of English, 22,* 281–309.

Clay, M. (1975). *What did I write?* Exeter, NH: Heinemann.

Clay, M. (2009). *An observation survey of early literacy achievement* (2nd ed). Portsmouth, NH: Heinemann.

Clay, M. M. (1991). Introducing a new storybook to young readers. *The Reading Teacher, 45,* 264–273.

Common Core State Standards for English Language Arts & Literacy in History/Social Studies, Science, and Technical Subjects.

(2010, March 10). Retrieved January 25, 2011, from www.corestandards.org/assets/CCSSI_ELA%20Standards.pdf

Conrad, N. J. (2008). From reading to spelling and spelling to reading: Transfer goes both ways. *Journal of Educational Psychology, 100*(4), 869–878.

Cunningham, A. E., & Stanovich, K. E. (2003). Reading matters: How reading engagement influences cognition. In J. Flood, D. Lapp, J. Squire, & J. Jensen (Eds.), *Handbook of research on teaching in the English language arts* (vol. 2, pp. 857–867). Mahwah, NJ: Lawrence Erlbaum.

Cunningham, P. (2005). *Phonics they use: Words for reading and writing* (4th ed.). Boston: Allyn & Bacon.

Cunningham, P. M. (2008). *Phonics they use* (5th ed.). Boston: Allyn & Bacon.

Dale, E., O'Rourke, J., & Bamman, H. (1971). *Techniques of teaching vocabulary.* Palo Alto, CA: Field Educational Publications.

Daniels, H. (2002). *Literature circles: Voice and choice in book clubs and reading groups.* Portland ME: Stenhouse Publishers.

Deacon, S. H., Conrad, N., & Pacton, S. (2008). Graphotactic and morphological regularities in spelling. *Canadian Psychology, 49*(2), 118–124.

Delpit, L. D. (1988). The silenced dialogue: Power and pedagogy in educating other people's children. *Harvard Educational Review, 58,* 280–298.

Diamond, L., & Gutlohn, L. (2006). *Vocabulary handbook.* Berkeley, CA: Consortium on Reading Excellence.

Diamond, L., & Gutlohn, L. (2007). *Vocabulary handbook.* Baltimore: Paul Brookes.

Dolch, E. W. (1942). *Better spelling.* Champaign, IL: The Garrard Press.

Dorr, R. E. (2006). Something old is new again: Revisiting language experience. *The Reading Teacher, 60*(2), 138–146.

Duffy, G. G. (2009). *Explaining reading: A resource for teaching concepts, skills and strategies* (2nd ed.). New York: Guilford Press.

Edwards, W. (2003). *Charting the orthographic knowledge of intermediate and advanced readers and the relationship between recognition and production of orthographic patterns.* Unpublished doctoral dissertation. University of Nevada, Reno, NV.

Ehri, L. (1992). Review and commentary: Stages of spelling development. In S. Templeton & D. Bear (Eds.), *Development of orthographic knowledge and the foundations of literacy: A memorial Festschrift for Edmund H. Henderson* (pp. 307–332). Hillsdale, NJ: Lawrence Erlbaum.

Ehri, L. C. (1997). Learning to read and learning to spell are one and the same, almost. In C. A. Perfetti, L. Rieben, & M. Fayol (Eds.), *Learning to spell: Research, theory, and practice across languages* (pp. 237–269). Mahwah, NJ: Lawrence Erlbaum.

Ehri, L. C. (1998). Grapheme-phoneme knowledge is essential for learning to read words in English. In J. L. Metsala & L. C. Ehri (Eds.), *Word recognition in beginning literacy* (pp. 3–40). Mahwah, NJ: Lawrence Erlbaum.

Ehri, L. C. (2000a). Learning to read and learning to spell: Two sides of a coin. *Topics in Language Disorders, 20,* 19–36.

Ehri, L. (2000b). Phases of acquisition in learning to read words and implications for teaching. *British Journal of Educational Psychology: Monograph Series, 1,* 7–28.

Ehri, L. C. (2005). Learning to read words: Theory, findings, and issues. *Scientific Studies of Reading, 9*(2), 167–188.

Ehri, L. C. (2006). Alphabetics instruction helps children learn to read. In R. M. Joshi & P. G. Aaron (Eds.), *Handbook of orthography and literacy* (pp. 649–678). Mahwah, NJ: Lawrence Erlbaum.

Ehri, L., & McCormick, S. (1998). Phases of word learning: Implications for instruction with delayed and disabled readers. *Reading and Writing Quarterly: Overcoming Learning Difficulties, 14,* 135–164.

Ehri, L., & McCormick, S. (2004). Phases of word learning: Implications for instruction with delayed and disabled readers. In R. B. Ruddell, M. R. Ruddell, & H. Singer (Eds.), *Theoretical models and processes of reading* (5th ed., pp. 365–389). Newark, DE: International Reading Assocation.

Ehri, L. C., & Roberts, T. (2006). The roots of learning to read and write: Acquisition of letters and phonemic awareness. In D. K. Dickinson & S. B. Neuman (Eds.), *Handbook of early literacy research* (vol. 2, pp. 113–131). New York: The Guilford Press.

Ehri, L. C., & Wilce, L. S. (1980). Do beginning readers learn to read function words better in sentences or lists? *Reading Research Quarterly, 15,* 675–685.

Elkonin, D. B. (1973). U.S.S.R. In J. Downing (Ed.), *Comparative reading.* New York: Macmillan.

Ellis, N., & Cataldo, S. (1992). Spelling is integral to learning to read. In C. M. Sterling & C. Robson (Eds.), *Psychology, spelling, and education* (pp. 112–142). Clevedon, UK: Multilingual Matters.

Estes, T., & Richards, H. (2002). Knowledge of orthographic features in Spanish among bilingual children. *Bilingual Research Journal, 26,* 295–307.

Farstrup, A. E., & Samuels, S. J. (Eds.). (2008). *What research has to say about vocabulary instruction.* Newark, DE: International Reading Association.

Fashola, O., Drum, P. A., Mayer, R.E., & Kang, S. J. (1996). A cognitive theory of orthographic transitioning: Predictable errors in how Spanish-speaking children spell English words. *American Educational Research Journal, 33,* 825–843.

Ferreiro, E., & Teberosky, A. (1982). *Literacy before schooling.* Portsmouth, NH: Heinemann.

Fisher, D., & Frey, N. (2008). Better learning through structured teaching: A framework for gradual release of responsibility. Alexandria, VA: Association for Supervision and Curriculum Development.

Flanigan, K. (2006). "Daddy, where did the words go?": How teachers can help emergent readers develop a concept of word in text. *Reading Improvement, 43*(1), 37–49.

Flanigan, K. (2007). A concept of word in text: A pivotal event in early reading acquisition. *Journal of Literacy Research, 39*(1), 37–70.

Flanigan, K., Hayes, L., Templeton, S., Bear, D. R., Invernizzi, M., & Johnston, F. (2011). *Words their way with struggling readers: Word study for reading, vocabulary, and spelling instruction, grades 4–12.* Boston: Allyn & Bacon.

Fresch, M. J., & Wheaton, A. F. (2004). *The spelling list and word study resource book.* New York: Scholastic.

Frith, U. (1985). Beneath the surface of developmental dyslexia. In K. Patterson, J. Marshall, & M. Coltheart (Eds.), *Surface dyslexia: Neuropsychological and cognitive studies of phonological reading* (pp. 301–330). London: Lawrence Erlbaum.

Fry, E. (1980). The new instant word list. *The reading teacher, 34*, 284–289.

Fry, E. B., & Kress, J. E. (2006). *The reading teacher's book of lists: K–12* (5th ed). San Francisco: Jossey-Bass

Fuchs, L. S., Fuchs, D., & Maxwell, L. (1988). The validity of informal reading comprehension measures. *Remedial & Special Education, 9*(2), 20–28.

Ganske, K. (1994). Developmental spelling analysis: A diagnostic measure for instruction and research (University of Virginia). *Dissertation Abstracts International, 55*(5), 1230A.

Ganske, K. (1999). The developmental spelling analysis: A measure of orthographic knowledge. *Educational Assessment, 6*, 41–70.

Gentry, J. (1980). Learning to spell developmentally. *Reading Teacher, 34*, 378–381.

Gibson, E. J. (1965). Learning to read. *Science, 148*, 1006–1072.

Gibson, J. J., & Yonas, P. M. (1968). A new theory of scribbling and drawing in children. In *The analysis of reading skill: A program of basic and applied research* (Final Report, Project No. 5-1213, Cornell University and the U.S. Office of Education, pp. 335–370). Ithaca, NY: Cornell University.

Gill, C. (1980). *An analysis of spelling errors in French.* Unpublished doctoral dissertation. University of Virginia.

Gill, C. H., & Scharer, P. L. (1996). Why do they get it on Friday and misspell it on Monday: Teachers inquiring about their students as spellers. *Language Arts, 73*, 89–96.

Gill, J., & Bear, D. (1988). No book, whole book, and chapter DR-TAs: Three study techniques. *Journal of Reading, 31*(5), 444–449.

Gillet, J. W., & Kita, M. J. (1979). Words, kids, and categories. *The Reading Teacher, 32*, 538–542.

Goswami, U. (1990). A special link between rhyming skill and the use of orthographic analogies by beginning readers. *Journal of Child Psychiatry, 31*, 301–311.

Goswami, U. (2008). Reading, complexity, and the brain. *Literacy, 42*(2), 67–74.

Goswami, U., & Mead, F. (1992). Onset and rhyme awareness and analogies in reading. *Reading Research Quarterly, 27*, 153–162.

Gough, P. B., & Hillinger, M. L. (1980). Learning to read: An unnatural act. *Bulletin of the Orton Society, 20*, 179–196.

Goulandris, N. K. (1992). Alphabetic spelling: Predicting eventual literacy attainment. In C. M. Sterling & C. Robson (Eds.), *Psychology, spelling, and education* (pp. 143–158). Clevedon, UK: Multilingual Matters.

Graham, S., Harris, K. R., & Chorzempa, B. F. (2002). Contribution of spelling instruction to the spelling, writing, and reading of poor spellers. *Journal of Educational Psychology, 94*, 669–686.

Graham, S., Harris, K. R., & Fink, B. (2000). Is handwriting causally related to learning to write? Treatment of handwriting problems in beginning writers. *Journal of Educational Psychology, 92*(4), 620–633.

Graham, S., Morphy, P., Harris, K. R., Fink-Chorzempa, B., Saddler, B., Moran, S., & Mason, L. (2008). Teaching spelling in the primary grades: A national survey of instructional practices and adaptations. *American Education Research Journal, 45*(3), 796–825.

Green, T. M. (2008). *The Greek and Latin roots of English* (4th ed). Lanham, MD: Rowman & Littlefield Publishers.

Hall, M. (1980). *Teaching reading as a language experience.* Columbus, OH: Merrill.

Hanna, P. R., Hanna, J. S., Hodges, R. E., & Rudorf, H. (1966). Phoneme-grapheme correspondences as cues to spelling improvement. Washington, DC: United States Office of Education Cooperative Research.

Harré, R., & Moghaddam, F. (Eds.). (2003). *The self and others: Positioning individuals and groups in personal, political, and cultural contexts.* Westport, CT: Praeger.

Harste, J. C., Woodward, V. A., & Burke, C. L. (1984). *Language stories and literacy lessons.* Portsmouth, NH: Heinemann.

Hart, B., & Risley, T. R. (1995). *Meaningful differences in the everyday experience of American children.* Baltimore: Paul C. Brookes.

Hasbrouck, J. E., & Tindal, G. (1992). Curriculum-based oral reading fluency norms for students in grades 2–5. *Teaching Exceptional Children, 24*(3), 41–44.

Hayes, D., & Ahrens, M. (1988). Vocabulary simplification for children: A special case of 'motherese'? *Journal of Child Language, 15*, 395–410.

He, T-h., & Wang, W-l. (2009). Invented spelling of EFL young beginning writers and its relation with phonological awareness and grapheme-phoneme principles. *Journal of Second Language Writing, 18*(1), 44–56.

Helman, L. (2004). Building on the sound system of Spanish. *The Reading Teacher, 57*, 452–460.

Helman, L. A. (Ed.). (2009). *Literacy development with English learners: Research-based instruction in grades K–6.* New York: Guilford Press.

Helman, L. A., & Bear, D. R. (2007). Does an established model of orthographic development hold true for English learners? In D. W. Rowe, R. Jimenez, D. L. Compton, D. K. Dickinson, Y. Kim, K. M. Leander, & V. J. Risko (Eds.), *56th Yearbook of the National Reading Conference* (pp. 266–280).

Helman, L., Bear, D. R., Invernizzi, M., Templeton, S., & Johnston, F. (2009). *Words their way: Emergent sorts for Spanish-speaking English learners.* Boston: Allyn & Bacon.

Helman, L. A., Bear, D. R., Templeton, S., Invernizzi, M., & Johnston, F. (2012). *Words their way with English learners* (2nd ed.). Boston: Pearson/Allyn & Bacon.

Henderson, E. H. (1981). *Learning to read and spell: The child's knowledge of words.* DeKalb: Northern Illinois Press.

Henderson, E. H. (1985). *Teaching spelling.* Boston: Houghton Mifflin.

Henderson, E. H. (1990). *Teaching spelling* (2nd ed.). Boston: Houghton Mifflin.

Henderson, E. H. (1992). The interface of lexical competence and knowledge of written words. In S. Templeton & D. R. Bear (Eds.), *Development of orthographic knowledge and the foundations of literacy: A memorial Festschrift for Edmund H. Henderson* (pp. 1–30). Hillsdale, NJ: Lawrence Erlbaum.

Henderson, E. H., & Beers, J. (Eds.). (1980). *Developmental and cognitive aspects of learning to spell.* Newark, DE: International Reading Association.

Henderson, E. H., Estes, T., & Stonecash, S. (1972). An exploratory study of word acquisition among first graders at midyear in a language experience approach. *Journal of Reading Behavior, 4*, 21–30.

Henderson, E. H., & Templeton, S. (1986). The development of spelling ability through alphabet, pattern, and meaning. *Elementary School Journal, 86*, 305–316.

Henry, M. (1988). Beyond phonics: Integrated decoding and spelling instruction based on word origin and structures. *Annals of Dyslexia, 38*, 258–275.

Henry, M. (1993). Morphological structure: Latin and Greek roots & affixes as upper grade code strategies. *Journal of Reading & Writing, 5*, 227–241.

Henry, M. (2003). *Unlocking literacy: Effective decoding and spelling instruction.* Baltimore: Paul H. Brookes.

Hiebert, E. H. (2005). In pursuit of an effective, efficient vocabulary curriculum for elementary students. In E. H. Hiebert & M. L. Kamil (Eds.), *Teaching and learning vocabulary: Bringing research to practice* (pp. 243–263). Mahwah, NJ: Lawrence Erlbaum.

Hiebert, E. H., & Bravo, M. (2010). Morphological knowledge and learning to read in English. In D. Wyse, R. Andrews, & J. Hoffman (Eds.), *The Routledge international handbook of English, language and literacy teaching* (pp. 87–97). London: Routledge.

Holdaway, D. (1979). *The foundations of literacy.* Portsmouth, NH: Heinemann.

Holmes, V. M., & Davis, C. W. (2002). Orthographic representation and spelling knowledge. *Language and Cognitive Processes, 17*, 345–370.

Horn, E. (1954). *Teaching spelling.* Washington, DC: National Education Association.

Invernizzi, M. (1985). *A cross-sectional analysis of children's recognition and recall of word elements.* Unpublished manuscript, University of Virginia, Charlottesville.

Invernizzi, M. (1992). The vowel and what follows: A phonological frame of orthographic analysis. In S. Templeton & D. Bear (Eds.), *Development of orthographic knowledge and the foundations of literacy: A memorial Festschrift for Edmund H. Henderson* (pp. 106–136). Hillsdale, NJ: Lawrence Erlbaum.

Invernizzi, M. (2002). Concepts, sounds, and the ABCs: A diet for a very young reader. In D. M. Barone & L. M. Morrow (Eds.), *Literacy and young children* (pp. 140–157). New York: Guilford Press.

Invernizzi, M. (2005, May). *The history and technical adequacy of qualitative spelling inventories.* Presentation for the Special Interest Group on English Orthography. International Reading Association (IRA), San Antonio, TX.

Invernizzi, M. (2009). Virginia's Early Intervention Reading Initiative (EIRI) and Response to Intervention (RtI). *Reading in Virginia*, 36–39.

Invernizzi, M., Abouzeid, M., & Gill, T. (1994). Using students' invented spellings as a guide for spelling instruction that emphasizes word study. *Elementary School Journal, 95*(2), 155–167.

Invernizzi, M., & Hayes, L. (2004). Developmental-spelling research: A systematic imperative. *Reading Research Quarterly, 39*, 2–15.

Invernizzi, M., & Hayes, L. (2010). Word recognition. In D. Allington & A. McGill-Franzen (Eds.), *Handbook of reading disabilities.* Newark, DE: International Reading Association.

Invernizzi, M., Juel, C., Swank, L., & Meier, J. (2006). *Phonological Awareness Literacy Screening for Kindergartners* (PALS-K). Charlottesville, VA: University Printing Services.

Invernizzi, M., Juel, C., Swank, L., & Meier, J. (2008). *Phonological Awareness Literacy Screening–Kindergarten (PALS-K): Technical Reference.* Charlottesville, VA: University of Virginia.

Invernizzi, M., Justice, L., Landrum, T., & Booker, K. (Winter, 2005). Early literacy screening in kindergarten: Widespread implementation in Virginia. *Journal of Literacy Research, 36*, 479–500.

Invernizzi, M., Meier, J., & Juel, C. (2003). *PALS 1–3 Phonological Awareness Literacy Screening* (4th ed.). Charlottesville, VA: University Printing Services.

Invernizzi, M., & Worthy, J. W. (1989). An orthographic-specific comparison of the spelling errors of LD and normal children across four levels of spelling achievement. *Reading Psychology, 10*, 173–188.

James, W. (1958). *Talks to teachers on psychology and to students on some of life's ideals.* New York: Norton. (Original work published 1899.)

Johnston, F. R. (1998). The reader, the text, and the task: Learning words in first grade. *The Reading Teacher, 51*, 666–675.

Johnston, F. R. (2000). Word learning in predictable text. *Journal of Education Psychology, 92*, 248–255.

Johnston, F. R. (2001). The utility of phonic generalizations: Let's take another look at Clymer's conclusions. *The Reading Teacher, 55*, 132–143.

Johnston, F. R. (2003, December). *The Primary Spelling Inventory: Exploring its validity and relationship to reading levels.* Paper presented at the National Reading Conference, Scottsdale, AZ.

Johnston, F. R., Invernizzi, M., & Juel, C. (1998). *Book buddies: Guidelines for volunteer tutors of emergent and beginning readers.* New York: Guilford Press.

Johnston, F., Invernizzi, M., Bear, D. R., & Templeton, S. (2009). *Words their way: Word sorts for syllables and affixes spellers.* Boston: Pearson/Allyn & Bacon.

Johnston, F., Invernizzi, M., Juel, C., & Lewis-Wagner, D. (2009). *Book buddies: A tutoring framework for struggling readers.* New York: Guilford Press.

Joseph, L. M. (2002). Facilitating word recognition and spelling using word boxes and word sort phonic procedures. *School Psychology Review, 3*, 122–129.

Joseph, L. M., & Schisler, R. (2009). Should adolescents go back to the basics? A review of teaching word reading skills to middle and high school students. *Remedial and Special Education, 30*(3), 131–147.

Juel, C. (1991). Beginning reading. In R. Barr, M. Kamil, P. Mosenthal, & P. D. Pearson (Eds.), *Handbook of reading research* (vol. II, pp. 759–788). New York: Longman Press.

Juel, C., Biancarosa, G., Coker, D., & Deffes, R. (2003). Walking with Rosie: A cautionary tale of literacy instruction. *Educational Leadership, 60*(7), 12–18.

Juel, C., & Deffes, R. (2004, March). Making words stick. *Educational Leadership, 61*(6), 30–34.

Juel, C., & Minden-Cupp, C. (2000). Learning to read words: Linguistic units and instructional strategies. *Reading Research Quarterly, 35*, 458–492.

Juel, C., & Roper-Schneider, D. (1985). The influence of basal readers on first grade reading. *Reading Research Quarterly, 18*, 306–327.

Justice, L. M. (2006). *Communication sciences and disorders: An introduction.* Upper Saddle River, NJ: Pearson/Merrill/Prentice Hall.

Justice, L. M., & Ezell, H. K. (2004). Print referencing: An emergent literacy enhancement technique and its clinical applications. *Language, Speech, and Hearing Services in Schools, 35*, 185–193.

Justice, L. M., Invernizzi, M., Geller, K., Sullivan, A. K., & Welsch, J. (2005). Descriptive-developmental performance of at-risk preschoolers in early literacy. *Reading Psychology, 26*(1), 1–25.

Justice, L. M., Kaderavek, J. N., Fan, X., Sofka, A., & Hunt, A. (2009). Accelerating preschoolers early literacy development through classroom-based teacher child story book reading and explicit print referencing. *Language, Speech, & Hearing Services in Schools, 40*, 67–85.

Justice, L. M., & Pullen, P. (2003). Promising interventions for promoting emergent literacy skills: Three evidence-based approaches. *Topics in Early Childhood Special Education, 23*, 99–113.

Justice, L. M., & Sofka, A. E. (2010). *Engaging children with print: Building early literacy skills through quality read alouds.* New York: Guilford Press.

Kaderavek, J. N., & Justice, L. M. (2004). Embedded-explicit emergent literacy: Goal selection and implementation in the early childhood classroom. *Language, Speech, and Hearing Services in Schools, 35*, 212–228.

Kim, Y., Petscher, Y., Foorman, B., & Zhou, C. (2010). The contributions of phonological awareness and letter name knowledge to letter-sound acquisition—a cross-classified multilevel model approach. *Journal of Educational Psychology,* 102, 313–326.

Kirk, C., & Gillon, G. T. (2009). Integrated morphological awareness intervention as a tool for improving literacy. *Language, Speech, and Hearing Services in Schools, 40*(2), 341–351.

Lane, H. B., & Allen, S. A. (2010). The vocabulary-rich classroom: Modeling sophisticated word use to promote word consciousness and vocabulary growth. *The Reading Teacher, 63*(5), 362–370.

Leong, C. K. (2000). Rapid processing of base and derived forms of words and grades 4, 5, and 6 children's spelling. *Reading and Writing: An Interdisciplinary Journal, 12*, 277–302.

Liberman, I., & Shankweiler, D. (1991). Phonology and beginning reading: A tutorial. In L. Rieben & C. Perfetti (Eds.), *Learning to read: Basic research and its implication.* Hillsdale, NJ: Lawrence Erlbaum.

Lubliner, S., & Scott, J. (2008). *Nourishing vocabulary: Balancing words and learning.* Thousand Oaks, CA: Corwin Press.

Lundberg, I., Frost, J., & Peterson, O. (1988). Effects of an extensive program for stimulating phonological awareness in preschool children. *Reading Research Quarterly, 23*, 267–284.

Mahony, D., Singson, M., & Mann, V. (2000). Reading ability and sensitivity to morphological relations. *Reading and Writing: An Interdisciplinary Journal, 12*, 191–218.

Malinowski, B. (1952). The problem of meaning in primitive languages. In C. K. Ogden & I. A. Richards (Eds.), *The meaning of meaning* (10th ed.). New York: Harcourt.

Markman, E. M., & Hutchinson, J. E. (1988). Children's sensitivity to constraints on word meaning: Taxonomic versus thematic relations. In M. B. Franklin & S. S. Barten (Eds.), *Child language: A reader* (pp. 137–157). New York: Oxford University Press.

Marzano, R. J. (1992). *A different kind of classroom: Teaching with dimensions of learning.* Alexandria, VA: ASCD.

Mashburn, A. J., Justice, L. M., Downer, J. T., & Pianta, R. C. (2009). Peer effects on children's language achievement during pre-kindergarten. *Child Development, 80*(3), 686–702.

Massengill, D. (2006). Mission accomplished . . . It's learnable now: Voices of mature challenged spellers using a Word Study approach. *Journal of Adolescent and Adult Literacy, 49*(5), 420–431.

Mathews, M. (1967). *Teaching to read: Historically considered.* Chicago: University of Chicago Press.

McCabe, A. (1996). *Chameleon readers: All kinds of good stories.* New York: Webster/McGraw-Hill.

McCandliss, B., Beck, I., Sandak, R., & Perfetti, C. (2003). Focusing attention on decoding for children with poor reading skills: Design and preliminary tests of the word building intervention. *Scientific Studies of Reading, 7*, 75–103.

McCarrier, A., Pinnell, G. S., & Fountas, I. C. (2000). *Interactive writing: How language & literacy come together, K–2.* Portsmouth, NH: Heinemann.

McCracken, M. J., & McCracken, R. A. (1995). *Reading, writing, and language* (2nd ed.). Winnipeg, Canada: Peguis.

McKenna, M. C., & Picard, M. C. (2006). Revisiting the role of miscue analysis in effective teaching. *Reading Teacher, 60*(4), 378–380.

McKenzie, M. G. (1985). Shared writing: Apprenticeship in writing. *Language Matters, 1–2*, 1–5.

Mesmer, H. A. E. (2006). Text decodability and the first-grade reader. *Reading & Writing Quarterly, 21*, 61–86.

Moats, L. (2000). *Speech to print: Language essentials for teachers.* Baltimore: Paul H. Brookes.

Moloney, K. (2008). *"I'm not a big word fan": An exploratory study of ninth-graders' language use in the context of word consciousness-oriented vocabulary instruction.* Unpublished doctoral dissertation, University of Nevada, Reno.

Morais, J., Cary, L., Alegria, J., & Bertelson, P. (1979). Does awareness of speech as a sequence of phonemes arise spontaneously? *Cognition, 7*, 323–331.

Morgan, R. K., & Meier, C. R. (2008). Dialogic reading's potential to improve children's emergent literacy skills and behavior. *Preventing School Failure, 52*, 11–16.

Morris, D. (1980). Beginning readers' concept of word. In E. Henderson & J. Beers (Eds.), *Developmental and cognitive aspects of learning to spell* (pp. 97–111). Newark, DE: International Reading Association.

Morris, D. (1981). Concept of word: A developmental phenomenon in the beginning reading and writing process. *Language Arts, 58*(6), 659–668.

Morris, D. (1982). "Word sort": A categorization strategy for improving word recognition ability. *Reading Psychology, 3*, 247–259.

Morris, D. (1993). The relationship between children's concept of word in text and phoneme awareness in learning to read: A longitudinal study. *Research in the Teaching of English, 27*(2), 133–154.

Morris, D. (1999). *The Howard Street tutoring manual.* New York: Guilford Press.

Morris, D. (2008). *Diagnosis and correction of reading problems.* New York: Guilford Press.

Morris, D., Blanton, L., Blanton, W. E., Nowacek, J., & Perney, J. (1995). Teaching low achieving spellers at their "instructional level." *Elementary School Journal, 92*, 163–177.

Morris, D., Blanton, L., Blanton, W., & Perney, J. (1995). Spelling instruction and achievement in six elementary classrooms. *The Elementary School Journal, 96*, 145–162.

Morris, D., Bloodgood, J. W., Lomax, R. G., & Perney, J. (2003). Developmental steps in learning to read: A longitudinal study in kindergarten and first grade. *Reading Research Quarterly, 38*, 302–328.

Morris, D., Nelson, L., & Perney, J. (1986). Exploring the concept of "spelling instructional level" through the analysis of error-types. *Elementary School Journal, 87*, 181–200.

Morris, D., & Perney, J. (1984). Developmental spelling as a predictor of first-grade reading achievement. *Elementary School Journal, 84*, 441–457.

Murray, B. A. (1998). Gaining alphabetic insight: Is phonemic manipulation skill or identity knowledge causal? *Journal of Educational Psychology, 90*, 461–475.

Nagy, W. (2007). Metalinguistic awareness and the vocabulary-comprehension connection. In R. K. Wagner, A. E. Muse, & K. R. Tannenbaum (Eds.), *Vocabulary acquisition: Implications for reading comprehension* (pp. 52–78). New York: Guilford Press.

Nagy, W., & Anderson, R. C. (1984). How many words are there in printed school English? *Reading Research Quarterly, 19*, 304–330.

Nagy, W., Berninger, V., Abbott, R., Vaughan, K., & Vermeulen, K. (2003). Relationship of morphology and other language skills to literacy skills in at-risk second-grade readers and at-risk fourth-grade writers. *Journal of Educational Psychology, 95*(4), 730–742.

Nagy, W., Berninger, V. W., & Abbott, R. D. (2006). Contributions of morphology beyond phonology to literacy outcomes of upper elementary and middle-school students. *Journal of Educational Psychology, 98*, 134–147.

Nash, R. (1997). *NTC's dictionary of Spanish cognates thematically organized.* Chicago: NTC Publishing Group.

Nathenson-Mejia, S. (1989). Writing in a second language: Negotiating meaning through invented spelling. *Language Arts, 66*, 515–526.

National Early Literacy Panel. (2008). *Report on a synthesis of early predictors of reading.* Louisville, KY: National Institute of Family Literacy.

National Reading Panel (NRP). (2000). *Teaching children to read: An evidence-based assessment of the scientific research literature on reading and its implications for reading instruction.* Washington, DC: National Institute of Child Health and Human Development.

Nessel, D., & Jones, M. (1981). *The language-experience approach to reading.* New York: Teachers College Press.

Nilsen, A. J., & Nilsen, D. L. F. (2004). *Vocabulary plus high school and up: A source-based approach.* Boston: Allyn & Bacon.

Nunes, T., & Bryant, P. (2006). *Improving literacy by teaching morphemes.* London: Routledge.

Nunes, T., & Bryant, P. (2009). *Children's reading and spelling: Beyond the first steps.* London: Wiley-Blackwell.

O'Connor, R. (2007). *Teaching word recognition: Effective strategies for students with learning difficulties.* New York: Guilford Press.

Ouellette, G. P., & Sénéchal, M. (2008). A window into early literacy: Exploring the cognitive and linguistic underpinnings of invented spelling. *Scientific Studies of Reading, 12*(2), 195–219.

Pearson, P. D., Hiebert, E. H., & Kamil, M. (2007). Vocabulary assessment: What we know and what we need to learn. *Reading Research Quarterly, 42*(2), 282–296.

Pense, K. L., & Justice, L. M. (2008). *Language development from theory to practice.* Upper Saddle River, NJ: Pearson/Merrill/Prentice Hall.

Perfetti, C., Beck, I., Bell, L., & Hughes, C. (1987). Phonemic knowledge and learning to read are reciprocal. *Merrill-Palmer Quarterly, 33*, 283–319.

Perfetti, C. A. (1997). The psycholinguistics of spelling and reading. In C. A. Perfetti, L. Rieben, & M. Fayol (Eds.), *Learning to spell: Research, theory, and practice across languages* (pp. 21–38). Mawah, NJ: Lawrence Erlbaum.

Phenix, J. (1996). *The spelling teacher's book of lists.* Ontario: Pembroke.

Pressley, M. (2006). *Reading instruction that works: The case for balanced teaching* (3rd ed.). New York: Guilford Press.

Proctor, C. P., August, D., Carlo, M. S., & Snow, C. (2006). The intriguing role of Spanish language vocabulary knowledge in predicting English reading comprehension. *Journal of Educational Psychology, 98*, 159–169.

Pufpaff, L. (2009). A developmental continuum of phonological sensitivity skills. *Psychology in the Schools, 46*(7), 679–691.

Pullen, P. C., & Justice, L. M. (2003). Enhancing phonological awareness, print awareness, & oral language skills in preschool children. *Intervention in School & Clinic, 39*(2), 87–98.

Purcell, T. (2002). *Linguistic influences on letter sound learning: Considering manner, place, and voicing.* Unpublished Doctoral Dissertation. University of Virginia, Charlottesville.

Purcell-Gates, V., Jacobson, E., & Degener, S. (2004). *Print literacy development: Uniting cognitive and social practice theories.* Cambridge, MA: Harvard University Press.

Raphael, T. E., Pardo, L. S., Highfield, K., & McMahon, S. I. (1997). *Book club: A literature-based curriculum.* Littleton, MA: Small Planet Communications.

Rasinski, T. V. (2008). *The fluent reader: Oral reading strategies for building word recognition, fluency, and comprehension.* New York: Scholastic.

Rasinski, T. (2010). *The fluent reader: Oral and silent reading strategies for building word recognition, fluency, and comprehension* (2nd ed.). New York: Scholastic.

Rastle, K., & Davis, M. H. (2008). Morphological decomposition based on the analysis of orthography. *Language and Cognitive Processes, 23*(7/8), 942–971.

Rayner, K., Foorman, B. R., Perfetti, C. A., Pesetsky, D., & Seidenburg, M. S. (2001). How psychological science informs the teaching of reading. *Psychological Science in the Public Interest, 2,* 31–74.

Read, C. (1971). Pre-school children's knowledge of English phonology. *Harvard Educational Review, 41*(1), 1–34.

Read, C. (1975). *Children's categorization of speech sounds in English.* Urbana, IL: NCTE Research Report No. 17.

Reed, D. K. (2008). A synthesis of morphology interventions and effects on reading outcomes for students in grades K–12. *Learning Disabilities Research & Practice, 23*(1), 36–49.

Richgels, D. J. (1995). Invented spelling ability and printed word learning in kindergarten. *Reading Research Quarterly, 30,* 96–109.

Richgels, D. J. (2001). Invented spelling, phonemic awareness, and reading and writing instruction. In S. B. Neuman & D. K. Dickenson (Eds.), *Handbook of early literacy research* (pp. 142–155). New York: Guilford Press.

Richgels, D. J., & McGee, L. (2007). *Literacy's beginnings: Supporting young readers and writers* (5th ed.). Allyn & Bacon.

Robb, L. (1999). *Easy mini-lessons for building vocabulary.* New York: Scholastic.

Roberts, B. S. (1992). The evolution of the young child's concept of word as a unit of spoken and written language. *Reading Research Quarterly, 27*(2), 125–138.

Rosenthal, J., & Ehri, L. (2008). The mnemonic value of orthography for vocabulary learning. *Journal of Educational Psychology, 100*(1), 175–191. Retrieved from Education Abstracts (H. W. Wilson) database.

Samuels, S. (1979). The method of repeated readings. *The Reading Teacher, 32,* 403–408.

Samuels, S. J. (1988). Decoding and automaticity: Helping poor readers become automatic at word recognition. *The Reading Teacher, 41,* 756–760.

Sawyer, D. J., Lipa-Wade, S., Kim, J., Ritenour, D., & Knight, D. F. (1997). *Spelling errors as a window on dyslexia.* Paper presented at the 1997 annual convention of the American Educational Research Association, Chicago.

Sawyer, D. J., Wade, S., & Kim, J. K. (1999). Spelling errors as a window on variations in phonological deficits among students with dyslexia. *Annals of Dyslexia, 49,* 137–159.

Schlagal, B. (2007). Best practices in spelling and handwriting. In S. Graham & C. MacArthur (Eds.), *Best practices in writing* (pp. 179–201). New York: Guilford Press.

Schlagal, R. (1989). Constancy and change in spelling development. *Reading Psychology, 10,* 207–232.

Schlagal, R. (1992). Patterns of orthographic development into the intermediate grades. In S. Templeton & D. Bear (Eds.), *Development of orthographic knowledge and the foundations of literacy: A memorial Festschrift for Edmund H. Henderson* (pp. 31–52). Hillsdale, NJ: Lawrence Erlbaum.

Schlagal, R. (2002). Classroom spelling instruction: History, research, and practice. *Reading Research and Instruction, 42,* 44–57.

Scott, J. A., Skobel, B. J., & Wells, J. (2008). *The word-conscious classroom: Building the vocabulary readers and writers need.* New York: Scholastic.

Sharp, A. C., Sinatra, G. M., & Reynolds, R. E. (2008). The development of children's orthographic knowledge: A microgenetic perspective. *Reading Research Quarterly, 43*(3), 206–226.

Shen, H., & Bear, D. R. (2000). The development of orthographic skills in Chinese children. *Reading and Writing: An Interdisciplinary Journal, 13,* 197–236.

Smith, M. L. (1998). Sense and sensitivity: An investigation into fifth-grade children's knowledge of English derivational morphology and its relationship to vocabulary and reading ability. University Microfilms No. AAM9830072. *Dissertation Abstracts International, 59* (4-A), 1111.

Smith, N. B. (2002). *American reading instruction* (special edition). Newark, DE: International Reading Association.

Smith, S. B., Simmons, D. C., & Kame'enui, E. J. (1995). *Synthesis of research on phonological awareness: Principles and implications for reading acquisition* (Tech. Rep. No. 21). Eugene, OR: University of Oregon, National Center to Improve the Tools of Educators.

Snow, C. E. (1983). Literacy and language: Relationships during the preschool years. *Harvard Educational Review, 53*(2), 165–189.

Snow, C. E., Burns, M. S., & Griffin, P. (Eds.). (1998). *Preventing reading difficulties in young children.* Washington, DC: National Academy Press.

Snowling, M. (1994). Towards a model of spelling acquisition: The development of some component skills. In G. D. A. Brown & N. C. Ellis (Eds.), *Handbook of spelling: Theory, process, and intervention* (pp. 111–128). Chichester, UK: John Wiley.

Spear-Swerling, L., & Sternberg, R. J. (Contributor) (1997). *Off track: When poor readers become "learning disabled."* Boulder, CO: Westview Press.

Stahl, S. A., & McKenna, M. C. (2001, August). The concurrent development of phonological awareness, word recognition, and spelling. CIERA Technical Report No. 01-07. Retrieved January 25, 2011, from www.ciera.org/library/archive/2001-07/200107.pdf

Stahl, S. A., & Nagy, W. E. (2006). *Teaching word meanings.* Mahwah, NJ: Lawrence Erlbaum.

Stanovich, K. (1986). Matthew effects in reading: Some consequences of individual differences in the acquisition of literacy. *Reading Research Quarterly, 21,* 360–406.

Stauffer, R. (1980). *The language-experience approach to the teaching of reading* (2nd ed.). New York: Harper & Row.

Steffler, D. J. (2001). Implicit cognition and spelling development. *Developmental Review, 21,* 168–204.

Sterbinsky, A. (2007). *Words their way spelling inventories: Reliability and validity analyses.* Memphis, TN: University of Memphis Center for Research in Educational Policy.

Strickland, D., & Morrow, L. (1989). Environments rich in print promote literacy behavior during play. *Reading Teacher, 43,* 178–179.

Sulzby, E. (1986). Writing and reading organization. In W. H. Teale & E. Sulzby (Eds.), *Emergent literacy: Writing and reading* (pp. 50–89). Norwood, NJ: Abex.

Swan, M., & Smith, B. (2001). *Learner English: A teacher's guide to interference and other problems* (2nd ed.). New York: Cambridge University Press.

Swank, L. (1991). A two-level hypothesis of phonological awareness (Doctoral dissertation, University of Kansas). *Dissertation Abstracts International,* 53-08A (2754).

Taft, M. (1991). *Reading and the mental lexicon.* London: Lawrence Erlbaum.

Taft, M. (2003). Morphological representation as a correlation between form and meaning. In E. G. H. Assink & D. Sandra (Eds.), *Reading complex words: Cross language studies* (pp. 113–137). New York: Kluwer Academic.

Temple, C. S. (1978). *An analysis of spelling errors in Spanish.* Unpublished doctoral dissertation, University of Virginia.

Templeton, S. (1979). Spelling first, sound later: The relationship between orthography and higher order phonological knowledge in older students. *Research in the Teaching of English, 13,* 255–264.

Templeton, S. (1980). Logic and mnemonics for demons and curiosities: Spelling awareness for middle- and secondary-level students. *Reading World, 20,* 123–130.

Templeton, S. (1983). Using the spelling/meaning connection to develop word knowledge in older students. *Journal of Reading, 27*(1), 8–14.

Templeton, S. (1989). Tacit and explicit knowledge of derivational morphology: Foundations for a unified approach to spelling and vocabulary development in the intermediate grades and beyond. *Reading Psychology, 10,* 233–253.

Templeton, S. (1991). Teaching and learning the English spelling system: Reconceptualizing method and purpose. *Elementary School Journal, 92,* 183–199.

Templeton, S. (1992). Theory, nature, and pedagogy of higher-order orthographic development in older children. In S. Templeton & D. Bear (Eds.), *Development of orthographic knowledge and the foundations of literacy: A memorial Festschrift for Edmund H. Henderson* (pp. 253–278), Hillsdale, NJ: Lawrence Erlbaum.

Templeton, S. (1996). *Children's literacy: Contexts for meaningful learning.* Boston: Houghton Mifflin.

Templeton, S. (1997). *Teaching the integrated language arts* (2nd ed.). Boston: Houghton Mifflin.

Templeton, S. (2002). Effective spelling instruction in the middle grades: It's a lot more than memorization. *Voices from the Middle, 9*(3), 8–14.

Templeton, S. (2003). Spelling. In J. Flood, D. Lapp, J. R. Squire, & J. M. Jensen (Eds.), *Handbook of research on teaching the English language arts* (2nd ed., pp. 738–751). Mahwah, NJ: Lawrence Erlbaum.

Templeton, S. (2004). The vocabulary-spelling connection: Orthographic development and morphological knowledge at the intermediate grades and beyond. In J. F. Baumann & E. J. Kame'enui (Eds.), *Vocabulary instruction: Research to practice* (pp. 118–138). New York: Guilford Press.

Templeton, S. (2010). Spelling–meaning relationships among languages: Exploring cognates and their possibilities. In L. Helman (Ed.), *Literacy development with English learners: Research-based instruction in Grades K–6* (pp. 196–212). New York: Guilford Press.

Templeton, S. (2011). Teaching spelling in the English/language arts classroom. In D. Lapp & D. Fisher (Eds.), *The handbook of research on teaching the English language arts* (3rd ed.). New York: Routledge.

Templeton, S., & Bear, D. (Eds.). (1992). *Development of orthographic knowledge and the foundations of literacy: A memorial Festschrift for Edmund H. Henderson.* Hillsdale, NJ: Lawrence Erlbaum.

Templeton, S., & Bear, D. R. (2006). *Spelling and vocabulary.* Boston: Houghton Mifflin.

Templeton, S., & Bear, D. R. (2011). Phonemic awareness, word recognition, and spelling. In T. Rasinski (Ed.), *Developing reading instruction that works.* Bloomington, IN: Solution Tree Press.

Templeton, S., Bear, D. R., Invernizzi, M., & Johnston, F. (2010). *Vocabulary their way: Word study with middle and secondary students.* Boston: Pearson/Allyn & Bacon.

Templeton, S., & Ives, R. T. (2007). The nature and development of spelling. In B. Guzetti (Ed.), *The encyclopedia of early childhood literacy education* (pp. 111–122). Westport, CT: Praeger.

Templeton, S., Johnston, F., Bear, D. R., & Invernizzi, M. (2009). *Words their way: Word sorts for derivational relations spellers* (2nd ed.). Boston: Pearson/Allyn & Bacon.

Templeton, S., & Morris, D. (1999). Questions teachers ask about spelling. *Reading Research Quarterly, 34,* 102–112.

Templeton, S., & Morris, D. (2000). Spelling. In M. Kamil, P. Mosenthal, P. D. Pearson, & R. Barr (Eds.), *Handbook of reading research* (vol. 3, pp. 525–543). Mahwah, NJ: Lawrence Erlbaum.

Templeton, S., & Scarborough-Franks, L. (1985). The spelling's the thing: Older students' knowledge of derivational morphology in phonology and orthography. *Applied Psycholinguistics, 6,* 371–389.

Templeton, S., Smith, D., Moloney, K., & Ives, B. (2007). The nature of morphology in a developmental model of word knowledge. Symposium presented at the 57th annual meeting of the National Reading Conference, Orlando, December.

Templeton, S., Smith, D., Moloney, K., Van Pelt, J., & Ives, B. (2009). Generative vocabulary knowledge: Learning and teaching higher-order morphological aspects of word structure in grades 4, 5, and 6. Symposium presented at the 59th annual meeting of the National Reading Conference, Albuquerque, December.

Templeton, S., & Spivey, E. M. (1980). The concept of "word" in young children as a function of level of cognitive development. *Research in the Teaching of English, 14*(3), 265–278.

Torgesen, J. K. (2004). Lessons learned from research on interventions for students who have difficulty learning to read. In P. McCardle & V. Chhabra (Eds.), *The voice of evidence in reading research* (pp. 355–382). Baltimore: Brookes.

Treiman, R. (1985). Onsets and rimes as units of spoken syllables: Evidence from children. *Journal of Educational Psychology, 77*(4), 417–427.

Treiman, R. (1993). *Beginning to spell.* New York: Oxford University Press.

Tunmer, W. E. (1991). Phonological awareness and literacy acquisition. In L. Rieben & C. A. Perfetti (Eds.), *Learning to read: Basic research and its implications* (pp. 105–120). Hillsdale, NJ: Lawrence Erlbaum.

Vallins, G. H. (1954). *Spelling.* London: Andre Deutsch.

Vellutino, F. R., Scanlon, D. M., Small, S., & Fanuele, D. P. (2006). Response to intervention as a vehicle for distinguishing between children with and without reading disabilities: Evidence for the role of kindergarten and first-grade interventions. *Journal of Learning Disabilities, 38,* 157–169.

Venezky, R. L. (1999). *The American way of spelling: The structure and origins of American English orthography.* New York: Guilford Press.

Viise, N. (1994). *Feature word spelling lists: A diagnosis of progressing word knowledge through an assessment of spelling errors.* Unpublished doctoral dissertation, University of Virginia.

Viise, N. (1996). A study of the spelling development of adult literacy learners compared with that of classroom children. *Journal of Literacy Research, 28*(4), 561–587.

Vygotsky, L. S. (1962). *Thought and language.* Cambridge, MA: MIT Press.

Ward, A. (2009). *A formative study investigating interactive reading activities to develop kindergartners' science vocabulary.* Unpublished dissertation, University of Virginia.

Wasik, B. A., Bond, M. A., & Hindman, A. (2006). The effects of a language and literacy intervention on Head Start children and teachers. *Journal of Educational Psychology, 98*(1), 63–74.

Welsch, J., Sullivan, A., & Justice, L. (2003). That's my letter: What preschoolers' name writing representation can tell us about emergent literacy knowledge. *Journal of Literacy Research, 35*(2), 757–776.

White, T. G. (2005). Effects of systematic and strategic analogy-based phonics on grade 2 students' word reading and reading comprehension. *Reading Research Quarterly, 40*(2), 234–255.

White, T. G., Sowell, J., & Yanagihara, A. (1989). Teaching elementary students to use word-part clues. *The Reading Teacher, 42,* 302–308.

Whitehurst, G. J. (1979). Meaning and semantics. In G. J. Whitehurst & B. J. Zimmerman (Eds.), *The functions of language and cognition* (pp. 115–139). New York: Academic Press.

Whitehurst, G. J., Arnold, D. S., Epstein, J. N., Angell, A. L., Smith, M., & Fiscehl, J. E. (1994). A picture book reading intervention in day care and home for children from low-income families. *Developmental Psychology, 30,* 679–689.

Worthy, M., & Viise, N. M. (1996). Morphological, phonological and orthographic differences between the spelling of normally achieving children and basic literacy adults. *Reading and Writing: An Interdisciplinary Journal, 8,* 138–159.

Worthy, M. J., & Invernizzi, M. (1989). Spelling errors of normal and disabled students on achievement levels one through four: Instructional implications. *Bulletin of the Orton Society, 40,* 138–149.

Wylie, R. E., & Durrell, D. D. (1970). Teaching vowels through phonograms. *Elementary English, 47,* 787–791.

Yang, M. (2005). Development of orthographic knowledge among Korean children in grades 1 to 6. (Doctoral dissertation, University of Virginia). *Dissertation Abstracts International,* 66/05, 1697.

Yopp, K. K. (1988). The validity and reliability of phoneme awareness tests. *Reading Research Quarterly, 23,* 159–177.

Zeno, S. M., Ivens, S. H., Millard, R. T., & Duvvuri, R. (1996). *The educator's word frequency guide.* New York: Touchstone Applied Science Associates.

Zutell, J. (1992). An integrated view of word knowledge: Correlational studies of the relationships among spelling, reading, and conceptual development. In S. Templeton & D. Bear (Eds.), *Development of orthographic knowledge and the foundations of literacy: A memorial Festschrift for Edmund H. Henderson* (pp. 213–230). Hillsdale, NJ: Lawrence Erlbaum.

Zutell, J. (1994). Spelling instruction. In A. C. Purves, L. Papa, & S. Jordan (Eds.), *Encyclopedia of English studies and language arts* (vol. 2, pp. 1098–1100). New York: Scholastic.

Zutell, J. (1996). The directed spelling thinking activity (DSTA): Providing an effective balance in word study instruction. *The Reading Teacher, 50,* 98–107.

Zutell, J. (1998). Word sorting: A developmental spelling approach to word study for delayed readers. *Reading & Writing Quarterly, 14,* 219–238.

Zutell, J., & Allan, V. (1988). The English spelling strategies of Spanish-speaking bilingual children. *TESOL Quarterly, 22,* 333–340.

Zutell, J., & Rasinski, T. (1989). Reading and spelling connections in third and fourth grade students. *Reading Psychology, 10,* 137–156.

Zwiers, J. (2008). *Building academic language: Essential practices for content classrooms.* San Francisco: Jossey-Bass.

Index